MTV

Ireland

1st Edition

**by Christi Daugherty, Olivia Edward &
Clare O'Connor**

Christi Daugherty

Christi Daugherty is a Texas expat living in London. While there she has discovered the joys of pubs and learned what bangers and mash are. Christi contributed to *MTV Europe* and is the author of several other Frommer's guides, including *Frommer's Ireland* and *Paris Day by Day*. Before emigrating to England, she attended Texas A&M University and worked as a freelance writer in Texas and New Orleans. Above all else she misses American football and tacos.

Olivia Edward

Olivia Edward is a British travel writer with a lust for adventure and new ideas. Beginning her career in Shanghai as Editor-in-Chief of China's first English-language travel magazine, *Asia and Away*, she went on to write for Time Out, DK, Luxe guides and over 50 other travel and lifestyle publications around the globe. Happiest when swimming in rough British seas, she is also extremely fond of fresh watermelon juice and Japanese all-you-can-eat-and-drink restaurants. With few such establishments in Ireland, her favorite stop-offs are Belfast—due to its hard edges and intense soul—and Bundoran, for the sea-bleached natives still living the surfing dream.

Clare O'Connor

Clare O'Connor is a global nomad, born in Bermuda and educated in England and Philadelphia, where she graduated from the University of Pennsylvania in 2005. She studied English literature and worked slavish hours for both school and local publications. She hopes to someday edit a travel magazine and retire to the Dalmatian coast, but for now she lives and works in London. Clare also contributed to *MTV Europe*.

Published by:
Wiley Publishing, Inc.
111 River St.
Hoboken, NJ 07030-5774

ISBN-13: 978-0-7645-8774-0

ISBN-10: 0-7645-8774-9

Editor: Caroline Sieg

Production Editor: Heather Wilcox

Cartographer: Roberta Stockwell

Photo Editor: Richard H. Fox

Cover & Interior Design: Eric Frommelt

Production by Wiley Indianapolis Composition Services

For information on our other products and services or to obtain technical support, please contact our Customer Care Department within the U.S. at 800/762-2974, outside the U.S. at 317/572-3993 or fax 317/572-4002.

Wiley also publishes its books in a variety of electronic formats. Some content that appears in print may not be available in electronic formats.

Manufactured in the United States of America

5   4   3   2   1

Table of Contents

Galway City   142

The Southeast   181

Cork City   229

County Kerry   279

CONTENTS

CONTENTS

List of Maps

An Invitation to the Reader

In researching this book, we discovered many wonderful places—hotels, restaurants, shops, and more. We're sure you'll find others. Please tell us about them, so we can share the information with your fellow travelers in upcoming editions. If you were disappointed with a recommendation, we'd love to know that, too. Please write to:

MTV Ireland, 1st Edition
Wiley Publishing, Inc.
III River St.
Hoboken, NJ 07030-5774

An Additional Note

Please be advised that travel information is subject to change at any time—and this is especially true of prices. We therefore suggest that you write or call ahead for confirmation when making your travel plans. The authors, editors, and publisher cannot be held responsible for the experiences of readers while traveling. Your safety is important to us, however, so we encourage you to stay alert and be aware of your surroundings. Keep a close eye on cameras, purses, and wallets, all favorite targets of thieves and pickpockets.

A Note on Prices

The MTV Guides provide exact prices in each destination's local currency. The rates of this exchange as this book went to press are listed in the table below. Exchange rates are constantly in flux; for up-to-the-minute information, consult a currency-conversion website such as www.oanda.com/convert/classic.

Euro €	US $	UK £	Canadian $	Australian $	New Zealand $
1€ equals	$1.20	£0.68	C$1.35	A$1.60	NZ$1.75

Star Ratings, Icons & Abbreviations

Every hotel, restaurant, and attraction listed in this guide has been ranked for quality, value, service, amenities, and special features using a **star-rating system.** Hotels and restaurants are rated on a scale of zero (recommended) to three stars (exceptional). Attractions, shopping, and nightlife are rated according to the following scale: zero stars (recommended), one star (highly recommended), two stars (very highly recommended), and three stars (must-see).

In addition to the star-rating system, we also use **three feature icons** that point you to great deals, in-the-know advice, and unique experiences. Throughout the book, look for:

Best — The most-happening restaurants, hotels, and things to do—don't leave town without checking these places out

FREE — When cash flow is at a trickle, head for these spots: no-cost museums, free concerts, bars with complimentary food, and more

MTV — Savvy advice and practical recommendations for students who are studying abroad

The following **abbreviations** are used for credit cards:

AE	American Express	DISC	Discover	V	Visa
DC	Diners Club	MC	MasterCard		

The Best of MTV Ireland

The Best Places to Have a Drink or Two

- **The Empire Music Hall** (Belfast): Launch yourself right into the center of student action at The Empire, a student den inside an old church where down-and-dirty youngsters go wild for cover bands and cheap drinks. Prepare to have your ears blown off. ☎ 028/9032-8110. See p. 431.
- **Sandino's** (Derry, County Derry): Definitely the hippest bar in Derry. Boho girls and boys clutter up the tiny inside, sipping on Euro-bottled beers, while soaking up some of the funkiest sounds in the North. Not to be missed. ☎ 028/7130-9297. See p. 470.
- **Sean's Bar** (Athlone, County Westmeath): Hunting for that quintessential Irish pub with sacks of atmosphere and a roaring fire? Try Sean's. Probably the oldest bar in the world, it also comes sprinkled with sawdust on the floor, impromptu jazz sessions, and a character-laden collection of locals. ☎ 090/649-2358. See p. 404.
- **Octagon Bar** (Dublin): Oooh, is that Bono from U2? Could well be; it's his bar in his hotel and he has been known to hang out here. An incredibly trendy drinkery where you don't have to be rich or beautiful to get through the door. It's not cheap but it is a fave celeb hangout. ☎ 01/670-9000. See p. 82.
- **Bodega** (Cork, County Cork): Hang with the hippest of Cork's university crowd as they slither past two-story mirrors and a capricious selection of automobile parts fixed to this bar's walls. Come as you are, but if you want to be in with the in-gang, the required uniform is boho chic. Go raid a granny's wardrobe. ☎ 021/427-2878. See p. 239.
- **Tatu** (Belfast): A huge minimalist cavern with a glass front to enable all the beautiful people to be seen. And my-oh-my are they beautiful. Somewhere to see and be seen. Expect to queue for the privilege. ☎ 028/9038-0818. See p. 434.

The Best Adrenaline Adventures

- **Surfing in Lahinch** (County Clare): Okay, so the water's freezing but the waves are mighty fine—especially between August and November when the Atlantic swell starts to make itself felt. Lahinch Surf School—run by a member of the Irish surf team—will get you hanging ten within 2 hours. ☎ 087/960-9667. See p. 340.

○ **Kitesurfing in Bundoran** (County Donegal): Of course, if you're really hip to what's happening on the waves, you'll know surfing is already passé and all the hot young things have moved on to kitesurfing. Have a go on the beautiful, flat sand-duned beach of Tullen Strand near Ireland's surfing HQ, Bundoran. The boys at Bundoran Surf Company will show you how it's done. ☎ **071/984-1968.** See p. 379.

○ **Kayaking at Union Hall** (County Cork): A little less action-packed than other sports in this section, Atlantic Sea Kayaking's Moonlight Adventure Trip will still get your blood pumping. Set off at dusk to explore the deserted craggy islands and tiny secluded coves of this stunning area all aglow with phosphorescent light. ☎ **028/33002.** See p. 267.

○ **A Ride in a Zapcat** (County Kerry): Zapcats are mini speedboats with Ferrari-style engines and the ability to jump 8m (26 ft.) in the air. Take a tour of the craggy Skellig Islands in one. If you can see past the spray, you may spot the dolphins, porpoises, killer whales, and turtles that live in the area. Activity Ireland are the guys to get you wet. ☎ **066/947-5277.** See p. 294.

○ **Coasteering off the Coast of Northern Ireland** (County Down): Do you fancy scrambling over endless rocks, jumping off high cliffs, and swimming in the icy cold seas around Northern Ireland? Well sign yourself up for a day's coasteering with the Mountain and Watersports Centre in Castlewellan Forest Park. A hardcore hit. ☎ **028/4377-0714.** See p. 494.

○ **Parachuting in Coleraine** (County Derry): Take to the sky—for a few brilliantly terrifying minutes—with Wild Geese Parachute Company. They will get you to fall from 1,050m (3,500 ft.) with a self-opening "static line," or from 3,900m (13,000 ft.) if you're happy to plummet attached to an instructor. ☎ **028/2995-8609.** See p. 482.

○ **Walking across the Carrick-A-Rede Rope Bridge** (County Antrim): It may not sound like much but when you look down and see you're 262m (80 ft.) above the crashing Atlantic and you've still got another 197m (60 ft.) until you reach the other side, your adrenaline level will probably start rising. Built by local fishermen to allow them to reach the island's salmon fishery from the mainland, this is a huge draw for visitors to the Antrim coast. ☎ **028/2073-1582.** See p. 485.

The Best Live Music Venues

○ **Spring and Airbrake** (Belfast): The little bro of the renowned Limelight club. While the older sibling gets the big acts like Oasis, Manic Street Preachers, and David Gray, Spring and Airbrake gets the up-and-coming and forever-hip acts like David Holmes and Gomez. ☎ **028/9032-5942.** See p. 438.

○ **The Casbah** (Letterkenny, County Donegal): Set to become the Northwest's best live music venue, this is a down-and-dirty underground music venue where

you'll get to hear independent Irish and international acts. From the moment you walk down the stairs, you know you've found somewhere exciting. No phone. See p. 382.

○ **The Nerve Centre** (Derry, County Derry): Oooh, this place is good. If there's not an exciting guitar band or singer-songwriter topping the bill most nights of the week—Damien Dempsey, The Editors, Idlewild, and Ash have all played here recently—you'll get a DJ set from the likes of Tall

Paul or an animation workshop or something else superb. ☎ 028/7126-0562. See p. 471.

○ **McGann's** (Doolin, County Clare): There are traditional Irish music pubs and then there is McGann's. It's a magnet for Irish musicians and consequently one of the best places on the island to get an earful of impromptu Irish trad. ☎ 065/707-4133. See p. 334.

○ **The Crane** (Galway, County Galway): Trad Irish music replete with old men dressed in tweed sporting scruffy old beards. This is the genuine article. Sessions can occur at any time, but the Sunday afternoon one is nigh-on a religious experience. Worship at the altar of folk. ☎ 091/567419. See p. 154.

○ **Crawdaddy** (Dublin): One of the country's most intimate live music venues and one of the hottest places in Dublin to catch a band. Expect fab acoustic and indie gigs set amidst a deeply casual atmosphere. Love it. ☎ 01/478-0166. See p. 86.

The Best Festivals

○ **Oxegen** (Punchestown Racecourse, County Kildare): One of Europe's hottest musical festivals. A huge weekend-long musical orgy with 100 acts smearing their talent over five stages. Headliners are usually rock divinities like Green Day and the Foo Fighters, but Coldplay and Snoop Dogg have also previously topped the bill. Early July. www.oxegen.ie. See p. 91.

○ **Celtronic Festival** (Derry, County Derry): Something for fans of the relentless beat. This is one of Ireland's biggest dance music parties and has it all from crowd-pleasers to out there sonic mysteries. A seriously high-energy event. Summer. www.celtronic.co.uk. See p. 472.

○ **Cathedral Quarter Arts Festival** (Belfast): From one of the coolest quarters in Belfast comes one of the country's top artsy festivals. It's all pretty cutting edge. Expect to encounter anything from Japanese punk rock to Canadian trip-hop. April or May. www.cqaf.com. See p. 440.

○ **The Puck Fair** (Killorglin, County Kerry): Enough of all that trendy stuff, get down with the goats at an outback town in the Irish countryside. Three days of drinking and dancing in celebration of the Celtic god Pan all topped off with the crowning of King Puck—the most eligible male goat in town. Get in. Early August. www.puckfair.ie. See p. 295.

○ **Tennent's Vital** (Belfast): Northern Ireland's big summer festival set in the lush surrounds of the Botanic Gardens. Previous acts have included Scissor Sisters, Franz Ferdinand, and Faithless. Not to be missed. August. www.vital05.com. See p. 440.

○ **Diversions Temple Bar** (Dublin): One for the paupers. The most important thing you need to know about this festival is it's free. Next up, it's an all-outdoor, all-ages, all-arts mix of dance, film, theatre, and music performances. Stretch those euros. May to August. www.temple-bar.ie. See p. 91.

○ **Murphy's Cat Laughs Comedy Festival** (Kilkenny, County Kilkenny): Laugh along with top international stand-up comedians and comediennes. Late May. www.wicklow.ie.tourism/events. See p. 218.

○ **Ocean Fest** (Bundoran, Donegal): A celebration of all things wet focusing on surfing. Indulge in free surf lessons during the day and extreme sports videos at night, plus lots of drinking and dancing, of course. Late September to early October. www.bundoranoceanfest.com. See p. 379.

The Best Bargain Places to Stay

○ **The Malin Head Hostel** (Malin Head, County Donegal): A budget travelers' paradise and possibly the most chilled hostel in Ireland. It's an oasis of comfort in one of the most wild and desolate regions of the country. Pick your pudding from the garden—fresh strawberries. Yummy. ☎ **074/937-0309**. See p. 386.

○ **Isaacs Hostel** (Dublin): A supernova hostel. Isaacs reinvents the hostel concept. Calling itself "Dublin's first V.I.P. hostel," it adds a full restaurant and an attractive sauna to the usual mix of TV rooms, lockers, and bunk beds. ☎ **01/855-6215**. See p. 66.

○ **Arnie's Backpackers** (Belfast): Like coming home to a mad crazy family. Cups of tea, a log fire, garden, and two dogs all await your arrival. With no curfew and a my-place-is-your-place beat up appeal, Arnie's really is the quintessential hostel. ☎ **028/9024-2867**. See p. 422.

○ **Sleepzone** (Galway): Is this really just a hostel? It's so damn plush it feels like you must be staying in a newly constructed motel at the very least. This is Galway's latest and greatest place to sleep. There's no curfew and free Wi-Fi throughout. Budget travel as it should be. Settle in. ☎ **091/566999**. See p. 148.

○ **The Bastion** (Athlone, County Westmeath): Okay, so it's not as cheap as a hostel, but for what you get for your buck it surely can't be beat. A boho B&B decorated with a spot-on mix of stripped floorboards and miscellaneous clutter like stuffed animals and pot plants. Seriously cool. ☎ **090/649-4954**. See p. 402.

○ **Macool's** (Portrush, County Derry): Right by the sea and run by the coolest couple and their handsome hound, Murphy. This is hostelling as you wish it always was, a bit like staying at a mate's house but a lot cleaner. Somewhere to stay while you learn to surf in Portrush. ☎ **028/7082-4845**. See p. 478.

○ **Walyunga B&B** (Kinsale, County Cork): It's a B&B, it's a garden, and it boasts views of the water. The beds are ultra-comfy, too, and you'll be kickin' back in plush country furniture. In short: It's heaven, and you'll still be able to afford dinner in the gourmet capital of Ireland. ☎ **021/477-4126**. See p. 252.

○ **The Saddler's House and the Merchant's House** (Derry, County Derry): It's not *that* much more than a hostel and it's worth it. Two big old 19th-century houses with stripped wooden floorboards, comfy checked dressing gowns hanging up on the back of the bedroom doors, the best breakfasts you'll eat in all of Northern Ireland, and an English bulldog called Bertie. If you need any more reasons, stay in bedroom number five in Merchant's House, which was once used by a sniper to attack a nearby police station. ☎ **028/7126-9691**. See p. 466.

The Best Dance Clubs

○ **Savoy Theatre** (Cork, County Cork): One of Cork's newest and coolest nightclubs. It used to be a cinema, hence the slinky hand-me-down red velvet curtains. It's already hosted some big-name music acts like Fun Loving Criminals and drum 'n' bass king DJ Hype, and the party looks set to continue. ☎ **021/425-3000**. See p. 242.

○ **Lillie's Bordello** (Dublin): Lillie's has been going for over a decade but the punters still can't get enough of her kitsch-cum-whorehouse decor dotted with nude paintings. The door policy can be fierce, so if you can't stand pretension find somewhere else to play. ☎ **01/679-9204.** See p. 86.

○ **Kelly's** (Portrush, County Derry): All the big boys have played here from Digweed to Judge Jules. It's a bit like Ibiza only without the sunshine. The dance night you're after is Lush. Just follow the crowds from Belfast and Derry. ☎ **028/7082-3539.** See p. 480.

○ **Shine** (Belfast): Unless something has gone horribly wrong by the time you're reading this, Shine is—without doubt—the hippest club night on the island of Ireland. Forget your designer clubwear, this is all about being edgy and underground with the über-cool set from Belfast Uni. It's their club night after all. ☎ **028/9032-3313.** See p. 436.

○ **The Potthouse** (Belfast): Currently being touted as one of western Europe's hottest new venues, The Potthouse is a frosted glass queen in Belfast's rapidly up-and-coming Cathedral Quarter. The crowd is hip without being haughty. A must. ☎ **028/9024-4044.** See p. 435.

○ **The Globe** (Limerick, County Limerick): Proving there's more to Limerick than drunken brawls, the Globe serves psychedelic-looking cocktails to the county's beautiful young things. Ooh and celebs like the Cranberries and U2 have been known to pop by. If it's good enough for them . . . ☎ **061/313533.** See p. 324.

○ **GPO** (Galway, County Galway): There's none of your chart nonsense here. In an inky cavelike interior small herds contort to fantastic soul and funk-infused house as well as hip-hop and drum 'n' bass. We like. ☎ **091/563073.** See p. 154.

The Best Websites

○ **www.knowhere.co.uk** Want to know the best place in town to find someone to get off with? Where to get a new pair of trainers or where the locals hang out? Take a look at knowhere.co.uk. Originally started by a bunch of skaters wanting to share info on where to do their thing, it's now expanded into a mob-ruled review of clothes, clubs, and so much more. Yes, the spelling is appalling but there's no better way of getting the truth about a town before you get a chance to chat with the locals yourself.

○ **www.ireland.ie** The Irish Tourist Board's official website. Or *Bord Failte* as it's known in Ireland. No, it's not wildly exciting, but it is comprehensive and enables you to search for available hostels and guesthouses across the country. And it doesn't do a bad job on the activities front either.

○ **www.freeflowmagazine.com** The website for what must be the hippest extreme sports magazine in Ireland, if not Europe. The website is expanding all the time. But pick up the mag and you not only get the low-down on new skate and BMX parks, you also get great photos and profiles of the country's top extreme scenesters.

○ **www.theaa.com** No, not Alcoholics Anonymous, this is the Automobile Association's website which does a fab job of giving you printout-able directions of tomorrow's route. Just plug in a starting point and a destination.

○ **http://entertainment.ie** A handy, exhaustive, searchable database including just about every event going on in Ireland, from museum exhibitions to indie gigs to hot new plays to club nights.

○ **www.anoige.ie** The Irish Youth Hostelling Association's website. Information on 24 affiliated youth hostels in the Republic, complete with star-ratings, prices, facilities, and photos. A great reference tool.

The Best Spots to Blow Your Budget

○ **A Bed at Malmaison** (Belfast): Northern Ireland's most luxe hotel—a seductive mix of old industrial stone and decadent velvet. Okay, so you might not be able to afford one of their enormous beds for the night, but you can spoil yourself with a meal in their divine restaurant or a cocktail at their minx of a bar. ☎ **028/9022-0200.** See p. 425.

○ **A Meal at Chapter One** (Dublin): Probably the city's most atmos-packed eatery, this stunner fills the vaulted basement space of the Dublin Writers Museum. On your plate you'll find modern Irish food made with local, organic ingredients. All around you are the city's movers and shakers. ☎ **01/873-2266.** See p. 77.

○ **A Gig at Slane Castle** (Slane, County Meath): David Bowie, U2, Paul Oakenfold, Iggy Pop, REM, and Madonna have all pumped out their tunes against the backdrop of Slane Castle. If your trip coincides with a gig here, go. The setting is stunning and the crowd usually goes wild. ☎ **041/988-4400.** See p. 138.

○ **A Flying Lesson** (Newry, County Down): Learn to fly in one of the most beautiful parts of Ireland. Okay, so you're not going to get your hands on a fighter jet, but for €75 per hour the boys and girls at Fly NI Airsports will teach you how to go solo in a microlight plane—if you can keep your eyes off the view. ☎ **07867/832185.** See p. 494.

The Best Gay Hangouts

○ **Mynt** (Belfast): A divine lounge bar with two club rooms and a chill-out area called Coolmynt. The dress code is funky and the vibe code is outrageous—stay at home if you're easily shocked. This place is seriously stylish, so don't expect to get in if you slob along in an old tracksuit. ☎ **028/9023-4520.** See p. 437.

○ **Garage** (Belfast): The usual sauna set-up: A Jacuzzi and steam room plus a video lounge and coffee bar. Open through the night on Fridays and Saturdays. "Prepare to have your nuts tightened." They said it. ☎ **028/9023-3441.** See p. 437.

○ **Howl** (Belfast): One for the girls. This group organizes a montly welcome-all alternative music night. Moon. Howl. Get it? They're strictly anti all phobias whether homo or hetero so check your prejudices in at the door. www.howlclub.com. The event takes place at **Pavilion.** ☎ **028/9028-3283.** See p. 438.

○ **The George** (Dublin): Dublin's most established gay bar is generally packed out with a chill crowd of locals and savvy travelers. It's coffee and chats during the day and dancing and DJs at night. A godsend. ☎ **01/478-2983.** See p. 90.

○ **GUBU** (Dublin): Okay, so it's not purely for a gay crowd but it's such fun here nobody should miss out. It's filled to the bursting most nights, with a casually, but beautifully, dressed, laid-back, enthusiastic crowd drawn by its party-pop music. Indulge. ☎ **01/874-0710.** See p. 90.

○ **Frankie's Guesthouse** (Dublin): Dublin's only exclusively gay guesthouse. Set on a quiet backstreet in a charming, mews-style building with a simple Mediterranean vibe. ☎ **01/478-3087.** See p. 68.

○ **Loafers** (Cork, County Cork): A relaxed and friendly venue stuffed full of the under-30s crowd. Summer sees everyone lounging around in the beer garden. On the weekends DJs get the crowd gyrating. ☎ **021/431-1612.** See p. 243.

The Best Bargain Meals

○ **Quay Co-Op** (Cork, County Cork): The place where Cork's veggie and vegan crowd hang out. Chow down on creamy lentil and coconut soup, homemade bread, and cakes. Food worth queuing for. ☎ **021/431-7026.** See p. 236.

○ **The Nerve Centre Café** (Derry, County Derry): The food here may be pretty run of the mill, but how often do you get to eat your budget quiche and chips alongside musical heroes like David Gray and Gomez? As this cafe is attached to Derry's top alternative music venue, you never know who might be sitting at your table. ☎ **028/7126-0562.** See p. 468.

○ **Foodies** (Athlone, County Westmeath): Exposed stone, bare-wood floors, a handsome manager, plenty of mags to read, and fantastic simple food. Stop by for a sandwich of brie with sun-blushed tomatoes and green salad or a special of smoked salmon with cream cheese. Almost everything's under €5. ☎ **090/649-8576.** See p. 403.

○ **Beshoffs** (Dublin): In a restaurant nearing 100 years old, this is fish and chips gone posh. Go for your usual cod or try a bite of shark—some days there are as many as 20 different types of fish to choose from. The chips (sorry, fries to the Americans) are crisp on the outside and soft in the center. Just as it should be. ☎ **01/677-8026.** See p. 72.

○ **Soup Dragon** (Dublin): When you've been bruised by a fall on Dublin's cobbles and soaked through by the Irish rain and are wondering what the hell you're doing here, pop along to Soup Dragon and get some internal central heating. All sorts of soups—from curried parsnip to sag aloo—are served up alongside instant-bum-and-tum desserts like bread and butter pudding. ☎ **01/872-3277.** See p. 75.

○ **The Winding Stair** (Dublin): A Dublin institution dove-tailing the pleasures of caffeine and literature. A self-service cafe serving simple whole foods and three floors of secondhand gems. Turn up after dark and you may find a poetry reading in progress. ☎ **01/873-3292.** See p. 76.

○ **Flour Crepe Room 46** (Belfast): A lush mint-green serving counter balances out just a handful of Scandinavian style dark-wood tables. Off these you'll find hip young things scoffing down crepes filled with lovely things like cottage cheese, pineapple, and tomato or Parmesan, or Mars bars and Baileys. Yes, please. ☎ **028/9033-9966.** See p. 427.

The Best Things to Do for Free

○ **Moone High Cross** (Moone, County Kildare): A top-of-the-range high cross that is nearly 1,200 years old. Look closely to see that naughty little nymphet Eve trying to tempt Adam with some fruit, the sacrifice of Isaac, and Daniel getting down with the lions. See p. 129.

○ **Monasterboice** (Collon, County Louth): One of the dreamiest ancient monastic sites in Ireland. Travelers will find a cemetery, one of the tallest round towers in Ireland, ancient church ruins, and two fab high crosses covered in carvings. Come at dawn or dusk to soak up the true atmos. See p. 140.

○ **Catch a Free Show on Grafton Street** (Dublin): On a sunny Saturday its mimes, musicians, and artists are legion. Just watching them interact with the hassled shoppers and baffled tourists is a joy. See "Dublin" section, p. 51.

○ **Spend a Day on the Beach** (Dingle Peninsula, County Kerry): Brandon Bay in County Kerry is both real pretty and a great place to go swimming. Other beaches on the Dingle Peninsula—including the brilliant dunes of Inch Strand—also offer up some stunning sights as the wild sea crashes into the land, but not all of them are safe for swimming. See p. 309.

○ **Get a Chance to Hang out with the Students at Trinity College** (Dublin): Although you do have to pay to sneak a peak at the original Book of Kells in the Old Library, there's no charge to look around the rest of the place. Spend a lazy afternoon watching cricket on campus. ☎ 01/6008-2308. See p. 100.

○ **Spend a Morning in one of Dublin's Public Galleries** (Dublin): Check out the art work of Yeats' often-overlooked brother Jack B. in the National Gallery of Ireland. ☎ 01/661-5133. Even better—and far funkier—is the Irish Museum of Modern Art. The traveling exhibitions are constantly changing so just stop by and see what's on. ☎ 01/612-9900. See p. 97 for both.

○ **Pay a Visit to the Void Gallery** (Derry, County Derry): Just opened in 2005, this is a gallery fuelled by passion, bringing the best of thought-provoking international art to Derry. Expect poetic video installations and images strong enough to incite a revolution. See p. 473.

○ **The Cliffs of Moher** (Liscannor, County Clare): Unmissable and totally breathtaking. The cliffs stretch for 8km (5 miles) about 210m (700 ft.) above the ocean. From O'Brien's Tower, a midway observation tower, you can see the Aran Islands, Galway Bay, and various other distant mountains. See p. 334.

The Best Sites to See

○ **Newgrange** (Slane, County Meath): Don't miss this one. It really is mind-blowing. Ireland's best-known prehistoric monument is one of the archaeological wonders of western Europe. Massive and mysterious, it was built as a burial mound more than 5,000 years ago. It's not one for claustrophobics but, if you're lucky, your guide will reenact the solstice light display inside the burial chamber. ☎ 041/988-0300. See p. 137.

○ **Dunluce Castle** (Bushmills, County Antrim): These ruins are great. Really, really great. See them at sunset and they appear as if from a film set, teetering on the top of the cliffs, black against the orange sky. Walk the 5km (3-mile) route up from Portrush to get yourself in the mood. ☎ 028/2073-1938. See p. 480.

○ **Skellig Michael** (The Skellig Islands, Iveragh Peninsula, County Kerry): Two crags jutting out of the violent sea acting as an eerie home to monastery ruins and thousands of gannets. The biggest isle, Skellig Michael, is ridiculously steep—the whole land mass is one sloping cliff face, with disued buildings perched precariously on its sides. Catch a boat across. ☎ 066/947-6306. See p. 293 and 294.

○ **The Giant's Causeway** (Bushmills, County Antrim): The Giant's Causeway is considered by many to be "The Eighth Wonder of the World." Thousands of hexagonal basalt pillars jut out from the sea all along the shoreline. Together they make a huge plane of geometrically pleasing steps. Has to be seen. ☎ 028/2073-1582. See p. 484.

○ **Cahir Castle** (County Tipperary—Southeast Chapter): This medieval fortress features fascinating features of the military architecture, tiny chambers, spiral staircases, and dizzying battlements. ☎ 052/41011. See p. 213.

The Best Brewery & Distillery Tours

○ **The Bushmills Distillery** (Bushmills, County Antrim): This is the oldest distillery in the world. It was licensed to distill spirits in 1608 but some say they were churning out alcoholic beverages as early as 1276. Watch and learn as they turn river water into fire water. Free samples at the end. ☎ **028/2073-1521.** See p. 483.

○ **Old Midleton Distillery** (Midleton, County Cork): See the largest pot still in the world—it holds 30,000 gallons of booze—and learn everything you ever wanted to know about whiskey but were afraid to ask. Many of the original build- ings from 1825 remain, including mills, corn houses, and a water wheel. And, yes, you get a glass of whiskey at the end of your tour. ☎ **021/4613594.** See p. 261.

○ **Guinness Storehouse** (Dublin): Ah, yes, we thought you'd be interested in this one. Founded in 1759, the Guinness Brewery is now world famous. Explore the Guinness Hopstore, Gilroy Gallery, and then comes the good bit: Stop in at the breathtaking Gravity Bar where you can grab a glass of the black stuff in this glass-enclosed bar 60m (200 ft.) above the city. ☎ **01/408-4800.** See p. 96.

○ **The Old Jameson Distillery** (Dublin): This museum tells the history of the stuff known in Irish as *uisce beatha* (the water of life). What you get is a film followed by a whiskey-making exhibition and right- in-front-of-your-eyes demonstrations. Finally, get your gob around the stuff itself and see what you think. Pretty good, eh? ☎ **01/807-2355.** See p. 98.

○ **St. Francis Abbey Brewery** (Kilkenny City): This brewery in a 12th-century abbey serves up free samples in the summer (Smithwick's, a popular local ale, is produced here). ☎ **056/772-1014.** See p. 226.

The Best Pickup Spots

○ **The Fly** (Belfast): If you're in Belfast and want to pick up someone half decent, The Fly is the place to head. Attracting a mix of up-for-it young professionals and non- skanky students, the vibe is fun-luvin' if a bit cheap and trashy but, hey, what's wrong with that? Hard-nut bouncers ensure there won't be any problems when you make a pass at someone else's girlfriend/boyfriend. ☎ **028/9023-5666.** See p. 432.

○ **Bambu Beach Club** (Belfast): Belfast natives say this is the place to go if you like sluts. So, there you have it, what fur- ther recommendation could you possibly need? ☎ **028/9046-0011.** See p. 435.

○ **Milk** (Belfast): If you're in the Northern Irish capital and want to get intimate with someone who isn't off their head, and perhaps even attractive, try Milk. You'll need to look good to get noticed here. It's one of *the* hottest dance clubs in town and hosts all the top international DJs. Bump and grind your way into someone else's affections. ☎ **028/9027-8876.** See p. 434.

○ **Bruxelles** (Dublin): One of Dublin's late- night bars. Pile in with a crowd of well- lubricated and friendly locals. It's not a beautiful place, but it's very popular with the natives. Somewhere to get off your face and embrace an Irish boy or girl you've never met before. Fantastic. ☎ **01/677-5362.** See p. 79.

○ **Copper Face Jacks** (Dublin): This is *the* Dublin pickup joint. Everybody here is on the make and image is all—it's not how smart you are that counts; it's how good you look. The young crowd (most are in their early 20s) are here to chat, drink, and—most importantly—meet members of the opposite sex. ☎ 01/475-8777. See p. 79.

○ **The Old Oak** (Cork, County Cork): The Oak packs out at the weekends and is considered a bit of a meat market—all those young fillies aren't wearing skintight jeans for nothing. Even if you don't pull, it's a friendly crowd, downing beer as U2 blasts out from the speakers. ☎ 021/427-6165. See p. 240.

○ **Padraigs Bar** (Galway): Galway's bars are notoriously friendly but if you're still desperate when the clock strikes 12, mosey on down to Padraigs where you'll find a bunch of hearty, salt-of-the-earth types exuding 80-proof perfume from every pore. Nice. It's down on the docks and a little sketchy, but if you can't pull one of the motley assortment of natives staggering in for "just the one more" you surely are a lost cause. Not one for girls

on their own. ☎ 091/563696. See p. 153.

○ **Sister Sara's** (Letterkenny, County Donegal): Sister Sara's draws partygoers in from across the local region usually keen for action of all sorts. Top nights are the commercial dance parties on the weekends and the wild Tuesdays and Thursdays when the students gather. There's usually some sort of drinks promotion every night of the week, making the crowd even more friendly. ☎ 074/912-2238. See p. 383.

○ **Earth Nite Club** (Derry, County Derry): Derry's top club is hugely popular with students from the nearby college and passing travelers. In fact, at the end of the night, you're likely to see almost everyone you took a passing fancy to earlier in the evening, turning up here. The music ranges from R&B to hip-hop and cheesy house. The clientele are notoriously youthful and up for whatever the DJ throws their way, and a lot more besides. ☎ 028/7136-0556. See p. 470.

The Best Tours Worth Taking

○ **A Paddywagon Tour** (countrywide): All aboard the big green bus for a hedonistic tour of Ireland with a bunch of other 20-somethings and a 100% Irish tour guide who's usually 100% up for fun. Billing themselves as "luxe budget tours of Ireland," they're a great way to get to know other travelers and are gentle on the wallet, too. Tours range from a 4-day weekend bender for £229 to a 10-day All Ireland tour for £309. All include beds, food, and entrance fees. A great way to get started. www.paddywagontours.com.

○ **A Free Derry Tour** (Derry, County Derry): Community-based tours of the city from a Republican perspective. Get the real lowdown on the historic persecution of Ireland's Catholic population, the IRA,

Bloody Sunday, and the city's moves toward peace. Highly recommended. ☎ 0781/208-4903. See p. 472.

○ **A Tour of West Belfast** (Belfast): There are various ways of touring the city's troubled West Belfast Area. You can either take a Black Taxi Tour (☎ 07751/565359), which—like it says on the tin—carries you around the area in a black cab; or you could explore the urban jungle with a Belfast Safari (☎ 028/9022-2925); or wander around with a member of the Republican community who has spent time locked away as a political prisoner (☎ 028/9020-0770). All will give you the lowdown on sectarian violence in the district and show you the "peace" wall and murals, plus tell you all the stuff you never heard on the news. See p. 441.

○ *A Titanic* **Boat Tour** (Belfast): The mighty *Titanic* was built in Belfast. It took I year to design and another year to build. The Lagan Boat Company takes passengers on a boat tour right up to the original slipways that launched the tragic sinker into the River Lagan and on to meet her icy reaper. ☎ **028/9033-0844.** See p. 441.

○ **A Historical & Mythological Cycling Tour** (Northern Ireland & the Republic of Ireland): A fantastic weeklong tour encompassing the legends and myths of both Northern Ireland and the Republic, taking in the Mournes and Cooley mountains, as well as Newgrange and the Hill of Tara, before finishing off in Drogheda. It's a great way to get a taste of the North and the South and an insight into all that divides and unites them. Unfortunately it ain't cheap at €1,200 but it does include bed and board. ☎ **041/685-3772.** See p. 450.

○ **An Outback Ireland Surf Tour** (Counties Galway & Clare): A beginners' surf tour starting off at the famous slow-rolling beach break at Lahinch in County Clare. An hour and a half of individual instruction is followed by a full day of surfing. The tour includes a beach barbecue lunch and a scenic return through the desolately beautiful landscape of the Burren. Of course, it would be plain rude not to stop at a pub or two on the way home. ☎ **091/84001;** ☎ **086/814-2661.** See p. 160.

The Best Places to Avoid the Crowds

○ **The Burren** (County Clare): This extraordinary landscape looks like something from another world—desolation and beauty combined in a killer cocktail. If looking out at this moonscape doesn't fire up your soul, you're possibly not a real human being. Ponder on the vastness of time as you meander between sheets of rock created about 300 million years ago. And you won't really be alone; some of Ireland's rarest creatures—including pine martens, stoats, and badgers—hang out here. See p. 335.

○ **Mourne Mountains** (County Down): A stunning collection of 12 peaks over 600m (2,000 ft.) including the hefty Slieve Donard, which at 839m (2,796 ft.) is Northern Ireland's highest mountain. Surrounding it are gentle rolling hills and lush majestic vistas, with more than enough barren stretches of uninhabited wilderness to discover the poet within. If you do go up here alone, better watch out as the weather can turn pretty nasty in the mountains. See p. 489.

○ **Connemara National Park** (County Galway): One of the best national parks in all of Ireland: over 2,000 hectares (4,940 acres) of still glacial lakes, towering mountains, and granite moorlands. Wild, barren, and almost eerie at times, a drive through this strange landscape will take your head places it has never have been before. Not a place to get lost hiking. See p. 169.

○ **Slieve League** (County Donegal): The cliffs of Slieve League are the highest in all of Europe, rising dramatically up from the turbulent Atlantic. Take in their knock-out nature from one of the view points or head out for a lonesome walk across the cliff tops. Guaranteed to make you tingle from your heart to your toe-tips. See p. 380.

The Best Oddities to Check Out

○ **Oliver Plunkett's Head** (Drogheda, County Louth): Yes, it really is a human head. Little Irish children would be brought here to see the mummified head of this 17th-century saint as a day out on their school holidays. It sits in a sealed glass container and is strangely serene but still really quite weird. Treat yourself. See p. 131.

○ **Ferret Racing** (Nohoval, County Cork): At Claybird you can watch furry little rodents Max, Champ, and his friends race each other down a track while you place bets. If that's not your bag, there are various shooting sports on offer, too. Something to get acquainted with the ways of the Irish countryside. ☎ 021/488-7149. See p. 258.

○ **The Wolfe Tone** (Letterkenny, County Donegal): Now, you're not going to want to spend all night in this bar, but if you're in the area do stop by. It is one of the most bizarre bars in Ireland. A full-on lesson in the history of the Republican struggle replete with a hunger strikers' corner and the medals of Irish revolutionaries. Needs to be done. ☎ 074/912-4472. See p. 383.

○ **Dzogchen Beara Retreat** (Centre Castletownbere, County Cork): A small town with a very un-Irish attraction: a secluded Tibetan Buddhist retreat overlooking the ocean. Sign up for a number of seminars all aimed at attaining "rigpa" or intelligence and awareness. Damn fine idea. ☎ 027/73032. See p. 265.

The
Basics

Chances are that you've been looking forward to this trip to Ireland for some time. You've probably set aside some hard-earned cash, taken time off from work, or other commitments, and now want to make the most of your vacation. So where do you start?

The aim of this chapter is to provide you with the information you need to make sound decisions when planning your trip: When should you go? How will you get there? Should you book a tour or travel independently? What should you pack? How much will it cost? You'll find all the necessary resources, along with addresses, phone numbers, and websites, here.

The Lay of the Land

The island of Ireland is comprised of the Republic of Ireland and Northern Ireland, with the Atlantic Ocean to the west and the Irish Sea to the east. Dublin, the capital city of the Republic, shares nearly the same latitude as Edmonton, Alberta, and Bremen, Germany, but its climate is much warmer, thanks to the presence of the Gulf Stream sending its warm currents northward.

With a landmass of approximately 84,434 sq. km (32,929 sq. miles), the island is roughly the same size as the state of Maine. In rounded figures, it is at most 484km (300 miles) north to south, and 274km (170 miles) east to west. No point in Ireland is farther than 113km (70 miles) from one of its encircling waters: the Atlantic Ocean, the Irish Sea, or the St. George and North channels.

Shaped like a saucer, Ireland's twisted, 3,228km (2,000-mile) coastline largely consists of rugged hills and low mountains, with sea cliffs to the west. Its interior is generally a rolling limestone plain of fertile farmland and peat bogs. Ireland's longest river is the Shannon, flowing 371km (230 miles) south and west across the midlands from its source in the Cuileagh Mountains of County Cavan to its estuary in County Limerick. The island's largest lake, Lough Neagh, occupies 396 sq. km (153 sq. miles) of counties Antrim and Armagh in the north.

Ireland

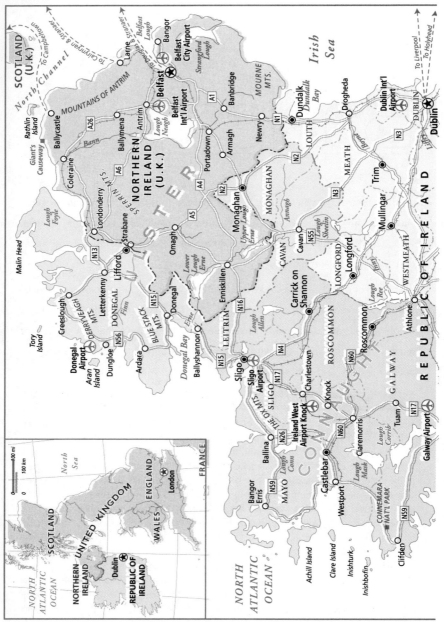

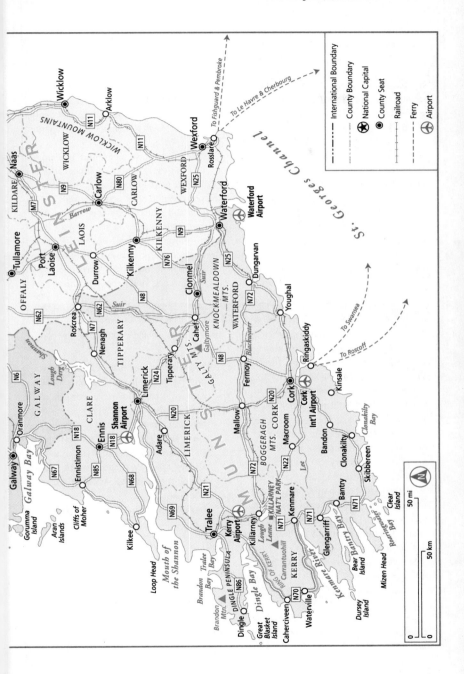

Technically speaking, Ireland has no mountains, only hills, although they call them mountains anyway because they are quite high—its highest peak, Carantuohill in County Kerry, reaches about 1,020m (3,346 ft.). Most of the heights, whether mountains or hills, were rounded off and smoothed into graceful slopes tens of thousands of years ago by receding glaciers.

One of Europe's least densely populated countries (third to last behind Finland and Sweden), Ireland is commonly described as unspoiled, even "untouched," but that's actually not true. The island was once entirely forested but—much like Scotland—has been almost completely cleared over time. Only about 1% of the hardwood forests survive, and Ireland has imported almost all its wood for the last 200 years. Relatively recently, there has been an effort to plant pine forests, and the government has created 60 forest parks.

Ireland has six national parks: Connemara National Park in County Galway, Glenveagh National Park in County Donegal, Killarney National Park in County Kerry, Wicklow Mountains National Park in County Wicklow, Burren National Park in County Clare, and Mayo National Park in County Mayo.

Many prehistoric bogs and limestone plains still survive, and the predominance of small-scale mixed agriculture contributes to the preservation of an unusually wide range of flora and fauna in the countryside, with the famous exception of snakes. As it happens, Mother Nature, not St. Patrick, deserves credit for Ireland's lack of snakes—all she gave to the island, herpetologically speaking, is one lonely common lizard.

The Regions in Brief

The island is divided into two major political units—Northern Ireland, which, along with England, Scotland, and Wales, forms the United Kingdom; and the Republic of Ireland. Of the 32 counties in Ireland, 26 are in the Republic. Of the four historic provinces, three and part of the fourth are in the Republic.

The line partitioning the land and people of Ireland into two separate entities became an official boundary in 1922, when the Republic became a free state. For some Irish on both sides of the border, the division of the island remains a matter of dispute, but in practical terms, the line between north and south represents a national border, although it is no longer unmarked.

Still very much alive to the Irish, however, is the ancient Gaelic set of divisions: Ulster is north, Leinster is east, Munster is south, and Connaught is west.

Newer divisions are provided by the 32 **counties.** Grouped under the four traditional provinces of Ireland cited below, the counties are:

> **In Ulster** (to the north): Cavan, Donegal, and Monaghan in the Republic; Antrim, Armagh, Derry, Down, Fermanagh, and Tyrone in Northern Ireland.
>
> **In Munster** (to the south): Clare, Cork, Kerry, Limerick, Tipperary, and Waterford.
>
> **In Leinster** (to the east): Dublin, Carlow, Kildare, Kilkenny, Laois, Longford, Louth, Meath, Offaly, Westmeath, Wexford, and Wicklow.
>
> **In Connaught** (to the west): Sligo, Mayo, Galway, Roscommon, and Leitrim.

DUBLIN & ENVIRONS With 40% of the Republic's population living within 97km (61 miles) of Dublin, the capital is the center of the profound, high-speed changes that have been transforming Ireland into a prosperous and increasingly European country, and it has been changed the most. Within an hour's drive of Dublin are Dalkey, Dùn Laoghaire, and many other engaging coastal towns, the rural beauty of the Wicklow Mountains, and the prehistoric ruins in County Meath.

THE SOUTHEAST   Boasting the warmest and driest weather in Ireland, heading to the southeast coast is one alternative to going to a pub to get out of the rain. Along with its weather, the southeast offers sandy beaches, Waterford's city walls and crystal works, Kilkenny and Cahir castles, the Rock of Cashel, the Irish National Heritage Park at Ferrycarig, and Ireland's largest bird sanctuary, on the Saltee Islands.

CORK & ENVIRONS   Cork, Ireland's second largest city, feels like a buzzy university town, and provides a congenial gateway to the south and west of the island. Within arm's reach of Cork are the famous Blarney Castle (with its more famous stone), the culinary and scenic delights of Kinsale, the Drombeg Stone Circle, Sherkin and Clear islands, and Mizen Head. Also in this region is the dazzling landscape of West Cork.

THE SOUTHWEST   The mountains and seascapes of the southwest, the wettest corner of Ireland, are also very pretty; there are more important things in life than staying dry. The once-remote splendors of County Kerry have long since ceased to be a secret, so at least during the high season, be prepared to share the view. Highlights are the Dingle Peninsula, and the Skellig and the Blaskett islands. Killarney was put on the map by its surrounding natural beauty, and is now synonymous with souvenir shops and tour buses. The "Ring of Kerry" (less glamorously known as N70 and N71), the circuit of the Iveragh Peninsula, is the most visited attraction in Ireland next to the Book of Kells. That's both a recommendation and a warning. Killarney National Park provides a dramatic haven from tour buses and the din of camera shutters.

THE WEST   The west of Ireland offers a first taste of Ireland's wild beauty and striking diversity for those who fly into Shannon Airport.

County Limerick has an array of impressive castles: Knappogue, Bunratty, King John's, Ashrod, and (just over the county line in Galway) Dunguaire. County Clare's natural offerings—the Cliffs of Moher and the lunar landscape of the Burren—are unforgettable. Farther up the coast to the north, past Galway, County Mayo is home of the sweet town of Westport on Clew Bay. Achill Island, Ireland's largest, is a favored vacation spot and is accessible by car.

GALWAY & ENVIRONS   Galway just may be the perfect small city. It is vibrant, colorful, and funky—a youthful, prospering port and university city, and the self-proclaimed arts capital of Ireland with theater, music, dance, and a vibrant street life. County Galway is the gateway to Connemara's moody, melancholy, magical landscapes. Here are the Twelve Bens mountains, Kylemore Abbey, and the charming town of Clifden. Offshore lie the mysterious Aran Islands—Inishmore, Inishmaan, and Inisheer—with their irresistible desolation.

THE NORTHWEST   In Ireland it's easy to become convinced that isolated austerity is beautiful, and nowhere is this more true than Donegal, with its jagged, desolate coastline that, if you don't mind the cold, offers some of the finest surfing in the world. Inland, the Glenveagh National Park offers as much wilderness as you could ever want. County Sligo has a dense collection of megalithic sites: stone circles, passage tombs, dolmens, and cairns at Carrowmore, Knocknarea, and Carrowkeel. This region inspired the poetry of W. B. Yeats.

THE MIDLANDS   The lush center of Ireland, bisected by the lazy River Shannon, is a land of pastures, rivers, lakes, woods, and gentle mountain slopes, a lush antidote to the barren beauty of Connemara and a retreat, in high season, from the throngs of tourists who crowd the coasts. The shores and waters of the Shannon and Lough Derg and of their many lesser cousins provide much of the lure. Outdoor pursuits—cycling, boating, fishing, and hiking—are the heart of the matter here. The midlands also hold remarkable sites— Birr Castle and its splendid gardens, and Clonmacnois, the evocative ruins of a famous Irish monastic center.

NORTHERN IRELAND   Across the border, Northern Ireland's six counties are undergoing a time of intense change, as peace has held there for nearly a decade. Still one of the most underrated parts of the island, the stunning Antrim coast (particularly between Ballycastle and Cushendum), the bizarre, octagonal basalt columns of the Giant's Causeway, and the alluring Glens of Antrim are unforgettable. The loveliness of the Fermanagh Lake District to the south is written in a minor key. The old city walls of Derry, the past glory of Carrickfergus Castle, and Belfast's elaborate political murals all make a trip across the border worthwhile.

Visitor Information

When you're first getting started, contact your local offices of the Irish Tourist Board and the Northern Ireland Tourist Board. They are eager to answer your questions and have stacks of helpful information, mostly free of charge.

After you've perused the brochures, check the appropriate websites for more information.

Note: While tourism offices should often be approached with caution—their unmitigated enthusiasm for *everything* can make their advice seem a bit suspect—the Irish versions are among the best of the lot. The tourism office in Dublin will do everything for you but your laundry (and they might do that, we've never asked). Their websites are handy methods for dipping your toe in the Irish traveling water.

In the United States

○ **Irish Tourist Board,** 345 Park Ave., New York, NY 10154 (☎ **800/223-6470** in the U.S. or 212/418-0800; fax 212/371-9052; www.tourismireland.com).

○ **Northern Ireland Tourist Board,** 551 Fifth Ave., Suite 701, New York, NY 10176 (☎ **800/326-0036** in the U.S. or 212/922-0101; fax 212/922-0099; www. discovernorthernireland.com).

In Canada

○ **Irish Tourist Board,** 2 Bloor St. W., Suite 1501, Toronto, ON M4W 3E2 (☎ **800/ 223-6470** or 416/925-6368; fax 416/ 929-6783; www.tourismireland.com).

○ **Northern Ireland Tourist Board,** 2 Bloor St. W., Suite 1501, Toronto, ON M4W 3E2 (☎ **800/576-8174** or 416/925-6368; fax 416/925-6033; www.discovernorthern ireland.com).

In the United Kingdom

○ **Irish Tourist Board,** 150 New Bond St., London W1Y 0AQ (☎ **020/7493-3201;** fax 020/7493-9065; www.tourismireland.com).

Frommers.com

www.frommers.com offers travel tips, reviews, monthly vacation giveaways, bookstore, and online booking. The Frommers.com Newsletter contains the latest deals, travel trends, and money-saving secrets; our Community area has message boards, where Frommer's readers post queries and share advice. The Online Reservations System (www. frommers.com/book_a_trip) takes you to Frommer's preferred online partners for booking.

Smoke Out

And everybody said it would never work. In 2004, Ireland passed a sweeping, nationwide, anti-smoking law banning cigarettes, pipes, and cigars in virtually all public places including bars, restaurants, shops—you name the place, you can't smoke there. They even toyed with the idea of banning smoking in hotel rooms, based on the argument that room cleaners should not have to breathe any residual smoke left behind after the residents move on, but they dropped that one. For now.

So strict was the anti-smoking edict that most of Europe predicted it could never work—the Irish are known to be a hard drinking, heavy smoking crew. But Ireland surprised them all by embracing the law. It's been hugely successful. The air in Ireland's bars and restaurants is as clear as a summer's day, and it's likely to stay that way.

Californians and New Yorkers will know the drill—no smoking with supper, no puffing with your pint, no lighting up before you've alighted from buses or trains. But smokers, don't despair. The Irish haven't given up on the old cancer sticks—they've just made smoking a bit of a moveable beast. Virtually every pub and restaurant have created a beer patio outside, and the best are covered and warmed by outside heaters. In fact, outside is the new inside in many bars. With all the smokers outside, nonsmokers quickly followed, and it is not that unusual to walk into a bar and find it completely empty—its crowds all having decamped to the beer garden to hang out with the smokers.

These beer gardens have also become the hottest pickup joints, where bumming a light is still a great way to look deep into a handsome stranger's eyes and . . . well, introduce yourself for a start.

Whatever you do, don't forget the law exists. Bartenders and waiters are pretty unforgiving, and the law is enforced strictly. Expected to be hustled right out of a place if you break the nonsmoking rules.

○ **Northern Ireland Tourist Board,** 24 Haymarket, London SW1 4DG (☎ 020/7766-9920; fax 020/7766-9929; www.discovernorthernireland.com).

In Australia

○ **All Ireland Tourism** (Republic and Northern Ireland), 36 Carrington St., 5th Level, Sydney, NSW 2000 (☎ 02/9299-6177; fax 02/9299-6323; www.tourismireland.com).

In New Zealand

○ **Irish Tourist Board,** Dingwall Building, Second Floor, 87 Queen St., Auckland (☎ 0064-9/379-8720; fax 0064-9/302-2420; www.tourismireland.com).

In Ireland

○ **Irish Tourist Board/Bord Fáilte,** Baggot Street Bridge, Dublin 2 (☎ 1890-525-525; fax 01/602-4100; www.ireland.travel.ie).

○ **Northern Ireland Tourist Board,** 16 Nassau St., Dublin 2 (☎ 01/679-1977; fax 01/679-1863; www.discovernorthern ireland.com).

In Northern Ireland

○ **Irish Tourist Board,** 53 Castle St., Belfast BT1 1GH (☎ 028/9032-7888; fax 028/9024-0201; www.tourismireland.com).

○ **Northern Ireland Tourist Board,** St. Anne's Court, 59 North St., Belfast BT1 1NB (☎ 028/9023-1221; fax 028/9024-0960; www.discovernorthernireland.com).

THE BASICS

Getting In & Out

Passports, Visas & Customs

This is one of the more critical areas of planning your trip. Getting your paperwork lined up is a very good idea, and it's usually fairly easy, depending upon where you live. For citizens of the United States, Canada, Australia, and New Zealand entering the Republic or Northern Ireland for a stay of up to 3 months, no visa is necessary, but a valid passport is required.

Tip: Allow plenty of time before your trip to apply for a passport; processing normally takes 4 weeks but can take longer during busy periods (especially spring). When traveling, guard your passport with your life. Those things are worth money on an international black market, and so there are people out there who would love to get their hands on it. Keep it tucked away in a money belt, and keep a separate photocopy of the pages with your photo and passport number. If you lose your passport, contact the nearest embassy as soon as possible.

What You Can Bring to Ireland

You can't just lug your kitchen with you into foreign countries, you know. There are rules. Still, you can bring a lot of stuff into Ireland. Overseas visitors, including U.S. and Canadian citizens, are allowed to bring in duty-free: 200 cigarettes (that's cigarettes themselves, not cigarette packs; don't get carried away), 1 liter of liquor, 2 liters of wine, and other goods (including beer) not exceeding a value of €150 ($181) per adult.

Don't even think about bringing any firearms, ammunition, explosives; narcotics; meat, poultry, plants, or their byproducts; or domestic animals from outside the United Kingdom.

What You Can Bring Home

On board the flight back home, you'll be given a Customs declaration to fill out. A few tips might be handy at this point, for those of you with trust funds: It's a good idea to keep receipts to prove your expenditures, just in case, although we've never been asked for them. If you owe duty, you must pay it on your arrival in the United States, either by cash, personal check, government or traveler's check, or money order, and in some locations, a Visa or MasterCard.

Sometimes—rarely—Customs can get a bit intense, so if you're going to be carrying a lot of electronics or fur coats or your Prada shoes, you might want to bring something that proves you owned it all before your trip, just to avoid any tension between you and the Customs agents. You can bring along an old receipt, insurance policy, jeweler's appraisal, or the like, if that's possible, which it probably isn't. Alternatively, you can register items with Customs before you leave, and get a serial number or marking for things like laptop computers, cameras, or CD players, which guarantees no hassle.

Take the items to any Customs office or register them with Customs at the airport from which you're departing. You'll receive, at no cost, a Certificate of Registration, which allows duty-free entry for the life of the item. It's a pain, and probably not necessary, but if you're freaking out about it, go ahead and do it.

If you've gone shopping crazy it's probably still okay, since U.S. citizens are allowed to bring back $800 worth of merchandise duty-free, but they're charged duty fees on anything above that. For more info on what you can bring back, download the free pamphlet *Know Before You Go* from www.cbp.gov. (Click on "Travel," and then click on "Know Before You Go.")

Canada allows its citizens a C$750 exemption, and you're allowed to bring back duty-free one carton of cigarettes, 1 can of tobacco, 40 imperial ounces of liquor, and 50 cigars per adult. In addition, you're allowed to mail gifts to Canada valued at less than C$60 a day, provided (weirdly) that they're unsolicited and (unsurprisingly) don't contain alcohol or tobacco (write on the package "Unsolicited gift, under $60 value"). All valuables should be declared on the Y-38 form before departure from Canada, including serial numbers of valuables you already own, such as expensive electronics. For a summary of Canadian rules, download the booklet *I Declare* from the Canada Border Services Agency (www.cbsa-asfc.gc.ca).

Citizens of the U.K. who are returning from Ireland go through a separate Customs Exit (called the "Blue Exit"). For you guys it's basically open season, since there is no limit on what you can bring back from an E.U. country as long as the items are for personal use, and you have already paid the necessary duty and tax. However, Customs law sets out "guidance levels" (uh-oh), and if you bring in more than those recommendations, you may get a few questions. Some of these "guidance levels" are 3,200 cigarettes, 200 cigars, 400 cigarillos, 3 kilograms of smoking tobacco, 10 liters of spirits, 90 liters of wine, and 110 liters of beer. Now, *that's* a party.

Passport Savvy

Allow plenty of time before your trip to apply for a passport; processing normally takes 4 weeks but can take longer during busy periods (especially spring). And keep in mind that if you need a passport in a hurry, you'll pay a higher processing fee. When traveling, safeguard your passport in an inconspicuous, inaccessible place like a money belt and keep a copy of the critical pages with your passport number in a separate place. If you lose your passport, visit the nearest consulate or embassy of your native country as soon as possible for a replacement.

The duty-free allowance in Australia is A$400 or, for those under 18, A$200. Aussies can bring in 250 cigarettes or 250 grams of loose tobacco, and 1,125 milliliters of alcohol. If you're returning with valuables you already own, such as foreign-made cameras, you should file form B263. Download the brochure *Know Before You Go* from Australian Customs Service (www.customs.gov.au).

THE BASICS

Money, Money, Money, Money (Money!)

The Republic of Ireland is part of the single European currency, the euro (€).

Euro notes come in denominations of €5, €10, €20, €50, €100, €200, and €500. The euro is divided into 100 cents; coins come in denominations of €2, €1, 50¢, 20¢, 10¢, 5¢, 2¢, and 1¢. It may seem awkward, particularly for Americans, but the terms "euro" and "cent" are never pluralized. That is, €50.25 is spoken as "50 euro, 25 cent."

Northern Ireland, as part of the U.K., uses the British pound (£). The British pound is not legal tender in the Republic, and the euro is not legal tender in the North—if you're traveling in both parts of Ireland, you'll need

some of both currencies, although shops right on the borderline tend to accept both.

The British currency used in Northern Ireland has notes in denominations of £5, £10, £20, £50, and £100. Coins are issued in £2, £1, 50p, 20p, 10p, 5p, 2p, and 1p denominations.

Note for U.S. Travelers: The value of the U.S. dollar has been fluctuating a great deal lately, so it is best to begin checking exchange rates well in advance of your visit to get a feel for where it will stand for your trip.

The best way to get cash is with your bank card in an automated teller machine (ATM), widely known as a "cashpoint" here. Any town large enough to have a bank branch (all

Online Traveler's Toolbox

Veteran travelers usually carry some essential items to make their trips easier. Following is a selection of handy online tools to bookmark and use.

→ **Airplane Seating & Food:** Find out which seats to reserve and which to avoid (and more) on all major domestic airlines at www.seatguru.com. And check out the type of meal (with photos) you'll likely be served on airlines around the world at www.airlinemeals.com.

→ **Hotel Room Emergencies:** If you arrive without a room, or find that your room booking has mysteriously disappeared, don't despair; this Irish tourism office website does an excellent job of finding available hotel space: www.gulliver.ie.

→ **Disabilities Issues:** People with disabilities may have questions or encounter problems and need somebody to talk to. An excellent place to turn to is Disability Information Ireland, where the website may have all the answers, **www.disability.ie**.

→ **Events & Attractions:** If you want to find out what's going on where you are, when you're there, the first place to look is the excellent Irish tourism website, which has an up-to-date calendar and loads of helpful info, **www.ireland.travel.ie**.

→ **What's Up in the North:** If you're headed to the North of Ireland, you can get the lowdown from the Northern Irish Tourism Office, which has an excellent site with plenty of good info at www.ni-tourism.com.

→ **Visa ATM Locator** (www.visa.com) or **MasterCard ATM Locator** (www.mastercard.com): Find ATMs in hundreds of cities in the United States and around the world.

→ **Intellicast** (www.intellicast.com) and **Weather.com** (www.weather.com): Gives weather forecasts for all 50 states and for cities around the world.

→ **Mapquest** (www.mapquest.com): This best of the mapping sites lets you choose a specific address or destination, and in seconds, it will return a map and detailed directions.

→ **Cybercafes.com** (www.cybercafes.com) or **Net Café Guide** (www. netcafeguide.com/mapindex.htm): Locate Internet cafes at hundreds of locations around the globe. Catch up on your e-mail and log on to the Web for a few dollars per hour.

→ **Travel Warnings** (http://travel.state.gov, www.fco.gov.uk/travel, www. voyage.gc.ca, www.dfat.gov.au/consular/advice): These sites report on places where health concerns or unrest might threaten American, British, Canadian, and Australian travelers. Generally, U.S. warnings are the most paranoid; Australian warnings are the most relaxed.

→ **Universal Currency Converter** (www.xe.com/ucc): See what your dollar or pound is worth in more than 100 other countries.

but the smallest villages) will have an ATM linked to an international network—Cirrus (☎ 800/424-7787) and PLUS (☎ 800/843-7587 in the U.S. or 1800/558 002 toll-free in Ireland) are the two most popular networks. *Tip:* Using ATMs gets you the best possible exchange rate.

Credit cards are a safe way to carry money and provide a convenient record of all your expenses, and they generally offer relatively good exchange rates. Cards are widely accepted, although small rural businesses and some B&Bs do not take them. **Warning:**

Many banks add a "currency conversion fee" (sometimes as high as 3%) to every transaction made in a foreign currency; check with your card's issuer before you leave to avoid a nasty surprise when you get your bill.

When to Go

Here's the deal: In summer, transatlantic airfares, car-rental rates, and hotel prices are highest and crowds at their most intense. But the days are long (6am sunrises and 10pm sunsets), the weather is warm, and every sightseeing attraction and hostel is open. In winter you can get rock-bottom prices on airfare, especially if you book a package through a good travel agent or Aer Lingus (see "Getting There," later in this chapter). But it will rain and the wind will blow, many rural sights will be closed, as will a fair proportion of the rural hostels and restaurants.

All things considered, the ideal time to visit is in spring and fall, when weather falls somewhere in between bad and not so bad, and you still get winter prices and no crowds.

Holidays

The Republic observes the following national holidays: New Year's Day (Jan 1), St. Patrick's Day (Mar 17), Easter Monday (variable), May Day (May 1), first Mondays in June and August (Summer Bank Holidays), last Monday in October (Autumn Bank Holiday), Christmas (Dec 25), and St. Stephen's Day (Dec 26). Good Friday (the Friday before Easter) is mostly observed, but not statutory.

In the North, the schedule of holidays is the same as in the Republic, with some

exceptions: The North's Summer Bank Holidays fall on the last Mondays of May and August; the Battle of the Boyne is celebrated on Orangeman's Day (July 12); and Boxing Day (Dec 26) follows Christmas.

Weather

Nowhere but Ireland will you hear the phrase, "Today we can expect showers, followed by periods of rain." In fact, rain is the constant in Irish weather, although brief moments of sunshine are usually just around the corner. The best of times and the worst of times are often only hours, or minutes, apart. It can be quite chilly when it rains, even in the summer, so think *layers* when you travel.

Winters can be quite brutal, as the wind blows in off the Atlantic with numbing constancy, and gales are common. But deep snow is rare, and temperatures rarely drop much below freezing. In fact, Ireland is a fairly temperate place: January and February bring frosts but seldom snow, and July and August are very warm, but rarely hot. The Irish consider any temperature over 68°F (20°C) to be "roasting," and below 34°F (1°C) as bone-chilling. For a complete online guide to Irish weather, consult **www.ireland.com/weather**.

THE BASICS

Average Monthly Temperatures in Dublin

	Jan	Feb	Mar	Apr	May	June	July	Aug	Sept	Oct	Nov	Dec
Temp (°F)	36–46	37–48	37–49	38–52	42–57	46–62	51–66	50–65	48–62	44–56	39–49	38–47
Temp (°C)	2–8	3–9	3–9	3–q	6–14	8–17	11–19	10–18	9–17	7–13	4–9	3–8

Health & Insurance

Travel insurance is a very good idea if things ever go wrong in your life. If you ever miss a plane or lose your tickets or forget important things (and who can say this never happens to them?), you might as well get it. It's not terribly expensive, and, while it is no panacea, it's useful. However, don't be too trusting. Insurance companies have to make money somehow, you know? Always check the fine print before you sign on; more and more policies have enormous built-in exclusions and restrictions that may leave you out in the cold if something goes wrong and you actually need to file a claim.

If you don't know where to go to get insurance, you might want to contact one of the following popular insurers:

○ Access America (☎ **800/284-8300;** www.accessamerica.com)
○ Travel Guard International (☎ **800/ 826-4919;** www.travelguard.com)
○ Travel Insured International (☎ **800/ 243-3174;** www.travelinsured.com)
○ Travelex Insurance Services (☎ **888/ 457-4602;** www.travelex-insurance.com)

Medical Insurance

Most health insurance policies cover you if you get sick away from home, but check, particularly if you're insured by an HMO because they don't seem to cover much of anything. Most out-of-country hospitals make you pay your bills upfront, and send you a refund after you've returned home and filed the necessary paperwork. Members of Blue Cross/Blue Shield can now use their cards at select hospitals in most major cities worldwide (☎ **800/ 810-BLUE** or www.bluecares.com for a list of hospitals).

If you don't have insurance at home, try one of the following companies for your trip:

○ MEDEX International, 8501 LaSalle Rd., Suite 200, Towson, MD 21286 (☎ **888/ MEDEX-00** or 410/453-6300; fax 410/ 453-6301; www.medexassist.com)
○ Travel Assistance International (☎ **800/ 821-2828;** www.travelassistance.com), P.O. Box 668, Mullersville, MD 21108 (for general information on services, call the company's Worldwide Assistance Services, Inc., at ☎ **800/777-8710**)

Safety & Scams

Dublin and Belfast have a small but steady problem with your typical urban crime: pickpockets, purse-snatchers, car thieves, and drugs. There's also quite a lot of drunks to be found staggering around on weekend nights, and that can be intimidating, if nothing else. To alert visitors to potential dangers, the Dublin Police (called the Garda) publish a small leaflet, *A Short Guide to Tourist Security,* which is available at tourist offices and other public places. It offers the usual (sound) advice: Don't carry large amounts of money or important documents like your passport or airline tickets when strolling around; don't

leave cars unlocked or cameras, iPods, or laptops unattended. Be alert and aware of your surroundings, and do not wander in lonely areas alone at night.

The north of Ireland, of course, has been infamous for political unrest and violence, but that situation has changed since the Good Friday Agreement brought a truce of sorts between the two factions. Occasionally, however, flare-ups do happen, especially during the Protestant "marching season" in the late summer. Still, visitors rarely, if ever, have problems with sectarian strife, since they are simply not the target of it. If you have any questions or concerns, contact the U.S. State Department to obtain the latest safety recommendations (☎ **202/647-5225;** http://travel.state.gov).

Getting Wired

These days it's hard to find a city of any size that *doesn't* have a cybercafe, and there are plenty in Dublin, Belfast, Derry, and Galway. Even some small towns have the occasional entrepreneur who has added a few computer terminals to a tea shop or pub.

Although there's no definitive directory for cybercafes—these are independent businesses, after all—two places to start looking are at www.cybercaptive.com and www.cybercafe.com.

Most youth hostels have at least one computer with Internet access, and public libraries offer Internet access free or for a small charge. Avoid hotel business centers unless you're willing to pay higher rates.

If you've got your laptop with you, you'll soon find that Wi-Fi (wireless fidelity) is not nearly as widespread in Ireland and the U.K. as it is in the U.S. In fact, it's still relatively rare to come across hotels that offer it, and virtually no coffee shops outside of inner-city Starbucks do at this time. Most business-class hotels do have dataports for laptop modems, and quite a few offer high-speed Internet access if you have an Ethernet cable.

If you're traveling outside the reach of your ISP, the iPass network has dial-up numbers in most of the world's countries. You'll have to sign up with an iPass provider, who will then tell you how to set up your computer for your destination(s). For a list of iPass providers, go to www.ipass.com and click on "Individuals Buy Now." One solid provider is i2roam (www.i2roam.com; ☎ **866/ 811-6209** or 920/235-0475).

Wherever you go, bring a connection kit of the right power and phone adapters, a spare phone cord, and a spare Ethernet network cable—or find out whether your hotel supplies them to guests. You might want to purchase a phone cord converter at the airport so that you can plug your phone cable into the wall using the U.K./Ireland-style plug, which is flatter than the U.S. and Canadian phone plugs.

Using a cellphone outside the U.S.

The three letters you want to hear your cellphone company say to you is GSM (Global System for Mobiles). That is the big, seamless network that makes for easy cross-border cellphone use throughout Europe and dozens of other countries worldwide. If your cellphone is on a GSM system, and you have a world-capable multiband phone, you can make and receive calls across the globe. Just call your wireless operator and ask for "international roaming" to be activated on your account, and you're underway. Unfortunately, international roaming charges can be astronomical—usually $1 to $1.50 per minute.

If you're going to be in Ireland long, consider buying an "unlocked" world phone, or just having your own phone unlocked ("locked" phones restrict you from using any other SIM cards than the one your phone company supplies). If your phone's unlocked, you can buy a cheap, prepaid SIM card from local cellphone shops in Ireland. You'll get a local phone number—and much lower calling rates.

Ireland Today

This is a fascinating time to visit Ireland, because it is deep in the midst of a transition that has brought tremendous wealth to this long-poor nation, particularly to its cities and towns, but also out in the countryside. With this wealth has come increasing stability. The violence in the north has calmed, and a recognizable democratic debate grips the land. There is much disagreement still between those who think it should stay as it is—with the North still under U.K. control, and the Republic fully independent—and those who believe it should be united. There is also still tension between Catholics and Protestants, who are learning to respect each other's views, but who still whisper the words "Catholic" and "Protestant" when talking in a public place, as if to avoid attracting attention. With all of the changes, this is still the kind of place where you look over your shoulder when you talk, even in the most benign and inoffensive terms, about religion.

But that factor is something the Irish themselves seem not even to notice. To them, looking over their shoulders when talking about religion is nothing compared to the past, when they waited for bullets to fly or bombs to drop. For them, this is real democratic peace. And there is so much joy in the Republic of Ireland right now about its prosperity, and a kind of intense pride that has not been seen in this country in some time, about its independence, its strong economy, and its place within the European Union.

All this despite the fact that the boom is on the wane.

In the late 1990s the Irish economy skyrocketed, and if you put a time-lapse camera on a street corner in Dublin—like the famous photos of the Eiffel Tower going up day by day—it would have recorded a quickly changing landscape, in which buildings, bridges, and monuments were raised, admired or despised, then taken down and moved, adjusted or polished, like a fussy housewife with new kitchen appliances.

The Irish economy was called the "Celtic Tiger" in the international press, and other nations looked on enviously as the country decided what to do with its income. It was a silly kind of wealth, as the E.U. lavished one of its poorest members with subsidies so vast that, at times, the Irish seemed not to know precisely what to do with all of the money. They built bridges and clocks while traffic in Dublin ground slowly to a standstill, brought to inertia by roads too old and insufficient to handle the city's new popularity.

Over the years, though, the country got a handle on its new situation, and poured money into public transportation in its capital—developing a new tram system and widening roads, work which is still underway (meaning that you can still expect traffic trouble). It refinished roads out in the countryside,

Getting There

By Air

When you're planning your trip, there are thousands of places you can look for info, from airline websites to Irish websites to,

well, *our* website. Take your time and browse around before you go anywhere.

The "big three" online travel agencies, Expedia.com, Travelocity.com, and Orbitz. com, sell most of the air tickets bought on invested in its farms and farming communities, and, in general, became wiser and more efficient.

When the E.U.—focusing now on its eastern European members, which have intense financial needs—made it clear that it considered Ireland strong enough to stand on its own two feet, though, there was widespread panic, as the residents feared that the bad old days would return as the European money went away. So far, though, there's been little sign of that. The silly money is gone, yes, but the Irish economy is, in fact, standing firmly.

Still, wealth brings problems of its own. While many people in Ireland have become very rich, many haven't, and the disparity between the haves and have-nots has widened. Property prices have skyrocketed, and those who didn't own property before the boom hit cannot afford to buy now, particularly in Dublin, where most of the workers come into town every day on public transportation from their small homes in the distant suburbs. Prices in the inner city are extremely high. This paradoxical situation—wealth accompanied by rising crime, rural poverty, teen drug use, and urban homelessness—is familiar to many "wealthy" nations, but it was new to Ireland, and it has come as a shock.

Still, the country is working through these growing pains, and even when the Irish complain about the changes in their country over the last few years, they do so with a kind of heartwarming pride. Heartwarming because, for so very long, there was little to be proud of in an Ireland torn apart by violence, and threatened by its own intrinsic inability to ever give way, even to itself.

Now the Irish have learned what you will find out for yourself on any visit here, and that is that the new Ireland is not incompatible with the old. The country has learned how to maintain and preserve the beautiful old buildings and quiet country lanes for which it is loved, while also growing, learning, and changing into a place that *it* can love. Modern new supermarkets stand beside Georgian town houses, and many of the old Irish shops have been replaced by European and British chain stores. But these changes are cosmetic, and the Irish always find a way to sell their wares in small boutiques and shops around the country, and to make the old new again (one of the most popular Irish chains—Avoca Weavers—uses old methods to make intensely modern products from Irish wool and clay).

Yes, the old Irish spirit is still here, beneath its new facade, behind the coffee shops, the juice bars, the pricey restaurants, and expensive cars. You'll find it in the pubs, and when walking in the hills, or sharing a laugh with someone in the post office, or as you stand under an awning in the rain.

THE BASICS

the Internet. (Canadian travelers should try Expedia.ca and Travelocity.ca; U.K. residents can go for Expedia.co.uk and Opodo.co.uk.) Of the smaller travel agency websites, SideStep (www.sidestep.com) gets good reviews but it's not perfect. It's a browser add-on that purports to "search 140 sites at once," but in reality beats competitors' fares about as often as other sites do.

For spur of the moment trips, site59.com and lastminutetravel.com in the U.S. and lastminute.com in Europe get good deals, while www.itravelnet.com lists bargain fares around the world.

Ireland has three major airports (Dublin Airport, Shannon Airport, and Belfast International Airport) and eight tiny ones (Cork, Donegal, Derry, Galway, Kerry, Knock, Sligo, and Waterford).

FOR STUDENTS

STA Travel is now the world's leader in student travel, thanks to their purchase of Council Travel. It also offers good fares for travelers of all ages. ELTExpress (☎ **800/TRAV-800;** www.eltexpress.com) started in Europe and has excellent fares worldwide, but particularly to that continent. It also has "local" websites in 12 countries. FlyCheap (☎ **800/FLY-CHEAP;** www.1800flycheap.com) is owned by package-holiday megalith MyTravel. Air Tickets Direct (☎ **800/778-3447;** www.airticketsdirect.com) is based in Montreal and leverages the currently weak Canadian dollar for low fares.

FROM THE UNITED STATES & CANADA

The Irish national carrier, Aer Lingus (☎ **800/474-7424** in the U.S. or 0818/365-000 in Ireland; www.aerlingus.ie) provides transatlantic flights to Ireland with scheduled, nonstop flights from New York (JFK), Boston, Chicago, Los Angeles, and Baltimore to Dublin, Shannon, and Belfast international airports.

American Airlines (☎ **800/433-7300;** www.aa.com) flies directly from New York (JFK) and Chicago to Dublin and Shannon. Delta Airlines (☎ **800/241-4141;** www.delta.com) flies directly from Atlanta to Dublin and Shannon. Continental Airlines (☎ **800/231-0856;** www.continental.com) offers nonstop service to Dublin and Shannon from its Newark hub.

From Canada, Air Canada (☎ **888/247-2262** in the U.S. and Canada; 0180/070-0900 in Ireland) runs frequent direct flights to Shannon and Dublin from major Canadian cities.

It's possible to save money by booking your air tickets through a consolidator (sometimes called a "bucket shop"). They work with the airlines to sell off their unsold air tickets at a cut price. Savings vary wildly from miniscule in the high season to substantial in the off season. UK Air (☎ **888/577-2900;** www.ukair.com) sells tickets to Britain, Ireland, and the rest of Europe on regular Delta, British Airways, and Continental flights. Start by looking in Sunday newspaper travel sections; U.S. travelers should focus on the *New York Times, Los Angeles Times,* and *Miami Herald.* **Beware:** Bucket shop tickets are usually nonrefundable or rigged with stiff cancellation penalties, often as high as 50% to 75% of the ticket price, and some put you on charter airlines, which may leave at inconvenient times and experience delays.

The following carriers offer direct flights from London: British Airways (☎ **800/247-9297** in the U.S. or 087/085-9850 in Britain; www.ba.com); Aer Lingus (☎ **800/474-7424** in the U.S. or ☎ 0818/365-000 in Ireland; www.aerlingus.ie); Lufthansa (☎ **800/581-6400** in the U.S.; www.lufthansa.co.uk); bmi baby (☎ **800/788-0555** in the U.S. or 01/242-0794 in Ireland; www.bmibaby.com); CityJet (☎ **0345/445588** in Britain); and Ryanair (☎ **01/609-7800** in Ireland; 0906/270-5656 in Britain; www.ryanair.com). Easyjet (☎ **1890/923-922;** www.easyjet.com) offers flights to Cork, Knock, Belfast, and Shannon from airports in London and the north of England.

Belfast has two airports, Belfast International Airport (☎ **028/9448-4848;** www.bial.co.uk) and Belfast City Airport (☎ **028/9093-9093;** www.belfastcityairport.com). Airlines flying directly from Britain to Belfast include British Airways (☎ **800/247-9297** in the U.S. or 087/085-0850 in Britain; www.ba.com) In addition, there is service by a range of discount carriers, including bmi (☎ **08702/642229** in Britain;

www.flybmi.com) from London Heathrow, and flybe (☎ 0871/700-0535 in Britain; www.flybe.com) from most airports in Britain.

By Ferry

If you're traveling to Ireland from Britain or the Continent, ferries can get you there in reasonable comfort. But the days when ferries were so cheap that backpackers piled on, going miles out of their way to take them, are long gone. These days flying can be as cheap, and certainly faster and less stomach-churning, so do some price comparison before you buy.

Prices fluctuate seasonally and depend on your route, your time of travel, and whether you are on foot or in a car, but just to give you an idea, the lowest one-way adult fare in high season on the cruise ferry from Holyhead to Dublin starts at around €31.

The websites given below have regularly updated schedules and prices.

FROM BRITAIN

Irish Ferries (www.irishferries.ie) operates from Holyhead, Wales, to Dublin, and from Pembroke, Wales, to Rosslare, County Wexford. For reservations, call Scots-American Travel (☎ 800/427-7268 in the U.S.; www.scotsamerican.com) or Irish Ferries (☎ 0870/517-1717 in the U.K. or 0818/300-400 in the Republic of Ireland; 00353/818-300-400 in Northern Ireland; www.irishferries.com). Stena Line (☎ 01/204-7777; www.stenaline.com) sails from Holyhead to Dun Laoghaire, 13km (8 miles) south of Dublin; from Fishguard, Wales, to Rosslare; and from Stranraer, Scotland, to Belfast, Northern Ireland. Brittany Ferries (☎ 021/427-7801 in Cork; www.brittany-ferries.com) operates from Holyhead to Dublin; from Fishguard and Pembroke to Rosslare; and from Stranraer to Belfast. Swansea/Cork Ferries (☎ 01792/456-116 in Britain; 0033/214-271-166 in Ireland; www.swansea-cork.ie) links Swansea, Wales, to Ringaskiddy, just outside Cork City, County Cork. P&O Irish Sea Ferries operates from Liverpool to Dublin and from Cairnryan, Scotland, to Larne, County Antrim, Northern Ireland. For reservations, call Scots-American Travel (☎ 561/563-2856 in the U.S., 0870/242-4777 in Britain, or 01/638-3333 in Ireland; www.poirishsea.com). Norse Merchant Ferries (☎ 0870/600-4321 in Britain or 01/819-2999 in Ireland; www.norsemerchant.com) sails from Liverpool to Belfast. Isle of Man Steam Packet Company/Sea Cat (☎ 08705/523-523 in Britain or 01/800-80-50-55 in Ireland; www.steam-packet.com) operates ferries from Liverpool to Dublin, and from Heysham and Troon, both in Scotland, to Belfast.

FROM CONTINENTAL EUROPE

Irish Ferries sails from Roscoff and Cherbourg, France, to Rosslare. For reservations, call Scots-American Travel (☎ 561/563-2856 in the U.S.; www.scotsamerican.com) or Irish Ferries (☎ 0870-5171717 in the U.K. or 01/638-3333 in Ireland). P&O Irish Sea Ferries operates from Cherbourg, France, to Rosslare. For reservations, call Scots-American Travel (☎ 561/563-2856 in the U.S., 0870/242-4777 in Britain, or 01/638-3333 in Ireland; www.poirishsea.com). Brittany Ferries (☎ 021/427-7801 in Cork; www.brittany-ferries.com) connects Roscoff, France, to Cork.

Note to Eurailpass holders: Because Irish Ferries is a member of the Eurail system, you can travel free between Rosslare and Roscoff or Cherbourg.

Staying There: Tips on Accommodations

Ireland is very tourist savvy and there's no shortage of places to stay. Even if you're on a budget, if you don't mind being a little creative, you can stay in the most amazing places

Gulliver.ie

For hotels rooms, the Irish tourism authority has an excellent online hotel booking service known as "Gulliver" (www.gulliver.ie), which includes hundreds of fully vetted hotels, B&Bs, and guesthouses in all price categories in the Republic and in Ulster. Because it's run by the tourism office, it offers both good prices and peace of mind.

here. Youth hostels are often in incredible locations or extraordinary historic buildings. Alternatively, if you're traveling with friends you can rent a cottage, house, or even castle for remarkably low rates when split between three or four people. If you're on a budget, probably the last thing you should do is rent a normal hotel room—in most of the country, hotels are the most expensive, and least rewarding, places to stay.

Youth Hostels

An Óige, the Irish Youth Hostel Association, 61 Mountjoy St., Dublin 7 (☎ **01/830-4555;** fax 01/830-5808; www.irelandyha.org), and, in the North, YHANI (Youth Hostels Association of Northern Ireland), 22–32 Donegall

Rd., Belfast BT12 5JN (☎ **028/9032-4733;** fax 028/9043-9699; www.hini.org.uk), run dozens of exquisitely located hostels in rural Ireland. Most are in drop-dead-beautiful spots and housed in buildings of real character. Regardless of whether or not you're trying to save money, check out the website—you won't believe the views.

Self-Catering/Do It Yourself

If you're in Ireland for a week or more, you might want to consider renting a cottage, country house, or for the ambitious, even a castle. What is hugely expensive in other countries is accessibly affordable here, and the range of available accommodations is impressive. The minimum rental period is usually 1 week, although shorter periods are available in the off season. Prices range from under €154 per week for a very tiny stone cottage in an isolated area to more than €1,538 per week for large houses nearer urban areas. Groups of friends traveling together often find this the best option.

Both the Irish Tourist Board and the Northern Ireland Tourist Board prepare helpful annual guides to self-catering cottages. But you can forge your own way by contacting companies such as Rent an Irish

King for a Day

Dream of spending your vacation like a king or queen? Two companies specialize in self-catering accommodations in Ireland's historic and architecturally significant properties—including elegant Georgian manor houses, stately country mansions, lighthouses, and castles. The Irish Landmark Trust, 25 Eustace St., Dublin 2 (☎ **01/670-4733;** fax 01/670-4887; www.irishlandmark. com), rescues historic but neglected properties all over the island and restores them into fabulous hideaways, complete with period furnishings. It's a not-for-profit institution, so prices are hard to beat. Elegant Ireland, 15 Harcourt St., Dublin 2 (☎ **01/475-1632;** fax 01/475-1012; www.elegant.ie), can put you up in anything from an upscale seaside bungalow to a medieval castle that sleeps 20. As most properties are privately owned, they are priced according to what the market will bear. Bargains are harder to come by, and deals are more likely in the off season; but if you split the price with friends, you'd be amazed what you can afford.

Booking a Room

The Irish use the phrase "en suite" to indicate a room with private bathroom. A "double" has a double bed, and a "twin" has two single beds. Queen- and king-size beds are limited to pricier hotels, inexplicably.

If you are traveling from abroad, you should always have at least your first night's room booked, not just because sleeping on the sidewalk sucks, but also because you will be required to give an address for where you're staying at immigration when you arrive at the airport. Call ahead and reserve a room or book via the Internet (you should look at a property's website anyway, as that's often where the best prices and last-minute deals are posted).

If, despite our advice, you arrive in Ireland without a room reservation, first call the hostels listed in this book, but if they're booked up head to the local tourist office, which can help with their computerized reservation service known as Gulliver. In Ireland or Northern Ireland, you can also call the Gulliver line directly (☎ **00800/668-668-66**). This is a nationwide and cross-border "free-phone" facility for credit card bookings, operated daily 8am to 11pm from Monday to Friday, and 8am to 10pm weekends. Gulliver is also accessible from the United States (☎ **011-800/668-668-66**) and on the Web at www.gulliver.ie.

Despite the various systems of approval, regulation, and rating, accommodations in Ireland are quite uneven in quality and cost. Often these variations are due to location; a wonderful, budget B&B in an isolated area of the countryside can be dirt cheap, whereas a mediocre guesthouse in Dublin or Cork can cost a comparative ransom.

In any given lodging, the size and quality of the rooms can vary considerably, often without any corresponding variation in cost. This is particularly true of single rooms, which can approach Dickensian garretlike status.

THE BASICS

Cottage (☎ **061/411109**; www.rentacottage.ie), Trident Holiday Homes (☎ **01/668-3534**; www.thh.ie), Cashelfean Holiday Houses (☎ **027/62000**; www.cashelfean.com), or Irish Country Holidays (☎ **067/27790**; www.country-holidays.ie). In Northern Ireland try Rural Cottage Holidays (☎ **028/9044-1535**; www.ruralcottageholidays.com).

Hotels & Guesthouses

Here as everywhere, hotels and guesthouses vary wildly. The really spectacularly expensive ones will answer your every desire for a price. They have slamming nightclubs, luscious spas, amazing restaurants, butlers, golf courses . . . you name it. But you'll pay for the privilege. If money is an object, though, there are mainly grim, rundown, chintzy, cheap places, where particle board seems to be the only kind of wood.

We're brutally honest in this guide to try to steer you away from the latter. Generally, if you're on a budget, B&Bs, guesthouses, and youth hostels are better options than cheap hotels.

Farmhouse Accommodations

If you really want a dose of country life, try staying at one of Ireland's small, family-run farms, where you can get your hands dirty and eat some really fresh eggs. The Irish Farm Holidays Association (www.irishfarmholidays.com) produces an annual guide to farmhouse accommodations.

Note: Many lodgings close for a few days or more on and around Christmas, even when they announce that they are open year-round. If you plan to visit Ireland during the Christmas holidays, double-check that the hotels, restaurants, and attractions you're counting on will be open.

Getting Around Ireland

By Air

Because Ireland is such a small country, it's unlikely you'll be flying from place to place. If you do require an air transfer, however, the main domestic carrier is Aer Arann (☎ 011/353-6170-44280 from the U.S.; ☎ 818/210210 from Ireland or ☎ 0800/587-23-24 from the U.K.; www.aerarann.com). It operates flights between Dublin and Belfast, Cork, Derry, Donegal, Galway, Kerry, Knock, Waterford, and Sligo, as well as from Galway to the Aran Islands.

By Train

Iarnrod Eireann (☎ 1850/366222 or 01/836-6222; www.irishrail.ie) operates the train services in Ireland. With the exception of flying, train travel is the fastest way to get around the country. Most lines radiate from Dublin to other principal cities and towns. From Dublin, the journey time to Cork is 3 hours; to Belfast, 2 hours; to Galway, 3 hours; to Limerick, $2^1/_4$ hours; to Killarney, 4 hours; to Sligo, $3^1/_4$ hours; and to Waterford, $2^3/_4$ hours.

Money-Saving Rail & Bus Passes

For extensive travel by public transport, you can save money by purchasing a rail/bus pass or a rail-only pass. The options include the following:

➜ **Eurailpass:** Of the dozens of different Eurailpasses available, some are valid for unlimited rail travel in 17 European countries—but none include Britain or Northern Ireland. Other passes let you save money by selecting fewer countries. In the Irish Republic, the Eurailpass is good for travel on trains, Expressway coaches, and the Irish Continental Lines ferries between France and Ireland. For passes that let you travel throughout continental Europe and the Republic of Ireland, first-class passes begin at $588 for 15 consecutive days of travel; youth passes (passengers must be under 26 years old) begin at $414 for 15 consecutive days of travel in second class. The pass must be purchased 21 days before departure for Europe by a non–European Union resident. For further details or for purchase, call **Rail Pass Express** (☎ 800/722-7151; www.eurail.com). It's also available from **STA Travel** (☎ 800/781-4040; www.sta.com) and other travel agents. You can also find more information online at www.eurail.com.

➜ **BritRail Pass + Ireland:** Includes all rail travel throughout the United Kingdom and Ireland, including a round-trip ferry crossing on Stena Line. A pass good for any 5 days of unlimited travel within a 30-day period costs $579 first class, $419 second class; 10 days of unlimited travel within a 30-day period costs $959 first class, $669 second class. It must be purchased before departure for Ireland or the United Kingdom. Available from **BritRail** (☎ 866/BRITRAIL; www.britrail.net).

Train Tips

When buying travel tickets—air, ferry, or train—ask for either a "single" (one-way) or a "return" (round-trip).

Iarnrod Eireann/Irish Rail also offers lots of weekend-to-weeklong holiday packages or RailBreaks to practically every corner of Ireland, north as well as south.

In addition to the Irish Rail service between Dublin and Belfast, Translink (☎ **028/9066-6630;** www.nirailways.co. uk) operates routes from Belfast that include Coleraine and Derry, in addition to virtually all 21 localities in Northern Ireland. The same organization runs the Belfast city service, called Citybus.

By Bus

Bus Eireann (☎ **01/830-2222;** www.bus eireann.ie) operates an extensive system of express bus service, as well as local service to nearly every town in Ireland. Express routes include Dublin to Donegal ($4^1/_4$ hr.), Killarney to Limerick ($2^1/_2$ hr.), Limerick to Galway (2 hr.), and Limerick to Cork (2 hr.). The Bus Eireann website provides the latest timetables and fares for bus service throughout Ireland. Bus travel is usually affordable, reliable, and comfortable. See Translink for detailed information on services within Northern Ireland (☎ **028/9066-6630;** www.nirailways.co.uk/atulsterbus.asp).

By Car

Note: For details on car rentals, see p. 35 later in this chapter.

Ireland is one of those countries where having your own car can be a really good thing. It gives you the freedom to travel when you want, and to go to all the sights that are too far off the beaten path to be reached by bus or train (castles are in the weirdest places). The disadvantages of having a car become apparent every time you have to fill the tank—gas prices in Ireland are triple what you pay in the United States. In high season, weekly rental rates on a manual-transmission compact vehicle begin at around €154.

Tip: While Ireland is a tiny country, the roads in the countryside can be so narrow and winding that getting from A to B rarely takes as little time as it looks. Allow yourself plenty of time to creep along.

Unless your stay in Ireland extends beyond 6 months, your own valid U.S. or Canadian driver's license (provided you've had it for at least 6 months) is all you need to drive in Ireland. Rules and restrictions for car rental vary slightly and correspond roughly to those in the United States, with two important distinctions. Most rental-car agencies in the Republic won't rent to you if you're under 23 or if your license has been valid for less than a year.

National (N) roads link major cities on the island. Though these are the equivalent of U.S. highways, they are rarely more than two lanes in each direction, and are sometimes one lane. Most pass directly through towns, making cross-country trips longer than you'd expect. Regional (R) roads have one narrow lane of traffic traveling in each direction, and generally link smaller cities and towns. Last, are the rural or unclassified roads, often the most scenic back roads. These can be poorly signposted, very narrow, and a bit rough.

In the North, there are two Major Motorways (M), equivalent to interstates, as well as a network of lesser A- and B-level roads. Speed limits are posted. In general, the limit for urban areas is 46kmph (30 mph), for open but undivided highways 95kmph (60 mph), and for major motorways 112kmph (70 mph).

Automatic Only?

Rental cars in Ireland are almost always equipped with standard transmissions. Automatics cost extra and they run out of them. Driving on the left side of the road and shifting gears with your left hand can take some getting used to. Then consider that another fact of life in Ireland is cramped roads. Even the major Irish motorways are narrow, with lanes made for horses, and best used by small cars. Off the motorways, it's rare to find a road with a hard shoulder—leaving precious little space when a bus or truck is coming from the opposite direction. So think small when you pick out your rental car. The choice is yours: room in the car or room on the road.

Tip: Both the North and the Republic have much more severe laws against drunk driving than the U.S. The general rule is: Don't drink and drive, or you could find yourself in serious trouble.

DRIVING IN IRELAND

Irish people drive like maniacs. Seriously. Zooming into your lane, coming right at you, ignoring the rules of the road—total maniacs. Ireland is ranked as the second-most-dangerous country in Europe in which to drive (Greece comes in at number one), so you have to drive defensively and stay alert. Keep an eye out for drivers headed right at you and be prepared to put it in a ditch if some moron is in the mood for a head-on collision. Buy all the insurance the rental agency will offer you.

As of 2005, all distances and speed limits on road signs in the Republic of Ireland were changed to kilometers, while in Northern Ireland they are still given in miles. Take extra care if you're driving around the borderlands—and there are no plans to harmonize the situation in the near future—as it's easy to get confused, particularly since the border is so ill-defined. There are no signs at all. Not that the signs wouldn't be confusing—"Thank you for visiting Ireland. Welcome to Ireland." But still.

To keep safe on these crazy, curvy roads with these bonkers local drivers, try to avoid driving late at night; get off the road when it's very rainy or fog rolls in. Don't be intimidated by drivers wanting you to go faster—if they tailgate you, pull over and let them pass. Until you've got the left-side, left-handed stick, narrow-road thing down, take your own sweet time. Consider driving only an hour or two on the first day, just far enough to get to a nearby hotel or bed-and-breakfast and to get a feel for the roads.

Instead of stop signs there are "roundabouts" (what Americans often call traffic circles or rotaries), and they take a little getting used to. Remember always to yield to traffic on the right as you approach a roundabout and follow the traffic to the left. If you have to go around the circle a few times to figure out which exit is yours, do it.

One signal that could be particularly misleading to U.S. drivers is a flashing amber light at a pedestrian crossing light. This almost always follows a red light and it means yield to pedestrians, but proceed when the crossing is clear.

Finally, traffic in Dublin provides its own frustration. Don't even think about renting a car for your time in the city. The pace of traffic in the capital's city center is around 8kmph (about 5 mph) because of ridiculous traffic congestion. In addition, a recent change has replaced many of the large English-language road signs with small, hard-to-read bilingual signs in which the Gaelic words are easier to read than the English (much to the annoyance of the local population, as well as visitors). Add to that

Road Rules in a Nutshell

1. Drive on the left side of the road.
2. Road signs are in kilometers, except in Northern Ireland, where they are in miles.
3. On motorways, the left lane is the traveling lane. The right lane is for passing and speeding like a lunatic.
4. Everyone must wear a seat belt by law.
5. Children under age 12 are not allowed to sit in the front seat.
6. When entering a roundabout (traffic circle), yield to traffic coming from the right.
7. The speed limits are 50kmph (31 mph) in built-up areas; 80kmph (50 mph) on regional and local roads, sometimes referred to as non-national roads; 100kmph (62 mph) on national roads, including dual carriageways; and 120kmph (75 mph) on motorways. There are no speed limit signs anywhere.

the one-way streets and dire lack of parking, and you're better off on foot.

PARKING

Yeah, we're going on and on about this but we can't say it often enough: Don't rent a car if you're staying in Dublin. Traffic, a shortage of parking places, and one-way streets conspire to make you regret having wheels.

Double yellow lines mean **don't park here.** Dublin, in particular, cracks down hard on offenders by booting or towing delinquent cars. It will cost you around €85 to have your car unclamped, or a whopping €165 to reclaim a towed car.

In most major cities, virtually all streets are pay-to-park. Look for signs to the ticket machines; there should be one on each block or so. Some larger towns also have multistory car parks; in central Dublin they average about €2 per hour and €20 for 24 hours. Night rates are about €6 to €9 per hour. In central Dublin, you'll find parking lots on Kildare Street, Lower Abbey Street, Marlborough Street, and St. Stephen's Green West.

Parking in most villages and small towns is easy and clear. Look out for public parking lots; they're usually free and clearly marked at the edge of villages.

In Belfast and other large cities in the North, certain security measures are in place. Control zone signs indicate that no unattended vehicle can be left there at any time. That means if you are a single traveler, you cannot leave your car; if you are a two-some, one person must remain in the car while it's parked. Also, unlocked cars anywhere in the North are subject to a fine, for security reasons.

CAR RENTALS

If you want to rent a car, book it early. Leave such arrangements until the last minute—or, worse, until you get to Ireland—and you could end up walking. This is a small country, and in high season it can literally run out of rental cars.

Most airports have major international car-rental firms represented at airports and cities throughout Ireland and Northern Ireland. They include Alamo-Treaty (☎ **800/462-5266** in the U.S.; www.goalamo.com); Auto-Europe (☎ **888/223-5555** in the U.S.; www.autoeurope.com); Avis (☎ **800/230-4898** in the U.S.; www.avis.com); Budget (☎ **800/527-0700** in the U.S.; www.budget.com); Hertz (☎ **800/654-3001** in the U.S.; www.hertz.com); Murrays Europcar

(☎ **800/800-6000** in the U.S.; www.europcar.ie); National (☎ **800/227-3876** in the U.S.; www.nationalcar.com); Payless/Bunratty (☎ **800/729-5377** in the U.S.; www.paylesscarrental.com); Dan Dooley/Kenning Rent-a-Car (☎ **800/331-9301** in the U.S.; www.dan-dooley.ie).

Tip: When comparing prices, always ask if the quoted rate includes the 13.5% government tax (VAT), the €15 airport pickup fee (assuming you pick up your car right upon arrival), CDW (collision damage waiver), or theft insurance. If you have your own auto insurance, you may be covered; check your existing policy before you pay for additional coverage you may not need.

Tips for Travel on the Cheap

Student Discounts

There are lots of travel discounts available to students, teachers (at any grade level, kindergarten through university), and youths (ages 12–25). Most attractions have a reduced student-rate admission charge, with the presentation of a valid student ID card.

Two popular student ID cards are the ISE Card (International Student Exchange Card) and the ISIC (International Student Identity Card). For a look at the various travel benefits that come with membership, go to www.isecard.com and www.isiccard.com.

The International Student Identity Card (ISIC) offers a range of benefits for students aged 12 and up, including store discounts and a 24-hour emergency helpline, as well as international recognition of your student status. They cost just $22 and are available through student travel offices, universities, and so forth. Check out the ISIC homepage (www.isic.com); you can also buy them from STA Travel (☎ **800/781-4040** in North America; www.sta.com or www.statravel.com), the biggest student travel agency in the world.

If you're no longer a student but are still under 26, you can get an International Youth Travel Card (IYTC) for the same price from the same group. It entitles you to some discounts (but not on museum admissions). Travel CUTS (☎ **800/592-CUTS**; www.travelcuts.com) offers similar services for both Canadians and U.S. residents.

Money-Saving Rail & Bus Passes

If you're not renting a car, you can save money by purchasing a rail/bus pass or a rail-only pass. The options include the following:

○ **Eurailpass:** Of the dozens of different Eurailpasses available, some are valid for unlimited rail travel in 17 European countries—but none include Britain or Northern Ireland. Other passes let you save money by selecting fewer countries. In the Irish Republic, the Eurailpass is good for travel on trains, Expressway coaches, and the Irish Continental Lines ferries between France and Ireland. For passes that let you travel throughout continental Europe and the Republic of Ireland, first-class passes begin at $588 for 15 consecutive days of travel; youth passes (passengers must be under 26 years old) begin at $414 for 15 consecutive days of travel in second class. The pass must be purchased 21 days before departure for Europe by a non–European Union resident. For further details or for purchase, call Rail Pass Express (☎ **800/722-7151;** www.eurail.com). It's also available from STA Travel (☎ **800/781-4040;** www.sta.com) and other travel agents. You can also find more information online at www.eurail.com.

○ **BritRail Pass + Ireland:** This option includes all rail travel throughout the United Kingdom and Ireland, including a round-trip ferry crossing on Stena Line. A pass good for any 5 days of unlimited travel within a 30-day period costs $579 first class, $419 second class; 10 days of unlimited travel within a 30-day period costs $959 first class, $669 second class. It must be purchased before departure for Ireland or the United Kingdom. Available from BritRail (☎ **866/BRITRAIL;** www.britrail.net).

Tips for Backpackers/Creative Packing

What to Carry & What Kind of Bag to Pack

Backpacker is a figurative term. You can be a young, carefree, budget-oriented traveler even if you carry a rolling suitcase. In most cases, a rolling bag is just as convenient to carry around as a backpack, if not more so, and it can be easier to keep organized. However, when it comes to climbing stairs and covering longer distances on foot, the classic backpack can't be beat.

To maximize the space in any bag, the key words are **rolling** and **compartmentalizing.** Rolling your clothes will keep you more space-efficient and you'll fit more. As for compartmentalizing, you want to be able to access readily those things that you need most and others not so much. Put toiletries near the top or in their compartment. Keep film, camera, and so on in a separate compartment that is easily accessible, and make sure you have a separate compartment for those dirty clothes.

Another thing to keep in mind is that **you don't have to look like a schlep to be a backpacker!** Nice(r) clothes don't necessarily take up more room in your bag, so ditch the hiking boots and pack some wrinkle-free clothes so that you can look presentable when you hit the town. The reality is, unless you're taking an extreme adventure/ecotourism tour, you won't *really* be hiking too much. Mostly, you'll be traipsing around cities where the locals look effortlessly chic year-round. Lastly, we all know that shoes can take up the most room in our bags. Keep this in mind and when choosing a backpack, make sure there are straps or compartments on the outside for larger items such as shoes, sweatshirts, coats, and blankets. Regardless of whatever else you pack, you'll want that favorite, flattering pair of jeans; sneakers (comfortable but cool); comfy, non-skimpy sleepwear (for those shared hostel rooms); and a pair of rubber flip-flops for the shared bathrooms and showers you'll encounter at hostels and other budget hotels. Keep the inside of your bag free for anything fragile that you might need to protect. And remember: Since you may want to bring a few things home, it doesn't hurt to leave a few compartments empty or pack an extra, empty bag for the goodies.

What to Bring?

○ Clothes. Check the weather, but the key here is a mix of comfortable city clothes, and casual country gear; always be prepared for rain—bring a rain jacket or windbreaker.

○ Comfortable shoes and sandals. You'll be doing a ton of walking.

○ Camera and memory card. Film and batteries can be easily purchased in Ireland.

○ Extra bag to bring stuff home in.

○ Electrical plug adapter (for computers and iPod and cellphone chargers).

○ Basic medicine kit (stomach medicine, pain relievers, diarrhea medicine).

○ Prescriptions.

○ Sunblock, sunglasses, and hat.

○ A change of clothes in your carry-on bag. (Luggage frequently misses its flight when you're connecting through another European airport.)

○ Passport (and visa if necessary).

○ ATM and/or credit cards, and some cash to keep you going upon arrival.

THE BASICS

Tips for Gay Travelers

There's a burgeoning gay community in Dublin. The *Gay Community News (GCN)* is a monthly free newspaper of comprehensive Irish gay-related information, available in gay venues and bookshops. *In Dublin,* the city's leading event listings guide, dedicates several pages to gay events, club info, and a helpful directory. Two minimagazines have recently emerged—*Free!* and *Scene City*—both contain city maps with gay venues highlighted.

Among the best resources on the web are Gay Ireland Online (www.gay-ireland.com) and Outhouse (www.outhouse.ie). These include events listings, advice sections, useful contacts, and discussion forums.

The following is a selection of organizations and help lines, staffed by knowledgeable and friendly people:

○ Outhouse Community & Resource Centre, 105 Capel St., Dublin 1 (☎ **01/873-4932;** fax 01/865-0900; www.outhouse.ie).

○ National Lesbian and Gay Federation (NLGF), 2 Scarlet Row, Dublin 2 (☎ **01/ 671-0939;** fax 01/671-3549; nlgf@tinet.ie).

○ Gay Switchboard Dublin, Carmichael House, North Brunswick Street, Dublin 7 (☎ **01/872-1055;** fax 01/873-5737; www. gayswitchboard.ie), Monday to Friday 7.30 to 9.30pm and Saturday 3:30 to 6pm.

○ Lesbian Line Dublin, Carmichael Centre, North Brunswick Street, Dublin 7 (☎ **01/ 872-9911**), Thursday 7 to 9pm.

○ LOT (Lesbians Organizing Together), the umbrella group of the lesbian community, has a drop-in cafe at 5 Capel St., Dublin 1 (☎/fax **01/872-7770**), open Monday to Thursday 10am to 6pm and Friday 10am to 4pm. LOT also sponsors LEA/Lesbian Education Awareness (☎/fax **01/872-0460;** leanow@indigo.ie).

Gay and lesbian travelers seeking information and assistance on travel abroad might want to consult the International Gay and Lesbian Travel Association (IGLTA; ☎ **800/448-8550** or 954/776-2626; fax 954/ 776-3303; IGLTA@iglta.org; www.iglta.org), the trade association for the gay and lesbian travel industry, which offers an online directory of gay- and lesbian-friendly travel businesses; go to their website and click on "Members."

Many agencies offer tours and travel itineraries specifically for gay and lesbian travelers. Above and Beyond Tours (☎ **800/397-2681;** www.abovebeyondtours.com) is the exclusive gay and lesbian tour operator for United Airlines. Now, Voyager (☎ **800/255-6951;** www.nowvoyager.com) is a well-known San Francisco–based gay-owned and -operated travel service.

You might also want to pick up a copy of *Frommer's Gay & Lesbian Europe* (Wiley Publishing, Inc.), which has a chapter on Dublin's GLBT scene.

Tips for Travelers with Disabilities

There are lots of stairs and lots of steep hills in Ireland, but there are also lots of people ready to help, so don't be afraid to come here. One of the best Irish-based online resources is www.disability.ie. Click on the "Holidays" button for good advice on traveling in Ireland with a disability, and companies that specialize in helping travelers with disabilities.

The Irish Wheelchair Association, Áras Chúchulainn, Blackheath Drive, Clontarf, Dublin 3 (☎ **01/833-8241;** www.iwa.ie), loans free wheelchairs to travelers in Ireland. A donation is appreciated. Branch offices are located in Carlow, Clare, Cork, Donegal, Dublin, Galway, Kavan, Kerry, Kildare, Kilkenny, Laois, Leitrim, Limerick, Longford, Louth, Mayo, Meath, Offaly, Roscommon, Sligo, Tipperary, Waterford, Westmeath, Wexford, and Wicklow. If you plan to travel by train in Ireland, be sure to check out Iarnrod Eireann's website (www.irishrail.ie), which includes services for travelers with disabilities. A Mobility Impaired Liaison Officer (☎ 01/703-2634) can arrange assistance for travelers with disabilities if given 24-hour notice prior to the departure time.

For advice on travel to Northern Ireland, contact Disability Action, Portside Business Park, 189 Airport Rd. West, Belfast BT3 9ED (☎ 028/9029-7880; www.disabilityaction. org). The Northern Ireland Tourist Board also publishes a helpful annual *Information Guide to Accessible Accommodation*, available from any of its offices worldwide.

Finding accessible lodging can be tricky in Ireland. As a historic country, where many of the buildings are hundreds of years old, older hotels, small guesthouses, and landmark buildings still have steps outside and in. The National Rehabilitation Board of Ireland, 24–25 Clyde Rd., Ballsbridge, Dublin 4 (☎ 01/608-0400), publishes several guides, the best of which is *Guide to Accessible Accommodations in Ireland*. Also, O'Mara Travel (disability@omara-travel. com), in association with the Disability.ie website (see above), often offers special deals on accommodations to travelers with disabilities.

Many travel agencies offer customized tours and itineraries for travelers with disabilities. Flying Wheels Travel (☎ 507/451-5005; www.flyingwheelstravel.com) offers escorted tours and cruises that emphasize sports and private tours in minivans with lifts. Access-Able Travel Source (☎ 303/232-2979; www.access-able.com) offers extensive access information and advice for traveling around the world with disabilities. Accessible Journeys (☎ 800/846-4537 or 610/521-0339; www.disabilitytravel.com) caters specifically to slow walkers and wheelchair travelers and their families and friends

For more information specifically targeted to travelers with disabilities, the community website iCan (www.icanonline.net/channels/travel/index.cfm) has destination guides and several regular columns on accessible travel.

Tips for Minority Travelers

Ireland has a very small but growing population of ethnic minorities; however it has a good record for interracial relations. Minorities are unlikely to encounter problems anywhere within the country, and are very unlikely to face violence or prejudice here in their travels. Most of the prejudice in Ireland is based on religion—tension between Catholics and Protestants—rather than ethnicity or skin color. If traveling in the north of Ireland, those who are either Catholic or Protestant would be wise not to get involved in political/religious discussions about the tensions between the two religions unless they are very comfortable with the people with whom they are talking. Generally people of all religions travel safely in Ireland, but the religious tensions that have tormented this country for centuries have not gone away just because peace has been declared, so do think before you speak.

Minorities traveling in Ireland may encounter isolated problems as they might in any other European country. In fact, there have been increasing reports of race-related incidents in Ireland over the last few years. Still, acts of outright racism or prejudice are quite atypical, and racial hate crimes are very rare. Thousands of ethnic minorities travel safely in Ireland every year.

THE BASICS

Tips for Solo Travelers

In cities, take a cab home at night, and follow all the usual advice of caution you get when you travel anywhere. Don't do anything in Ireland you would not do at home.

Men

Foreign men should encounter few problems traveling in Ireland. The Irish are very familiar with international travelers, and are generally savvy about tourists and tourism. There is a bit of a macho culture out in the countryside—particularly in the north—and men should avoid getting involved in any local tensions by staying clear of discussions of politics or religion. Otherwise, though, you're likely to find that interactions with local residents are friendly and relaxed. In the end, the simple fact is that being male and foreign will neither hurt you nor help you as you wander the countryside. While Ireland is a conservative country, it is not backward, and you should feel comfortable striking up conversations with men and women precisely as you would at home.

Women

Women should expect few if any problems traveling in Ireland. The country's views on women are much more advanced now than they were even a couple of decades ago. Women traveling alone or in groups are accepted in virtually every environment, and gone are the days when women were expected to order half-pints of beer in pubs, while men were allowed to order the bigger, more cost-effective pints of brew. In fact, the only time you're likely to attract any attention at all is if you eat alone in a restaurant at night—a sight that is still relatively uncommon in Ireland outside of the major cities. Even then, you'll not be hassled. If you drink in a pub on your own, though, expect all kinds of attention, as a woman drinking alone is still considered to be on the market—even if she's reading a book, talking on her cell phone to her fiancé, and doing su doku at 100 miles per hour. So be prepared to fend them off. Irish men almost always respond well to polite rejection, though.

Specialized Tours & Resources

When you're booking a tour, think about what you want out of it. Do you want to be busy all day? Do you want a lot of free time? Decide, and then get all the info you can in advance so you know what you're getting yourself into. Ask for a complete schedule of the trip to find out how much sightseeing is planned each day and whether enough time will be left for chilling or necessary isolationism.

It's also good to know how big the group will be. Generally, the smaller the group, the more flexible the itinerary, and the less time you'll spend waiting for people to get on and off the bus. Find out the demographics of the group as well. What is the age range? What is the gender breakdown? Is this mostly a trip for couples or singles? We're not ageist or anything, but this is good information to know.

Discuss what is included in the price. You may have to pay for transportation to and from the airport. A box lunch may be included in an excursion, but drinks might cost extra. Tips may not be included. Find out if you will be charged if you decide to opt out of certain activities or meals.

Finally, if you plan to travel alone, you'll need to know if a single supplement will be charged and if the company can match you up with a roommate.

Special-Interest Tours

You can take a trip to do just about anything—see ghosts, see saints, see rocks—you name it. It all comes down to: What do you feel like doing?

The Dublin bus company, Dublin Bus (☎ 01/873-4222; www.dublinbus.ie), operates several excellent tours of Dublin and the coast to Malahide, all of which depart from the Dublin Bus office at 59 Upper O'Connell St., Dublin 1. Check out the Ghost Tour—it's both funny and a bit spooky. You can buy your ticket from the bus driver or book in advance at the Dublin Bus office or at the Dublin Tourism ticket desk on Suffolk Street.

Summer School

Got a yearning for learning? Choose from a raft of short summer courses on Irish history and culture.

Get in on the secrets of Ireland's most famous chef, Darina Allen, at **Ballymaloe Cookery School,** in Shanagarry, County Cork (☎ 021/464-6785; fax 021/464-6909; www.cookingisfun.ie).

Spend a week in Glencolmcille, County Donegal, studying the Irish (Gaelic) language, dancing, archaeology, Celtic pottery, or tapestry weaving at **Oideas Gael** (☎ 074/973-0248; fax 074/973-0348; www.oideas-gael.com).

Discover the four greatest Irish playwrights—Synge, O'Casey, Beckett, and Friel—in a 3-week course with the **Irish Theatre Summer School** and the **Gaiety School of Acting** at University College Dublin. Contact the North American Institute for Study Abroad (☎ 570/275-5099; fax 570/275-1644; www.naisa.com) for details.

For more on summer study in Ireland, get in touch with the Irish Tourist Board (p. 18).

Gray Line (☎ 01/605-7705) offers a range of full-day and multiple-day excursions from Dublin, to Glendalough, Newgrange, and Powerscourt, around the Ring of Kerry, and down to Kilkenny. For day trips adult fares range from €20 to €30.

The national bus company, Bus Eireann (☎ 091/562000; www.buseireann.ie), offers a surprisingly good range of tours throughout Ireland. You can tour Dublin and around to Glendalough or Newgrange by bus, or by boat to Waterford, and it also offers good tours of Galway, taking in the Maam Cross, Recess, Roundstone, and Clifden. Day tours start at around €22.

There are also a number of smaller tour companies, often run by locals, that offer excellent tours to various regions. Some of those are listed here.

For touring the Wicklow Mountains and Glendalough, try Aran Tours (☎ 01/280-1899; www.wildcoachtours.com), which offers a tour it has dubbed the "Wild Wicklow Tour." Wild might be too strong a word, but it is cheery, and includes visits to Avoca and Sally Gap.

A slightly less wild tour, with a more historical, intellectual approach to Ireland is Mary Gibbons Tours (☎ 01/283-9973), which offers absorbing, in-depth tours of Dublin and Glendalough.

Finally, in Belfast, do take one of the amazing Black Cab Tours (☎ 0800/052-3914; www.belfasttours.com), which are one-on-one tours with somebody affected by the "Troubles." They drive you through the Catholic and Protestant areas, show you the murals, and answer any of those pesky questions you're afraid to ask anybody else. It's real, and it's intense.

Adventure Tours

There are plenty of options for taking a more boots-on-the-ground approach to travel in Ireland. You can explore the country on foot, by bicycle, on horseback, or even by surfboard. Here are a few places to get started.

If you want to explore Ireland by bike, Backroads (☎ **800/GO-ACTIVE** or 510/527-1555; www.backroads.com) and VBT (☎ **800/BIKE-TOUR;** www.vbt.com) are both well-regarded companies offering all-inclusive bicycle trips in Ireland. Included are bikes, gear, luggage transportation via a support van, good food, and accommodations in local inns and hotels of character—everything bundled into one price.

If you want to design your own itinerary and bike independently, several rental agencies with depots nationwide permit one-way rental. They include Eurotrek Raleigh (Ireland's largest), Longmile Road, Dublin 12 (☎ **01/465-9659;** www.raleigh.ie); and Rent-A-Bike Ireland, 1 Patrick St., Limerick, County Limerick (☎ **061/416983;** www.irelandrentabike.com). Mountain and cross-country bike rental rates average €20 per day, €80 per week, and €100 for a one-way rental. You'll also have to fork up a refundable deposit of €80 per bike.

If you want your cycling trip to be orchestrated and outfitted by affable local experts, consider Irish Cycling Safaris, Belfield Bike Shop, Belfield House, University College Dublin, Dublin 4 (☎ **01/260-0749;** fax 01/716-1168; www.cyclingsafaris.com). It's run by Marian Ryan and family, who offer trips to practically every part of Ireland suitable for two wheels.

For independent cycling adventures in the southeast of Ireland, contact Celtic Cycling, Lorum Old Rectory, Bagenalstown, County Carlow (☎ **059/977-5282;** fax 059/977-5455; www.celticcycling.com). On the opposite side of the island, Irish Cycling Tours (Derrynasliggaun, Leenane, Connemara, County Galway, Ireland; ☎ **095/42302;** fax 095/42314; www.irishcyclingtours.com), offers guided and self-guided tours in the west—specifically Kerry and Connemara—for everyone from honeymooners to families to seniors to singles.

To see the country on foot, Hidden Trails (☎ **888/9-TRAILS;** www.hiddentrails.com) offers 7-day guided and self-guided hiking tours of six regions in Ireland, including the Wicklow Mountains, West Cork, the Burren, and Connemara. The tours are graded "easy," "moderate," or "challenging," and include lodging, meals (breakfast, picnic lunch, and dinner), and luggage transport to and from the trail heads. Rates average $563 per person, double occupancy, for a week.

In the west of Ireland, there's a wide selection of guided walks in the Burren, from 1 day to a week or more. Contact Burren Walking Holidays, with the Carrigann Hotel, Lisdoonvarna (☎ **065/707-4036;** fax 065/707-4567). In the southwest, contact SouthWest Walks Ireland, 6 Church St., Tralee, County Kerry (☎ **066/712-8733;** fax 066/712-8762; www.southwestwalksireland.com). For a full walking holiday package to County Kerry or County Clare and Connemara, consult BCT Scenic Walking, 227 North El Camino Real, Encinitas, CA 92024 (☎ **800/473-1210;** www.bctwalk.com).

On the Northern Ireland Tourist Board's website (www.discovernorthernireland.com/walking.aspx), there is a walking and hiking page that lists self-guided tours, 14 short hikes along the Ulster Way, and names and addresses of organizations offering guided walks throughout the North.

Ireland is a horse-loving country, with a plethora of stables and equestrian centers offering trail rides and instruction. The Association of Irish Riding Establishments (www.aire.ie) is the regulatory body that accredits stables, ensuring adequate safety standards and instructor competence. Riding prices range from €15 to €35 per hour; expect to pay €20 on average. A list of accredited stables throughout the country is available from the Irish Tourist Board (www.equestrian.travel.ie).

Equestrian Holidays Ireland (www.ehi.ie) is a collection of some 37 riding centers, each registered with the Association of Irish Riding Establishments, offering a wide variety of accommodations and riding holiday experiences. EHI properties include Dingle Horse Riding, Ballinaboula, Dingle (☎ **066/915-2199;** www.dinglehorseriding.com); and Drumindoo Stud & Equestrian Centre, Knockranny, Westport, County Mayo (☎ **098/25616**).

To hit the water, check out the Irish Canoe Union (www.irishcanoeunion.com). Kayaking and other aquatic vacations are also available at Delphi Adventure Centre, Leenane,

County Galway (☎ **095/42307;** fax 095/42303), and National Mountain and Whitewater Centre, Tiglin, Ashford, County Wicklow (☎ **0404/40169;** www.tiglin.com).

Irish dive centers and schools include The National Diving School, Malahide Marina Village, County Dublin (☎ **01/845-2000**); Oceantec Adventures, Dun Laoghaire, County Dublin (☎ **01/280-1083;** http://indigo.ie/oceantec); Baltimore Diving & Watersport Centre, Baltimore, County Cork (☎/fax **028/20300;** www.baltimorediving.com); and Scubadive West, Renvyle, County Galway (☎ **095/43922;** fax 095/43923; www.scubadivewest.com).

I Don't Want to Leave! Staying in Ireland Beyond a Mere Holiday

Study Abroad

Considering the sheer number of language schools, business colleges, and universities in Dublin alone, it's not surprising the country's student population is considerable. If you're interested in studying here, contact your university to find out if they have a partnership program in Ireland. To get basic info on whether or not you need a student visa and how to get one, consult the website www.irlgov.ie/iveagh, or get in touch with the Irish Department of Foreign Affairs Visa Section, Hainault House, 69–71 St. Stephen's Green, Dublin (☎ **01/408-2374**). U.S. firms offering educational travel programs to Ireland include Academic Travel Abroad (☎ **800/556-7896** or 202/785-9000; www.academic-travel.com), and North American Institute for Study Abroad (☎ **570/275-5099** or 570/275-1644; www.naisa.com).

If you do spend a semester or two in Ireland, contact the Union of Students in Ireland Travel (☎ **02/602-1600;** www.usit.ie). They're great for arranging travel from and around Ireland at the cheapest rates. Its

notice boards are filled with flatshares, language classes, jobs, and cheap flights.

If you're looking for less structured knowledge, try spending a week in Glencolmcille, County Donegal, studying the Irish (Gaelic) language, dancing, archaeology, Celtic pottery, or tapestry weaving at Oideas Gael (☎ **074/973-0248;** fax 074/973-0348; www.oideas-gael.com).

Discover the four greatest Irish playwrights—Synge, O'Casey, Beckett, and Friel—in a 3-week course with the Irish Theatre Summer School and the Gaiety School of Acting at University College Dublin. Contact the North American Institute for Study Abroad (☎ **570/275-5099**; fax 570/275-1644; www.naisa.com) for details.

Work Abroad

Getting permission to work in Ireland as a non-citizen is relatively easy if you have the skills and background the Irish government is looking for. Ireland has a large number of immigrant workers and has a long history of welcoming them. There are rumors of changes ahead however, and a possibility that immigration rules could be tightened in the future, so it's a good idea to stay in contact with the Irish government if you're considering moving to the country permanently.

E.U. citizens and people from Norway, Iceland, Switzerland, and Liechtenstein need no work permits. Everyone else will need to apply for one. To find out how to apply and to get further information on whether or not you'll qualify, visit the website of the **Department of Enterprise, Trade and Employment** (www.entemp.ie/labour/workpermits). Another great website to consult for information is the Irish e-government website **Information on Public Services** (http://oasis.gov.ie/employment), and you can find more forms and information at a government Web page devoted to documents for International workers (http://www.movetoireland.com).

WORK PERMITS

There are two types of work permits. The standard permit allows you to work in Ireland for only 1 year at a time. You cannot apply for this work permit yourself—you're perspective employer must apply for it and pay for it.

The other type of work permit—the working visa or work authorization—is much more coveted. It's directed at those with high-end skills in demand in Ireland. These include computer professionals, construction engineers, architects, and surveyors, as well as most medical positions. Ireland is always desperate for nurses, and makes it very easy for those with nursing qualifications to get work permits.

There are many rules and exceptions to the various limitations and requirements, so read the websites and applications thoroughly.

For more information about work permits contact **Ireland's Work Permits Division,** Department of Enterprise, Trade & Employment, Davitt House, 65a Adelaide Road, Dublin 2 (1/631 3333) or consult the websites listed above.

Eating Your Way through Ireland

Ireland has an admirable range of restaurants in all price categories. The settings range from old-world hotel dining rooms, country mansions, and castles to sky-lit terraces, shop-front bistros, riverside cottages, thatched-roof pubs, and converted houses. Lately there has been a new appreciation for creative cooking here, with an emphasis on local produce and meat.

Before you book a table, here are a few things you should know:

RESERVATIONS   Except for self-service eateries, informal cafes, and some popular seafood spots, most restaurants encourage reservations, and most expensive restaurants require them. In the most popular eateries, Friday and Saturday nights are often booked up a week or more in advance, so have a few options in mind if you're booking at the last minute and want to try out the hot spots in town.

Tip: If you stop by or phone a restaurant and find that it is booked from 8 or 8:30pm onward, ask if you can dine early (at 6:30 or 7pm), with a promise to leave by 8pm. You will sometimes get a table.

PRICES   Meal prices at restaurants include taxes (13.5% VAT in the Republic of Ireland and a 17.5% VAT in Northern Ireland). Many restaurants include the tip as a service charge added automatically to the bill (it's usually listed at the bottom, just before the bill's total). It ranges from 10% to 15%, usually hovering around 12%. When no service charge is added, tip up to 15% depending on the quality of the service. But do check your bill, as some unscrupulous restaurants do not make it clear that you have actually already tipped,

Dining Bargains

Restaurant prices in Ireland have gone up dramatically—in many cases by 20% to 25%—in recent years. Nobody is more aware of this than the Irish themselves, who are furious. Some people blame the price hikes on the changeover from the punt to the euro, some blame general inflation, and still others cite bald-faced greed on the part of restaurateurs. But there are some strategies you can use to keep your meal costs down:

If you want to try a top-rated restaurant but can't afford dinner, have your main meal there in the middle of the day by trying the set-lunch menu. You'll experience the same great cuisine at half the price of a nighttime meal.

As a final suggestion, try an inexpensive lunch in a cafe or pub. Pub food is usually a lot better than its name suggests; the menu usually includes a mix of sandwiches and traditional Irish food including stews and meat pies. In recent years, many pubs have converted or expanded into restaurants, serving excellent, unpretentious meals at reasonable prices.

thus encouraging you to accidentally do so twice.

DINING TIPS   If you splurge at an upscale restaurant, don't be surprised if you are not ushered to your table as soon as you arrive. This is not a delaying tactic—many of the better dining rooms carry on the old custom of seating you in a lounge or bar area while you sip an aperitif and peruse the menu. Your waiter then comes to discuss the choices and to take your order. You are not called to the table until the first course is about to be served.

Irish Pubs: My Home away from Home . . .

The pub continues to be a mainstay of Irish social life. There are pubs in every city, town, and hamlet, on every street and at every turn. Most people have a "local"—a favorite pub near home—where they go for a drink and some conversation with neighbors, family, and friends. Pubs are more about socializing than drinking—many people in the pub are just having a soft drink (lime and soda is a particular favorite, or orange juice and soda water). So feel free to go to the pub, even if you don't drink alcohol.

PUB HOURS   The Republic of Ireland's drinking hours were extended in the year 2000, a mere 2 centuries after they were introduced. Hours are 10:30am to 11:30pm Monday to Wednesday, 10:30am to 12:30am Thursday to Saturday, and 12:30 to 11pm Sunday (pubs previously had to close between 2–4pm). After normal drinking hours, there are always nightclubs and discos, which close at 3am.

You'll notice that when the dreaded "closing time" comes, nobody clears out of the pub. That's because the term is a misnomer. The "closing time" is actually the time when the barmen must stop serving alcohol, so expect to hear a shout for "Last orders!" or, occasionally, the marvelous but un-p.c., "Time, gentlemen, please!" Anyone who wants to order his or her last drink does so, and the bars don't actually shut their doors until up to an hour later.

In the North, pubs are open year-round from 11:30am to 11pm Monday to Saturday, and 12:30 to 2pm and 7 to 10pm on Sunday.

THE BASICS

Recommended Books, Movies & Music

Books

Ireland is one of the most written about places in the world. You've probably been reading about it all your life. If you're especially ambitious, you could bite off James Joyce's *Ulysses,* a classic to be certain, but one that is famously impenetrable. Some Joycean classics that are a bit easier to dip into include *Dubliners,* a book of short stories about the titular city, and *A Portrait of the Artist as a Young Man.*

Dive into the absorbing books and plays of Brendan Behan by finding a copy of *Borstal Boy,* his breakthrough semi-autobiographical book about growing up a member of the I.R.A. Also good is his play *Quare Fellow.*

If you're headed out into the Irish countryside, you might want to pick up a copy of W.B. Yeats *Collected Poems,* since the view you're about to see is the same one that inspired him.

Of modern writers, among the best-loved are Maeve Binchy *(Dublin 4),* J. P. Donleavy (whose book, *The Ginger Man,* about a drunken Trinity College student, was banned by the Catholic church), Roddy Doyle (whose book, *The Commitments,* about aspiring Irish musicians, became a top-grossing film), and Jennifer Johnston, who addressed the tension between Protestants and Catholics in *How Many Miles to Babylon?* There's also Edna O'Brien *(The Country Girls)* for bawdy laughs, Flann O'Brien *(At-Swim-Two-Birds)* for hilarious writing about . . . writing, and Liam O'Flaherty, whose *The Informer* is a tense thriller about a veteran of the civil war.

When it comes to nonfiction, two excellent books by Tim Pat Coogan, *The Irish Civil War* (Seven Dials, 2001), and *The Troubles: Ireland's Ordeal 1966–1996 and the Search for Peace* (National Book Network, 1997), are essential reading for anyone wanting to understand the complexities of 21st-century Ireland. For a look at modern Ireland, try John Ardagh's *Ireland and the Irish,* or F. S. Lyons, *Ireland Since the Famine.* To understand more about the Famine, try Cecil Woodham-Smith's *The Great Hunger.* It's viewed as the definitive, dispassionate examination of what really happened.

Film

Although lots of movies have been made about Ireland, not very many *good* movies have been made about Ireland. Here are a few exceptions. *Michael Collins* (Neil Jordan, 1996) is a fine biopic about the Irish rebel, filmed largely on location. *Nora* (Pat Murphy, 2000) is a good biographical film about James Joyce's fascinating and long-suffering wife. *Maeve* (John Davis/Pat Murphy, 1982) is widely viewed as one of Ireland's first proper independent films. It addresses the lives of the young amid sectarian violence. *Veronica Guerin* (Joel Schumacher, 2003) is a dark, fact-based film with Cate Blanchett about a troubled investigative reporter. *Bloom* (Sean Walsh, 2004) is a brave adaptation of *Ulysses,* with Stephen Rea. *Intermission* (John Crowley, 2003) has Colin Farrell talking in his real accent, in this Irish romance.

Music

Here are a few top Irish bands you're not likely to see playing in a bar any time soon. Damien Rice *(O)*—he did play in bars until he became a superstar a couple of years ago. The Irish folk singer Christy Moore *(Live at the Point)* is still widely viewed as one of the greatest ever. Barry McCormack has been winning accolades from critics for his *We Drank Our Tears.* David Kitt is one of Dublin's top songwriters, and you cannot go wrong with his *The Big Romance.* The Frames have been playing on the Dublin scene for years, and you can join their devoted followers by buying *Set List.* Finally, Adrian Crowley's *When You Are Here, You Are Family,* is a warm and delightful folky album well worth having in your collection.

Nuts & Bolts

American Express   The American Express offices in Ireland are in Dublin at 41 Nassau St. (☎ 1890/205511) and in Killarney on East Avenue Road (☎ 066/35722). There are no longer branches in the North. In an emergency, traveler's checks can be reported lost or stolen by dialing collect (to the U.S.) ☎ 00-1-336-333-3211.

ATM Networks   See "Money," p. 21.

Business Hours   **Banks** are open 10am to 4pm Monday to Wednesday and Friday, and 10am to 5pm Thursday.

Post offices (known as **An Post**) in city centers are open from 9am to 5:30pm Monday to Friday and 9am to 1:30pm Saturday. The GPO on O'Connell Street in Dublin is open 8am to 8pm Monday to Saturday, and 10:30am to 6:30pm Sunday (for stamps only). Post offices in small towns often close for lunch from 1 to 2:30pm.

Museums and sights are generally open 10am to 5pm Tuesday to Saturday, and 2 to 5pm Sunday.

Shops generally open 9am to 6pm Monday to Friday, with late opening on Thursday until 7 or 8pm. In Dublin's city center, most department stores and many shops are open noon to 6pm Sunday.

In **Northern Ireland,** bank hours are Monday to Friday 9:30am to 4.30pm. Post offices are open 9:30am to 5:30pm Monday to Friday and Saturday 9am to 1pm. Some in smaller towns close for an hour at lunchtime. Shopping hours are much the same as in the Republic with some smaller shops closing for an hour at lunchtime.

Car Rentals   See "Getting Around Ireland," p. 32.

Currency   See "Money," p. 21.

Driving Rules   See "Getting Around Ireland," p. 32.

Drugstores   Drugstores are called "chemist shops" and are found in every city, town, and village. Look under "Chemists—Pharmaceutical" in the Golden Pages of the Irish telephone book or "Chemists—Dispensing" in the Yellow Pages of the Northern Ireland telephone book.

Electricity   The Irish electric system operates on 220 volts with a plug bearing three rectangular prongs. The Northern Irish system operates on 250 volts. To use standard American 110-volt appliances, you'll need both a transformer and a plug adapter. Most new laptops have built-in transformers, but some do not, so beware. Attempting to use only a plug adapter is a sure way to fry your appliance or, worse, cause a fire.

Embassies & Consulates   The **American Embassy** is at 42 Elgin Rd., Ballsbridge, Dublin 4 (☎ 01/668-8777); the **Canadian Embassy** at 65–68 St. Stephen's Green, Dublin 2 (☎ 01/678-1988); the **British Embassy** at 31 Merrion Rd., Dublin 2 (☎ 01/205-3700); and the **Australian Embassy** at Fitzwilton House, Wilton Terrace, Dublin 2 (☎ 01/676-1517). In addition, there is an **American Consulate** at 14 Queen St., Belfast BT1 6EQ (☎ 028/9032-8239).

Emergencies   For the **Garda (police),** fire, or other emergencies, dial ☎ 999.

Holidays   See "When to Go," p. 23.

Information   See "Visitor Information," p. 18.

Internet Access   Public access terminals are no longer hard to find in Ireland; they're now in shopping malls, hotels, and even hostels, especially in the larger towns and more tourist-centered areas. Virtually every town with a public library offers free Internet access, though you may have to call ahead to reserve time on a PC. (For a list of public libraries in Ireland, visit **www.libdex.com/country/Ireland.html**.) Additionally, there are an increasing number of Internet cafes sprouting up across the island. We list many of these in the chapters that follow.

Liquor Laws   Individuals must be age 18 or over to be served alcoholic beverages in Ireland. For pub hours, see "Irish Pubs: My Home away from Home . . .", on p. 45. Restaurants with liquor licenses are permitted to serve alcohol during the hours when meals are served. Hotels and guesthouses with licenses can serve during normal hours to the public; overnight guests, referred to as "residents," can be served after closing hours. Alcoholic beverages by the bottle can be purchased at liquor stores, at pubs displaying OFF-LICENSE signs, and at most supermarkets.

Ireland has very severe laws and penalties regarding driving while intoxicated, so don't even think about it.

Lost & Found   Be sure to tell all of your credit card companies the minute you discover your wallet has been lost or stolen and file a report at the nearest police precinct. Your credit card company or insurer may require a police report number or record of the loss. Most credit card companies have an emergency toll-free number to call if your card is lost or stolen; they may be able to wire you a cash advance immediately or deliver an emergency credit card in a day or two. For American Express call ☎ 01/617-5555 in Ireland, for MasterCard call ☎ 1-800/557378 toll-free in Ireland, and for Visa call ☎ 1-800/558002 toll-free in Ireland.

Identity theft or fraud is a potential complication of losing your wallet, especially if you've lost your driver's license along with your cash and credit cards. Notify the major credit-reporting bureaus immediately; placing a fraud alert on your records may protect you against liability for criminal activity. The three major U.S. credit-reporting agencies are **Equifax** (☎ 800/766-0008; www.equifax.com), **Experian** (☎ 888/397-3742; www.experian.com), and **TransUnion** (☎ 800/680-7289; www.transunion.com). Finally, if you've lost all forms of photo ID, call your airline and explain the situation; they might allow you to board the plane if you have a copy of your passport or birth certificate and a copy of the police report you've filed.

Mail   In Ireland, mailboxes are painted green with the word POST on top. In Northern Ireland, they are painted red with a royal coat-of-arms symbol. From the Republic, an airmail letter or postcard to the United States or Canada, not exceeding 25 grams, costs €.65 and takes 5 to 7 days to arrive. Prestamped aerogrammes or air letters are also €.65. From Northern Ireland to the United States or Canada, airmail letters cost 45p and postcards 35p. Delivery takes about 5 days to a week.

Passports   For Residents of the United States: Whether you're applying in person or by mail, you can download passport applications from the U.S. State Department website at **http://travel.state.gov**. To find your regional passport office, either check the U.S. State Department website or call the **National Passport Information Center** toll-free number (☎ 877/487-2778) for automated information.

For Residents of Canada: Passport applications are available at travel agencies throughout Canada or from the central **Passport Office,** Department of Foreign Affairs and International Trade, Ottawa, ON K1A 0G3 (☎ **800/567-6868;** www.ppt.gc.ca).

For Residents of the United Kingdom: To pick up an application for a standard 10-year passport (5-year passport for children under 16), visit your nearest passport office, major post office, or travel agency or contact the **United Kingdom Passport Service** at ☎ **0870/521-0410** or search its website at www.ukpa.gov.uk.

For Residents of Australia: You can pick up an application from your local post office or any branch of Passports Australia, but you must schedule an interview at the passport office to present your application materials. Call the **Australian Passport Information Service** at ☎ **131-232,** or visit the government website at www.passports.gov.au.

For Residents of New Zealand: You can pick up a passport application at any New Zealand Passports Office or download it from their website. Contact the **Passports Office** at ☎ **0800/225-050** in New Zealand or 04/474-8100, or log on to www.passports.govt.nz.

Police   In the Republic of Ireland, a law enforcement officer is called a **Garda,** a member of the *Garda Siochana* ("Guardian of the Peace"); in the plural, it's *Gardai* (pronounced *Gar*-dee) or simply "the Guards." Dial ☎ **999** to reach the Gardai in an emergency. Except for special detachments, Irish police are unarmed and wear dark blue uniforms. In Northern Ireland you can also reach the police by dialing ☎ **999.**

Restrooms   Public restrooms are usually simply called "toilets" or are marked with international symbols. In the Republic of Ireland, some of the older ones still carry the Gaelic words *Fir* (men) and *Mna* (women). Among the newest and best-kept restrooms are those found at shopping malls and at multistory parking lots. Free restrooms are available to customers of sightseeing attractions, museums, hotels, restaurants, pubs, shops, theaters, and department stores. Most of the newer gas stations have public toilets, and some even have baby-changing facilities.

Safety   See "Safety & Scams," p. 24.

Smoking   See "Smoke Out" box on p. 19.

Taxes   As in many European countries, sales tax is called VAT (value-added tax) and is often already included in the price quoted to you or shown on price tags. In the Republic, VAT rates vary—for hotels, restaurants, and car rentals, it is 13.5%; for souvenirs and gifts, it is 21%. In Northern Ireland, the VAT is 17.5% across the board. VAT charged on services such as hotel stays, meals, car rentals, and entertainment cannot be refunded to visitors, but the VAT on products such as souvenirs is refundable.

Telephone   In the Republic, the telephone system is known as Eircom; in Northern Ireland, it's British Telecom. Phone numbers in Ireland are currently in flux, as digits are added to accommodate expanded service. Every effort has been made to ensure that the numbers and information in this guide are accurate at the time of writing. If you have difficulty reaching a party, the Irish toll-free number for directory assistance is ☎ **11811.** From the United States, the (toll) number to call is ☎ **00353-91-770220.**

Local calls from a phone booth require a Callcard (in the Republic) or Phonecard (in the North). Both are prepaid computerized cards that you insert into the phone instead of coins. They can be purchased in a range of denominations at phone company offices, post offices, and many retail outlets (such as newsstands). There's a local and international phone center at the General Post Office on O'Connell Street in Dublin.

Overseas calls from Ireland can be quite costly, whether you use a local Phonecard or your own calling card. If you think you will want to call home regularly while in Ireland, you may want to open an account with **Vartec Telecom Ireland** in Ireland (☎ **1800/4110077;** www.vartec.ie). Its rates represent a considerable savings, not only from Ireland to the United States but vice versa (handy for planning your trip as well as keeping in touch afterward).

To place a call from your home country to Ireland, dial the international access code (011 in the U.S., 0011 in Australia, 0170 in New Zealand, 00 in the U.K.), plus the country code (**353** for the Republic, **44** for the North), and finally the number, remembering to omit the initial 0, which is for use only within Ireland (for example, to call the County Kerry number 066/00000 from the United States, you'd dial 011-353-66/00000).

To place a direct international call from Ireland, dial the international access code (**00**) plus the country code (U.S. and Canada 1, the U.K. 44, Australia 61, New Zealand 64), the area or city code, and the number. For example, to call the U.S. number 212/000-0000 you'd dial ☎ 00-1-212/000-0000. The toll-free international access code for **AT&T** is ☎ 1-800-550-000; for **Sprint** it's ☎ 1-800-552-001; and for **MCI** it's ☎ 1-800-55-1001. *Note:* To dial direct to Northern Ireland from the Republic, simply replace the 028 prefix with 048.

Time   Ireland follows Greenwich Mean Time (1 hr. earlier than Central European Time) from November to March, and British Standard Time (the same as Central European Time) from April to October. Ireland is 5 hours ahead of the eastern United States.

Ireland's latitude makes for longer days and shorter nights in the summer, and the reverse in the winter. In June the sun doesn't fully set until around 11pm, but in December, it is dark by 4pm.

Tipping   Most hotels and guesthouses add a service charge to the bill, usually 12.5% to 15%, although some smaller places add only 10% or nothing at all. Always check to see what amount, if any, has been added to your bill. If it is 12.5% to 15%, and you feel this is sufficient, then there is no need for more gratuities. However, if a smaller amount has been added or if staff members have provided exceptional service, it is appropriate to give additional cash gratuities. For porters or bellhops, tip €1 per piece of luggage. For taxi drivers, hairdressers, and other providers of service, tip as you would at home, an average of 10% to 15%.

For restaurants, the policy is usually printed on the menu—either a gratuity of 10% to 15% is automatically added to your bill or it's left up to you. Always ask if you are in doubt. As a rule, bartenders do not expect a tip, except when table service is provided.

Water   Tap water throughout the island of Ireland is generally safe. If you prefer bottled water, it is readily available at all hotels, guesthouses, restaurants, and pubs.

Yellow Pages   The classified section of telephone books in the Republic of Ireland is called the **Golden Pages** (www.goldenpages.ie). In the North, it's called the **Yellow Pages.**

Dublin

Funky, trendy, modern, sophisticated . . . Dublin? Oh, yes.

Don't tell us, let us guess—the picture of Dublin you have in your head is of a kind of rock-solid, old-fashioned, quaint place, where Irish colleens smile shyly as they pour you a pint of Guinness, and men in wool caps sit at the bar, a pipe clenched between their teeth as they talk about the horse races.

Please. That's so 1930. Things have changed around here, you know.

Twenty-first-century Dublin is a rocking place, one of Europe's top city-break destinations, a favorite place for European urbanites, who come for a weekend of drinking, dining, and partying, and then jet off back home. It's a place where property sells for millions of euros for even the tiniest closet-size flat, where millionaires sip vintage champagne in private clubs with supermodels, where dinner out in even a casual-nice restaurant will set you back €77.

But don't let that intimidate you. It's also a young city, ambitious and energetic, packed with international students here to study at its many universities and language schools. Along with that inevitably comes a youth culture of great bars, cheap hostels, nightly gigs, slammin' dance clubs, and lots of free stuff to do with your time.

This town is compact and walkable—you can easily stroll from Parnell Square in the north down to the Grand Canal on the south side without breaking a sweat—and it's as friendly as an international city can be. Give yourself a few days to get your bearings and you'll be navigating the place like a pro.

In the summertime its lush, green squares and parks open up as vast, breezy picnic grounds, where you can loll in the sunshine and watch the girls and boys go by. In the winter the pubs look particularly inviting, as fires roar and crackle at the grate, and you can settle down into an easy chair with a creamy pint of stout and read the local papers.

So, whatever you like, and whatever brought you here, get ready to have a great time. This is a buzzing, happening, *living* city. You're going to have a great time.

Best of Dublin

○ **A Pint of Guinness in the Long Hall:** With its old-fashioned bar, fancy Victorian decor, and quirky paraphernalia—check out those muskets and chandeliers—there are few better places to sup a pint of the black stuff with some new-found friends. See p. 85.

○ **A Bargain Meal at the Porterhouse:** When you get caught out in a Dublin rain shower—trust me, you will—warm up with a bowl of steaming Irish stew at The Porterhouse for only €6. It's a great big rambling pub, with wooden floors and endless rooms. See p. 75.

○ **A Bed with Extras at the Isaacs Hostel:** No, dirty minds, not *those* sorts of extras. Taking the novel approach that cheap doesn't need to mean grim, Isaacs has lots of frills including a sauna and a restaurant. Add in a bright and friendly atmosphere and it's easy to forget this is just a hostel. See p. 66.

○ **A Snog at Zanzibar Nightclub:** Enrobed in a decor designed, surely, to summon images of naughty harems, this nightclub fulfills its purpose of providing a place for young professionals to meet other young professionals and fall helplessly in lust. See p. 83.

○ **A Shopping Spree at Cow's Lane:** The many tiny, quirky boutiques on this little lane are owned by locals, who design and make the one-of-a-kind fashions. Whatever you buy here, you're unlikely to ever run into someone else wearing the same thing. See p. 109.

○ **A Free Show on Grafton Street:** On a sunny Saturday its mimes, musicians, and artists are legion, and just watching them interact with the hassled shoppers and baffled tourists is a joy. See p. 58.

○ **A Gig at Whelans:** Everybody who was ever anybody has played in this historic music pub—and when they're not playing, they're hanging out at the bar. With its rock-cool attitude and reasonably priced pints, there isn't a better place to catch a gig. See p. 86.

Getting Around/Getting into Town

BY PLANE **Aer Lingus** (☎ **800/474-7424;** www.aerlingus.com), Ireland's national airline, operates regularly scheduled flights into Dublin International Airport from Chicago, Boston, Los Angeles, Baltimore, and New York's JFK. **Delta Airlines** (☎ **800/241-4141;** www.delta.com) flies to Dublin from Atlanta and New York, and Continental Airlines (☎ **800/231-0856;** www.continental.com) flies to Dublin from Newark. Charters also operate from a number of U.S. and Canadian cities. You can also fly from the United States

County Dublin

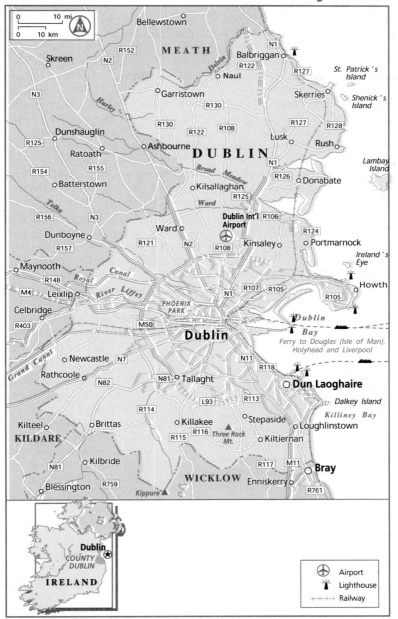

to London or other European cities and back-track to Dublin (see "Getting There," in chapter 2).

Dublin International Airport (☎ 01/814-1111; www.dublin-airport.com) is 11km (6³/₄ miles) north of the city center. A Travel Information Desk in the Arrivals Concourse provides information on public bus and rail services throughout the country.

An excellent airport-to-city shuttle bus service called AirCoach operates 24 hours a day, making runs at 15-minute intervals. Its buses run direct from the airport to Dublin's city center and south side, stopping at O'Connell Street, St. Stephen's Green, Fitzwilliam Square, Merrion Square, Ballsbridge, and Donnybrook—that is, all the key hotel and business districts. The fare is €7 one-way or €12 round-trip (children under 12 travel free); buy your ticket from the driver. Although **AirCoach** (☎ 01/844-7118; www.aircoach.ie) is slightly more expensive than the Dublin Bus (see below), it is faster because it makes fewer intermediary stops and speeds you right into the hotel districts.

If you need to connect with the Irish bus or rail service, the **Airlink Express Coach** (☎ 01/844-4265) provides express coach service from the airport into the city's central bus station, Busáras, on Store Street, and on to the two main rail stations, Connolly and Heuston. Service runs daily from 7am until 11pm (Sun 7:30am–8:30pm), with departures every 20 to 30 minutes. One-way fare is €5 for adults.

Finally, **Dublin Bus** (☎ 01/872-0000; www.dublinbus.ie) runs services between the airport and the city center from 6am to 11:30pm. The one-way trip takes about 30 minutes, and the fare is €5. Nos. 16a, 33, 41, 41a, 41b, 41c, 46x, 58x, 746, 747, or 748 all serve the city center from Dublin Airport. Consult the Travel Information Desk in the Arrivals Concourse to figure out which bus will bring you closest to your hostel.

For speed and ease—especially if you've bought all your extreme sports kit—a taxi is the best way to get directly to your hostel or hotel. Depending on your destination in Dublin, fares average between €18 and €25. Surcharges include €.50 for each additional passenger and for each piece of luggage. Depending on traffic, a cab should take between 20 and 45 minutes to get into the city center. A 10% tip is standard. Taxis are lined up at a first-come, first-served taxi stand outside the arrivals terminal.

Major international and local car-rental companies operate desks at Dublin Airport. For a list of companies, see "Getting Around," below.

BY FERRY   Passenger and car ferries from Britain arrive at the Dublin Ferryport (☎ 01/855-2222), on the eastern end of the North Docks, and at the Dun Laoghaire Ferryport (☎ 01/204-7700). Call Irish Ferries (☎ 01/661-0511; www.irishferries.ie), P&O Irish Sea (☎ 01/800-409-049; www.poirishsea.com), or Stena Line (☎ 01/204-7777; www.stenaline.com) for bookings and information. There is bus and taxi service from both ports.

BY TRAIN   Irish Rail (☎ 01/836-6222; www.irishrail.ie), also called Iarnród Éireann, operates daily train service to Dublin from Belfast, Northern Ireland, and all major cities in the Irish Republic, including Cork, Galway, Limerick, Killarney, Sligo, Wexford, and Waterford. Trains from the south, west, and southwest arrive at Heuston Station, Kingsbridge, off St. John's Road; from the north and northwest at Connolly Station, Amiens Street; and from the southeast at Pearse Station, Westland Row, Tara Street.

BY BUS   Bus Eireann (☎ 01/836-6111; www.buseireann.ie) operates daily express coach and local bus service from all major cities and towns in Ireland into Dublin's central bus station, Busárus, Store Street.

DUBLIN

Are We Lost Yet?

In the town center just south of the river, Dame Street, which changes its name to College Green, Westmoreland Street, and Lord Edward Street at various points, is the main east-west artery connecting Trinity College with Dublin Castle and Christ Church Cathedral. On one side of Dame Street the winding medieval lanes of Temple Bar are jam-packed with nightclubs, pubs, and bars. This is Dublin's party central, and we have a feeling you'll spend some time here at one point or another.

On the other side of Dame Street are lots of tributary streets lined with shops and cafes—the best of these is Great St George's Street, which arcs off toward the south, with lots of good coffee shops and a few bars.

Where Dame turns into College Green, the sturdy gray stone walls of Trinity College make an excellent landmark and a great place to hang out, watching Irish students walk by on their way to class. At its southwest corner is the top of Grafton Street—a crowded pedestrianized shopping lane inevitably filled with tourists, musicians, and artists. It leads on to the peaceful statue-filled park, St Stephen's Green.

From there, heading back up via Kildare Street will take you past Leinster House, where the Irish parliament meets, while a turn to the right brings you to Merrion Square, another of Dublin's extraordinarily well-preserved Georgian Squares, with a *louche* statue of Oscar Wilde, who once lived there.

To get to the Northside, most visitors choose to walk across the pretty arch of the Ha'penny Bridge, but most locals take the less attractive, but more convenient O'Connell Bridge nearby, as it leads directly onto O'Connell Street, a wide, bustling boulevard that is the north's main thruway.

O'Connell Street runs north to Parnell Square (which holds a couple of great museums), passing along the way a lot of workaday shops, and historic Clery's department store—which is sort of like Macy's, only with history. From the bottom to the top, O'Connell Street is lined with workaday shops and fabulous statues, starting with an outrageously ornate statue of the politician, Daniel O'Connell, who gave the street its name. He's surrounded by angels (one of which still has bullet holes left from the Easter Uprising).

The street running along the Liffey's embankment is generally referred to as the North Quays, although it changes its name virtually every block reflecting the long-gone docks that once lined it. This is an increasingly hip area for pubs, hotels, and restaurants.

DUBLIN

BY CAR If you are arriving by car from other parts of Ireland or on a car ferry from Britain, all main roads lead into the heart of Dublin and are well signposted to An Lar (City Centre). To bypass the city center, the East Link (toll bridge €1.50) and West Link are signposted, and M50 circuits the city on three sides.

Orientation

Dublin is sliced down the middle by the River Liffey, which empties into the sea at the city's farthest edge. To the north and south, the city center is encircled by canals: The Royal Canal arcs across the north, and the Grand Canal through the south. For years, the section just south of the river has been Dublin's

Dublin Orientation

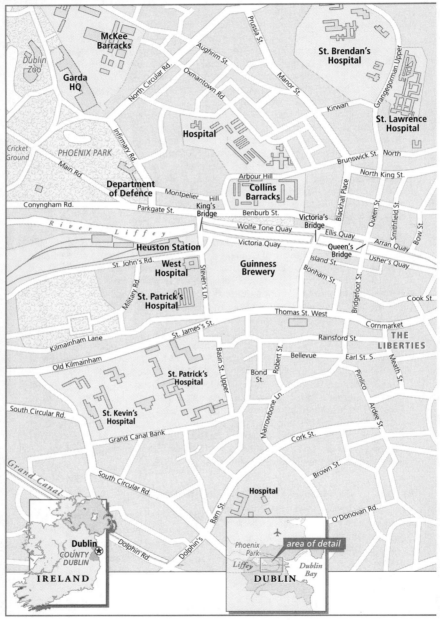

McKee Barracks

Dublin Zoo

Garda HQ

St. Brendan's Hospital

Grangegorman Upper

Prussia St.

Aughrim St.

Oxmantown Rd.

North Circular Rd.

Manor St.

Kirwan

St. Lawrence Hospital

Cricket Ground

PHOENIX PARK

Main Rd.

Infirmary Rd.

Hospital

Brunswick St. North

North King St.

Department of Defence

Montpelier Hill

Arbour Hill

Collins Barracks

Blackhall Place

Queen St.

Smithfield St.

Bow St.

Conyngham Rd.

Parkgate St.

King's Bridge

Benburb St.

Victoria's Bridge

River Liffey

Wolfe Tone Quay

Ellis Quay

Arran Quay

Victoria Quay

Queen's Bridge

Heuston Station

St. John's Rd.

West Hospital

Steven's Ln.

Guinness Brewery

Island St.

Usher's Quay

Bonham St.

Bridgefoot St.

Cook St.

Military Rd.

St. Patrick's Hospital

Thomas St. West

Cornmarket

THE LIBERTIES

Kilmainham Lane

St. James's St.

Rainsford St.

Old Kilmainham

Basin St. Upper

St. Patrick's Hospital

Bond St.

Robert St.

Bellevue

Earl St. S.

Meath St.

Pimlico

South Circular Rd.

St. Kevin's Hospital

Marrowbone Ln.

Ardee St.

Grand Canal Bank

Cork St.

Grand Canal

South Circular Rd.

Bard St.

Brown St.

Hospital

O'Donovan Rd.

Dolphin Rd.

Dolphin's

IRELAND

Dublin

COUNTY DUBLIN

Phoenix Park

area of detail

Liffey

DUBLIN

Dublin Bay

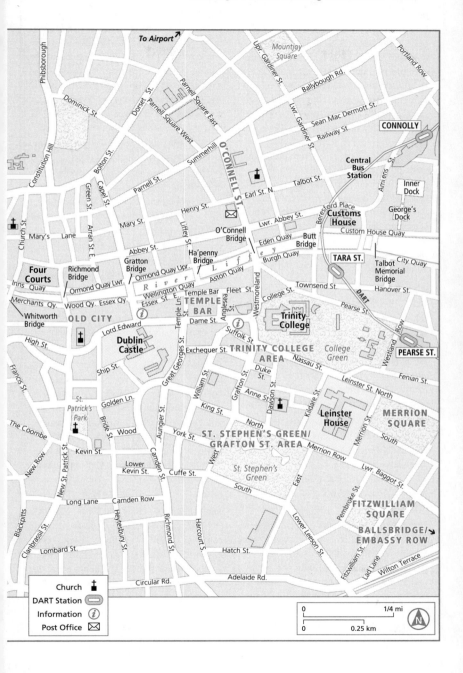

To Airport ↗

Mountjoy Square

Phibsborough

Upr. Gardiner St.
Ballybough Rd.
Portland Row

Dominick St.

Dorset St.
Parnell St.
Parnell Square East
Parnell Square West

Constitution Hill

Bolton St.
Green St.
Capel St.

Sean Mac Dermott St.
Lwr. Gardiner St.
Railway St.

CONNOLLY

O'CONNELL ST.

Summerhill

Central
Bus
Station

Amiens St.

Inner
Dock

Earl St. N.
Talbot St.

Mary's Lane
Church St.
Arran St. E.

Mary St.
Henry St.
Liffey St.

Earl St. N.

Beresford Place

George's
Dock

**Customs
House**

Custom House Quay

Abbey St.
Gratton
Bridge
Ormond Quay Upr.

O'Connell
Bridge

Lwr. Abbey St.
Eden Quay
Butt
Bridge

Ha'penny
Bridge

Burgh Quay

TARA ST.

Talbot
Memorial
Bridge

City Quay

**Four
Courts**

Richmond
Bridge

Inns Quay
Ormond Quay Lwr.
Merchants Qy.
Wood Qy. Essex Qy.

River   *Liffey*

Aston Quay
Wellington Quay

Essex St. E.
Temple Ln.
Temple Bar
Fleet St.
College St.

Townsend St.

Hanover St.

Whitworth
Bridge

OLD CITY

ⓘ

**TEMPLE
BAR**

Anglesea
Westmoreland

Pearse St.

DART

PEARSE ST.

High St.

Lord Edward
Dame St.
Suffolk St.
ⓘ

**Trinity
College**

Westland Row

Dublin
Castle**Dublin
Castle**

Great Georges St.

Exchequer St.

**TRINITY COLLEGE
AREA**

*College
Green*

Fenian St.

Francis St.

Ship St.

William St.
Grafton St.
Anne St.
Dawson St.

Duke
St.

Nassau St.

Leinster St. North

Kildare St.

**MERRION
SQUARE**

St.
Patrick's
Park

Golden Ln.
Bride St.
Wood

King St.
York St.

North

**Leinster
House**

Merrion St.

South

The Coombe

Kevin St.

Aungier St.

**ST. STEPHEN'S GREEN/
GRAFTON ST. AREA**

West

Merrion Row

Pembroke St.

Lwr. Baggot St.

New Row
New St. Patrick's St.

Lower
Kevin St.
Cuffe St.
Camden St.

*St. Stephen's
Green*

East

Lower Leeson St.

**FITZWILLIAM
SQUARE**

Long Lane
Camden Row
Heytesbury St.

South

**BALLSBRIDGE/
EMBASSY ROW** ↘

Blackpitts
Clanbrassil St.

Richmond St.

Harcourt St.

Hatch St.

Fitzwilliam St.

Lad Lane

Wilton Terrace

Lombard St.

Circular Rd.
Adelaide Rd.

Church	✝
DART Station	⬭
Information	ⓘ
Post Office	✉

0   1/4 mi
0   0.25 km

buzzing, trendy hub. It still holds most of the best hotels, restaurants, shops, and sights, but the Northside is on the move, with hip new bars and chic hotels making it the new cool place to hang. Both north and south, Dublin is compact and easily walked in an hour. In fact, a 25-minute walk from the bucolic peace of St Stephen's Green, up Grafton Street, and across the Liffey to the top of O'Connell Street offers a good overview of the city's prosperous present and troubled past.

Don't overlook the city's waterfront suburbs, easily reached by tram. These are (headed north on the tram) Drumcondra, Glasnevin, Howth, Clontarf, and Malahide; and (heading south) Ballsbridge, Blackrock, Dun Laoghaire, Dalkey, Killiney, Rathgar, and Rathmines.

THE NEIGHBORHOODS

TRINITY COLLEGE AREA On the south side of the River Liffey, Trinity College is an Ivy League–style university with shady quadrangles and atmospheric stone buildings. It's virtually the dead center of the city, and is surrounded by bookstores, shops, and noisy traffic. It's a handy meeting place, fun to wander and sort of the center of everything.

TEMPLE BAR Wedged between Trinity College and the Old City, this is Dublin's party hub, packed with noisy bars, clubs, and pubs. There are also a few good shops, two worthwhile art galleries, recording studios, and theaters. This is largely the stomping ground of young people on the hunt for lots of alcohol.

OLD CITY Dating from Viking and medieval times, the cobblestone streets of this historic area include Dublin Castle, the remnants of the city's original walls, and Christ Church and St. Patrick's cathedrals. Recently, Old City has also gained cachet for its hip boutiques, mostly on Cow Lane, where local designers sell their clothes. It encompasses the Dublin 8 and 2 zones.

THE LIBERTIES Adjacent to Old City, the Liberties district takes its name from the fact that it was once just outside the city walls, and, therefore, exempt from Dublin's jurisdiction. Although it prospered in its early days, Liberties fell on hard times in the 17th and 18th centuries and is only now feeling a touch of urban renewal. Its main claim to fame is the Guinness Brewery.

ST. STEPHEN'S STREET/GRAFTON STREET AREA The biggest tourist draw in town, this district is home to Dublin's finest (and priciest) hotels, restaurants, and shops. The neighborhood is filled with impressive Georgian architecture, and is primarily a business and shopping zone.

FITZWILLIAM & MERRION SQUARE These two little square parks between Trinity College and St. Stephen's Green are surrounded by grand Georgian town houses. Some of Dublin's most famous citizens once lived here; today many of the houses are offices for doctors, lawyers, and government agencies. This area is part of the Dublin 2 zone.

O'CONNELL STREET (NORTH OF THE LIFFEY) The epicenter of Dublin's stormy political struggles, the north was once a fashionable area, but it lost much of its charm and became rundown in the 20th century. Now it's rebounding with high-profile hotels, plenty of shops, and a few top-rated restaurants. With four theaters in walking distance of O'Connell Street, this is Dublin's theater district.

NORTH QUAYS (THE LIFFEY RIVERBANKS ON THE NORTHSIDE) Once the grubby center of Dublin's shipping industry, this is now one of Dublin's trendier addresses for hotels, bars, and clubs. The quays are actually a series of streets named after the wharves that once stood at the water's edge, starting near the mouth of the Liffey and ending in the green peace of Phoenix Park.

Stand on Your Own Two Feet

....

While driving in the city is intimidating, in general, getting around Dublin is not at all daunting. Public transportation is good and getting better, taxis are plentiful and reasonably priced, and your own two feet can easily carry you from one end of town to the other. In fact, with its current traffic and parking problems, it's a city where the foot is mightier than the wheel. If you can avoid it, don't use a car while you're in the city.

BALLSBRIDGE/EMBASSY ROW Immediately south of the Grand Canal, this wealthy residential suburb is just barely within walking distance of the city center. Primarily a prestigious residential area, it is also home to expensive hotels, restaurants, and embassies, including the U.S. embassy.

Public Transportation/ Getting Around

BY BUS Dublin Bus operates a fleet of green double-decker and single-deck buses, and cute little minibuses called "imps." Most originate on or near O'Connell Street, Abbey Street, and Eden Quay on the north side, and at Aston Quay, College Street, and Fleet Street on the south side. Bus stops, which resemble big blue or green lollipops, are located every 2 or 3 blocks on main thoroughfares. To tell where the bus is going, look at the destination streets and bus numbers above each bus's front window; those heading for the city center say so, but in Gaelic: VIA AN LAR.

Bus service runs daily throughout the city, starting at 6am (10am on Sun), with the last bus at 11:30pm. On Thursday, Friday, and Saturday nights, the Nitelink night buses take over, ferrying people from the city center to the suburbs from midnight to 3am.

Buses operate every 10 to 15 minutes for most runs; schedules are posted on revolving notice boards at bus stops.

Inner-city fares are based on distances traveled. The minimum fare is €.90; the maximum fare for journeys in the city center is €1.85. The Nitelink fare is a flat €4. Buy your tickets from the driver as you enter the bus; exact change is required, so have some change available. Notes of €5 or higher may not be accepted. Discounted 1-day, 3-day, 5-day, and 7-day passes are available in advance. The 1-day bus-only pass costs €5; the 3-day pass costs €10; the 5-day pass goes for €16; and the 7-day pass costs €19. For more information, contact **Dublin Bus,** 59 Upper O'Connell St., Dublin 1 (☎ **01/873-4222;** www.dublinbus.ie).

BY DART While Dublin has no subway in the strict sense, there is an electric rapid-transit train, known as the **DART** (Dublin Area Rapid Transit). It travels mostly at ground level or on elevated tracks, linking the city-center stations at **Connolly Station, Tara Street,** and **Pearse Street** with suburbs and seaside communities as far as Malahide to the north and Greystones to the south. Service operates roughly every 10 to 20 minutes Monday to Saturday from 7am to midnight and Sunday from 9:30am to 11pm. The minimum fare is €1. One-day and 10-journey passes, as well as student and family tickets, are available at reduced rates from ticket windows in stations. For further information, contact **DART,** Pearse Station, Dublin 2 (☎ **1850/366222** in Ireland, or 01/836-6222; www.irishrail.ie).

BY TRAM The newest addition to Dublin's public transportation network, the sleek light-rail tram system known as **LUAS** first opened in the summer of 2004. With trams on two lines traveling at a maximum speed of 70kmph (45 mph) and departing every 5 minutes in peak hours, LUAS has already made an impact on Dublin's appalling traffic congestion. The lines link the city center at **Connolly Station** and **St. Stephen's Green** with the suburbs of Tallaght in the southwest and Dundrum and Sandyford to the south. For visitors, one of the handiest reasons to use the LUAS is to get between Connolly and Heuston stations. The one-way fare within the city center is €1; 1-day and multiple-day passes are also available. For further information, contact **LUAS** (☎ **01/703-2029;** www.luas.ie).

BY FOOT Marvelously compact, Dublin is ideal for walking, as long as you remember to look right and then left (in the direction opposite your instincts if you're from North America) before crossing the street. Pedestrians have the right of way at specially marked, zebra-striped crossings (there are usually two flashing lights at these intersections).

BY TAXI You don't usually hail taxis on the street here; instead, they line up at taxi stands (called "ranks") outside major hotels, at bus and train stations, and on prime thoroughfares such as Upper O'Connell Street, College Green, and the north side of St. Stephen's Green.

You can also phone for a taxi. Some of the companies that operate a 24-hour radio-call service are **Co-Op** (☎ **01/676-6666**), **Shamrock Radio Cabs** (☎ **01/855-5444**), and **VIP Taxis** (☎ **01/478-3333**).

Taxi rates are fixed by law and posted in each vehicle. The following are typical travel costs in the city center: A 3.25km (2-mile) journey costs €8 by day and €10 at night; an 8km (5-mile) journey runs €10 by day and €12 at night; and a 16km (10-mile) journey costs €20 by day and €22 at night. There's an additional charge of €.50 for each extra passenger and for each suitcase. And it costs an extra €1.50 for a dispatched pickup. **Be warned:** At some hotels, staff members will tack on as much as €4 for calling you a cab, although this practice violates city taxi regulations.

RENTING A CAR We can't say it often enough: If you'll be spending all of your time in Dublin, it is very unlikely you'll really need to rent a car. In fact, getting around the city is much easier without one.

If you must drive in Dublin, remember to keep to the *left-hand side of the road,* and don't drive in bus lanes. The speed limit within the city is 46kmph (30 mph), although you'll be very unlikely ever to reach it, and seat belts must be worn at all times by driver and passengers.

Most major international **car-rental firms** have branches here, as do many Irish-based companies. They have desks at the airport, full-service offices downtown, or both. Rates vary greatly according to company, season, type of car, and duration of rental. In high season, the average weekly cost of a car, from subcompact standard to full-size automatic, ranges from €200 to €1,525; you'll be much better off if you've made your car-rental arrangements well in advance from home.

Rental agencies in Dublin include **Avis,** 1 Hanover St. E., Dublin 1, and at Dublin Airport (☎ **01/605-7500;** www.avis.ie); **Budget,** in Dublin (☎ **01/662-7711;** www. budget.ie), and at Dublin Airport (☎ **01/ 844-5150**); **Hertz,** 149 Upper Leeson St., Dublin 4 (☎ **01/660-2255;** www.hertz.ie), and at Dublin Airport (☎ **01/844-5466**); and **Murray's Europcar,** Baggot Street Bridge, Dublin 4 (toll-free ☎ **1850/403803;** www. europcar.ie), and at Dublin Airport (☎ **01/ 812-0410**).

PARKING During normal business hours, free parking on Dublin streets is virtually nonexistent, but throughout the city there are "pay and display" **parking** facilities. If you do manage to park on the street, look around for a meter (there's usually one on every block), as street parking is not free here—you pay coins into the machine for however many hours you expect to be there, and stick a ticket in the front window of your car to prove you've done it. Expect to pay around €2 per hour. The best places to park are surface parking lots and multistory car parks in central locations such as Kildare Street, Lower Abbey Street, Marlborough Street, and St. Stephen's Green West. Expect to pay €1.90 per hour and €19 for 24 hours. Night rates run €6 to €9 per hour. The bottom line here is that you're better off without a car. Sorry, are we getting boring?

Never park in bus lanes or along a curb with double yellow lines. City officials will either clamp or tow errant vehicles. To get your car declamped, the fee is €85; if your car is towed away, it costs €165 to reclaim it.

BY BICYCLE   The relentless flow of Dublin traffic rushing down one-way streets might look a little scary for most cyclists, but there are many opportunities for more chill pedaling in residential areas and suburbs, along the seafront, and around Phoenix Park. The Dublin Tourism office can supply you with bicycle touring information and suggested routes.

Bicycle rental averages €20 per day, €80 per week, with a €65 deposit. The one-way rental fee is €100. In the downtown area, bicycles can be rented from **Raleigh Ireland,** Kylemore Road, Dublin 10 (☎ **o1/ 626-1333**).

Basics

Tourist Offices

Dublin Tourism operates six useful walk-in visitor centers in greater Dublin, and they're open every day except Christmas. The biggest is on Suffolk Street near Trinity College, and it has a decent currency exchange counter, a car-rental counter, an accommodations-reservations service, bus and rail information desks, desks where you can book tickets to upcoming events, tour operators, helpful people wandering around who can give you directions or advice, a gift shop with reasonable prices, and a cafe. It's open from June to August Monday to Saturday from 9am to 8:30pm, Sunday and national holidays 10:30am to 3pm, and the rest of the year Monday to Saturday 9am to 5:30pm, Sunday and national holidays 10:30am to 3pm.

The five other centers are in the Arrivals Hall of Dublin Airport; at Exclusively Irish, O'Connell Street, Dublin 1; at the Baggot Street Bridge, Baggot Street, Dublin 2; at The Square Towncentre, Tallaght, Dublin 24; and in the ferry terminal at Dun Laoghaire Harbor. All centers are open year-round with at least the following hours: Monday to

Friday 9am to 5:30pm and Saturday 9am to 5pm. To reach any of them, call ☎ **o1/605-7700** or check out www.visitdublin.com.

For information on Ireland outside of Dublin, call **Bord Fáilte** (☎ **1850/230330** in Ireland; www.travel.ireland.ie).

At any of these centers you can pick up the free *Tourism News;* or the free *Event Guide,* a biweekly entertainment guide, online at www.eventguide.ie. Alternatively, you could do what the locals do and pick up a copy of *In Dublin,* a very useful arts-and-entertainment magazine that sells for €3 at most newsstands.

Youth Information Service Offices

Contact the Union of Students in Ireland Travel (☎ **02/602-1600**; www.usit.ie). They're great for arranging travel from and around Ireland at cheaper rates, and their notice boards are filled with flatshares, language classes, jobs, and cheap flights. Their offices are on Aston Quay (on the South side of the Liffey about 45m/150 ft. from the O'Connell Street Bridge).

Recommended Websites

To find out what's going on in Dublin, check out www.eventguide.ie for up-to-date local listings for gigs, theater, clubs, and restaurants. Similarly, www.hotspots.ie lists clubs and pubs and gives good descriptions and basic guidance for most worthwhile places in the city. If you need advice on possible cheap places to stay, check out www.hostel.ie.

Nuts & Bolts

Banks   Nearly all banks are open Monday to Friday 10am to 4pm (to 5pm Thurs) and have ATMs that accept Cirrus network cards as well as MasterCard and Visa. Convenient locations include the Bank of Ireland, at 1 Ormond Quay, Dublin 7, and 34 College Green, Dublin 2; and the Allied Irish Bank, at 64 Grafton St., Dublin 2, and 37 O'Connell St., Dublin 1.

Cellphone Providers   There are companies selling cellphones (called "mobile phones" here) and related equipment all over town. Try **Carphone Warehouse,** 30 Grafton St., Dublin 2 (☎ 01/670-5265; www.carphonewarehouse.ie), or **Vodafone,** 55 Grafton St., Dublin 2 (☎ 01/679-9938; www.vodafone.ie).

Currency Exchange   Currency-exchange services, signposted as BUREAU DE CHANGE, are in most Dublin banks and at many branches of the Irish post office system, known as An Post. A bureau de change operates daily during flight arrival and departure times at Dublin airport; a foreign currency note-exchanger machine is also available on a 24-hour basis in the main arrivals hall. Some hotels and travel agencies offer bureau de change services, although the best rate of exchange is usually when you use your bank card at an ATM.

Dentists   For dental emergencies, contact the Eastern Health Board Headquarters, **Dr. Steevens Hospital,** Dublin 8 (☎ 01/679-0700), or try **Molesworth Clinic,** 2 Molesworth Place, Dublin 2 (☎ 01/661-5544). See also "Dental Surgeons" in the Golden Pages (Yellow Pages) of the telephone book. The American Embassy (see "Embassies & Consulates," below) can provide a list of dentists in the city and surrounding areas. Expect to be charged upfront for services.

Doctors   If you need to see a physician, most hostels and guesthouses should be able to contact a doctor for you. The American Embassy (see "Embassies & Consulates," below) can provide a list of doctors in the city and surrounding areas and you should contact them first. Otherwise, you can call either the **Eastern Health Board Headquarters,** Dr. Steevens Hospital, Dublin 8 (☎ 01/679-0700), or the **Irish Medical Organization,** 10 Fitzwilliam Place, Dublin 2 (☎ 01/676-7273). As with dentists, expect to pay for treatment upfront and when you return home, contact your insurance company to see if you are eligible for reimbursement.

Embassies & Consulates   The **American Embassy** is at 42 Elgin Rd., Ballsbridge, Dublin 4 (☎ 01/668-8777); the **Canadian Embassy** at 65–68 St. Stephen's Green, Dublin 2 (☎ 01/417-4100); the **British Embassy** at 31 Merrion Rd., Dublin 2 (☎ 01/205-3700); and the **Australian Embassy** at Fitzwilton House, Wilton Terrace, Dublin 2 (☎ 01/664-5300). In addition, there is an **American Consulate** at 14 Queen St., Belfast BT1 6EQ (☎ 028/9032-8239).

Emergencies   For police, fire, or other emergencies, dial ☎ **999.**

Gay & Lesbian Resources   Contact the **Gay Switchboard Dublin,** Carmichael House, North Brunswick Street, Dublin 7 (☎ **01/872-1055**); the **National Lesbian and Gay Federation (NLGF),** 6 S. William St., Dublin 2 (☎ **01/671-0939**); or the **LOT** (Lesbians Organizing Together), 5 Capel St., Dublin 1 (☎ **01/872-7770**).

Hospitals   For emergency care, two of the most modern are **St. Vincent's University Hospital,** Elm Park (☎ **01/269-4533**), on the south side of the city, and **Beaumont Hospital,** Beaumont (☎ **01/837-7755**), on the Northside.

Information   For directory assistance, dial ☎ **11811.** For visitor information offices, refer to the Tourist Information offices listed earlier in this chapter.

Internet Hotspots   Internet access is everywhere in Dublin; look for signs in cafes, pubs, shopping malls, hotels, and hostels. Like all of Dublin's public libraries, the **Central Library,** in the ILAC Centre, off Henry Street, Dublin 1 (☎ **01/873-4333**), has a bank of PCs with free Internet access. Three centrally located cybercafes are the **Central Cybercafe,** 6 Grafton St., Dublin 2 (☎ 01/677-8298); **Planet Cyber Café,** 13 St. Andrews St., Dublin 2 (☎ **01/670-5182**); and **The Connect Point,** 33 Dorset St. Lower, Dublin 1 (☎ **01/834-9821**). A half-hour online averages €3.50. Students might want to pop in at the **Oz Cybercafé** (39 Abbey St. on the North Side, Dublin 1), as they get Internet access for €1 per hour, while mere mortals must pay double that.

Laundry   **Laundrette** (Pearse St., Dublin 2) is where most Trinity College students get their laundry done. It's not self service—expect to pay €5 to €10 to have your clothes washed, dried, and folded.

Luggage Storage   The best places to store luggage are at the main bus station, **Busárus,** Store Street (☎ **01/703-2436**), at **Connolly Station** (the "left luggage" office is on platform two), at Heuston Station (left luggage is near the ticket office), and at **Dublin Airport** (☎ **01/814-4633**).

Pharmacies   Centrally located drugstores, known locally as pharmacies or chemist shops, include **Dame Street Pharmacy,** 16 Dame St., Dublin 2 (☎ **01/670-4523**). A late-night chemist shop is **Hamilton Long & Co.,** 5 Lower O'Connell St. (☎ **01/874-8456**), and its sister branch at 4 Merrion Rd., Dublin 4 (☎ **01/668-3287**). Both branches close at 9pm on weeknights and 6pm on Saturday.

Police   Dial ☎ **999** in an emergency. The metropolitan headquarters for the **Dublin Garda Siochana** (Police) is in Phoenix Park, Dublin 8 (☎ **01/666-0000**).

Post Office   The Irish post office is best known by its Gaelic name, An Post. The **General Post Office (GPO)** is located on O'Connell Street, Dublin 1 (☎ **01/705-7000;** www.anpost.ie). Hours are Monday to Saturday 8am to 8pm, Sunday and holidays 10:30am to 6:30pm. Branch offices, identified by the sign OIFIG AN POST/POST OFFICE, are open Monday to Saturday only, 9am to 5pm.

Telephone Tips   The dialing code for Dublin is 01, but you don't need to dial the prefix if you're calling from within Dublin itself. Local phone numbers all consist of seven digits, although elsewhere in Ireland phone numbers may be shorter or longer. If you are calling from outside Ireland, add the international dialing code for

DUBLIN

Ireland—353—then 1 for Dublin (omitting the o), then the subsequent seven digits. To make an international call from within Ireland, dial oo, then the country code, then the number itself. Here are some country codes to get you started: Australia 61, U.K. 44, U.S. and Canada 1, South Africa 27, New Zealand 64. Local calls cost money here, so if you're borrowing somebody's phone, realize they have to pay for that call by the minute. If you need to make international calls, get a phone card—you'll see them in newsagents and shops. They allow you to talk for much less than phoning direct.

Tipping   The standard tipping rate in restaurants is 12%. You don't tip in pubs, but you do in upscale bars, about the same rate as you would back home. Cab drivers should get 10% to 12%, although most people just add a euro to their fare and call it even. If anybody helps with your bags, tip whatever your conscience tells you to—just how heavy are your bags, anyway?

Sleeping

Dublin is packed with housing options, from cheap hostels to moderately priced B&Bs and on to lavishly expensive boutique hotels. Aside from the hostels, prices can be a bit painful, but there are good deals to be had—keep an eye on the hotel websites in the months before you book your trip.

In general, hotel rates in Dublin do not vary as much with the seasons as they do in the countryside, although some charge slightly higher prices during special events, such as St. Patrick's Day and the Dublin Horse Show. The money savings here comes by the day of the week: If you're looking for the best deal, some hotels cut their rates by as much as 50% on Friday and Saturday nights, when business traffic is low. Other hotels offer midweek specials.

It pays to book well in advance; either call and book before you come, or do it online—many hotels and some B&Bs offer Web-only special deals.

Most luxury hotels are on the south side of the river in Temple Bar and around Trinity College, but some are springing up on the Northside. Places like the boutique U2-owned **Clarence** hotel in Temple Bar are stylish indicators of how far Dublin has come, while the celebrity hangout **Morrison** hotel just across the river from it proves that the north bank is on the upswing. There are

lots of excellent midrange hotels around St. Stephen's Green, and most budget hotels are in the north, where affordable guesthouses cluster around funky Lower Gardiner Street and near the North Quays.

Hostels

→ **Dublin International Hostel**   Open year-round and run by An Óige, the Irish Youth Hostel Organization, this hostel is in a historic stone building smack in the city center. Good looking public rooms feature stripped wooden floor boards, a huge old kitchen, an Internet cafe, newly renovated TV/game room, garden, laundry, and a handsome restaurant where a continental breakfast is served for free (if you want the full Irish version it will cost you extra). Dinner is available June through August. Rooms are small and basic but clean. The hostel is open 24 hours and the front desk is always staffed. Members of An Óige/Hostelling International will receive a €2 discount on the rates listed here. *61 Mountjoy St., Dublin 1.* ☎ *01/830-4555. www.irelandyha.org €18–€21 dorm, €48–€52 double. Rates include continental breakfast. Bus: Any city-center service. Amenities: Restaurant; Internet; kitchen; laundry; TV/game room.*

→ **The Four Courts**   Set in some mighty pretty Georgian buildings overlooking the

Sleeping in Dublin

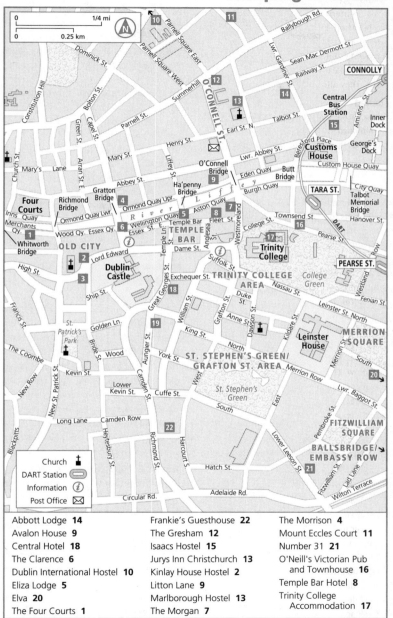

Abbott Lodge **14**	Frankie's Guesthouse **22**	The Morrison **4**
Avalon House **9**	The Gresham **12**	Mount Eccles Court **11**
Central Hotel **18**	Isaacs Hostel **15**	Number 31 **21**
The Clarence **6**	Jurys Inn Christchurch **13**	O'Neill's Victorian Pub
Dublin International Hostel **10**	Kinlay House Hostel **2**	and Townhouse **16**
Eliza Lodge **5**	Litton Lane **9**	Temple Bar Hotel **8**
Elva **20**	Marlborough Hostel **13**	Trinity College
The Four Courts **1**	The Morgan **7**	Accommodation **17**

Liffey, this friendly hostel has all the basics, and a few frills. Its setting, at the edge of the river, is top-notch. Inside, the rooms have big windows, stripped wooden floor boards, desks, and other sweet touches that make the plain, metal bunk beds slightly more bearable. It has 24-hour access, free continental breakfast, good security, laundry facilities, a game room, free Internet access, a place to park your car, and, in general, more than most hostels will give you for your dosh. *15–17 Merchants Quay, Dublin 8.* ☎ *01/672-5839. www.fourcourtshostel.com. €10–€19 dorm; €48 double. Rates include free continental breakfast. Bus: Any city center service. Amenities: Game room; Internet; laundry.*

📺 **Best** ➔ **Isaacs Hostel** This is the champagne of hostels. Isaacs is turning the backpacker concept of cheap and cheerful right on its head. Calling itself "Dublin's first V.I.P. hostel," it adds to the usual mix of bunk beds, lockers, and TV rooms a heady cocktail of extras including a full restaurant and, the newest addition, an attractive sauna. It's a thoughtful hybrid hostel, then, with a laid-back atmosphere. *2–5 Frenchman's Lane, Dublin 1.* ☎ *01/855-6215. www.dublinbackpacker.com. €12–€25 dorm); €58–€72 double, twin; €32–€39 single. Amenities: Restaurant; Internet; kitchen; pool tables; sauna; TV room.*

➔ **Kinlay House Hostel** Open year-round and run by USIT, Kinlay House occupies a beautiful red brick town house in one of Dublin's oldest neighborhoods, which the oldies will tell you is steps from Christ Church Cathedral, but who cares about that when it's right on the edge of the trendy Temple Bar area. There's a large self-catering kitchen and dining room, a TV room, and colorful hangout room. Dorm rooms are small but clean, and the front desk is open 24 hours. Toast and coffee are served each morning until 9:30am. *2–12 Lord Edward St., Dublin 2.* ☎ *01/679-6644. www.kinlayhouse.ie. €16–€20 dorm; €40–€50 single; €50–€62 double. Rates*

include continental breakfast. *Bus: 21A, 50, 50A, 78, 78A, or 78B. Amenities: TV room; kitchen.*

➔ **Litton Lane** Just a 2-minute walk across the river from Temple Bar, this hip hostel was once a recording studio where legends like Van Morrison, Sinéad O'Connor, Bob Geldof, and others recorded their tunes. Today it's a small hostel in a cute row of stone buildings, just off O'Connell Street and handy for everything. Rooms are tiny but neatly furnished. Along with 8- and 10-bed dorms, there are twin and double rooms. There's a kitchen, so you can avoid eating out every night, telephones, 24-hour reception, space to park your car, and bedding is included in the price. *2–4 Litton Lane, Dublin 1.* ☎ *01/872-8389. www.littonlanehostel.com. €12–€19 per person dorm. €70–€80 double, twin. Bus: All O'Connell St. buses. Amenities: Kitchen.*

➔ **Marlborough Hostel** This handy, northside hostel doesn't look like it's up to much from the outside, but inside is a good, sound hostel, with plenty of extras for the underfunded but fussy international traveler. There are dorms with eight beds, or four beds, as well as a few private rooms. It's clean, there's a lovely garden, and for those about to rock—no curfew. *81–82 Marlborough St., Dublin 1.* ☎ *01/874-7629 or 01/874-7812. www.marlboroughhostel.com. €15–€20 dorm. €51–€60 twin, double. Bus: All O'Connell Street buses. DART: Connolly. Amenities: Garden; Internet; kitchen; TV (in common room).*

➔ **Mount Eccles Court** This is a beautiful small hostel in a Georgian building on the north side of the river—a great option for those who find themselves freaked out by the bigger facilities. Its 10 bedrooms and 10 dorms are secured with keycard locks and neatly decorated with neutral walls and homely touches, like plants flourishing in pots. All the extras are there—24-hour access; bedding, including sheets, provided; luggage lockers; Internet access; bike storage; free hot showers; TV and music lounges. *42 N.*

Great Georges St., Dublin 1. ☎ *01/873-0826. www.eccleshostel.com. €12–€18.50 dorm. €42– €70 double, twin. Bus: All O'Connell Street buses. Amenities: Internet; TV.*

➔ **Trinity College Accommodation**
During the summer months Trinity College rents student rooms to visitors by the night, putting you right in the center of the city's action. Forget ivy-league and get a load of the ivy-covered Trinity College, the oldest university in the country. Most of its rooms are inside the college grounds. Ask if you can go in the 19th-century buildings; otherwise, you might get put in the new dorms built in 1990. Most rooms have a twin bed, a desk, plenty of built-in cupboards, and a compact bathroom with shower. Other room breeds include suites with two (or four) single rooms, a living room, one (or two) shared bathrooms, and minimal kitchen facilities (perfect for friends traveling together). The best rooms are in the Graduate Memorial Building—prepare for buckets of character, high ceilings, and views across the green to the Old Library. The biggest rooms can be found in Goldsmith Hall, the newest dorm on campus. A generous continental breakfast is served cafeteria-style in The Buttery, a student eatery. *Trinity College, Dublin 2.* ☎ *01/608-1177. www.tcd.ie. €42–€69 per person. Rates include continental breakfast. Discounted rates at nearby parking garage. Rooms available June 7–Sept 30. Bus: All city center buses.*

Cheap

➔ **Abbott Lodge** Budget travelers just keep on trotting through the Abbott Lodge's doors. Pop by and you'll see why. The place fairly brims with historical atmosphere, from the huge high ceiling and original cornices to the mahogany beds. And the best bit, it's really near all the bars and eateries of the city center. If you can't decide where to go, the staff will point you in the direction of their favorites. *87–88 Lower Gardiner St.,*

Dublin 1. ☎ *01/836-5548. www.abbott-lodge. com. €45 single; €90 double. Rates include full Irish breakfast. Parking €5 per night. DART: Connolly. Bus: All An Lar (cross-city) buses. Amenities: Lounge. In room: TV (cable).*

➔ **Avalon House** This warm and friendly guesthouse in a beautiful old red brick building is well known among those who travel to Dublin on a budget. Its pine floors, high ceilings, and open fireplace make it a top chill out spot, and its cafe is a popular hangout for international travelers. Rooms range from dorms to doubles, and it's got all you really need—clean, cheerful rooms in a safe location at a cheap price. *55 Aungier St., Dublin 2.* ☎ *01/475-0001. www.avalon-house. ie. €30–€74 double. AE, MC, V. Bus: 16, 16A, 19, 22, or 155. Amenities: Cafe; nonsmoking rooms; TV lounge; currency exchange; cooking facilities; Internet; luggage storage; safe.*

➔ **Elva** If you can't get in anywhere else and/or you're missing home, Sheila Matthews will look after you in her old Victorian home, 15 minutes from the city center. Tuck yourself up in one of the three en suite bedrooms filled with mismatched furniture. Then snuggle down under your floral bedspread. You'll have to kiss yourself goodnight. *5 Pembroke Park, Ballsbridge, Dublin 4.* ☎ *01/660-2931. €50 single; €80 double. No credit cards. Free private parking. Closed Dec–Feb. DART: Lansdowne Rd. Station. Bus: 10. In room: TV.*

➔ **O'Neill's Victorian Pub and Townhouse** Perched Victorian style above a pub, this inn has been putting up budget travelers for more than a century. The location, just across from Trinity College, can't be beat, although some older travelers have complained about street noise in the past. But, hey, if you're out most of the night, what do you care? Otherwise, shove in some earplugs. The eight rooms are tiny but neat, and the full Irish breakfast in the morning will see you through the day. *36–37 Pearse St., Dublin 2.* ☎ *01/6714074. www.oneillsdublin.com. Rates* include full Irish breakfast. €35–€65 per person double, twin. (Rate depends on room, time of week, and season.) Buses: All cross-town buses. Amenities: Restaurant; bar; central heating.

Doable

→ **Eliza Lodge** This bijou hotel opened a few years ago right beside the Liffey and immediately staked out a place among the coolest options in Temple Bar. Okay, so it looks like a motel from the outside and the reception rooms aren't much to write home about, but the 18 guest rooms are just fine in neutral creams and blond wood, with big floor-to-ceiling windows—all the better to take in the riverside views. 23 Wellington Quay, Dublin 2. ☎ 01/671-8044. www.dublin lodge.com. €110–€130 double. Bus: 51B, 51C, 68, 69, or 79. Amenities: Restaurant; bar; non-smoking rooms. In room: A/C, TV, tea/coffeemaker, hair dryer, iron.

[MTV] (Best) → **Frankie's Guesthouse** Billed as Dublin's only guesthouse exclusively for lesbians and gays, Frankie's is a charming, mews-style building with a wonderful address in the heart of Georgian Dublin. Set on a quiet back street, the house has a Mediterranean feel, with fresh whitewashed rooms and simple furnishings. Book well in advance, especially for a weekend stay. 8 Camden Place, Dublin 2. ☎/fax 01/478-3087. www. frankiesguesthouse.com. €100 double with private bathroom; €82 double with shared bathroom. Rates include breakfast. Bus: 16, 16A, 16C, 19A, 22, or 22A. Amenities: Roof terrace; sauna; TV lounge. In room: TV, tea/coffeemaker.

→ **Jurys Inn Christchurch** A fab location in the Old City, near all the nightlife, and frequent special offers that keep the price in the bargain basement arena make this a budget option. The rooms are larger than many in the city, though the decor disappoints with the same naff polyester floral bedspreads and framed watercolors as every other chain hotel you've ever visited. Make your reservations early and request a fifth-floor room facing west for a view to remember. Christ Church Place, Dublin 8. ☎ 800/44-UTELL in the U.S. or 01/454-0000. www.jurysdoyle.com. €117–€130 double. Service charge included. Breakfast €9.50. Discounted parking available at adjacent lot. Bus: 21A, 50, 50A, 78, 78A, or 78B. Amenities: Restaurant (Continental); bar; laundry/dry cleaning; non-smoking rooms. In room: A/C, TV, coffeemaker, hair dryer.

Splurge

→ **Central Hotel** This rambling, eccentric old hotel has enough quirky personality to make up for what it lacks in modernity. The public areas have a laid-back, Victorian atmosphere enhanced by a divine collection of original Irish art. Bedrooms have high ceilings and carved cornices but are let down by cheep-and-cheerful fabrics. Its atmospheric Library Bar is your new favorite place—a truly cool haven for a cappuccino or a pint and a bit of calm. 1–5 Exchequer St. (at the corner of Great Georges St.), Dublin 2. ☎ 800/780-1234 in the U.S. or 01/679-7302. www.centralhotel.ie. €135–€175 double. Rates include service charge and full Irish breakfast. AE, DC, MC, V. Discounted parking in nearby public lot. Bus: 22A. Amenities: Restaurant (Irish/Continental); bar; lounge; nonsmoking rooms; room service. In room: TV, garment press, hair dryer, iron, minibar, tea/coffeemaker, voice mail.

→ **The Clarence** This has been the most famous hotel in Dublin since 1992, when U2's Bono and the Edge bought it. Its rock 'n' roll pedigree aside, this is also the most stylish hotel in the city. Rooms are designed with lush fabrics in neutral tones of oatmeal and chocolate, light Shaker-style oak furniture, and ultracomfy, king-size beds. Suites and deluxe rooms have balconies, some with views over the Liffey. It may be expensive, but it's not snobby—the hip staff are on top of things, and always seem to remember who you are. The Tea Room restaurant, is one of the best in town for contemporary Irish cuisine, while the Octagon Bar is a favorite with visiting celebrities. *6–8 Wellington Quay, Dublin 2.* ☎ *01/670-9000. www.theclarence.ie. €330 double; €640 1-bedroom suite. Valet parking/service. Bus: 51B, 51C, 68, 69, or 79. Amenities: Restaurant (eclectic Continental); bar; concierge; salon; 24-hr. room service; babysitting; laundry/dry cleaning; nonsmoking rooms; foreign-currency exchange; study. In room: A/C, hair dryer, interactive TV/DVD/broadband system, minibar.*

→ **The Gresham** This big, historic hotel has been here for nearly 200 years, and it's one of the city's most famous hotels. It's a relaxing place to hang out even if you're not staying here—the vast lobby is ideal for a cup of tea or a pint of beer and people-watching. The whole place is currently undergoing a much-needed makeover. What's done is good; what's not is not. If you're thinking of staying here, make sure to ask for a renovated room, then you'll get a huge bathroom. *Note:* Breakfast is a cafeteria-style meal in the fusty Aberdeen Restaurant, where customers are largely of the gray-haired variety. Still, overall this is a great hotel, and booking online often yields steep discounts. *23 Upper O'Connell St., Dublin 1.* ☎ *01/874-6881. www.gresham-hotels.com. €150–€220 double. AE, DC, MC, V. Parking €10 per night. Bus: 11 or 13. Amenities: 2 restaurants (contemporary Irish, traditional international); 2 bars; concierge; laundry/dry cleaning; nonsmoking floors; room service. In room: A/C, TV, dataport (wireless in some rooms), hair dryer, minibar (some rooms), safe.*

→ **The Morgan** Sitting coolly amid Temple Bar's revelry, this trendy boutique hotel has a bit of a cult following among those in the fashion and music industries, so you never know who might sit next to you in the lobby. It's easy to see what attracts them: Rooms have a minimalist vibe, with light beech-wood furnishings; crisp, white bedspreads; and creamy neutral walls; topped off with funky Irish artworks. The effect is elegance with a decadent twist. *10 Fleet St., Dublin 2.* ☎ *01/679-3939. Fax 01/679-3946. www.themorgan.com. 66 units. €140–€165 double. Bus: 78A or 78B. Amenities: Cafe; bar; fitness center; room service; aromatherapy/masseuse; babysitting; laundry/dry cleaning; video/CD library. In room: TV/VCR, dataport, tea/coffeemaker, iron, safe, CD player, garment press, voice mail.*

→ **The Morrison** This is really an oversize boutique hotel with an ideal location just across the Liffey from Temple Bar. Fashion fans will be in heaven in design star John Rocha's creation—he is responsible for everything from the blood red crushed velvet bed throws to the Waterford crystal vases. Guest rooms are minimalist but kitted out with stereos, Egyptian-cotton linens, and cool Portuguese limestone in the bathrooms. The stylish atrium-style restaurant, Halo, is one of the most talked-about eateries in town. *Lower Ormond Quay, Dublin 1.* ☎ *01/887-2400. www.morrisonhotel.ie. €220–€450 double. DART: Connolly. Bus: 70 or 80. Amenities: 2 restaurants (fusion, Asian); 2 bars; concierge; room service; babysitting; dry cleaning; video/CD library. In room: A/C, dataport, minibar, hair dryer, safe, CD player, voice mail.*

→ **Number 31** You know you've found a good hotel when it doesn't even need to bother with a sign. A discreet plaque outside a locked gate is the only pointer you get at Number 31. Made up of two buildings—one a grand Georgian town house, the other a more modern coach house—this place has some fab bits, like a sunken living room with seating arranged around a peat-burning fireplace.

Spot the Celeb

When it comes to star-spotting, Ireland has one advantage over most other countries—it's relatively easy. This is a tiny place, and there are a few places where celebrities gather.

There's no place to hide.

The only downside is, most of the celebrities in Ireland are either Irish or British and you've probably never heard of half of them. So here is a brief list of places to go to run into a star or two whose names you might actually know.

The most likely place to stumble into the lifestyles of the rich and famous is Dublin. It's hugely trendy these days, and has plenty of chic hotels, night-clubs, and restaurants, making it a bit of a star magnet. You need only the smallest bit of luck to run into some of its own stars, like the members of U2, who are regularly spotted shopping in the Old City or having a cup of coffee in Temple Bar at The Clarence, the swanky boutique hotel co-owned by Bono and The Edge. In fact, the Octagon Bar in the Clarence is always a good place to look out for stars, although looking for stars in a hotel owned by stars is kind of like cheating.

Another hotel with star status is the Morrison Hotel, just across the Liffey from the Clarence on Ormond Quay. It made headlines a few years ago when Christina Aguilera raised eyebrows by "partying" so noisily in her room that other guests (including British television personality Lloyd Grossman) complained. Designed very nearly to death by John Rocha, its lavish Halo restaurant and slamming Lobo nightclub are frequented by pop stars and boy-bands like Westlife. Still, it all held no allure for Britney Spears, as when she was in Dublin in 2004 she stayed at the Westbury Hotel, which, by the way, gets its share of star guests as well.

Owner Noel Comer is a friendly chap always up for a chat, while his gentle dog, Homer, pads around at breakfast time looking hopeful. In the main house, rooms are large and classy but simple with white walls and high ceilings; in the coach house rooms go sleek and modern, some with their own patios. Breakfast here is something else— think mushroom frittatas, fresh-baked cranberry bread, homemade granola, and crisp potato cakes. *31 Leeson Close, Lower Leeson St., Dublin 2.* ☎ *01/676-5011. Fax 01/676-2929. www.number31.ie. €150–€240 double. Rates include breakfast. Free parking. Bus: 11, 11A, 11B, 13, 13A, or 13B. Amenities: Bar; lounge. In room: TV, hair dryer.*

→ **Temple Bar Hotel** It may be twice as big and half as stylish as the Morgan, but this is still a solid option. The Art Deco lobby is warmed by a cast-iron fireplace, and guest rooms are filled with trad mahogany furnishings, with heaps of extras. The sky-lit, garden-style Terrace Restaurant serves sandwiches and pasta while the hotel bar is a heaving local nightspot called Buskers. *Fleet St., Temple Bar, Dublin 2.* ☎ *800/44-UTELL in the U.S. or 01/677-3333. www.towerhotelgroup.ie. €142–€182 double. Rates include full Irish breakfast. DART: Tara St. Bus: 78A or 78B. Amenities: Restaurant (light meals); bar; access to a nearby health club; concierge; room service; foreign-currency exchange. In room: TV, tea/coffeemaker, hair dryer, garment press.*

Outside the hotels, it's not a bad idea to go shopping, and Dublin's new posh department store, Harvey Nichols, is a good place to start. This upscale British outpost of London's glitzy Harvey Nicks is in a class of its own with designer clothes, bars (multiple), and an in-house nightclub. Marilyn Manson's sleek wife Dita Von Teese hangs out there when she's in town.

For her part, when she was here in 2005, Britney preferred a quieter incognito wander through the more mainstream shops on Grafton Street.

To find more Irish celebrities head to the seaside suburb of Dalkey, which along with the nearby town of Howth is home to so many stars that the locals jokingly call it "Bel Eire." Celebs in residence include Bono, Lisa Stansfield, film-director Neil Jordan, and novelist Maeve Binchy. These are tiny towns, though, so it's a little difficult to go unnoticed as you gaze hopefully at every passing person looking for recognizable facial features.

Out in the countryside, it's harder to track anybody down, but one good way to find them is to go where they go. When Paul McCartney and Heather Mills married in 2004, they honeymooned at the gorgeous manor house hotel known as Castle Leslie, in County Monaghan, about 70 miles from Dublin.

A few years before that Pierce Brosnan and Keeley Shay Smith were married at the equally gorgeous manor house Ashford Castle in County Mayo, and they were in good company, as dozens of celebrities—from the members of the rock band Oasis on down to the actress Christina Ricci—have spent time at this luxurious hotel. Unfortunately, room prices start at €360 per night. Which is a bit of a high price to pay to get an autograph.

Eating

Let's just say it plain: Eating out in Dublin is expensive. Most restaurants are pricey, and even restaurants that *should* be cheap—Chinese restaurants, Indian restaurants, and the like—cost more than you might expect them to. In fact, restaurant prices in Dublin are considerably more than you'd pay in a comparable U.S. city, or even in Paris or London. The problem, it seems, is a pesky combination of high taxes and a bit of nouveau riche overenthusiasm among restaurant owners for charging a lot. There is a kind of expensive = good ethos in Dublin sometimes, that can hit a budget traveler's wallet where it hurts.

Luckily, you can get a cost break in the city's many cafes and coffee shops, where you can pick up sandwiches and hot lunches at reasonable prices, as well as from pubs, which offer big Irish lunches (stews, meat pies, sausages, and mashed potatoes) at more old-fashioned prices. If you really want to save money, try buying sandwiches to go in grocery stores or street-corner delis at lunchtime and only eat out one meal a day. Or, if you don't mind eating this way, make lunch your big meal of the day (since lunchtime menus are much cheaper than dinner menus), and just grab a sandwich at dinner time. However you do it, don't fall prey to the city's obsession with spending money. Read menus before you go in, and order carefully. Wine, in particular, can really raise the bottom line.

Cheap

- - - - - - - - - - - - - - - - - - -

🎬 (**Best**) → **Beshoffs** FISH AND CHIPS
This is fish and chips gone up in the world.
Ivan Beshoff hopped over from Russia in 1913,
starting a fish business that developed into
this top-notch eatery. Recently renovated in
Victorian style, it has a chill atmosphere and
a simple self-service menu. Crisp chips are
served with a choice of fresh fish, from the
trad cod to classier options using salmon,
shark, prawns, and other local sea life—some
days there are as many as 20 different varieties. The potatoes are grown on a 120-
hectare (300-acre) farm in Tipperary and
freshly cut each day. A second shop is just
south of the Liffey at 14 Westmoreland St.,
Dublin 2 (☎ 01/677-8026). *6 Upper O'Connell
St., Dublin 1. ☎ 01/872-4400. All items €3–€7.
No credit cards. Mon–Sat 10am–9pm; Sun
noon–9pm. DART: Tara St. Bus: Any city-center
bus.*

→ **Cafe Bell** IRISH/SELF-SERVICE   In the
cobbled courtyard of early-19th-century St.
Teresa's Church, this gem of a place has high
ceilings and an old-world decor, providing
calm after the bustle of Grafton Street just a
block away. The menu changes daily but usually includes thick and tasty homemade
soups, thick-cut sandwiches, fresh salads,
quiches, lasagna, sausage rolls, scones, and
other baked goodies. *St. Teresa's Courtyard,
Clarendon St., Dublin 2. ☎ 01/677-7645. All
items €3–€6. No credit cards. Mon–Sat
9am–5:30pm. Bus: 16, 16A, 19, 19A, 22A, 55,
or 83.*

→ **Chompy's** BREAKFAST/LUNCH   Perched
high above the attractive Powerscourt Centre,
this is a favorite place for many Americans
living in Dublin to stop in for a familiar breakfast of pancakes with maple syrup, French
toast, eggs Benedict, or bagels. It's a brill
lunch spot too, churning out big, fresh sandwiches and soups. *Powerscourt Townhouse
Centre, Clarendon St., Dublin 2. ☎ 01/*
679-4552. *Main courses €4–€9. Daily noon–
5:30pm. Bus: Any city-center bus.*

→ **Cornucopia Wholefood Restaurant**
VEGETARIAN   This little cafe just off
Grafton Street is one of the best veggie
restaurants in the city. It also serves wholesome meals for people on various restricted
diets (vegan, nondairy, low sodium, low fat).
Soups are particularly good here, as are the
salads and the hot dishes, like the baked
lasagna made with eggplant. A delish healthy
alternative. *19 Wicklow St., Dublin 2. ☎ 01/
677-7583. Main courses €4–€10. Mon–Thurs
8am–7pm; Fri–Sat 8am–10pm. Bus: Any city-
center bus.*

→ **Elephant & Castle** AMERICAN   You
might think you could find this kind of food—
burgers, chicken wings, omelets—at any old
Yankee-style joint, but Noel Alexander lifts
everyday American cooking to an art form,
working a stove like he was raised in American
diners. His chicken wings are admired city-
wide and his burgers are out of this world.
This place fills up fast for breakfast, brunch,
lunch, afternoon nibble, dinner, and late
dinner. Expect to wait for a table. *18 Temple
Bar, Dublin 2. ☎ 01/679-3121. Main courses
€8–€22. Mon–Fri 8am–11:30pm; Sat 10:30am–
11:30pm; Sun noon–11:30pm. Bus: 51B, 51C, 68,
69, or 79.*

→ **Epicurean Food Hall** GOURMET FOOD
COURT   This first-rate food hall sells mountains of yummy artisan foods, local Irish
meats, and regional dishes. Shops to keep
an eye out for include **Caviston's,** Dublin's
fave deli, for smoked salmon and seafood;
Itsabagel, for just-like-home bagels, imported
from H&H Bagels in New York City; **Crème de
la Crème,** for French-style pastries and
cakes; **Missy and Mandy's,** for American-
style ice cream; **Nectar,** for a flood of healthy
juice drinks; and **Aroma Bistro** for Italian
paninis. There is limited seating but this place
gets jammed during lunchtime midweek, so

Eating in Dublin

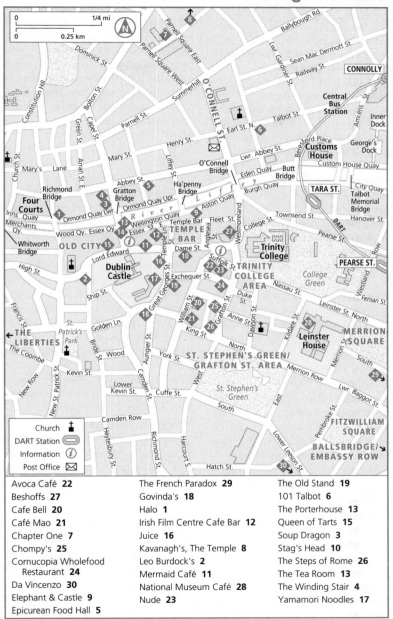

Avoca Café **22**	The French Paradox **29**	The Old Stand **19**
Beshoffs **27**	Govinda's **18**	101 Talbot **6**
Cafe Bell **20**	Halo **1**	The Porterhouse **13**
Café Mao **21**	Irish Film Centre Cafe Bar **12**	Queen of Tarts **15**
Chapter One **7**	Juice **16**	Soup Dragon **3**
Chompy's **25**	Kavanagh's, The Temple **8**	Stag's Head **10**
Cornucopia Wholefood Restaurant **24**	Leo Burdock's **2**	The Steps of Rome **26**
Da Vincenzo **30**	Mermaid Café **11**	The Tea Room **13**
Elephant & Castle **9**	National Museum Café **28**	The Winding Stair **4**
Epicurean Food Hall **5**	Nude **23**	Yamamori Noodles **17**

go off peak if possible. *Middle Abbey St., Dublin 1. No phone. All items €2–€12. No credit cards. Mon–Sat 10am–6pm. Bus: 70 or 80.*

➔ **Govinda's** VEGETARIAN The motto here is healthy square meals on square plates for very good prices. The meals are generous, belly-warming concoctions of vegetables, cheese, rice, and pasta. Every day, 10 main courses are offered cafeteria-style. Some are always Indian; others are your usual Euro dishes like lasagna or macaroni and cheese. Veggie burgers are prepared to order. For dessert, try a rich wedge of carrot cake with a dollop of cream or homemade ice cream. *4 Aungier St., Dublin 2. ☎ 01/475-0309. Main courses €8–€13. Mon–Sat noon–9pm. Closed Dec 24–Jan 2. Bus: 16, 16A, 19, or 22.*

➔ **Irish Film Centre Cafe Bar** IRISH/ INTERNATIONAL One of the hottest drinking spots in Temple Bar, the hip Cafe Bar (in the lobby of the city's coolest place to watch a movie) also features an excellent, good-deal menu that changes daily. Expect plenty of veg dishes and a smattering of Middle Eastern attitude. *6 Eustace St., Temple Bar, Dublin 2. ☎ 01/677-8788. Lunch and dinner €6–€10. Mon–Fri 12:30–3pm; Sat–Sun 1–3pm; daily 6–9pm. Bus: 21A, 78A, or 78B.*

➔ **Juice** VEGETARIAN If nobody told you Juice was a veggie restaurant, you'd probably never guess. Yes, the food is *that* good. The interior is also beautifully designed, with soaring 9m (30-ft.) ceilings and oh-so-classy decor. Brunch is classic here: Pancakes, huevos rancheros, and French toast topped with fresh fruit or organic maple syrup. The rest of the day you can sample the homemade dips—hummus, baba ghanouj, tapenade, roasted carrot pâté—with crudités and pita-bread strips. And, yes, there are about 30 different types of juices and smoothies on offer. *Castle House, 73 S. Great Georges St., Dublin 2. ☎ 01/475-7856. Reservations recommended Fri–Sat. Main courses €7–€10. AE, MC, V. Daily 11am–11pm. Bus: 50, 54, 56, or 77.*

➔ **Kavanagh's, The Temple** TRADI-TIONAL Situated on the corner of Dorset and Temple Street on the Northside, this pub has a real turn-of-the-20th-century feel to it. Come around lunch time and you'll find it packed out with office suits, but it's well worth the 15-minute stroll from O'Connell Street. Take your pick from daily specials, soup, or sandwiches. The toasted sandwich (turkey, ham, tomato, and onion) on chunky white bread is a particular winner. *71 Upper Dorset St. ☎ 01/874-1570. Pub food €5–€12. No credit cards. Mon–Fri 12:30–2:30pm. DART: Connolly. Bus: 11, 13, 16, 41, 33, or 33B.*

➔ **Leo Burdock's** FISH AND CHIPS From the first fish slapped in batter in 1913, this Irish takeaway shop across from Christ Church Cathedral is a Dublin institution. Cabinet ministers, university students, and businesspeople can all be spotted at the counter waiting for fish bought fresh that morning and good Irish potatoes, both cooked in "drippings" (none of that modern cooking oil nonsense here). There's no seating, but you can grab a nearby bench or stroll down to the park at St. Patrick's Cathedral. *2 Werburgh St., Dublin 8. ☎ 01/454-0306. Main courses €6–€7. No credit cards. Mon–Sat noon–midnight; Sun 4pm–midnight. Bus: 21A, 50, 50A, 78, 78A, or 78B.*

➔ **National Museum Café** CAFETERIA A great place to nab a cheap meal. The cafe is pretty casual but not ugly thanks to a mosaic floor, marble tabletops, and tall windows looking across the cobbled yard. Everything is made fresh: beef salad, chicken salad, quiche, an Everest of pastries. The soup of the day is often veggie, always good. Admission to the museum is free, so you can take a tour for afters. *National Museum of Ireland, Kildare St., Dublin 2. ☎ 01/677-7444. Soup €3; lunch main courses under €8. Tues–Sat 10am–5pm; Sun 2–5pm. Bus: 7, 7A, 8, 10, 11, or 13.*

→ **Nude** VEGETARIAN This small chain with sleek little outlets all around town is an excellent place to grab lunch or a snack without blowing your diet. The emphasis here is on healthy, from the freshly squeezed juices down to the wraps (chickpea and chili is a longtime favorite), sandwiches, soups, salads, and sweets. The prices aren't too chunky either. Other branches are at: 103 Lower Leeson St., 38 Upper Baggot St., and 28 Grafton St. *1 Suffolk St., Trinity College, Dublin 2. ☎ 01/ 67704804. www.nude.ie. Main courses €5–€6. No credit cards. Mon–Sat 7:30am–8:30pm; Sun 10am–6pm. Bus: 50, 54, or 56.*

→ **The Old Stand** TRADITIONAL One hundred fifty years ago this was a forge; now the horses have gone and been replaced with sporting celebs munching on pub grub. Choose from a daily special of soup, meat, vegetables, with tea or coffee, or omelets, salads, chicken, steak, or fish. *Note:* This is one of the few pubs serving food during evening hours. *37 Exchequer St. (just off Great George's St.), Dublin 2. ☎ 01/677-7220. www. theoldstandpub.com. Lunch main courses €10; dinner main courses €8–€13. Daily noon– 9pm. DART: Pearse or Tara St. Bus: Any city-center bus.*

Best → **The Porterhouse** TRADITIONAL One of Dublin's first microbrewery pubs and still a star. Bang in the middle of the Temple Bar action, prepare to get your lips round a constantly changing range of home-brewed ales, lagers, and stouts, all served up in a laid-back folksy atmosphere. Pull up one of the many pews and order some traditional chow. Irish stew, bangers and mash, and steak pie are all for the taking at rather attractive prices. *16–18 Parliament St., Temple Bar, Dublin 2. ☎ 01/679-8847. www.porterhouse brewco.com. Pub food €5–€14. Daily 11am– midnight. Any city-center bus.*

→ **Queen of Tarts** TEA SHOP A top spot to blow your diet on decadent cakes and cookies. The cake counter is dizzying—we

challenge you to try to come here and not order something sweet, like the luscious blackberry pie or the rich chocolate cake, with cream bursting from its seams. The scones are tender and light, dusted with powdered sugar and accompanied by little pots of jam. *4 Corkhill, Dame St., Dublin 2. ☎ 01/ 670-7499. Baked goods and cakes €1.25–€4. No credit cards. Mon–Fri 7:30am–7pm; Sat 9am–6pm; Sun 10am–6pm. Bus: Any city-center bus.*

Best → **Soup Dragon** SOUPS Soup has become the healthy, hip alternative to stodgy sandwiches and fast food, and the Soup Dragon leads the way for cheap and cheerful chow in Dublin. It's a tiny place, with less than a dozen stools alongside a bar, but it's big on drama. Think blue walls, black and red mirrors, orange slices and spice sticks flowing out of giant jugs, and huge flower-filled vases. The menu changes daily, but usually features a few traditional choices (potato and leek, carrot and coriander) as well as the more exotic (curried parsnip and sag aloo, a spicy Indian spinach and potato concoction). It's also a good place for dessert. Try the bread-and-butter pudding or the yummy banana bread. *168 Capel St., Dublin 1. ☎ 01/ 872-3277. All items €3–€8. Mon–Sat 9:30am– 6pm; Sun 1–6pm. Bus: 70 or 80.*

→ **Stag's Head** TRADITIONAL Built in 1770, the Stag's Head had its last "modernization" in 1895. Wrought-iron chandeliers, stained-glass skylights, huge mirrors, gleaming wood, and mounted stags' heads set the mood. Plump for soup and toasted sandwiches or heaping platters of bacon, beef, or chicken plus two veg. The pub is just off Exchequer Street (from Great George's St.)— look for the mosaic depicting a stag's head, embedded in the sidewalk of Dame Street, in the middle of the second block, on the left side coming from College Green, then turn onto the small lane that leads to Dame Court—a complicated journey, but worth the effort. *1 Dame Court, Dublin 2.* ☎ *01/679-3701. Main courses €5–€11. No credit cards. Mon–Fri 12:30–3:30pm and 5–7pm; Sat 12:30–2:30pm. DART: Pearse or Tara St. Bus: Any city-center bus.*

➔ **The Steps of Rome** ITALIAN/PIZZA Word is out that this restaurant—just off the busy shopping thoroughfare of Grafton Street—offers some of the best simple Italian fare in Dublin. Large, succulent pizza slices available for takeout are one way to enjoy the wonders of this authentic Italian kitchen when the dining room is full—the seven tables huddled within this tiny restaurant seem to be forever occupied. The potato, mozzarella and rosemary pizza, with a thick crust resembling focaccia, is particularly delish. Although the pasta dishes are also quite good, nothing tops those pizzas. *Chatham Court, off Chatham St., Dublin 2.* ☎ *01/670-5630. Main courses €8–€11; pizza slices €3.50. No credit cards. Mon–Sat 10am–midnight; Sun 1–11pm. DART: Pearse. Bus: Any city-center bus.*

MTV Best ➔ **The Winding Stair** HEALTH FOOD This relaxing bookshop is a great place to hang out with like-minded literature and caffeine fans, and its self-service cafe is a real refuge from the noisy street below. Indulge in a snack while browsing for secondhand gems among the three floors of books, all connected by the winding 18th-century staircase. Tall windows provide light and expansive views of the Ha'penny Bridge and River Liffey, and the food is simple and healthy—sandwiches made with additive-free meats or fruits (such as banana and honey), organic salads, homemade soups, and natural juices. If you come in the evening you might catch a poetry reading or recital. *40 Lower Ormond Quay, Dublin 1.* ☎ *01/873-3292. All items €2–€8. Mon–Sat 9:30am–6pm; Sun 1–6pm. Bus: 70 or 80.*

➔ **Yamamori Noodles** JAPANESE This Japanese restaurant is so fun and bouncy you might just be startled by how good the food

is. Prices range from bargain to splurge-for dishes like chili chicken ramen, and the yamamori yaki soba with a mound of wok-fried noodles, piled high with prawns, squid, chicken, and roast pork. Vegetarians aren't overlooked as there are plenty of veggie options. Lunch specials are outstanding here; work your day around it. *71–72 S. Great George's St., Dublin 2.* ☎ *01/475-5001. Reservations only for parties of 4 or more. Main courses €11–€18. Sun–Wed 12:30–11pm; Thurs–Sat 12:30–11:30pm. Bus: 50, 50A, 54, 56, or 77.*

Doable

➔ **Avoca Café** MODERN IRISH A polished, casual cafe perched above the vibrant pinks and reds of the knitted wools and painted doo-dads in the cutesy Avoca shop near Trinity College is one of Dublin's fave lunch spots. If you can rip yourself away from the shops, there are thick homemade soups, fresh salads, and chunky sandwiches in this buzzing cafe. *11–13 Suffolk St., Trinity College, Dublin 2.* ☎ *01/672-6019. www.avoca.ie. Main courses €9–€13. Mon–Wed and Fri 10am–6pm; Thurs 10am–8pm; Sat 10am–6:30pm; Sun 11am–6pm. Bus: 50, 54, or 56.*

➔ **Café Mao** ASIAN Dubliners have beaten a path to this place since it opened a few years back. It's already an icon. This is where to go for Asian cooking laced with attitude. An exposed kitchen lines an entire wall, and the rest of the space is wide open—tops for people-watching on weekends. The menu reads like a "best of Asia": Thai fish cakes, nasi goreng, chicken hoisin, salmon ramen. Everything is lush—you can't go wrong. There's a branch in the Pavilion in Dún Laoghaire now as well (☎ *01/214-8090). 2 Chatham Row, Dublin 2.* ☎ *01/670-4899. Reservations recommended. Main courses €13–€18. Mon–Wed noon–10:30pm; Thurs–Sat noon–11:30pm; Sun 1–10pm. DART: Pearse. Bus: 10, 11A, 11B, 13, or 20B.*

→ **Da Vincenzo** ITALIAN Occupying a storefront within a few minutes of St. Stephen's Green, this friendly, owner-run bistro creates a chill atmosphere with brick fireplaces, pine walls, dried flower arrangements, modern art, and a busy open kitchen. Pizza, with a light, pita-style dough cooked in a wood-burning oven, is a specialty here. Other main courses range from pastas to veal and beef dishes, including an organically produced filet steak. *133 Upper Leeson St., Dublin 4. ☎ 01/660-9906. Reservations recommended. Fixed-price lunch €11; dinner main courses €12–€22. Mon–Fri 12:30–11pm; Sat 1–11pm; Sun 3–10pm. Bus: 10, 11A, 11B, 46A, or 46B.*

→ **The French Paradox** FRENCH/WINE BAR Ooh we like this one, a lovely little bistro and wine bar that's endeared itself to Dublin thanks to its low prices. The wine's the thing here and you get a free glass when you order a main course. There are some scrummy cheese and ham plates too or, if you're feeling more peckish, what about that Bistro classic confit of duck with vegetables. A mighty fine choice. *53 Shelbourne Rd., Dublin 4. ☎ 01/660-4068. www.thefrench paradox.com. Reservations recommended. All items €10–€20. Mon–Sat noon–3pm and 2 evening sittings at 6 and 9pm. DART: Lansdowne Rd. Bus: 5, 6, 7, 8, or 18.*

→ **Mermaid Café** MODERN Owned by a chef and an artist, this fashionable eatery is a mixture of good restaurant and classy hangout. A lunchtime favorite of local professionals, and a good place to take a date in the evening, dishes often found on the frequently changing menu range from slow-roasted pork belly, to an array of first-rate seafood dishes, including a luxe Atlantic seafood casserole. *70 Dame St., Dublin 2. ☎ 01/670-8236. www.mermaid.ie. Reservations required. Dinner main courses €18–€30. Mon–Sat 12:30–2:30pm and 6–11pm; Sun* 12:30–3:30pm (brunch) and 6–9pm. Bus: 50, 50A, 54, 56A, 77, 77A, or 77B.

→ **101 Talbot** INTERNATIONAL This second-floor eatery above a shop might not look like much from the outside but don't be conned—it's actually a bright beacon of good cooking on the Northside. The menu features light, healthy food, with a focus on veg dishes. These change all the time but could include seared filet of tuna, roast duck breast, or Halloumi cheese and mushroom brochette. The dining area is casually funky, with contemporary Irish art, big windows, and newspapers scattered about. The staff is effortlessly friendly. *101 Talbot St. (at Talbot Lane near Marlborough St.), Dublin 1. ☎ 01/874-5011. Reservations recommended. Dinner main courses €14–€19. AE, MC, V. Tues–Sat 5–11pm. DART: Connolly. Bus: 27A, 31A, 31B, 32A, 32B, 42B, 42C, 43, or 44A.*

Splurge

📺 Best → **Chapter One** MODERN IRISH Arguably the city's most atmospheric restaurant, this stunner fills the vaulted basement space of the Dublin Writers Museum. Artfully lighted and tastefully decorated, it's one of the top restaurants in town. Meals are prepared with local, organic ingredients, all cleverly used in incredible dishes like the ravioli with Irish goat cheese and warm asparagus, and the Irish beef with shallot gratin. *18–19 Parnell Sq., Dublin 2. ☎ 01/873-2266. www.chapteronerestaurant.com. Reservations recommended. Main courses €20–€35; fixed-price dinner €52. Tues–Fri 12:30–2:30pm and 6–11pm; Sat 6–11pm. Bus: 27A, 31A, 31B, 32A, 32B, 42B, 42C, 43, or 44A.*

→ **Halo** FRENCH/FUSION This is easily one of the hippest, hottest places to eat in Dublin—so book your table before you leave home. The room is buzzy and stylish—the perfect backdrop for chef Jean-Michel Poulot's elaborate cooking. The food is French fusion—strange combinations of taste and texture that manage to be elegant as well as a bit far-flung. There's loin of venison with sweet potato fondant and braised cabbage, or fillet of beef with shallots tatin and smoked bacon *jus*. Fans believe there's no place like it; detractors dismiss it as snobby and unimpressive. Decide for yourself. *Morrison Hotel, Ormond Quay, Dublin 1.* ☎ *01/878-2999. www. morrisonhotel.ie. Reservations required. Dinner main courses €32–€45. Daily 7–10:30pm; Sat–Sun noon–3:30pm. DART: Connolly. Bus: 70 or 80.*

→ **The Tea Room** INTERNATIONAL   This ultrasmart restaurant, ensconced in the U2-owned Clarence hotel, is guaranteed to deliver one of your most memorable meals in Ireland. This gorgeous room's soaring yet understated lines are the perfect backdrop for Antony Ely's complex but controlled cooking, which takes form in dishes like loin of Finnebrogue venison with celeriac puree, or the roasted organic salmon with lentils and red wine *jus*. Desserts can wax creative, as in the basil crème brûlée. *In The Clarence, 6–8 Wellington Quay, Dublin 2.* ☎ *01/670-9000. Reservations required. Fixed-price 2-course dinner €48; 3-course dinner €55. Mon–Fri 12:30–2pm; Mon–Sun 6:30–9:45pm. Bus: 51B, 51C, 68, 69, or 79.*

Partying

Nightlife in Dublin is a well shaken cocktail of traditional pubs, where the Irish music swirls and jangles, and cool modern bars, where the latest techno rhythms fill the air, and the crowd knows more about Prada than the Pogues. There's little in the way of crossover, although there are a couple of quieter bars and a few pubs with a rock music angle, should you be in a hybrid mood.

If you're here to dance, keep an eye on local listings magazines and websites, since things change constantly. The same club could be a gay fetish scene one night and techno-pop dance the next, so you have to stay on your toes. The first rule is to get the latest listings from local magazines or websites—pick up a copy of *In Dublin* and the *Event Guide* at local cafes and shops if you're looking for the latest on the club scene. Or check out the website of the *Irish Times* (www.ireland.com), which offers a "what's on" daily guide to cinema, theater, music, and whatever else you're up for. The *Dublin Events Guide* (www.dublinevents. com) also provides a comprehensive listing of the week's entertainment possibilities.

The hottest clubs have a "strict" (read: unfriendly) door policy of admitting only "regulars." Your chances of getting past the door increase if you're female and wear your hippest clothes.

Cover charges tend to fluctuate from place to place and from night to night and even from person to person (some people can't buy their way in, while others glide in gratis). Cover charges range from nothing to €15.

One key difference between pubs, bars, and clubs is open hours. Pubs tend to be open all day and virtually all close at 11pm, based on long-standing tradition, more than anything else. Bars and music clubs usually open at 7pm and stay open until 2am, while nightclubs open even later, and stay open as late as there are dancers on the floor.

Bars & Winebars

Going to a bar is the best way to get a cocktail you'll recognize from home—in fact, bars here are cocktail crazy. Flaming Nipples and Curvy Hips—if it has a dumb name, it's going to be on the menu. To help you decide what to order, most bars have "drinks menus" which will guide you to the house specials (often the most expensive items, strangely enough). Usually it's cheaper to order traditional drinks (martinis, Bloody Marys, and so on) than the latest drink craze. Prices have risen in recent years, so expect to pay anything from €4.50 for a basic gin and tonic to €12 for a fancy tall cocktail with a fruity umbrella.

→ **Ba Mizu** This bar draws the young, glamorous set. The clientele includes a regular smattering of models (both male and female) and trendy urbanites. *Powerscourt Townhouse Centre, S. William St., Dublin 2.* ☎ *01/674-6712.*

→ **The Bank** As the name implies, this bar is in a converted bank building, and that is somehow appropriate, given that the crowd is made up largely of professionals in very expensive shoes. It's got a good reputation, and it's a gorgeous, vast space. *20—22 College Green, Dublin 2.* ☎ *01/677-0677.*

[MTV] [Best] → **Bruxelles** This is one of Dublin's late-night bars, staying open until 2:30am on weekends, and its crowd tends to be well lubricated and therefore somewhat overly friendly. It's not a beautiful place, but it's very popular with locals. Somewhere to get off your face and embrace someone you've never met before. *7—8 Harry St., off Grafton St., Dublin.* ☎ *01/677-5362.*

→ **Café en Seine** This vast bar packs in thousands of young, well-dressed, well-paid local professionals, and yet it never seems crowded. It's a gorgeous turn-of-the-century building, with plenty of architectural detail, but nobody who comes here regularly much cares. They're here for the booze and each other. Get a load of both. *40 Dawson St., Dublin 2.* ☎ *01/677-4567.*

→ **Capitol Lounge** A bland, modern bar, the Capitol is a favorite with young partiers getting a bit liquored up before heading out to the clubs. Thus its happy hour specials often run until 11pm, pushing the limits of the whole happy *hour* thing. Downstairs has a small dance floor and a more frenetic vibe; upstairs there's a slightly more chilled out groove. Open Mon—Thurs 10:30am—2:30am;

Fri—Sat 10:30am—2:30am; Sun noon—2:30am. *18-19 Lr. Stephens St., Dublin 2.* ☎ *01/475-7166.*

→ **Cocoon** This is a small, minimalist space with lots of straight lines and open spaces, and with big windows designed so that those outside can admire your new outfit. The color scheme is chocolate and cream; it's filled with low tables, tiny candles, and leather stools; and it's only for the beautiful people. *Royal Hibernian Way, off Grafton St., Dublin 2.* ☎ *01/679-6259. www. cocoon.ie.*

[MTV] [Best] → **Copper Face Jacks** Locals believe this busy club is *the* Dublin pickup joint. Everybody here is on the make, they say, and everything is physical—it's not how smart you are that counts; it's how good you look. The young crowd (most are in their early 20s) are here to chat, drink, and meet members of the opposite sex. It's loud, steamy, and crowded, but my-oh-my it's a fine looking place. Open daily 10pm to 3am. *29 Harcourt St., Dublin 2.* ☎ *01/475-8777. www. jackson-court.ie/copper.html.*

→ **Karma** In the George Frederic Handel Hotel at the edge of Temple Bar, Karma is easy to find, and hugely popular for such a small club. Its DJ lineup is solid, and wall-to-wall—this place is serious about music and dancing. Karma is a favorite of expats and students, so it's a good place to meet other Americans. Those in the know often stop in for dinner between 5:30—8:30pm, and the food is okay, as are the prices. *George Frederic Handel Hotel, 16—18 Fishamble St., Temple Bar, Dublin 2.* ☎ *01/670-9400. Mon—Wed noon—11:30pm; Thurs—Sat noon—3am; Sun noon—11pm.*

→ **The Market Bar** This is what they call around here a "superpub." It's not really a pub at all, just a big, laid-back bar, with a soaring ceiling, gorgeous design, a good beer and wine list, and friendly bar staff. This is the kind of place where you could sit in the late afternoon and have a solitary pint and

DUBLIN

Partying in Dublin

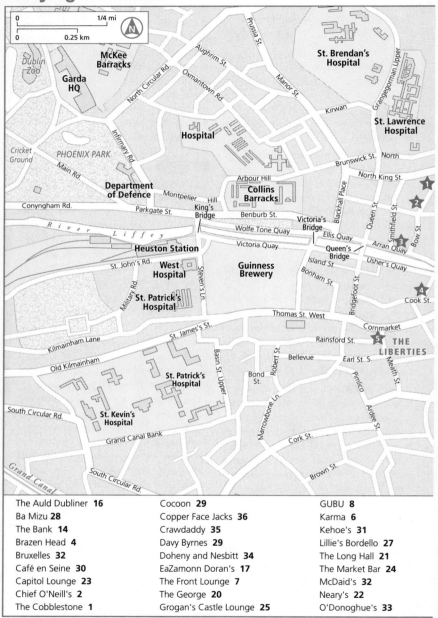

The Auld Dubliner **16**	Cocoon **29**	GUBU **8**
Ba Mizu **28**	Copper Face Jacks **36**	Karma **6**
The Bank **14**	Crawdaddy **35**	Kehoe's **31**
Brazen Head **4**	Davy Byrnes **29**	Lillie's Bordello **27**
Bruxelles **32**	Doheny and Nesbitt **34**	The Long Hall **21**
Café en Seine **30**	EaZamonn Doran's **17**	The Market Bar **24**
Capitol Lounge **23**	The Front Lounge **7**	McDaid's **32**
Chief O'Neill's **2**	The George **20**	Neary's **22**
The Cobblestone **1**	Grogan's Castle Lounge **25**	O'Donoghue's **33**

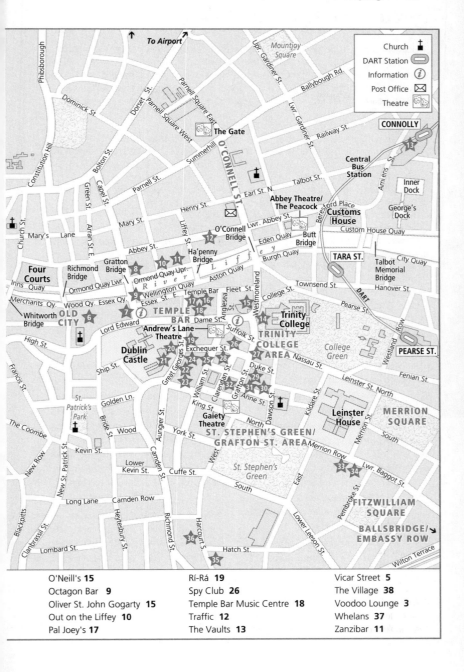

old Enough to Know Better

Dublin may be a party town, but Ireland's a conservative country, and you need to bear that in mind. Given its reputation as a fun-loving, hard-drinking place, this island just might surprise you with its collective habit of looking at the world over the top of its metaphorical glasses and clucking its tongue. A combination of strong religious mores and a largely rural environment make this a cautious, old-fashioned place.

Luckily for you, though, this is Europe.

We say luckily for you, because even the most conservative country in Europe is going to be more liberal than the big killjoy the U.S. has turned into lately, so conservative as it is, Ireland has a lower age limit for just about everything.

When was the last time 18 was the legal drinking age in your hometown? The 1980s, that's when. But that's what it is in Ireland. From 18 on you can buy alcohol in liquor stores (which are called "off-licenses" here), and drink in pubs. Some nightclubs are exceptions to that rule, though, and voluntarily set higher age limits of 21 or even 23, so check with the venue before you go if you're at the lower end of the age range.

Other age limits are similarly promising for the young and hopeful—you must be at least 16 to buy cigarettes, and 17 to drive.

You can legally have sex at 17, but you can't get married until you're 18. Hey! What kind of message are they sending here?

Do you think we should point that out to them?

Nah, nevermind.

DUBLIN

nobody would bother you. Its no-music policy means it's quiet enough to hear yourself drink. *Fade St., off South Great George's St., Dublin 2.* ☎ *01/613-9094. www.marketbar.ie.*

→ **McDaid's** This was Brendan Behan's favorite pub—well, one of them at least; he had so many—back in his Dublin drinking days, and it still has a literary bent, although it's well on the tourist track these days, and thus has lost some of its cool cache. Still, it's got a good atmosphere. *3 Harry St., off Grafton St., Dublin 2.* ☎ *01/679-4395.*

📺 (Best) → **Octagon Bar** This incredibly trendy bar on the ground floor of the Clarence Hotel is one of the hottest places in town. It's got an eight-sided bar, which the bartenders handle with aplomb, and you don't have to be rich or beautiful to get in the door. There's a quieter back room, and prices are not as high as they might be. A fave celeb hangout. *Clarence Hotel, 6–8 Wellington Quay, Dublin 2.* ☎ *01/670-9000.*

→ **O'Donoghue's** Tucked between St. Stephen's Green and Merrion Street, this touristy, smoke-filled enclave is the grand-daddy of traditional music pubs in Dublin, and it's usually packed with Americans. A spontaneous session is likely to erupt at almost any time of the day or night. *15 Merrion Row, Dublin 2.* ☎ *01676-2807.*

→ **Voodoo Lounge** Partly owned by New York's Fun Lovin' Criminals, this hip, North-side joint is a hardcore music and dance bar, and a popular late-night hangout for those who are not into the normal techno-pop mix. Given its roots, it's unsurprising that the music here is the latest and best stuff around, with an emphasis on hip-hop and R&B. This place isn't pretty, but it's cool. *38 Arran Quay, Dublin 7.* ☎ *01873-6013.*

The Talk of the Town

Five Ways to Start a Conversation with a Local

The main thing you need to do to strike up a conversation in Dublin is to ask a question. Any question, generally, will do. Avoid politics (you never know what side somebody's on), but just about anything else is open season. Ask for advice (you know you need it), and odds are the conversation will take off from there. Here are a few topics to get you started.

1. The Irish are very proud of their famous fellow-citizens, especially the musicians, so ask about somebody you've heard of. This could include Bono's international peace-keeping penchant, Sinéad O'Connor's strangeness, just how good are the Thrills anyway? And so on.

2. "What's your favorite pub?" Ask for advice on where to go, or, if you're already there, ask for advice on what to order. It doesn't always work (Dubliners in pubs are a bit savvy to this one), but they're often patient and helpful. Once they know you're friendly and curious about all things Ireland, conversation should come easy.

3. Ask just what the heck Gaelic football and hurling are. Locals love the games, so their enthusiasm should propel the conversation.

4. The weather is a bit of a national obsession. It's predictably unpredictable, and dull though this conversation might seem, everybody's always willing to tell you, "You think this is cold? This is nothing! You should have been here last winter. Now *that* was cold!"

5. Ireland itself seems an inexhaustible subject for the locals. Ask what anybody's favorite region is—What should you absolutely not miss?—and expect to be listening for some time.

DUBLIN

Best → Zanzibar This, like the Market Bar, is one of Dublin's "superpubs"—a big, sleek bar, with a relaxed publike atmosphere. In its extravagant, vaguely North African–style setting, a huge crowd of young professionals mixes with local university students, and looking good is what it's all about. It's a well-known "meat market," so be prepared for that level of interaction. You can't miss its huge purple facade on Ormond Quay—inside it has multiple levels, multiple bars, and DJs spinning tunes every night from 9pm. Open daily 5pm to 2:30am. *Ormond Quay, Dublin 1.* ☎ *01/878-7212.*

Pubs

See also "Pubs for Traditional & Folk Music," below.

Pubs generally serve beer and liquor, but most don't do much in the way of cocktails beyond a vodka tonic or rum and coke. Ask for a cosmopolitan, and you'll likely get a blank stare. Beer is generally sold by the pint and half-pint. Prices are pretty uniform in the city center: A shot of whiskey runs around €3.50, a pint of stout about €3.50, and lager €3.70.

→ Davy Byrnes In *Ulysses,* Leopold Bloom describes this place as a "moral pub," and stops in for a Gorgonzola sandwich and a glass of burgundy. It has drawn poets, writers, and readers ever since. It dates from 1873, when Davy Byrnes first opened the doors—he presided over it for more than 50 years, and visitors can still see his likeness on one of the turn-of-the-20th-century murals hanging over the bar. *21 Duke St. (off Grafton St.), Dublin 2.* ☎ *01/677-5217. www.davybyrnes.com*

You Make Me Want to Hurl

This country is sports crazy. Absolutely nuts for athletic events.

The only problem is, most of the sports they're crazy for, you've never heard of. Consider this: the number one sport in Ireland? Hurling. Number two? Gaelic football. Soccer's a weak number three.

Still, if you're a sporty type yourself, don't be put off by the unfamiliarity of the games. These are wild and crazy sports, and a hurling match or a Gaelic football game will just about put hair on your chest, and they're well worth seeing. Gaelic football is a cross between rugby and soccer, while hurling closely resembles a kind of hockey hybrid. Both games are fast, furious, and not for the faint of heart. And, this is no laughing matter—as Ireland's national sports, they are treated with near-reverence.

The rules are fairly simple: In both games, teams of 15 players compete on a playing field with both rugby goalposts and soccer nets. Getting the ball in the net is worth three points (a goal) while putting it over the crossbar earns one point. Just how players in each sport achieve this, however, is where the games differ.

Gaelic football's closest living relative is Australian Rules Football—like soccer on speed with referees in weird hats, which gives you an idea of what to expect there.

Hurling is much more ancient and just as fast. In hurling games the ball, or *slíothar,* is hit or carried along by a hurley stick. Along the way the clash of the ash and the aggressive momentum of the game make the whole thing ludicrously exhilarating to watch.

Reference is made to hurling in Ireland's ancient Brehon laws, which date to the 8th century, so this is a truly old, truly Irish sport. It was so popular during the English occupation that it was banned for a time by the British killjoys, who thought if it was popular it must be subversive, but in villages around the country the playing never really stopped.

Today, both sports are played in every county in the country, and the All-Ireland Championship played out each summer is a series of games of such quintessential Irishness that if you are lucky enough to see one, you're likely never to forget it.

On game nights you'll see the locals streaming into pubs in their team colors, chanting and singing, and, win or lose, you'll likely see them later, celebrating or drowning their sorrows—you'll be able to tell by looking at them how their team fared.

If you want to find out more, check out the Gaelic Athletic Association website (www.gaa.ie). It oversees all the major teams in the country.

MTV Best →**Doheny and Nesbitt** Competition is stiff, but this may well be the best looking traditional pub in town. The Victorian bar houses two fine old "snugs"—small rooms behind the main bar where women could have a drink out of the sight of men in days of old—and a restaurant that's good for traditional Irish food. *5 Lower Baggot St., Dublin 2.* ☎ *01/676-2945.*

→**Grogan's Castle Lounge** This eclectic place is a bit rundown around the edges, but it's a proper local pub, not heavily frequented by tourists. Its crowd includes local writers and artists, as well as people who just live around the corner. It's a good place to get in touch with local nightlife. *15 William St. S., Dublin 2.* ☎ *01/677-9320.*

→ **Kehoe's** This tiny traditional bar is best during the day when it's not too crowded and you can take in its old-fashioned character, eavesdrop on its chatty regulars, and settle in for a pint or two in its comfortable snugs. *9 S. Anne St., Dublin 2.* ☎ *01/677-8312.*

📺 Best → **The Long Hall** This is Doheny and Nesbitt's main competition in the Prettiest Pub Contest. With a beautiful Victorian decor of filigree-edged mirrors, polished dark woods, and traditional snugs, this place is like a theater of beer. The atmosphere is great, and bartenders pour a good pint. *51 S. Great George's St., Dublin 2.* ☎ *01/475-1590.*

→ **Neary's** Adjacent to the back door of the Gaiety Theatre, this celebrated enclave is a favorite with stage folk and theatergoers. Its pink-and-gray marble bar and Victorian touches, like the brass hands that support the globe lanterns by the entrance, give it a touch of class. *1 Chatham St., Dublin 2.* ☎ *01/677-7371 or 01/677-8596.*

→ **O'Neill's** This friendly place is the pub equivalent of quicksand—you walk in for a quick pint, and before you know it, it's midnight and you've got 20 new best friends. It's big and noisy, but it's made up of a series of smaller rooms, and that makes it a pleasant place for conversation. Gets boisterous at the weekends. *2 Suffolk St., Dublin 2.* ☎ *01/679-3671. www.oneillsbar.com*

Pubs for Traditional & Folk Music

If you're here for the more old-fashioned Irish music, there are quite a few alternatives. Generally the band plays in the main bar for tips, although sometimes there's a separate room for music, and the entrance fee is paid at the door (in cash)—usually €5 to €8.

Pub Hours

Remember: Almost ALL pubs close at 11:30pm Monday through Wednesday, 12:30am Thursday through Saturday, and 11pm Sunday.

→ **The Auld Dubliner** A pub for people who don't normally go to pubs. It's in Temple Bar, so it's central. It's completely relaxed, with bands playing traditional music upstairs, Irish stew on the stove, and quiet pints at the downstairs pub. *17 Anglesea St., Dublin 2.* ☎ *01/677-0527.*

→ **Brazen Head** In its time, revolutions were plotted in this brass-filled, lantern-lit pub. The Head was first licensed in 1661, which makes it one of the oldest pubs in Ireland. Nestled on the south bank of the River Liffey, it is at the end of a cobblestone courtyard and was once the meeting place of rebels Robert Emmet and Wolfe Tone. Trad music sessions start at 9:30pm nightly. *20 Lower Bridge St., Dublin 8.* ☎ *01/677-9549.*

→ **Chief O'Neill's** This Northside pub in a hotel of the same name is a serious music-lovers option. The hotel has a music theme, and the pub is one of the best places in town to catch gimmick-free traditional music. *Smithfield Village, Dublin 7.* ☎ *01/817-3838. www.chiefoneills.com. Bus: 25, 25A, 66, 67, or 90.*

→ **The Cobblestone** This is the most Irish of Irish pubs, with a musicians' corner downstairs where trad Irish music is played for free, and a proper music hall upstairs where you have to buy tickets but the bands are top-notch. It's one of the places the locals go to hear music, so expect to find none of what they call "paddy-whackery." *77 King St. N., Dublin 7.* ☎ *01/872-1799.*

→ **Oliver St. John Gogarty** In the heart of Temple Bar and named for one of Ireland's literary greats, this pub has an inviting old-world atmosphere, with shelves of empty bottles, stacks of dusty books, a horseshoe-shaped bar, and old barrels for seats. There are traditional-music sessions most every night from 9 to 11pm, as well as Saturday at 4:30pm, and Sunday from noon to 2pm. *57–58 Fleet St., Dublin 2. ☎ 01/671-1822.*

Music Clubs

The best place in town to catch an up-and-coming band is always going to be in one of these music bars. Most have been around for years, and all have excellent reputations for attracting bands with a top potential to rock your world.

📺 **Best** ➔ **Crawdaddy** Dublin's most intimate live music venue, Crawdaddy has a classy look—like a chilled-out House of Blues. Its good acoustics and fab indie gigs make it one of the hottest places in town to catch a band. The staff is friendly. The atmosphere is deeply casual. Open nightly from 5pm. *Old Harcourt Station, Harcourt St., Dublin 2. ☎ 01/478-0166.*

➔ **Eamonn Doran's** This Temple Bar hefty is one of the city's top music bars, with regular gigs by local and national acts. Rock music dominates here, but you can also catch cool jazz from time to time. A great place to hang out and catch an up-and-coming act. *3A Crown Alley, Temple Bar, Dublin 2. ☎ 01/679-9114.*

➔ **Pal Joey's** This place is hit or miss—it all depends when you get here. Come early to watch in horror as limp couples linger around the piano bar for shows at 8pm and 10:30pm. Come later—we're talking after 2am—to dive into the crowds at one of Dublin's favorite late-night bars. Yes, the drinks are a little pricey, but where else are you going to get a pint of Warshteiner at this hour? Open daily 8pm to 4am. *15–16 Crown Alley, Temple Bar, Dublin 2. ☎ 01/671-7288. www.paljoey.ie.*

➔ **Temple Bar Music Centre** One of Dublin's hugest names in music, the TBMC attracts both Irish and international bands.

The emphasis here is vaguely on indie sounds, but its booking policy is wide ranging, so arrive open-minded. Late on weekend nights it converts into a dance club, while on Saturday afternoons it features local musicians. *Curved St., Temple Bar, Dublin 2. ☎ 01/670-9202. www.tbmc.ie.*

➔ **Vicar Street** Part of the holy music trilogy (along with Whelans and The Village), Vicar Street is a busy, multifarious bar and music club, with a constant stream of Irish, British, and international bands gracing its stage. A great place to know about, and even better place to hang out. *99 Vicar St., Dublin 8. ☎ 01/454-5533. www.vicarstreet.com.*

➔ **The Village** This modern music venue and bar within stumbling distance of Whelans is a first-rate place to have a drink and chill, and maybe catch some amazing new Irish band. The very best Irish and international indie bands play here, so you can hardly go wrong popping by to see who's on stage. *26 Wexford St., Dublin 2. ☎ 01/475-8555. www.thevillagevenue.com.*

📺 **Best** ➔ **Whelans** This relaxed, colorful bar has been nurturing young musicians for decades now, and it's still one of the top three places in Dublin for live gigs by Irish bands. In a pre-Victorian building decorated inside with murals inspired by the Book of Kells, it packs in crowds to hear acts with the potential to make it big. It's also a friendly place, and a top spot for meeting locals. *25 Wexford St., Dublin 2. ☎ 01/478-0766. www. whelanslive.com.*

Clubs

The area around Grafton Street remains the hottest section of town for nightclub action, which is handy as there are ample bars and pubs around there if you want to gather with friends first before heading out to the nightclub.

📺 **Best** ➔ **Lillie's Bordello** Open more than a decade and still the hippest of them all, Lillie's breaks the rule that you've got to be new to be hot. Paintings of nudes hanging on whorehouse-red walls is the look that's made Lillie's a surprisingly unraunchy icon of kitsch. There's a well-deserved reputation for posers and boy-band celebrities, and the door policy can best be described as callous, except on Sundays. If you don't feel like dancing, head for "The Library," whose floor-to-ceiling bookcases and well-worn leather Chesterfields evoke a Victorian gentlemen's club. Open daily from 11pm to 3am. *Adam Court, off Grafton St., Dublin 2.* ☎ *01/679-9204.*

➔ **Rí-Rá** The name means "uproar" in Irish. It fits. Though trendy, Rí-Rá has a friendlier door policy than most of its competition, so this may be the place to try first. Open nightly from 11:30pm to 4am or later. *1 Exchequer St., Dublin 2.* ☎ *01/677-4835.*

➔ **Spy Club** Fashionable 30-somethings love this lounge bar, where the emphasis is firmly on socializing. The look begins with a classical, 18th-century town house with mile-high, corniced ceilings. Next, add Greco-Roman friezes and pared-down, contemporary furnishings. Need more drama? The VIP room's focal point is a photo of a woman in the buff riding a tiger pelt—an in-your-face wink at the Celtic tiger. Saturday is electric pop night; Sunday is gay night. Open nightly from 7pm to 3am. *Powerscourt Townhouse Centre, S. William St., Dublin 2. No phone.*

➔ **Traffic** Located opposite Arnott's department store, this urban-cool bar and club covers three floors. Music is provided by a mix of Dublin DJs and international talent. By day, the mood is fresh and funky; after hours things get hotter. *54 Middle Abbey St., Dublin 1.* ☎ *01/873-4800.*

➔ **The Vaults** This is a double-edged club—fave lunch spot for local office workers by day, crowded dance club by night. Set in the heart of Dublin's booming financial district, it's fantastically atmospheric, with polished floors and low brick arches under which bar tables and stools are arranged. Unfortunately as it's close to no other nightlife, any bar-hop that starts here usually ends here, too. Open nightly from 10pm to 3am or later. *Harbourmaster Place, IFSC, Dublin 1.* ☎ *01/605 4700. www.thevaults.ie.*

Performance Halls

Bigger, international bands and classical music orchestras generally play in a handful of larger venues scattered around the city and its suburbs. Check local magazines and newspapers to see what's coming up. For most of these performances, tickets need to be purchased weeks, if not months, in advance.

➔ **The Helix** This massive auditorium at University College Dublin hosts many concerts throughout the year. The box office is open Monday to Saturday 10am to 6pm. *Collins Ave., Glasnevin, Dublin 9.* ☎ *01/700-7077. www.helix.ie. Tickets €13–€60.*

➔ **National Concert Hall** This 1,200-seat hall is home to the National Symphony Orchestra and Concert Orchestra, and hosts dozens of international orchestras and performing artists. In addition to classical music, there are Broadway-style musicals, opera, jazz, and recitals. The box office is open Monday to Friday from 10am to 3pm and from 6pm to close of concert. Open weekends 1 hour before concerts. Parking is available on the street. *Earlsfort Terrace, Dublin 2.* ☎ *01/417-0000. www.nch.ie. Tickets €10–€35. Lunchtime concerts €5.*

➔ **The Point Depot** With a seating capacity of 3,000, The Point is one of Dublin's larger indoor theater/concert venues, attracting Broadway-caliber shows and international stars such as Justin Timberlake and Tom Jones. The box office is open Monday to Saturday 10am to 6pm. Parking is €4 per car. *East Link Bridge, North Wall Quay.* ☎ *01/836-3633. Tickets €13–€65.*

DUBLIN

Up & Coming
••

There must be something in the water. What is it about Ireland and music? This place is, and always has been, lousy with musicians. Good musicians. Innovative bands. An endless array of gigs. If you like music, this is heaven.

Obviously most people have heard of the most famous Irish bands—U2, Sinéad O'Connor, Van Morrison—but there's a younger generation that fewer have yet discovered, but which music aficionados know all about. Led by Snow Patrol, the Northern Ireland band whose catchy ballad "Run" was a hit on U.S. college radio in 2003, and the Thrills, whose California-style sound propelled the album *So Much for the City* up the charts in 2004, these bands all seem to be headed for the big time, and if you see them playing around, get your tickets early as they're certain to sell out.

The band Bell X1 plays music with a soft lyrical grace that has earned them awards, U.S. tours, and a stint on the California radio station KCRW's influential "Morning Becomes Eclectic" show. Their album *Neither Am I* played well on college radio in the U.S., and its sound has been described as "sweet, emotive ballads teetering on the edge of sonic paroxysms." Which about sums them up.

Based in Dublin, Blink is a jobbing band with a gentle indie sound and sharply creative lyrics. Their records are popular in Ireland, Europe, and the U.K., and they've had four Irish top 10 singles.

Loud, brash, and defiant, the three-piece Dublin-based band Future Kings of Spain has been receiving critical acclaim since it formed in 2000. Its songs of love, fear, anger, and hope strike a note with college students in Ireland and the U.K. who keep them touring almost constantly.

The Kings are virtually spring chickens compared to The Frames—as their website sums it up, "Fourteen years old. Fourteen years of Dublin. Fourteen years of touring America, Europe, the East. Six record companies. Four managers. Many big loans. A hundred songs. No press." Indeed, and those songs are intelligent and beautifully crafted, and increasingly popular with music fans around the world. Check them out if you get the chance.

Another to check out is the tousle-haired singer-songwriter Damien Dempsey, whose alt-country sound gets quite a bit of airtime in Ireland and the U.K. If you like Dempsey's thoughtful lyrics, you should also track down the Dublin-based singer-songwriter Paddy Casey, who's rockin' 2005 album *Amen (So Be It)* was a hit with European music critics.

This is in no way all of the acts you should look out for, but if you see one of these bands playing, you can hardly go wrong.

Comedy Clubs

Along with the clubs listed below, **Vicar Street** (p. 86) tends to get many of the international comics. As always, check the latest listings magazines for details. Admission ranges from €5 to €20 depending on the act and the night.

➔ Ha'Penny Laugh Comedy Club

Ha'Penny plays host to some of Ireland's funniest people, many of whom are in theater. The Battle of the Axe is a weekly show in which comedians, singers, songwriters, musicians, actors, and whoever storms the open mic in pursuit of the Lucky Duck Award.

Ha'penny Bridge Inn, Merchant's Arch, 42 Wellington Quay, Dublin 2. ☎ *01/677-0616.*

→ **International Bar** This virtually legendary bar hosts comedy clubs 3 nights a week: Thursdays and Saturdays it's Murphy's International Comedy Club, and Wednesdays it's the Comedy Cellar (which, you'll be unsurprised to learn, is held upstairs). While Murphy's International is more established comedians, the Cellar is young and unpredictable. *23 Wicklow St., Dublin 2.* ☎ *01/677-9250.*

Classical Concerts, Dance & Theater

The online booking site **Ticketmaster** (www.ticketmaster.ie) is an excellent place to get a quick look at what's playing where and also to buy tickets. In addition to the major theaters listed below, other venues present fewer, although on occasion quite impressive, productions. They also book music and dance performances. They include the **Focus Theatre,** 12 Fade St., Dublin 2 (☎ **01/671-2417**); the **Olympia,** 72 Dame St., Dublin 2 (☎ **01/679-3323**); **Project: Dublin,** 39 E. Essex St., Dublin 2 (☎ **01/679-6622**); and the **Tivoli,** 135–138 Francis St., opposite Iveagh Market, Dublin 8 (☎ **01/454-4472**).

→ **Abbey Theatre** For more than 90 years, the Abbey has been the national theater of Ireland. The original theater, destroyed by fire in 1951, was replaced in 1966 by the current functional, although uninspired, 600-seat house. The Abbey's artistic reputation in Ireland has risen and fallen many times, but is reasonably strong at present. *Lower Abbey St., Dublin 1.* ☎ *01/878-7222. www.abbeytheatre.ie. Tickets €15–€26. Student discounts.*

→ **Andrews Lane Theatre** This relatively new venue has a rising reputation for fine theater. It consists of a 220-seat main theater where contemporary work from home and abroad is presented, and a 76-seat

studio geared for experimental productions. *9–17 St. Andrews Lane, Dublin 2.* ☎ *01/679-5720. Tickets €13–€20.*

→ **Gaiety** The elegant little Gaiety holds a varied array of performances, including everything from opera to classical Irish plays to Broadway-style musicals and variety acts. *King St. S., Dublin 2.* ☎ *01/677-1717. Tickets €21–€25 or €15 for previews.*

→ **The Gate** Just north of O'Connell Street off Parnell Square, this recently restored 370-seat theater was founded in 1928 by Hilton Edwards and Michael MacLiammoir to provide a venue for a broad range of plays. That policy prevails today, with a program that includes a blend of modern works and the classics. Although less known by visitors, The Gate is easily as distinguished as the Abbey. *1 Cavendish Row, Dublin 1.* ☎ *01/874-4368. Tickets €21–€25 or €15 for previews.*

→ **The Peacock** In the same building as the Abbey, this 150-seat theater features contemporary plays and experimental works. It books poetry readings and one-person shows, as well as plays in the Irish language. *Lower Abbey St., Dublin 1.* ☎ *01/878-7222. www.abbeytheatre.ie. Tickets €10–€20.*

Gay & Lesbian Clubs & Bars

The gay scene in Dublin has expanded by leaps and bounds in the last decade, from absolutely nothing at all, to small but determined. Due to the country's traditional conservatism, it's unlikely this will ever be a Miami-level gay zone, but at least there are high-quality gay bars, and regular gay nights at local dance clubs. Hotels accept same-sex couples without raising an eyebrow, unlike in years past. However, the aforementioned conservatism means that it's not a great idea for same-sex couples to hold hands or cuddle on the street, and keeping a low profile when wandering with your gay friends from restaurant to bar isn't a bad idea. Think small-town

DUBLIN

America, and you'll get the zeitgeist. The tolerance here only goes so far.

Cover charges range from €5 to €15, depending on the club or venue, with discounts for students and seniors.

Check the *Gay Community News, Free!,* and *Scene City* to find out what's going on in town. The most comprehensive websites for gay organizations, events, issues, and information are **Gay Ireland Online** (www.gay-ireland.com) and **Outhouse** (www.outhouse.ie); another good resource is the site **Ireland's Pink Pages** (www.pink-pages.org). Folks on the help lines **Lesbians Organizing Together** (☎ 01/872-7770) and **Gay Switchboard Dublin** (☎ 01/872-1055) are also extremely helpful in directing you to activities of particular interest. (See "Specialized Tours & Resources," in chapter 2, for details on many of these resources.)

→ **The Front Lounge** This big, modern bar sprawls across several floors, with wide windows overlooking the hustle and bustle of Temple Bar outside. The crowd is a friendly, mixed gay/straight clientele. The look here is nice shoes, just the right amount of stubble, and expensive hair gel. *33–34 Parliament St., Temple Bar, Dublin 2.* ☎ *01/670-4112.*

📺 Best → **The George** This is Dublin's most established gay bar, and it tends to be packed most nights with a laid-back, cheerful crowd, mixing mostly locals with savvy tourists. It's a quiet haven during the day, and a good place to sit and have a coffee, but late at night there's a DJ, and tables are pushed back for dancing. If you're gay and visiting Dublin, this is the place you're looking for. *89 S. Great George's St., Dublin 2.* ☎ *01/478-2983.*

📺 Best → **GUBU** This mixed gay/straight Northside dance club, with an emphasis on gay, is filled to bursting most nights, with a casually, but beautifully, dressed, laid-back, enthusiastic crowd drawn by its party-pop music and "it's a gay thing" attitude. *7–8 Capel St., Dublin 7.* ☎ *01/874-0710.*

→ **Out on the Liffey** This relaxed, friendly pub caters to a balance of gays and lesbians (except for Sat, which is men only) and serves up pub food with good conversation. In 1998, "Out" expanded to include a happening late-night venue, Oscar's, where you can dance (or drink) until you drop. *27 Upper Ormond Quay, Dublin 1.* ☎ *01/872-2480. DART: Tara St. Walk up the Liffey and cross at Parliament Bridge. Bus: 34, 70, or 80.*

Sightseeing

The best way to really discover Dublin is to get out of your hotel room, grab a map, and start walking. This city was made for aimless strolling. It's small, neatly divided into bite-size chunks, and, given its size, filled with an enormous array of museums, castles, and magnificent cathedrals. If you want to find out more about the minutia of the city's history and lore, take one of the many excellent tours that wander across it every day.

Don't worry too much about cost—many of its museums and sights are free, and all of those that charge have student discounts. Bring your international student cards, or hostel IDs, with you just in case. Remember,

we'll steer you right, and give you the real lowdown on what you can expect to see, and whether individual sights are worth your time and money.

Tickets for everything can be purchased at the sight in question, or you could purchase tickets in advance for most sights at the main Dublin Tourist Office.

Festivals

○ **Funderland:** Royal Dublin Society, Ballsbridge, Dublin 4. An annual indoor funfair, complete with white-knuckle rides, carnival stalls, and family entertainment

(☎ 061/419988; www.funfair.ie). December/January.

○ **Six Nations Rugby Tournament:** Lansdowne Road, Ballsbridge, County Dublin. This annual international tourney features Ireland, England, Scotland, Wales, France, and Italy. It's a brilliant atmosphere, be it at Lansdowne Road or a neighborhood pub. Contact Irish Rugby Football Union, 62 Lansdowne Rd., Dublin 4 (☎ 01/668-4601). Alternate Saturdays, early February to April.

○ **St. Patrick's Dublin Festival:** Held around St. Patrick's Day itself, this massive 4-day festival is open, free, and accessible to everyone. Street theater, carnival acts, sports, music, fireworks, and other festivities culminate in Ireland's grandest parade, with marching bands, drill teams, floats, and delegations from around the world (☎ 01/676-3205; www.stpatricksday.ie). On and around March 17.

○ **Dublin Film Festival:** Irish Film Centre, Temple Bar, Dublin 2, and various cinemas in Dublin. More than 100 films are featured, with screenings of the best in Irish and world cinema, plus seminars and lectures on filmmaking (☎ 01/679-2937). March/April.

○ 📺 Best **Diversions Temple Bar:** Dublin 2. This is an all-free, all-outdoor, all-ages cultural program, featuring a combination of day and night performances in dance, film, theater, music, and visual arts. Beginning in May, the Diversions program includes live music, open-air films, and a circus (☎ 01/677-2255; www.temple-bar.ie). May to August.

○ **Bloomsday Festival:** Various venues in Dublin. This unique day of festivity celebrates Leopold Bloom, the central character of James Joyce's *Ulysses.* Every aspect of the city, including the menus at restaurants and pubs, duplicates the aromas, sights, sounds, and tastes of

Joyce's fictitious Dublin on June 16, 1904, the day when all of the action in *Ulysses* takes place. Ceremonies are held at the James Joyce Tower and Museum, and there are guided walks of Joycean sights. Contact the James Joyce Centre, 35 N. Great George's St., Dublin 1 (☎ 01/878-8547; fax 01/878-8488; www.jamesjoyce. ie). June 16.

○ 📺 Best **Oxegen:** Punchestown Racecourse, County Kildare. This (mainly rock) music festival is now one of Europe's premier summer music fests, with nearly 100 acts playing on five stages over the duration of a weekend. Previous headliners have included Coldplay and Counting Crows. For tickets contact **www.ticket master.ie**. Early July.

○ **All-Ireland Hurling and Gaelic Football Finals:** Croke Park, Dublin 3. The finals of Ireland's most beloved sports, hurling and Gaelic football, are Ireland's equivalent of the Super Bowl. If you can't be at Croke Park, experience this in the full bonhomie of a pub. Tickets can be obtained through Ticketmaster at www. ticketmaster.ie (☎ 01/836-3222). September.

○ **Dublin Theatre Festival:** Theatres throughout Dublin. Showcases for new plays by every major Irish company (including the Abbey and the Gate), plus a range of productions from abroad (☎ 01/677-8439; www.dublintheatrefestival. com). First 2 weeks in October.

○ **Dublin City Marathon:** On the last Monday in October, more than 5,000 runners from both sides of the Atlantic and the Irish Sea participate in this popular run through the streets of the capital (☎ 01/626-3746; www.dublincity marathon.ie). Late October.

The Top Attractions

→ **Bank of Ireland Centre/Parliament House** Another one for history buffs. This

DUBLIN

Dublin Attractions

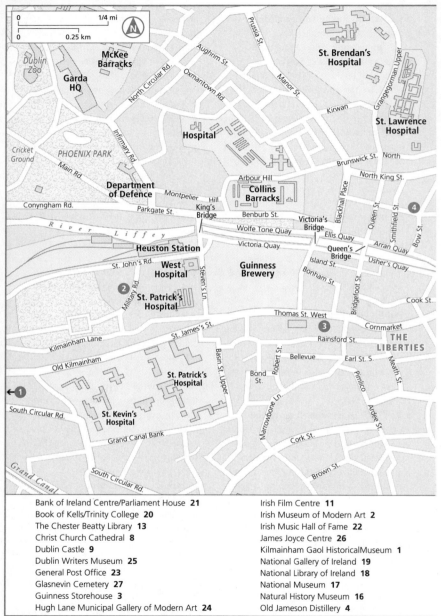

Bank of Ireland Centre/Parliament House **21**
Book of Kells/Trinity College **20**
The Chester Beatty Library **13**
Christ Church Cathedral **8**
Dublin Castle **9**
Dublin Writers Museum **25**
General Post Office **23**
Glasnevin Cemetery **27**
Guinness Storehouse **3**
Hugh Lane Municipal Gallery of Modern Art **24**

Irish Film Centre **11**
Irish Museum of Modern Art **2**
Irish Music Hall of Fame **22**
James Joyce Centre **26**
Kilmainham Gaol HistoricalMuseum **1**
National Gallery of Ireland **19**
National Library of Ireland **18**
National Museum **17**
Natural History Museum **16**
Old Jameson Distillery **4**

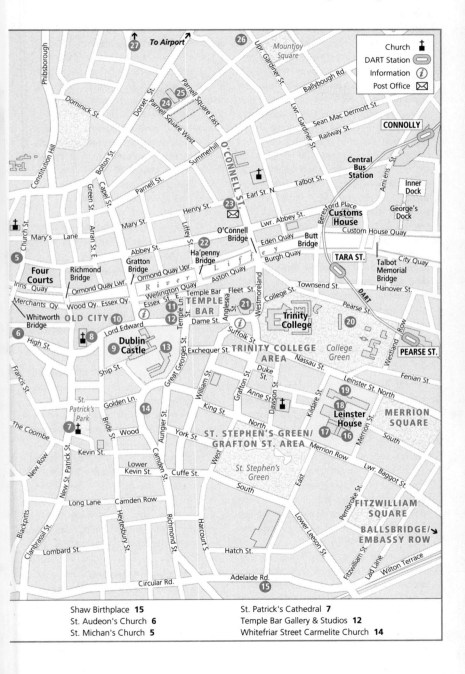

Shaw Birthplace **15**
St. Audeon's Church **6**
St. Michan's Church **5**
St. Patrick's Cathedral **7**
Temple Bar Gallery & Studios **12**
Whitefriar Street Carmelite Church **14**

building was built in 1729 to house the Irish Parliament. It did so for less than a century. In 1797 the British Prime Minister William Pitt decided the only way to end religious violence in Ireland was to close the Irish Parliament and merge it with the English. The Irish Parliament members weren't too keen on the idea. Pitt bought them off with cash titles and promises of the end of anti-Catholic laws if they voted an end to themselves. They did. Big mistake. King George III decided to keep the anti-Catholic laws but didn't give the Irish back their government. They are the only parliament ever to have voted themselves out of existence. The building became a bank. You can still see bits from its heyday like the windowless front portico, built to avoid distractions from the outside when Parliament was in session. Inside is also the **Bank of Ireland Arts Centre,** where there are free art exhibitions, concerts, and literary readings. 2 *College Green, Dublin 2.* ☎ *01/661-5933, ext. 2265. Free admission. Mon–Wed and Fri 10am–4pm; Thurs 10am–5pm. Guided 45-min. tours of House of Lords chamber Tues 10:30, 11:30am, and 1:45pm (except holidays). DART: Tara St. Bus: Any city-center bus.*

➔ **The Book of Kells**   This extraordinary hand-drawn manuscript of the four Gospels, dating back to the year 800, is one of Ireland's true jewels, and with elaborate scripting and colorful illumination, it is undeniably magnificent. Unfortunately, the need to protect it for future generations means that there's little for you to see. It's very small, and displayed inside a wooden cabinet shielded by bulletproof glass. So what you really see here are the backs of a lot of tourists, leaning over a small table, trying to see two pages of an ancient book. Along with another early Christian manuscript, the Book of Kells is on display at Trinity College in the Colonnades, an exhibition area on the ground floor of the Old Library. It's quite disappointing because of the unavoidable viewing

restrictions, and it seems to be overpriced given what is on offer, and the student discount is barely noticeable it's so small. Still, if you're a literary type you will be dazzled by the Library's Long Room (which your ticket also gives you access to). Inside the grand, chained library many rare works on Irish history are displayed. Also housed in the Old Library is the **Dublin Experience,** a multimedia introduction to the history and people of Dublin, which is informative, if a bit basic. *College Green, Dublin 2.* ☎ *01/608-2320. www.tcd.ie/Visitors/attractions.html#book. Admission to Book of Kells €7.50 adults, €6.75 seniors/students. Combination tickets for the Library and Dublin Experience also available. Mon–Sat 9:30am–5pm; Sun noon–4:30pm (opens at 9:30am June–Sept).*

`FREE` ➔ **Chester Beatty Library**   Sir Alfred Chester Beatty was an Irish-American who made a fortune in the mining industry, and spent his spare time collecting rare manuscripts. In 1956 he left his extensive collection to Ireland, and this fascinating museum inside the grounds of Dublin Castle was the ultimate result of that gift. The awesome array of early illuminated gospels and religious manuscripts outshines the Book of Kells, and there are endless other goodies here: ancient editions of the Bible and other religious books, beautiful copies of the Koran, and endless icons from Western, Middle Eastern, and Far Eastern cultures. Best of all: It's free. *Clock Tower Building, Dublin Castle, Dublin 2.* ☎ *01/407-0750. Free admission. Tues–Fri 10am–5pm; Sat 11am–5pm; Sun 1–5pm. Free guided tours Wed and Sat 2:30pm. DART: Sandymount. Bus: 5, 6, 6A, 7A, 8, 10, 46, 46A, 46B, or 64.*

➔ **Christ Church Cathedral**   This magnificent cathedral is difficult to appreciate fully if you walk up the street that runs in front of it, as it is actually below street level. It was designed to be seen from the river, so walk to it from the river side in order to truly

ⓤ Hanging Out with Dublin's Students
M T V

Students are everywhere in town, but there are a few places where you can almost always find them. They catch bands at Whelan's and The Village (see Music Clubs, above), as well as at a bar called **The Lower Deck,** 1 Portobello Harbour (☎ 01/475-2041), this is a newish place on the scene, but it's becoming increasingly hip.

On weekend nights you're likely to find a youngish crowd in the **Dice Bar,** the sister bar to the **Voodoo Lounge** (p. 82; 79 Queen St.; ☎ 01/674-6710), and at the **Octagon Bar at The Clarence Hotel** (p. 82), as well as at **Carnival,** 11 Wexford St. (☎ 01/405-3604), which has guest DJs, and packs in the Whelan's crowd before or after a gig. Cow Lane's many tiny boutiques and markets draw students in for the good deals on one-of-a-kind fashions, and they keep record and book stores like **Road Records,** 16b Fade St. (☎ 01/671-7340), and **The Secret Book and Record Store,** 15A Wicklow St. (☎ 01/679-7272), alive and kicking. Finally, students get their cheap vintage clothing at shops like **Harlequin,** Castle Market (☎ 01/478-4122), and the **Eager Beaver,** 17 Crown Alley (☎ 01/677-4332).

appreciate its size and the way in which it dominates the neighborhood. It dates from 1038, when Sitric, Danish king of Dublin, built the first wooden Christ Church here. In 1171 the original foundation was extended into a cruciform and rebuilt in stone by the Norman warrior Strongbow. The present structure dates mainly from 1871 to 1878, when a huge restoration took place that is controversial to this day, as much of the old detail was destroyed in the process. Still, there's magnificent stonework and graceful pointed arches. There's also a statue of Strongbow inside, and some believe his tomb is here as well, although historians are not convinced. The best way to get a glimpse of what the building must originally have been like is to wander the crypt, which is original to the 12th century structure, and thus designed by Strongbow himself. Things to look out for include a heart-shaped iron box in the southeast chapel which is believed to contain the heart of St. Laurence O'Toole. *Lovely. Christ Church Place, Dublin 8.* ☎ *01/677-8099. Admission €5 adults, €2.50 students. Daily 10am–5:30pm. Closed Dec 26. Bus: 21A, 50, 50A, 78, 78A, or 78B.*

→ **Dublin Castle** This 13th-century structure was the seat of British power in Ireland for more than 7 centuries, until the new Irish government took it over in 1922. You can walk the grounds for free, although as this is largely municipal office space now, it's a bit disappointingly dominated by parking lots. Still, it's worth a wander. If it's open, check out the Undercroft, an excavated site on the grounds where an early Viking fortress stood, and the Treasury, built in the early 18th century. Follow the courtyard through to find the fab Chester Beatty Library. There's also a vaguely interesting on-site craft shop, heritage center, and restaurant. *Palace St. (off Dame St.), Dublin 2.* ☎ *01/677-7129. Admission €4.50 adults, €3.25 students. No credit cards. Mon–Fri 10am–5pm; Sat–Sun and holidays 2–5pm. Guided tours every 20–25 min. Bus: 50, 50A, 54, 56A, 77, 77A, or 77B.*

→ **Dublin Writers Museum** This place is for everybody who ever paid attention in English class. The attraction is more than just seeing Joyce's typewriter, or reading early playbills for the Abbey Theatre when Yeats was involved in running it; the draw is also long letters from Brendan Behan talking

DUBLIN

about parties he was invited to with the Marx Brothers in Los Angeles after he hit the big time, and scrawled notes from Behan, Joyce, and Beckett about work, life, and love. This museum opens a window and lets light in on Ireland's rich literary heritage, and it is wonderful to walk in that glow. *18–19 Parnell Sq. N., Dublin 1.* ☎ *01/872-2077. www.writersmuseum.com. Admission €6.50 adults, €4 students. Mon–Sat 10am–5pm (until 6pm June–Aug); Sun and holidays 11am–5pm. DART: Connolly Station. Bus: 11, 13, 16, 16A, 22, or 22A.*

→ **General Post Office (GPO)** Ah, yes. It looks just like a post office and it was once a post office. So why have we brought you here? Because it's also a symbol of Irish freedom. It was the main stronghold of the Irish Volunteers during the Easter Uprising in 1916. On Easter Sunday Patrick Pearse stood on its steps and declared a free Irish Republic beginning, "In every generation the Irish people have asserted their right to national freedom and sovereignty." Then he and his army barricaded themselves inside the post office. A siege followed and the building was pretty much destroyed. Just when it was looking good again, the Civil War broke out in 1922 and beat it up some more. Today you can put your fingers into the bullet holes that riddle its columns, lingering reminders of the Irish struggle. Even today its steps are a rallying point for demonstrations and protests. In the vast, somber interior, a series of paintings tell the tale of the Easter Uprising. A massive bronze statue of Cúchulainn, the legendary knight of the Red Branch who is used as a symbol by both Loyalist and Republican paramilitary groups, stands proudly in the middle of things. *O'Connell St., Dublin 1.* ☎ *01/705-8833. www.anpost.ie. Free admission. Mon–Sat 8am–8pm; Sun 10:30am–6:30pm. DART: Connolly. Bus: 25, 26, 34, 37, 38A, 39A, 39B, 66A, or 67A.*

→ **Glasnevin Cemetery** Somewhere to hang out with the Irish celebs without spending a cent. The only thing is they're dead. Residents include former Irish Taoiseach Eamon de Valera and national hero Michael Collins. Literary biggies include the writers Christy Brown (the subject of the film *My Left Foot*) and Brendan Behan (at whose funeral, in 1964, his coffin was escorted by an IRA honor guard). A heritage map, on sale in the flower shop at the entrance, serves as a guide to who's buried where, or you can take a free 2-hour guided tour. *Finglas Rd., Dublin 11.* ☎ *01/830-1133. Free admission. Daily 8am–4pm. Free guided tours Wed and Fri 2:30pm from main gate. Map €3.50. Bus: 19, 19A, 40, 40A, 40B, or 40C.*

Ⓜ **Best** → **Guinness Storehouse** Skip the dull old churches and head here to find out how that distinctive dark stout, with its thick, creamy head, is actually made. Founded in 1759, the Guinness Brewery is now world famous. You can explore the Guinness Hopstore, a 19th-century building with multimedia lessons on Guinness brewing, then move on to the Gilroy Gallery, to check out the graphic design work of John Gilroy. Then comes the good bit: Stop in at the breathtaking Gravity Bar where you can grab a glass of the black stuff in this glass-enclosed bar 60m (200 ft.) above the ground with knock-you-over views of the city. *St. James's Gate, Dublin 8.* ☎ *01/408-4800. www.guinness-storehouse.com. Admission €14 adults, €9 students. Daily 9:30am–5pm. Guided tours every half-hour Bus: 51B, 78A, or 123.*

→ **Hugh Lane Municipal Gallery of Modern Art** This cute but hard-hitting gallery has a brilliant collection of Impressionist works including Degas' *Sur la Plage* and Manet's *La Musique aux Tuileries,* and also holds sculptures by Rodin and lots of other stuff by modern Irish artists. One room holds the complete studio of the Irish painter Francis Bacon, which the gallery purchased and moved to Dublin piece by piece from London, then reconstructed it behind glass.

Everything was moved, right down to the dust. *Parnell Sq. N., Dublin 1.* ☎ *01/874-1903. www.hughlane.ie. Free admission to museum; Francis Bacon studio €7.50 adults, €3.50 students. Tues–Thurs 9:30am–6pm; Fri–Sat 9:30am–5pm; Sun 11am–5pm. DART: Connolly or Tara stations. Bus: 3, 10, 11, 13, 16, or 19.*

➜ **Irish Film Centre** This art-house film institute is a hip hangout for cinephiles in Dublin's artsy Temple Bar district, housing two cinemas, the Irish Film Archive, a library, and a small but comprehensive bookshop. The cafe here is a great place for a cup of coffee on a cold afternoon, and the busy bar is one of the city's coolest hangouts. *6 Eustace St., Dublin 2.* ☎ *01/679-5744, or 01/679-3477 for cinema box office. www.irishfilm.ie. Free admission; cinema tickets €6.50–€8. Centre open daily 10am–11pm; cinemas daily 2–11pm; cinema box office daily 1:30–9pm. Bus: 21A, 78A, or 78B.*

📺 Best FREE ➜ **Irish Museum of Modern Art (IMMA)** This stunner of a 17th-century building known as the Royal Hospital, the IMMA holds heaps of theatrical and musical events. The small permanent collection contains some great works by Irish artists, but the big draws are the numerous temporary exhibitions that pass through. Outside, the formal gardens have been restored to stellar condition. *Military Rd., Kilmainham.* ☎ *01/612-9900. www.modernart.ie. Free admission. Tues–Sat 10am–5:30pm; Sun noon–5:30pm. Bus: 79 or 90.*

➜ **Irish Music Hall of Fame** Music heads go crazy, this museum takes you through the entire history of Irish music, from traditional and folk through pop, rock, and dance. There are bits and pieces from U2, Van Morrison, Christy Moore, the Chieftains, the Dubliners, Thin Lizzy, Bob Geldof, Enya, the Cranberries, and Sinéad O'Connor, right up to Boyzone, Westlife, and Samantha Mumba. *57 Middle Abbey St., Dublin 1.* ☎ *01/878-3345. Admission €7.60. Daily 10am–5:30pm. DART:*

Connolly. Bus: 25, 26, 34, 37, 38A, 39A, 39B, 66A, or 67A.

➜ **James Joyce Centre** This is a funny old place; there's not much in the way of real Joyce memorabilia except a writing table Joyce used in Paris when he was working on *Finnegan's Wake,* and early copies of his work, including a *Ulysses* inscribed by Brendan Behan, "I wish that I had written it." There's a trippy display on that confusing novel where the structure is explained by drawing it on a wall (apparently the characters represent body parts, natural elements, *and* places in Dublin). If you're a big Joyce fan you'll love it; otherwise, you're best off only coming here if there's someone interesting giving a talk. *35 N. Great George's St., Dublin 1.* ☎ *01/878-8547. www.jamesjoyce.ie. Admission €5 adults, €4 students. Separate fees for walking tours and events. Mon–Sat 9:30am–5pm; Sun 12:30–5pm. Closed Dec 24–26. DART: Connolly. Bus: 3, 10, 11, 11A, 13, 16, 16A, 19, 19A, 22, or 22A.*

➜ **Kilmainham Gaol Historical Museum** If you're interested in Ireland's fight for freedom from British rule, you've got to stop by this museum. Within these walls political prisoners were incarcerated, tortured, and killed from 1796 until 1924. The leaders of the 1916 Easter Uprising were executed here, along with many others. Future *Taoiseach* (Prime Minister) Eamon de Valera was its final prisoner. To walk along these corridors, through the grim exercise yard, or into the walled compound is a moving experience that lingers in your memory. *Kilmainham, Dublin 8.* ☎ *01/453-5984. www.heritageireland.ie. Guided tour €5 adults. Apr–Sept daily 9:30am–4:45pm; Oct–Mar Mon–Fri 9:30am–4pm, Sun 10am–4:45pm. Bus: 51B, 78A, or 79.*

📺 Best FREE ➜ **National Gallery of Ireland** This museum is where you'll find Ireland's national art collection, along with a pile of great European art from the last 600 years. All the top schools of art are represented from Italian Renaissance artists (especially Caravaggio's *The Taking of Christ*) to French Impressionists, and Dutch 17th-century masters. The highlight of the Irish collection is the room dedicated to the mesmerizing works of Jack B. Yeats, brother of the poet W. B. Yeats. All public areas are wheelchair accessible. The museum has a shop and a first-rate help-yourself **National Museum Café** (see "Eating," above). *Merrion Sq. W., Dublin 2.* ☎ *01/661-5133. www.national gallery.ie. Free admission. Mon–Sat 9:30am–5.30pm (Thurs until 8.30pm); Sun noon–5.30pm. Closed Dec 24–26; Good Friday. Free guided tours (meet in the Shaw Room) Sat 3pm, Sun 2, 3, and 4pm. Closed Good Friday and Dec 24–26. DART: Pearse. Bus: 5, 6, 7, 7A, 8, 10, 44, 47, 47B, 48A, or 62.*

FREE → **National Library of Ireland**
If you're coming to Ireland to find out if you're a Celt in blood as well as heart, this library is a good place to start. Inside are thousands of volumes and records packed full of ancestral information. Opened here since 1890, this is the main library for Irish studies. Particularly special are its first editions and the papers of Irish writers and political figures, such as W. B. Yeats, Daniel O'Connell, and Patrick Pearse. It also has a top collection of maps of Ireland. *Kildare St., Dublin 2.* ☎ *01/603-0200. www.nli.ie. Free admission. Mon–Wed 10am–9pm; Thurs–Fri 10am–5pm; Sat 10am–1pm. DART: Pearse. Bus: 10, 11A, 11B, 13, or 20B.*

FREE → **National Museum** This museum is like a tutorial in ancient Irish history. It holds the country's most amazing historical finds, including a huge collection of Irish Bronze Age gold and the Ardagh Chalice, Tara Brooch, and Cross of Cong, as well as artifacts from the Wood Quay excavations of the Old Dublin Settlements. The only place where it falls flat is on interactive exhibits, which are not as loved as they could be. The museum has a shop and a cafe. *Note:* The National Museum includes two other sites,

Collins Barracks and the Natural History Museum; see their separate listings. *Kildare St. and Merrion St., Dublin 2.* ☎ *01/677-7444. Free admission. Tours (hours vary) €2 adults, free for seniors and children. Tues–Sat 10am–5pm; Sun 2–5pm. DART: Pearse. Bus: 7, 7A, 8, 10, 11, or 13.*

FREE → **Natural History Museum**
They're watching you. Inside this cold, stone building are thousands of stuffed and mounted creatures stored inside polished wooden cabinets, just as they would have been in the 19th century. Fascinating and absolutely bizarre. It contains examples of major animal groups killed all around the world. Many are now rare or extinct—perhaps they wouldn't be if you hadn't . . . oh, nevermind. *Merrion St., Dublin 2.* ☎ *01/677-7444. www.museum.ie. Free admission. Tues–Sat 10am–5pm; Sun 2–5pm. DART: Pearse. Bus: 7, 7A, 8, or 13A.*

📺 Best → **The Old Jameson Distillery** Irish whiskey is considered by many the best in the world. Learn to love it at this museum telling the history of the stuff known in Irish as *uisce beatha* (the water of life). Take as much as you can bear of the inevitable film, then move on to the whiskey-making exhibition and right-in-front-of-your-eyes demonstrations. Finally, get your gob around the firewater yourself and see what you think. Pretty good, eh? *Bow St., Smithfield Village, Dublin 7.* ☎ *01/807-2355. Admission €8 adults, €6.25 students. Mon–Sat 9:30am–6pm (last tour at 5pm); Sun 11am–7pm. Bus: 67, 67A, 68, 69, 79, or 90.*

→ **Phoenix Park** The vast green expanses of Phoenix Park are Dublin's playground. It's easy to see why. This is a brilliantly designed park, scored with roads and pedestrian walkways cutting right into the heart of its 704 hectares (1,739 acres). Rows of oaks, beech trees, pines, and chestnut trees make for shady hideaways, or you can bronze up in the broad expanses of grassland. It's a gorgeous place to spend a restful afternoon, but there's plenty to do here if you're itchy for activities. The homes of the Irish president and the U.S. ambassador are both in the park, as is the Dublin Zoo. Livestock graze peacefully on pasturelands, deer roam the forested areas, and horses romp on polo fields. The Phoenix Park Visitors Centre, adjacent to Ashtown Castle, has an audiovisual presentation on the park's history, for the particularly curious. The cafe/restaurant is open 10am to 5pm weekdays, 10am to 6pm weekends. Free car parking is adjacent to the center. The park is 3km (2 miles) west of the city center on the north bank of the River Liffey. *Phoenix Park, Dublin 8.* ☎ *01/677-0095. www.heritage ireland.ie. Visitors Centre admission €2.75 adults, €2 students. June–Sept 10am–6pm (call for off-season hours). Bus: 37, 38, or 39.*

➔ **St. Audeon's Church**   You need to be quite a church fan to bother with this one. Bits of the really old St Audeon's Church, built in the 12th and 13th century, survive near the Old City walls. Nearby is the "new" St. Audeon's Church, this one Catholic and built in 1846. It was here Father "Flash" Kavanagh used to say the world's fastest mass so his congregation was out in time to catch the football matches. Visits to the ancient church are by guided tour. Open in high summer only. *Cornmarket (off High St.), Dublin 8.* ☎ *01/677-0088. Admission and tour €2 adults, €1 students. June–Sept daily 9:30am–5:30pm. Last admission 45 min. prior to closing. Bus: 21A, 78A, or 78B.*

➔ **St. Michan's Church**   This is the church that inspired Bram Stoker to write *Dracula.* St. Michan's has a burial vault where, because of the dry atmosphere, bodies have lain for centuries without really decomposing. Little Bram was brought to the spooky vaults filled with perfect corpses as a child and, unsurprisingly, the experience stayed with him. School trips just ain't as good as they used to be. *Church St., Dublin 7.* ☎ *01/*

872-4154. Free admission. Guided tour of church and vaults €3.50 adults, €3 students. Nov–Feb Mon–Fri 12:30–2:30pm, Sat 10am–1pm; Mar–Oct Mon–Fri 10am–12:45pm and 2–4:45pm, Sat 10am–1pm. Bus: 134 (from Abbey St.).

➔ **St. Patrick's Cathedral**   This is the largest church in Ireland, and quite a beauty. St Patrick is thought to have wandered through Ireland on his travels, baptizing new converts in a nearby well. A little wooden church was built on this site, which was then turned into the present cathedral in 1190. Though thanks to fires and 14th-century renovators not much remains. Now the building acts as a memorial to Irish war dead (check out the banners and flags throughout the building, some literally rotting away on their poles) and is also very much a working church, holding services twice a day. St. Patrick's is also closely associated with the writer Jonathan Swift, who was dean here from 1713 to 1745, and he is buried here alongside his longtime partner, Stella. St. Patrick's is the national cathedral of the Church of Ireland. *21–50 Patrick's Close, Patrick St., Dublin 8.* ☎ *01/475-4817. www.stpatrickscathedral.ie. Admission €4 adults, €3 students. Year-round Mon–Fri 9am–6pm; Nov–Feb Sat 9am–5pm, Sun 9am–3pm. Closed except for services Dec 24–26 and Jan 1. Bus: 65, 65B, 50, 50A, 54, 54A, 56A, or 77.*

➔ **Shaw Birthplace**   George Bernard Shaw, author of *Pygmalion, Man and Superman,* and *John Bull's Other Island,* was born here in 1856 and lived here until his twenties when he moved to London. See how he would have lived before he became one of Dublin's three winners of the Nobel Prize for Literature. It's decorated in early Victorian style. Rooms to nose about in include the kitchen, the maid's room, the nursery, the drawing room, and a couple of bedrooms, including young Bernard's. The house is a 15-minute walk from St. Stephen's Green.

33 Synge St., Dublin 2. ☎ 01/475-0854. Admission €6 adults, €5 students. Discounted combination ticket with Dublin Writers Museum and James Joyce Museum available. May–Oct Mon–Tues and Thurs–Fri 10am–1pm and 2–5pm, Sat–Sun 2–5pm. Closed Nov–Apr. Bus: 16, 19, or 22.

FREE → **Temple Bar Gallery and Studios** More than 30 Irish artists work here at a variety of contemporary visual arts, including sculpture, painting, printing, and photography. Only the gallery section is open to the public, but you can make an appointment in advance to view individual artists at work. *5–9 Temple Bar, Dublin 2. ☎ 01/671-0073. Free admission. Tues–Wed 11am–6pm; Thurs 11am–7pm; Sun 2–6pm. Bus: 21A, 46A, 46B, 51B, 51C, 68, 69, or 86.*

MTV **Best** → **Trinity College** The oldest university in Ireland, Trinity was founded in 1592 by Queen Elizabeth I to educate the children of the upper classes and protect them from the "malign" Catholic influences elsewhere in Europe. Luckily it didn't quite work. It's now simply the top uni in Ireland. Ex-students include Bram Stoker, Jonathan Swift, Oscar Wilde, and Samuel Beckett, and an array of rebels and revolutionaries who helped create the Republic of Ireland. The campus bulges out into central Dublin just south of the River Liffey, with cobbled squares, gardens, a sweet quadrangle, and lots of buildings, some over 300 years old. This is also where you'll find the Book of Kells (p. 94). *College Green, Dublin 2. ☎ 01/6008-2308. www.tcd.ie. Free admission.*

FREE → **Whitefriar Street Carmelite Church** Believe it or not, this Byzantine-style church is one of the city's most romantic spots. Loved-up couples flock to the 19th-century church because it contains relics of St. Valentine given to the church by Pope Gregory XVI. They're kept in a casket on an altar to the right of the main altar, and you'll often see couples praying in front of it. If that doesn't get your partner going we don't know what will. *56 Aungier St., Dublin 2. ☎ 01/475-8821. Free admission. Mon and Wed–Fri 8am–6:30pm; Sat 8am–7pm; Sun 8am–7:30pm; Tues 8am–9:30pm. Bus: 16, 16A, 19, 19A, 83, 122, or 155.*

Organized Tours

BUS TOURS

Not got the energy to trot around the streets? The city bus company, **Dublin Bus** (☎ 01/873-4222; www.dublinbus.ie), operates several tours of Dublin, all departing from the Dublin Bus office at 59 Upper O'Connell St., Dublin 1. Buy a ticket from the bus driver or book in advance at the Dublin Bus office or at the Dublin Tourism ticket desk on Suffolk Street. The following are the best options:

The 75-minute guided **Dublin City Tour** does the hop-on, hop-off thing, connecting 10 major interesting spots, including museums, art galleries, churches and cathedrals, libraries, and historic sites. Rates are €13 for adults, €11 students. Tours operate daily from 9:30am to 6:30pm.

The 2-hour-15-minute **Dublin Ghost Bus** is a spooky evening tour run by Dublin Bus, departing Monday to Friday at 8pm and Saturday and Sunday at 7 and 9:30pm. The tour does the rounds of felons, fiends, and phantoms. You'll see haunted houses, learn of Dracula's Dublin origins, and even get a crash course in body snatching. Fares are €22 for adults only.

The 3-hour **Coast and Castle Tour** departs daily at 10am, traveling up the north coast to Malahide and Howth. Fares are €20 for adults. Visiting Malahide Castle will require an additional charge.

The 3-hour-45-minute **South Coast Tour** departs daily at 11am and 2pm, traveling south through the seaside town of Dun Laoghaire, through the upscale "Irish Riviera" villages of Dalkey and Killiney, and farther south to visit the vast Powerscourt Estate. Fares are €22 for adults.

Around Dublin

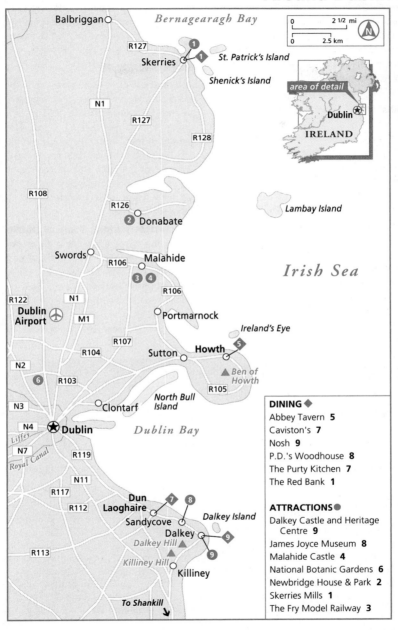

DINING ◆
Abbey Tavern **5**
Caviston's **7**
Nosh **9**
P.D.'s Woodhouse **8**
The Purty Kitchen **7**
The Red Bank **1**

ATTRACTIONS ●
Dalkey Castle and Heritage
   Centre **9**
James Joyce Museum **8**
Malahide Castle **4**
National Botanic Gardens **6**
Newbridge House & Park **2**
Skerries Mills **1**
The Fry Model Railway **3**

Gray Line (☎ 01/605-7705; www.guide friday.com) does a similar thing to the Dublin City Tour above. The first tours leave at 10am from 14 Upper O'Connell St., running every 10 to 15 minutes afterwards. The last departures are 4:30pm. You can also join the tour at any of a number of pickup points along the route and buy your ticket from the driver. Gray Line's Dublin city tour costs €14 for adults, €12 for students. Gray Line also does day trips from Dublin to nearby sights like Glendalough, Newgrange, and Powerscourt. Fares stretch from €20 to €30.

HORSE-DRAWN-CARRIAGE TOURS

Come on, you know you want to do it. It's the quintessential tourist thing: You can tour Dublin in a handsomely outfitted horse-drawn carriage with a driver who will comment on the sights as you clip-clop through the streets and squares. Drivers are stationed with carriages at the Grafton Street side of St. Stephen's Green. Rides range from a short swing around the green to an extensive half-hour Georgian tour or an hour-long Old City tour. Rides are on a first-come, first-served basis from approximately April to October (weather permitting) and will run you between €15 and €50 for one to four passengers.

WALKING TOURS

Small and compact, Dublin was made for walking. If you prefer to set off on your own, the **Dublin Tourism Office,** St. Andrew's Church, Suffolk Street, Dublin 2, has maps for four tourist trails signposted throughout the city: Old City, Georgian Heritage, Cultural Heritage, and the "Rock 'n Stroll" music tour.

If you'd like more guidance, more info, or just some fellow walkers to chat with, try one of the following.

→ Historical Walking Tours of Dublin

Tours with this award-winning outfit are like cheat sheets on Dublin's history. Lasting 2 hours, they take in medieval walls and Viking remains, posh Georgian houses, and the juiciest bits of Irish history. Guides are historians who like to be pumped for extra info. No need to call ahead, just wander along to

MTV ⓤ Dublin's Universities

Dublin is a busy college town with four major universities and a number of smaller arts colleges and international schools keeping the place young, and creating a lively and constantly metamorphosing nightlife. The most famous school in town is **Trinity College (www.tcd.ie),** Ireland's oldest university, right at the heart of the city. It's like Ireland's Harvard, and has stringent admission codes and high fees. Trinity has a great vibe, with its ivy-covered stone buildings, but it is besieged by tourists.

Looming larger on the student scene is **University College Dublin (www.ucd.ie),** the country's biggest university. It has a broad prospectus and is located in Belfield, about 15 minutes by bus from the city centre. Compared to Trinity, UCD is more of a "normal" university, an oasis of youth, dorms, and classrooms.

Dublin City University (www.dcu.ie) is the youngest of Dublin's universities. It specializes in Business, Science, and Engineering, and is located in Glasnevin, about 25 minutes by bus from the centre. The **Dublin Institute of Technology (www.dit.ie)** is actually several colleges scattered around the city, while the **Institute of Technology Tallaght (www.it-tallaght.ie)** offers mostly technology and business courses in suburban Tallaght.

the gate outside Trinity College. ☎ 01/878-0227. www.historicalinsights.ie. Tickets €10 adults, €8 students. May–Sept daily 11am and 3pm; Oct–Apr Fri, Sat, Sun noon.

→ **Literary Pub Crawl** Walk in the footsteps of Joyce, Behan, Beckett, Shaw, Kavanagh, and other Irish literary giants. This tour joins up the dots between Dublin's pubs and its writers. Actors do some funny stuff and there is a literary quiz throughout the evening. The tour assembles at the Duke Pub on Duke Street (off Grafton St.). The Duke Pub, 9 Duke St., Dublin 2. ☎ 01/670-5602. www.dublinpubcrawl.com. Tickets €10. Apr–Nov Mon–Sat 7:30pm, Sun noon and 7:30pm; Dec–Mar Thurs–Sat 7:30pm, Sun noon and 7:30pm.

→ **1916 Rebellion Walking Tour** This rebellion known as the Easter Rising had a massive effect on Dublin. Head into the heat of the action at the General Post Office; find out how the anger rose until the rebellion exploded on Easter Sunday in 1916. The tour is run by local historians whose vast knowledge shines through and makes things interesting. The International Bar, 23 Wicklow St., Dublin 2. ☎ 086858347. www.1916rising.com. Tickets €10. Mar–Nov Tues–Wed 11:30am; Thurs–Sat 11:30am and 2:30pm; Sun 1pm. Phone or check the website for the winter schedule.

→ **Traditional Irish Musical Pub Crawl** If you can handle the embarrassment, this tour explores and samples the traditional music scene, and the price includes a songbook. Two prof musicians sing as you make your way from one famous pub to another—are you cringing yet?—in Temple Bar. Yes, it is touristy but the music's good. It lasts 2¹/₂ hours. Leaves from Oliver St. John Gogarty pub and restaurant (upstairs), 57–58 Fleet St. (at Anglesea St.), Temple Bar. ☎ 01/478-0193. Tickets €12 adults, €10 students. Apr–Oct daily 7:30pm; Nov–Mar Thurs–Sat 7:30pm. Tickets on sale at 7pm or in advance from Dublin Tourist Office.

→ **Walk Macabre** The Trapeze Theatre Company offers this 90-minute walk past the homes of famous writers around Merrion Square, St. Stephen's Green, and Merrion Row, while reconstructing scenes of past murder and intrigue. It includes some of the darker pages of Yeats, Joyce, Bram Stoker, and Oscar Wilde. Would get an "R" for violent imagery, back home. Advance booking is essential. Tours leave from the main gates of St. Stephen's Green. ☎ 087/677-1512 or 087/271-1346. Tickets €12 adults, €10 students. Daily 7:30pm.

→ **The Zozimus Ghostly Experience** A "cocktail mix" of ghosts, murderous tales, horror stories, humor, circus, history, street theater, and whatever's left, all within the precincts of medieval Dublin. The blind and aging Zozimus is your storyteller and you help guide him down the dark alleyways. It's essential to book in advance, when you'll receive the where (outside the pedestrian gate of Dublin Castle, opposite the Olympia Theatre) and the when (time varies according to nightfall). The experience lasts approximately 1¹/₂ hours. 28 Fitzwilliam Lane, Dublin 2. ☎ 01/661-8646. www.zozimus.com. €10. Daily at nightfall, by appointment.

DUBLIN

Playing Outside

From late spring to early fall, all of Dublin prefers to be out of doors. Summer here is glorious, warm but not hot, breezy and pleasant. For the rest of the year, however, forget about it. Outdoors might as well not exist. However, for obvious reasons, we'll focus here on things that are fun to do when the weather cooperates.

Sitting at the edge of the sea, Dublin has plenty of beach-bound activities, from sunbathing and swimming to kitesurfing and kayaking. On dry land there's horseback riding and hiking to get the sweat flowing. Go get sticky.

BEACHES   Plenty of fab beaches are accessible by city bus or DART, which follows the coast from Howth, north of the city, to Bray, south of the city in County Wicklow. Some popular beaches include Dollymount, 5km (3 miles) away and Sutton, 11km (6³/₄ miles) away. But the most popular beaches for the young, tanned, and fit are to be found at Howth, 15km (9¹/₃ miles) away and Malahide 11km (6³/₄ miles) away. Arguably the most popular is in the southern suburb of Dun Laoghaire, 11km (6³/₄ miles) away, at Sandycove Beach, which can get really packed on warm weekend afternoons. Prepare to get close.

BICYCLING   If you want to get out from the smoke, hire a bike from **Irish Cycle Hire** (☎ **041/685-3772;** www.irishcyclehire.com) for €70 for the week or €15 for the day. You can take a spin around the local area or for an extra €20 you can ride it on to one of their other depots across Ireland in Drogheda, Donegal, Westport, Galway, Ennis, Dingle, Killarney, or Cork. They've got mountain bikes and touring bikes and they're all usually new. A good way to go.

FISHING   Wanna hook your supper from the deep blue sea? Charles Weston's guide service (☎ **01/843-6239**) will take you out to fish the depths off the shores of Malahide, just north of the city. In addition, the **Dublin Angling Initiative,** Balnagowan, Mobhi Boreen, Glasnevin, Dublin 9 (☎ **01/837-9209**), will take you out for a bit of deep-sea fishing in Dublin Bay from Dun Laoghaire. Or you can pick up their brochure—the *Dublin Freshwater Angling Guide,* available for €2— to learn all you need to know about local fishing. Agency prices start at around €50 per person.

GO-KARTING   You can race in a very small car at rather high speeds on the 347m (1,155 ft.) indoor circuit at Kylemore Karting in

suburban Dublin (Killeen Rd., Dublin 10; ☎ **01/626-1444**).

HORSEBACK RIDING   It's easy to put your legs on either side of a pony near Dublin. Prices start from €25 an hour, with or without instruction. Many stables offer guided trail riding. To do this through Phoenix Park, **Ashtown Riding Stables** (☎ **01/838-3807**) is ideal. They're in the village of Ashtown, adjoining the park and only 10 minutes by car or bus (no. 37, 38, 39, or 70) from the city center. Among the other riding centers within easy reach of downtown Dublin are **Calliaghstown Riding Centre** (Calliaghstown, Rathcoole, County Dublin; ☎ **01/458-8322**), and **Carrickmines Equestrian Centre** (Glenamuck Rd., Foxrock, Dublin 18; ☎ **01/295-5990**).

ICE SKATING   The **Dublin Ice Rink,** Dolphin's Barn, South Circular Road, Dublin 8 (☎ **01/453-4153**), will have you skidding across the rink on your behind in no time flat. A quick lesson (€4 for a 20-min. session) should see your behind less bruised.

PAINTBALLING   Most paintballing centers are elsewhere in rural Ireland, but Dublin does have one facility, **Paintball Pursuit,** which offers a bit of chasing and shooting for those who like that sort of thing (Gerardstown House, Ballyboughal, Dublin 2; ☎ **01/843-3510**).

PITCH & PUTT   There are plenty of places to get a bit of pitch and putt in around Dublin. The most central option is the Old County **Pitch and Putt Club** (Lorcan O'Toole Park, Kimmage, Dublin 2), then there's the RGSC Pitch and Putt Club (Naas Rd., Dublin 22), and **CPM Pitch and Putt Club** (Nangor Rd., Clondalkin, Dublin 22; ☎ **01/459-2937**).

SKATEBOARDING   Skateboarders in Ireland get quite intense when asked about persecution of the sport in the country. Ireland is the only country in Europe without a public skateboarding park. Since skateboarders tend to be harassed when skateboarding on public streets, this seems to set them up for trouble. Plans are underway to build a skatepark at **Bushy Park** on the southside, but recent controversy has slowed the process, as locals fret and worry about what skateboarders will do to the neighborhood. It's all very 1995, but if plans go ahead, by the time you arrive in Dublin, there *should* be a skatepark at Bushy Park. Until then, most skateboarding in Dublin is done at Phoenix Park to the north of the city center.

SWIMMING   Dublin has a number of public pools, should the heat affect you and the chilly ocean waters not lure you to try swimming in the sea. Here are some spots where you can go for a dip for a few euros: **Markiewicz Centre** (Townsend St., Dublin 2; ☎ 01/672-9121), and **Sean McDermott Street Pool** (Sean McDermott St., Dublin 1; ☎ 01/872-0752). Commercial pools, which cost slightly more, include **Oasis Swimming Pool** (River Court, 17/19 Rogerson's Quay, Dublin 2; ☎ 01/670-9778), and **St. Paul's Swimming Pool** (Sybil Hill, Raheny, Dublin 5; ☎ 01/831-4011).

WALKING   So, you're hung over and need to get some fresh air? The Royal Canal and Grand Canal, skirting the north and south city centers, are ideal. Both make for effortless, flat trails and they are marked so there's no brainpower involved. Both routes pass some small towns and villages where you can start or stop, or just sneak in a quick beer. For more information, contact the Waterways Service at **Dúchas the Heritage Service** (☎ 01/647-6000).

If you're after something a little more bracing, the walk from Bray (the southern terminus of the DART) to Greystones along the rocky promontory of **Bray Head** is great with beautiful views back toward Killiney Bay, Dalkey Island, and Bray. Follow the beachside promenade south through Bray; at the outskirts of town, the promenade turns left and up, beginning the ascent of Bray

Head. Shortly after the hill begins, a trail branches to the left—this is the cliffside walk, which continues another 5km (3 miles) along the coast to Greystones. From the center of Greystones, a train will take you back to Bray. This is an easy walk, about 2 hours each way. In bad weather or strong winds, the cliffside path can be dangerous. Seriously.

Dalkey Hill and **Killiney Hill** drop steeply into the sea and give stunning views of Killiney Bay, Bray Head, and Sugarloaf Mountain. To get there, leave the Dalkey DART station, head into the center of Dalkey, and then south on Dalkey Avenue (at the post office). About 1km (½ mile) from the post office, you'll pass a road going up through fields on your left—this is the entrance to the Dalkey Hill Park. From the parking lot, climb a series of steps to the top of Dalkey Hill; from here you can see the whole bay, the Wicklow Hills in the distance, and the obelisk topping nearby Killiney Hill. If you continue on to the obelisk, there is a trail leading from there down the seaward side to Vico Road, another top place for a windblown seaside walk. It's about 1km (½ mile) from the parking lot to Killiney Hill.

WATERSPORTS   Sign up for certified level-one and level-two instruction and equipment rental for kayaking, sailing, and windsurfing at the **Surfdock Centre,** Grand Canal Dock Yard, Ringsend, Dublin 4 (☎ 01/668-3945; www.surfdock.ie). It offers surfing weekends, where small groups of would-be surfers spend a weekend learning the art of surfing a wave—prices start at around €180. Dublin Bay is filled with sea-life and old wrecks, making it ideal for cold-water diving. To try it out, get in touch with **Oceantec Adventures** in Dun Laoghaire (☎ 01/280-1083; toll-free within Ireland 1800/272-822). It offers a five-star PADI diving school and arranges dive vacations on the west coast. Or try the **National Diving School,** 8 St. James Terrace, Malahide, County Dublin (☎ 01/845-2000; www.nds.ie), or **Irish Divers** (www.

DUBLIN

Time to Get Dirty

Does Dublin leave you yearning for the great outdoors? Then get out of town with **Dirty Boots Treks** (☎ 01/623-6785; www.dirtybootstreks.com), an outfit offering full-day excursions into the mountains south of Dublin. These guys really know what they're doing—they know the hills like the backs of their hands, and they'll take you to places you would never find without them.

They've thought of everything. After a 9am pickup at the gates of Trinity College, your group (maximum eight people) will be transported in a 4×4 Land Rover deep into Wicklow Mountains National Park. Highlights of the easy-to-moderate hike might include spotting a herd of wild deer or taking a dip in a mountain stream, or coming across an ancient monastery long since abandoned. Treks are typically 4 to 5 hours of trail walking, with plenty of stops for conversation, photo opportunities, admiring the scenery, and a homemade picnic lunch. The day is capped off with a quick pint in a local country pub before returning to Dublin around 6pm.

Later on, you can download photos from your trek from the Dirty Boots website and send them to friends back home. A full-day trek, including round-trip transportation and lunch, costs €45 for adults, €39 for students. Didn't pack your hiking gear? No worries. For €11 Dirty Boots will provide hiking boots, gaiters, and waterproofs—all in your size. It's essential to book ahead, either by phone or online.

irishdivers.com; ☎ 01/278-2732) which offers guided wreck dives in Dublin bay, as well as guided dives all around the country. If **kitesurfing** is your thing, check out the website www.kitesurfing.ie. It offers advice on where to buy or rent boards, the best locations, weather conditions, and hooks you up with other kitesurfers.

You can spend a day on a high-speed boat, jetting around the bay for glimpses of seals, porpoises, and dolphins, as well as roaring past cormorants and kittiwakes. One of the most popular boating companies is **Sea Safari** (www.seasafari.ie; ☎ 01/806-1626). Prices vary depending on the trip involved, but start at around €25 per person.

Shopping

In recent years Dublin has surprised everyone by becoming an excellent shopping city. This is surprising because, frankly, it used to be rubbish. A sort of wasteland of chunky white sailor sweaters and bad Irish joke T-shirts. But those days are so over. Now you won't find many bargains, but you will find great designer gear, fab vintage items, and some decent well-made knickknacks to take back home to grandma. The student population also ensures there are plenty of thrift, book, and record stores scattered across town.

The area of little streets around **Grafton Street** is definitely the city's coolest shopping zone. If you're looking for hip clothes, the latest jewelry, used books, shoes, check out **William Street South, Castle Market,** and **Drury Street,** all of which have tiny boutiques and lots of funky little shops. The hottest address in the city for shopping right now is **Cow's Lane,** in the Old City, behind Christ Church Cathedral. It's filled with great local boutiques.

On William Street South, pop into the **Powerscourt Townhouse Centre** (59 S.

William St., Dublin 2; ☎ **01/679-4144**), which is like a little shopping mall in a big Georgian town house—it's got some of the city's trendiest cafes, cheap antiques shops, good shoe stores, and, on the top floor, the Design Centre, which sells jewelry and clothes by young Irish designers, often at reasonable prices.

If you're looking for used books, cheap vintage clothes, and the latest boho jewelry, pop into the **George's Street Arcade,** which is just a few minutes' walk from the Powerscourt Townhouse.

If you need to do major industrial shopping (like if you forgot your underwear), go to **Marks and Spencer** on Grafton Street, or dive into one of the city's big(ish) department stores: On the Northside there's **Arnotts** (12 Henry St., Dublin 1; ☎ **01/805-0400**), and **Clerys** (Lower O'Connell St., Dublin 1; ☎ **01/878-6000**). If you have money to burn (and lucky you) and you feel like hitting a department store, you'll definitely want to darken the doorway at **Brown Thomas** (15–20 Grafton St., Dublin 2; ☎ **01/605-6666**).

Dublin also has a slew of charity secondhand shops. There are a couple just around the corner from Trinity College including **Oxfam** (S. Great George's St.). On the north side, there's **C.A.S.A.** (26 Capel St.; ☎ **01/872-8538**), which benefits the Caring and Sharing Association. Sounds nice, doesn't it?

There are even a couple of cheap secondhand shops in touristy Temple Bar. **The Eager Beaver** (17 Crown Alley) has two floors of unisex secondhand. **Damascus** (2 Crown Alley) has men's and women's secondhand, plus some weird totems from Indonesia and a fleet of wind chimes that's threatening to collapse the ceiling.

If you're headed out with your credit card and a plan for some retail therapy, bear in mind that Dublin shops are open from 9am to 6pm Monday to Saturday, and Thursday until 9pm. Many of the larger shops also have Sunday hours from noon to 6pm, but most small shops are closed Sundays.

Art

→ **Green on Red** Okay, so you're going to be unlikely to snap up a painting at these prices, but the top level local and international contemporary artists represented at this gallery make it definitely worth a browse. Prepare to see some hot works by Fergus Feehily, Martin & Hobbs, Gerard Byrne, and Bridget Riley. *26 Lombard St., Dublin 2.* ☎ *01/671-3414. www.greenonredgallery.com. DART: Pearse.*

Books

→ **Hodges Figgis** Bookworms, you've found a juicy fruit here. This enormous bookstore has books on virtually every topic and is Dublin's go-to store for absolutely everything literary. It's so big you can almost get lost in it. Well worth an afternoon wander. *56–58 Dawson St., Dublin 2.* ☎ *01/677-4754. DART: Pearse. Bus: 10, 11A, 11B, 13, or 20B.*

→ **Greene's Bookshop Ltd.** Established in 1843, this shop near Trinity College is one of Dublin's treasures for scholarly bibliophiles. It's chock-full of new and secondhand books on every topic from religion to the modern novel. A catalog of Irish-interest books is issued five to six times a year. *16 Clare St., Dublin 2.* ☎ *01/676-2554. www. greenesbookshop.com. DART: Pearse. Bus: 5, 7A, 8, or 62.*

🎬 **Best** → **The Winding Stair** This charming, rambling store is Dublin's best-loved bookseller. You'll see why the minute you walk in the door. The towering shelves of new and used books fill three floors, and there's a laid-back cafe upstairs overlooking the river (a top spot for lunch or a coffee; see "Eating," above). *40 Ormond Quay Lower, Dublin 1.* ☎ *01/873-3292. Bus: 70 or 80.*

DUBLIN

Clothes

FOR MEN

➜ **Alias Tom** This was Dublin's best small, men's designer shop until BT2 opened. The emphasis is Italian (Gucci, Prada, Armani), but if that's not your bag there are designers from the rest of Europe and America, too. Don't even bother coming through the door if you're wallet's not bulging—prices are exorbitant. *Duke House, Duke St.,* ☎ *01/671-5443.*

➜ **BT2** This offshoot of Brown Thomas, the high-end department store across the street on Grafton, is Dublin's top shop for hip designer labels for both boys and girls. The look is sporty, chill, and geared to the hopelessly cool. The prices are nearly as crazy as in BT. *Grafton St., Dublin 2.* ☎ *01/605-6666. Bus: All cross city buses.*

➜ **Flip** This little gem was one of the first Temple Bar shops, and it's still whacking out a great line in vintage clothing from the fifties and the sixties. Popular with students and hip out-of-towners. Does boys' and girls' gear. *4 Fownes St., Opposite Central Bank, Temple Bar, Dublin 2.* ☎ *01/671-4299.*

FOR WOMEN

➜ **BT2** Brown Thomas's sister shop, located across the street, is the best place in town for A-list designer labels. BT2 targets a younger but no less label-conscious crowd than BT—think style-obsessed Trustifarians and yuppies and you've got the clientele in a nutshell. *Grafton St., Dublin 2.* ☎ *01/605-6666. Bus: All cross city buses.*

➜ **Jenny Vander** This is where actresses and supermodels come to find extraordinary and stylish antique clothing. Dream of grabbing yourself a bejeweled frock, then take a peek at the price tag and back away in shock. If you've got the cash, this is a fabulous place to find a one-of-a-kind stunner. If not it's still worth a saunter. *20 Georges St. Arcade, S. Great Georges St., Dublin 2.* ☎ *01/677-0406. DART: Pearse. Bus: 10, 11A, 11B, 13, or 20 B.*

➜ **Tulle** A small but hugely hip shop selling contemporary clothing designs. It's filled with scrummy works by hot new designers like Joanne Hynes and international designers like Pink Soda and Stella Forest. Still not cheap. *28 George's St. Arcade, Dublin 2.* ☎ *01/ 679-9115. Bus: 10, 11A, 11B, or 13.*

Comics

➜ **Forbidden Planet** Cartoon and sci-freaks can let out a squeal of joy There's a Forbidden Planet store—just like the one in New York—here in Dublin. Yes, it's a chain but we think it's a good one. There's more than enough merchandise and role-playing gear here to satisfy even the most ardent fantasist. *5–6 Crampton Quay, Dublin 2.* ☎ *01/ 671-0688. Bus: 50, 50A, 54, 56, or 77.*

Music

➜ **Big Brother Records** Calling all vinyl junkies and beat freaks, Big Bro sells hip-hop, jazz, techno, funk, reggae, electronica, and so much more. Snuggled in a basement underneath Selectah records in the midst of all the Temple Bar action, the staff really know their stuff and owner Gerry will always tell you what's rockin' his world that week. *4 Crow St., Dublin 2.* ☎ *01/672-9355. www.bigbrother records.com. Bus: 50, 50A, 54, 56, or 77.*

➜ **The Celtic Note** It's all about trad here. Second only to the mighty Claddagh Records (below), this is where you'll get some Celtic tunes to take back home. The staff is experienced and helpful, and you can listen to a CD before shelling out for it. You'll pay full whack here, but you're likely to find what you're looking for. *14–15 Nassau St., Dublin 2.* ☎ *01/670-4157. DART: Pearse. Bus: 5, 7A, 15A, 15B, 46, 55, 62, 63, 83, or 84.*

➜ **Claddagh Records** Traditional Irish musicians get excited when you mention this shop; this is the real deal in Celtic music and the place to find yourself a new favorite band. Not only is the staff knowledgeable and

This Little Piggy Went to Market

Back in the day Dubliners would buy everything at the weekly market and then sneak in a few pints afterwards. There were weekly vegetable markets, bread markets, meat markets, fish markets . . . . Look around sleek, modern, retail-loving, credit card–wielding Dublin, and it appears those times are all in the past, but don't be fooled—Dubliners still love a good market. In fact, there are some hugely good markets around town, if you just know where to look.

There are workaday markets like the **Moore Street Market,** where fruit, vegetables, fish, and bread are sold every weekday from 10am to 2pm, on Moore Street on the Northside (a great place to pick up some hostel provisions). Then there are more upscale, gourmet markets, like the **Temple Bar Food Market** every weekend from 10am to 5pm in Meeting House Square. Here you can nab yourself some splurge picnic supplies like farmhouse cheeses and fresh, homemade breads, jams, and chutneys. For books, try the **Temple Bar Book Market** weekends in Temple Bar Square from 11am to 4pm—every imaginable topic is wrapped in its pages, and prices are very good.

If you're looking for bargain antiques, head south of the city center to the **Blackberry Fair** (42 Rathmines Rd., south of the Grand Canal). Every weekend from 10am to 2pm this market gathers equal amounts of discoveries and discardables, and weeding through it all is half the fun.

For a genuine flea market, stroll over to the "mother of all markets," **Mother Red Caps Market** (Back Lane, off High St., Dublin 8; ☎ 01/453-8306). You know the drill: stalls selling the usual garage-sale junk mixed in with the occasional treasure (some more in hiding than others), including antiques, old books, coins, silver, leather stuff, clothes, music, and furniture. There's even a fortuneteller.

Finally, if it's all about fashion for you, try the **Cow's Lane Market** on Cow's Lane in the Old City. Here local designers try out their work on a savvy crowd, who pack in knowing they'll get the clothes at much lower prices than in a boutique. It's held every Saturday from 10am to 4pm.

DUBLIN

enthusiastic about new artists, but they'll tell you the best place to head for live music that week. *Dame St., Dublin 2.* ☎ *01/677-3644.*

www.claddaghrecords.com. Bus: 50, 50A, 54, 56, or 77.

Around Dublin: Southern Suburbs

Heading southward along the bay, the bustling harbor town of **Dùn Laoghaire** (pronounced "Dun Leary") is quickly followed by ever more upscale seaside towns of **Dalkey** and **Killiney.** All have been labeled "Bel Eire" for their beauty and the number of Irish celebs in residence. You could spend an afternoon wandering all three, or just pick one and linger for the day. Dùn Laoghaire has lots of shopping, as well as a promenade to parade along and a fab park for lounging. Killiney has a stunning cliff-backed expanse of beach, and pretty little Dalkey is a heritage town with two tiny castle towers, a sweet medieval streetscape, and lots of old-world pubs, gourmet restaurants, and pricey little boutiques.

Eating

→ **Caviston's** SEAFOOD It's all about fresh, fresh fish at this tiny lunch spot in Sandycove, run by the Caviston family, next to their legendary fish shop. The menu changes daily, but could include roast monkfish with pasta in a saffron-and-basil sauce, chargrilled salmon with béarnaise, or marinated red mullet with roasted red peppers. *59 Glasthule Rd., Sandycove, County Dublin. ☎ 01/280-9120. Reservations recommended. Main courses €13–€28. Tues–Fri 3 sittings: noon, 1:30, 3pm; Sat noon, 1:45, and 3:15pm.*

→ **Nosh** INTERNATIONAL This bright, buzzing restaurant is so laid-back it has plastic chairs, but it still dolls out the sort of hit-the-spot food you wish you could get every day: French toast with bacon, bananas, and maple syrup; scrumptious soups; and chunky club sandwiches or salads. For dinner there are things like grilled filet of plaice with crabmeat or some fancy fish and chips. Weekend brunch here is the business. Like it says, "Wickedly good food." *111 Coliemore Rd., Dalkey, County Dublin. ☎ 01/284-0666. www. nosh.ie. Reservations recommended. Main courses €17–€25. Tues–Sun noon–4pm and 6–10pm. DART: Dalkey.*

→ **P.D.'s Woodhouse** IRISH/MEDITER-RANEAN The first and only oak-wood barbecue bistro in Ireland, P.D.'s Woodhouse cooks everything over oak chips, and the flavor it bestows is stratospheric. The wild Irish salmon is always good, although you will rarely go wrong with the catch of the day. *1 Coliemore Rd., Dalkey center, County Dublin. ☎ 01/284-9399. Reservations recommended. Main courses €15–€23. Mon–Sat 6–11pm; Sun 4–9:30pm. DART: Dalkey.*

Partying

→ **P. McCormack and Sons** You're out in the suburbs now so don't be expecting too many hip night clubs. What you'll get here is an old-fashioned feeling pub with stained-glass windows, filled with nooks and crannies, and crammed full of books and jugs. Outside is a beer garden. The pub grub here is top-notch, with a pick 'n' mix of salads and meats for lunch at decent prices. *67 Lower Mounttown Rd. (off York Rd.), Dun Laoghaire, County Dublin. ☎ 01/280-5519.*

→ **The Purty Kitchen** Housed in an old building dating from 1728, this pub has a homey atmosphere, with an open brick fireplace, cozy alcoves, a large fish mural, and pub poster art on the walls. There's always something going on—be it a session of Irish traditional music in the main bar area, blues upstairs in the Loft, or a DJ spinning dance music. *Old Dunleary Rd., Dun Laoghaire, County Dublin. ☎ 01/284-3576. No cover for traditional music; cover €6–€8 for blues in the Loft.*

Sightseeing

→ **Dalkey Castle and Heritage Centre** Set in a little 16th-century tower house, the center tells the story of Dalkey in some sweet, if unsophisticated, displays. There are tours, too, but they can get a little crazy, with interpretive dancers occasionally getting involved. Hilarious stuff. If you prefer to make your own jokes, climb the battlements and lap up the view. Adjoining the center is a medieval graveyard and the very old Church of St. Begnet, Dalkey's patron saint. *Castle St., Dalkey, County Dublin. ☎ 01/285-8366. Admission €6 adults, €5 students. Apr–Oct Mon–Fri 9:30am–5pm, Sat–Sun 11am–5pm; Nov–Mar Sat–Sun 11am–5pm. DART: Dalkey. Bus: 8.*

→ **Dalkey Island** Young Aidan Fennel rows visitors out to the Island, just like his father did before him and his grandfather did before that. There's not much life out there, only a small herd of wild goats and the occasional seal. The island was settled in 6000 B.C. so does have a few ruins: a thousand-year-old church, some 15th-century battlements, and a tower built in 1804 to scare off

Napoleon. Impress your gal (or boy) by rowing out to the island in one of Aidan's homemade boats. *Coliemore Rd. (at stone wharf, adjacent to a seaside apt complex).* ☎ *01/283-4298. Island ferry round-trip €10 adults; rowboat rental €16/hr. June–Aug, weather permitting.*

→ **James Joyce Museum** This museum sits in another tower built to make Napoleon think twice. When the danger passed, lots of them were made into homes. James Joyce lived here in 1904 as a guest of Oliver Gogarty, who,

himself, rented the tower from the Army for an annual fee of IR£8 (€10). Joyce put the tower in the first chapter of *Ulysses,* and it has been known as Joyce's Tower ever since. Its collection of Joycean memorabilia includes letters, documents, first and rare editions, personal possessions, and photographs. *Sandycove, County Dublin.* ☎ *01/ 280-9265. Admission €6.50 adults, €6 students. Apr–Oct Mon–Sat 10am–1pm and 2–5pm; Sun 2–6pm. Closed Nov–Mar. DART: Sandycove. Bus: 8.*

Around Dublin: Northern Suburbs

The towns on Dublin Bay to the north of the city are slightly less posh than those to the south, but there's still plenty to keep you busy including castles and the beach itself. **Howth** and **Malahide** are really cuties, and offer stunning views of Dublin Bay, sweet gardens, and some fine seafood restaurants. Both are easily reached on the DART. Farther north along the coast, but only 20 minutes from Dublin Airport, lies the buzzy and handsome harbor town of **Skerries.** Skerries is a good spot to spend your first or last night in Ireland; or stay longer and get to know the resident colony of gray seals.

Eating & Partying

→ **Abbey Tavern** SEAFOOD/INTERNA-TIONAL Dinner is pretty pricey here. If you can't afford the scrumptious mains like scallops *ty ar mor* (with mushrooms, prawns, and cream sauce), *crepes fruits de mer* (seafood crepes), poached salmon, duck with orange and Curaçao sauce, and veal a la crème, take a sniff and head downstairs for the music. This 16th-century tavern is well known for its nightly traditional-music ballad sessions. Don't be surprised when things turn lively. *Abbey St., Howth, County Dublin.* ☎ *01/ 839-0307. www.abbeytavern.ie. Reservations necessary. Fixed-price dinner €35. Mon–Sat 7–11pm. DART: Howth. Bus: 31.*

→ **The Red Bank** SEAFOOD This place is strictly old-skool. Your waiter takes your order in the cozy lounge, where you wait with a drink until your appetizers are ready and you're brought to your table. Chef Terry McCoy is a top-of-the-class chef, who gets his fish straight from the local sea. This place is at its best with old classics like scallops in butter, cream, and white wine, or the divine lobster Thermidor. Service is correct and respectful, highlighted when the dessert trolley is wheeled in, laden with confections. Sit up straight, hold your knife and fork properly, and you might get to come again. *7 Church St., Skerries, County Dublin.* ☎ *01/849-1005. www.redbank.ie. Reservations required. Dinner main courses €16–€30; fixed-price dinners €45–€48. Mon–Sat 7–9:30pm; Sun 12:30–4pm. Suburban rail. Bus: 33.*

Sightseeing

→ **The Fry Model Railway** This one's arguably mostly for the kids, but it's still quite cool in a quirky way. On the grounds of Malahide Castle (see listing below), this is an exhibit of handmade models of more than 300 Irish trains. The trains were built in the 1920s and 1930s by Cyril Fry, a railway engineer, draftsman, and man with a lot of time on his hands. Prepare for models of stations, bridges, trams, buses, barges, boats, the River

DUBLIN

12 Hours in Dublin: A Walking Tour

Start with a wander around the ivy-covered buildings of historic Trinity College, and pop in to see the Old Library, with its vast rows of antiquarian books. There's usually an excellent display on some element of Irish history or literature on offer, too.

Afterward, grab some lunch at the Avoca Café, and do a bit of shopping at the Avoca store, which has colorful knits in funky fashions, and covetable handmade jewelry—souvenirs you'll actually wear.

When you've worn out your credit card, head on down Dame Street to the City Hall—you can wander its marvelously symmetrical lobby for free—try standing in the middle and looking straight up at the domed ceiling to really appreciate the artwork here.

The noble stone walls of Dublin Castle are right next door, and you can wander through the courtyard at will. The ambitious may want to take a tour (they're relatively infrequent, and you usually have to wait a while); others will follow signs around to the next courtyard to visit the outstanding Chester Beatty Library, which has an extensive collection of gorgeous illuminated manuscripts and is free of charge.

Once you're fully versed on biblical history, stroll down South Great George's Street to Exchequer Street; along the way you'll pass shops and coffee shops that are well worth your time, and eventually you'll come to the hustle and bustle of Grafton Street. You can wander the chain shops and good bookstores, relish the fact that you are not a mime, and then at the foot of the street you'll arrive at St. Stephen's Green. If it's a sunny day, stretch out in the park and rest your toes, or stroll around taking in its craggy statues of James Joyce and Wolfe Tone. If it's cold and rainy, turn left and head to the Shelbourne Hotel for a cup of tea in its comfortable lobby—locals have been popping in here for a warming cup for more than a century. Grab one of the free newspapers lying around, and chill out.

Liffey, and the Hill of Howth. *Malahide, County Dublin.* ☎ *01/846-3779. Admission €6 adults, €5.25 students. Apr–Oct Mon–Sat 10am–5pm, Sun 2–6pm; Nov–Mar Sun 2–5pm. Tours closed for lunch 1–2pm year-round. Suburban Rail to Malahide. Bus: 42.*

→ **Malahide Castle**   Now *this* is a castle. Most castles still open to the public in Ireland are ruins, but this one stands so solidly you can really get the picture—it's what a castle should be. Founded in the 12th century by Richard Talbot, it was occupied by his descendants until 1973. The fully restored interior is chock-full of antiques. After touring the house, explore the vast estate—it's the perfect place for a picnic on a sunny

day. The Malahide grounds also contain the **Fry Model Railway** museum (see above) and **Tara's Palace,** an antique dollhouse and toy collection. *Malahide, County Dublin.* ☎ *01/846-2184. Admission €6.50 adults, €5 students, gardens free. AE, MC, V. Combination tickets with Fry Model Railway and Newbridge House available. Apr–Oct Mon–Sat 10am–5pm, Sun 11am–6pm; Nov–Mar Mon–Fri 10am–5pm, Sat–Sun 2–5pm; gardens May–Sept daily 2–5pm. Castle closed for lunch 12:45–2pm (restaurant remains open). DART: Malahide. Bus: 42.*

→ **National Botanic Gardens**   If you think you've got a green thumb, you ain't seen nothin' yet. With more than 20,000 varieties of plants, a Great Yew Walk, a bog garden, a water garden, a rose garden, and an herb garden, this shows you what a garden could be. Stylish Victoriana glass houses are filled with tropical plants and exotic species. A top spot for chilling on a summer day, although you won't be alone. *Botanic Rd., Glasnevin, Dublin 9.* ☎ *01/837-7596. Free admission. Guided tour €2. Apr–Oct Mon–Sat 9am–6pm, Sun 11am–6pm; Nov–Mar Mon–Sat 10am–4:30pm, Sun 11am–4:30pm. Bus: 13, 19, or 134.*

➜ **Newbridge House and Park** This country mansion 19km (12 miles) north of Dublin will make you think your own apartment is far, *far* too small. Dating from 1740, this was once the "modest" home of Dr. Charles Cobbe, an archbishop of Dublin, and it was occupied by his descendents until 1984. Today it's packed out with family memorabilia: hand-carved furniture, portraits, daybooks, and dolls, plus a museum of objects collected on world travels. The house sits in a vast park, with picnic areas and walking trails. The grounds also include a working Victorian farm, as well as a craft shop and a coffee shop. *Donabate, County Dublin.* ☎ *01/843-6534. Admission €2.50 adults, €1.50 students. Apr–Sept Tues–Sat 10am–1pm and 2–5pm, Sun 2–6pm; Oct–Mar Sat–Sun 2–5pm. Suburban rail to Donabate. Bus: 33B.*

➜ **Skerries Mills** Get grinding. Last known as the Old Mill Bakery, when it provided loaves to the local north coast, this mill was burnt down in 1986 and lay ruined until 1999. Then a restoration plan brought two windmills and a water mill back into operation. There's even an adjoining field of grains—barley, oats, and wheat, all that's needed for the traditional brown loaf—sown, harvested, and threshed using traditional implements and machinery. The result is not only the sweet smell of fresh bread, but also an intriguing glimpse into the past, brought to life by guided tours and the chance to put your hand to the stone and grind a bit of flour. Hungry yet? No problem, there's a tearoom out back. *Skerries, County Dublin.* ☎ *01/849-5208. Admission €5.50 adults, €4 students. Apr–Sept daily 10:30am–6pm; Oct–Mar daily 10:30am–4:30pm. Closed Dec 20–Jan 1. Suburban Rail. Bus: 33. Skerries town and the Mills signposted north of Dublin off the N1.*

Road Trips from Dublin

You don't have to go very far out of Dublin to swap urban views for gorgeous green valleys. Just an hour's drive south of the city, the Wicklow Mountains offer up some supreme off-roading with a heady mix of hiking, mansions, and ancient monastic sights.

To the north of Dublin prepare to be blown away by the mysterious ruins left by ancient civilizations at prehistoric sites Newgrange and Knowth. Not far off, the smooth green hills of the Valley of the Boyne are where the Irish kings once reigned with a killer cocktail of fairy dust and force. To the east, the flat plains of County Kildare are not as dull as they first might seem. This is Ireland's horse country.

Make no mistake, this is real countryside—no cities, and only a few towns of any size. Nightlife is largely restricted to pubs, and eateries are . . . how should we put this . . . rural. On the bright side, it's beautiful, and everything is cheaper than in the cities—pints, food, sights—you name it, it's cheaper out here. You can reach all the towns mentioned here by public transport, but many of the sights are out in the countryside and cannot be reached except by car or tour bus. In an ideal world, you would rent a car and pick up a good map at the tourist office in Dublin before setting out. Yeah, yeah, we know we said not to drive in Dublin, but this is different. It's time for a road trip. Put your foot down, boys and girls; we're going for a ride.

County Wicklow & County Carlow

Sitting at a seaside cafe in buzzy Bray at the very edge of Dublin's suburbs, you can see the mountains of County Wicklow off in the distance. Stunning, mountainous, rural Wicklow is just a dozen or so miles south of central Dublin, making it one of the easiest and quickest day trips. There's plenty to do there—pig out with a picnic by the river in the **Vale of Avoca** or hike through the isolation around **Glendalough,** this is real country living.

A raised granite ridge runs through the county, peaking at two of the highest mountain passes in Ireland—the **Sally Gap** and the **Wicklow Gap**—making for some highly dramatic views. Once you're among the mountains, the best way to really see them is to strike out on foot on the well-marked **Wicklow Way,** which wanders past mountain tarns and secluded glens. You can pick up a map at any tourism office, and then choose a stretch of the path to explore. If you've got a car, head down to the choccy-box villages of **Roundwood, Laragh,** and **Aughrim.**

Just over the border of County Wicklow, little County Carlow doesn't have such a huge bundle of offerings for travelers. Hemmed in by the scenic **Blackstairs Mountains** to the east, and the Barrow Valley and Killeshin Hills to the west, its hugest feature is the 5,000-year-old granite burial site known as **Browne's Hill Dolmen.** It is the largest capstone in Europe, weighing a colossal 100 tons. How did they lift . . .? Who? Don't ask us—nobody knows. It's right up there with Stonehenge.

GETTING THERE & GETTING AROUND

BY TRAIN & BUS   **Irish Rail** (☎ 01/836-6222; www.irishrail.ie) provides daily train service between Dublin and Bray and Wicklow, but you'll have to hop on to local buses to get to smaller towns, and most rural sights are not served by public transport at all. **Bus Eireann** (☎ 01/836-6111) operates daily express bus service to Arklow, Bray, and Wicklow towns. **St. Kevin's Bus Service** (☎ 01/281-8119) travels from Dublin through Bray twice daily on the way to Glendalough, and twice headed back to Dublin. Call for exact times and pickup locations. Both Bus Eireann and **Aran Tours** (☎ 01/280-1899; www.wildcoachtours.com) offer an excellent tour dubbed the "Wild Wicklow Tour." It may not be wild, exactly, but it's lively and thorough, and includes visits to Avoca and Sally Gap. Another tour option is the **Mary Gibbons Tours** (☎ 01/283-9973), offering a meaty tour of Glendalough.

Given all of that, the best way to see Wicklow is by car, as that's the only way that you can take in all the little villages not well served by bus or train. The Dublin Tourist Office has excellent road maps for all of Ireland. Take the N11 south from Dublin City and follow turnoff signs for major attractions.

You can reach **Carlow** on **Bus Éireann,** route 4 on the Dublin-Waterford line, with connections to Athlone and Kilkenny. The bus stops at Barrack Street eight times a day, four times on Sunday, on the way to Waterford. The **Carlow Train Station** (Railway St., NE of Carlow; ☎ 0503/31633) is on the Dublin-Waterford route as well, making three to five stops daily. It's a bit of a walk (about 20 min.) from the train station into the center of town: From the station, walk straight down Railway Road, make a left onto Dublin Road, and another left onto College Street.

BY BICYCLE   Pedal your cares away at **Coleman Cycles in Carlow** (19 Dublin St.; ☎ 0503/31273; €5 per day, €25 per week, €40 deposit).

BASICS

TOURIST INFORMATION   The **Wicklow Tourist Office,** Fitzwilliam Square, Wicklow

Road Trips from Dublin

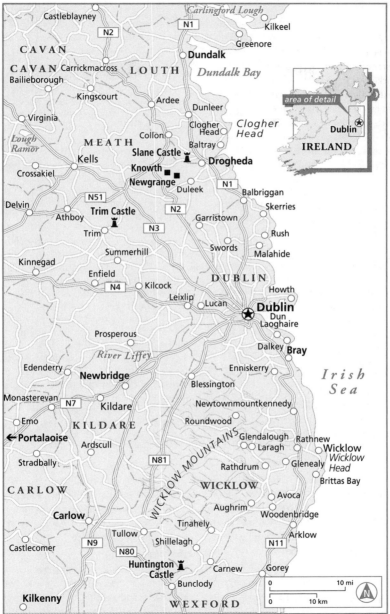

Getting from A to B via X, Y & Z

Ireland's convoluted and limited public transportation routes don't allow you to just hop on a bus or train and go wherever you please whenever you please, and that will definitely shape your itinerary to a large degree. As for heading out to the smaller towns in each county, buses are the only way to go . . . unless you like to cycle. Bicycling is ideal for village-hopping. Of course, if you have a car you can go wherever you please; the cost of rentals can sound like a lot, but if you can split it with friends, it's often cheaper than train tickets. Although if you think gas is expensive in the States, wait till you start forking over the big bucks for Irish petrol, sold not by the gallon but by the tiny little liter.

Other transport options include taking a private bus service. **St. Kevin's Bus Service (☎ 01/281-8119)** runs from Dublin to Glendalough, where you can gaze at shimmering lakes and walk amid forested ruins. However, its route is limited, so if you want to get around the rest of Wicklow, you'll have to take St. Kevin's back up to Bray, and then Bus Éireann or Irish Rail down to Wicklow Town. In fact, if you want to get anywhere from Glendalough you'll pretty much have to head back north to Bray or Dublin first. Once you're in Wicklow Town, though, you can take the train or the bus to Wexford Town—Wicklow and Wexford are both Irish Rail stops. From Wexford, Rosslare Harbour's ferries are just a short train trip away, but you won't be heading there until you're ready to take on the rest of Europe.

Beyond this region, things remain complicated. From Wexford, you can take the train or the bus to Waterford; if you'd rather skip Waterford and head on to Kilkenny instead, you're still going to have to stop in Waterford, because there's no direct route from Wexford to Kilkenny. After you've spent time in Kilkenny, where to next? Options are back to Waterford (again) or Dublin, or to Carlow Town to see Browne's Hill Dolmen, which is on the Waterford-Dublin bus route.

Going from Wicklow to Kilkenny involves another complicated route—as we've said, you'll find a lot of those in this country—so you've got to study the train and bus schedules and maps carefully before deciding on an itinerary. And if you want to get to Cork from the Southeast, don't take the train; taking the bus is a lot easier.

Town, County Wicklow (☎ **0404/69117;** www.wicklow.ie), is open Monday to Friday year-round, Saturday during peak season. The **Carlow Tourist Office,** Presentation Buildings, Tullow Street, Carlow Town, County Carlow (☎ **059/913-1554;** www.countycarlow.com), is open Monday to Friday year-round, 10am to 1pm and 2 to 6pm.

SLEEPING

Generally speaking, your chance of finding a great hostel with amazing views multiply massively the second you step out of Dublin's boundaries. There's plenty to pick from in Wicklow, which is a kind of hostel paradise. Other guesthouses and B&Bs are also well represented, although there are fewer traditional hotels, which you'll find is typical around the Irish countryside.

Hostels

The hostels in this area are gorgeous, but be a bit careful in choosing yours—several well established and reliable Wicklow hostels have closed down rather suddenly in the last few years. It is always a good idea to give them a call the day before you head out (particularly if you'll be hiking) and make sure that your planned lodging hasn't suddenly gone belly-up. All of these hostels were open and flourishing as this book was going to press.

→ An Óige Glendaloch Lodge Hostel
Location, location, location—this An Óige hostel has a spectacular location right near the Glendalough ruins and lakes, with extraordinary views. It was renovated a few years ago, so everything's clean and comfortable, if a tad sterile, and there's no curfew. Breakfast is available for €3–€5 and dinner for €6.50; if you'd rather cook for yourself you'll have to walk to nearby Laragh for groceries, which is a mile away. The Irish Writers' Centre of Dublin hosts traditional music and poetry sessions here three times a week during the summer months. It's got a great vibe, and it's very big with hikers. *Glendalough. Follow the signs for Glendalough; the hostel is on the road to the upper lake.* ☎ *0404/45342. www.anoige.ie. €10–€12 dorm, quad. €40 double, twin. Lockout noon–5pm. Amenities: Restaurant; Internet; kitchen; laundry; bureau de change. St Kevin's Bus (*☎ *01/281-8119) twice daily from Dublin.*

→ An Óige Knockree Hostel This old farmhouse sits in gorgeous countryside with top-notch views of Glencree and the mountains around it. From here you have easy access to Powerscourt, the German War Cemetery, and the Wicklow Way, which passes right by the hostel. It's a small, casual place with a fire burning cheerily in the lounge, and just a few dorm rooms. There's a kitchen (which is good, because there's no restaurant or breakfast); otherwise, amenities are few. As this place is right on the Wicklow Way, it tends to be filled with hikers. By bus, take the 185 from Bray Dart station, then get off at the River Shop on Glencree Road; from there it's a walk of several miles to the hostel (follow the signs). By car, follow

the Glencree Road from Enniskerry for 3 miles, and then follow the hostel signs. *Glencree.* ☎ *01/830-4555. www.anoige.ie. €11–€14 dorm. No credit cards. Lockout 10am–5pm. Amenities: Kitchen; laundry; luggage storage; parking; safe.*

→ An Óige Tiglin Hostel Slap-bang in the middle of the lush greenery of Wicklow national park, the Tiglin Hostel is a sweet old stone building right next to the National Outdoor Training Centre. The folks at the center can hook you up with an expedition doing just about anything in the mountains—hiking, canoeing, rock climbing, fishing. . . . Whatever you choose to do, you're in the right location for outdoor life, as you're right next to Devil's Glen—you can hear the rush and gurgle of the Devil's Punchbowl from the front porch. There's no place to get food within an hour's walk, unfortunately, but the hostel does have a small store, and breakfast is served each morning. The public transportation options here are slightly better: From Dublin, you can take Bus Éireann toward Wicklow to Ashford (or from Wicklow to Ashford, only a 10-min. ride), and then it's about a 3-mile walk west to the hostel on a tiny, unmarked road. If you're hiking from Glendalough, the hostel is about a 4-mile walk to the northeast. Drivers should take the R763 off of the N11 to find the hostel. *Devil's Glen, Ashford.* ☎ *0404/40259. www.anoige.ie. €11–€15 dorm. No credit cards. Amenities: Breakfast included in the price; Internet; lockers.*

Doable
→ Abhainn Mor House A handsome Georgian-style house on the Rathdrum-Avoca road. There's no reason to come out of your way to stay here. It's a quiet little place, nothing particularly fancy, but it is handy for heading to Glendalough and Avoca. There is a great garden for picnics and lounging about on summer days. *Corballis, Rathdrum, County Wicklow.* ☎ *0404/46330. €60 double. Rates*

include full breakfast. Open year-round. In room: Tea/coffeemaker.

→ **Ashdene Country Home** A modern house decorated in an old-aunt style near the Avoca Handweavers, not far from Glendalough. Oldies seem to love this place. Youngsters may feel a bit out of their environment, but owner Jacki Burns is a friendly sort and the views all around are great. If you fancy a knockabout, there's even a grass tennis court. All bedrooms are nonsmoking so tuck those cowboy killers away. Knockanree Lower, Avoca, County Wicklow. ☎ 0402/35327. www.ashdeneavoca.com. €65 double. Discount for 3 nights or more. Rates include full breakfast. Closed Nov–Easter. Amenities: Lounge; tennis court.

→ **Sherwood Park House** This one is a true stunner. As they say, it's "an accessible country retreat for anyone who enjoys candlelit dinners and brass and canopy beds"— don't we all? Prepare to be wowed by an imposing gray-stone 18th-century Georgian country house and working farm. The views, as you can imagine, are inspirational. There are only four guest rooms here, and all of them are quite large—two on the second floor also have small, adjoining twin rooms, which make them perfect for small groups. In the grand sitting room a peat fire burns and an old piano sits in the corner. Dinner is served in the high-ceilinged dining room, and it's a fancy affair where conversation is encouraged as everyone sits together at a long polished table. Kilbride, Ballon, County Carlow (off the N80, 3km/2 miles south of Ballon). ☎ 059/915-9117. www.sherwoodparkhouse.ie. €90 double. Dinner €35. Amenities: Sitting room. In room: TV.

→ **Tudor Lodge** Well located on the slopes of the Wicklow Mountains, this guesthouse makes a good base for ramblers, and a chill retreat for those wanting to get away from it all. Outside it looks a little like a Swiss ski lodge; inside it's all white and the bedrooms

have plenty of room. There's also a desk in each one, in case you're moved by the landscape to scribble down some poetry. The dining room and living room have large windows overlooking green meadows and mountains. There is a yummy array of breakfast choices, and the restaurants and pubs of Laragh are only a short and scenic walk away. Laragh, County Wicklow. ☎ 0404/45554. www. tudorlodgeireland.com. €70–€80 double. Amenities: Nonsmoking rooms; living room; sunroom. In room: TV, tea/coffeemaker, hair dryer.

Do It Yourself

If you don't plan to be wandering around too much, consider renting a self-catering cottage for the week—split between a group of friends, it's cheaper than a hostel for 7 days, and oh so much nicer.

→ **Fortgranite** Fortgranite is—and has been for hundreds of years—a working farm in the rolling foothills of the Wicklow Mountains, with three loveable stone cottages, once home to farm workers, available for rent by the week. Two gatehouses each have a double bedroom, while the lodge sleeps four. All have open fireplaces and their own garden—perfect for those summer BBQs. There's no luxury here, but lots of character instead. Hiking and horse riding can both be found nearby. They're not too keen on smokers. Baltinglass, County Wicklow (4.8km/3 miles southeast of Baltinglass on R747). ☎ 059/648-1396. 3 cottages. €300–€600 per week. No credit cards. In room: TV, kitchen, no phone.

→ **Manor Kilbride** A grand Wicklow manor house and manicured grounds stretching across two small lakes and along a stretch of the River Brittas. On a budget you won't get the house, but you could get one of four stone cottages available for rent: two courtyard cottages and a river lodge each sleeping four, as well as a gate lodge perfect for two. All the cottages are packed out with modern amenities, hidden beneath their old beamed ceilings. If split three or four ways, these houses are incredibly cheap, especially given how cute they are. *N. Blessington, County Wicklow (on N81 6.5km/4 miles north of Blessington, take Kilbride/Sally Gap turn, then left at sign for Sally Gap).* ☎ *01/458-2105. Cottages €400–€650 per week year-round. In room: TV, kitchen, microwave, washing machine.*

➜ **Tynte House** Now, these are pretty tasty. Whereas with so many Irish hotels and guesthouses you despair at the decor, here you get the feeling you wouldn't mind making this place your home. It's a 19th-century family farm complex near the tiny town of Dunlavin in western Wicklow with rooms, apartments, and self-catering cottages all available. The overall feeling is fresh and contemporary with light-wood furniture and huge bathrooms. The no. 3 mews house and the open-plan apartment are favorites, but none will disappoint. There's a grassy picnic area, a barbecue grill and picnic tables, tennis courts, and a game room with Ping-Pong and pool tables. Prices depend on the season and the size of the cottage. Short stays and weekend discounts are available in the off season. *Dunlavin center, County Wicklow.* ☎ *045/401561. www.tyntehouse.com. B&B €70 double; self-catering units €230–€520 per week. Dinner €25. In room: TV, kitchen, dishwasher, microwave, washer/dryer.*

Splurge
➜ **Brook Lodge Hotel & Wells Spa** Brook Lodge is a revolutionary idea in Ireland—not so much a hotel as a whole village with guest rooms, eateries, pubs, a bakery, shops, and even a chapel. The hotel itself is luxurious and comfortable, licked out in warm, energized colors. Rooms have king-size four-poster beds, deep tubs, and a contemporary vibe. Service is excellent—even going as far as a very Irish nightly turndown: chocolates on your pillow and a hot-water bottle between the sheets. The hotel restaurant is **The Strawberry Tree**—gourmet and all-organic. The latest addition to this holistic oasis is **The Wells,** a spa with Finnish baths, mud baths, hot tubs, indoor and outdoor pools, a flotation room, and all sorts of therapies and skin treatments. You can often get good discounts by booking online. Otherwise, you'll have to hope someone will treat you. *Macreddin Village (between Aughrim and Aghavannagh), County Wicklow.* ☎ *0402/36444. www.brooklodge.com. €170–€240 double. Rates include service charge and full Irish breakfast. Fixed-price 4-course dinner €55. Amenities: 2 restaurants (organic, cafe); 2 pubs; full-service spa; laundry service. In room: TV, hair dryer.*

EATING
You have to look around a bit, but there are a few cheap places in this area. On the other hand, B.Y.O. is a mighty fine idea as there are endless places to indulge in an al fresco feast. When it hits lunch o'clock, remember that pubs are cheaper than most restaurants in the area and more atmospheric.

Cheap
➜ **Avoca Handweavers Tea Shop** BISTRO/VEGETARIAN Try to forget this is essentially a cafe packed full of tourists. It's also a great place to eat and dishes out sound, healthy meals. The menu is forever changing, but starters might include pea-and-mint soup or a crunchy Caesar salad. Main courses could be sesame-glazed chicken, honey-roasted ham, Mediterranean sweet frittata, or smoked Wicklow trout. The tea shop attracts pastry junkies. *Avoca, County Wicklow.* ☎ *0402/35105. Lunch €4–€10. Daily 9am–5pm.*

Doable
➜ **Hungry Monk Wine Bar** INTERNATIONAL Yes, the monk motif can be a little bit overwhelming here. If you can handle that, this eatery has a little bit of something for everyone. It's nothing outstanding but it

will fill you up without robbing you of the entire contents of your wallet. Prepare for seafood chowder, spring rolls, fried plaice, and scampi. Upstairs you'll get a three-course meal. Downstairs you can get a nibble at the wine bar. The food is good, honest, and average. The service is unobtrusive; the crowd is cheerful. *Church Rd., Greystones, County Wicklow.* ☎ *01/287-5759. Main courses €13–€18. Wed–Sat 7–11pm; Sun 12:30–8pm.*

➜ **Poppies Country Cooking** IRISH   As the name implies, this is a friendly, casual place to get a bite to eat in Enniskerry. The food is simple stuff (stews, sandwiches, soups, and meat pies), but it is homemade, and a cut above what you normally find in these places. The cakes are delish, so stop by for a tea break. *The Square, Enniskerry, County Wicklow.* ☎ *01/282-8869. Main courses €11–€15. Daily 9:30am–6pm.*

➜ **Roundwood Inn** IRISH/CONTINENTAL   A brill old 18th-century coaching inn in the middle of Roundwood's mountain beauty. Step in from the wilds to discover a pub packed with old-world atmosphere, where regulars sit on antique furnishings warmed by open log fires. Nearly everything on the menu is home-baked or locally grown—from steaks and sandwiches to Irish stew, fresh lobster and salmon, and seafood pancakes. In the summer grab a seat in the beer garden. There's fab pub grub in the bar between meal times. *Main St. (R755), Roundwood, County Wicklow.* ☎ *01/281-8107. Reservations recommended for dinner. Main courses €20–€30. Wed–Fri 7–9:30pm; Sat–Sun 1–2:30pm.*

➜ **Rugatino's River Café** SEAFOOD   Sit yourself down by the river in Wicklow town and get some chops round some incredibly fresh fish. Most of it is right off the boat. Specials include grilled and sautéed seafood friends. *Schooner House, South Quay, Wicklow Town, County Wicklow.* ☎ *0404/61900. Main courses €15–€21. Daily 9:30am-6pm.*

Splurge

➜ **The Strawberry Tree** GOURMET ORGANIC   Only wild and organic foods are served in the chic dining room at this rave-reviewed eatery. And only rather moneyed types tend to eat here. Starters might include Macreddin smoked salmon with wild sorrel, or wild wood pigeon terrine. Then there could be beef filet with beetroot, in a balsamic *jus,* or wild guinea fowl with dried fruit compote. From Rathdrum, follow signs for Aughrim and then 3km (2 miles) to Macreddin Village and the Brook Lodge Hotel. *Macreddin Village (between Aughrim and Aghavannagh), County Wicklow.* ☎ *0402/36444. www.brooklodge. com. Reservations required. Fixed-price dinner €55; Sun lunch €35. Wed–Sat 7–9:30pm; Sun 1–2:30pm.*

PARTYING

In terms of general nightlife, you'll find live trad very nearly nightly at **Philip Healy's** in Wicklow Town (Fitzwilliam Sq.; ☎ **0404/ 67380**), which serves up good pub grub and has the busiest social scene in town. This place packs itself to the rafters every night with young and old, local and tourist—all are welcome. Also in Wicklow Town, the **Bridge Tavern** (Bridge St.; ☎ **0404/67718**) offers live music—country, trad, or pop—every night of the week at "The Crow's Nest" (reached through another doorway on the cross street, although it's the same pub).

Adorned with hanging flowerpots, the Tudor-style **Coach House** (Main St., Roundwood; ☎ **01/281-8157;** www.thecoach house.ie) is marvelously twee, surrounded by mountains, in the picturesque village of Roundwood. In Bray, the **Harbour Bar** (Seapoint Rd., Bray; ☎ **01/286-2274**) is a terrific pub near the seafront—it's essentially two places in one: One half is a traditional pub with a stone floor and an eclectic collection of memorabilia, the other a kind of 1970s lounge, with velvet curtains and wall hangings (including one donated by Peter O'Toole, an occasional patron). The crowd is laid-back and a bit bohemian. In little Glencullen, **Johnnie Fox's** (Main St., Rathdrum; ☎ 0404/46774) is endlessly popular—as much for its seafood as for its nightly sessions of traditional Irish music. It can get quite steamy when it fills out at the weekends, but the food is good and the crowd is friendly.

In the Vale of Avoca, **The Meetings** (Avoca; ☎ 0402/35557) stands idyllically at the "Meeting of the Waters." More importantly, it serves good pub grub daily.

SIGHTSEEING

➔ **Avondale House & Forest Park** It's back to the history folks. Built in 1779 and set in a lush forest valley, this house was the birthplace and home of one of Ireland's top leaders, Charles Stewart Parnell (1846–91). When he wasn't strolling around his humongous pad he fought for Irish home rule and land reform. Inside you get a grand old house filled with Georgian furniture and displays on the life and times of old Charlie himself. Outside, take a wander along some nature trails including a rather lovely wooded number following the river for 5.5km (3.5 miles). There's a cute cafe serving tea and light lunches, as well as homemade breads and pastries. *Off R752, Rathdrum, County Wicklow.* ☎ *0404/46111. Admission €5 adults, €4.50 seniors and children under 12, €15 families. Mid-Mar to Oct 31 daily 11am–6pm. Parking €5.*

➔ **Browne's Hill Dolmen** Also known as the Druid's Altar—doesn't that sound good?—nobody really knows what this 5,000 year-old capstone was used for. Most likely it marks the burial place of a long-dead king, but over the years many myths and legends have sprung up around the old stone. As with all dolmens, the Irish see them as sacred, so don't even think of sneaking a stone into your pocket. You will, apparently, be cursed. *Off Rathvilly Rd., Carlow, County Carlow. Free*

admission. Daily year-round. Access via car park and enclosed pedestrian pathway.

FREE ➔ **Glendalough** This evocative, misty glen is a magical place. You gotta see it. An old, abandoned monastery built around two dark lakes, surrounded by towering forests. Its name is derived from the Irish *Gleann Da Locha,* meaning "The Glen of the Two Lakes." Wander the rocky paths beside the ancient chapels, and lap up the feeling of pure spirituality.

The ruins date back to the 5th century, when St. Kevin chose this setting, already used as a Bronze Age tomb, for his home. For 7 years he fasted, prayed, slept on the hard ground, and ate only what he could catch or find. His self-deprivation and fervor gained attention from passing hunters and peddlers, and soon he'd gathered quite a crowd of fellow masochists.

Over the next 4 centuries, Kevin's church became a center of religious learning, attracting thousands of students from all over Europe. Unfortunately, its success, as with so many early Irish religious sites, was its downfall, and Glendalough came to the attention of those wicked Vikings, who pillaged it repeatedly between 775 and 1071. But it was always rebuilt, stronger than ever, until 1398, when it was virtually wiped out by English forces. Attempts were made to bring it back to life, and it limped on in some form until the 17th century when it was abandoned altogether.

When you get here, stop by the visitor center behind the Glendalough Hotel near the entrance to the valley, and pick up a map. There are heaps of walking trails, each one taking in different ruins, as the chapels and houses were scattered over miles around the glen. The oldest ruins, the Teampall na Slellig, can be seen across the lake at the foot of towering cliffs, but as there's no ferry there's no way of getting out there.

DUBLIN

There's also a cave known as Kevin's Bed, which is believed to be where he lived when he first arrived at Glendalough. Follow the path from the upper lake to the lower lake and walk through the remains of the monastery complex. Although much of the monastic city is in ruins, there's a nearly perfect round tower, 31m (102 ft.) high, as well as hundreds of timeworn Celtic crosses and several chapels. One of these is St. Kevin's chapel, often called St. Kevin's Kitchen.

The only drawback of the whole gorgeous place is that, once again, it is a victim of its own success, and in the summer it tends to be overrun with tourists, which rather defeats the purpose. In the high season, it's best to arrive very early in the morning, or after 5pm (it stays light until 9pm at least) in order to see it at its best. If you stay at the nearby hostel, that's an easy thing to do. *County Wicklow (11km/6[bf]3/4 miles east of Wicklow on T7 via Rathdrum). Visitor Center:* ☎ *0404/45325 or 0404/45352. Free admission; exhibits and audiovisual presentation €2.75 adults, €1.25 students. Mid–Oct to mid–Mar daily 9:30am–5pm; mid–Mar to mid–Oct daily 9am–6pm.*

➜ **Glenmacnass Waterfall**   The River Glenmacnass rushes south across the highest mountain in Western Wicklow, Mt. Mullaghcleevaun (848m/2,781 ft.). At one point it reaches the edge of a plateau and plunges spectacularly off the edge. There's a parking lot near the top, and a path to the falls. Watch out on those there rocks; they can be treacherous. *Follow the Military Rd. through the Sally Gap and Laragh to the top of Glenmacnass Valley, and then watch for signs to the waterfall. Free admission.*

➜ **Huntington Castle**   This one is spooktastic. Built in 1621 on the site of an abbey, which was itself built on the site of a druid temple—doesn't that just get the hairs on the back of your neck quivering already?—this rambling, old manor house is said to be one

of the most haunted places in Ireland. It was originally the home of Lord Esmonde (English majors might like to know he was the inspiration behind Thackeray's novel *Henry Esmonde*). Esmonde's descendants still live in the main building. Other less corporeal forms spotted about the house and grounds include quite a few monks and the grieving first wife of Lord Esmonde who combs her hair in the moonlight still waiting for him to return from the wars. There's also an Irish soldier who dressed up to infiltrate Cromwell's forces and was shot through the castle grille as his mates didn't recognize him when he tried to get back in. Watch out for his face floating about outside. Inside, Barbara St. Lege, a woman who married into the family in the 18th century, still sweeps around the house jangling her keys. Behind her follows her maid, Honor Byrne, polishing door handles with her hair. To top off the party, the 18th century Bishop Leslie of Limerick has taken a liking to the Four Poster Room—guests say they've woken in the middle of the night to see him grinning at them from the end of their bed. Such shenanigans have attracted both Stanley Kubrick and Mick Jagger who have stayed here at one point or another (Kubrick filmed *Barry Lyndon* here). You can rent out one wing of the castle, with space for up to five people, for €650 a week. If you think you're hard enough. *Clonegal, County Carlow (off N80, 6.5km/4 miles from Bunclody).* ☎ *054/77552. Guided tour €6 adults, €4 seniors. June–Aug daily 2–6pm; May and Sept Sun 2–6pm; other times by appointment.*

➜ **Powerscourt Gardens, House Exhibition, and Waterfall**   If you like gardens, this is a magnificent one. Prepare to be stunned by half-naked Greek- and Italian-inspired statues, a shady grotto made of petrified moss, a serene Japanese garden, and a way-over-the-top fountain with statues of winged horses.

The house, on the other hand, is not so magnifico. It was designed in the 18th century by Richard Cassels (also called Richard Castle), the architect of Russborough House (see below) and Dublin's Parliament building. The same family lived in the building for 350 years, until the 1950s. When they moved out it took 20 years to restore the place. Then, in 1974, on the day before it was finally scheduled to open to the public, it caught fire. The interior was completely destroyed. It's been closed ever since, as a slow and, um, well, just plain slow renovation has been underway. In essence, the renovation here has already taken half a century. And counting. Tell your grandkids to pop by if they're in the area in 50 years time.

If you want a hike, follow the well-marked path over 7km (4⅓ miles) to the picturesque Powerscourt Waterfall. It's the highest in Ireland, at 121m (397 ft.), and a great place to do lunch. If you're not feeling energetic, you can drive, following signs from the estate. *Be warned:* Nothing comes cheap here—going to visit the waterfall will cost you extra.

Back on base, the cafe at Powerscourt is run by the brilliant Avoca chain. It serves up rich cakes, hot soups and stews, and healthy salads at bargain prices with breathtaking views thrown in for free. *Enniskerry, County Wicklow (off the N11).* ☎ *01/204-6000. www.powerscourt.ie. Gardens €9 adults, €5.50 students; waterfall €4 adults, €3.50 students. Gardens and house exhibition Mar–Oct daily 9:30am–5:30pm, Nov–Feb daily 9:30am–dusk; waterfall Mar–Oct daily 9:30am–7pm, Nov–Feb daily 10:30am–dusk.*

→ Russborough House One for the art lovers. Built between 1741 and 1751, and designed by the great Richard Cassels, Russborough was bought in the 1950s by Sir Alfred Beit, a member of the de Beers diamond family, who inherited a massive collection of art, which he shipped here. The paintings include some lovelies from Vernet, Vermeer, Guardi, Goya, Gainsborough, and Rubens.

Word soon got round about what was inside, attracting some unwanted attention. In 1974 an IRA gang stole 19 paintings worth nearly €12 million. They knocked Sir Alfred over the head with a revolver, tied him up in the library, and left him watching as they cut the paintings from their frames with a screwdriver. In 1986 Dublin master thief Martin Cahill found his way in and out with nearly €45 million worth of paintings. Most of these works of art were hauled in by police but, unsurprisingly, you can now only see the house by guided tour. The gallery was closed in 2005 but expected to be open in 2006. *Blessington, County Wicklow (off N81).* ☎ *045/865239. Admission to main rooms €6 adults, €4.50 students. Apr–Sept daily 10am–5pm. Tours given on the hour. Closed Oct–Mar.*

FREE → St. Mullin's Monastery This little gem is a well-kept secret. On a sunny day its divine setting—in a sleepy village beside the River Barrow—is reason enough for a visit. Whatever the weather, it's a fascinating spot, an outdoor museum of sorts, spanning Irish history from the early Christian period to the present, over the course of a few acres. It all begins with the ruins of a monastery founded by St. Moling (Mullin) in roughly A.D. 614. Plundered again and again by the Vikings in the 9th and 10th centuries, it was annexed in the 12th century by a nearby Augustinian abbey. You can also see bits of a Norman castle here, too. In the Middle Ages, the monastery ruins became a hot travel spot, especially during the height of the Black Death in 1348. Then pilgrims would cross the river barefoot, mutter prayers as they circled the burial spot of St. Mullin, add some small stones to the cairn marking the spot, and drink from the healing waters of the saint's well. Sound a bit old-fashioned? You might be surprised to find out people still make the pilgrimage to the ruin and waters today, near or on July 25. Next to the monastery buildings is an ancient cemetery, still in use, where, unusually, Protestants and Catholics have

DUBLIN

long been buried side by side. Even if the Heritage Centre is closed (it opens at the discretion of the caretaker, Seamus Fitzgerald), there's a map and brief history at the entrance to the cemetery. *On the scenic Barrow Dr., 12km (7[bḟ]l1/2 miles) north of New Ross, St. Mullins, County Carlow. Free admission.*

→ **Vale of Avoca** Basically a peaceful riverbank, the Vale of Avoca was made famous by 19th-century poet Thomas Moore. Apparently the poet sat under "Tom Moore's Tree" looking for inspiration before scribbling down the lines, "There is not in the wide world a valley so sweet / as the vale in whose bosom the bright waters meet . . ." The tree itself is a sorry sight—it's been picked almost bare by naughty souvenir hunters—but the place is still worth a visit. *Rte. 755, Avoca, County Wicklow.*

→ **Wicklow Mountains National Park** Hikers' heaven: tens of thousands of hectares of forest stretching for kilometers across County Wicklow. The main area surrounds Glendalough, including the Glendalough Valley and Glendalough Wood Nature Reserves. Hardcore hikers will be pleased to hear the most mountainous stretch of the Wicklow Way cuts through this park (www.irishwaymarkedways.ie). You'll find an info station at the Upper Lake at Glendalough. Here you can find out about hiking in the Glendalough Valley and surrounding hills, including maps and descriptions of routes. Free guided nature walks—mainly through rolling woodland—begin from the center on Tuesdays (departing 11am and returning 1:30pm) and Thursdays (departing 3pm and returning 4pm). The closest parking is at Upper Lake, where you'll pay €2 per car; instead, just walk up from the Glendalough Visitor Centre, where the parking's free. *Glendalough, County Wicklow.* ☎ *0404/45425. Visitor center free admission. Park admission €2.75 adults, €1.25 students. May–Aug daily 10am–6pm; Apr and Sept weekends only 10am–6pm. Closed Oct–Mar.*

→ **Wicklow's Historic Gaol** Given the archaic look of the place, it is impossible to believe that this old jail operated until 1924, the end of a terrifying career that spanned 2 centuries. It's all cheesy fun: After passing under the hanging beam, visitors are lined up against the wall of the "day room" and confronted with some dark facts of prison life in 1799, when more than 400 prisoners, most of them rebels, occupied the jail's 42 cells. After years of being fed once every 4 days and allowed to walk in the prison yard for 15 minutes a month, prisoners must have warmed to the idea of hanging. Within the main cellblock, you can roam the cells and visit informative exhibitions. Many prisoners were sent from here to penal colonies in Australia and Tasmania; that story, too, is told here, with the help of a stage-set wharf and prison ship. There's an in-house cafe, but if you've still got an appetite after all that, you're doing better than us. *Kilmantin Hill, Wicklow Town, County Wicklow.* ☎ *0404/61599. www.wicklows historicgaol.com. Tour €6.80 adults, €4.90 students. Apr 17–Sept daily 10am–6pm (last admission at 5pm).*

PLAYING OUTSIDE

BICYCLING The Lorum Old Rectory is also the base for **Celtic Cycling** (☎ **059/977-5282;** www.celticcycling.com), which offers a wide variety of 1- and 2-week cycling tours, or you can hire the gear you need from them and go it alone. In the summer, this area, with its rolling hills (although things get a bit steep in Wicklow) and gentle breezes, is great cycling country, and this outfit will help you make the most of it. In addition, **Cycling Safaris** (☎ **01/260-0749;** www.cycling safaris.com) offers a weeklong tour of the area for €590 per person, including accommodations, food, and luggage transfers.

HIKING Hikers and ramblers go wild about the isolation and sheer beauty of the **Wicklow Way,** a 132km (82-mile) signposted walking path following forest trails, sheep paths, and country roads from the suburbs south of Dublin, up into the Wicklow Mountains, and then down through country farmland to Clonegal, where the path ends. It takes about 5 to 7 days to walk the whole lot, with overnight stops at B&Bs and hostels along the route. Most people choose to walk sections as day trips.

The most spectacular places to walk in Wicklow are in the north and central parts of the county, which is overrun with short trails. One first-rate walk on the Wicklow Way begins at the **Deerpark parking lot** near the Dargle River and continues to Luggala, passing Djouce Mountain; the next section, between Luggala and Laragh, cuts across some wild country around Lough Dan. Recommended.

St. Kevin's Way, one of the oldest pilgrim routes in Ireland (dating back more than 1,000 years), has recently been restored. You don't have to have your halo firmly in place to walk the path running for 30km (18 miles) from Hollywood to Glendalough. It follows the rural route taken by pilgrims visiting the ancient monastic city of Glendalough, and winds its way through a combination of roads, forest paths, and open mountainside. Along the way you can stop at historical sites linked to St Kev, who traveled this route in search of a mountain hermitage.

Those of us you who want a softer option can follow the paths around the lakes at beautiful **Glendalough,** or join the southern section of the **Wicklow Way,** through Tinahely, Shillelagh, and Clonegal. Not as rugged as the terrain in central Wicklow, the gentle hills roll through gorgeous glens. Through much of this section, the path follows country roads chosen for their lack of traffic. Consider treating yourself to a night at **Park Lodge B&B,** Clonegal, Shillelagh (☎ 055/29140; parklodge@hotmail.com), near the trail's end; double rooms run €70 per night. If you're on foot, the hospitable Osborne family can arrange to pick you up at one of several points along the trail between Shillelagh and Clonegal.

You can pick up information and maps at the Wicklow National Park center at Glendalough, or at any local tourist office. Information on less strenuous walks can be found in the **Wicklow Trail Sheets,** also from tourist offices. It provides a map and route descriptions for several good short walks along the Way.

HORSEBACK RIDING   The secluded hillside paths of Wicklow are perfect for horseback riding. More than a dozen stables and equestrian centers offer horses for hire and instructional programs. Rates for horse hire average €25 per hour. Among the leading venues are **Broomfield Riding School,** Broomfield, Tinahely (☎ 0402/38117), and **Brennanstown Riding School,** Hollybrook, Kilmacanogue (☎ 01/286-3778). At the **Paulbeg Riding School,** Shillelagh (☎ 055/ 29100), experienced riders can explore the beautiful surrounding hills, and beginners can receive expert instruction from Sally Duffy, a friendly woman who gives an enthusiastic introduction to the sport.

Devil's Glen Holiday and Equestrian Village, Ashford, County Wicklow (☎ 0404/ 40637; www.devilsglen.ie), at the edge of the wilderness of the Devil's Glen, offers a full range of equestrian opportunities, from lessons to jumping to trekking cross-country. Prices hover at around €30 per hour, per person. Once your behind is sore you can also stay in spotless, spacious, fully equipped, self-catering two-bedroom apartments, two-bedroom bungalows, and three-bedroom cottages. These make a great base from which to explore the Wicklow Mountains and coastline, whether or not you ever swing your leg over a pony. Weekly rates run from €355 to €875, depending on season and size of bungalow. Weekend (Fri–Sun) and midweek (Mon–Thurs) rates are also available. Both the equestrian center and the self-catering village are open year-round.

DUBLIN

Spotting a Cute Whore

A number of words and phrases in Ireland have meanings quite different to other parts of the world, like the one above. Don't be disappointed. Here's a helpful list:

➜ **Cute hoor** (pronounced whore): This one has a very different meaning than it does in other countries. In Ireland, cute is often used to mean someone sly or devious and a *cute hoor* is a devious person. It's generally used to describe a man rather than a woman. You'll probably hear pub regulars shouting it at the TV when a politician comes on screen.

➜ **Fag:** Cigarette.

➜ **Fanny:** Female genitalia.

➜ **Ride:** Sex or an attractive person. So ask for a lift if you're looking for someone to drive you somewhere.

➜ **Take the piss out of** (as in: We were just taking the piss out of him"): Messing with you, teasing you. Another phrase for this is "slagging you."

Curses are used liberally in Ireland (those from Brooklyn will feel right at home). You'll no doubt encounter people saying "shite" as they drop something or "for feck's sake" (the equivalent of "for God's sake" when their football team misses a goal).

Another thing to look out for is the hand symbol you make when you hold your pointer and middle fingers up in a V with your palm facing inwards. This is nearly as fierce as raising your middle finger to someone. Watch out when ordering a couple of pints.

HUNTING Go leaping across the hedges with the **Broomfield Riding School,** Broomfield, Tinahely (☎ 0402/38117), which offers access to the hunt for those who can demonstrate adequate equestrian skills, especially jumping. The riding school is open year-round for lessons and trail rides.

WATERSPORTS & ADVENTURE SPORTS Deep in the Wicklow Mountains, the Blessington Lakes are a playground of clean, speedboat-free water. Less than an hour's drive from Dublin center, and signposted on the N81, the **Blessington Adventure Centre,** Blessington, County Wicklow (☎ 045/865800), offers all you need to get going canoeing, kayaking, sailing, or windsurfing, as well as equipment for land-based sports such as archery, orienteering, and pony trekking. Some picked-at-random prices per hour for adults include €15 for canoeing and kayaking, €20 for sailing, windsurfing,

and pony trekking. Full- and half-day multi-activity prices are also available. Open daily 10am to 5pm.

For the more adventurous, the **National Mountain and Whitewater Centre,** The Devil's Glen Forest, Ashford, County Wicklow (☎ 0404/40169; www.tiglin.com), is an innovative state-funded facility offering weekend courses in white-water kayaking, mountaineering, and rock climbing. Basic equipment is provided; fees for 1- to 5-day courses range from €80 to €450. The centre caters for a lively, young crowd, usually staying in hostels nearby.

County Kildare

This county is all about horses, and you'll see why if you come here—the low rolling hills of Kildare are a bit like the blue-green pastures of Kentucky. The soil is lush and fertile, producing miles of fields perfect for raising

DUBLIN

horses, and the population is one of the wealthiest in Ireland, with plenty of cash for buying and selling prime horseflesh. This is also the home of the Curragh, the racetrack where the Irish Derby is held, and of smaller tracks at Naas and Punchestown. To sum it up, this is a quiet, wealthy place, with few major sights. Most people who come here are horse-lovers, or race-lovers. Everybody else tends to ride on by.

GETTING THERE

BY TRAIN & BUS   Irish Rail (☎ 01/836-6222; www.irishrail.ie) provides daily train service to Kildare from Dublin Heuston station—the journey takes about an hour-and-a-half. DART trains run as far as Newbridge, but then you have to skip onto a bus from Newbridge to Kildare. **Bus Eireann** (☎ 01/836-6111; www.buseireann.ie) operates daily express bus service to Kildare. It takes an hour for the No.12 bus to get from Dublin to Kildare on the Dublin-Limerick-Ennis line; buses depart Dublin hourly every day. Heading back to Dublin, the ride takes 10 minutes longer because the 12 line adds a couple of stops, but it leaves Kildare hourly every day.

BY CAR   Take the main Dublin-Limerick road (N7) west of Dublin from Kildare, or the main Dublin-Galway road (N4) to Celbridge, turning off on local road R403.

BASICS

TOURIST INFORMATION   Contact the **Wicklow Tourist Office,** Wicklow Town (☎ 0404/69117). It's open year-round Monday to Friday, and Saturday during peak season. There is also a seasonal (mid-May to Sept) information office on The Square, Kildare Town, County Kildare (☎ 045/522696).

SLEEPING

In theory you won't be spending the night here as you're a very short distance from Dublin, but if you do, there are only a few options in any price range.

Doable

➔ **Castle View Farm**   If horses turn you on, try Liz and Ned Fitzpatrick's farmhouse. They don't breed horses, but at their sweet little farmhouse it's a short walk down a hedge-trimmed path to their working dairy farm. Hey, it's a farm. With animals. And delicious home-cooked meals. 4km (2.5 miles) from Kildare town; signs are posted all along the way from the center of town. ☎ 045/521-816. www. castleviewbb.com. €26–€30 per person. Open Mar–Nov. Amenities: Community TV; lounge.

➔ **Tonlegee House**   This country house in chill-out Athy has a cult following among Dubliners who come down for a few days of the three Rs (in Kildare, that's rest, relaxation, and racing). The house is an elegant 18th-century manor filled with antiques and roaring fires. Guest rooms are country style, with very large bathrooms (some with claw-foot tubs). The in-house restaurant is a destination on its own, and breakfasts here are memorable. Athy is a handsome town on the Grand Canal with some good easygoing walks. Athy, County Kildare (leave Athy by Barrow Bridge and Canal Bridge, then pass Tergal and take next left). ☎ 059/863-1473. €130 double. Dinner Mon–Sat €35. Amenities: Restaurant (country style); drawing room. In room: TV, hair dryer.

Splurge

➔ **Barberstown Castle**   This sturdy castle has overlooked Kildare for more than 750 years. Its five segments—constructed in the 13th, 16th, 18th, 20th, and 21st centuries—fuse together to form a highly satisfying whole. Each luxe guest room is named after one of the castle's former lords or proprietors—ranging from Nicholas Barby, who constructed the battlemented rectangular keep in the 13th century, to previous owner and guitarist Eric Clapton. This is real rich living. Prepare to be wowed with four-poster beds, chandeliers, and enormous bathrooms. From Dublin, drive south on N7, take a turn for Straffan at Kill; from west on N4, then turn for Straffan at Maynooth. *Straffan, County Kildare. ☎ 800/323-5463 in the U.S. or 01/628-8157. www.barberstowncastle.ie. €220 double; €270 4-poster bed. Service charge 10%. Closed Jan–Feb. Amenities: Restaurant (Continental); lounge; laundry service; nonsmoking rooms. In room: TV, hair dryer, garment press.*

EATING & PARTYING

There's not much in the way of restaurants in Kildare, and what there is isn't very cheap. If you're on a shoestring budget, try to have lunch in one of the pubs. Nightlife is about talking and tipping back those pints.

Doable

→ **Silken Thomas** GRILL   When you've won on the horses, this is somewhere to come and spend your cash. An old-world pub with an atmospheric eatery with wooden floors and fires crackling in the hearth. On the menu are plenty of soups, sandwiches, burgers, and salads, as well as steaks, roasts, mixed grills, and fresh seafood platters. *The Square, Kildare, County Kildare. ☎ 045/521264. Reservations recommended for dinner. Main courses €14–€28. Mon–Sat 12:30–2:30pm and 6–10pm; Sun 12:30–3pm and 6–9pm.*

Splurge

→ **Ballymore Inn** INTERNATIONAL   Looking like just another ordinary country restaurant, this place truly surprises with its inspired cooking. Each dish is a thing of beauty. And that's no exaggeration. The menu is varied and unpretentious—chic pizzas topped with oven-dried tomatoes, linguini with mussels, sautéed beef with mushrooms and paprika-laced sour cream. The only downer is the prices—they're high. *Ballymore Eustace, County Kildare (off the N81, southeast of Blessington). ☎ 045/864585. Reservations required. Main courses €23–€27. Mon–Thurs 12:30–3pm;*

Tues–Thurs 6–9pm; Sat 12:30–9:30pm; Sun 12:30–7pm.

Pubs

→ **The George Inn**   The back room of this pub is what makes it such a winner. Guessers say it was the kitchen of the original cottage, which would explain the huge fireplace with warm inglenooks. Now there's also a brass-and-leather horse harness hanging over the mantel. Seating is a random hodgepodge of cozy pine tables and chairs, and the atmosphere is come-on-in-and-have-a-pint-with-the-locals. *Prosperous, County Kildare. ☎ 045/861041.*

→ **The Moone High Cross Inn**   This big, 18th-century pub is ideal for a pint stop. There's genuine hospitality and excellent pub food—toasted sandwiches, shepherd's pie, all the old Irish classics—not to mention an open fire, finely pulled pints, and endless conversation. Get to know the Kildare locals. *Moone, County Kildare. No phone.*

SIGHTSEEING

→ **Castletown**   A grand mansion designed by Italian architect Galilei for Irish MP William Connolly (1662–1729). It set the fashion for big houses across Ireland for the next couple of hundred years. Inside is grand and there are two glorious follies on the grounds—both commissioned by William Conolly's wife, Louisa, when it was necessary to make work for the starving population of Ireland during the Famine. One is an obelisk, the other a quirky barn, shaped like an ever-so-slightly crooked funnel, around which winds a stone staircase. Its name, fittingly, is the "Wonderful Barn." *R403, off main Dublin-Galway Rd. (N4) Celbridge, County Kildare. ☎ 01/628-8252. Admission (including guided tour) €3.50 adults, €1.25. Easter day to Sept Mon–Fri 10am–6pm, Sat–Sun 1–6pm; Oct Mon–Fri 10am–5pm, Sun 1–5pm; Nov Sun 1–5pm. Closed Dec–Easter.*

→ **The Curragh**   This is the country's best-known racetrack, majestically placed at the

The Black Stuff

The pints of Guinness in Ireland taste a million times better than they do anywhere else in the world. Call it the home-court advantage, or credit it to the fact that it doesn't come any fresher than when you're in Ireland, but it's a fact that the Guinness you drink in Ireland is a cut above what you'll get served in Irish bars around the globe.

When Arthur Guinness took over a small brewery in Dublin, he had his sights set on the future. He may not have known then that his brew would account for one of every two pints sold in Ireland or would be sold in more than 150 countries, but he definitely was going for longevity—in 1979 he signed a 9,000 year lease on the brewery's site.

And let's get a few things cleared up about Guinness. Some slanderous troublemakers have dared to say it's packed full of calories. Nonsense. Actually, a pint of Guinness has about as many calories as a pint of orange juice—around 260. Another misconception is that Guinness is a particularly heavy drink, an idea that probably comes from the look of it. Again, not true. Really, Guinness is very easy to drink and refreshing—don't be scared off by that thick, creamy head.

Finally, five words to live by in Ireland: A good pint takes time. Bar girls and boys draw the pint about three-quarters and let it sit for about 2 minutes. Then, by pushing the tap forward so the stout comes out even more slowly than the first draw, they fill the glass the rest of the way (some even do it in a three-step process). They're not trying to be cruel; it's how a real pint is pulled and how you get the best creamy, white head on top.

When you do finally get your grubby hands around the glass, don't drink it just yet. Wait until it's turned almost black. To see if it's really ready, take a coin and tap it against the glass, working upward. When the coin makes a heavy thud through the glass, rather than a tinny tap, your pint is ready. You can also tell a good pint of Guinness by the circle of foam it leaves on the inside of the glass with each sip. Those with hairy faces be warned: That foam won't look so good on your goatee.

DUBLIN

edge of Ireland's central plain, and home to the **Irish Derby,** held every spring. Races are on at least 1 Saturday a month from March to October. The track has rail links with all major towns, and Irish Rail runs directly to it from Dublin (Heuston Station) for around €15, including courtesy coach to the main entrance. There's also a "Racing Bus" from Dublin (Busárus) each race day. Call Bus Eireann for details (☎ 01/836-6111; www.buseireann.ie). *Dublin-Limerick Rd. (N7), Curragh, County Kildare. ☎ 045/441205. www.curragh.ie. Admission €15 for most days of racing; €20–€50 on Derby days. Hours vary; 1st race usually 2pm but check newspaper sports pages.*

→ **Irish National Stud with Japanese Gardens & St. Fiachra's Garden** No, ladies, not those sort of studs. These are horses. But they have raised some of the fastest in Ireland on this government-sponsored farm. Wander around the 383-hectare (946-acre) grounds and watch the handsome devils being trained. A converted groom's house has exhibits on racing, steeplechase, hunting, and show jumping, plus a rather macabre display featuring the skeleton of Arkle, one of Ireland's most famous horses. Included is a peaceful **Japanese garden** dating to 1906, with pagodas, ponds, and trickling streams. There's also a visitor center with a restaurant and shop. **The Commemorative Garden of St. Fiachra,** in a natural setting of woods, wetlands, lakes, and islands, opened in 1999. The reconstructed hermitage has a Waterford crystal garden of rocks, ferns, and delicate glass orchids. Interesting. *Off the Dublin-Limerick Rd. (N7), Tully, Kildare, County Kildare.* ☎ *045/522963. Admission €9 adults, €7 students. Jan–Nov 12 daily 9:30am–6pm. Bus: From Busárus, Dublin, each morning, returning each evening.*

FREE → **The Irish Pewtermill** Ireland's oldest pewter mill. An 11th-century building. Show up in the morning to watch up to six craftsmen casting pewter in antique molds, some up to 300 years old. Casting takes place most days. The showroom has lots of pewter things for sale, from bowls to reproductions of parts of the Moone High Cross (see the listing below). *Timolin-Moone (signposted off N9 in Moone), County Kildare.* ☎ *059/862-4164. Free admission. Mon–Fri 10am–4:30pm; Sat–Sun 11am–4pm.*

→ **Larchill Arcadian Garden** Not to be missed if you're in the area. This unusual farm garden is the only surviving "ornamental farm" in Europe and it was nearly lost forever—it had fallen into decay in the 1970s and 1980s, but was restored in the late 1990s. Products of the Romantic Movement, these hybrid farms were all the rage in Europe in the 18th century. Larchill is a first-rate example of art for art's sake. All around the working farm are little things of beauty: a lake dotted with delightful Gothic follies; miles of wooded nature trails; meadows stocked with emus and llamas; a walled garden filled with goats, geese, and peacocks. There's even a resident ghost haunting a medieval tower. It's all very family-oriented, but still quite cool. Snacks and ice cream are available in the tearoom. *Kilcock, County Kildare (signposted off N4 near Maynooth).* ☎ *01/628-7354. www.larchill.ie. Admission €7.50 adults. May and Sept Sat–Sun noon–6pm; June–Aug Tues–Sun noon–6pm.*

MTV **Best** → **Moone High Cross** Amid the awesome ruins of Moone Abbey stands this top-of-the-range high cross that is nearly 1,200 years old. The abbey, established by St. Columba in the 6th century, lies in ruins around it. The cross features some mighty fine Celtic designs and good old-fashioned biblical storytelling. Look closely to see that naughty little nymphet Eve trying to tempt Adam with some fruit, the sacrifice of Isaac, and Daniel getting down with the lions. Among the carvings are several surprises— no not Noah getting frisky with his missus, but actually something even more bizarre— there's a Near Eastern fish that reproduces when the male feeds the female her own eggs, which eventually hatch from her mouth. Hmmm. What can that mean? *Moone, County Kildare (signposted off N9 on southern edge of Moone village).*

FREE → **St. Brigid's Cathedral** When you wish upon a stone . . . This 13th-century church isn't going to set the world of youth on fire, but it does have a 10th-century round tower that is second tallest in the country (33m/108 ft.). If the groundskeeper is in, he'll let you climb the stairs to the top for €3.20. Watch out for a strange looking stone with a hole at the top near the tower; it's known as the "wishing stone." According to legend, if you put your arm through the hole and touch your shoulder, your wish will come true. Or are the locals just enjoying making muppets of the tourists? We'll leave that up to you. *Market Sq., Kildare Town, County Kildare.* ☎ *045/521229. Free admission. May–Oct Mon–Sat 10am–1pm and 2–5pm; Sun 2–5pm.*

PLAYING OUTSIDE

BICYCLING Kildare's flat-to-rolling landscape is perfect for gentle cycling. Sadly, most organized tours bypass Kildare for regions with more diverse scenery, but you can always plan your own route.

HIKING The way-marked **Grand Canal Way** is a long-distance walking path that cuts through part of Kildare. Its flatness makes it ideal for beginners, walkers who lack ambition, and drink-soddled layabouts. The canal passes through plenty of scenic towns, such as Sallins, Robertstown, and Edenderry, where you can find a room and stock up on provisions. For more information, contact the tourist office.

HORSEBACK RIDING Visitors can expect to pay an average of €25 per hour for trekking or trail riding in the Kildare countryside. To arrange a ride, contact the **Kill International Equestrian Centre,** Kill (☎ 045/877208), or the **Abbeylands Equestrian Centre,** Clane (☎ 045/868188).

Counties Meath & Louth— The Boyne River Valley

With its quiet hilly pastures dotted with fluffy white sheep, Meath may look like your typical Irish county, but keep very still and you may feel a hint of mystery in the air. This is home to tons of ancient historical sites.

First up is the **Hill of Tara**—the Olympus of early Ireland where the kings of Ireland ruled 1,000 years ago, protected—so they said—by fairies. Some old men with long beards even believe the Holy Grail may be hidden underneath it.

In the role call of ancient sites Tara is a mere babe, Meath's rich soil had already been attracting settlers for more than 8,000 years. Archaeologists have uncovered vast burial grounds and ruined settlements showing this region was humming even then.

The most intriguing is **Newgrange,** with its mysterious carvings and huge stone passage tombs you can stroll inside. Nearby, the **Hill of Slane** overlooks the beautiful Boyne Valley. On this hill a Welsh priest named Patrick is said to have lit a Christian fire defying rules put down by the pagan Irish King Laoghaire, starting off the first of many fights between Ireland's religious orders.

Elsewhere is **Kells.** Yep, that's right, where the famous Book of Kells came from. It's all ruins now but there are some bits worth seeing although the traffic rather distracts from the air of mystery. Nearby is **Bective Abbey,** another ruined monastery.

Most of Meath is inland, but it's got its own coastline and two fine beaches, **Bettystown** and **Laytown.**

Louth is Ireland's tiniest county and even its largest towns (**Drogheda** and **Dundalk**) are quite small. With about 24,000 people, Drogheda is the largest and most happening town in the area. But remember, we're out in the country, where "happening" is a relative term. It has miniscule nightlife and a few decent restaurants, but it's really a lazy place. This town won't keep you here for long—although you absolutely must swing by the cathedral to get an eyeful of ▮▮ Best Oliver Plunkett's shrunken head kept in a glass container, and to hear about the keeper's ongoing battle with munching mites—but it's close to many of the ancient spots in the Boyne Valley and Louth areas, and will keep you busy, if not exhilarated, till the wee hours. The most compelling reasons to come here are the nearby sites, Newgrange and **Monastaireboice.** Dundalk is worth a stop for the **Harp Lager Brewery** or a pub lunch at the old-world-style **Windsor Pub** on Dublin Street.

The heritage town of **Carlingford** is easily the cutest in Louth, on a spur of the Cooley Mountains, overlooking glassy Carlingford Lough. Carlingford still follows its ancient street patterns, and is overseen by a massive 13th-century castle. On the heights above the town, the ancient Irish folk hero Cùchulainn is said to have single-handedly defeated the armies of Ulster in an epic battle.

Between Carlingford Lough and Dundalk Bay, the **Cooley Peninsula** is the scenic setting for many of Ireland's myths and legends. Its mountains, rivers, and woodlands cast a

DUBLIN

spell on many travelers. And if you're not swayed by these old tales it's also a fab place to go out into the Cooley Mountains either by foot or bike.

GETTING THERE

BY RAIL & BUS **Irish Rail** (☎ 01/836-6222; www.irishrail.ie) has several trains headed to Drogheda from Dublin and Belfast every day. **Bus Eireann** (☎ 01/836-6111; www.buseireann.ie) operates daily express bus service to Slane and Navan in County Meath, and Collon and Drogheda in County Louth. Bus Eireann and **Gray Line Tours** (☎ 01/605-7705; www.guidefriday.com) offer seasonal sightseeing tours to Newgrange and the Boyne Valley.

BY CAR Take the N1 north from Dublin City to Drogheda, then the N51 west to Boyne Valley; the N2 northwest to Slane and east on the N51 to Boyne Valley; or the N3 northwest via Hill of Tara to Navan, and then east on the N51 to Boyne Valley.

BASICS

TOURIST INFORMATION Contact the **Dundalk Tourist Office,** Jocelyn Street, County Louth (☎ 042/933-5484); the **Drogheda Tourist Office,** Headfort Place (behind the town hall), Drogheda, County Meath (☎ 041/984-5684); or the **Bru na Boinne Center,** Newgrange, Donore, County Meath (☎ 041/988-0300).

FESTIVALS

Locals in the region go crazy for the **Tain Festival** (www.tainfestival.ie; ☎ 042/9392919), a weekend-long rhythm and roots festival normally held around the end of October featuring piles of top Irish talent.

SLEEPING

Hostels

→ **Green Door Hostel** This bright hostel is a local fave for backpackers in the know. Strolling into its sun-filled lounge, with blonde-wood floors, a big brick fireplace, and bright cushions chucked about, you have to remind yourself you're in a hostel, it feels more like a friend's oversize home. Rooms come in a variety of sizes from doubles and triples to dorms, and the staff seems to be hired for its friendliness. Beds are comfy, and private rooms have TVs and tea-making facilities, while dorm residents can hang out in the laid-back Salt House restaurant, gabbing over endless cups of tea. There are lots of bargain tours on offer, making a good alternative to going it alone. All in all, this is the best hostel in the area. *47 John St., a block from the bus station, Drogheda.* ☎ *041/983-4422. www.greendoor.hostel.com. €17 dorm, €28 triple. No credit cards. Amenities: Restaurant; kitchen; linen provided; security lockers; TV lounge.*

→ **Harpur House Hostel** A small independent hostel in a gorgeous old house at the edge of central Drogheda. Rooms range from dorms to doubles and triples, and the quads they call "family rooms." **Be warned:** There is a midnight curfew. The place is also basic and in need of a spruce up, but it's handy to know about when other hostels are full. A few readers have described the owners as less than friendly, and there's the eternal irony of the sign outside reading "Harpur Bed & Breakfast" when no breakfast is provided. Let us know what you think. From the town center, take Shop Street to Peter Street and take a right onto William Street. The hostel is the last house on the right. *William St., Drogheda.* ☎ *041/983-2736. www.harpurhouse. com. €20—€35 per person. No credit cards. Amenities: Kitchen; lockers; linens included; 24-hr. reception.*

→ **Kells Hostel** This recently renovated, family-owned hostel is friendly and fun. Run entirely by locals it's got all the information you could ever want, and they're happy to part with it. There are four-bed and eight-bed dorms as well as private en suite rooms available, and all kinds of extras, including a kitchen for guests to use, large TV room, free showers, and bed linens. The pub next door is usually packed with travelers. There are also camping facilities if you *really* want to save some money. *Carrick St.* ☎ *046/924-9995. www.kellshostel.com. €14 per person dorm; €19 per person double; €8 per person camping. No credit cards. Amenities: Kitchen; linens; TV lounge.*

Cheap

→ **Delamare House** Eileen McGeown runs this modern bungalow overlooking Carlingford Lough and the Mourne Mountains. The view is amazing, and McGeown welcomes singles, which makes a change. The house is 5km (3 miles) from Carlingford and 1km ($\frac{1}{2}$ mile) from Omeath on the Carlingford-Omeath Road, opposite Calvary Shrine. Call for information on how to get there by public transport. *Ballyoonan, Omeath, County Louth.* ☎ *042/937-5101. eileenmcgeown@eircom.net. €28 single without bathroom, €30 single with bathroom; €50 double without bathroom, €54 double with bathroom. Rates include full breakfast. No credit cards. Closed Nov–Mar. In room: TV, tea/coffeemaker, hair dryer.*

→ **Harbour Villa** This Victorian harbormaster's house, surrounded by gardens, sits on the River Boyne. Bedrooms are the usual mix of floral bedspreads and pine furniture. If you can stomach those, the beach is 2km (1'l₂ miles) away, and the house has its own tennis court. Breakfast is also a bit of a treat with freshly baked bread or scones and scrambled eggs with salmon, fruit salad, or local cheeses; herbal teas are also offered. *Mornington Rd., Drogheda (1.6km/1 mile from town off the main Dublin road), County Louth.* ☎ *041/983-7441. €60 double with bathroom. Rates include full breakfast. No credit cards. Amenities: Tennis court.*

→ **Headfort Arms Hotel** This simple, central hotel offers all you need, but don't come expecting any frills. Rooms are small but comfortable, while the furnishings are a little rough around the edges. The in-house

restaurant serves your usual Irish nosh with an emphasis on roasted meat at okay prices to a largely gray-haired crowd. The coffee shop is a bit of a local hangout for salt-of-the-earth types. *John St., Kells.* ☎ *046/924-0063. €40 per-person double. No credit cards. Amenities: Restaurant.*

→ **Tara Guesthouse** The main reason to stay at this friendly, clean guesthouse is its location at the edge of the sea. Tara Guesthouse sits so close to the water that sand might blow into your room. The bedrooms are well laid out, and the sea breezes make for a chill atmosphere. Breakfast isn't included in the room price. *Beachfront, Laytown, County Meath.* ☎ *041/982-7239. €65 double. No credit cards. Amenities: Lounge. In room: TV, hair dryer.*

Doable

→ **Jordan's Townhouse & Restaurant** A 16th-century town house right in the center of Carlingford. The food and decor are both well done. The mood is chill, and the service is friendly. A good option, if you've got a budget that will stretch this far. *Newry St., Carlingford, County Louth.* ☎ *042/937-3223. 5 units. €115 double. Rates include full breakfast. Amenities: Restaurant (bistro/seafood). In room: TV, hair dryer.*

Splurge

→ **Ghan House** You're going to love this place. Imagine a Georgian country house left just as it was hundreds of years ago. An old rocking horse in the hall, a classic bicycle leaning up against a wall. Dotted around the place are stuffed birds in glass cases. The common rooms are so gorgeous they'll have to drag you out when it comes time to leave. They are all unique, but all have creaking antique beds, jazz put on the CD player for your arrival, a collection of well-thumbed secondhand books, and a soon-gone collection of homemade biscuits waiting in a glass jar. The rooms are just a tiny bit scruffy but that's half the charm. It really does feel like someone's home. And you gotta dress for dinner. Take cocktails in the drawing room in front of the fire, or sitting on the old tractor seats in the lush bar before sitting up around the candlelit table and tucking into some of the best organic food in the region. If you're booking, make sure to ask to go in the old house as the new wing just ain't the same. Upon entering Carlingford from the south, look out for "Carlingford-Medieval Heritage Town" and turn left 10m after that. Ghan House is the big white one. ☎ 042/937-3682. *www.ghanhouse.com. Double €170; single €65. Rates include full Irish breakfast. Free parking. Amenities: Bar/lounge. In room: CD player/ radio, TV, tea- and coffeemaking kit (including cookies).*

EATING

Generally speaking, good restaurants are few and far between in this rural area. Your best chances are in Drogheda and Kells. You can pick up makings of a picnic in Kells at the **Tesco Supermarket** (across the street from the Kells Hostel). **Pebbles** (Newmarket St, Kells.; 9am–5:30pm Mon–Sat) is a decent greasy-spoon diner popular with the locals. In Drogheda, **Monks Espresso Bar/Cafe** (Shop St. near river; ☎ **041/984-5630**) is a cool cafe good for lunch or coffee drinks while **La Pizzeria** (St. Peter's St.; ☎ **041/ 983-4208;** Mon–Sat till 11pm; dinner €8–€12) is popular with locals and is a good bet for dinner with tasty pizza and pasta dishes. Many pubs in town have good lunches on offer as well. Backpackers hang out at the cheap and cheerful **Salt House** restaurant at the Green Door Hostel (see p. 132), and at **Weavers** pub on West Street for the cheap, good lunches.

Doable

→**The Brake** SEAFOOD/STEAKS/SAND-WICHES Sit yourself down at this rustic restaurant, directly on the seafront, to chow down on seafood (crab claws, prawns, lobster in summer) and steaks, as well as porc

a la crème and home-cured ham on the bone. It's been run by the Smyth family for nearly 25 years, and inside the stone walls are a crazy jumble of old prints, lamps, jugs, old posters, and other "artifacts." Service is as warm as the glowing, open fireplace. *Main St. on Seafront, Blackrock, County Louth. ☎ 042/ 932-1393. Main courses €9–€20. Mon–Sat 6:30–10:30pm; Sun 6–9:30pm.*

→**Vanilla Pod** MODERN IRISH This is a modern, creative little restaurant in the center of Kells, where fresh local ingredients are the center of attention. The menu features light dishes prepared with fresh herbs and local poultry and meat, and it's all served up in a cheerful dining room, with a friendly touch. *John St., Kells, County Meath. ☎ 046/ 40084. Main courses €11–€17. Mon–Fri 5:30– 10pm; Sat–Sun 6–11pm.*

Splurge

→**Mountainstown House** MODERN IRISH One of the region's top restaurants, set in an old Queen Anne house, the dining room is pure indulgence with heavy furniture and lots of lavish art. The food, first-rate variations on trad Irish food such as herb-encrusted rack of lamb, and Wicklow venison, is really rather good. The manor house itself is set on country grounds, populated by horses and the odd peacock. If you've got the cash you could stay the night in one of their divine rooms (€95–€150). *Castletown, Navan, County Meath. ☎ 046/905-4154. Reservations required Fri–Sat. Main courses €22–€33. Service charge 10%. Daily 7–11pm.*

PARTYING

Drogheda offers a couple of popular pub-cum-disco places that are actually a lot of fun—especially once you accept the fact that they are your only options. **Peter Mathew's** (9 Lawrence St., Drogheda; ☎ **041/983-7371**) is a popular pub with the local young people and plays indie music to lure them in. **Fusion** (12 George St., Drogheda) spins mostly Top-40 remixes and funky classic-rock-type grooves for the uninhibited local youths. A clubby pub where you can dance and drink, **The Earth** (Westcourt Hotel on West St., Drogheda; ☎ 041/983-0969) features a cool stone-age motif. **Number 4** (Stockwell Lane, Drogheda; ☎ 041/984-5044; €1–€5 cover on weekends; open late) goes for a slicker look; and is your best bet for late-night fun. Plus they have DJs and live music on weekends.

You should also check out the town's friendly pubs. **Carbery's** on the North Strand is probably the best-known gathering place on this part of the east coast, especially for the traditional sessions on Tuesday nights (from 9pm) and Sunday lunchtimes (12:30–2:30pm). To get a seat on Sunday make sure you're there by noon. **Clarkes,** on the corner of Fair and Peter streets, is quiet and old-fashioned during the week, popular with the local literary set, but on Saturday nights is a fashionable meeting place.

Kells is quieter, but **O'Shaughnessy's** (Market St., Kells; ☎ 012/664-1110) is a decent pub in the traditional vein, while **Monaghan's** attracts all the backpackers in town, since it's in the same building as the Kells Hostel (see p. 132).

If you find yourself in Dudalk you absolutely must spend a night in **The Spirit Store** (George's Quay; ☎ 042/935-2697; www.spiritstore.ie), a hip hangout blasting out live music from top local and international indie bands, as well as trad music performances and sets from first-rate comedians. If a band's being talked about by the cool young things in Louth and Meath, it will often play here, but usually to a sold-out crowd so phone ahead.

SIGHTSEEING

→ **Hill of Tara**   This hill doesn't look like much—just a green hill, really—but the legends and folklore that surround it place it at the center of early Irish history. Something about this nondescript green hill has always attracted people for reasons of spiritualism. Ancient tombs have been discovered on the hill that date back to the Stone Age. Pagans believed that the goddess Maeve lived and reigned from here. By the 3rd century, it was home to the most powerful men in Ireland—the high kings. They had a ceremonial residence on the hill, and ruled as much by myth as by military strength. Every 3 years a *feis* (a banquet reaching the proportions of a great national assembly) was held. It's said that more than 1,000 princes, poets, athletes, priests, druids, musicians, and jesters celebrated for a week. A *feis* wasn't all fun and games: Laws were passed, disputes settled, and matters of defense decided. The last *feis* was held in A.D. 560, and afterwards, Tara went downhill as the power and popularity of Christianity rose. What's left of all of this is not physically impressive—grassy mounds, some ancient pillar stones, and depressions where the Iron Age ring forts stood. All the wooden halls rotted long ago, so you'll have to rely on your imagination. But it's still a magnificent spot, with the hill rising 90m (295 ft.) above the surrounding countryside, and beautiful views. Plus there are always some weirdoes wandering around who usually have some wacky Tara philosophies they're more than happy to chat about. A visitor center, with exhibits and a stirring film, is in the old church beside the entrance to the archaeological area. There's no picnicking, but there is a coffee shop/tearoom. *Off the main Dublin road (N3), Navan, County Meath.* ☎ *046/902-5903. Admission €2 adults, €1 students. Mid-May to mid-Sept daily 10am–6pm. Closed mid-Sept to mid-May.*

→ **Knowth**   Is Newgrange more historically important than Knowth? Who gives a sheep's bottom. Both are mightily impressive Stone Age burial grounds, with complex passage tombs. Knowth's tomb was closed to the public for many years as archaeologists plunged its depths, but is now open, at least in part. It is a massively long passage—at 34m (112 ft.) it is longer than the one at Newgrange.

What Does It All Mean?

....

Zipping around the Irish countryside you're likely to spot some strange old place names. Use the following list to mix and match and get their Irish Gaelic meaning. For example, Tullamore translates into Great Small Hill (tul + mor), which, come to think of it, doesn't make a lot of sense either but, hey, that's Ireland for you. Mysterious.

- → Ard: Height, hill
- → Aw, ow: River
- → Bal, bally: Town
- → Bawn: White
- → Beg: Small
- → Carrick, carrig: Rock
- → Cloch: Stone
- → Derg: Red
- → Doo, du: Black
- → Drom, drum: Ridge
- → Dun: Fort
- → Glen, glas: Valley
- → Innis, ennis, inch: Island

- → Kil, kill: Church
- → Knock: Hill
- → Lis, liss: Fort
- → Lough: Lake
- → Mone, mona: Bog
- → Mor: Great, large
- → Owen, avon: River
- → Rinn, reen: A point
- → Ross: Peninsula
- → Shan, shane: Old
- → Tra, traw: Beach
- → Tul, tulagh: Small hill

In 1968, archaeologists discovered a second passage tomb on the opposite side of the mound that was 6m (20 ft.) longer. In the mound itself scientists found the largest collection of passage tomb art uncovered so far in Europe, as well as a number of underground chambers, and 300 carved slabs. The mound itself is surrounded by 17 satellite graves in a complex pattern. The meaning of it all remains shadowed in mystery, and even now all of Knowth's secrets have not been uncovered—excavation work ploughs on and you'll probably get a chance to see the archaeologists at work. All tickets are issued at the visitor center. Combined tickets with Newgrange are available. *Drogheda, County Meath (1.6km/1 mile northwest of Newgrange, between Drogheda and Slane).* ☎ *041/988-0300. www.knowth.com. Admission to Knowth and Bru na Boinne Centre €4.25 adults, €1.50 students. Nov–Feb daily 9:30am–5pm; Mar–Apr and Oct daily 9:30am–5:30pm; May daily*

9am–6:30pm; June to mid-Sept daily 9am–7pm; mid- to late Sept daily 9am–6:30pm.

→ **Loughcrew** *Slieve na Calliaghe,* or "The Hill of the Witch," has 30 passage tombs on top of three hills in western Meath. From their peaks, the views of the plains of Meath and of the lake lands of Cavan will blow you away on a clear day. Not literally, we hope. Two of the cairns—decorated with funky Neolithic carvings—can be entered with a key. Guided tours of the eastern cairn are offered from mid-June to mid-September, and a key is available at the office for the western tomb (the more intriguing of the two). A €25 deposit is required for the key. From October to May the keys to both cairns are available from Mrs. Basil Balfe (☎ 049/854-1256), whose home is the first house on your right after turning into the Loughcrew drive. *Outside Oldcastle, County Meath. Admission €1.50 adults, €.50 students. Mid-June to mid-Sept daily 10am–6pm. Other times:*

key is available (see above). From N3, take R195 through Oldcastle toward Mullingar. 2.4km (1½ miles) out of Oldcastle, look for a signposted left turn. The next left turn into Loughcrew is also signposted.

MTV Best → **Newgrange** Don't miss this one. It really is mind-blowing. Ireland's best-known prehistoric monument is one of the archaeological wonders of western Europe. Built as a burial mound more than 5,000 years ago—long before the Egyptian Pyramids or Stonehenge—it sits atop a hill near the Boyne, massive and mysterious. The mound is 11m (36 ft.) tall, but is approximately 78m (256 ft.) in diameter. It consists of 200,000 tons of stone, a 6-ton capstone, and other stones weighing up to 16 tons each, many of which were hauled from as far away as County Wicklow and the Mountains of Mourne. Each stone fits perfectly in the overall pattern, and the result is a watertight structure, an amazing feat of engineering. The question remains, though: Who was it for? Even as archaeologists found more elaborate carvings in the stones—spirals, diamonds, and concentric circles—they got no clues as to whether it was for kings, political leaders, or for a long-lost ritual. Inside, a passage 18m (59 ft.) long leads to a central burial chamber that sits in pitch darkness all year, except for 5 days in December. During the winter solstice (Dec 19–23), a shaft of sunlight travels down the arrow-straight passageway for 17 minutes, until it hits the back wall of the burial chamber. You can register to be in the tomb for this extraordinary event, but the waiting list is already booked several years ahead. As part of the tour, you can walk down the passage, past elaborately carved stones and into the chamber, which has three sections, each with a basin stone that once held cremated human remains. It's not one for claustrophobics but, if you're lucky, your guide will reenact the solstice light display. So simple yet so astounding. *Tips:* Admission

to Newgrange is by guided tour only. It's 3km (2 miles) east of Slane. Get there early. All tickets are issued at the visitor center, Bru na Boinne. Combined tickets with Knowth, another nearby megalithic passage tomb, are available. Because of the great numbers of visitors, especially in the summer, expect delays; access is not guaranteed. The last tour is given at 4:30pm. Newgrange lies just north of the River Boyne, about 13km south of Drogheda and 5km southeast of Slane. Knowth is about 1km northwest of Newgrange or almost 4km by road. There are no direct buses to either of the sites. During most of the week, the closest you'll get is Slane, which is served by up to six buses daily Monday-Saturday from Drogheda. On Saturday, the bus from Drogheda stops at Donore, closer to the visitor's center (see below), on its way to Slane. *Off N51, Slane, County Meath. ☎ 041/ 988-0300. www.knowth.com/newgrange.htm. Guided tour and admission to Bru na Boinne Centre €5.50 adults, €2.75 students. Nov–Feb daily 9:30am–5pm; Mar–Apr and Oct daily 9:30am–5:30pm; May daily 9am–6:30pm; June to mid-Sept daily 9am–7pm; mid- to late Sept daily 9am–6:30pm.*

FREE → **St. Colmcille's House** Sitting strangely in a row of modern houses, St. Colmcille's House is all that's left of an old monastic settlement that once stood where modern homes are now built. Most of the building is 10th century, although some parts are a century older. Like so many other old buildings in these counties, what exactly it was built for is unknown, although some experts believe it was once a scriptorium—where the monks wrote and illuminated their dazzling books. Step inside the first room to see an ancient fireplace and entrance. A narrow metal staircase goes up to a dark vault just under the roof. The small two-roomed space is where some folks think the Book of Kells was completed. *About 180m (about 590 ft.) northwest of St. Columba's Church, Church*

Mel Gibson woz 'ere

There's just something about Ireland that Hollywood cannot resist. As long as there have been films, they've been filming here. It can't be the weather that brings them in—it's usually terrible. It could be the hilly green countryside, mountains, and seaside views, of course. Or, call us cynical but, could it be the generous tax breaks and the low wages for which locals were willing to work that drew filmmakers irresistibly to this Tinsel Village? No, surely not.

These days wages may be a bit higher, but the tax breaks are still good, and international films are still made here fairly steadily. In 2004, Jerry Bruckheimer filmed his blockbuster *King Arthur* here with Keira Knightly and Clive Owen as Guin and Art, and County Kildare doing an (arguably better) impression of a stormy and ominous Camelot.

Of course, everyone knows that parts of *Braveheart* were filmed in Ireland, with lots of scenes being shot at Trim Castle. What people don't know is that the extras used in the battle scenes were largely from the Irish territorial army. Local rivalry between different companies is often intense and the extras were plucked from many different companies. Consequently, some of those violent battle scenes you see on screen are more realistic than you might think, with rival soldiers taking the opportunity to bash the bejesus out of each other.

That Ireland could stand in for England or Scotland is hardly surprising, but from time to time filmmakers have used Ireland as a stand-in for quite surprising places. In *Saving Private Ryan* the Wexford Coast stood in for Normandy, and who noticed the difference? Nobody, that's who. In a kind of spectacular example of filmic contortions, on more than one occasion Georgian Dublin has even managed to stand in for modern New York. In Jim Sheridan's *In America* (which arguably should have been called "In Ireland") and Pierce Brosnan's *Laws of Attraction,* Dublin did Manhattan. The irony cuts both ways, though—the archetypal 1990s Irish comedy *Waking Ned Devine* was actually filmed on Britain's Isle of Man. For tax purposes, naturally.

In *Ella Enchanted,* County Wicklow made a lovely fairy-tale land that suited its princess, Anne Hathaway, but that was not the first time the green countryside of Eire was used as a backdrop to fairy-tale lore—in the late 1980s *The Princess Bride* was filmed in County Clare around the Cliffs of Moher. Similarly (well, kind of), in 2002's *Reign of Fire* the fire-breathing dragons wheeled in the skies above picturesque Glendalough in County Wicklow.

Still, most of the time in films, Ireland is Ireland. The dark bio-pic *Veronica Guerin* was shot on location in Dublin and in County Kildare, *Angela's Ashes* was filmed in villages in Counties Cork and Limerick, all as you might expect.

Lane, Kells, County Meath. Free admission. Mon–Sat 10am–5pm. Ask for key from caretaker Mrs. B. Carpenter, next door to the oratory on Church Lane.

📺 Best → **Slane Castle** David Bowie, U2, Paul Oakenfold, Iggy Pop, REM, and Madonna have all pumped out their tunes against the backdrop of Slane Castle. You can even see clips of Madonna's concert and the

castle in her 2005 film *I'm Going to Tell You a Secret.* If you can catch a gig here, do. The setting is stunning and the crowd usually goes wild. By day, this 18th-century castle is a big tourist draw. The original building was made even grander in the early 19th century prior to a visit by the naughty King George IV. Gossip has it Lady Conyngham—who lived here then—was his mistress, and the road from Dublin to

Slane was only built to make George's journeys to her home a little less bumpy. A fire in 1991 burned most of the castle's art and antiques. After major renovations, the castle is now open again for visits. *Just west of Slane (signposted off the Navan road), County Meath.* ☎ *041/988-4400. www.slanecastle.ie. Admission €7 per person. May–Sept Mon–Thurs noon–5pm.*

→ **Trim Castle** "They may take our lives, but they'll never take our Freedom." Yep, the immortal words of one of Hollywood's more miniature men, Mel Gibson, when he was playing the Scottish legend William Wallace, in *Braveheart*. That film really put Trim Castle on the travel map. Before then, despite being built in the 12th century by Norman Lord Hugh de Lacy, it fell into disrepair in the 17th century and nobody really bothered with it until Mel left. Afterwards it was restored as a "preserved ruin." Now the crowds can't keep away. You can take the guided tour, but you'll have to arrive early. It's usually a sellout but can't be booked in advance. Note that this tour is unsuitable for anyone afraid of formidable heights. *Trim, County Meath.* ☎ *046/943-8619. Admission to grounds and tour of keep €3.50 adults, €1.25 students; admission to grounds only €1.50 adults, €.75 students. Easter–Oct daily 10am–5pm (last admission at 4:15pm). Tours every 30 min.: 1st tour at 10:15am and last tour at 4:15pm. Closed Nov–Easter.*

→ **Holy Trinity Heritage Centre** In a restored medieval church, this center runs through Carlingford's history. If you book ahead, your visit can include a free guided walking tour of the town. Worth it just to hear about the origin of our modern wardrobes. Apparently, the town's local guards would hang their clothes up above the guardhouse's pile of stinking human effluent, believing the strong stench kept their clothes "disinfected." This area was known as the guardrobe, later morphing into the modern wardrobe. And

that's not all: More grizzly, gory bits of the tour include a look at where local fiends were strung up for their misdemeanors and a guide to old-fashioned home security—simply pour anything from urine to boiling oil down onto intruders below. Brilliant stuff. *Carlingford, County Louth.* ☎ *042/9373454. Admission €2 adults, €1 students. Sept–May Sat–Sun noon–5pm; June–Aug daily 10am–4:30pm.*

→ **Mellifont Abbey** More than 400 monks once lived and worked within these walls. Founded in the 12th century, this was the most spectacular Cistercian (a particular order of monks) monastery on the island. Enough is left of the abbey buildings, just a few miles north of Drogheda, to give you an idea of what Mellifont was like in its day, when it was the center of Cistercian faith in Ireland. You can see the outline of various buildings including an old octagonal wash room and a warming room, which was the only place those poor masochistic monks would have been able to warm their toes—their faith required them to live a life of suffering without heating. *Off the R168, Tullyallen, County Louth.* ☎ *041/982-6459. Admission €2 adults, €1 students. June–Sept daily 9:30am–6:30pm; Oct–May daily 10am–5pm.*

→ **Millmount Museum and Martello Tower** In the courtyard of 18th-century Millmount Fort, this strange little museum tells the history of Drogheda and the Boyne Valley. The collection includes Bronze Age finds, medieval tiles, and 18th-century banners. The mishmash display also includes random domestic items: looms, brewing equipment, gramophones, and, strangely, mousetraps. A geological exhibit contains specimens of stone from every county in Ireland, every country in Europe, and beyond. *Duleek St., off the main Dublin road (N1), Drogheda, County Louth.* ☎ *041/983-3097. Admission museum and tower €5.50 adults, €3 students; tower only €3.50 adults, €2.50 students. Mon–Sat 10am–5:30pm.*

DUBLIN

Spirit in the Stone

In ancient Irish churches you may see huge lumps of rock scattered in parts of the graveyard. These mark very old graves. In olden-day Ireland it was believed stones could capture spirits. So even though granny may have died, it was thought the only way to get her ghost out of the house was to take a stone from the house and place it on her grave, hopefully taking her spirit with it and moving it on to the next world.

Best **FREE** → **Monasterboice**

This is one of the dreamiest ancient monastic sites in Ireland. Travelers will find a cemetery, one of the tallest round towers in Ireland, ancient church ruins, and two fab high crosses. It all gives a real sense of this being a peaceful place of prayer. The original site was set up in the 4th century by a St. Patrick devotee named St. Buithe. The "Buithe" name mutated into Boyne over the years, so the whole region is named after him. The small monastic community was eventually invaded and occupied by Vikings in the 10th century. They were then defeated by the Irish high king of Tara, Donal, who is said to have single-handedly killed 300 of them. Go Donal go. Today there's little left, but the Muiredeach's High Cross is worth the trip alone. Dating from 922, the near-perfect cross is covered in biblical cartoons featuring all the top New and Old Testament starlets.

You may notice that on two separate places on the cross, Christ's wound is in different places. This apparent mistake may be attributed to a simple mistake on the part of the sculptor, or could be the work of two different artists with poor communication skills, or it could be something else entirely. Vanity was considered a major sin to the 10th-century monks who lived and worked here, and it's very likely the mistake was made intentionally to avoid making the cross perfect, in case viewers thought the monks were getting a bit full of themselves.

The round tower at Monasterboice is impressive as well. There's nothing in the tower anymore, though it was once used as a storehouse and possibly a refuge from invading bands of thugs. Built to have an entrance 14 feet off the ground, you may notice that the doorway is now much closer to the earth. What made the entrance lower? Well, for hundreds of years, people were buried around the tower, and as time went on, they began burying people on top of each other, gradually raising the ground level. Kind of gruesome. *Off the main Dublin road (N1), 9.7km (6 miles) northwest of Drogheda, near Collon, County Louth. Free admission. Daily dawn–dusk.*

FREE → **St. Peter's Church of Ireland**

An 18th-century church with some heavily carved tombs, including a rather spooky one featuring skeletons wearing shrouds. Those in the know say it's all about the Black Death. St. Peter's is infamous for an incident that occurred here during the battle of Drogheda in 1641 as Cromwell's men were rampaging through Ireland. A group of Irish men, fleeing the losing battle, sought refuge in this protestant church. When Cromwell's forces invaded the church, the men climbed into the steeple. Cromwell used the pews as timber to start a fire, and the men were burned alive. This is the second reincarnation of St. Peter's since that horrible event. *William St., Drogheda, County Louth. No phone. Free admission. Daily 10am–3pm.*

PLAYING OUTSIDE

BICYCLING   You can rent bikes by the day from **Clarke's Sports** at the back of the Navan Indoor Market (39 Trimgate St.; ☎ **046/902-1130**). Rates are around €14 per day. If you want to head out into the countryside from Drogheda, think about renting a bike from **Irish Cycle Hire** (☎ **041/685-3772;** www.irishcyclehire.com) for €70 for the week or €15 for the day. You can ride it on to one of their other depots across Ireland in Dublin, Westport, Donegal, Galway, Ennis, Dingle, Killarney, or Cork. They've got mountain bikes and touring bikes, and they're all new each season.

HORSEBACK RIDING   There are a few trail riding and trekking operations around the region—expect to pay an average of €25 per hour to trek through the countryside. To arrange a ride, contact the **Kells Equestrian Centre**, Kells (☎ **046/924-6998**).

Galway City

Artsy, funky, laid-back Galway is to Dublin what San Francisco is to New York. On a much smaller scale, of course. Sitting on one of Ireland's most dramatic stretches of coastline, tucked between the Atlantic and the blue waters of Lough Corrib, Galway's setting could not be better, and the sheer beauty of the place has attracted a burgeoning community of artists, writers, and musicians to the west coast town. They feed its lively arts scene and funky nightlife, and keep the city youthful and constantly changing. They also ensure that the bars stay open late at night.

In fact, the little city (pop. 70,000) has some of the best bars and cafes in Ireland, as well as tons of live music, jam-packed clubs, internationally renowned theaters, and a summer-long schedule of kick-ass events including the Galway Arts Festival—one of the most energetic and down-to-earth arts fests in Europe.

Still, even with all that, the pubs are the heart of this city, and you'll find them full of former travelers who came here for a weekend, and loved the vibe so much they never left.

The Best of Galway City

○ **A Gig at the Roísín Dubh:** The excellent Roísín Dubh is *the* place to go to hear the best music on the Irish and international scene. This is one of the country's top venues—not to be missed. See p. 154.

○ **A Show Put on by the Druids:** Don't get too excited. You're not going to get a weird pagan ritual performed for you. But you will get the world-renowned Druid Theatre group, home to some of Ireland's top actors. See p. 155.

○ **A Lazy Afternoon in Eyre Square:** The most happening outdoor gathering place is always Eyre Square. On a sunny

Galway City

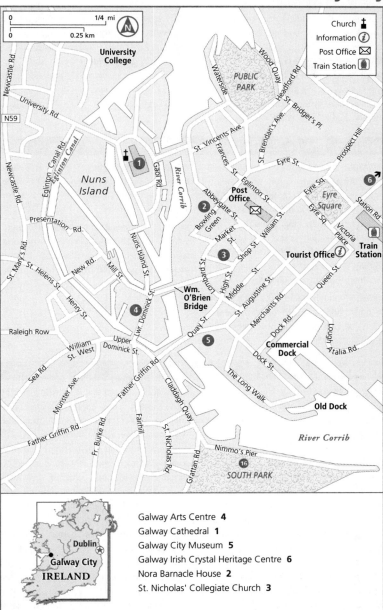

Map legend:
- Church ✝
- Information (i)
- Post Office ✉
- Train Station 🏠

Galway Arts Centre **4**
Galway Cathedral **1**
Galway City Museum **5**
Galway Irish Crystal Heritage Centre **6**
Nora Barnacle House **2**
St. Nicholas' Collegiate Church **3**

IRELAND
Dublin
Galway City

afternoon, locals gather here in droves to throw around a kite, kick around a ball, play guitar, flirt, and gab. You can almost always count on a good vibe and a spontaneous guitar or drum session. See p. 158.

○ **A Day in Galway during the Arts Festival:** To be in Galway in July for the massive Galway Arts Festival is unforgettable. Famous for its street carnival, music, theater, and great atmosphere. Possibly the best all 'round summer festival in Europe. See p. 157.

○ **An Adrenaline Adventure with Delphi Adventure Holidays:** Hook up with Delphi Adventure Holidays, which offers plenty to set your hair on end, from sailing to sea kayaking to water-skiing, by way of abseiling, archery, and pony trekking. See p. 159.

Getting There & Getting into Town

BY PLANE **Aer Aran** flies from Dublin into Galway Airport (Carnmore, about 16km/ 10 miles east of the city; ☎ 091/755569; www.galwayairport.com) five times daily, two times a day to London, and once a day to Birmingham and Edinburgh. A taxi to the city center costs about €16; the occasional bus, if it coincides with your arrival, costs €4 and drops you off at Galway Rail Station.

BY TRAIN **Irish Rail** trains from Dublin and other points arrive daily at Ceannt Station (☎ 091/561444; www.irishrail.ie), off Eyre Square, Galway.

BY BUS **Buses** from all parts of Ireland arrive daily at **Bus Éireann Travel Centre,** Ceannt Station, Galway (☎ 091/562000; www.buseireann.ie).

BY CAR As the gateway to west Ireland, Galway is the terminus for many national roads. They lead in from all parts of Ireland, including N84 and N17 from the north points, N63 and N6 from the east, and N67 and N18 from the south.

Orientation

Galway is small, but all the streets are winding ancient paths and you'll get disoriented in no time, so get yourself a good street map from the tourist office as soon as you can. The hub of the city is the big bustling park in **Eyre Square** (pronounced *Air* Square), officially called the John F. Kennedy Park in commemoration of his visit here in June 1963, a few months before his assassination. A bust of JFK shares space in the park with hundreds of people relaxing, flying kites, kicking balls around, busking—just generally kicking back.

Shop Street at the center of town is, as the name implies, loaded with shops. It's a good place to look for just about anything. It's also dominated by **Lynch's Castle,** which dates to 1490 and is watched over by excellently hideous gargoyles. One block away on Market Street the **Lynch Memorial Window** above a built-up Gothic doorway commemorates the tragic story of a 16th-century Galway mayor, who condemned his son to death for the murder of a wealthy Spanish man. After finding no one to carry out the deed, he executed his own son.

Heading down to the city docks, you can still see the area where Spanish merchants once unloaded cargo from their galleons. The **Spanish Arch** down there is another local gathering place (it dates to 1594), and just by it the **Spanish Parade** is a small open square that is one of the city's most popular hangouts.

Getting Around

BY BUS   Galway has excellent local bus service. Buses run from the **Bus Éireann Travel Centre** (☎ **091/562000**) or Eyre Square to various suburbs, including Salthill and the Galway Bay coastline. The flat fare is €1.20.

BY TAXI   There are taxi ranks at Eyre Square and all the major hotels in the city. If you need to call a cab, try **Abbey Cabs** (☎ **091/569369**), **Cara Cabs** (☎ **091/563939**), or **Galway Taxis** (☎ **091/561112**).

BY CAR   If you must bring your car into the center of town, park it and then walk. There is free parking in front of Galway Cathedral, but most street parking is not free. Drivers will need parking "disks" (which can be purchased from the tourism office) in order to park on the street. Expect to pay €.60 per hour. Multistory parking garages average €1.50 per hour or €11 per day.

To rent a car, contact one of the following firms: **Avis Rent-A-Car**, Higgins Garage, Headford Road (☎ **091/568886**; www.avis. ie); **Budget Rent-A-Car**, Galway Airport (☎ **091/556376**; www.budget.ie); or **Murrays Rent-A-Car**, Headford Road (☎ **091/562222**; www.europcar.ie).

BY BICYCLE   Cycling is a bit tough in the city itself because of the rough stone roads; however, all around the edges conditions are outstanding. Most hostels, including Kinlay House and Salmon Weir Hostel, rent bicycles. If you need to rent a bike, check out the Mountain **Trail Bike Shop** (St. Augustine St.; ☎ **091/569888**), **Celtic Cycles** (Queen St., Victoria Place; ☎ **091/566606**), or **Europa Cycles** (☎ **091/563355**) across from the Galway Cathedral. Rates start at around €10 for 24 hours.

Basics

TOURIST OFFICE   When you first arrive in Galway, drop by the **Ireland West Tourism office (Aras Fáilte)**, Foster Street (☎ **091/537700**; www.westireland.travel.ie), and pick up a map and brochures about what's on in town during your stay. Hours are May, June, and September daily 9am to 5:45pm; July and August daily 9am to 7:45pm; October to April Monday to Friday 9am to 5:45pm, Saturday 9am to 12:45pm.

YOUTH INFORMATION SERVICE OFFICES You can get help and check out the bulletin boards at **Galway Youth Information Centre** (Ozanam House, St. Augustine St., ☎ **091/562434**), which also has a "Eurodesk Information point" with info on traveling and working in Europe, as well as Internet access and the like. Open Monday through Friday 9am to 4:45pm.

RECOMMENDED WEBSITE   www.galway. net.

Nuts & Bolts

Cellphone Providers/Service Centers   Carphone Warehouse represents most major cellphone rental companies and can get you a good deal on phones and sim cards. There's one handily in Eyre Square (☎ **0818/270370**).

Crisis Centers   The Galway Rape Crisis Centre at 7 Claddagh Quay (☎ **091/589495**). For information, gay and lesbian travelers might contact the Galway Gay Help Line (☎ **091/566134**), Tuesday and Thursday 8 to 10pm; or Galway Lesbian Line (☎ **091/566134**), Wednesday 8 to 10pm.

Currency Most of the banks in the center of town have bureaus de change and ATMs. Bank of Ireland has two branches on Eyre Square, while Allied Irish Bank has branches in Lynch's Castle and on Shop Street. There's an American Express on the north side of Eyre Square (☎ 091/562316).

Drugstore If you need a drugstore, try Flanagan's Pharmacy, 32 Shop St. (☎ 091/562924), Matt O'Flaherty Chemist, 16 William St. (☎ 091/561442 or after hours 091/525426), or Whelan's Chemist, Williamsgate Street (☎ 091/562291).

Emergencies In an emergency, call ☎ 999. You can also go to Galway University College Hospital (Newcastle Rd.; ☎ 091/580-580), or Merlin Park Regional Hospital (Merlin Park; ☎ 091/757-631).

Internet Access Despite the inevitable silly name, Net@ccess Cyber Café (The Olde Malte Arcade, High St.; ☎ 091/569-772; 10am–10pm Mon–Fri, 10am–7pm Sat, noon–6pm Sun; www.netaccess.ie; €4 per hour, €3.50 students) is a central spot to log on. They also sell international calling cards with good rates. There's free Internet access at the Galway Public Library (Cathedral Sq.; ☎ 91/562471), but you have to book a day in advance, and you only get the computer for an hour. Hotlines, 4 High St. (☎ 091/562838), offers Net access and low-cost international phone calls and is open 7 days a week.

Laundromats Wash and fold service costs about €7 per load at Laundrette (4 Sea Rd; ☎ 091/584524) and Bubbles Laundrette (19 Mary St; ☎ 091/563434).

Luggage Storage The best (and possibly only) option for luggage storage is at the train station.

Post Offices The Post Office, Eglinton Street (☎ 091/562051), is open Monday to Saturday 9am to 5:30pm.

Safety Galway has a very low crime rate, and no particular hotspots. Follow the usual safety advice, and don't leave your purse lying around unwatched during the Galway Arts Festival, when most people in town are from out of town.

Telephone Tips Galway dialing code is 091; information can be gained by dialing ☎ 1190; while the international operator is on 114. International and local phone cards can be purchased in almost any shop. The green-and-pink "Spirit" cards have the best international rates. There are pay phones in the main pedestrian mall and on the south side of Eyre Square. Eircom calling cards are sold in convenience stores and supermarkets.

Sleeping

Given its funky atmosphere and bohemian spirit, it's unsurprising that Galway has a wide range of good digs, from super-cheap to absolutely opulent. But don't be too complacent—you're not the only one who wants to hang out in this cool city, so you definitely need to book ahead, especially during the high season, and even in the off season for weekends and during festivals—otherwise, you might end up in some dingy dive.

Most hostels are clustered near Eyre Square in the city center, as are most expensive hotels. Most cheaper guesthouses are to be found in the Salthill neighborhood, a couple of miles from the city center, down by the seafront.

The Talk of the Town

5 Ways to Start a Conversation with a Local

1. "How about those horse races?" The Galway Races is one of the biggest events of the year for locals. Find out more about it.

2. "What's your favorite band?" This town's nuts about music. Bands play constantly. Ask around for the best options, and who knows where the conversation might lead.

3. "What's up with this town's obsession with JFK and Ché Guevara?" Parks are named after the former and murals abound of the latter— what's that about?

4. "Anyone for surfing?" The coast around Galway is great for surfing, and young locals are really into it.

5. "Who's your favorite Irish artist?" With one of the biggest annual arts festivals in Europe, Galway knows its way around a contemporary art museum. Brush up before you come.

If you find yourself bedless on a packed weekend, give your feet a rest and try the reservations center upstairs at the tourist office. For a few euros they'll call around until they find you something.

Hostels

For the most part, the hostels in Galway are clean and well run. The ones listed here all have laundry services, comfy TV lounges, and well-equipped kitchens.

→ **Barnacles Quay Street House** This is an attractive and clean hostel right on the main pub drag. Most rooms are bright, spacious (by hostel standards), and airy with polished wood floors, and the added ambience of busker music drifting up from the street. There are international payphones, free toast and tea in the morning, and no curfew or lockout. *10 Quay St.* ☎ *091/568-644. www. barnacles.ie. €11–€13 per person dorm, €13–€16 per person twin, double. Bike storage, bureau de change, Internet access, kitchen, laundry service.*

→ **Corrib Villa** This chilled-out hostel epitomizes the laid-back, boho lifestyle for which Galway is known. A Georgian town house with neat, simple rooms, cool artwork,

a cozy atmosphere, and a friendly staff, Corrib Villa is located on the river on the grounds of Galway University a couple of miles from the city center. It has a regular crowd of devoted regulars who make the place warm and homey. Open 24 hours. *4 Waterside.* ☎ *091/ 562892. €10–€14 per person dorm. No credit cards. Amenities: Kitchen; Internet access.*

→ **Great Western House** Directly opposite the train station, this is a welcoming place with neat, clean rooms and access for disabled travelers. There's no curfew, and the desk is staffed 24 hours. The crowd can be a little older here, and it's not the hottest place in town as it once was, but it's still a good, handy option. *Frenchville Lane, Eyre Sq.* ☎ *091/561139. €8–€11.50 dorm, €29–€40 per person double, single. Amenities: Kitchen; dining room; TV lounge; laundry service; pool room.*

→ **Salmon Weir Hostel** One of the city's quirkier hostels, Salmon Weir has a cheery, party-loving atmosphere. This place has such a good vibe, one-time guests long since settled into Galway regularly come by just to hang out. It's a clean and cozy converted house with free-flowing tea and coffee, and mucho mayhem. Be warned, though, the dorm rooms here are so tiny, not only is there no room to swing a cat, you'd do damage if you tried to swing a *kitten*. The whole place, including the slacker-paradise TV room with VCR/DVD, is totally nonsmoking. Not for introverts or claustrophobics. *3 St. Vincent's Ave., Woodquay.* ☎ *091/561133. www.salmon weirhostel.com. €10–€17 per person dorm; €18–€20 per person double, twin. No credit cards. Amenities: Kitchen; Internet access; laundry service.*

📺 Best → **Sleepzone** This is the latest and greatest hostel in Galway. A few minutes walk from the train and bus terminals, Sleepzone is one of the new "superhostels," meaning it's big, it's attractive, and it has plenty of extras. Private rooms are as good as any you're likely to find in a B&B, and the staff is unfailingly friendly; there's no curfew or lockout. Recent visitors have raved about the place. *Bothar Na mBan, Woodquay.* ☎ *091/566999. www.sleepzone.ie. €13–€20 dorm; €18–€50 per person triple, double, single. Amenities: Free Wi-Fi; electronic lockers; kitchen; laundry; safe-deposit boxes.*

Cheap

→ **Clare Villa** This spacious, modern house steps from the beach is very popular in summer, and that's as it should be. Its six pleasant rooms all have firm, comfortable beds, and the owners are as helpful as they can be. The biggest attraction, though, is waking up so close to the seafront, and taking in that fresh salt air every morning. *38 Threadneedle Rd., Galway, County Galway.* ☎ *091/ 522520. clarevilla@yahoo.com. €60 double. Rates include full breakfast. No credit cards. Amenities: Sitting room. In room: TV, hair dryer.*

→ **Devondell** You'd be hard-pressed to find a better B&B in Galway than Berna Kelly's popular house in the Lower Salthill residential area, about 2km (just over a mile) from Galway's city center. It's a modern house, and the four guest rooms are spacious and

done up with period furnishings and crisp Irish linens. Breakfasts are big enough to get you through the day, with cereals and fresh fruit, yogurt and cheese, hash browns and kippers, and eggs and French toast. Devondell is walking distance from the seafront. *47 Devon Park, Lower Salthill, County Galway.* ☎ *091/528306. www.devondell.com. €80 double. Rates include full breakfast. Free parking. Closed Nov–Feb. Amenities: Sitting room. In room: TV.*

→ **Knockrea Guest House** On a commercial street in Salthill, just outside Galway City center and 5 minutes from the waters of Galway Bay, this attractive guesthouse is friendly and beautifully maintained. The six large guest rooms are furnished in simple pine furniture with polished pine floors and light-colored walls. Two family rooms offer more space and lots of beds for those traveling with groups of friends. *55 Lower Salthill, Galway, County Galway.* ☎ *091/520145. www. knockrea.com. €60–€70 double with shared bathroom; €90 double with private bathroom. Rates include full breakfast. Free parking. Amenities: Nonsmoking rooms; 3 sitting rooms; use of kitchen. In room: TV.*

Doable

→ **Brennans Yard Hotel** One of the cleverest restorations in Galway's historic area, right next to the Spanish Arch, this four-story stone building was formerly a warehouse. It has compact, skylit public areas enhanced by modern Irish art. The 45 guest rooms overlook the city's Spanish Arch area and are decorated in a hip, contemporary style, with Irish pine furnishings, designer fabrics, and locally made pottery. *Lower Merchant's Rd., Galway, County Galway.* ☎ *800/44-UTELL in the U.S., or 091/ 568166. www.brennansyardhotel.com. €95– €137 double. Rates include full breakfast. Free parking at nearby car park. Amenities: Restaurant (modern Continental); bar. In room: Phone, TV, tea/coffeemaker, hair dryer.*

➜ **Cregg Castle** This is a grand place—a huge, ivy-covered, turreted castle built in the 1600s, set amid sprawling farmland. Owners Ann-Marie and Pat Broderick are the unstuffiest most hands-on hosts you're likely to come across. Both musicians, they often play traditional music in the drawing room. The nine bedrooms vary in size and design, but all are wonderfully decorated (room 12 feels like a cozy cave) and immensely comfortable. The only problem is it's 9 miles outside the city, and you need a car to get here. *9 miles north of Galway City on N84 at Cloonboo Cross, then signposted from Regan's Bar. Corrandulla, County Galway.* ☎ *091/791434. www. creggcastle.com. €100–€120 double. Rates include full breakfast. Amenities: Drawing room. In room: Hair dryer.*

➜ **Eyre Square Hotel** This place is a great find: It's not as expensive as some of the other hotels in this section and has a convenient address (right on Eyre Square), spacious rooms, helpful staff, and a good Irish breakfast each morning. The decor in the 60 bedrooms is a little boring, with lots of dark wood and unimaginative patterned bedcovers, but the place is kept in good condition with frequent refurbishments, and feels well tended. This hotel has the most central location of the recommended less-expensive hotels. *Forster St., Galway, County Galway.* ☎ *091/569-6333. www.eyresquarehotel.com. €80–€130 double. Rates include full breakfast. Amenities: Restaurant (Irish); bar; nightclub. In room: TV, tea/coffeemaker.*

➜ **Skeffington Arms Hotel** Another central hotel overlooking Eyre Square, the Skeffington is useful to know about. While its rooms may be mostly functional, it has a good restaurant, and an attractive pub, so it's a particularly handy place for those who've been doing a lot of traveling and don't want to wander around looking for places to eat and drink at the end of the day. The 23 guest rooms are large and pleasant enough, and a recent refurbishment has left them all with neutral decor—creamy walls and carpet and pale blue bedcovers. The staff is friendly, and the atmosphere in the pub is jovial. *Eyre Sq., Galway, County Galway.* ☎ *091/563173. www.skeffington.ie. €118–€130 double. Rates include full breakfast. Free parking. Amenities: Restaurant (Irish); bar; nightclub. In room: TV, tea/coffeemaker.*

Splurge

➜ **Galway Great Southern Hotel** Dating from 1845 and built as a resting place for train travelers, this five-story hotel is the grande dame of Galway. In the heart of the city, overlooking Eyre Square, its location couldn't be more central—next to the bus and rail station and within walking distance of all the major sights. The spacious public areas have high ceilings, elaborate plasterwork, crystal chandeliers, and original Connemara marble fireplaces. The 99 guest rooms are elegant in beige and cream, with modern furniture and designer fabrics. The public areas are a favorite meeting place for Galwegians, and the hotel is always buzzing. *15 Eyre Sq., Galway, County Galway.* ☎ *800/44-UTELL in the U.S. or 091/564041. www.gshotels.com. €230–€300 double. Rates include service charge and full Irish breakfast. Street parking only. Amenities: 2 restaurants (seafood, Continental); bar; sauna/steam room; concierge; room service; babysitting; laundry service. In room: TV, tea/coffeemaker, hair dryer, garment press, radio.*

Eating

Galway is the west coast's foodie capital, so it's jammed with good restaurants, bakeries, and cafes, providing a wide variety of food at varied prices. Its proximity to the sea means seafood is very big here—and it's hard to go wrong when you can get a huge order of fish

James Joyce Makes Me Sleepy

When you go to Ireland, everybody says the same things: "Read up on Joyce, Yeats, and old George Bernard Shaw. Pack in a little Jonathan Swift while you're at it." Let's be honest: Joyce is almost impenetrable (what *was* he talking about?), and everybody else . . . well, they're dead. You might ask yourself, doesn't anybody in this country write anymore? Where's a young person supposed to turn when they want to read something written by somebody . . . alive?

To us, that's where.

Ireland is loaded with good, living writers, and they all merit your attention just as much as its classical writers do (and you should, actually, read some Swift and Brendan Behan, if you don't mind us saying so—you'll love them).

A good place to start if you're milling about aimlessly in the Irish literary waters is with Roddy Doyle. His novels are clever, quick, and often hilarious. If you haven't discovered *The Commitments, The Van,* and *The Snapper* yet, you really should.

If you've been there and read that, move on to Colm Tóibín. One of Ireland's leading journalists and best young writers, he's written two books in recent years that were received with acclaim by reviewers around the globe. *The Blackwater Lightship,* which tells the fictional history of a young Irishman's family as he dies of AIDS, was short-listed for Britain's Booker prize, and is beautifully written in a short, spare, honest style. His other book is a kind of shortcut to Irish writing, the *Penguin Book of Irish Fiction,* a massive 1,000-page anthology of Irish lit. Read some of it, and you'll make just about everyone happy.

Another writer to look out for as you make your way through the shelves of the Winding Stair bookshop in Dublin is Dermot Bolger, a Dublin native who has written numerous books, plays, and film scripts. His latest novel, *The Family on Paradise Pier,* took more than 4 years to write, and has been very well received.

Colum McCann is another Irish writer worth tracking down, as his award-winning novels have wowed the critics. Frank McCourt, who wrote *Angela's Ashes,* was clearly blown away. He wrote, "The language you find in Colum McCann's novel, *This Side of Brightness,* makes you claw at yourself with pleasure." Gosh, could it be *that* good?

Other writers making (slightly less gushing) headlines include playwright Marina Carr, who wrote *Portia Coughlan* and *By the Bog of Cats,* and novelist Anne Enright whose quirky novels *What Are You Like?* and *The Pleasure of Eliza Lynch* are both enjoyable reads.

Finally, Sean O'Reilly has been creating a real stir with his angry, clever Dublin thriller *The Swing of Things.* Just about everybody believes he's the next big thing.

So, warm up that Itty Bitty Booklight and get reading.

and chips for under €6. The best seafood is to be found at places down by the waterfront, while the cheapest food is found in cafes and bakeries scattered around Eyre Square and near the hostels.

Cheap

→ **Busker Brown's** CAFE/BAR   A modern cafe in a medieval building, Busker Brown's is a favorite of locals and travelers for its funky decor that mixes ancient stonework with modern tables and art, as well as for its big breakfasts and homemade, inexpensive lunches and dinners. It offers everything from hamburgers and sandwiches to fresh stews and pasta. It also stays open late—one of few Galway eateries that do. *Upper Cross St., Galway, County Galway.* ☎ *091/563377. Main courses €5–€12. Mon–Sat 10:30am–11:30pm; Sun 12:30–11:30pm.*

➔ **The Cobblestone** VEGETARIAN Tucked away on a winding, medieval lane, this casual eatery is a bright light on Galway's cuisine scene. Proprietor Kate Wright serves up excellent fresh salads, soups, quiches, and pastas. There are plenty of vegetarian dishes (try the "beanie shepherd pie") and fresh croissants, breads, muffins, cakes, and cookies. Head here when you're in the mood for a light meal or snack. *Kirwan's Lane, Galway, County Galway.* ☎ *091/567227. Main courses €6–€15. Daily 9am–7pm.*

➔ **Couch Potatas** CAFE With homemade soups and big baked potatoes stuffed with a ton of different fillings, this place is a good, warming option on a rainy day. Try the Hawaii 5-0, with ham, onion, pineapple, peppers, and melted cheddar cheese. Every 'tater comes with a generous side salad, as well. It's a great spot for lunch, although it does get quite crowded at midday. *Upper Abbeygate St.* ☎ *091/561664. Noon–10pm Mon–Sat; 1–10pm Sun. All items under €7. No credit cards.*

➔ **Da Tang Noodle House** NOODLES This tiny place on a quiet street off Shop Street, has just a few tables inside, but it's got that great hole-in-the-wall atmosphere. The menu here is all about cheap, tasty noodles. Everything is simple but good, and there are plenty of veggie options. *2 Middle St.* ☎ *091/561443. Mains €7–€12. Mon–Thurs noon–3pm, 5:30–10pm; Fri–Sat till 10:30pm; Sun 5:30–10pm.*

➔ **G.B.C. (Galway Bakery Company)** BAKERY/BISTRO This place is two eateries

in one. The ground-level coffee shop is cheap and cheerful, with steaming fresh coffee and melt-in-your-mouth pastries. Upstairs is a bistro offering quiches, omelets, salads, and plates of stir-fried veg. The coffee shop gets packed at peak breakfast and lunch times. *7 Williamsgate St.* ☎ *091/563087. www.gbc-galway.com. Coffee-shop items under €7; dinner main courses €10–€20. Coffee shop daily 8am–10pm; restaurant daily noon–10pm.*

➔ **Goya's** TEAROOM/BAKED GOODS This small, casual place has a great bakery, so it's always crowded with locals lining up for the fresh pastries and desserts. Stop in for tea and a scone, or buy a loaf of the rich soda bread for lunch. *Kirwan's Lane, Galway, County Galway.* ☎ *091/567010. All items under €8. No credit cards. Mon–Sat 10am–6pm.*

➔ **Home Plate Organics** Possibly the most popular place for travelers to have lunch in Galway. Huge, fresh, tasty helpings of organic pasta, burgers, or sandwiches in a homey little place across from the post office with friendly staff and good service. There are lots of veggie options here as well. *13 Mary St.* ☎ *091/561475. €3.50–€7 lunch; €5.50–€12 dinner. No credit cards. Daily 10:30am–2:30pm.*

➔ **McSwiggans** A big, friendly pub with good, Irish lunches at reasonable prices, so just about everybody comes here for lunch at one point or another. *3 Eyre St., Woodquay.* ☎ *091/568917. €5–€10. Daily 10:30am–11pm.*

➔ **Scotty's Sunset Grill** Run by a jocular Ohioan expat, Scotty's is a little island of Americana amid all the Irish stews and bangers and mash. Here hotdogs sell for €2.50, and quarter-pound burgers for €4.50, fries are €1.99, and the Cokes are ice cold. The deli sandwiches are similarly delicious. It's moved around town a bit over the years, but Scotty's has been a favorite of local students and savvy international travelers for more than a decade. *Glasán Village, Ballybane*

GALWAY CITY

Rd., opposite GMIT. ☎ 091/768344. www.scottys sunsetgrill.com. €2–€8. Daily 10am–10pm.

Doable

→ **Conlon** SEAFOOD   If you love seafood, head here to find Galway's seafood specialists. The house specialties are wild salmon and oysters, so that's not a bad place to start. Entrees include grilled wild salmon, steamed Galway Bay mussels, and fishermen's platters with a bit of everything—smoked salmon, mussels, prawns, smoked mackerel, oysters, and crab claws. Eglinton Court. ☎ 091/ 562268. Seafood bar items €4–€8; main courses €7–€25. Mon–Sat 11am–midnight; Sun 5pm–midnight.

→ **McDonagh's** FISH AND CHIPS/SEAFOOD For seafood straight off the boats, served up in an authentic maritime atmosphere, this is Galway's best choice. The place is divided into three parts: a cheap "chippy" for fish and chips, a smart restaurant in the back, and a fish market where you can buy raw seafood. The McDonaghs buy direct from local fishermen every day, and it shows; crowds line up every night to get in. In the back restaurant, you can crack your own prawns' tails and crab claws in the shell, or tackle a whole lobster. 22 Quay St. ☎ 091/565001. Reservations not accepted June–Aug. Main courses €8–€34. Daily noon–10pm.

→ **The River God Cafe** IRISH/CONTINENTAL   The portions are huge and the prices are small at this chill cafe. The River God is all about Irish comfort food. The casserole of cod and potatoes Connemara style will put color back in your cheeks, while the large slab of wild-mushroom tart with paprika potatoes will rejuvenate vegetarians. Quay St. (at Cross St.). ☎ 091/565811. Reservations not accepted. Fixed-price 3-course dinner €16; dinner main courses €10–€18. Daily 5– 10:30pm.

Splurge

→ **Nimmo's** WINE BAR/CONTINENTAL Galway's trendy young things all head here. It might look like just another historic building, but pass the stone facade, climb a winding stairway, and you'll find yourself in the most romantic dining room in Galway, particularly on a starry night when you can see the moon through the skylights. Start with the zesty fish soup or the smoked-salmon salad, then move on to the delicious Parmesan chicken or beef bourguignon. Make a reservation in advance to be sure of getting a table. Long Walk, Spanish Arch. ☎ 091/ 561114. Reservations recommended. Main courses €12–€24. Tues–Sun 12:30–3pm and 7–10pm.

Partying

In Galway, there's no such thing as a dead night out, and there's never a night without music. Just about every pub in town hosts nightly gigs, usually trad sessions or cover bands. Most young travelers in Galway gravitate toward the tourist-oriented "superpubs" of Shop and Quay streets. Sardine-packed with drunken hordes of university students in winter months and tipsy tourists in summer, they're definitely good, in that beer-blast kind of way. For a more mellow, local feel, try the cluster of bars around Dominick Street, on the west side of the River Corrib.

Galway's drink prices are country-cheap compared with Dublin. The general price for a pint in a pub hovers around €3, or €2.75 for a shot. Drink prices at clubs are a bit higher across the board. Bring cash—most bars and pubs don't take cards.

Pub hours are the same here as in the rest of Ireland (10:30am–11pm Mon–Sat or till 11:30pm in summer, and 12:30–2pm/4–11pm

Sun year-round), but it's standard publican practice to shut the front doors at the pre-scribed closing time, then let the party roll on inside for another hour or so. You won't get in off the street anywhere after legal closing, so if you're still doing the crawl at 11pm, give it up quick and settle into your favorite pub.

Bars & Pubs

Despite its ground-zero location in Galway's teeming tourist hub, scrappy little **Tigh Neachtain** (17 Cross St.; ☎ 091/568820) attracts a nice mix of locals and scruffy beatnik travelers. Allen Ginsberg was known to enjoy a pint (and maybe an occasional joint) here, when in town, and that should give you an idea of what kind of fashions (casual) and attitudes (laid-back) to expect. On warm afternoons, drinkers take to the tables outside, to drink in the sun.

The **Hole in the Wall** (9 Eyre St.; ☎ 091/586146), right on Eyre Square, is the kind of chilled out, friendly pub where you wish you could be a regular: low-beamed ceiling, a jukebox with the standard rock classics, a sunny beer garden out to the side, and just enough off the beaten track so you can always find a seat. The Hole ain't fashion-able, but it fits. *One warning:* The owner is big into horses, so madness reigns during the July races.

Just to confuse you, the **Front Door** (Cross St.; no phone) announces itself as "Tomás ó Riada: Draper, Grocer, Matchmaker" over its other entrance on High Street (which turns into Shop St.). The best bar in town for playing hide-and-seek with its mazelike lay-out, it's also the mellowest of the superpubs, catering to an unpretentious just-post-university crowd.

The other "superpubs" include **The Quays** (Quay St.; ☎ 091/568347), which looks like a church at sea, and frequently hosts tradi-tional Irish music; the **King's Head,** which also often has bands playing; **The Skeff**

(Eyre Sq.; ☎ **091/563173**) with six different bars on two floors; and **Busker Brownes** (Cross St.; ☎ **091/563377**) with its medieval "Hall of Tribes." These are the pubs with the highest pickup potential.

On the alternative side of town, **Le Graal** (38 Lower Dominick St.; ☎ **091/567614**) is popular with Galway's international and gay crowds, who come to drink wine and lounge about on the red felt couches while cande-labras flicker against the rough stone walls. Dance to sounds of Latin, jazz, salsa, and world music, or grab a bite—the relaxed staff also serve up food until last call. Sometimes there's a cover of €2 to €3.

In the same neighborhood, the **Blue Note** (William St. West; ☎ **091/568347**) is the committed clubber's pre-club hangout. Here, as local DJs spin the sounds, you'll find the town's greatest density of hair gel. Go for the great BBQ deal on Tuesday nights in the sum-mer: Buy a Heineken, get a free burger, repeat.

Best **Padraigs Bar** (The Docks; ☎ **091/563696**) right on the docks, maybe a little sketchy, and always full of hearty, salt-of-the-earth types exuding 80-proof per-fume from every pore. Best in the wee hours on a weekend, when all walks of life can be seen crawling in for "just the one more" under the smoke-stained collection of clas-sic film posters. There's a pool table in the back and a spinning ceiling fan to help patrons further lose their bearings.

Live Music

For the most part, trad rules the night in Galway. The remaining slots on local dance cards tend to be filled with your standard rock cover bands. It's sort of like college par-ties all over again—which makes sense, given the overwhelming size of the university crowd in Galway. No matter what's play-ing, everyone's out for a good time. One exception to the cover-band rule is **Roísín Dubh** (see below), a live joint with enough character (and incoming talent) to stand out in any city. **Cuba** (see "Clubs," below) spices up the week with jazz on Saturdays and occasional imported Latin-flavored bands.

You can hear your basic trad Irish music almost anywhere in town, but the place to go for the real stuff is 🎬 Best **The Crane** (2 Sea Rd.; ☎ **091/567419**). It's what the Irish would call an "old man's pub" a little out on the west side of town, so the dress code is a lot of old tweed and a scruffy beard. A session could occur at any time, but a good bet is the one casually "scheduled" nightly at 9:30pm. The Sunday afternoon session here can be a religious experience.

The wood-lined 🎬 Best **Roísín Dubh** (Dominick St.; ☎ **091/586540**; www.roisin dubh.net; free–€25; www.roisindubh.net)— that's "rawsheen dove" to you—happens to be one of the best places in Ireland for all that other music, hosting local and international names in rock, folk, indie, blues—and trad—on the little stage in back. Definitely a musicians' hangout, the pub fills with a good, healthy bohemian blend every night. Check out the website to see listings for what's coming up.

The King's Head (High St.; ☎ **091/566630**) is elbow-to-elbow most nights with the young and drunk, all staggering along to the daily parade of (actually, pretty good) cover bands. A summer meat market is provided courtesy of weekly tour bus shipments of eager young backpackers. The chilled out Dixieland jazz session summer Sunday afternoons at 12:30pm is a local institution.

Catch an excellent (and very well attended) set-dancing session at **Monroe's** (Upper Dominick St.; ☎ **091/583397**) every Tuesday night. You can hear trad, trad, and more trad every night of the week, beginning at 9:30pm Irish time, which is to say "sometime after dark." Although relatively spacious for a pub (and charming, too, with murals covering the walls), there's almost never any room to sit down when the music starts, so get here early, around 8 to 9pm, for a seat. Monroe's

also serves good pub grub at breakfast and lunch times, and you can get above-average pizzas beginning at 4pm at the little hole-in-the-wall pizzeria next door. Aside from a few well-informed hostellers, the crowd here's exclusively local.

Clubs

Like the town itself, Galway's clubs are a no-stress affair. Some fashion victims (ladies, you know who you are) don the full get-up, but the guy in Birks just behind them gets in, too. With a little straightening, your grungy travel gear might even pass muster. Sounds too good to be true, but bouncers are (relatively) mellow, and the mainly undergrad clubbers are out to drink, dance, drink some more, then hook up—not pose or critique. The size of these places may surprise you—there's no shortage of floor space here. For a night-by-night breakdown, pick up the ever-present *Galway List*. Covers run from €5 mid-week to €8 weekends. Clubs are open from 11pm till 2am, but the crowds, and the lines, arrive as soon as the pubs clear out at midnight. Make an early dash out of the pub on weekends, or take the chance of waiting outside in a line half the night.

🎬 Best **GPO** (Eglinton St.; ☎ **091/563073**) does its best to keep the western flame of trendiness alive, trying just a little harder than the rest to be hip. Wear black to match the inky dark interior and the rest of the patrons. The "Drum Bar" is downstairs, a dance space the size of a four-car garage is upstairs. Home of local heroes, the Disconauts duo, spinning soul and funk-infused house to loving crowds, GPO also regularly hosts hip-hop and drum 'n' bass nights. Daytime bar staff often have free passes hidden behind the jungle-gym piping—just ask sweetly.

Big, blue, and three stories high, **Cuba** (Eyre Sq.; ☎ **091/565991**) has a lounge bar on one, DJs on two, and live bands on three. Indie Mondays; Latin jazz, funk, and soul Saturdays; and a healthy mix of chart, disco, and dance for the rest of the week. This place is hot with the cool crowd, and the blue lighting and Latin rhythms get the co-eds *en fuego*. Public displays of lust abound. Passes behind the bar during daytime hours; ask the bartender to give you a few.

The **Alley** (Ball Alley Lane, off Williamsgate St.; ☎ 091/563173) is youth-quake central in a converted warehouse. At the door they claim to be over-21-only, but the dance floor and three bars are packed with the youngest club crowd in town—seems to be a don't-ask-don't-tell policy. Once in, you don't have to be off your face, but it would definitely help you blend . . . Mostly college pop tunes (the cheesier the better—the theme from *Friends* gets everybody dancing—Yikes!) early on, with the dance stuff coming on later in the night.

Central Park (36 Upper Abbeygate St.; ☎ 091/565974; www.centralparkclub.com) is one of the city's most obvious meat markets—lots of makeup, lots of very short skirts, *hundreds* of bellybuttons . . . you get the picture. The music is cool, and the look of the place is space-age. Remember, pretty is as pretty does.

Gay Scene

Galway's no gay mecca, but it does have a small (Okay, *tiny*) scene. If what you're looking for is a comfortable place to meet locals and to just be yourself, check out **Le Graal** (see "Bars & Pubs," above). It balances friendly with cool in a good way.

Keepers of the faith often congregate in other hip spots, such as **Café du Journal** (The Halls, Quay St.; ☎ 091/568426), a chilled out coffee bar filled with chaotic piles of books and daily papers stacked on wooden church pews. It's a bit literary for some—big with grad students and journalists—but pretty much everybody (straight and gay) hangs out here at some point or another. **Apostasy** (56 Little Dominick St.; ☎ 091/561478) is another funky little coffee shop that attracts a delightfully mixed up crowd. You might also check out **Nimmo's Long Walk Wine Bar** (Spanish Arch; ☎ 091/561114); this is a romantic little bistro to take your Irish love when you find him/her.

The **Galway Gay Help Line** (☎ 091/566134) and **Galway Lesbian Line** (☎ 091/564611) are good resources, or check out the monthly freesheet, GCN (Gay Community News) and look for Galway listings in the back.

If you happen to be here on a weekend, Friday and Saturday nights Club Mix in The Attic at **Liquid** (Salthill; ☎ 088/2691412; doors open 10:30pm; €5 cover) draws every lonely farm boy and maybe an incognito village priest or two from the western hinterlands. It's not only *the* place to meet other guys, it's kind of the *only* place to be guaranteed a meeting with other guys, since just about every other gathering spot is mixed.

Performing Arts

For such a small town, Galway's theater scene is kickin'. Some of Ireland's finest have come out of this artistic hotbed. If you're lucky enough to be in Galway when the 📺 **Best Druid Theatre Company** is here, go to a show. They're old hands in London and on Broadway, have won several Tonys, and are considered by many to be the best theater company in Ireland. Their own theater is pretty small, so the Town Hall Theatre on Courthouse Square usually hosts their larger productions.

Based in Galway but traveling worldwide, **Macnas** (Fisheries Field, Salmon Weir Bridge; ☎ 091/561462) is another company you should catch if they're in town when you are. Known for mind-blowing costumes and sets, these are the people who put on the surreal parade at Galway Arts Fest.

Town Hall Theatre (Courthouse Sq.; ☎ 091/569777) is the big theater in town, just across from the courthouse. It hosts anything that fills seats: Irish or international theater, dance, opera, music, and readings,

Going Gay in Ireland

You want the good news first, or the bad? Let's start with the good news: Ireland has come a very long way in terms of accepting homosexuality. The bad news is that it started out *way* behind most of Europe on this one. In fact, homosexuality was a crime in Ireland until 1993. That, as you might imagine, put quite a damper on coming out parties.

Obviously a law making being gay illegal couldn't last forever, and after Ireland joined the E.U. things began to change. Once gay sexuality was decriminalized, gay bars could finally come out of the closet, and there are quite a few of them now. Still, it's a very small gay scene, and, by U.S. standards, equivalent to the rural Midwest in both size and scope.

Unsurprisingly given its size, Dublin is the country's most emotionally advanced city on this issue, but you should also encounter little in the way of trouble in cities of any size. Generally speaking, you should not be hassled when asking for a room with a double bed for you and your partner in Galway, Belfast, Tipperary, or any major tourist town.

The problems might come in smaller towns or out in the countryside, although, even then, in most cases it should be of the raised eyebrow, tut-tut variety.

Still, it is crucial that you're aware this isn't San Francisco. Ireland is a deeply conservative country, and for your trip to go smoothly we recommend you keep a low profile and respect that fact. Even in Dublin, which has Ireland's best gay bars (the George and GUBU), you can get into trouble if you so much as kiss your same-sex partner on the street. Our gay friends there highly recommend no public hand-holding, definitely no public kissing, and don't even think about ass-grabbing or any other extreme displays of affection. Unfortunately, there have been incidents of attacks on same-sex couples who didn't abide by these rules, and although such crimes are rare, we don't want anybody to get hurt.

Pretend you're in your grandmother's front yard—all the time—and if you behave accordingly all should be fine.

and serves as the main venue for the Cúirt Festival. The box office is open Monday to Saturday, 10am–7:30pm. The Town Hall people also run the Studio (on the same site), for smaller productions, and the **Black Box** (Dyke Rd.; ☎ 091/568151), which does everything from theater to music to comedy to circus in a big school gymnasium—looking space.

The main theatre groups are listed below.

→ **Druid Theatre** This creative theatre group performs in two venues in Galway—in a converted grain warehouse at Chapel Lane (☎ 091/568617), and at the Town Hall Theatre (☎ 091/569777). Performances are unique and original, focusing on Irish folk dramas and Anglo-Irish classics. The Druids are frequently either sold out or on tour, so book well in advance. *www.druidtheatre.com. Evening tickets €11–€20.*

→ **Siamsa, The Galway Folk Theatre** This touristy blend of traditional Irish music, dance, and folk drama is a kind of guilty pleasure. It's like Riverdance . . . but it's not Riverdance. Shows take place June through early September, Monday to Friday at 8:45pm. *Claddagh Hall, Nimmos Pier, Galway, County Galway.* ☎ 091/755479. *http://home page.tinet.ie/~siamsa. Tickets €20.*

ᴹ ᵀ ᵛ 🎧 coffeehouses & Late-Night Bites

Two cafes reign over Galway's late-night scene. Both serve good cafe food, with soundtrack, to a student/backpacker crowd. **Apostasy** (56 Lower Dominick St.; ☎ **091/561478**) is a funky little chamber with a wall shrine to the genius of espresso. It's open until 4am, as is **Java** (17 Upper Abbey St.; ☎ **091/567-400**), which takes up two floors. The long kitchen-style tables upstairs are great if you're doing the late shift with posse in tow. Do not be surprised if a soft-spoken guy wearing a spiked dog collar serves you your skim latte.

For late-night wine, candles, and weirdness, try **O'Ché's** (3 Francis St.; ☎ **091/585126**), also open until 4am. This place is a remnant of Galway's bizarre Ché obsession—check out the cosmic-erotic entrance mural starring the "Commie Christ" and his pal Fidel, then submerge yourself in the slightly eerie underground atmosphere of this up-all-night wine bar. The two candlelit rooms won't fill up with the usual revolutionary leftists until well after midnight. Glasses of house wine run €3.50, pitchers of sangria keep the crowd happy, and the little stage hosts live acts almost every night, starting around midnight.

→ **Taibhdhearc Theatre** Pronounced Thive-yark, this is a 108-seat, year-round venue for Irish-language plays. In the summer it presents a program of traditional music, song, dance, and folk drama. It is possibly the most touristy thing in western Ireland. Your parents will want you to go there. We're not so sure if that's a good idea. The box office is open Monday to Saturday from 1 to 6pm (until 8pm on show nights); most shows start at 8pm. *Middle St., Galway, County Galway.* ☎ *091/563600. Tickets €10–€15.*

Sightseeing

The absolute best way to explore Galway is on foot. It's too small to justify tour buses, and the winding, narrow streets are a nightmare if you're driving. So get a good map at the tourism office and put feet to concrete. Or cobblestones, really. It's a bit easy to get lost here, but the town's so small that just about the time you're thinking, "Uh-oh, I have no idea where I am . . ." you come out into a little alley onto Eyre Square again. Which is great.

Festivals

○ **Cúirt International Festival of Literature** (Apr, flexible dates; most events in Town Hall Theatre, Courthouse Sq.; ☎ **091/569777**): An eclectic migration of world-renowned scribblers telling you how they did it. Past greats to speak here have included Seamus Heaney and Allen Ginsberg, presumably stoking the flames of culture, creativity, and lust.

○ **Galway Early Music Festival** (3 days in mid-May; ☎ **091/846366**): Pageantry, theater, and music from those vibrant Dark Ages.

○ **Galway Film Fleadh** (early July; ☎ **091/569777**): Your standard film festival, with past appearances by famous Irish actors, including Gabriel Byrne.

○ 🎬 Best **Galway Arts Festival** (mid-July; ☎ **091/562480**; www.galwayarts festival.ie): This is the Big One. Famous for its street carnival, music, theater, and much more. Could be the best summer festival in Europe. Like Mardi Gras with art instead of parades.

○ **Galway Races** (late July; ☎ 091/
753870): A Bukowski-like horse-racing
bacchanal that utterly transforms the
town. Many businesses shut down for
the week as everybody goes to the track
and/or pub. You won't find a vacancy in a
Limerick broom closet, let alone in
Galway.

○ **Galway International Oyster Festival**
(late Sept; ☎ 091/527-282): Besides lots
of oyster-eating, this festival includes,
among other things, a golf tournament
and yacht race to celebrate Ireland's
favorite bottom-feeding mollusk.

Museums/Art Galleries/ Historic Buildings/ Gardens & Parks

Many of Galway's top attractions are outdoors and free of charge—you can have the
most fun just strolling around the Spanish
Arch and through the shops around Eyre
Square and chilling in the John F. Kennedy
Park. An afternoon picnicking on the banks
of the River Corrib is always free.

FREE → **Galway Arts Centre** Once
the home of W. B. Yeats's patron, Lady
Gregory, this attractive town house for many
years housed local governmental offices. Now
that those have been kicked out, it's all about
posh concerts, readings, and exhibitions by
Irish and international artists. Lady Gregory
would surely have approved. *47 Dominick St.
and 23 Nuns Island. ☎ 091/565886. Free
admission to exhibits. Mon–Sat 10am–6pm.*

FREE → **Galway Cathedral** It's easy
to understand why they gave this church
such a short nickname when you learn that
its official name is "Cathedral of Our Lady
Assumed into Heaven and St. Nicholas." Its
walls are fine-cut limestone from local quar-
ries, and its floors are Connemara marble.
It's not particularly old, as it was built in the
1960s, but it's attractive—contemporary
Irish artists designed the statues, stained-
glass windows, and mosaics. *University and*

MTV U → Hanging Out

The most unoriginal, and yet best,
outdoor gathering place is Eyre
Square. On a sunny afternoon,
droves of merry Galwegians join a
cast of students, resident winos, and
Australian backpackers and stretch
out on the grass. You can almost
always count on a good vibe and a
spontaneous guitar or drum session.

Otherwise, you can do a lot of
good people-watching down at the
riverside park and plaza, and the
crowd inevitably hanging out by the
Spanish Arch usually seem deeply
mellowed, perhaps lulled by the
drifting swans, swirling seagulls,
and beautiful view of Galway Bay.

If the weather's not conducive to
picnics on the grass, join the other
gracefully disheveled 20-somethings,
local students, and bermudas-and-
baseball-cap-wearing tourists outside Tigh Neachtain (see "Bars &
Pubs," earlier)—one of the best
pubs in Galway. If you're not up
for a boozy mood, head to **Café
du Journal** (The Halls, Quay St.;
☎ **091/568426**), where the stone-
topped cafe tables and wooden
church pews are usually piled high
with books and newspapers, and
the crowd leans toward the grad-
student-Jim-Morrison-type.

*Gaol rds., beside the Salmon Weir Bridge on the
river's west bank. ☎ 091/563577. Free admission; donations welcome. Daily 8am–6pm.*

→ **Galway City Museum** This little
museum offers a fine collection of local
documents, photographs, city memorabilia,
examples of medieval stonework, and
revolving exhibits. *Off Spanish Arch, Galway,
County Galway. ☎ 091/567641. Admission
€1.30 adults, €.75 students. Apr–Sept daily
10am–1pm and 2–5pm; Oct–Mar Tues–Thurs
10am–1pm and 2–5pm.*

FREE →Galway Irish Crystal Heritage Centre Don't go swinging your arms wildly in this place, where craftsmen blow, shape, and hand-cut the glassware. Pick up a few pieces for the parents in the shop, or hang out and watch those glassmakers do their thing. The shop and restaurant are open daily. *East of the city on the main Dublin road (N6), Merlin Park, Galway, County Galway. ☎ 091/ 757311. Free admission. Guided tour €4 adults, €3 students. Year-round Mon–Fri 9am– 5:30pm; Sat 10am–5:30pm; Sun 11am–5pm.*

→ Nora Barnacle House Just across from the St. Nicholas church clock tower, this restored 19th-century terrace house was once the home of the fabulously named Nora Barnacle, who later would become the wife of James Joyce. It contains letters, photographs, and other exhibits on the lives of the Joyces and their connections with Galway. *Bowling Green, Galway, County Galway. ☎ 091/ 564743. Admission €1.60. Mid-May to mid-Sept Mon–Sat 10am–5pm (closed for lunch), and by appointment.*

→ St. Nicholas' Collegiate Church This is Galway's oldest church—it's said that Christopher Columbus prayed here in 1477 before setting out for the New World. Established about 1320, it has changed from Roman Catholic to Church of Ireland and back again at least four times and is currently the latter. Inside are a 12th-century crusader's tomb with a rare Norman inscription, a carved font from the 16th or 17th century, and a stone lectern with barley-sugar twist columns from the 15th century. Guided tours, conducted by Declan O Mordha, a knowledgeable and enthusiastic church representative, depart from the south porch according to demand, except on Sunday morning. *Lombard St., Galway, County Galway. ☎ 091/564648. Free admission to church; donations of €2 adults, €1.30 students requested. Tours €3—reservations required. Mid-Apr to Sept Mon–Sat 9am–5:45pm, Sun 1–5:45pm; Oct to mid-Apr Mon–Sat 10am–4pm, Sun 1–5pm.*

Playing Outside

BEACHES If beaches good for prancing and showing off your nonexistent tan will satisfy, you can take a 20-minute walk out to Salthill, a hotel- and amusement-gorged suburb west of the city center and across the bridge, home to Galway's closest beach. It's almost always teeming with humanity's ritzier half. That said, you can probably find nicer strands among Galway's outermost reaches, or try the beach at Spiddal, a short Bus Éireann (Rte. 424) ride west of Galway, past Salthill. It's actually nicer than Salthill's beach: clean, sandy, and perfect for swimming.

BOATING You can take some friends and head up the River Corrib in a rented boat on a sunny afternoon. Just stop by **Corrib Boat Hire** (Brando Screen Printing, Waterside St. across from the old Galway Rowing Club; no phone; 9am–8pm daily; rowboats €8 per

hour; no credit cards). Row up the river to the ruins of an old castle surrounded by fields of grazing horses, then drop anchor and picnic in the sunshine.

If you prefer more powerful vessels, and more exhilarating options, contact ▨ Best **Delphi Adventure Holidays** (☎ 095/ 42208; www.delphiadventureholidays.ie), which offers a wide variety of activities, from sailing to sea kayaking to water-skiing, by way of abseiling, archery, and pony trekking.

If sailing is your thing, contact the **Galway Sailing Centre** (☎ 091/794527) for advice on the best rates for renting sailing boats in the area. One option is **Bow Waves,** the Galway sailing and powerboat school (Galway Mayo Institute of Technology, Renmore, Galway; ☎ 091/560560; www. bowwaves.com), which offers an adventurous

GALWAY CITY

introduction to cutting through the ocean waves.

CYCLING   Most hostels rent bicycles, particularly Salmon Weir Hostel. For a bigger selection of bikes contact **Richard Walsh Cycles** (Headford Rd., Woodquay; ☎ **091/565710**). You can also try **Europa Bicycles** (Hunters Building, Earls Island, across from Galway Cathedral; ☎ **091/563355**). Prices average €15 per day or €75 per week.

FISHING   Dotted beside the River Corrib, Galway City and nearby Connemara are popular fishing centers for salmon and sea trout. For the latest information on requirements for licenses and local permits, check with the **Western Regional Fisheries Board (WRFB),** Weir Lodge, Earl's Island, Galway (☎ **091/563118**; www.wrfb.ie), which also offers free consultation on where to go for salmon or trout, where to find the best *ghillies* (guides), and which gear to use. Maps and brochures are available on request. For gear and equipment, try **Duffys Fishing,** 5 Main Guard St. (☎ **091/562367**), or **Freeney Sport Shop,** 19 High St. (☎ **091/568794**).

Deep-sea fishing is famously good off the Galway Coast. Numerous boat companies offer fishing tours. If there's a group of you, try the *Immigrant,* berthed at the Galway Docks, where a half-day tour is €120 (☎ **086/812-0916**; immigrant@netaccess. ie). For more options, ask at your hostel or hotel, or stop by the tourist office, which will have loads of brochures for you to choose from.

GO-KARTING   For those of you who need to feel the wind in their . . . rented helmets, **Pallas Karting** will fill those speed gaps in your life with its two tracks (500m for slow people, 1,500m for pros), dozens of karts to choose from, and general appreciation of the need for speed (Tynagh, Loghrea, Co. Galway; ☎ **0509/45147**; www.pallaskarting.com). Prices start at €15 for 15 minutes.

HORSEBACK RIDING   To take a turn on one of those famed Galway horses, try **Aille Cross Equestrian Centre** (Aille Cross, Loughrea, County Galway; ☎ **091/841216**; www.aille-cross.com), about 32km (20 miles) east of Galway. Run by personable Willy Leahy, this facility is one of the largest in Ireland, with 50 horses and 20 Connemara ponies. For about €25 to €35 an hour, you can ride through nearby farmlands, woodlands, forest trails, and beaches.

SURFING   Since Ireland hosted the European surfing championship in '98, word's gotten around about the good Irish surf. The Atlantic swells come year-round, but the best are in April/May and September/October. Sampling Ireland's tubular bounty is easy in Galway: Just call Bryan Redmond at ⓂBest **Outback Ireland Surf Tours** (☎ **091/84001**, ☎ **086/814-2661**). For beginners, usually in groups of five, Bryan and his staff will pick you up at 8:30am, transport you to the slow-rolling beach break at Lahinch, County Clare, and provide you with board, wetsuit, and an hour and a half of individual instruction followed by a full day of surfing. The tour includes a beach barbecue lunch and a scenic return through the desolately beautiful landscape of the Burren. Of course, a pub stop or two is always an option before returning to Galway in the evening. Bryan offers more experienced surfers a choice of breaks from Dingle to Donegal, and will arrange custom tours of 1 to 3 days for surfers of any level.

For the lowdown on surfing from Galway locals, do your research in advance on the **Irish Surfing Association** website (☎ **096/49428**; www.isasurf.ie). For gear, check out the **Lahinch Surf Shop** (The Promenade, Lahinch; ☎ **065/708-1543**; www.lahinch surfshop.com). Owners Tom and Rosemarie Buckley rent and sell beginner surfboards, boogie boards, and full-length wetsuits. They also offer lessons and give a daily surf report on the phone (☎ **0818/365180**).

WINDSURFING If you feel like you're tough enough for Ireland's vicious cold-water windsurfing, check out **Rusheen Bay Windsurfing** (☎ 087/260-5702; www.rusheen bay.com), which offers advice, equipment, lessons, and an introduction to the bitchin' conditions on the waves off the Galway coast. Lessons start at €40 per hour.

Spectator Sports

GREYHOUND RACING The hounds race year-round every Tuesday and Friday at 8:15pm at the **Galway Greyhound Track,** College Road, off Eyre Square (☎ 091/562273). Admission is €5.

HORSE RACING This is one of the most famous racetracks in Europe—the subject of fable and song—and when (in July, Sept, and Oct) horses pound the track at the **Galway Racecourse,** Ballybrit (☎ 091/753870; www.galwayraces.com), less than 3km (2 miles) east of town, it's an event known simply as the **Galway Races.** It brings in horse lovers and high rollers from around the country. Tickets aren't expensive and it's a truly Irish event well worth catching if you happen to be in town when the races are on. Admission is €10 to €15, depending on the event and the day of the week.

Shopping

This is a deeply cool town, and with that comes deeply cool shopping. You can get funky clothes, beautiful antiques, and original artworks at vaguely reasonable prices. And it's just a lot of fun to shop here, through the tiny malls of small shops clustered in historic buildings, such as the **Cornstore** on Middle Street, the **Grainstore** on Lower Abbeygate Street, and the **Bridge Mills,** a 430-year-old mill building beside the River Corrib. **Eyre Square Centre,** the downtown area's largest shopping mall, with 50 shops, is where you go when you actually *need* something.

Most shops are open Monday to Saturday 9 or 10am to 5:30 or 6pm. In July and August, many shops stay open late, usually until 9pm on weekdays, and some also open on Sunday from noon to 5pm.

Here's a sampling of some of Galway's coolest shops.

If you're here on a weekend, start at the **Galway Market** (Market St.; 9am–5pm Sat) for stands of fruit, organic veggies, pottery, clothes, jewelry, and trinkets. They've got good eats here: Look for the "Curryman" and the stand selling sweet and savory crêpes.

In the taxi rank area at the top of Eyre Square, stalls sell clothes, jewelry, and even horse and bridle stuff from 9am till 5pm every Monday through Saturday.

Don't let the slightly precious exterior fool you, 'cause **Kenny's Book Shop and Gallery** (Corner Middle and High sts.; ☎ 091/562507) is the grand old man of Galway books. The three floors are packed with all sorts of subjects and titles, both rare and budget-bin, with a specialty in (what else?) Irish literature.

Conveniently opposite the back door of Kenny's, there's **Charlie Byrne's Bookshop** (The Cornstore, Middle St.; ☎ 091/561766). Just a big, comfy ol' horde of used, remaindered, and discounted books. Books, books, and more books, from Behan to Dewey, line every inch of wall space. This is the one in town with that stay-all-day vibe. Mmm . . . it even smells like a good bookshop.

Besides being the only place in town where you can score secondhand vinyl, **Mulligan** (5 Middle St. Court, Middle St.; ☎ 091/564961) boasts of having "everything" in Irish and Scottish trad, along with respectable collections of jazz, blues, soul, and ethnic music. Tickets for Roisín Dubh (see "Live Music," earlier) shows, other biggish local gigs, and charity events are all on sale here.

12 Hours in Galway City

After getting a map from the tourist office, head out to the town center. Start on Shop Street at **Lynch's Castle** (now a bank), and take a few pictures of its fantastically gloomy exterior, and crazy gargoyles. Head a block away to Market Street to see the **Lynch Memorial Window,** which tells the city's saddest tale. Around Shop and Market streets are lots of shops and boutiques to distract you—pop into **Zhivago Records** at No.5 (see below), or head over to Middle Street to find **Kenny's Book Shop and Gallery** (see above). After a bit of shopping and wandering, pop into **Home Plate Organics** (see "Eating," earlier) on Mary Street for some fresh sandwiches or burgers for lunch. Once you're fortified, head down toward the docks to the Spanish Arch to see what's happening on the Parade. If it's a sunny day, there will definitely be a crowd gathering, and the people-watching will be excellent. If not, head to Eyre Square to see if a band is jamming. Then over to **Café du Journal** (see "Hanging Out," earlier) for some coffee, and to catch up on the International Herald Tribune. When the dinner grumbling starts, it's got to be burgers and fries at **Scotty's Sunset Grill** (see "Eating," earlier), where you'll probably run into other people from the hostel. Then later, head down to the **Roísín Dubh** (see "Live Music," earlier) to see who's playing. You can kick back there for the rest of the night.

Half-looking like yet another cheesy tourist-drag souvenir shop, **Zhivago Records** (5 Shop St.; ☎ **091/509960**) has the Ticketmaster outlet for all major shows nationwide. And you can pick up a "Guinness Is Good For You" T-shirt while you're getting your tix.

If you want a glittering souvenir to take home with you, stop in at **Fallers of Galway** (Williamsgate St., ☎ **091/561226;** www.fallers.com), which has been a prime source of Claddagh rings, many made on the premises, since 1879. It also sells Celtic crosses and contemporary Irish jewelry designs.

If that doesn't do it for you, pop in to **Hartmann & Son Ltd.** (29 William St.; ☎ **091/562063;** www.hartmanns.ie), which has had a shop just off Eyre Square since 1942. See how their Claddagh rings compare to Fallers'.

Road Trips from Galway City

The Galway Bay Coast

Whether you do it in a bus, on a bike, or in a car of your own, a trip up the Galway Bay coast is one of those things that travelers tell each other they must not miss. It's spectacular and almost mystical, with the Aran Islands looming up out to sea in soft focus, and the barren, fierce hills of Connemara nearby. Heading out of Galway, you immediately feel like you're really heading out into the wild west. The landscape just looks so remote, melancholy, and moody. And it's not a long trip at all: It takes about 40 minutes by car or bus from Galway to Rossaveal, and another 40 minutes to Carna, at the northernmost tip of the bay.

Head west into Connemara, following signs for the coast road (R336), which winds its way along the edge of the headland to the busy, modern beach resort, Salthill, which is packed with Irish families in the summertime, and feels like nothing so much as the New Jersey shore in the United States, or Blackpool in England. It has a boardwalk and a fine beach, plus lots of bars, fast food, amusement rides, and game arcades. Keep going down the road if what you're looking for is charming little historic towns. Up ahead is the charming Gaelic-speaking Spiddal (An Spidéal), where they make those big, chunky white Aran sweaters and other artsy things.

Note, though, if you look for Connemara on road signs, you may be looking forever because it's not a city or county, but an area or region, like the Burren in County Clare. The boundaries are a bit hazy, but most agree that Connemara is west of Galway City, starting at Oughterard, and continuing toward the Atlantic. You know it when you see it, as it is gorgeous and unique, with dark bogs and tall jagged mountains punctuated by glassy lakes.

The road continues as far as Inverin, then turns northward, with signposts for Rossaveal. From Rossaveal, you can make the shortest sea crossing from the Galway mainland to the Aran Islands (see p. 173), and on a sunny day you might want to head out there to see the historical remains.

If you continue on R336, you'll leave the Galway Bay coast and travel past the rocky and remote scenery approaching the center of Connemara. Casla (Costelloe) is an Irish-language town, while Rosmuc is the site of the Padraic Pearse Cottage, where Pearse (1879–1916), one of the leaders of Ireland's 1916 Easter Rising, once lived. It's now a national monument.

Along the way, there's loads to do. At Killary Harbour you can take your pick of just about every adventure sport there is, from diving to kayaking to rock-climbing. If ancient ruins are your thing, you'll also want to check out the Aran Islands, which have preserved Stone Age dolmens and wedge tombs. As you pass a small traditional cottage alongside a weird maze of stones laid down thousands of years ago, you wouldn't be the first visitor to feel a shiver of awe at the sight of all the layers of history unfolding before you.

GETTING THERE & GETTING AROUND

BY CAR   The best way to see the sights along the Galway Bay coast is by car or bike. From Galway City, follow the coast road (R336). From Galway City to Inverin, it's about 32km (20 miles).

BY BUS OR TRAIN   Unfortunately, it's nearly impossible to get around if you're relying on public transportation. While Bus Éireann (☎ **091/562000;** www.buseireann. ie) provides daily service to Clifden and other small towns en route from Galway City, it still bypasses many beaches and tiny villages. As with the coast, the best way to get around Connemara is to drive or bike, following N59 from Moycullen and Oughterard. Or you can take a guided tour. Clifden is 65km (40 miles) west of Galway City.

BASICS

TOURIST INFORMATION   Contact or visit **Ireland West Tourism,** Aras Fáilte (Foster St., Galway, County Galway; ☎ **091/563081;** www.westireland.travel.ie). It's open year-round; see p. 144 for hours. Seasonal offices, open from late April through September, are at **Clifden** (☎ **095/21163**) and **Salthill** (☎ **091/520500**).

The **Oughterard Tourist Office,** Main Street, Oughterard (☎ **091/552808**), is open year-round Monday to Friday from 9am to 5pm, with extended hours in the summer season. In addition, a seasonal office, open Monday to Saturday 9am to 5pm between March and October, is maintained at **Clifden** (☎ **095/21163**).

TOURS

Some of the bigger hostels in Galway City offer good, reasonably priced tours. If you're not staying at a hostel, pop into one and ask if they're organizing a tour during your time in the city.

Otherwise **Bus Éireann** has regular tours departing from the bus station in Galway, taking an 8-hour tour through Connemara including Maam Cross, Recess, Roundstone, and Clifden, as well as Kylemore Abbey, Leenane, and Oughterard. It's available in the summertime only. (Ceannt Station, Galway, County Galway. ☎ **091/562000.** www.buseireann.ie. Tour average €22 adults, €16 students.)

Connemara Walking Centre has expert local guides lead walking tours of Connemara, with an emphasis on history and archaeology as well as scenery. All walks assemble at Island House in Clifden and include bus transportation to the walking site. Advance reservations are required. (The Island House, Market St., Clifden, County Galway. ☎ **1-877 WALK IRELAND** from the U.S.; in Ireland 095/21379. www.walkingireland.com. Tours from €20.)

Corrib Cruises depart from the pier at Oughterard and travel across Lough Corrib, stopping at some of its 365 islands. One visits Inchagoill Island, with a 12th-century monastery. Another trip goes to Cong in County Mayo, site of Ashford Castle (p. 70). There's also an evening Irish Hour (happy hour) cruise. (Oughterard, County Galway. ☎ **092/46029** or 092/46292. www.corrib cruises.com. 90-min. round-trip cruise to island €12 adults/students. Be sure to book ahead and to confirm times.)

SLEEPING
Hostels

➜ **Killary Harbour Youth Hostel** This is the perfect base for explorations in this wild and scenic region of Ireland. When the German philosopher Ludwig Wittgenstein lived here during the summer of 1948, the house had only two rooms and no electricity or running water. He still managed to get some writing done, and maybe you, too, will find inspiration here. The hostel is gorgeously located on a pier near the mouth of Killary

Harbour. The "green road" (see Walking Killary Harbour—The Green Road, p. 170) passes the hostel on its way to Leenane and makes a great walk. There are six dorms inside, all with eight beds and no bathrooms. *Rosroe, Renvyle, County Galway.* ☎ *095/43417. €14 dorm. No credit cards. Closed Oct–Feb. Amenities: Common room.*

➜ **Old Monastery Hostel** Location is a plus at this personable hostel, tucked into an old grove of trees a stone's throw from the Connemara National Park interpretive center—the Ellis Wood nature trail passes nearby on its way through the fine old forest. Stephen Gannon is an outgoing host who also runs the vegetarian restaurant serving up a buffet-style dinner each night. The food may not be memorable, but it certainly is filling. The complimentary continental breakfast includes homemade scones, porridge, and organic coffee. The hostel is in a handsome stone building set into the steep hillside. The kitchen is small but well stocked, and there's a bright, spacious sitting room with a fireplace. There are eight rooms inside. None with bathroom. Two are doubles and the rest are dorms. You can rent bikes for €10 per day. *Letterfrack, County Galway.* ☎ *095/41132. www.oldmonasteryhostel.com. €12–€14 per person dorm; €32 double. Rates include continental breakfast. Dinner €10. Follow signs on N59 for Connemara National Park; hostel is a few hundred yards from interpretive center. Amenities: Restaurant (vegetarian); sitting room; kitchen; laundry; bike rental.*

Cheap

➜ **The Anglers Return** This 18th-century sporting lodge was once part of the Ballynahinch Castle estate, and it sits in a grove of trees. The house feels lived in and has many great details, including a stove in the spacious dining room for warmth on cool mornings. The beds are unique: One room has an ornately carved Tudor headboard while in another room the bed is nearly 2m

County Galway

0   10 mi
0   10 km

M A Y O

Ballyhaunis

R395   Sheffrey Hills   Claremorris

N59   Lough Cara

Lough Mask

Inishbofin   Killary Harbour   Leenane   Ballinrobe   Dunmore

Inishark   Renvyle   Lough Fee   Maamturk Mountains   Cong

Cleggan

Letterfrack   CONNEMARA NATIONAL PARK

Omey Island   Clifden   Maam Cross   Lough Corrib   Tuam

Ballyconneely   Recess   N59   Oughterard   Headford

R342   Screeb   N17

Roundstone   R340   Lettermore   G A L W A Y

Carna   Costelloe   Galway   Athenry

Lettermore   Rossaveel   R336   Bearna   Salthill   N6

Inverin   Spiddal

Galway Bay   N18

Inishmore   Inishmaan   Kinvarra

COUNTY GALWAY   ARAN ISLANDS   Inisheer   Gort

Dublin   Doolin

IRELAND   C L A R E

Ferry Route

(6 ft.) wide. The extensive and delicious breakfast ensures veggies leave with their bellies full, too. *Toombeola, Roundstone, County Galway.* ☎ *095/31091. www.anglersreturn. itgo.com. €75 double. Rates include full breakfast. No credit cards. Closed Dec–Jan. 6.4km (4 miles) east of Roundstone on R341. In room: Hair dryer, iron.*

→ **Ardmore Country House** This modern bungalow overlooks the bay and the Aran Islands; check out the fab views through the large windows. You can chill out in the landscaped gardens or on the terrace. Guest rooms are spacious and attractively decorated, and in the morning you're offered a menu that has won the Galtee Irish Breakfast Award three times. *Greenhill, Spiddal, County*

Galway. ☎ *091/553145. €48 single; €71 double. Rates include full breakfast. Closed Jan–Feb. On the Galway Bay coastal road 1km (2/3 mile) from Spiddal. Amenities: Laundry facilities. In room: TV, hair dryer.*

→ **Bay View** The view over Streamstown Bay from this modern bungalow has got to be one of the best in the area. The four guest rooms are just fine, and you're likely to find a peat fire glowing in the lounge, which also has a TV for guest use. Bridie knows the area well, is always helpful in planning sightseeing for her guests, and can arrange a day's deep-sea fishing if that's your bag. All rooms have showers. *Westport Rd., Clifden, County Galway.* ☎ *095/21286. €26 single; €54 double. Closed*

Dec–Jan. Amenities: Sitting room. In room: TV, tea/coffeemaker, hair dryer.

➜ **Cloch na Scíth, Kellough Thatched Cottage** The trio of guest rooms in Nancy Hopkins Naughton's centuries-old thatched farmhouse are warm and welcoming, with antique pine furniture, polished wood floors, and patterned quilts. The whole house is open to guests and packed full of old curiosities. Tomas Naughton, Nancy's man, is a talented painter and an all-Ireland sean-nos (traditional a cappella Gaelic) singer. Nancy bakes a fresh corn cake in the open hearth each day and leaves it out for her guests to have with tea. A small sandy beach is minutes away by foot. In addition, there is an inviting self-catering thatched stone cottage, built by Tomas's great-grandfather. It rents for €210 to €560 per week, depending on the season. It has two bedrooms, a kitchen-dining-living room with a woodstove, a spacious sunroom, and 1¹/₂ bathrooms. *15km (9¹/₃ miles) from Galway center, just east of Spiddal, Coast Rd., Kellough, Spiddal, County Galway.* ☎ *091/553364. www.thatchcottage.com. €70 double. Rates include full breakfast. No credit cards. Amenities: Nonsmoking rooms. In room: No phone.*

➜ **Errisbeg Lodge** Right next door to Roundstone and beautifully wedged between mountainside and sea, Errisbeg Lodge is somewhere to get away from the bars and back to nature. Jackie and Shirley King's family land, reaching high onto the slopes of Errisbeg Mountain and sloping down to the sea, is a haven for rare wildflowers and birds, while the Atlantic is spread out before you, with two divine white sand beaches a few hundred yards away. Guest rooms are rustic and spare, with stucco walls and light pine furniture, with either mountain or ocean views. Muy tranquilo. *Just over 1.6km (1 mile) outside of Roundstone on Clifden Rd., Roundstone, County Galway.* ☎ *095/35807. www.connemara.net/errisbeg-lodge. €70–€80*

double. *Rates include full breakfast. No credit cards. Closed Dec–Jan. Amenities: Nonsmoking rooms.*

➜ **Glen Valley House and Stables** At the base of a remote glaciated valley, this award-winning B&B redefines "isolation." The drive follows the valley for over a mile before you arrive at the house, with its grab-your-camera views across to the far line of hills. The owners, the O'Neills, are helpful without being in your face, and their home attracts people looking to listen to the whistling wind for a day or two. The spectacular Western Way walking trail passes near the house and follows the hills along Killary Harbour, with unforgettable views of the harbor mouth. A top spot to watch the sun set. *Signposted 5.6km (3¹/₂ miles) west of Leenane on the Clifden Rd., Glencroff, Leenane, County Galway.* ☎ *095/42269. 4 units, 2 with private bathroom. €60 double with shared bathroom; €70 double with private bathroom. Closed Nov–Feb. Amenities: Sitting room. In room: Tea/coffeemaker.*

➜ **Knockferry Lodge** This lodge is set in a secluded spot on the Connemara shores of Lough Corrib, 23km (14 miles) northwest of Galway City. There are turf fires in both of the large lounges, and there's a spacious dining room. A game room has table tennis and bar billiards. Motorboats are available for hire for €40 per day plus fuel. Guest rooms are great—most have lake views. *Knockferry, Roscahill, County Galway.* ☎ *091/550122. www.knockferrylodge.com. €70 double. Rates include full breakfast. 21km (13 miles) from Oughterard; take N59 to Moycullen, turn left onto a small, unclassified road (the lodge is signposted) and then drive 9.5km (6 miles). Amenities: Restaurant (Continental); game room; massage; fishing-boat rental. In room: Phone, hair dryer.*

Doable

➜ **Doonmore Hotel** This waterfront hotel stakes out a prime location on Inishbofin, with amazing views of the open sea—a seal colony barks grumpily just beyond the hotel's front doors. The appealing, unpretentious rooms are clean and tastefully furnished with simple pine furniture. The hotel offers equipment for sea angling and scuba diving, and is a short walk from the ferry. It will provide van service to and from the main harbor on request. *Inishbofin Island, County Galway.* ☎ *095/45804. www.doonmorehotel.com. 25 units. €80–€110 double. Rates include full breakfast. Closed Nov–Mar. Amenities: Restaurant (Continental); bar; sitting room. In room: TV, tea/coffeemaker.*

Splurge

→ **Abbeyglen Castle**   On a hilltop overlooking Clifden and the bay, this property dates from the 1820s, although it only gained its castlelike facade 2 decades ago. This is a splendidly informal Irish hotel—the kind of place where a parrot in reception confuses staff by mimicking the telephone. In the evening, the piano bar brings guests together in a laid-back house party atmosphere. Guest rooms are large and comfortable, as are many of the guests. The smiling staff can arrange fishing trips, packed lunches, and local activities. One for the wealthy. *Note:* Rates are half-board and include bed, breakfast, and dinner. *Sky Rd., Clifden, County Galway.* ☎ *800/447-7462 in the U.S. or 095/21201. www.abbeyglen.ie. €200–€300 double. Half-board rates include full breakfast and dinner. Closed early Jan to Feb. Amenities: Restaurant (Continental); bar; outdoor swimming pool; tennis court; Jacuzzi; sauna; miniature golf; solarium. In room: TV.*

→ **Delphi Lodge**   Play at being an Irish country gent or lady. Delphi Lodge is a vast country house in a breathtaking, wild setting at the foot of towering mountains. Built in the early 19th century as a sportsman's hideaway, it occupies a landscape of crystal-clear lakes and rivers, dark-green hardwood forests, and near-vertical mountain slopes. All that, plus there are salmon and sea trout waiting to be caught. The rooms are big and kitted out with tasteful antiques giving a simple, elegant vibe. Owner and fly fisherman Peter Mantle can supply you with everything you need—permits, licenses, and equipment rental. The kitchen staff can prepare your catch of the day, or send it to you at home, smoked, after you return. *The Delphi Estate and Fishery, Leenane, County Galway.* ☎ *095/42222. www.delphilodge.ie. €150–€190 double. Rates include full Irish breakfast. 2- and 3-bedroom self-catering cottages €400–€1,000 per week. Closed Christmas and New Year's holidays. Amenities: Sitting room. In room: TV.*

EATING

This is a very rural area, with only tiny villages and small towns. Outside of the town of Clifden, food is not easily found, and good food is even rarer. If you're visiting the area on a day trip, which is likely, pack a picnic lunch. Otherwise, here are the few options in the area. There's also good cheap food on offer at the **Killary Harbour Youth Hostel** (p. 164), and at the **Avoca Café** inside the Avoca shop in Clifden (see "Shopping," below), and you can get a cheap veggie dinner at the **Old Monastery Hostel** (p. 164).

Cheap

→ **The Central** TRADITIONAL IRISH   This large bar/lounge is made cozy by lots of dark wood and a cheerful open fire (especially welcome on cool, dull days). The seafood chowder is especially good. Hot meals might include bacon and cabbage, lasagna, chicken curry, sandwiches, and soups. There's often traditional music in the bar, especially on summer nights. *Main St., Clifden, County Galway.* ☎ *095/21430. Sandwiches €3–€4; hot plates €7–€9.*

→ **Paddy Burke's** SEAFOOD   Platters of local oysters and mussels are served throughout the day at this homey and thatched roof tavern. Pick a quiet spot amid the half-dozen rooms and alcoves with stone walls, open fireplaces, potbellied stoves, and traditional *sugan* chairs (wood chairs with twisted rope seats). In good weather, soak up the sun in the back garden. Lunch and snack items range from seafood soups and chowders to sandwiches, salads, and omelets. In the evening, you can also order full meals, including Atlantic plaice and crab with prawn sauce. The tavern is on the main road, 16km (10 miles) south of Galway City. *Ennis-Galway Rd. (N18), Clarenbridge, County Galway.* ☎ *091/796226. Reservations recommended for dinner. Main courses €14–€25.*

→ **Two Dog Café** MEDITERRANEAN   This bright, smoke-free cafe is a great place to relax and enjoy homemade soups, fresh sandwiches (on baguettes, tortillas, and ciabatta), salads, pastries, tea, and Italian coffee. The baguette with goat's cheese and grilled red peppers is particularly enticing. Wine is served by the glass or bottle. There is also an Internet cafe on the second floor. You pay €2 for the first 15 minutes, €.65 for each additional 5 minutes, or €8 per hour, with discounts for students. *Church St., Clifden, Connemara, County Galway.* ☎ *095/22186. www.twodogcafe.ie. All items €3–€7. June–Sept daily 9:30am–10pm; Oct–May Tues–Sun 10:30am–6:30pm.*

Doable

→ **High Moors** MODERN CONTINENTAL   Just outside of Clifden, a narrow country road leads to this modern bungalow-style restaurant, high on a hill with panoramic views of the Atlantic and the wild countryside. It's a little like being in someone's dining room, and the food is simple, based on whatever is fresh at the markets—chicken with basil and tomato; roast leg of Connemara lamb with red currant and rosemary. *Off the Bally-coneely Rd., Dooneen, Clifden, County Galway.* ☎ *095/21342. Reservations recommended. Main courses €14–€20. Wed–Sun 6:30–10pm. Closed Nov–Easter.*

→ **O'Dowd's Seafood Restaurant** SEAFOOD   This homey, traditional restaurant overlooking the harbor has been serving up meals since 1840 and delivers perhaps the best seafood in Roundstone at near-budget prices. Top of the menu are seafood chowder, crab claws in garlic butter, fresh oysters, steamed mussels, and piled-high fishermen's platters. *Roundstone Harbour, Connemara, County Galway.* ☎ *095/35809. www.odowd srestaurant.com. Reservations recommended. Main courses €8–€20.*

→ **Twelve Pins** SEAFOOD   Named for the famous mountain range of Connemara, this old-world roadside inn is known for its fresh oysters and the humongous size of its seafood dishes (oysters, mussels, smoked salmon, and prawns). Other top options include scallops en croûte and trout Oisin (stuffed with almonds and prawns). For non–fish eaters, the menu offers a traditional roast of the day, plus steaks, rack of lamb, duckling, vegetarian stir-fry, and lasagna. (Rooms from €90 double.) *Coast Rd., Barna, County Galway.* ☎ *091/ 592368. Reservations recommended. Dinner main courses €8–€35. Daily 8am–9pm.*

Splurge

→ **The Signal** MODERN CONTINENTAL   Foodies flock to this restaurant, hidden away in the courtyard at the rear of the Clifden Station House Hotel. The draw is the cooking of Mr. Stefan Matz, a superchef who makes even the dullest dish twinkle with zest and originality. He loves to chargrill and smoke, which heightens the taste of the rich flavors he favors in dishes like the blackened turbot, served with smoked oysters and grilled mushrooms. Desserts are a must-have, too. *At the rear of the Station House Hotel, on the N59, Clifden, Connemara, County Galway.* ☎ *095/ 22946. Reservations recommended. Main courses €18–€26. Closed Oct–Apr.*

SIGHTSEEING

The capital of Connemara is Clifden, with a brill location at the top of pretty-as-a-picture

The Bogs

There's an awful lot of bog in County Galway. Today, one-third of Connemara is classified as bog lands. They began forming 2,500 years ago and have been put to good use ever since. During the Iron Age, the Celts preserved their butter in the bog. Now the turf (or peat) cut from bog remains an important source of fuel. Cutting and drying turf is part of the rhythm of the seasons in Connemara. It requires a special tool, a spade called a slane, which slices the turf into bricks about 46cm (18 in.) long. The bricks are first spread out flat to dry, and then stacked in pyramids for further drying. You'll see them as you whiz by on the roads. And if you spend any time in the Irish country, you'll get used to the strong, smoky smell of burning turf. You can always tell when a home's burning turf—the smoke coming out of the chimney is blue and sweet-scented. You'll leave loving it.

Clifden Bay. It's an attractive town with tall church steeples and Victorian architecture at the edge of thick forests. It's got loads of restaurants, hotels, and pubs, so makes a handy base for exploring the area.

But, it's a busy tourist town these days, so if you prefer something a little chiller, you might want to look at one of its many smaller towns and villages in the area, such as the small fishing port of Roundstone, which, while still pretty quiet, is also kitted out with all of the essentials: pristine beaches, good eateries, some fine places to stay, and more than its share of natural charm.

From Roundstone you can head on to the little community of Letterfrack at the edge of Connemara National Park, close to Kylemore Abbey. The tiny village, founded by Quakers, has a handful of pubs and B&Bs, in a glorious

natural setting. It's near Glassillaun Beach, with its bright white sand.

→ **Aughnanure Castle**   Standing on a rocky island close to the shores of Lough Corrib, this decaying fortress is a well-preserved example of a six-story Irish tower castle, with an unusual double bawn (a fortified enclosure) and a watchtower. It was built around A.D. 1500 as a stronghold of the "Fighting" O'Flaherty clan. *32km (20 miles) west of Galway City, signposted off N59, Clifden Rd., Oughterard, County Galway.* ☎ *091/ 552214. Admission €2.50 adults, €1.30 students. Mid-June to mid-Sept daily 9:30am– 6:30pm.*

🎬 Best → **Connemara National Park**   This has got to be one of the best national parks in all of Ireland: Over 2,000 hectares (4,940 acres) of mountains, bogs, and grasslands. It's really wild, desolate, and almost other-worldly at times. Not a place to get lost. There's a great visitor center just south of the crossroads in Letterfrack, which should stop that happening, and can give you tips and general info on the park's landscape, population of wild things, and scenic walking trails. It's worth taking one of these up some of the Twelve Bens, or through the peaceful Gleann Mór (Big Glen), with its River Polladirk. The center also offers sustenance in the form of tea, sandwiches, and freshly baked goodies. *Clifden-Westport Rd. (N59), Letterfrack, County Galway.* ☎ *095/41054. Admission €2.75 adults, €1.25 children and students. Visitor center closed mid-Oct to Mar.*

→ **Coole Park**   Now a national forest and wildlife park, Coole Park was once the setting for Coole House, the stately home of Lady Gregory, a big supporter of the arts and a founder of the Abbey Theatre. At this house she entertained W. B. Yeats, George Bernard Shaw, and Sean O'Casey, as well as Douglas Hyde, the first president of Ireland. The house no longer stands, its site marked only by ruined walls and stables; however, you can

Walking Killary Harbour—The Green Road

Not just a dull old harbor, **Killary Harbour** is also Ireland's only fjord; really remote and wild at its western, seaward end. To suck out its full flavor, take a hike along the **green road.** Now used mainly by sheep, it was once the fast track from the Rinvyle Peninsula to Leenane. The famine devastated this area; you'll pass an abandoned prefamine village on the far side of the harbor, the fields rising at a scarily steep slope from the ruined cottages, down by the water's edge. This is a walk into Ireland's recent past, when many lived by subsistence farming and fishing, always perilously close to disaster.

The walk begins at the **Killary Harbour Youth Hostel** (p. 164). Heading away from the hostel on the local access road, take a left on a grassy path just before the first house on the left. This path continues all the way to **Leenane,** a distance of about 13km (8 miles), but the most beautiful part is the first 3km (2 miles) from the youth hostel. If you don't want to return the way you came, look for the second of two roofed but abandoned houses on the right; it's right next to the trail, and partially obscured by rhododendrons. Just past this house is a path, scarcely discernible, that heads up the slope, veering back the way you've come. If you can find this track, it's easy to follow as it climbs gradually to the ridge top, which it meets at a curious notch cut in the hillside. (Marks left by the devil, apparently, when he tried to pull a local saint into hell, using a long iron chain for the purpose.) Descending on the other side of the notch, make your way down to the hostel access road. This will take you back to the starting point. Total distance for the loop is about 8km (5 miles). Get your boots on.

still see the famous "Autograph Tree," on which many of them carved their initials. There's a great atmosphere about the place that sets the imagination to work. The visitor center has an audiovisual presentation, exhibitions, and a tea shop. *Gort, County Galway.* ☎ *091/631804. www.heritageireland.ie. Admission €2.75 adults, €1.25 students. Park year-round; visitor center Easter to mid-June Tues–Sun 10am–5pm; mid-June to Aug daily 9:30am–6:30pm; Sept daily 10am–5pm. Last admission 1 hr. before closing. 3km (2 miles) north of Gort, due west of N18.*

→ **Dan O'Hara's Homestead Farm** See how the Irish used to live. This teeny farm is set up as it would have been before the famine conditions and shows how rural folk lived in the 1840s, with local people using traditional tilling and farming methods. There are also some cleverly designed reconstructions of ancient dwellings and fortifications

giving real insight into how things looked way back then. And, as ever in Ireland, hidden away on the land is an authentic megalithic tomb and a dolmen. For those who like the peace and quiet here too much to tear themselves away, there is a farmhouse B&B and some self-catering cottages. *About 6.5km (4 miles) east of Clifden off the main N59 Rd., Lettershea, Clifden, County Galway.* ☎ *095/ 21246. Admission €7 adults, €6 students. Closed Nov–Mar.*

→ **Dunguaire Castle** This beaut of a castle is situated on the south shore of Galway Bay. It was erected in the 16th century by the O'Hynes family and early in the 20th century, Oliver St. John Gogarty, the Irish surgeon and author, purchased and restored it. The decor is not exactly medieval so you'll have to use your imagination. You can, however, still see the impression left in the ground-floor vaulted ceiling by the wicker supports used in the vault's construction. And the *machicolation* (a bit that stuck out from the top of the castle wall to allow soldiers to drop rocks and boiling oil onto attacking forces below) placed at roof level above the door to the castle is still there. You might want to see the castle by coming to an evening medieval banquet. Then again, you might not. *Kinvara, County Galway.* ☎ *061/360788. www.shannonheritagetrade.com Admission* €4 *adults,* €3 *students. No credit cards. May–Oct daily 9:30am–5:30pm. From Galway City, take N18 south, then take road toward Doolin. Well signposted.*

→ **Inishbofin Island** A small emerald-green gem 11km (6¹⁄₄ miles) off the northwest coast of Connemara. It offers little more than seclusion and spectacular beauty, and unforgettable views from its shores. This was the lair of pirate queen Grace O'Malley, and later became Cromwell's infamous priest prison. It's currently home to 180 year-round residents. Numerous ferries to the island leave from and return to the sleepy port of Cleggan (13km/8 miles northwest of Clifden off N59) daily April through October. *Inishbofin Island Tours, Kings of Cleggan, Cleggan, County Galway* (☎ *095/44878), operates the largest, newest, and fastest boat, the Island Discovery. Tickets cost* €17 *per adult/student from the company office in Cleggan. Book in advance.*

→ **Kylemore Abbey** This is a stunningly beautiful place on the side of a wooded hill overlooking Kylemore Lake. The main building is a 19th-century house, and a splendid example of the neo-Gothic style for all your architecture fans. In 1920 its owners donated it to the Benedictine nuns who still run a convent boarding school here, but have opened the grounds and part of the house to the public. The complex includes a restaurant, which serves produce grown on the nuns' farm; a shop with a working pottery studio; and a visitor center. *Kylemore, County Galway.* ☎ *095/41146. www.kylemoreabbey.com. Admission* €10 *adults,* €6.50 *students. Open year-round daily 9am–5:30pm.*

PLAYING OUTSIDE

ADVENTURE SPORTS **The Delphi Adventure Centre** (Leenane, County Galway; ☎ **095/42307;** www.delphiadventure holidays.ie), is one of the best of the many adventure centers in Ireland. Courses are available in kayaking, wind-surfing, surfing, as well as in mountaineering, abseiling, hiking, and pony trekking. Accommodations are in bright, simply furnished single or dorm-style rooms. The food in the dining room is good and plentiful, and vegetarian meals can be arranged. All that fun doesn't come cheap though—weekend prices for room, full board, and activities begin at €185 for an adult. The nonresidential activities fee for 1 full day is €45.

BICYCLING Bicycles can be rented year-round from **Mannion Cycles,** Bridge Street, Clifden, County Galway (☎ **095/21160**). The rate for a regular touring bike in high season is €9 per day. Mountain bikes can be hired from May through October at **Killary Adventure Company,** Leenane, County Galway (☎ **095/43411;** www.killary.com). They go for €20 per day, and road bikes for €14 per day. If you don't want to go it alone, check out **Irish Cycling Tours** (☎ **095/42302;** www.irishcyclingtours.com), which offers guided and self-guided bike tours.

FISHING Grab your rod; it's time to hook something tasty. This area is prime territory for deep-sea fishing, especially mackerel, pollock, cod, turbot, and shark. To find a boat in the area where you plan to stay, contact the **Western Regional Fisheries Board,** the Weir Lodge, Earl's Island, County Galway (☎ **091/563118;** www.wrfb.ie), for recommendations, or ask at your hotel or hostel.

Lough Corrib is renowned for brown-trout and salmon fishing. Brown-trout fishing is usually good from the middle of February, and salmon is best from the end of May. The mayfly fishing begins around the middle

GALWAY CITY

of May and continues for up to 3 weeks. Angling on Lough Corrib is free, but a state license is required for salmon. For expert advice and rental equipment, contact the **Cloonnabinnia Angling Centre,** Moycullen, County Galway (☎ **091/555555**).

HIKING If you feel like stretching your legs, head to the town of Leenane, which is the start of any number of lung-pumping walks. One of the best takes you to the brill Aasleagh Waterfall (Eas Liath) east of the Killary Harbor. Another walk around that harbor, Ireland's only fjord, follows the Green Road. It was once the primary route from the Rinvyle Peninsula to Leenane, and is now largely a sheep track. The path passes a ghost town (an abandoned pre-famine village) on the far side of the harbor, where the fields rise at a devilishly steep slope from the ruined cottages, clustered at the water's edge (see "Walking Killary Harbour—The Green Road," p. 170). There are excellent walking trails in the Connemara National Park, some of which lead up the sides of the Twelve Bens. You can get maps at the park's visitor center.

Lough Inagh, nestled between the Maumturk and The Twelve Ben Mountains in the heart of Connemara, is in a spectacularly beautiful valley, where mountain slopes rise abruptly from the valley floor, and small streams cascade into the lake in a series of sparkling waterfalls. The R344 cuts through the valley, linking Recess to the south and Kylemore Lake to the north.

The Western Way, a walking route traversing the high country of Galway and Mayo, follows a quiet country road above the R344 through the Lough Inagh Valley. To reach the beginning of the walk, drive north on the R344, turning right on a side road—sign for Maum Ean—about 200m (656 ft.) before the Lough Inagh Lodge Hotel. Continue on this side road for about 6km (3³/₄ miles) to a large gravel parking lot on the left. Park here, and follow the well-worn

trail 2km (1.3 miles) to the top of the pass, through glorious mountain scenery.

This short (4km/2.5-mile) walk follows the Western Way to the top of a mountain pass that has long been associated with St. Patrick, and that is now the site of a small oratory, a hollow in the rock known as Patrick's Bed, a life-size statue of the saint, and a series of cairns marking the Stations of the Cross. Together, these monuments make a striking ensemble, strangely eerie when the mists descend and conceal the far slopes in their shifting haze. On a clear day there are great views from here, with the Atlantic Ocean and Bertraghboy Bay to the southwest and another range of mountains to the northeast. The round-trip walking time is about 1 hour.

HORSEBACK RIDING See the beaches of Connemara from horseback on a trek with the **Cleggan Riding Centre** (Cleggan, County Galway; ☎ **095/44746;** www.clegganriding centre.com). The center offers beach and mountain treks, and the most popular is a 3-hour ride to Omey Island at low tide. Prices start at €50. Or explore with **Connemara and Coast Trails** (Loughrea, County Galway; ☎ **091/841216;** www.connemara-trails.com). Rides are offered for both experienced and beginning riders. Riding costs €20 per person per hour.

SWIMMING The Silver Strand at Barna and the beach at Spiddal are clean, sandy, and ideal for swimming.

WATERSPORTS Hobie Cat sailing and sailboarding can be arranged at the **Killary Adventure Company** (Leenane, County Galway; ☎ **095/43411;** www.killary.com). Rates are €60 per day (two sessions), which entitles you to use the watersports equipment and participate in all the center's supervised sporting activities, including kayaking, water-skiing, hill and coastal walking, rock climbing, archery, and more. For diving, you can rent equipment and receive instruction at **Scubadive West,** Renvyle, County Galway (☎ 095/43922; www.scubadivewest.com).

SHOPPING

The busy little town of Clifden and the bustling village of Spiddal are both great for shopping. Lots of artsy stuff as well as chunky knit Irish fishermen sweaters and warm hats—good fun and cheap options abound.

As ever, one of the best is **Avoca Handweavers** (Clifden—Leenane Rd. (N59), Dooneen Haven, Letterfrack, County Galway; ☎ 095/41058). The Connemara branch of the famous Wicklow weavers is about 10km (6¼ miles) north of Clifden on an inlet of the bay, in a picturesque location. Inside are colorful woven clothes and blankets, as well as candles, jewelry, and music. There's an excellent cafe as well, which makes a good place for lunch.

Elsewhere in Clifden is the **Celtic Shop & Tara Jewelry** (Main St., Clifden, County Galway; ☎ 095/21064). This is a good place to pick up souvenirs, including gold and silver Celtic jewelry, hand-woven Irish rugs, knitwear, ceramics, and crystal, as well as a good selection of Irish books. For more jewelry pop in at **O'Dalaigh Jeweller** (Main St., Clifden, County Galway; ☎ 095/22119; www.celticimpressions.com), a family-run jewelry shop with handmade, one-of-a-kind pieces with a lovely Celtic theme. Along with affordable silver pieces, there is some gorgeous gold jewelry, some based on designs found carved on stones at Newgrange.

Go to the **Connemara Marble Visitor Centre** (13km (8 miles) west of Galway City on Galway-Clifden Rd. (N59), Moycullen, County Galway (☎ 091/555102) to find Connemara's unique green marble—quarried, cut, shaped, and polished here. Estimated by geologists to be about 500 million years old, the marble ranges from lime green to dark emerald. On weekdays you'll see craftspeople at work hand-fashioning jewelry, paperweights, ashtrays, Celtic crosses, and other such items.

Fuchsia Craft (The Square, Oughterard, County Galway; ☎ 091/552644). Wedged in the center of Oughterard's main thoroughfare, this small shop is a treasure trove of unusual, hard-to-find crafts, produced by more than 100 craftspeople throughout Ireland including recycled art cards of Connemara scenes, pottery, crystal, jewelry, and knitwear.

In Spiddal, the **Ceardlann an Spideil/ Spiddal Craft Village** (Coast Rd., Spiddal, County Galway; ☎ 091/553041) is actually a cluster of cottage shops for local craftspeople, and a good place to find unique pottery, woven wool, and jewelry. The art galleries feature hand-carved stone crafts, sculpture, paintings, and posters, and there's a good coffee shop on the premises. For a snack, lunch, or light meal, Jackie's Bistro, in a rustic cottage at the Craft Village, offers highly recommended fare. Another fixture on the Connemara coast for decades, **Standun** (Coast Rd., Spiddal, County Galway; ☎ 091/553108) has long been known as a good source for authentic *bainin* sweaters, handcrafted by local women from the nearby Aran Islands and the surrounding Connemara countryside. Oh go on, you'd look lovely in one. Along with these chunky white knits it also offers tweeds, sheepskins, linens, glassware, china, pottery, jewelry, books, and maps. It also has a good cafe with great views of Galway Bay and the Aran Islands.

The Aran Islands

When you see the ghostly shapes of the islands floating just off the Galway shore, you instantly understand why the Aran Islands have been the subject of fable and lore for thousands of years. Today the three islands— Inis Mór (*Inishmore*), Inis Meain (*Inishmaan*), and Inis Oírr (*Inisheer*)—continue to be outposts of Gaelic culture and language. Not only do these islands look damn good, they are also where heaps of rare animals and birds call home. Altogether it's an intoxicating and incredibly isolated landscape. To this day, many of the 1,500 inhabitants of the islands still live a traditional Aran Island life—fishing from currachs (small crafts made of tarred canvas stretched over timber frames), living in little stone cottages, relying on pony-drawn wagons to get around, and speaking Gaelic (although they all speak English as well). The classic hand-knit *bainin* sweaters originating here are still worn by the locals (not just tourists).

The islands are an easy trip from Galway, and many folks go for only an afternoon. Chances are that if you have time for only one of the islands, you'll be visiting Inis Mór. It's the largest and the easiest to get to from Galway, and the one that best handles the large groups of tourists. Its easy transport means you can escape the crowds if you wish, or, if you play well with others, there are plenty of pubs and restaurants to keep you busy.

But if you do have time, consider visiting Inis Oírr, which is perfect for long romantic walks with your gal or boy. It's not as touristy as Inis Mór either but there are enough B&Bs (and one well-above-average hostel) to choose from, and they're all within a horseshoe's toss of the pier. Getting around is as easy as putting one foot in front of another, since you can easily walk from one end of the island to the other (it's only 3 miles long), through mazes of ancient stone walls fencing in a few bored-looking cows. You may not see a single soul all afternoon, and when you do, it'll be a farmer driving by in his tractor. Plop yourself down on the large rocks—perfect for sunbathing, were there ever any sun—and watch the tide rush in. You could easily fool yourself into believing you were the tiny island's sole inhabitant. If you are looking to do a little soul-sifting, this is the place.

Most visitors arrive on ferries at Kilronan, Inishmore's main town and a very easy place

How to Catch a Leprechaun

You'll know a lot about these folk already. They're 3 feet tall. They wear cute little green suits. And, you should know if you watched that cheesy mid-1990s flick *Leprechaun* with Jennifer Aniston, they're not always friendly. More importantly, every leprechaun has a stash of gold hidden someplace, and if you can catch hold of one of the little fellows long enough to ask the right questions, it's yours for the taking. Easier said than done, though.

The only time you can catch a leprechaun is if he's sitting down to mend his shoes. Should be easy enough. But keeping hold of him is another matter. Don't take your eyes off him for a minute or he'll be gone in a track of dust. Ask where the gold is. He'll deny he has any. Keep asking—a threatening tone of voice wouldn't hurt, y'know, put the ol' "fear of God" into 'im for a bit. And don't trust his word—make him show you *exactly* where it is. These little critters are more slippery than Smeagol. And if you ever get any of this to actually benefit you somehow, be sure to let us know.

in which to arrange or rent transportation. The mode is up to you: Horse-pulled carriages can be hailed like taxis as you step off the boat, minivans stand at the ready, and bike rental shops are within sight.

On all the islands, everything is within walking distance, but on Inis Mór it's easier and faster to rent a bike. As for Inis Meáin and Inis Oírr, bikes aren't necessary. You can cover the whole of each island in a matter of a couple of hours by foot. Bring a picnic lunch, sturdy shoes, and your idle curiosity, and you're all set for a lovely afternoon.

GETTING THERE & GETTING AROUND

BY PLANE   The fastest way to get from the mainland to the Aran Islands is on the local airline, **Aer Aerann** (Connemara Airport, Inverin, County Galway; ☎ **091/593034;** www.aerarann.ie; €44 adult round-trip), which has small planes departing from Connemara Airport, approximately 29km (18 miles) west of Galway City to the islands every day in the high season. Flight time is 10 minutes, and bus service between Galway City and the airport is available. You can book your flight at the Galway Tourist Office or at Aer Arann Reservations. A range of specials is usually on offer, combining flights with bus/accommodations, and so forth.

BY BOAT   **Aran Island Ferries** (Victoria Place, off Eyre Sq., Galway, County Galway; ☎ **091/568903;** www.aranislandferries. com; round-trip fare €20 adults, €15 students), with a number of offices in Galway center, offers extensive, year-round daily service to all three Aran Islands. Most boats leave from Rossaveal in Connemara, 37km (23 miles) west of the city, for the 40-minute trip. Island Ferries provides bus connection service from its Victoria Place office 90 minutes before sailing time. During peak summer season there are daily excursions from Galway Dock, which cost up to €6.50 more than tickets from Rossaveal.

BY BUS   There are plenty of buses, both tour and transport, all over Inis Mór, lots parked right at the pier (they aren't shy about soliciting your business, either); tickets are around €8 return to Dún Aengus. One of these bus lines is **Noel Mahon Mini Bus** (☎ **099/61213,** mobile 086/877-3766), offering tours and taxi service.

BASICS

TOURIST INFORMATION   **The Inishmór tourist office** (☎ **099/61263**) is on the waterfront near the ferry pier in Kilronan. They can help you book a room if you haven't

booked in advance. **On Inis Oírr, the Tourist Office** (☎ **099/75008;** 10am–6pm July–Aug) is in a little hut right on the pier; you can also call the **Inisheer Island Cooperative** (☎ **099/75008**) for information.

SLEEPING

There are quite a few hostels on Inis Mór, and some of them are excellent. On Inis Oírr, Brú Radharc Na Mara is the only hostel, but it's a good one, and very little in the way of choice on Inis Meáin, which is the emptiest of all the islands.

Hostels

→ **An Áharla Hostel**   Along with the Artist's Lodge Hostel, this is one of the friendliest, most comfortable places to stay on Inis Mór. Here, roaring fires greet you on cold days, as do the three comfy guest rooms (with space for two, four, and six people, respectively) and the friendly and colorful owner, Colm Conneely, who will tell stories and crack jokes by the fireside at night. The cozy atmosphere brings one-time lodgers back again and again. Book well ahead during the summer months just as you would anywhere else that's especially small. *Off the main road, signposted; St. Rónáins Rd., Kilronan, Inis Mór.* ☎ *099/61305. €12–€17 per person. Amenities: Common room with fireplace.*

→ **The Artist's Lodge Hostel**   We just can't say enough about this place. It has only 10 beds in the whole place, and the building itself is a cozy little cottage with a fantastic sitting room, lovely views, and a fire going all afternoon and long into the night. Residents from all over the island come to borrow from the sitting-room bookshelves, and you can take and leave good books here. Owner Marion Hughes makes you feel even more comfortable than you would in your own home—write your address in the guest book and she'll even send you a Christmas card. The price includes toast and tea for breakfast (and anything else around the kitchen that

Sweater Story

Aran sweaters may be one of Ireland's hottest exports today, but they came from humble beginnings. Originally, the almost-waterproof wool sweaters were knitted together by the women of the Aran Islands to ensure their men folk stayed warm and dry when they went out fishing (the waterproofing comes from natural oils from the sheep's skin, which remain on the wool even when it's washed). The wives and mothers of the fishermen created a different pattern for each family. Sadly, one of the reasons these patterns were created was to help the islanders identify fishermen who had drowned off this dangerous coast. Buy one here on the Aran Islands. Sure, you can buy them anywhere in Ireland but they're not all the genuine handmade article you get here. Look for a tag signed by the woman who knitted it—the best sweaters will have one attached. It will set you back about €90 but it will last forever and your granny will love you in it.

you can get your hands on). On top of all that, the beds are incredibly comfortable; you'll remember them longingly for the rest of your stay in Ireland. *Off the main road, signposted; St. Rónáins Rd., Kilronan, Inis Mór.* ☎ *099/61457. €12–€15 per person. Amenities: Common room.*

➜ **Brú Radharc Na Mara** On Inis Oírr, this is an excellent choice—okay, it's the *only* choice if you're looking to stay in a hostel. But it's quite a nice one, actually, so you're lucky. There's a nice big kitchen, and a cozy sitting room with fireplaces overlooking the ocean. The skylit guest rooms on the upper floor are perfect for bedtime stargazing. Given the island's general isolation, it's a good thing that the hostel also serves meals: continental breakfast for a few euros, Irish breakfast for a couple more, and dinner for about €10. Handily, there's a cheerful pub next door where bands frequently play unannounced gigs of traditional Irish music. *Strand Rd., short walk from the pier, to the right, Inis Oírr.* ☎ *099/75024. €11 per person. Amenities: Kitchen; TV room; fireplace.*

➜ **Kilronan Hostel** It doesn't get much more convenient than this mint green hostel. Not only is it located right on the pier, but there's a pub on the floor below it. That said,

this shouldn't be your top choice. Reception is chilly and so's the atmosphere. On its website it calls itself the "most picturesque hostel in Ireland." Tsk. Their nose will grow. But the place is clean, and it's big enough that you're pretty much guaranteed a bed. Should you arrive on a ferry dead tired in the pouring rain, it'll do just fine. *At the pier, Kilronan, Inis Mór.* ☎ *099/61255. www.kilronanhostel.com. €14 per person dorm. Amenities: Kitchen, TV room.*

➜ **Mainstir House Hostel** This is the other popular option, about a 15-minute walk from the pier, on the left side. While it has a reputation as a haven for artists, writers, musicians, and backpackers alike, there have been complaints about morose staff and less-than-clean facilities. What really gives Mainstir House its international renown is the restaurant, overseen by Joel D'Anjou, who cooks up organic vegetarian feasts for a laid-back dining room. He's not exactly known for his sunny demeanor, though, so stay on his good side. Be sure to make a reservation; the food is popular, and deservedly so. As for the hostel itself, well—let's just say we've seen better. *On the main road, Inis Mór;* ☎ *099/61169. www.mainistirhousearan.com. €15 per person dorm, €35 single, €25 per person double. Breakfast included. Dinner €15.*

Cheap

➜ **Radharc An Chlair** Leaving the ferry on the island of Inis Oírr, and walking onto tiny Inisheer, you're met by Peadar Poil and given a lift up to the house—wait for it—on his tractor. That's worth the price in itself! The Poils run a spit-and-polish B&B operation and the guest rooms are all comfortable and cozy. Brigid Poil is a superb cook and a terrific baker, so even a scone and a cup of tea here is a pleasure. *Inis Oírr, Aran Islands, County Galway.* ☎ *099/75019. www.radharc anchlair.com. €56 double. Rates include full breakfast. Amenities: Sitting room. In room: TV, tea/coffeemaking facilities, iron, hair dryer (on request).*

➜ **Tigh Ruairí** Is there anything the folks at Tigh Ruairí can't do? In addition to serving up great dinners, running a cozy little pub, and keeping the island stocked through their convenience store, they also run a good B&B. All rooms have their own bathroom, and the whole place is clean and airy. There's a lovely sitting room for when it's chilly outside, and when it's sunny it's just a few minutes walk from here to the beach. *The Strand, Inis Oírr.* ☎ *099/75002. €20–€30 per person double. Amenities: TV lounge; kitchen; breakfast included in price.*

Doable

➜ **Kilmurvey House** This 18th-century stone building holds 12 diverse rooms, all comfortable and impeccably clean. It's a friendly place, and an array of delights awaits you at breakfast. Kilmurvey House lies just below Dún Aengus, Inishmore's prime attraction. A handful of shops, cafes, and restaurants, as well as a blue flag (safe to swim) white sand beach, are within a short stroll. *8km (5 miles) from the ferry on the Coast Rd., Kilmurvey, Kilronan, Inis Mór, Aran Islands, County Galway.* ☎ *099/61218. www.kilmurvey house.com. €80 double. Rates include full breakfast. Closed Nov–Easter. Sitting room.*

➜ **Man of Aran Cottage** In the traditional thatched seaside cottage constructed in 1934 for the filming of *Man of Aran,* this cozy B&B overlooking Kilmurvey Bay is friendly and unpretentious, with comfortable rooms—decorated with simple pine furniture and whitewashed walls—and tranquil views. The biggest draw may well be its first-class restaurant (see "Eating"), where the menu draws upon the organic vegetables and herbs grown in the cottage garden, and fresh seafood. *Kilmurvey, Kilronan, Aran Islands, County Galway.* ☎ *099/61301. www.manofaran cottage.com. €70. Rates include full breakfast. Reservations required for dinner. Fixed-price dinner €30. No credit cards. Amenities: Restaurant; sitting room.*

EATING

If you'd rather do it yourself, head to the **Spar Supermarket** on Inis Mór (☎ **099/61203**). It's on the main road that heads out from the pier. Stock up on groceries if you're heading out to the other islands later on, as they haven't got grocery stores. On Inis Oírr, Tigh Ruairí (see "Sleeping," above), along with a pub and B&B, also has a small convenience store.

There are several simply decorated little cafes on Inis Mór, all essentially interchangeable. Each offers sandwiches, soups, and other light fare for around €4, as well as meat or fish dishes for around €8. There's **Lios Aengus,** next to the Spar supermarket, **An Sean Cheibh,** across the street and right behind the Aran Sweater Market, and a few farther out on the island. **An Sunda Cáoch** (☎ **099/61218;** no credit cards) or "The Blind Sound," is a cafe and coffee shop outside the entrance to Dún Aengus—it serves coffee, sandwiches, and cake, all for under €4. **Tigh Nan Phaidt** (just off the main road, at the turnoff to Dún Aengus; ☎ **099/ 61330;** no credit cards), is in a cute little thatched-roof cottage, where it serves smoked salmon sandwiches made with homemade bread for under €8.

Man of Aran (past Kilmurvey Beach, on the right of the main road, Inis Mór; ☎ **099/61301;** no credit cards) is in a small traditional cottage where the movie of the same name was filmed back in 1934. Here you can fill up with tea and tasty organic lunches for under €6. Man of Aran also is a B&B with a charmingly authentic location (and amazing breakfasts), although the location is a bit out of the way.

Less rustic is the **Bay Café** (at the pier, Kilronan), part of the brightly painted Bayview Guesthouse overlooking the dock. Prices and menus are the same as Man of Aran's, but the decor's a bit spiffier, all done in bright colors that somehow manage to keep from looking gaudy.

For dinner on Inis Mór, there are several good choices. The organic vegetarian meals at **Mainstir House Hostel** always receive glowing reports. Bring a bottle of wine from the supermarket and you're all set. At the **Aran Fisherman** (near the pier, Kilronan, Inis Mór; ☎ **099/61104**) the menu's filled with—you guessed it—seafood, and so fresh you might want to check first to make sure it won't bite you back. For fishphobics, it also has pizza, burgers, and vegetarian dishes.

On Inis Oírr, one of the best places for dinner is **Tigh Ruairí** (The Strand Rd., Inis Oírr; ☎ **099/75002**). Yeah, it's pub grub, but it's extremely good pub grub. The chef's special recipe for making fish and chips (€7.50 for a huge portion) is so good, he's been pestered by foodie magazines to reveal his recipe. The soups are excellent as well: Try the tomato basil or clam chowder for just a few euros.

PARTYING

There's something about the Aran Islands that makes you think you'll be surrounded by guitar-picking, accordion-squeezing musicians

the moment you arrive. But you won't. Whether that's a good thing or not is up to you, but to us it's a bit disappointing that a place that cries out for a Hollywood-esque rollicking music scene in a small, stone pub, has little of that. Still, look around a bit, and you'll find things to do. Most pubs on the islands open around 10am, and close around 11pm.

If, by chance, you came to Inis Mór specifically to hear Irish guys singing Garth Brooks and blink-182 tunes, **Joe Watty's** (Kilronan, main road, left side, past the post office and bank; no phone) is the place. Watty's isn't your typical Irish pub—it's brightly lit and may remind you of a makeshift bar in someone's basement game room. The music's nightly, and this bar stays open later than normal, till 1:30am. The two-man band stops playing sometime around half-past midnight, but if you beg for an encore, they'll play another song or two before packing it in. Watty's serves good pub grub until 8pm in summertime.

Don't look for Budweiser at the **American Bar** (Kilronan, Inis Mór, at the pier, behind Bayview House; ☎ **099/61130**)—it got its name only because it has a pool table in the back room and rock music playing on the loudspeaker. It's got more of a "real pub" feel than Joe Watty's, and there's live trad music here most nights in the summer, and no cover.

Elsewhere, the action is at **Tí Joe Mac** (at the pier, Kilronan, Inis Mór; no phone). Just below the Kilronan Hostel (p. 176), it's usually the most crowded pub on Inis Mór on chilly moonlit nights — so crowded, in fact, that the musicians barely have room to play. Tí Joe Mac is also the most touristy of the three Kilronan pubs, since the hostel is right upstairs and there are so many B&Bs nearby. There's a good mix of locals here, as well as Irish people on their holidays.

Care to dance the night away on Inis Mór? Every Friday, Saturday, and Sunday night a *céilí* (*kay*-lee)—that's a traditional Irish music and dancing session—is held at the **dance hall,** beginning at midnight. Admission is €5–€7; storytelling and ballads precede the dance. Ask any of the locals at the bars around closing time; chances are a lot of them are heading to the *céilí.* (In the winter, the sessions are held only on Sat.)

Inis Meáin's got only one pub, **Teach Ósta Inis Meáin** (about a half-mile straight on away from the pier; no phone; no cover; no credit cards), but don't go in there expecting a party—this is a bit of an isolationist place, and you'll be lucky if you can elicit a single grunt from the weather-beaten locals at the bar.

You might have better luck at **Tigh Ruairí** (The Strand Rd., Inis Oírr; ☎ **099/75002**)—a cozy little place for a pint and a bit of Irish gab. The food's excellent, and there are trad sessions most nights in summer, although there's no established schedule. The sea winds will chill you at sunset, so after that romantic stroll to the other end of Inis Oírr and back, get yourself a delicious steaming mug of Bailey's coffee at Tigh Ruairí.

The pub at Hotel Inis Oírr, **O'Flaherty's** (on the Strand Rd. leading to Tigh Ruairí, Inis Oírr; ☎ **099/75020**), is much more spacious than the other two bars on the island, but there's not too much going on here besides a few musicians engaged in a too-casual-to-be-entertaining jam session. It's not the best pub on the island, but okay for a pint before heading to Tigh Ned's. Note the trophy and American license plate collections above the bar.

Were O'Flaherty's and Tigh Ruairí a wee bit quiet for you? Wondering where everybody went? Try **Tigh Ned** (Inis Oírr, on the Strand Rd., a short walk from the pier, next door to Brú Radharc Na Mara (p. 176; no phone). Everyone and their brother's here, and everybody's young—and surprisingly hip, too, for such an out-of-the-way place. It's got comfy booths, walls covered with old photographs, and truckloads of rugby boys swarming around the dartboard. There's traditional music here most nights in the summer (beginning around 9:30pm, as is customary in Irish pubs); but there is no definite schedule—these sessions are always impromptu.

SIGHTSEEING

All of the islands are weird-looking, with a ring of rocks around their outer edges, and, inside, small farms cozied down on nests of soft green grass and wildflowers. For high drama head to the western sides where huge cliffs plummet down into the frothing sea below.

For history boffins, there are some excellent archaeological sights out here, including the magnificent **Dún Aengus,** a vast stone cliff fortress on Inishmór, dating back 2,000 years on the edge of a cliff dropping 90m (295 ft.) to the sea. Its original purpose is unknown—some think it was a military structure, others say it was a vast ceremonial theater. From the top there are spectacular views of Galway Bay, the Burren, and Connemara.

Also on Inishmór a heritage center, **Ionad Arann,** Kilronan (☎ **099/61355**), explores the history and culture of the islands. Exhibits examine the harsh landscape, Iron Age forts, and early churches. In addition, the 1934 film *Man of Aran,* directed by Robert Flaherty, is shown six times daily. This is an amazing documentary showing how the islanders used to live, but sadly without a whisper of the Gaelic language as it was all narrated in English for the audience at the time. Stars include Colman "Tiger" King and Big Patcheen' Conneely of the West. They are either shark hunters or canoeists. You get the picture. The center is open March to May and October daily 10am to 5pm, and from June to September daily 10am to 7pm. Admission to the center is €4.50 for adults, €3 for students. Discounted combination tickets to the center and film are available. The cafe serves soups, sandwiches, and pastries throughout the day.

The
Southeast

So you've done Dublin, have you? And you're thinking, what next? The scenic coast of western Cork? The tourist-crunched Ring of Kerry? The spectacular Cliffs of Moher?

Well, hold on a minute. Before you zip over to the west of Ireland to take in those popular travel destinations, don't bypass the Southeast, because it's worth your time.

If you skip a visit to the medieval castle town of Kilkenny, or bypass the enormous fortress on the Rock of Cashel, or pass on a chance to scuba dive in the caves off of Hook Head, we just don't know what you're thinking.

In the less touristy climes of Kilkenny, Wexford, and Waterford, you'll see the countryside without the crowds and ubiquitous, smog-spewing tour buses. You'll wander along city walls built a thousand years ago, climb hills where rebels fought for freedom, and visit pubs that are older than America. Toss back a pint in a pub rich with history, like Kilkenny's Kyteler's Inn, which dates to 1324 and was once the home of alleged witch Dame Alice Kyteler.

The larger towns of southeastern Ireland have a distinctly historic flavor. Wexford and Waterford suffered heavily from Viking invasions, and you can still see signs of the Viking's presence in the region in the names of the streets.

There's plenty to see here, not only because the region has such a long and violent history. The Hook Peninsula was famous for shipwrecks, despite the fact that it has a lighthouse dating to the 13th century.

Walk around the monuments in Wexford Town on a cool summer evening, or stand in the shadow of 12th century St. Canice's Cathedral in Kilkenny City (or Jerpoint Abbey) and you'll see what we mean.

The Best of the Southeast

○ **Filling Up Your Memory Card in Inistioge:** Nestled in the Nore River Valley, surrounded by undulating hills, this riverfront village with two spacious greens and a host of pubs cries out to be photographed. Its rivers and lakes are swimming with fish and attract hosts of anglers. See p. 216.

○ **Pondering the Art Scene in Kilkenny:** Kilkenny is a charming medieval town. Its city walls, splendidly restored castle, and renowned arts scene draw visitors from across Ireland and abroad. The combination of the historic feel and the modern arts movement makes this an especially rewarding town to discover. See p. 216.

○ **Admiring Cahir Castle:** One of the largest of Ireland's medieval fortresses, this castle is in an extraordinary state of preservation. Tours explain some fascinating features of the military architecture, and then you're free to roam through a maze of tiny chambers, spiral staircases, and dizzying battlements. See p. 213.

○ **Exploring Kilkenny Castle:** Although parts of the castle date from the 13th century, the existing structure has the feel of an 18th-century palace. There have been many modifications since medieval times, including the addition of colorful landscaping, and the old stables now hold numerous art galleries and shops. See p. 225.

○ **Tooling Around the Rock of Cashel:** In name and appearance, "the Rock" suggests a citadel, a place designed more for power than prayer. In fact, Cashel (or *Caiseal*) means "fortress." The rock is a huge outcropping—or an *up*cropping—of limestone topped with spectacularly beautiful ruins, including what was formerly the country's finest Romanesque chapel. This was the seat of clerics and kings, a power center to rival Tara. Now, however, the two sites vie only for tourists. See p. 214.

County Wexford/Wexford Town

It's often overlooked by the tourists who pass hurriedly through it on their way to or from the ferry port at Rosslare Harbour, but Wexford radiates its own laid-back charm, with extra-friendly locals, charming towns and villages, and relaxed pubs and restaurants.

This town of 10,000 is well known in some circles: Wexford's fame originates from its annual **Opera Festival** (see "Performing Arts," below) in October, which attracts thousands of fans from all over the world, as well as its typically bloody Irish past. Over the centuries, Vikings, Gaels, and Normans all struggled for control of the little harbor, and Oliver Cromwell, needless to say, left his mark in County Wexford. The historians in Enniscorthy have some interesting stories to tell. Although the waterways that once made this town a busy port are now filled with silt thanks to the River Slaney, the waterfront and miles of coastline still define Wexford.

Getting There

BY BUS **Bus Éireann** operates daily bus service to Wexford and Rosslare from throughout the Southeast, into O'Hanrahan Station and Bus Depot, Redmond Square, Wexford (☎ **053/33114;** www.buseireann. ie). It's easy to get to Enniscorthy from Wexford Town via Bus Éireann Route 2. The ride lasts 25 minutes, and there are at least seven buses every day.

BY CAR The best way to visit the area is generally in a car. Some of the sights are nowhere near towns, and even some towns are not well served by public transport. If you're driving from Dublin and points north, take the N11 or N80 to Wexford; if you're coming from the west, take the N25 or N8. Two bridges lead into Wexford from the north—the Ferrycarrig Bridge from the main Dublin road (N11) and the Wexford Bridge from R741. The Ferrycarrig Bridge takes you into town from the west. The Wexford Bridge leads right to the heart of town along the quays.

BY FERRY Ferries from Britain run to Rosslare Harbour, 19km (12 miles) south of Wexford Town. **Stena Line** (☎ **053/61597;** www. stenaline.com) handles service from Fishguard, Wales. **Irish Ferries** (☎ **053/33158;** www.irishferries.com) has a route between Rosslare and Pembroke, Wales. (Irish Ferries also provides service from Le Havre and Cherbourg, France.)

If you're traveling between County Wexford and County Waterford, there's a waterborne shortcut. The **Passage East Car Ferry Ltd.,** Barrack Street, Passage East, County Waterford (☎ **051/382488**), operates a car-ferry service across Waterford Harbour. It links Passage East, about 16km (10 miles) east of Waterford, with Ballyhack, about 32km (20 miles) southwest of Wexford. The shortcut saves about an hour's driving time between the cities. Crossing time averages 10 minutes. It offers continuous drive-on, drive-off service, with no reservations required. Fares are €6.50 one-way and €9.50 round-trip for car and passengers; €1.50 single trip for foot passengers and €2 round-trip; €2.50 one-way and €3.50 round-trip for cyclists. It operates April to September, Monday to Saturday 7am to 10pm, Sunday 9:30am to 10pm; October to March, Monday to Saturday 7am to 8pm, Sunday 9:30am to 8pm.

BY TRAIN There's daily train service to Wexford's O'Hanrahan Station (Redmond Sq.; ☎ **053/33162;** www.irishrail.ie) from Dublin, and to Rosslare Pier by Irish Rail.

Getting Around

There is no in-town bus service in Wexford Town, but **Bus Éireann** (☎ **051/22522;** www.buseireann.ie) operates daily service between Wexford and Rosslare. Other local services operate on certain days only to Kilmore Quay, Carne, and Gorey.

The best way to see Wexford Town is to walk it. Park your car along the quays. Parking operates according to the disc system, at €.40 per hour. Discs are on sale at the tourist office and many shops. Get oriented by walking the entire length of North and South Main Street, taking time to detour up and down the alleys and lanes that cross the street. The tourist office can supply you with a free map. You may want to start out by visiting the Westgate Heritage Tower (see below), which will provide you with valuable context and background information before you explore the rest of the city.

BY BIKE Both **Haye's Cycle Shop** (108 S. Main St.; ☎ **053/22462;** 9am–6pm Mon–Sat; bikes also available Sun; €15 per day, cash deposit or ID required) and **The Bike Shop** (N. Main St.; ☎ **053/22514;** 9am–6pm Mon–Sat; €14 per day, cash deposit required) offer rentals.

THE SOUTHEAST

The Southeast

R430
N9
Carlow Town
R726
Tullow
WICKLOW
Woodenbridge
Leighlinbridge
Shillelagh
Arklow
Old Leighlin
R. Barrow
Muine Bheag
(Bagenalstown)
Bunclody
Gorey
N10
St. George's
Channel
N9
R705
CARLOW
Ferns
Borris
Graiguenamanagh
Thomastown
R. Nore
R729
Enniscorthy
St. Mullins
R. Slaney
N11
Blackwater
KILKENNY
New
Ross
N79
Clonroche
Oylgate
WEXFORD
John F.
Kennedy Park
N25
N25
Wexford
Town
Wexford
Harbour
Mullinavat
Dunganstown
R738
Cheekpoint
Ballyhack
Wellington Bridge
Rosslare
Rosslare
Harbor
Waterford
City
Passage
East
R733
Duncannon
Duncormick
To Fishguard & Pembroke →
Tramore
Fethard-on-Sea
R736
Tomhaggard
Lady's Island
Dunmore
East
Waterford Harbour
Baginlown
Head
Fornlorn Pt.
Kilmore Quay
To Roscoff & Cherbourg →
HOOK
PENINSULA
SALTEE ISLANDS

Celtic Sea

IRELAND
area of detail
Dublin

Ferry Route

0   10 mi
0   10 km

BY CAR   If you need to rent a car, contact **Budget** at the Quay, New Ross (☎ **051/421670**), Rosslare Harbour, Wexford (☎ **053/33318**), or Waterford Airport, Waterford (☎ **051/421670**); **Murrays Europcar,** Rosslare Ferryport, Rosslare (☎ **053/33634**); or **Hertz,** Ferrybank, Wexford (☎ **053/23511**), or Rosslare Harbour, Wexford (☎ **053/33238**).

BY TAXI   If you want a cab, call **Wexford Cabs** (☎ **053/23123**) or **Wexford Taxi** (☎ **053/53999**).

Basics

EMERGENCIES   In an emergency, dial ☎ **999**. The **Garda Station** (police) is on Roches Road, Wexford (☎ **053/22333**). **Wexford General Hospital** is on Richmond Terrace, Wexford (☎ **053/42233**).

INTERNET   Like most towns in Ireland today, Wexford offers free Internet access in its **Public Library** (☎ **053/21637**), which is in Selskar House, off Redmond Square just in from Commercial Quay. Its hours are Tuesday 1 to 5:30pm; Wednesday 10am to 4:30pm and 6 to 8pm; Thursday and Friday 10am to 5:30pm; and Saturday 10am to 1pm. The demand is so great, however, that it's usually necessary to call in advance to reserve time on a PC. Otherwise, Monday to Saturday between 9am and 5pm, you can go to the **Westgate Computer Centre,** Westgate (☎ **053/46291**), next to the Heritage Tower. The center offers Internet access for €3 per 30 minutes online.

LAUNDRY   Head to **Padraig's Laundrette Ltd.** (4 Mary St., next to Kirwan House; 9:30am–6:30pm Mon–Fri; Sat 9am–9pm) for the old fluff and fold.

NEWSPAPERS   The weekly *Wexford People* covers town and county events and entertainment.

PHARMACY   If you need a drugstore, try **John Fehily/The Pharmacy,** 28 S. Main St.,

Wexford (☎ **053/23163**); **Sherwood Chemist,** 2 N. Main St., Wexford (☎ **053/22875**); or **Fortune's Pharmacy,** 82 N. Main St., Wexford (☎ **053/42354**).

POST OFFICE   The **General Post Office** on Anne Street, Wexford (☎ **053/22587**), is open Monday to Saturday 9am to 5:30pm.

TOURS   Walking Tours of Wexford The Old Wexford Society is a group of locals who offer tours for €2.50 per person—check in at the tourist office to see if any are heading off soon. All tours depart from Westgate Heritage Tower.

VISITOR INFORMATION   Contact the **Wexford Tourist Office,** Crescent Quay, Wexford (☎ **053/23111**); the **Gorey Tourist Office,** Town Centre, Gorey (☎ **055/21248**); and the **Rosslare Harbour Tourist Office,** Ferry Terminal, Rosslare Harbour (☎ **053/33232**), or visit the website at www.wexford tourism.com. The Wexford and Gorey Town offices are open year-round Monday to Saturday 9am to 6pm. The Rosslare Harbour office opens daily to coincide with ferry arrivals. Seasonal offices, open June to August, are at **Enniscorthy Town Centre** (☎ **054/37596**), and at **New Ross Town Centre** (☎ **051/421857**).

Sleeping
HOSTELS

➜ **Kirwan House**   This is a famously friendly hostel, and the common rooms are just as comfortable as your family room at home. Owner Richard Barlow makes it a personal mission to keep all of his guests at ease and informed about everything there is to do and see in Wexford Town. The social vibe here can't be beat; you'll never want for a drinking buddy (or two, or more). If you're lucky, you'll catch an informal Irish language lesson going on as well. Rooms have beds for three to eight people. Two rooms have private baths; everything else is communal. There is no curfew. *3 Mary St., Wexford, County*

Wexford Town

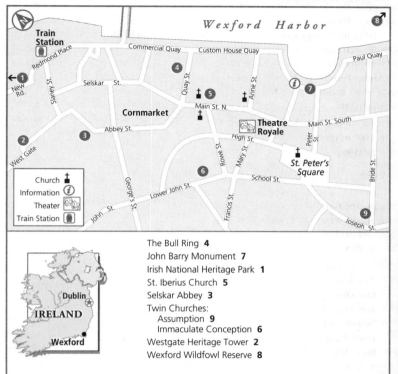

The Bull Ring **4**
John Barry Monument **7**
Irish National Heritage Park **1**
St. Iberius Church **5**
Selskar Abbey **3**
Twin Churches:
Assumption **9**
Immaculate Conception **6**
Westgate Heritage Tower **2**
Wexford Wildfowl Reserve **8**

Wexford. ☎ *053/21208. Dorms €14–€18. No credit cards. Amenities: TV lounge; kitchen.*

➜ Rosslare Harbour Hostel Sitting on a hill overlooking the ferry port, this hostel has a midnight curfew, but why would you be out later than that in this town, anyway? The facilities are purely utilitarian: sufficient, but by no means fantastic. The reception desk is open during the night to accommodate people getting off the ferries. The hostel is up the hill from the ferry port; walk up the steps from the terminal, make an immediate left after Hotel Rosslare. You can call the hostel if a pickup is necessary. *Goulding St., Rosslare Harbour, County Wexford.* ☎ *053/33399. €14–€18 dorm. Amenities: TV lounge; kitchen.*

CHEAP/DOABLE

➜ Clonard House Set on a hillside overlooking Wexford Town, Clonard House is a Georgian country home with a marvelous historic feel. At night you can unwind over an Irish coffee in the drawing room before retiring to one of the nine bedrooms, most of which have four-poster beds. Breakfast is big enough to see you through the day. *Clonard Great, Wexford Town, County Wexford.* ☎ *054/43141. €70–€80 double. Rates include full breakfast. No credit cards. Amenities: Lounge. In room: TV, hair dryer.*

➜ Clone House This 250-year-old farmhouse makes a great getaway at the edge of Enniscorthy, but you'll need a car to get here. The friendly owners know everything about

Wexford, and they'll answer all of your questions. The place is lovely and lived in. You can walk through the fields to the bank of the River Bann. *Ferns, Enniscorthy, County Wexford.* ☎ *054/66113. €80–€90 double. Rates include full breakfast. No credit cards. Closed Nov–Apr. Amenities: Nonsmoking rooms. In room: TV in 3 rooms.*

➔ **The Iona** If you choose to spend the night out in Rosslare, the best place to lay your head would have to be at this ample white Victorian. Staying here is like sleeping over at your grandma's house—that is, providing your grandma had a nice house and was fun to stay with. Everything has that lovely worn-in, well-loved feeling. The Iona offers full breakfast, and all rooms have bathrooms and televisions—but why bother with the remote when that lovely golden strand awaits? Turn left onto the main Rosslare Strand Road from the train station road; it's on the right. *Rosslare, County Wexford.* ☎ *053/32116. €80 double. Rates include full breakfast. No credit cards. Amenities: Lounge. In room: TV.*

➔ **McMenamin's Townhouse** At the edge of Wexford Town, opposite the railroad station, this Victorian-style town house is well worth the price. Guest rooms are individually furnished with Irish antiques and comfortable beds. (Not all of them have TVs, so if this is important to you, ask.) McMenamin's is run by Seamus and Kay McMenamin, who once ran a restaurant, and Kay puts her cooking skills to work on the huge, gourmet breakfasts complete with homemade bread and cereal. *3 Auburn Terrace, Redmond Rd., Wexford, County Wexford.* ☎ *053/46442. €90 double. Rates include full breakfast. Amenities: Babysitting; nonsmoking rooms. In room: TV in some rooms, tea/coffeemaker.*

SPLURGE

➔ **Woodbrook House** Hidden away at the end of a long drive through farmland and rolling hills a few miles outside of Enniscorthy, this 17th-century country house looks as if it stepped out of a Jane Austen novel. In the vast hall a wrought iron "flying staircase" curves upward with no support. Walls are done with *trompe l'oeil.* Owners Giles and Alexandra FitzHerbert run the place with calm skill, while raising four children. It's affordable elegance. *Kilnane, Enniscorthy, County Wexford.* ☎ *054/55114. www.woodbrookhouse.ie. €140 double. Closed Nov–Apr. Rates include full breakfast. Amenities: Lounge with fireplace. In room: Hair dryer, radio.*

Eating

Wexford has a great reputation for fine dining, but there aren't a ton of cheap places to eat if you're on a budget. Save money by eating in local pubs—check out the excellent (and affordable) pub menu at Tim's Tavern (p. 189) or at any of the other pubs in town.

CHEAP

➔ **The Bohemian Girl** PUB GRUB Named for an opera written by one-time Wexford resident William Balfe, this is a handsome Tudor-style pub, with lantern lights and barrel-shaped tables; this pub has excellent lunches that include fresh seafood, sandwiches, and homemade soups. *2 Selskar St., Wexford, County Wexford.* ☎ *053/24419. Main courses €2.50–€10. Daily 10:30am–11pm.*

➔ **Rendezvous Coffee and Grill** TRADITIONAL IRISH Tucked away in a dinky little mall called Lowney's, this casual diner offers the best cheap breakfast in town. It's usually packed with families with young children drawn by the good, basic food and low prices. Plunk down €4.50 for a generous plate of bacon and cabbage along with potatoes and veggies, or pay less for sandwiches and french fries. It's cheap, authentically Irish, and highly recommended by the local bacon-and-cabbage set. *In Lowney's Mall, S. Main St., Wexford, County Wexford.* ☎ *053/22220. Main courses under €8. Daily 7am–3pm.*

➜**Robertino's** ITALIAN   This cheap and cheerful diner offers all the familiar pasta and pizza dishes you would expect for around €8. Good, but not exactly a taste of Roma. *19 S. Main St., Wexford, County Wexford* ☎ *053/23334. Main courses €7–€12. Daily 11:30am–9:30pm.*

DOABLE

➜**Mangé** FRENCH FUSION   This attractive restaurant does French cooking with a global twist. The mix won't be for everybody, but many will love the roasted red pepper and fennel samosa with baby beets, or the pine-nut fritter that accompanies the filets of sole, or the roast breast of chicken with thin strips of pan-fried chorizo and savory cabbage. *100 S. Main St., Wexford, County Wexford.* ☎ *053/44033. Reservations recommended. Dinner main courses €17–€24. Tues–Fri and Sun 12:30–2:30pm; daily 6–10:30pm.*

SPLURGE

➜**Forde's Restaurant** IRISH   This place right on Wexford's lovely waterfront is an Irish bistro. Expect Dublin Bay prawns with garlic, beignets of fresh crabmeat with ginger and basil, and an excellent sirloin with garlic butter. The wine list is well chosen, the crowd happy, the service professional. *The Crescent, Wexford, County Wexford.* ☎ *053/23832. Reservations recommended. Main courses €17–€22. Daily 6–10:30pm.*

Partying

PUBS

Dim, youthful, and lively, **The Centenary Stores** (Charlotte St. near Commercial Quay, Waterford Town; ☎ **053/24424**) meets with the approval of even the hippest travelers. Chill to the strains of some kick-ass trad on Monday and Wednesday nights and on Sunday afternoons. Later on Thursday through Sunday nights the lights go down and the music goes up as it converts itself into a nightclub, spinning the usual techno and pop

(11pm–2am; cover €8). Not surprisingly, this pub's most popular with the "I've-been-living-out-of-my-backpack-for-the-past-3-months" crowd.

The next best nightspot has got to be **Mooney's Lounge** (Commercial Quay; ☎ **053/24483**). A popular pub with cheap lunches, Mooney's has live bands and frenzied dancing Thursday through Sunday nights. Most of the time there's no cover charge. Oh, and don't worry about that sign stating that only over-21s are allowed—as you'll find in many pubs and clubs in Ireland, it's just a lot of blarney.

An older, quieter, more local crowd predominates at **The Sky and Ground** (112 S. Main St. near King St., Wexford Town; ☎ **053/21273**), where you can hear live trad Sunday through Thursday nights, and sometimes Friday nights in the summertime. The music, the locals, and the quintessential Irish pub ambience make it a must.

Best known for its awesome award-winning pub food, **Tim's Tavern** (51 S. Main St., Wexford Town; ☎ **053/23861**) offers only occasional live trad sessions. Come for the delicious munchies and the colorful local crowd.

The rafters and floorboards at **Ó'Faolain's** (11 Monck St.; ☎ **053/23877**) are constantly vibrating with live music. You'll find trad on Sundays at noon, and on Friday, Saturday, and Sunday nights there's a nightclub with the typical trad music, decor, and characters swinging until 1:30am. Cover's €7, but you pay less if you've been in the pub first.

About 2 miles north of Wexford Town, the **Oak Tavern** (Wexford-Enniscorthy Rd. [N11], Ferrycarrig, County Wexford; ☎ **053/20922**) dates back over 150 years. Originally a toll-house, it overlooks the River Slaney near the Ferrycarrig Bridge. There is a riverside patio for fine days, and traditional music sessions are held most evenings in the front bar.

THE SOUTHEAST

Performing Arts

Opera fans troop to little Wexford each fall for the Wexford Festival Opera in October, but you can catch interesting theatrical performances here all year-round. Wexford is a town with a fine tradition of music and the arts. **The Theatre Royal,** High Street, Wexford (☎ 053/22144), is an ornate 19th-century theater that makes an ideal setting for opera. The festival is a unique experience, and opera lovers will be in heaven; booking for the **Opera Festival** (www.wexford opera.com) opens in June each year. Tickets range from €10 to €85.

Sightseeing

At the edge of the River Slaney, Wexford Town is a compact and congested town with quaint narrow streets—successors of the 9th-century market trails—lined with 18th-century houses and workaday shop fronts. Four quays (Custom House, Commercial, Paul, and the semicircular Crescent) run beside the water. Crescent Quay marks the center of town. One block inland Main Street is a long, narrow thoroughfare that you can easily walk. Wexford's shops and businesses are on North and South Main Street and the many smaller streets that fan out from it.

The best way to see the town is to walk it. Park your car along the quays. You'll probably need to pay to park; look for parking meters on the street (marked with big blue "P" signs) and have some coins ready. There is free parking off Redmond Square, beside the train and bus station. You'll need a car to reach County Wexford attractions outside of town.

Get started exploring by walking the length of North and South Main Street, taking time to detour up and down the alleys and lanes that crisscross it. The tourist office can supply you with a free map if you want some guidance. You may want to start out by visiting the Westgate Heritage Tower (see below), which gives you a good rundown on the history of the area.

Wexford's streets can get a little confusing; the Normans, Vikings, and Irish weren't exactly doing any city-planning together. Kinda-but-not-really parallel to the Quays, Selskar Street becomes North Main Street, which turns into South Main Street. The old Cornmarket is just off the intersection where Selskar becomes North Main, and inland of that you'll find Abbey Street. Several side streets branching off the main street lead into the residential areas, where you might find children playing with hurly sticks in the streets on warm dusky evenings.

If you have a car, or have enough time to wait for a bus, head out of Wexford Town to see sights in the surrounding area (see "Sightseeing Beyond Wexford Town," p. 192). Nearby is the Ring of Hook, which is ideal for hiking and sunbathing (see "Hiking Ring of Hook," p. 192); as well as Enniscorthy, where the ill-fated 1798 Rebellion took the lives of thousands, making it Ireland's Alamo.

FREE ➔ **The Bull Ring** In 1798 the first declaration of an Irish Republic was made here, and a statue memorializes the Irish pikemen who fought for the cause. Earlier, in the 17th century, the town square was a venue for bull baiting, a sport introduced by the butcher's guild. Tradition maintained that, after a match, the hide of the ill-fated bull was presented to the mayor and the meat was used to feed the poor. Today, activity at the ring is much tamer: a weekly outdoor market, open Friday and Saturday from 10am to 4:30pm. *Off N. Main St., Wexford, County Wexford. Free admission.*

➔ **Irish National Heritage Park** This 35-acre living-history park on the banks of the River Slaney outside of Wexford Town provides a good, if a bit plastic, introduction to life in ancient Ireland, from the Stone Age to the Norman invasion. It's deeply touristy, but generally well done. The 20-minute video you can watch at the start is engaging and informative, but can't hold a candle to a guided tour by head guide Jimmy O'Rourke, who really brings it all to life. There's also a nature trail and interpretive center, gift shop, and cafe. *Off the Dublin-Wexford Rd. (N11), Ferrycarrig, County Wexford.* ☎ *053/20733. www.inhp. com. Admission €7.50 adults, €6 students. Mar–Oct daily 9:30am–6:30pm.*

→**John Barry Monument** This bronze statue, a gift from the American people in 1956, faces out to the sea as a tribute to John Barry, a favorite son who became the father of the American navy. Born at Ballysampson, Tacumshane, 16km (10 miles) southeast of Wexford Town, Barry emigrated to the colonies while in his teens and volunteered to fight in the American Revolution. One of the U.S. Navy's first commissioned officers, he became captain of the *Lexington.* In 1797 George Washington appointed him commander-in-chief of the U.S. Navy. *Crescent Quay, Wexford, County Wexford.*

FREE →**St. Iberius Church** Erected in 1660, St. Iberius was built on hallowed ground—the land has been used for houses of worship since Norse times. *N. Main St., Wexford, County Wexford.* ☎ *053/43013. Free admission; donations welcome. May–Sept daily 10am–5pm; Oct–Apr Tues–Sat 10am–3pm.*

FREE →**Selskar Abbey** This abbey dates from early in the 12th century, and it has often been the scene of synods and parliaments. The first Anglo-Irish treaty was signed here in 1169, and it's said that Henry II spent the Lent of 1172 at the abbey doing penance for having Thomas à Becket beheaded. Although the abbey is mostly in ruins, its choir is part of a Church of Ireland edifice, and a portion of the original tower is a vesting room. The adjoining graveyard has suffered a disturbing amount of vandalism over the years. The entrance most likely to be open is to the left of Westgate. *Off Temperance Row at Westgate St., Wexford, County Wexford. Free admission.*

FREE →**The Twin Churches: Church of the Assumption and Church of the Immaculate Conception** These twin Gothic structures (1851–58) were designed by architect Robert Pierce, a pupil of Augustus Pugin. Their 69m (226-ft.) spires dominate Wexford's skyline. Mosaics on the main door of both churches list relevant names and dates. *Bride and Rowe sts., Wexford, County Wexford.* ☎ *053/22055. Free admission; donations welcome. Daily 8am–6pm.*

→**Westgate Heritage Tower** Westgate once guarded the western entrance of Wexford Town. Sir Stephen Devereux built it in the 13th century on instructions from King Henry. Like other town gates, it consisted of a toll-taking area, cells for offenders, and accommodations for guards. Fully restored and reopened in 1992 as a heritage center, it presents artifacts and displays that delve into Wexford's complex and turbulent history. If you see this presentation prior to exploring the city, your ambles will likely be a good deal more meaningful. *Westgate St., Wexford, County Wexford.* ☎ *053/46506. Audiovisual show €3 adults, €1.50 students. May–Aug Mon–Fri 10am–6pm, Sat–Sun noon–6pm; Sept–Apr Mon–Fri 10am–5pm.*

FREE →**Wexford Wildfowl Reserve** This national nature reserve is part of the unfortunately named North Slob, adjacent to Wexford Harbour, 5km (3 miles) east of Wexford Town. About 10,000 Greenland white-fronted geese—more than one-third of the world's population—spend the winter here, as do brent geese, Bewick's swans, and wigeons. The reserve has a visitor center, an audiovisual program, a new exhibition hall, and an observation tower and blinds. *North Slob, Wexford, County Wexford.* ☎ *053/23129. Free admission. Apr 16–Sept daily 9am–6pm; Oct–Apr 15 daily 10am–5pm.*

Hiking Ring of Hook

The Hook Peninsula in southwest County Wexford is a favorite of walkers, hikers, and beach lovers, and it's easy to see why. It's a gorgeous setting of rocky headlands and secluded beaches stretching between Bannow Bay and Waterford Harbour. In medieval times these were critical harbors for travelers from Britain, and plenty of archaeological sites remain as memorials to that. The route described below will guide you through a driving or biking tour, and hikers can see most of the places listed from the Wexford Coastal Pathway.

Start your exploration of the peninsula at the town of Wellington Bridge. Just west of town on R733 is a roadside stop on the left by a cemetery; from here you can look across Bannow Bay to the ruins of Clonmines—a Norman village established in the 13th century. It's a fine example of a walled medieval settlement, with remains of two churches, three tower houses, and an Augustinian priory. You can drive to the ruins—just follow R733 another mile west to a left turn posted for the Wicklow Coastal Pathway, and continue straight on this road where the Coastal Pathway turns right. The ruins are on private land, so you should ask permission at the farmhouse at the end of the road.

Continuing west on R733, turn left on R734 at the sign for the Ring of Hook, and turn right at the sign for Tintern Abbey (see below). The abbey was founded by the monks of Tintern in South Wales in the 13th century. The grounds are beautiful and contain a lovely stone bridge across a narrow stretch of sea that cries out to be photographed.

At Baginbun Head there's a great secluded beach nestling against the cliffs from which you can see the outline of the Norman fortifications on the head.

The tip of the peninsula, with its line of low cliffs, eroded in places for blowholes, has been famous for shipwrecks since Norman times. There has long been a lighthouse on this site; the present structure consists of a massive base, built in the early 13th century.

The Ring of Hook road returns along the western side of the peninsula, passing the beaches at Booley Bay and Dollar Bay. On a hilltop overlooking the town of Duncannon is a fort built in 1588 to protect Waterford Harbour from the Spanish Armada. Just north of Duncannon, along the coast at the village of Ballyhack, a ferry runs to County Waterford, and at Ballyhack, a Knights Hospitallers castle stands on a hill.

A visit to the Hook Peninsula wouldn't be complete without a stop at Dunbrody Abbey, in a field beside the road about 6.5km (4 miles) north of Duncannon. The abbey, founded in 1170, is a magnificent ruin and one of the largest Cistercian abbeys in Ireland. Tours are sometimes available; ask at the visitor center across the road.

Sightseeing Beyond Wexford Town

➜ **Ballyhack Castle**   On a steep slope overlooking the Waterford estuary, about 32km (20 miles) west of Wexford, this large tower house was built around 1450 by the Knights Hospitallers of St. John, one of the two great military orders of the Crusades. The castle has been restored and turned into a heritage information center, with displays on the Crusader knights, medieval monks, and Norman nobles. *Off R733, Ballyhack, County Wexford.* ☎ *051/389468. Admission €1.50.*

€.75 *students. June–Sept daily 9am–6pm. Closed Oct–May.*

➔**Enniscorthy Castle/Wexford County Museum** Overlooking the River Slaney at Enniscorthy, 24km (15 miles) north of Wexford Town, this rugged castle tower was built by the Prendergast family in the 13th century. It's said that the poet Edmund Spenser once owned it briefly. Remarkably well preserved, it's now home to the Wexford County Museum, which focuses on the area's history and traditions. Displays include an old Irish farm kitchen, early modes of travel, and items connected with Wexford's role in Ireland's struggle for independence, especially the 1798 and 1916 risings. *Castle Hill, Enniscorthy, County Wexford.* ☎ *054/35926. Admission €4.50, €3.50 students. June–Sept daily 10am–6pm; Oct–Nov and Feb–May daily 2–5:30pm; Dec–Jan Sun 2–5pm.*

FREE ➔**Ferns Castle** These atmospheric ruins are all that's left of a once-grand castle built in 1221. Sitting at the north end of the village of Ferns, the castle is believed to have been the old fortress of Dermot Mac-Murrough. There's still a moat and walls, as well as a tower, which offers excellent views from the top. If you do climb up, check out the hole at the top just to the left of the door— it was a murder hole, through which defenders could pour hot oil or drop heavy stones onto invaders below. The castle was destroyed in the mid–17th century by Parliamentarians led by Sir Charles Coote, who also ordered almost all of the local residents killed. *Ferns, County Wexford. Free admission. Open dawn–dusk, year-round.*

➔**Irish Agricultural Museum and Famine Exhibition** The importance of farming in Wexford's history is the focus of this museum, on the Johnstown Castle Demesne 6km (3³/₄ miles) southwest of Wexford Town. In historic farm buildings, the museum contains exhibits on planting, and the diverse activities of the farm household.

Sadly, the 19th-century Gothic Revival castle on the grounds is not open to the public beyond the entrance hall, which holds an information booth. Still, the grounds are perfect for picnics. *Johnstown Castle, Bridgetown Rd., off Wexford-Rosslare Rd. (N25), Wexford, County Wexford.* ☎ *053/42888. Admission to museum €5, €3 students; gardens €2, €.50 students. No credit cards. Museum June–Aug Mon–Fri 9am–5pm, Sat–Sun 11am–5pm; Apr–May and Sept–Nov Mon–Fri 9am–12:30pm and 1:30–5pm, Sat–Sun 2–5pm; Dec–Mar Mon–Fri 9am–12:30pm and 1:30–5pm. Gardens year-round daily 9am–5:30pm.*

➔**J.F.K. Trust Dunbrody** Housed in twin 18th-century grain mills, this intelligent, absorbing center tells the story of the Irish diaspora, beginning with the monks who went to Europe in the 6th century and continuing to the present day, using a variety of interactive and live-action methods. It is an interesting and sometimes heartbreaking tale. A section of the center is devoted to John Kennedy, who was (in case you haven't noticed yet) descended from a County Wexford family.

The magnificent tall ship *Dunbrody*—458 tons and 53m (174 ft.) long—is also here, moored on the New Ross quays as a floating exhibition center. *The Quay, New Ross, County Wexford.* ☎ *051/425239. www.dunbrody.com. Admission €6.50, €4 students. Sept–June Mon–Fri 10am–5pm, Sat–Sun noon–5pm; July–Aug daily 9am–6pm.*

➔**John F. Kennedy Arboretum** As the name implies, this arboretum, about 20 miles west of Wexford, is dedicated to the former U.S. President. The hook is that the property overlooks the simple thatched cottage where JFK's great-grandfather was born. Plants and trees from five continents grow here. A hilltop observation point (at 266m/872 ft.) presents a sweeping view of County Wexford and five neighboring counties, the Saltee Islands, the Comeragh Mountains, and parts

THE SOUTHEAST

The Rebellion at Vinegar Hill

Of the many rebel groups that took hold in the late 18th century, the Society of United Irishmen, founded in 1791, was the most ahead of its time. Led by Wolfe Tone, it welcomed Catholics, Protestants, and dissenters alike in its effort to free Ireland from England's yoke. The British were deeply suspicious of the group's motives, not least because Tone was not shy about involving the French, England's enemy, in the battle. In fact, in 1796, the French government sent 14,000 soldiers to join a United Irishmen uprising, but poor weather forced the boats back.

In 1798, the group tried again. Battles were fought in Kildare, Carlow, Wicklow, and Meath, and quickly won by English forces. In Wexford, though, feelings were very high, and the rebels were victorious. A detachment of 100 English-led soldiers was cut down at Oulart, and the city of Wexford burned. Wexford became the center of the battle in part because of the behavior of English-led forces. Throughout that spring there had been fury in Wexford because of torture of residents, and house burnings conducted by the loyalist North Cork Militia. Once the rebellion began, Wexford residents heard of summary executions of suspected United Irishmen in Wicklow and at the edge of Wexford. In the end, they knew they were fighting for their lives.

On May 29, led by Father John Murphy, a priest who reluctantly agreed to take over the leadership of the group, insurgents headed to Wexford Town. The group, armed with muskets and pikes, gathered size as it moved, and by the time it reached the town it had 15,000 fighters. The town fell quickly. Exhilarated, the group attempted to take the entire county, but its efforts to take other towns failed in places like Arklow and New Ross.

of the rivers Suir, Nore, and Barrow. This one's for true JFK fans. *Off Duncannon Rd. (R733), New Ross, County Wexford.* ☎ *051/388171. Admission €2.75, €1.25 students. Apr and Sept daily 10am–6:30pm; May–Aug daily 10am–8pm; Oct–Mar daily 10am–5pm.*

→ **The National 1798 Visitor Centre** It's a bit kid-targeted, but this center is still a good place to learn about what happened in the Vinegar Hill Rebellion of 1798. It uses interactive displays to give insight into the birth of modern democracy—in Ireland and elsewhere. Computers, a surprisingly moving film about the doomed uprising, and an array of artifacts help bring the events home in an interesting way. *Millpark Rd., Enniscorthy, County Wexford.* ☎ *054/37596. Admission €6, €3.50 students. Mon–Fri 9:30am–6pm; Sat–Sun 11am–6pm.*

→ **SS *Dunbrody* Emigrant Ship** A full-scale reconstruction of a ship built in 1845 and ultimately used to carry emigrants to the U.S. at the height of the Great Famine, this is an interesting way to step back into that turbulent history. There's a visitor center on board that explains the ship and the story of the mass migration in which it took part. There's also a database of Irish immigration to the U.S., and you can look your family up. *On the quay, New Ross, County Wexford.* ☎ *051/425239. Admission €6 adults, €3.50 students. Apr–Sept daily 9am–5pm; Oct–Mar daily noon–5pm.*

→ **Tintern Abbey** In a lovely rural setting overlooking Bannow Bay, Tintern Abbey was founded in the 12th century by William Marshall, the Earl of Pembroke, as thanks to God after he nearly died at sea. The early monks

The English were shocked by the rebels' success at Wexford Town, but were soon emboldened by their subsequent failures, and they marched out to take them on. The troops arrived at the rebel encampment, on Vinegar Hill at the edge of Enniscorthy, on June 21. The rebels knew they were coming, and they prepared to take them on. Battle began at dawn, and lasted less than 2 hours. The rebels were mercilessly shelled, and their poor weapons were no match for the English artillery. More than 500 died in the battle, but that was nothing compared to what happened next.

Weeks of murder and atrocities followed, as loyalist troops raped and pillaged ruthlessly, killing an estimated 25,000 men, women, and children. Protestant leaders of the rebellion were beheaded, and their heads mounted on spikes outside the courthouse in Wexford Town. Father Murphy was stripped, flogged, hanged, and beheaded. His corpse was burned in a barrel. His head was spiked outside the local Catholic church, and Catholics in town were forced to open their windows so they could smell his body burn.

The horrific massacre became a rallying cry for all subsequent Irish rebellions, and Wexford is forever associated with sacrifice and violence.

Vinegar Hill is at the east end of Enniscorthy, and although there's little there to memorialize the rebellion, it's a peaceful place with beautiful views. You reach it by crossing the bridge in town, and taking the first right after Treacy's Hotel, then following the signs. There's also an excellent hour-long walking tour that includes the 1798 history, with lots of fascinating details. Contact **Castle Hill Crafts** (☎ **054/36800**) for details, or ask at the tourist office in Wexford Town.

THE SOUTHEAST

were Cistercians from Tintern in South Wales (hence the name). The parts that remain—nave, chancel, tower, chapel, and cloister—date from the early 13th century, though they have been much altered since then. The grounds are extraordinarily beautiful and include a stone bridge spanning a narrow sea inlet. There's a small coffee shop on the premises if the caffeine situation gets desperate. *Saltmills, New Ross, County Wexford.* ☎ *051/562650. Admission €5, €1 students. Mid-May to mid-Oct daily 10am–6pm. Signposted 19km (12 miles) south of New Ross off of R733.*

➜ **Yola Farmstead** A voluntary community project, here's yet another historic learning center/theme park, this one depicting a Wexford farming community as it would have been 200 or more years ago. It has the obligatory thatched-roof buildings, bread- and butter-making demonstrations (in the summer), and craftspeople at work blowing and hand-cutting crystal at Wexford Heritage Crystal, a glass-production enterprise. It's undeniably touristy but can be interesting. The Genealogy Center (☎ 053/31177) is open daily 9am to 5pm. Knowledge doesn't come cheap—to search the history of your Irish name will cost €25. *16km (10 miles) south of Wexford Town, 2.4km (1½ miles) from Rosslare Ferryport, Wexford-Rosslare Rd. (N25), Tagoat, County Wexford.* ☎ *053/32610. Admission €6 adults, €4.50 students. June–Sept daily 10am–5pm; Mar–Apr and Nov Mon–Fri 9:30am–4:30pm. Closed other months.*

Playing Outside

BEACHES County Wexford's beaches at Courtown, Curracloe, Duncannon, and Rosslare are ideal for walking, jogging, and swimming. Ever see *Saving Private Ryan?*

Remember that pretty beach where the D-Day troops landed in the extremely bloody first scene? No, it's not actually in Normandy. It's Curracloe Beach, at 19km (12 miles) long the longest beach in Ireland. Walking out to Curracloe from town takes about 4 hours, but it's assuredly lovely; you can also bike out, or take a taxi one or both ways. For directions, check with the Wexford Tourist Office or ask at Kirwan House, the local hostel (see "Sleeping," p. 186). Kirwan House also offers guided walks from town to other scenic areas around Wexford.

BICYCLING   You can rent mountain bikes in Wexford Town at **Hayes Cycle Shop,** 108 S. Main St. (☎ **053/22462**). From Wexford, the road north up the coast through Curracloe to Blackwater is a scenic day trip. For complete 1- or 2-week cycling holidays in the Southeast, contact Don Smith at **Celtic Cycling,** Lorum Old Rectory, Bagenalstown (☎ **059/977-5282**).

DIVING   The Kilmore Quay area, south of Wexford Town, offers some of the most spectacular diving in Ireland, especially around the Saltee Islands and Conningbeg rocks. For all your diving needs, consult the **Pier House Diving Centre** (☎ **053/29703**).

FISHING   The town of Kilmore Quay, south of Wexford Town on R739, is a center for sea angling in Wexford. Several people offer boats for hire, with all the necessary equipment; Dick Hayes runs Kilmore Quay Boat Charters (☎ **053/29704**) and is skipper of the Cottage Lady. The most popular rivers for fishing are the Barrow and the Slaney, where the sea trout travel upstream from mid-June to the end of August.

HANG-GLIDING   The rounded granite form of Mount Leinster, the highest in Wexford, is a landmark throughout the region. A popular hang-gliding spot, the summit is always windy, and often shrouded in clouds. If you can get to the top on a clear day, however, it

will be an experience you won't soon forget. To get there, follow signs for the Mount Leinster Scenic Drive from the sleepy town of Kiltealy on the eastern slopes of the mountain. Soon you will begin climbing the exposed slopes; don't get too distracted by the dazzling views because the road is twisting and quite narrow in places. There's a parking area at the highest point of the auto road, and a paved access road (closed to cars) continues for over 2km (1 1/4 miles) to the summit. From the top you can scramble along the ridge to the east, known as Black Rock Mountain. To return, continue along the Scenic Drive, which ends a few miles outside the town of Bunclody. The only catch is you either have to have a hang glider of your own, or know somebody who does.

HIKING   Along the entire coastline, you'll see brown signs with a picture of a hiker on them. The signs mark the Wexford Coastal Path, along which you can walk the coast via pristine beaches and country lanes. Unfortunately, the roads are often too busy for it to be a good idea to walk the whole route—especially on the bypass around Wexford Town. The markers are handy, however, for shorter walks between Wexford's beaches. In the northern part of the county, the section of beach from Clogga Head (Co. Wicklow) to Tara Hill is especially lovely, as is the walk to the top of Tara Hill, which offers views across sloping pastures to the sea. Farther south, the path veers off the roads and sticks to the beach from Cahore Point south to Raven Point and from Rosslare Harbour to Kilmore Quay.

There's a lovely coastal walk near the town of Wexford in the Raven Nature Reserve, an area of forested dunes and uncrowded beaches. To get there, take R741 north out of Wexford, turn right on R742 to Curracloe just out of town, and in the village of Curracloe turn right and continue for just over a mile to the beach parking lot. The nature reserve is to your right. You can get there by car, driving a half-mile south, or walk the distance along the beach. The beach extends another 5km (3 miles) to Raven Point, where at low tide you can see the remains of a shipwreck, half-buried in the sand.

On the border between counties Wexford and Carlow the long, rounded ridge of peaks are the Blackstairs Mountains, which offer plenty of walks in an area remarkably unspoiled by tourism. As of yet, these mountain trails are completely unspoiled by tourism, and there are beautiful walks in several directions. Pick up a guide called *Walking the Blackstairs* at the Wexford tourist office that includes trail descriptions along with information about plant and wild life.

Blackstairs is a vast landscape flooded with peaceful farming communities. The best walks in the area are the "Blackstairs Walk" (10km round-trip) or the "Sculloge Gap" walk (26km round-trip). Half- or full-day walks can be planned. To join in guided walks, ask at the Wexford Tourist office.

The Blackstairs reward you not only with virgin forest walks but also with panoramic views in most directions. About 3 miles upriver of Graiguenamanagh is the hamlet of Borris, a good center for exploring the mountains. There are rugged heathery slopes in all directions, and the most luxuriant forest cover on the eastern slopes.

The area is presided over by Mount Leinster at 783m (2,610 feet). If you have a car, you can actually follow the roadway right up the summit of Mount Leinster, but the Wexford Walking Club strongly encourages people to hike up instead. Most trails are rated easy, but there are challenging routes if you are so inclined.

HORSEBACK RIDING   Horsetown House ✻, Foulksmills (☎ **051/565771**), offers riding lessons by the hour or in a variety of packages that include meals and lodging. One of the better residential equestrian centers in Ireland, it caters particularly to families and children. For more experienced riders, lessons in jumping and dressage are available, as is a game called "polocross," which combines polo and lacrosse. Training in hunting and admission to the hunt can also be arranged. Riding is €25 per hour; accommodations start at €100 for a double room, including an all-organic breakfast.

Shopping

Shops in Wexford are open Monday to Thursday 9am to 5:30pm, Friday and Saturday 9am to 6pm; some shops stay open until 8pm on Friday.

➜**Barkers**   Established in 1848, this shop has an admirable selection of Waterford crystal, Belleek china, and Royal Irish Tara china, as well as Irish linens and international products such as Aynsley, Wedgwood, and Lladró. *36–40 S. Main St., Wexford, County Wexford.* ☎ *053/23159.*

➜**Byrne's Wexford Bookshop**   This extensive and bustling emporium—spread out across three levels—offers much more than books. There's a long wall full of magazines and newspapers, a selection of stationery, and a slew of toys. *31 N. Main St., Wexford, County Wexford.* ☎ *053/22223.*

➜**Wexford Silver**   Pat Dolan and his sons create gold, silver, and bronze pieces by hand using traditional tools and techniques. They trace their silversmithing connections back to 1647. Open 10am to 5:30pm. *115 N. Main St., Wexford, County Wexford.* ☎ *053/21933.*

➜**The Wool Shop**   If you still haven't found your hand-knitted souvenirs, head here. The selection runs from caps to sweaters and jackets, with tweeds, linens, and knitting yarns. *39 S. Main St., Wexford, County Wexford.* ☎ *053/22247.*

County Waterford/Waterford City

If you're headed for Waterford, chances are—well, it's as certain as the Irish love their Guinness, really—that you're here for the crystal. Most travelers, and natives for that matter, find this major working port city of the Southeast cloaked in a vague cloud of drabness, and nobody really opts to linger for too long. The industrial waterfront does hide a charming old, narrow-laned town center with an identifiable youth scene, but Waterford is hardly the most exciting or colorful city in Ireland—not by a long shot. You probably won't spend more than a day here; you'll soon be off to prettier scenery and livelier goings-on, though very likely laden down with the crystal vase you promised to buy for your grandma (although it'd probably be better to get it shipped home—or to buy it at your last shopping stop before you leave the country, as you can find it everywhere, and at the same price).

The Crystal Factory does have an incredible staff of craftspeople, and you can watch them working their glassblowing magic on factory tours. Founded in 1783, the place supplied all the decanters the British aristocracy could hoist until the Famine hit; the factory closed in 1851 and wasn't reopened until 1947.

There are also a few great pubs around here worth checking out, and the Waterford coastline makes a nice side trip. It might not have all the charm of Kilkenny, but Waterford City's air is also distinctly medieval. Chunks of the original city wall, built by the Vikings in the 700s, are still standing, and one of the coolest pubs in town, T & H Doolan's (see below), actually incorporates the battlements into its building structure.

If you have a car you can head south of Waterford to the pretty village of Dunmore East and nearby Portally Cove, Ireland's only Amish-Mennonite community; Dungarvan, a major town with a fine harbor; Ardmore, an idyllic beach resort; and Passage East, a tiny seaport from which you can catch a ferry across the harbor and cut your driving time from Waterford to Wexford in half. Of all the coastal towns in County Waterford, Ardmore stands out as the perfect getaway. It has an ancient monastic site, a pristine blue-flag beach, a stunning cliff walk, a fine crafts shop, an excellent restaurant, and comfortable seaside accommodations.

In northwest County Waterford, the Comeragh Mountains are a favorite with hikers and bikers—they have beautiful trails, especially the short trek to Mahon Falls.

Getting There & Getting Around

To see most of Waterford's sights (except the Waterford Crystal factory), it's best to walk. You can park along the quays, and pay at the nearest machine. You'll need a car to reach the Waterford Crystal and County Waterford attractions outside of town.

BY PLANE   **Little Waterford Airport,** off R675, Waterford (☎ 051/875589; www.fly waterford.com), is served by **Aer Arran** (☎ 011/353-6170-44280 from the U.S., 818/210210 from Ireland, or 0800/587-23-24 from the U.K.; www.aerarann.com) from London's Luton airport.

BY BUS   **Bus Éireann** operates daily service into Plunkett Station Depot, Waterford (☎ 051/879000; www.buseireann.ie), from Dublin, Limerick, and other major cities throughout Ireland.

Bus Éireann operates daily bus service within Waterford and its environs. The flat fare is €1.10. Taxi ranks are outside Plunkett Rail Station and along the Quay opposite the Granville Hotel. If you need to call a taxi, try **Rapid Cabs** (☎ 051/858585), **Metro Cabs** (☎ 051/857157), or **Waterford Taxi Co-op** (☎ 051/877778).

BY CAR Four major roads lead into Waterford: N25 from Cork and the south, N24 from the west, N19 from Kilkenny and points north, and N25 from Wexford.

To rent a car, contact **Budget Rent A Car,** Waterford Airport (☎ **051/421670**).

BY FERRY The **Passage East Car Ferry Ltd.,** Barrack Street, Passage East, County Waterford (☎ **051/382480** or 051/382488), operates a car-ferry service across Waterford Harbour. It links Passage East, about 16km (10 miles) east of Waterford, with Ballyhack, about 32km (20 miles) southwest of Wexford. This shortcut saves about an hour's driving time. The crossing time averages 10 minutes. It's continuous drive-on, drive-off service, with no reservations required.

BY TRAIN **Irish Rail** offers daily service from Dublin and other points into Plunkett Station, at Ignatius Rice Bridge, Waterford (☎ **051/873401;** www.irishrail.ie).

Basics

EMERGENCIES Dial ☎ **999** in an emergency. **Garda Headquarters** (☎ **051/305300**) is the local police station. **Holy Ghost Hospital** is on Cork Road (☎ **051/374397**), and **Waterford Regional Hospital** is on Dunmore Road (☎ **051/848000**).

INTERNET The **Voyager Internet Cafe,** Parnell Court, off Parnell Street (☎ **051/843843**), isn't actually a cafe, but it does provide high-speed access with all the peripherals for €1.80 per 15 minutes. Open Monday to Saturday 11am to 11pm. You can use the computers at the **Waterford Library** (Ladylane, no street number; ☎ **051/873-506;** 11am–1pm 2:30–5:30pm Tues, Thurs, Sat; 2–8pm Wed, Fri; closed Mon) for free, but you've got to book at least an hour in advance. The computers aren't as speedy as those at the Voyager, but large windows letting in natural light and potted plants on the windowsill make a considerably nicer environment in which to immerse yourself in cyberspace.

PHARMACY If you need a drugstore, try **Gallagher's Pharmacy,** 29 Barronstrand St. (☎ **051/878103**); or **Mulligan's Chemists,** 40–41 Barronstrand St. (☎ **051/875211**).

POST OFFICE The **General Post Office** on Parade Quay (☎ **051/317312**) is open Monday to Friday 9am to 5:30pm, Saturday 9am to 1pm.

VISITOR INFORMATION The **Waterford Tourist Office** is at 41 The Quay, Waterford (☎ **051/875788;** www.waterfordtourism. com). It's open April to September, Monday to Saturday 9am to 6pm; October, Monday to Saturday 9am to 5pm; November to March, Monday to Friday 9am to 5pm. The year-round office in The Courthouse, off the Square in Dungarvan (☎ 058/41741), keeps comparable hours. The seasonal tourist office on the Square at Tramore (☎ 051/381572) is open from mid-June to August, Monday to Saturday 10am to 6pm.

Sleeping

Waterford is very much lacking in good, affordable accommodations, perhaps because there's just not enough demand. You can choose between a few really fancy (and really expensive) hotels, a small handful of mostly mediocre B&Bs, or a couple of lukewarm hostels, but that's about it. You probably won't be spending more than a night here anyway, though, so it's not such a big deal.

HOSTELS

➔**Barnacle's Viking House Hostel** This is the comfiest and biggest hostel in town. And given that it has 100 beds, it's unlikely you'll be turned away. It's the main attraction for backpackers when it comes to places to stay in the area, so it's a good place to meet other travelers. Its size means there are plenty of extras: continental breakfast is included, along with 24-hour reception, a bureau de change, relatively spacious dorm rooms (many with en suite bathrooms), and a

THE SOUTHEAST

nice common room with a 16th-century fireplace the owners unearthed while setting up the place. *Greyfriars/Coffee House Lane, The Quay, Waterford, County Waterford.* ☎ *051/ 853-827. €14–€17 dorms. Amenities: Bureau de change; kitchen; laundry; TV lounge.*

→ **Waterford Hostel** This tiny little hostel only has 22 beds, and is only open in the summer, but it's a good alternative if the Viking House just seems too big for you. Its small and simple rooms are tiny but clean. There is no lockout or curfew, and the hostel is a 5-minute walk from the city center. *70 Manor St., Waterford, County Waterford.* ☎ *051/850-163. €12–€15 dorm. Amenities: TV lounge.*

CHEAP/DOABLE

→ **Aglish House** You need a car to stay here; if you have one, it's worth driving out of town to find this B&B in a 17th-century manor home, alongside a working dairy farm. Tom and Teresa Moore are the friendly owners, and breakfast is especially fresh and good. This is a favorite place for cyclists, as the Moores are avid cyclists, well versed in local routes. A short walk from the house are the Kiltera Ogham stones, ancient inscribed pillars; also nearby is the lovely Blackwater estuary. A short drive brings you to the coast or the Knockmealdown Mountains. *Aglish, Cappoquin, County Waterford.* ☎ *024/96191. www.aglishhouse.com. €80 double. Rates include full breakfast. In room: TV.*

→ **An Bohreen** This little B&B is sweetly done, with a fire in the lounge, excellent food, and charming guest rooms with pine furniture, polished wood floors, and white bed covers. In fact, if you can afford it, don't miss dinner. You'll feast on Dungarvan Bay fish soup, prawns and crab on brown bread, roasted lamb and homemade desserts. *Killineen W., Dungarvan, County Waterford.* ☎ *051/291010. www.anbohreen.com. €68– €72 double. Rates include full breakfast.*

Dinner €32. Amenities: Sitting room. In room: Tea/coffeemaker.

→ **Beechwood** This place is among the best of the bed-and-breakfasts in Waterford City, for several reasons: The charming, traditional rooms are quiet, thanks to a good old-fashioned home-and-B&B combo; and the square, spread out in front of Christ Church Cathedral, allows only pedestrian traffic. The owners are friendly, the beds are comfortable, and the breakfasts are excellent. Surely you don't want more than that? *7 Cathedral Sq. Follow Henrietta St. off the Quay, Waterford, County Waterford.* ☎ *051/876-677. €60 double. No credit cards. Breakfast is included in the rate. Amenities: TV lounge; hair dryer.*

→ **Brown's Townhouse** This friendly Victorian town-house B&B is a good value within walking distance of the center of Waterford town. Owners Leslie and Barbara Brown collect Irish modern art, and colorful paintings hang in every room. Bedrooms are spacious, with big windows and pleasant, if slightly worn, decor. The best room has a roof garden terrace. Breakfast is a grand affair, with pancakes, homemade breads and preserves, fruit salad, and a full Irish breakfast. *29 S. Parade, Waterford, County Waterford.* ☎ *051/870594. www.brownstownhouse.com. €90–€100 double. Rates include full breakfast. Amenities: Nonsmoking rooms. In room: TV.*

SPLURGE

→ **Waterford Castle** There's something magical about taking a boat back home to your castle at the end of the night. And this is an outstanding castle: along with a Norman keep it also has two Elizabethan wings, leaded roof, mullioned windows, and fairy-tale turrets. Dating back 800 years, it's a deeply secluded place, on a private island in the River Suir, surrounded by woodland . . . and an 18-hole championship golf course. It's 3km (2 miles) south of Waterford, accessible only

Waterford City

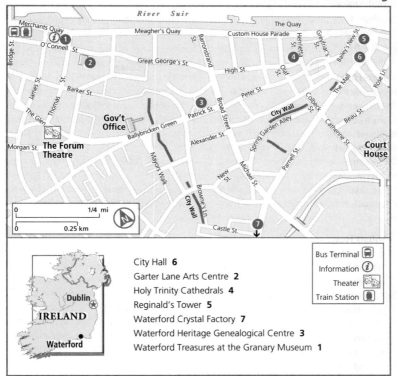

City Hall **6**
Garter Lane Arts Centre **2**
Holy Trinity Cathedrals **4**
Reginald's Tower **5**
Waterford Crystal Factory **7**
Waterford Heritage Genealogical Centre **3**
Waterford Treasures at the Granary Museum **1**

Bus Terminal
Information
Theater
Train Station

by the castle's private boat. Inside are oak-paneled walls, colorful tapestries, and huge stone fireplaces. Rooms have four-poster or canopied beds and claw-foot bathtubs. Despite all that, the atmosphere is not over the top; staff are friendly and will (for a fee) arrange horseback riding, fishing, watersports, and other local activities. *The Island, Ballinakill, Waterford, County Waterford.* ☎ *051/878203. www.waterfordcastle.com. €195–€265 double. Breakfast €16. Amenities: Restaurant (international); bar; concierge; 18-hole championship golf course; laundry and valet service; room service; tennis courts. In room: TV, CD player, hair dryer, radio.*

Eating

There's not exactly an abundance of inexpensive places to eat in this city. Well, there are several places, but most lack atmosphere—unless you consider the Golden Arches to be atmosphere. The eminently classy Café Luna and the California Café are your best choices if you don't want fries with that. You can also find cheap but yummy pub grub anywhere on Barronstrand Street. Try Egan's, T & H Doolan's, or Muldoon's on John Street.

Generic but inexpensive spots for lunch include the two locations of the local chain **Pages** (upstairs at **The Book Centre,** Barronstrand St.; 5 S. Main St.; ☎ **051/873-823**).

CHEAP

➜ **Café Luna** CAFE   Generally known as Waterford's hippest spot for coffee, salad, or a sandwich, and some laid-back conversation, Luna attracts what few bohemians there are in this city—and a few wannabes, too. Don't come exclusively for the food, though; while it's decent, by the end of the day the kitchen can be out of whatever it is you want to order—and this place is open till 3:30am most nights of the week. And you'll have to order something else, too, if you're going to stay long enough to hear that Eric Clapton CD on the stereo revert back to track one—they don't like loiterers here. *53 John St., Waterford, County Waterford.* ☎ *051/834-539. Main courses €5–€12. Mon-Wed 7am-midnight; Thurs-Sun 7am-3:30am.*

➜ **Café Suí Síos** CAFE   Try "sitting down" (that's what the name means in Irish) at this cafe, which offers an inexpensive yet thorough breakfast menu; lunch and dinner options consist mainly of sandwiches and pasta. Set on the town's main street, it's a sunny, bustling spot, ideal for a healthy breakfast of muesli, yogurt, and fresh fruit for a few euros. Carnivores will want to order the typical full Irish breakfast for a couple euros more. *54 High St., Waterford, County Waterford.* ☎ *051/841-063. All items under €12. Daily 6:30am–9:30pm.*

➜ **California Café** CAFE   Chill to the strains of Tracy Chapman and soak up the bright decor at this casual cafe, which offers tasty food at dirt cheap prices. Try a sandwich named "Hollywood," "Beverly Hills," or "Los Angeles" (the menu's as cheesy as Monterey Jack), or try the potato and leek soup for €4.50—the chef'll ask you if you liked it. This would be the perfect place to hang out, read a book, or chat with a friend, except that it closes way too early. *8 The Mall, Waterford, County Waterford.* ☎ *051/855-525. Main courses €5–€12. Daily 11am-7pm.*

DOABLE

➜ **Bodega!** CONTINENTAL   If you're looking for the party place in Waterford, you just found it. This place draws a young (20-something) crowd for the great food, lack of volume control, and convivial atmosphere. Choose from specials chalked onto the blackboard menu, which tends to be heavy on the fish and seafood. Everything's tasty, so just go for what you like: There's sea bass with string beans and ratatouille, or a fish medley of cod, salmon, crab ravioli, and mussels. The coffee and desserts are excellent, too, so leave room to relax at the end of the meal with something sweet. *54 John St., Waterford, County Waterford.* ☎ *051/844177. Lunch main courses €5–€10; dinner main courses €14–€21. Mon–Fri noon–2:30pm; Mon–Wed 6–10pm; Thurs–Sat 6–10:30pm.*

➜ **Buggy's Glencairn Inn** COUNTRY IRISH   This upscale place is all about grilled steak perfectly cooked, and the freshest smoked salmon expertly prepared. The atmosphere is casual, but upscale, so don't wear your dirty hiking boots. *Glencairn, County Waterford (5km/3 miles from Lismore).* ☎ *058/56232. www.buggys.net. Reservations recommended. Main courses €15–€22. Wed–Mon 7:30pm.*

➜ **The Wine Vault** WINE BISTRO   The food here is great, and the wines are excellent, but the real draw is that the place is so welcoming, with red brick walls and wood paneling—like your favorite trattoria. The herb-crusted salmon with peppered cucumber and cabernet sauvignon dressing is simple and perfect, the marinated squid with garlic and ginger a memorable delicacy. Desserts, such as the Chocolate Nemesis and homemade lemon-curd ice cream are fantastic. *High St., Waterford, County Waterford.* ☎ *051/853444. www.waterfordwinevault.com. Reservations recommended. Main courses €10–€18. Mon–Sat 12:30–2:30pm and 5:30–10:30pm.*

SPLURGE

→ **Coast** INTERNATIONAL   This is the top eatery du jour in the area, and when you walk in it's easy to see why—its decor is as chic and understated as the menu is outspoken. Start with smoked Barbary duck salad, or goat's cheese tart, and move on to fillet of Angus beef, herb-crusted lamb with mustard cream sauce, or sweet potato fishcakes. Desserts are similarly dreamy. If you feel like drifting from the dinner table to your bed, there are also four smartly turned-out double guest rooms upstairs, available for €100 to €160 per night. *Upper Branch Rd., Tramore, County Waterford.* ☎ *051/393646. www.coast. ie. Reservations recommended. Dinner main courses €19–€26. Tues–Sun 6:30–10:30pm; Sun 1–2:30pm. Closed Dec 24–Jan 1.*

Partying

The intensity of Waterford's youth vibe, orbiting around the Waterford Institute of Technology, on Cork Road, just off the eastern end of the main highway, almost makes up for its minuscule size.

Supposedly the oldest pub in the city, and with a chunk of the original Viking-built city wall to prove it, **T & H Doolan's** (32 George's St.; ☎ 051/841-504), right in the town center northwest of the cathedral, is a venerable mainstay in Waterford City. Once a stagecoach stop it's fabulously traditional and a great spot for live music sessions: An as-yet-undiscovered Sinéad O'Connor once played in this cryptlike space, and the crowd is just as bold and on the lookout for new phenoms today.

A splendid pub (and a good spot for inexpensive pub grub), **Egan's** (36–37 Barronstrand St.; ☎ 051/875-619) is similar to T & H Doolan's, but not as old. You probably won't find any trad here, but be forewarned: There is the occasional karaoke session.

All the beautiful 20-somethings in Waterford City make appearances at **Geoff's**

(9 John St.; ☎ **051/874-787**), a 5-minute walk south of the town center. It's the city's hippest bar by general consensus. The surging vibe makes Geoff's the best place in Waterford for a little local cruising action, at least.

Right next door to Geoff's, **The Pulpit** (John St.; no phone) brims with Waterford's trendiest mid-20s every night of the week. It also hosts a nightclub upstairs, Preacher's (see "Clubs," below), which is a trippy ascent into a weird Gothic fantasy—though one with a mixed-ages crowd of easy-to-meet locals.

Muldoon's (John St.; ☎ **051/856-924**), just a few steps from Geoff's, has a dark spacious sports-bar feel and good pub food. There are occasional folk and trad sessions, and it's open the latest of all the pubs—1:30am or later. You can get free basic bar snacks after 11:30pm.

Jack Meade (Cheekpoint Rd., Halfway House, County Waterford; ☎ **051/8509500**) is a unique option tucked beneath an old stone bridge in an area known as Halfway House, about 6km ($3^3/_4$ miles) south of Waterford City. Dating from 1705, the pub is widely known by the locals as Meade's Under the Bridge. It was once a stopping-off point for coach travelers between Waterford and Passage East. The facade and interior—wooden beams and open fireplaces—haven't changed much over the years. Impromptu evening music sessions can spring up at a moment's notice. In summer good bar food is served daily.

MUSIC SCENE

The King's Bar (8 Lombard St.; ☎ 051/870-949), just off the Mall, dates from 1776, when it was a sending-off point for emigrants leaving Ireland. Today it retains its Georgian facade and old-world charm, particularly in the cozy front bar. It offers a trad session every Friday night, and all musicians are welcome. Take Parnell Street, which becomes the Mall; turn right on Lombard Street. This historic landmark pub, which has an old wood-burning fireplace, is popular not only with music lovers but also among the kind of sportsmen who like to place bets on horse races and then watch them on wide-screen TVs. Also check out Doolan's (above) for nightly folk or traditional music; it's got solid cred. There's also trad on Sunday nights at The Woodman, the bar at Ruby's (see "Clubs," below).

CLUBS

Probably the liveliest club in town and definitely the most bizarre, **Preacher's** (upstairs at the Pulpit, John St.; 11pm—2am Wed—Sun) has this Goth thing going on in the decorating scheme that some would think fabulous and others downright scary. Take your pick. At any rate, the club goers are, in contrast, upbeat and unpretentious.

Continuing with the pub-cum-club thing, **Snag's** (upstairs at Egan's, 36—37 Barronstrand St.; ☎ 051/875-619; usual club hours Fri—Sun) is more of a generic nightspot, but still good for laughs.

"Neat dress essential" at **Ruby's** (Parnell House, Parnell St.; ☎ 051/858-128; 11pm—2am daily; cover €5—€10) means sport jackets for guys and skintight black leather for girls. It's a decent, if undistinctive, nightspot overall, though, with handy utilitarian food available at the adjoining bar, The Woodman, during daylight hours and still more trad by night. No teenyboppers need apply: Supposedly they're pretty strict about the over-23-only rule.

PERFORMING ARTS

Waterford has two main entertainment centers. The 170-seat **Garter Lane Theatre** (22a O'Connell St.; ☎ 051/855038), presents the work of local production companies and visiting Irish troupes. Performances are usually Tuesday to Saturday, and tickets average €10 to €13 for most events. The box office is open

Tuesday to Saturday noon to 6pm, and accepts MasterCard and Visa.

When big-name Irish or international talents come to Waterford, they usually perform at the **Forum Theatre at the Glen** (☎ 051/871111), a 1,000-seat house off Bridge Street. Tickets average €13 to €20, depending on the event. The box office is open Monday to Friday 11am to 1pm and 2 to 4pm. The Forum opens a late-night bar, Deja Vu, every Friday and Saturday, but the crowd's a little on the 30-plus side.

From May to September, on Tuesday, Thursday, and Sunday evenings at 8:45pm, the historic Waterford City Hall hosts the Waterford Show, an intensely touristy evening of music, storytelling, song, and dance. Admission is €10, which includes a preshow drink and a glass of wine during the show.

Sightseeing

Waterford is a commercial city focused on its waterfront. The city center sits on the south bank of the River Suir. Traffic from the north, west, and east enters from the north bank over the Ignatius Rice Bridge and onto a series of quays (Grattan, Merchants, Meagher, and Parade), although most addresses simply say "The Quay." Shops and attractions are concentrated near the quay area or on two thoroughfares that intersect it: The Mall and Barronstrand Street (changing their names to Broad, Michael, and John sts.). These streets were once rivers flowing into the Suir and, in fact, the original waterways continue to flow beneath today's pavement.

FREE ➔ **City Hall** Headquarters of the local city government, this late-18th-century building houses local memorabilia, including the city's charter, granted in 1205. There's an absorbing display on the incredible life of Thomas Francis Meagher, a leader in an Irish insurrection in 1848; he was sentenced to death, but escaped to America. There he fought in the Civil War, earned the rank of brigadier general, and was eventually appointed governor of Montana. City Hall's other treasures include an 18th-century Waterford glass chandelier and priceless antique Waterford glasses. *The Mall, Waterford, County Waterford.* ☎ *051/73501. Free admission. Mon–Fri 9am–1pm and 2–5pm.*

FREE →**Garter Lane Arts Centre** One of Ireland's largest arts centers, the Garter Lane occupies two buildings on O'Connell Street. No. 5, the site of the former Waterford Library, holds exhibition rooms and artists' studios, and no. 22a, the former Friends Meeting House, is home of the Garter Lane Theatre, with an art gallery and outdoor courtyard. The gallery showcases works by contemporary and local artists. *5 and 22a O'Connell St., Waterford, County Waterford.* ☎ *051/855038. Free admission to exhibitions. Gallery Tues–Sat noon–6pm.*

→**Holy Trinity Cathedrals** Waterford has two impressive cathedrals, one Catholic and the other Protestant, both built by one equal opportunity architect, John Roberts (1714–96), who lived 82 years, fathered 22 children, and built nearly every significant 18th-century building in and around Waterford. Holy Trinity on Barronstrand is the only baroque cathedral in Ireland and has 10 Waterford Crystal chandeliers. It's open daily 7:30am to 7pm. The Anglican or Church of Ireland Holy Trinity Cathedral (conveniently nicknamed Christ Church) on Henrietta Street has a most peculiar spire and only clear glass because its first bishop and rector disliked stained glass. *Barronstrand and Henrietta sts., Waterford, County Waterford.*

→**Reginald's Tower** Circular, topped with a conical roof, and with walls 3m (10 ft.) thick, this mighty tower stands at the eastern end of the Quay beside the river. It's said to have been built in 1003 by a Viking governor named Reginald and has never fallen into ruin. Still dominating the Waterford skyline,

it's particularly striking at night when fully floodlit. Over the centuries, it's been a fortress, a prison, a military depot, a mint, an air-raid shelter, and now a museum. *The Quay, Waterford, County Waterford.* ☎ *051/73501. Admission €2. June–Aug daily 9:30am–9pm; May and Sept daily 9:30am–6pm; Oct–Apr daily 10am–5pm.*

→**Waterford Crystal Factory and Gallery** For obvious reasons, this is Waterford's number-one attraction. Since it was founded in 1783, Waterford has been a byword for crystal. The gallery contains a glittering display of crystal, with elaborate confections like trophies, globes, and chandeliers. In the shop you can spend your way into the poorhouse in no time at all (don't look for any discounts at the factory—there are no seconds to be had—the main advantage in shopping here is simply the wide selection). True fans will take the excellent, 35-minute tour of the factory to see the work firsthand. *Cork Rd., Waterford, County Waterford.* ☎ *051/373311. Tour €8, €3.50 students. Free admission to gallery. Tours Mar–Oct daily 8:30am–4:15pm; Nov–Feb Mon–Fri 9am–3:15pm. Reservations not required. Showrooms Mar–Oct daily 8:30am–6pm; Nov–Feb Mon–Fri 9am–5pm.*

FREE →**Waterford Heritage Genealogical Centre** Did your ancestors come from Waterford? If so, follow the small lane between George's and Patrick streets to this historic building adjoining St. Patrick's to get the trained staff to trace your County Waterford ancestry. Church registers dating from 1655, surveys, rolls, and census lists are used as resources. *St. Patrick's Church, Jenkins Lane, Waterford, County Waterford.* ☎ *051/876123. Fax 051/850645. www.waterfordheritage.ie. Free admission; basic search fee €80 (by appointment only). Mon–Thurs 9am–5pm; Fri 9am–2pm.*

→**Waterford Treasures at the Granary Museum** This impressive heritage center and museum, housed in a converted granary, unfolds Waterford's history from its earliest Viking origins. Along with an exceptional collection of Viking and medieval artifacts recovered in the region, there's also an ambitious state-of-the-art multimedia show including a three-dimensional film. There's plenty to see and do, and it's well designed to make it all worthwhile. *Merchant's Quay, Waterford, County Waterford.* ☎ *051/304500. www.waterfordtreasures.com. Admission €4, €3 students. Combined ticket with Reginald's Tower available. June–Aug daily 9:30am–9pm; Apr–May and Sept daily 9:30am–6pm; Oct–Mar daily 10am–5pm.*

Sights Beyond Waterford City

FREE ➔ **Ardmore High Cross** Ardmore (Irish for "the great height") is a very ancient Christian site—St. Declan, its founder, is said to have been a bishop in Munster as early as the mid–4th century, well before St. Patrick came to Ireland. Tradition has it that the small stone oratory in a cemetery high above Ardmore marks his burial site. St. Declan's Oratory is one of several stone structures here composing the ancient monastic settlement. The most striking is the perfectly intact 30m (98-ft.) high round tower. There are also ruins of a medieval cathedral and, nearby, St. Declan's well and church. *Ardmore, County Waterford. Free admission.*

➔ **Lismore Castle** High above the River Blackwater, this turreted castle dates to 1185, when Prince John of England built a similar fortress on this site. Local lore says that Lismore Castle was once granted to Sir Walter Raleigh for IR£12 (€15) a year, although he never occupied it. One man who did live here was Richard Boyle, the first Earl of Cork. He rebuilt the castle, including the thick defensive walls that still surround the garden, in 1626, but most of the present structure was rebuilt in the mid–19th century. You're free to wander the 3,200-hectare (7,904-acre) estate of gardens, forests, and farmland, but

not the castle itself. It is the Irish seat of the duke and duchess of Devonshire who won't let the general public in, but they're not above making a bit of money off of them. In fact, if you've got money to burn, you can see it all, since the castle can be rented, complete with the duke's personal staff, to private groups for a minimum of €24,500 per week. Included in the price are dinners, afternoon teas, breakfasts, and staff. *Lismore, County Waterford.* ☎ *058/54424. Admission to gardens €4. Mid-Apr to mid-Oct daily 1:45–4:45pm. From Cappoquin, take N72 6.5km (4 miles) west.*

➔ **Lismore Heritage Centre** This interpretative center, in the town's Old Courthouse, tells the history of Lismore, a charming town founded by St. Carthage in the year 636. There's an interesting multimedia display on the town's unique treasures, including the Book of Lismore, which dates back 1,000 years, and the Lismore crosier (1116). Both were discovered hidden in the walls of Lismore Castle in 1814. The presentation also provides an excellent introduction to the surrounding area and its attractions. The center also offers tours of the Lismore town and cathedral. *Lismore, County Waterford.* ☎ *058/ 54975. www.lismore-ireland.com/heritage/index. htm. Admission €4, €3.50 students. Apr–Oct daily 10am–5:30pm. Closed Nov–Mar.*

Playing Outside

BEACHES There are wide sandy beaches at Tramore, Ardmore, Clonea, and Dunmore East.

BICYCLING From Waterford City, you can ride 13km (8 miles) to Passage East and take the ferry (€3 with a bicycle) to Wexford and the beautiful Hook Peninsula. Or continue on from Passage East to Dunmore East, a picturesque seaside village with a small beach hemmed in by cliffs. The road from there to Tramore and Dungarvan is quite scenic. For a complete 1- or 2-week biking vacation in the Southeast, contact Don Smith at **Celtic Cycling,** Lorum Old Rectory, Bagenalstown,

County Carlow (☎/fax **059/977-5282;** www.celticcycling.com).

FISHING The Colligan River is excellent for sea trout and salmon. For permit information, contact **Baumann's Jewellers,** 6 St. Mary St., Dungarvan (☎ **058/41395**). For sea angling, there are plenty of licensed charter-boat companies operating out of Kilmore Quay, roughly 24km (15 miles) southwest of Wexford. One such operation is **Kilmore Quay Boat Charters;** contact Dick Hayes (☎ **053/29704**). For landlubbers, the River Slaney, brimming with salmon and sea trout, can be fished from the old bridge in Enniscorthy.

HIKING Mahon Falls is in the Comeragh Mountains, on R676 between Carrick-on-Suir and Dungarvan. At the tiny village of Mahon Bridge, 26km (16 miles) south of Carrick-on-Suir, turn west on the road marked for Mahon Falls, then follow signs for the falls and the "Comeragh Drive." In about 5km (3 miles), you reach a parking lot along the Mahon River (in fact, just a tiny stream). The trail, indicated by two boulders, begins across the road. Follow the stream along the floor of the valley to the base of the falls. From here you can see the fields of Waterford spread out below you, and the sea a glittering mirror beyond. Walking time is about 30 minutes round-trip.

HORSEBACK RIDING Arrange to ride at **Killotteran Equitation Centre,** Killotteran, Waterford (☎ **051/384158**). Fees average around €25 per hour.

SAILING, WINDSURFING & SEA KAYAKING From May to September, the **Dunmore East Adventure Centre,** Dunmore East (☎ **051/ 383783**), offers courses of 1 to 4 days that cost €30 to €45 per day, including equipment rental. Summer programs for children are also available. This is a great spot for an introductory experience, but there isn't much wave action around here for thrill-seeking windsurfers.

Shopping

Most come to Waterford for the crystal, but there's plenty of unbreakable stuff to shop for around here, especially in the three multilevel enclosed shopping centers: **George's Court,** off Barronstrand Street, **Broad Street Centre,** on Broad Street, and **City Square,** off Broad Street. Hours are usually Monday to Saturday from 9 or 9:30am to 6 or 6:30pm. Some shops are open until 9pm on Thursday and Friday.

Beside the Granville Hotel, **Aisling** (61 The Quay, Waterford, County Waterford; ☎ **051/873262**), an interesting shop, offers an assortment of handmade crafts, from quilts, tartans, and kilts to floral art, miniature paintings, and watercolors of Irish scenes and subjects.

➔**The Book Centre** This huge, four-level bookstore has all the books, newspapers, and magazines you need, as well as useful maps and CDs. You can also make a photocopy here or zap off a fax. *5 Barronstrand St., Waterford, County Waterford.* ☎ *051/873823.*

➔**Kelly's** Dating from 1847, this shop offers a wide selection of Waterford crystal, Aran knitwear, Belleek and Royal Tara china, Irish linens, and other souvenirs. *75–76 The Quay, Waterford, County Waterford.* ☎ *051/ 873557.*

➔**Penrose Crystal** Established in 1786 and revived in 1978, this is Waterford's other glass company, which turns out delicate hand-cut and engraved glassware carved with the stipple engraving process. A retail sales outlet is at Unit 8 of the City Square Shopping Centre. Both are open the usual hours, but the factory is also open Sunday from June to August, 2 to 5:30pm. *32A Johns St., Waterford, County Waterford.* ☎ *051/ 876537.*

checking out the comeragh Mountains

In the center of County Waterford, Comeragh attracts climbers and hill walkers with its rich variety of terrain—everything from the precipitous Knock-anaffrin Ridge to the glacial amphitheater of Lough Coumshingaun. The highlight of this area is Mahon Falls.

You can walk around the entire lake at Coumshingaun, in the eastern part of the mountains. It is surrounded by dramatic rock faces known for excellent climbing routes.

For a deeper exploration of the mountains—where the going gets rougher, steeper, and tougher—a guide is recommended. The **Dungarvan Walking Group** is willing to show you the Comeraghs. Organizer Michael Powers (who can be reached at Powers Book Shop, ☎ **058/41617,** in Dungarvan) will brief you on all of the provisions you might need for a day in the great outdoors, and then lead you out into the wild. The group meets at the TSB Bank on Main Street in Dungarvan for its 10am Sunday walks. These walks, lasting about 5 hours and covering rugged terrain, are not for the faint of heart.

If this sounds like altogether too much walking, you can also explore the mountains on horseback. We've gone horseback riding in the Comeraghs, and you can too if you call **Melody's** in Ballymacarbry (☎ **052/36147**), where horses can be rented at the rate of €22 per hour. Ballymacarbry is northwest of the park, halfway between Clonmel and Dungarvan.

It's possible, and not illegal, to go camping in these mountains, although locals tell us this is almost never done. If you do decide to camp out on the land, you of course have to bring your own provisions and gear. And be sure to carry away any litter that might pile up around your tent.

Instead of camping, a more viable option might be to stay at the tiny **Coumshingaun Lodge** at Kilclooney (☎ **051/646-238;** €60), lying at the base of the mountains. "Lodge" is a bit of an exaggeration: There are only three rooms, each containing one queen-size and one single bed. It's bone-bare but clean and comfortable, and lies only 200 yards from the base of the Comeraghs, so there are views in all directions. The price includes an Irish breakfast made in the old-fashioned kitchen.

Note: The Comeragh Mountains are a 7-mile drive north of Dungarvan on the N25. The road is flat for most of the way except for three hills. You can walk it but it's a bit of an effort, especially if you want to conserve energy for hiking the mountains themselves. Unfortunately, there are no buses.

South Tipperary

South Tipperary is one of Ireland's best-kept secrets. Here, far from the tour buses and the clicking of camera shutters, you may just find the Ireland everyone is looking for: welcoming, unspoiled, and splendidly beautiful.

Clonmel, the capital of Tipperary, is the unassuming gateway to the region. A working town, as yet unspoiled by massive tourism, Clonmel (whose delightful name in Gaelic, Cluaín Meala, means "Meadows of Honey") makes a strategic, pleasant base in the Southeast. Looking at the pretty rural town, poised on the banks of the Suir, it's hard to believe that it once withstood a Cromwellian siege for 3 brutal months.

Scenic Drives

Whether you're staying in Clonmel or moving on, several marvelously scenic drives converge and present themselves here: the Comeragh or Nire Valley Drive deep into the Comeragh Mountains, which rise from the south banks of the Suir; the Suir Scenic Drive; and the Knockmealdown Drive, which passes through the historic village of Ardfinnan and on through the Vee. These are all signposted from Clonmel.

Whether you're staying in Clonmel or just passing through, several scenic drives converge here: the Comeragh or Nire Valley Drive deep into the Comeragh Mountains, which rise from the south banks of the Suir; the Knockmealdown Drive, through the historic village of Ardfinnan and the Vee (see below); and the Suir Scenic Drive. All are signposted from Clonmel.

North of Clonmel and deep in the Tipperary countryside, Cashel, with its Rock of Cashel and cluster of monastic buildings in a dramatic setting, is the reason most people make their way to Tipperary. Because it's on the main N8 road, most people pass through en route from Dublin to Cork. If your travels don't take you to Cashel, a side trip from Waterford is worth the drive. In particular, two scenic routes are well worth a detour:

At Cahir, you can head north through the Galtee Mountains, Ireland's highest inland mountain range, to the Glen of Aherlow. The pristine 11km (7-mile) Glen of Aherlow is a secluded and scenic pass between the plains of counties Tipperary and Limerick.

If you're driving south into Waterford, head for the "Vee." This 18km-long (11-mile) road winds through the Knockmealdown Mountains from Clogheen to Lismore and

Cappoquin in County Waterford. It's one of the most dramatic drives in the Southeast—and the high point is at the Tipperary-Waterford border, where the two slopes of the pass converge to frame the patchwork fields of the Galtee Valley far below. From there, numerous walking trails lead to the nearby peaks and down to the mountain lake of Petticoat Loose—named after a, shall we say, less-than-exemplary lady. A more edifying local character was Samuel Grubb, of Castle Grace, who so loved these slopes that he left instructions that he should be buried upright overlooking them. And so he was. The rounded stone cairn you might notice off the road between Clogheen and the Vee is where he stands in place, entombed, facing the Golden Vale of Tipperary.

Getting There & Getting Around

BY CAR Major roads that lead south to Tipperary are the N8 and the N24.

BY BUS The best way to get around is by bus. **Bus Éireann** (☎ 062/62121) runs four buses per day from Main Street, Cashel, to Dublin; three per day to Cork (two on Sun); four per day to Cahir; and four per day to Limerick. Four or five buses also leave for Waterford every day from Cahir. The bus stop in Cahir is at Cahir Castle. In addition, **Kavanagh's** buses (☎ 062/51563) travel Monday through Saturday between Cashel and Dublin, making stops at Tipperary and Cahir.

BY TRAIN The **Cahir Train Station** (off Cashel Rd.; call the Thurles station at ☎ 0504/21733 for information) has one daily train, Monday through Saturday, on the Waterford-Limerick Junction line.

Basics

VISITOR INFORMATION The **Clonmel Tourist Office** is on Sarsfield Street, Clonmel (☎ 052/22960). It's open year-round Monday to Saturday, 9:30am to 5:30pm. Seasonal offices, open June to August Monday to Saturday, 9:30am to 6pm, are at Castle Street, Cahir (☎ 052/41453), and at the Town Hall, Cashel (☎ 062/61333). The website for all Southeast Tourism is www.southeastireland.travel.ie. To get the latest on news, listings, and events in Clonmel and the surrounding area, buy a copy of the local *Nationalist*, which hits the stands every Saturday. Among other things, it will tell you what's on at the Regal Theatre or the White Memorial Theatre, Clonmel's principal venues for the arts.

Sleeping

HOSTELS

→ **Cashel Holiday Hostel**   This place is handy—it's close to both the Rock of Cashel and the bus stop. If you book far enough in advance, you can get a room with a private bathroom; otherwise, you'll have to share. The hostel has a big kitchen for guests to use and a comfy lounge/TV room to hang out in. There is no curfew or lockout. Two thumbs up. *6 John St., Cashel, County Tipperary. ☎ 062/62330. Dorms €12–€16. Amenities: Kitchen; TV lounge; lockers.*

→ **O'Brien's Holiday Lodge**   A charming converted stone barn with an attached coach house, O'Brien's is a safe pick. It's practically right under the Rock, just across the street from Hore Abbey, and you can camp outside and rent bikes there. There's no curfew, and there is a kitchen and dining/lounge area. Staff are really friendly, and the other backpackers are very cool. Call ahead; it's only got 14 beds. *St. Patrick's Rock, Dundrum Rd, Cashel, County Tipperary. ☎ 062/61003. Dorms €12–€15.*

CHEAP/DOABLE

→ **Bansha House**   The town of Bansha sits at the base of the magnificent Galtee Mountains, making this an ideal base for walking, cycling, or just taking in the scenery. The guest rooms in this small Georgian manor house are nicely done, with sturdy country

furniture and perhaps a bit too much pink in the color scheme. Nearby, the self-catering Primrose Cottage, which sleeps five, is a cheaper option for groups traveling together. *Bansha, County Tipperary. ☎ 062/54194. www.tipp.ie/banshahs.htm. €70–€90 double. Rates include full breakfast. Cottage €300–€450 per week. Amenities: Sitting room.*

→ **Kilmaneen Farmhouse**   This cleverly decorated, relaxing farmhouse B&B is a real find. Set amid a beautiful mountainous terrain, it's run by Kevin and Ber O'Donnell. Those who love fishing, love Kilmaneen, as you can cast for trout here, into either the Suir or the Tar without any permit required, and there's even a fisherman's hut for tying flies, storing equipment, and just hanging out looking knowledgeable. Kevin is trained in mountaineering and leads trekking and walking tours into the nearby Knockmealdowns, Comeraghs, or Galtee mountains. If you're with a group and you want to stay a week, there's a fully equipped guest cottage, with space for five. It rents for anywhere from €150 to €350 depending on the season. Finding your way here can be tricky, so call ahead and ask for detailed directions. *Newcastle, County Tipperary. ☎ 052/36231. €75 double. Rates include full breakfast. In room: Tea/coffeemaker.*

→ **Mr. Bumbles**   Above Declan Gavigan's Mr. Bumbles restaurant, with their own exterior staircase, these four rooms are basic but bright and simple. They are meticulously clean and have firm beds. The restaurant downstairs is a bit pricey, but very good. *Richmond House, Kickham St., Clonmel, County Tipperary (top of Clonmel Market Place). ☎ 052/29380. €70 double. Rates include full breakfast. Amenities: Restaurant (international). In room: TV.*

SPLURGE

→ **Dundrum House Hotel**   Located 10km (6¼ miles) northwest of Cashel, this Georgian country manor is nestled in the fertile Tipperary countryside, surrounded by sprawling grounds and gardens. Originally built as a residence in 1730 by the earl of Montalt, it was later used as a convent school, then transformed into a hotel in 1978. It is furnished with heirlooms and reproductions. Each room is individually decorated with a traditional and slightly dated feel, some with four-poster beds or hand-carved headboards, armoires, vanities, and other traditional furnishings. Look for exceptional weekend specials on offer all year. The hotel's bar is especially appealing, in a former chapel with vivid stained-glass windows. *Dundrum, County Tipperary.* ☎ *800/447-7462 in the U.S. or 062/71116. www.dundrumhousehotel.com. €160 double. Weekend discounts available. Amenities: Restaurant (Irish/Continental); bar; 18-hole championship golf course; gym; horseback riding; indoor pool; sauna; trout fishing privileges. In room: TV, hair dryer, radio.*

DO IT YOURSELF

→**Coopers Cottage** This adorable Victorian cottage is perfect for a group of friends wanting to explore the southeastern counties of Tipperary, Waterford, and Kilkenny. It's been lovingly restored and renovated into a comfortable, tasteful hideaway. With exposed beams and polished wood floors, it's full of light, with spectacular views of the Galtee Mountains. The house has three bedrooms and sleeps six, and comes with absolutely everything—there's even a barbecue and a patio for sunny days. *1.6km (1 mile) off N24 at Bansha, Raheen, Bansha, County Tipperary.* ☎ *062/54027. Fax 062/54027. www.dirl.com/tipperary/coopers.htm. 1 cottage. €349–€450 per week. No credit cards. Amenities: Dishwasher; dryer; kitchen; microwave; patio; TV; washing machine.*

Eating

If you're here on a budget, there are a few fairly simple options, but most of the restaurants are in the more expensive categories.

Still, as long as there are cafes, you won't starve. Come to think of it, your best bet might be to make good use of the hostel kitchen. If you're looking for groceries, the SuperValu on Main Street has the largest selection; the Centra Supermarket on Friar Street is fine but smaller.

CHEAP/DOABLE

→**Angela's Wholefood Restaurant** CAFETERIA This laid-back, low-key cafe is a favorite with locals and backpackers for its good food and good prices. The blackboard menu might include breakfast omelets, spicy Moroccan lamb stew, homemade soup, sandwiches to order, and crisp salads. The food is vibrant, fresh, and the place is packed with patrons who line up with trays in hand, from barristers to babysitters. *14 Abbey St., Clonmel, County Tipperary.* ☎ *052/26899. Main courses €2.50–€9. No credit cards. Mon–Fri 9am–5:30pm; Sat noon–5pm.*

→**The Coffee Shop** INTERNATIONAL This second floor joint may not have a very evocative name, but it offers good quiches, lasagna, sandwiches, and pie for under €8. It's a decent spot for a late lunch if you're waiting for the bus—which stops right outside. *Main St., Cashel, County Tipperary.* ☎ *062/61680. Main courses €5–€10. No credit cards. Daily 7am–4pm.*

→**Pasta Milano** ITALIAN This simple, friendly trattoria has the usual pizza and pasta options at affordable prices. The food is good, and the atmosphere is cheery. *Ladyswell St., Cashel, County Tipperary.* ☎ *062/62729. Main courses €7–€14. Daily 11am–9pm.*

SPLURGE

→**Chez Hans** CONTINENTAL/SEAFOOD In a former Gothic chapel in the shadow of the mighty Cashel Rock, this restaurant's cathedral-style ceiling, stone walls, and candlelight create a dramatic setting. The menu features the likes of Dublin Bay prawn bisque, cassoulet of seafood, herb-crusted roast Tipperary lamb, and free-range duck with honey and thyme. A really romantic place. *Rockside, Cashel, County Tipperary.* ☎ *062/61177. Reservations required. Main courses €26–€32. Tues–Sat 6:30–10pm. Closed last 2 weeks in Jan and last 2 weeks in Sept.*

Partying

There's generally not much a booming nightlife scene in this region. There is, though, a low-key pub culture, and lots of good Irish music.

Cashel's center for traditional Irish music, **Brú Ború** (Rock Lane; ☎ **062/61122;** free admission to center; €10 per show), looks like a fairly dull community center but offers ripping music performances from mid-June to mid-September on Tuesday through Saturday nights at 9pm. You can have a big ole traditional Irish lamb platter spread during the show for an additional fee. The admission price may seem hefty, but it's some of the best live music around, and it makes for a foot-stomping night. Brú Ború also has a heritage center with a minimuseum, self-service cafe, and gift shop peddling fortress-y sorts of wares. Dress nice.

Although Cashel won't win any awards for its pub scene, there are still several places to drink the evening away if you'd rather not fork over the bucks for the Brú Ború show. **Ryan's** (76 Main St.; ☎ 062/61431) has a really cool beer garden and live trad or rock most nights. **Feehan's** (Main St.; ☎ **062/61929**) is a lively little pub with trad on Thursday nights only. Some folks say comfortable **Dowling's** (also on Main St.; ☎ 062/62130) serves the best pints in town. Heck, pick any old pub on Main Street and you'll be doing fine. These are all a good deal more relaxed and low-key than Brú Ború, so showing up in your jeans is fine.

Here are some other Tipperary options:

→ **Gerry Chawkes** Chawkes is a Clonmel landmark, a shrine not so much to stout as to sport. A fanatic of hurling and racing (dogs and horses), Gerry Chawke has made his pub a cult place, lined with sports memorabilia. *3 Gladstone St. Upper, Clonmel, County Tipperary.* ☎ *052/21149.*

→ **Railway Bar** You'll need on-the-ground directions to find Kitty's, which is what locals call this pub in a cul-de-sac behind the train station. Your efforts will be rewarded, especially on weekends, when a traditional-music session is likely to break out. No one is paid or even invited to play here; they just show up. Often, there are so many musicians and so many wanting to hear them that the music spills outside, down the lane. No frills here—just the best Irish music around, and a pub out of the who-knows-when past. *Clonmel, County Tipperary. No phone.*

→ **The Ronald Reagan** This place is very strange—a kind of shrine to the former U.S. president, right in the middle of the town that was home to his great-grandfather, Michael Reagan. The place is filled with pictures and mementos of the president's June 3, 1984, visit to Ballyporeen, and the back wall is devoted to a mural of the original Reagan homestead. *Main St., Ballyporeen, County Tipperary.* ☎ *052/67133.*

→ **Tierney's** This is a classy boozer, with dark carved wood, shiny brass railings, and stained glass. It goes on and on from one level to another, with small lounges, big dining rooms, and little nooks. Upstairs, there is a full-service restaurant with several dining rooms, each with its own character, and outside there's a walled beer garden for times when the weather is kind. *13 O'Connell St., Clonmel, County Tipperary.* ☎ *052/24467.*

Sightseeing

→ **Ahenny High Crosses** You're likely to have this little-known and rarely visited site to yourself, except for the cows whose pasture you will cross to reach it. The setting is idyllic and, on a bright day, gorgeous. The well-preserved Ahenny high crosses date from the 8th or 9th century. Tradition associates them with seven saintly bishops, all brothers who were said to have been waylaid and murdered. Their unusual stone "caps," thought by some to be bishops' miters, more likely suggest the transition from wood crosses, which would have had small roofs to shelter them from the rain. Note, too, their intricate spiral and cable ornamentation in remarkably high relief, which may have been inspired by earlier Celtic metalwork. *Kil Crispeen Churchyard, Ahenny, County Tipperary. 8km (5 miles) north of Carrick-on-Suir, signposted off R697. Open site. Box for donations.*

➔**Athassel Priory**   Although it is in ruins, many delightful details from the original medieval priory that once stood here still remain. This was an Augustinian priory, founded in the late 12th century, and it was once elaborately decorated. The main approach is over a low stone bridge and through a gatehouse. The church entrance is a beautifully carved doorway at its west end, while to the south of the church is the cloister, its graceful arches eroded by time. Look for a carved face protruding from the southwest corner of the chapel tower, about 9m (30 ft.) above ground level, 3km (2 miles) south of Golden, County Tipperary. *Take signposted road from Golden, on the N74; the priory is in a field just east of the road. Open site.*

➔**The Bolton Library**   In this library, you'll see the smallest book in the world, as well as other rare, antiquarian, and unusual books dating from as far back as the 12th century. The works by Dante, Swift, Calvin, Newton, Erasmus, and Machiavelli are displayed alongside silver altarpieces from the original cathedral on the Rock of Cashel. *On the grounds of St. John the Baptist Church, John St., Cashel, County Tipperary. ☎ 062/61944. Admission €2 adults, €1.30 seniors and*

students, €.70 children. Mon–Fri 9:30am–5:30pm; Sun 2:30–5:30pm. Closed Mon Mar–Sept.

FREE ➔**Brú Ború Heritage Centre**   At the foot of the Rock of Cashel, this modern complex adds a musical element to the historic Cashel area. Operated by Comhaltas Ceoltoiri Eireann, Ireland's foremost traditional-music organization, Brú Ború presents daily performances of authentic Irish traditional music at an indoor theater. Many summer evenings feature concerts in the open-air amphitheater. A gift shop, restaurant, and self-service snack bar are also on hand. *Rock Lane, Cashel, County Tipperary. ☎ 062/61122. Free admission to center; show €15; 7pm dinner and show €40. Oct–Apr daily 9am–5:30pm; May–Sept daily 9am–5pm. Shows mid-June to mid-Sept Tues–Sat 9pm.*

MTV Best ➔**Cahir Castle**   On a rock in the middle of the River Suir, this medieval fortress can trace its history to the 3rd century, when a fort was first built on the rock—hence the town's Gaelic name, "City of the Fishing Fort." The present structure, which belonged to the Butler family for 600 years, 1375 to 1961, is Norman. It has a massive keep, high walls, spacious courtyards, and a great hall, all fully restored. The interpretive center has an engaging 20-minute video introduction to the region's major historic sites, as well as guided tours of the castle grounds. Take the time to walk through the castle buildings, which are not included in the tour. *Cahir, County Tipperary. ☎ 052/41011. Admission €2.75 adults, €1.25 students. Mid-Mar to mid-June and mid-Sept to mid-Oct daily 9:30am–5:30pm; mid-June to mid-Sept daily 9am–7pm; mid-Oct to mid-Mar daily 9:30am–4:30pm.*

➔**Ormond Castle**   The mid-15th-century castle built by Sir Edward MacRichard Butler on a strategic bend of the River Suir has lain in ruins for centuries. What still stands, attached to the ancient battlements, is the last surviving Tudor manor house in Ireland.

THE SOUTHEAST

Trusting that "if he built it, she would come," Thomas Butler constructed an extensive manor in honor of his most successful relation, Queen Elizabeth I—whose mother, Anne Boleyn, is rumored to have been born in Ormond Castle. She never came, but many others have, especially since the Heritage Service partially restored this impressive piece of Irish history. Current plans include an elaborate furnishing of the Earl's Room in period style. The manor's plasterwork, carvings, period furniture, and startling collection of original 17th- and 18th-century royal charters will make you glad you bothered to visit and wonder why Queen Elizabeth never did. *Signposted from the center of Carrick-on-Suir, Carrick-on-Suir, County Tipperary.* ☎ *051/640787. Admission €2.75 adults, €1.25 students. June–Sept daily 9:30am–6:30pm. Closed Oct–May.*

📺 **Best** ➜ **The Rock of Cashel** When you reach the town of Cashel, look for signs to the Rock of Cashel, which dominates the Tipperary countryside for miles. An outcrop of limestone reaching 60m (197 ft.) into the sky, "the Rock" tells the tales of 16 centuries. It was the castled seat of the kings of Munster at least as far back as A.D. 360, and it remained a royal fortress until 1101, when King Murtagh O'Brien granted it to the church. Among Cashel's many great moments was the legendary baptism of King Aengus by St. Patrick in 448. Remaining on the rock are the ruins of a two-towered chapel, a cruciform cathedral, a 28m (92-ft.) round tower, and a cluster of other medieval monuments. The views of and from the Rock are spectacular. Forty-five-minute guided tours are available on request. *Cashel, County Tipperary.* ☎ *062/61437. Admission €5 adults, €2 students. Mid-June to mid-Sept daily 9am–7pm; mid-Sept to mid-Mar daily 9am–4:45pm; mid-Mar to mid-June daily 9am–5:30pm. Last admission 45 min. before closing.*

➜ **Swiss Cottage** The earls of Glengall used the Swiss Cottage as a hunting and fishing lodge as far back as 1812. It's a superb example of cottage orné: a rustic house embodying the ideal of simplicity that so appealed to the Romantics of the early 19th century. The thatched-roof cottage has extensive timberwork, usually not seen in Ireland, and is believed to have been designed by John Nash, a royal architect. The interior has some of the first wallpaper commercially produced in Paris. A guided tour (the only way to see the building) lasts approximately 40 minutes. *Off Dublin-Cork Rd. (N8), Cahir, County Tipperary.* ☎ *052/41144. Guided tour €2.75 adults, €1.25 students. Late Mar and mid-Oct to Nov Tues–Sun 10am–1pm and 2–4:30pm; Apr Tues–Sun 10am–1pm and 2–6pm; May to mid-Oct daily 10am–6pm. Closed Dec to late Mar.*

➜ **Tipperary Crystal** This crystal factory is laid out in the style of traditional Irish cottages, complete with a thatched roof. Visitors are welcome to watch master craftspeople as they mouth-blow and hand-cut crystal. *Waterford-Limerick Rd. (N24), Ballynoran, Carrick-on-Suir, County Tipperary.* ☎ *051/641188. Free admission. Mon–Fri 9am–5:30pm; Sat. 9:30am–6pm; Sun 11am–5pm.*

Playing Outside

BICYCLING For complete 1- or 2-week cycling holidays in the Southeast, contact Don Smith at **Celtic Cycling,** Lorum Old Rectory, Bagenalstown, County Carlow (☎/fax **059/977-5282**). If you just need to rent a bike for a few days, try **McInerney's** (Main St., Cashel; ☎ **062/61225**).

FISHING The River Suir, from Carrick-on-Suir to Thurles, was once one of the finest salmon rivers in Europe, but recent excessive trawling at its mouth has threatened its stock. It's still a decent salmon river, especially in the February run and from June to September. Trout (brown and rainbow) are in abundance here in the summer. Here you'll find some of the least expensive game fishing in Ireland; single weekday permits cost €20 to €32 for salmon, €7 for trout. They are available from **Kavanagh Sports**, Westgate, Clonmel, County Tipperary (☎/fax **052/21279**), as is everything else you'll need. Manager Declan Byrne can outfit you with all of the essentials and more. To orient yourself and to consider your options, pick up a copy of Angling on the Suir, a helpful pamphlet put out by the Tourist Office. The River Nore and the nearby River Barrow are also known for good salmon and trout fishing.

For deep-sea fishing, picturesque Dunmore East, 13km (8 miles) south of Waterford, is a good bet. Contact **John O'Connor** (☎ **051/383397**) to charter a boat for reef, wreck, and shark fishing. Boat charter rates are around €400 per day.

HORSEBACK RIDING For trekking and trail riding on the slopes of the Comeragh Mountains, you can't do better than **Melodys Nire Valley Equestrian Centre,** Nire View, Ballycarbry, Clonmel (☎ **052/36147**).

HIKING R668 between Clogheen and Lismore is a scenic stretch of road, and some great walks begin at the Vee Gap, a dramatic notch in the Knockmealdown Mountains. About 2km (1¼ miles) north of R669 and R668, you reach the highest point in the gap; there is a parking lot, as well as a dirt road continuing down to a lake nestled into the slope below. This is Bay Lough, and the dirt road used to be the main thoroughfare over the gap; it now offers a fine walk to the shores of the lake, with outstanding views of the valley to the north. For a panoramic perspective of the region, start walking due east from the gap parking lot to the summit of Sugarloaf Hill; the hike is extremely steep, but well worth the effort—the views from the ridge are superb.

In the Clonmel area, there are excellent river and hill walks, some more challenging than others. The most spectacular is the ascent of famed Slievenamon, a mountain rich in myth. Inexpensive, detailed trail maps for at least a half-dozen walks are available at the Clonmel Tourist Office on Sarsfield Street, Clonmel. Also available is a free leaflet guide to the Wilderness Gorge.

The Galtee Mountains, northwest of the Knockmealdowns, offer some great long and short walks. One beautiful route on a well-defined trail is the circuit of Lake Muskry, on the north side of the range. To get there, take R663 west out of Bansha, and follow signs for the town of Rossadrehid. To get to the trail, ask for directions in Rossadrehid; there are several turns, and the landmarks change frequently because of logging. The trail leads you up a glaciated valley to the base of a ring of cliffs where the crystalline waters of Lake Muskry lie; from here you can walk around the lake, take in the tremendous views of the valley, and return the way you came. Walking time to the lake and back is 3 hours.

Another option on this walk is to continue up past the lake to the top of the ridge, and from there along the ridge top to Galtymore, a prominent dome-shaped peak about 5km (3 miles) west of Lake Muskry. It is a beautiful but extremely demanding walk, about 6 hours to Galtymore and back. This is only one of many extraordinary walks in the Glen of Aherlow. Trail maps and all the information and assistance you could think of asking for are available at the **Glen of Aherlow Failte Centre,** Coach Road, Newtown (☎ **062/56331**). It's open daily June to October from 9:30am to 5:30pm.

SWIMMING If you're staying in the area, you're welcome to swim at the **Clonmel Civic Swimming Pool** (☎ **052/21972**), near the Market Place. It's open Monday to Friday 9am to 9:45pm, Saturday and Sunday 10am to 7:45pm. Call for specific public swimming hours.

THE SOUTHEAST

County Kilkenny/Kilkenny City

With its remarkable collection of well-preserved castles, churches, monastic sites, and winding narrow lanes, lovely Kilkenny City is a graceful medieval town. It's also a national hub for crafts and design, and its streets are lined with shops selling pottery, woodwork, paintings, and jewelry. You just can't help falling in love (or at least in some serious like) with Kilkenny's quaint little streets, imposing old stone structures, and fantastic pub scene. If you're going to linger in the Southeast, make it a point to spend a good-size chunk of your time here.

Its many charms make it popular with travelers, and it's certainly not untouched by tourism, but it's in no way as overrun as Kerry, and in the off season it reverts to its normal, sleepy self (its normal population is just 11,000), and you can wander its streets in peace.

Like so many Irish towns, Kilkenny stands on the site of an old monastery from which it takes its name. A priory was founded here in the 6th century by St. Canice—in Gaelic, Cill Choinnigh means "Canice's Church." As the monastery grew, the town sprang up around it and prospered. It owes its graceful appearance to its success in the Middle Ages. Then it was a prosperous walled city, and it served as an important governmental center during the 14th century. Much of its medieval architecture has been skillfully preserved, and the basic town plan has not changed much in the last 600 years.

The oldest house in town may well be Kyteler's Inn on St. Kieran Street. It was once the home of Dame Alice Kyteler, a wealthy woman accused of witchcraft in 1324. She escaped and disappeared into the countryside, but her maid, Petronilla, was burned at the stake. Her home is now a pub and restaurant, decorated with effigies of witches.

Another building that stands out on the streetscape is the Tholsel, on High Street, with its curious clock tower and front arcade. It was originally (in 1761) a tollhouse or exchange. Milk and sugar candy were sold here, and dances, bazaars, and political meetings were held here. Today, completely restored, it houses municipal archives.

The surrounding County Kilkenny countryside is dotted with rich river valleys, green pastures, hills, and picture-postcard villages. If you like monastic sites, make the time to see the Jerpoint Abbey, on the River Nore just southwest of Thomaston on N9. It's an extraordinary Cistercian ruin that still has many elaborate medieval carvings on its walls; some even have traces of the original pigment. Also on the Nore is the picturesque village of 📺 Best **Inistioge,** about 24km (15 miles) southeast of Kilkenny City, with a tree-lined square and stone bridge with nine low arches spanning the river.

Abbey lovers will want to continue on to the tongue-twister town of Graiguenamanagh (its name means "Village of the Monks"), which holds the Duiske Abbey. Surrounded by peaceful views of Brandon Hill and the Blackstairs Mountains, Graiguenamanagh is at a bend of the River Barrow, about 32km (20 miles) southeast of Kilkenny City.

Kells, about 10km (6¼ miles) south of Kilkenny City (and not to be confused with the town of the same name in County Meath), is the only completely walled medieval town in Ireland. The thick city walls, seven towers, and some of the monastic buildings have all been well preserved.

GETTING THERE

BY BUS **Bus Éireann,** McDonagh Station, Dublin Road, Kilkenny (☎ **056/776-4933;** www.buseireann.ie), operates daily service from Dublin and all parts of Ireland.

There's also private bus: **JJ Kavanagh's Rapid Express** (depart from The Parade;

☎ 01/679-1549 in Dublin, 056/31106 in Kilkenny) has several buses running daily between Kilkenny and Dublin.

BY CAR Many roads pass through Kilkenny, including the N9/N10 from Waterford and Wexford, the N8 and N76 from Cork and the southwest, the N7 and N77 from Limerick and the west, and the N9 and N78 from Dublin and points north and east.

BY TRAIN **Irish Rail** provides daily service on the Dublin to Waterford line into the McDonagh Station, Dublin Road, Kilkenny (☎ 056/772-2024; www.irishrail.ie).

Getting Around

There is no bus service within Kilkenny. Local buses run to nearby towns on a limited basis, departing from the Parade. Check with **Bus Éireann** (☎ 056/776-4933; www.bus eireann.ie).

TAXIS It's unlikely you will, but if you need a taxi, call **Nicky Power Taxi** (☎ 056/776-3000), **Billy Delaney Cabs** (☎ 056/772-2457), or **Kilkenny Taxi Service** (☎ 056/776-3017).

It's best not to drive once you're in town—Kilkenny's narrow medieval streets are only really navigable by locals, and you'll almost certainly get stuck. Park at one of the designated parking areas at the Parade, at the rail station, or at one of the shopping centers. Some parking is free, and other spaces have coin-operated machines, usually for €.50 per hour. There's also a central multistory car park on Ormonde Street, which costs €1 per hour until you reach €8, which will last you for 24 hours. If you need to rent a car to see the surrounding countryside, call **Barry Pender,** Dublin Road, Kilkenny (☎ 056/776-5777 or 056/776-3839).

The best way to see Kilkenny City is on foot. Plot your own route or join a guided walking tour.

Basics

EMERGENCIES Dial ☎ **999.** The local **Garda Station** is on Dominic Street (☎ 056/772-2222).

INTERNET If you need to access the Internet, try the **Kilkenny Library** at 6 John's Quay (☎ 056/772-2021), open Tuesday to Saturday 10:30am to 1pm, Tuesday to Friday 2 to 5pm, and Tuesday and Wednesday 7 to 9pm. **Web-Talk,** Rose Inn Street (no phone), is an Internet cafe with ISDN Internet access; open Monday to Saturday 10am to 10pm and Sunday 2 to 8pm, for €1.50 every 10 minutes and €6.50 an hour.

PHARMACY If you need a drugstore, try **John Street Pharmacy,** 47 John St. (☎ 056/776-5971); **John O'Connell,** 4 Rose Inn St. (☎ 056/772-1033); or **White's Chemist,** 5 High St. (☎ 056/772-1328).

POST OFFICE The **Kilkenny District Post Office,** 73 High St. (☎ 056/772-1813), is open Monday to Friday 9:30am to 5:30pm, Saturday 9:30am to 1pm.

RECOMMENDED WEBSITES For information on upcoming events and festivals, visit www.kilkenny.ie or www.kilkennycityonline. com. When you're in town, check out the weekly *Kilkenny People* (www.kilkenny people.ie), which also covers local happenings.

TOURS **Tynan's Walking Tours** Local historian Pat Tynan leads you through the streets and lanes of medieval Kilkenny, providing historical facts and anecdotes along the way. Tours depart from the tourist office, Rose Inn Street, 10 Maple Dr., Kilkenny, County Kilkenny (☎ 056/776-5929). Tickets €4.50 adults, €3.80 students.

VISITOR INFORMATION For information, maps, and brochures about Kilkenny and the surrounding area, contact the **Kilkenny Tourist Office,** Shee Alms House, Rose Inn Street, Kilkenny (☎ 056/775-1500). It's open April to October, Monday to Saturday 10am to 6pm; November to March, Monday to Saturday 9am to 1pm and 2 to 5pm.

Festivals

Kilkenny Arts Week (mid-Aug; ☎ 056/ 63663; http://www.kilkennyarts.ie; tickets free—€15 per event, some student discounts) is Ireland's longest-established and best arts festival, drawing all ages to its program of street theater, classical and contemporary music, jazz, and film events. There are innumerable art exhibitions. Young people from all over Ireland and Britain, including many international travelers, show up here as well, not just for the main festival itself, but for "The Fringe Festival" that has grown up in recent years around the main festival. The Fringe Festival is more cutting edge and youth-oriented. Amateur musicians show up; there is spontaneous open-air theater, poetry readings, displays of provocative art, and a general sense of fun and outrageousness. The town is booked to the gills during the festival and advance reservations are important. Festival time is the most fun and happening time for a young budget traveler to show up.

⚑ Best Murphy's Cat Laughs Comedy Festival (early June; ☎ 056/63416 for info, 056/63837 for booking; www.murphyscat laughs.com) is Kilkenny's best-loved comedy venue that brings you Kilkenny's best-loved comedy festival early every summer. It brings together some of Ireland's funniest comedians as well as several from abroad. Comedians perform throughout various locations in town. Don't wait to get your tickets, and book your room way in advance even if you aren't into stand-up—plenty of other people are, and they'll all be here.

Sleeping

While there's no shortage of B&Bs, there aren't a lot of hostels to choose from in Kilkenny, although the ones that are here are better than average. Hotels get extremely pricey here—luckily a lot of the guesthouses are less expensive and just as luxurious. During the summer and comedy and arts festival weeks, they can fill up; try to book in advance.

HOSTELS

➜Foulksrath Castle Hostel Foulksrath is Ireland's oldest hostel in two ways: the Norman-style tower house dates from the 15th century. This place is absolutely beautiful, a proper castle in every way, but the tower, huge dining hall, fireplaces, and spiral staircase come with a price: The dorm rooms can be cold and echoey. You'll deal with it for the sake of the authentic atmosphere. **Buggy's Coaches** (Castlecomer; ☎ 056/ 41264) runs a shuttle service to the castle every day but Sunday. Don't stay here if you want to do a pub crawl; there's a 10:30pm curfew and the shuttle doesn't run late anyway. *Jenkinstown, 13km (8 miles) north of Kilkenny, County Kilkenny. ☎ 056/67144 or 056/67674. Open Mar–Oct. €12–€16 dorm. Amenities: Kitchen; lounge.*

➜Kilkenny Tourist Hostel In an 18th-century Georgian town house within spitting distance of a half-dozen of the best pubs in the city, the KTH has a bright, comfortable decor, friendly staff, clean spacious dorms, and a spirited social vibe. An excellent and informative events board in the front room, updated daily, will tell you where to find trad sessions, plays, and whatever else is going on that night. Most hostellers prefer to cook in the bright, airy kitchen and eat in the dining room that's always abuzz with activity, even impromptu music sessions. It's always got mellow music on the CD player and incense burning in the comfortable sitting room. There's always a fire burning in the fireplace on a cold, rainy night. Hostels don't get much better than this. *35 Parliament St., Kilkenny, County Kilkenny. ☎ 056/63541. http://home page.eircom.net/~kilkennyhostel. Dorm €12– €18. Amenities: Kitchen; laundry; TV room.*

Kilkenny City

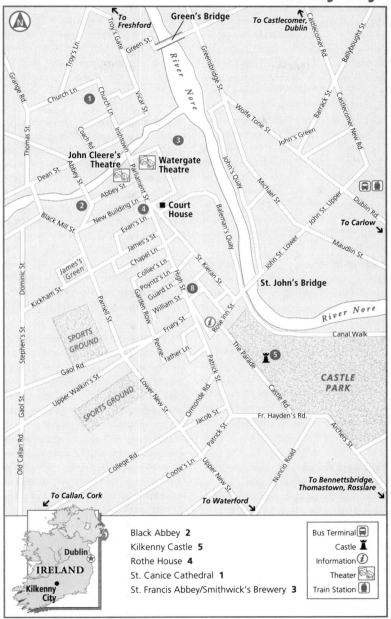

To Freshford
Troy's Gate
Green St.
Troy's Ln.
Grange Rd.
Church Ln.
Thomas St.
Church Ln.
Coach Rd.
Vicar St.
Irishtown
Green's Bridge
River Nore
Greensbridge St.
To Castlecomer, Dublin
Castlecomer Rd.
Ballybought St.
Wolfe Tone St.
Barrack St.
Castlecomer New Rd.
John's Green

John Cleere's Theatre
Watergate Theatre
Abbey St.
Dean St.
Abbey St.
Parliament St.
Black Mill St.
New Building Ln.
■ **Court House**
Evan's Ln.
John's Quay
Michael St.
Balenan's Quay
John St. Upper
Dublin Rd.
To Carlow
John St. Lower
Maudlin St.

James's St.
Chapel Ln.
Collier's Ln.
Poyntz's Ln.
Guard Ln.
William St.
Friary St.
St. Kieran St.
High St.
St. John's Bridge
Dominic St.
James's Green
Kickham St.
Parnell St.
Garden Row
Penney's
father Ln.
Rose Inn St.
River Nore
Canal Walk
Stephen's St.
SPORTS GROUND
Gaol Rd.
Upper Walkin's St.
SPORTS GROUND
Lower New St.
Patrick St.
The Parade
Castle Rd.
CASTLE PARK
Gaol St.
Old Callan Rd.
College Rd.
Coote's Ln.
Upper New St.
Ormonde Rd.
Jacob St.
Patrick St.
Fr. Hayden's Rd.
Nuncio Road
Archers St.
To Callan, Cork
To Waterford
To Bennettsbridge, Thomastown, Rosslare

Dublin
IRELAND
Kilkenny City

Black Abbey **2**
Kilkenny Castle **5**
Rothe House **4**
St. Canice Cathedral **1**
St. Francis Abbey/Smithwick's Brewery **3**

Bus Terminal 🚌
Castle ♟
Information ⓘ
Theater 🎭
Train Station 🚉

CHEAP

➜**Abbey House** This pretty Georgian building alongside the Little Argile River was once part of the Jerpoint Abbey's estate. The front garden is a perfect spot to relax, and the sitting room, with piano and stacks of books, is perfect for relaxing on a rainy afternoon. The owner, Helen Blanchfield, serves you tea and scones when you arrive, and then directs you to one of the comfortable rooms. The nearby town of Thomastown is tiny and quiet. This is not the place if you're looking for a party scene. *Thomastown, County Kilkenny. On the N9, directly across from Jerpoint Abbey.* ☎ *056/7724166. www.abbey housejerpoint.com. €90–€160 double. Rates include service charge and full Irish breakfast. Amenities: Sitting room. In room: TV on request, tea/coffeemaker.*

➜**Ballyduff House** This is a fine B&B, with big, comfortable rooms filled with sunlight and decorated with antiques in a rambling old house. Owner Brede Thomas worked in the U.S. for 10 years, and has a marvelous relaxed approach—you're welcome to chill out just about anywhere, although the library is the best place of all, with shelves filled with enticing books, and lots of soft sofas to sink into. The grounds have streams for fishing. *Thomastown, County Kilkenny. On R700, 5km (3 miles) from New Ross.* ☎ *056/775-8488. €90 double. Rates include full breakfast. No credit cards. Amenities: Library; lounge.*

➜**Cullintra House** You need a car to get to this slightly bohemian guesthouse. It's a historic country farmhouse on a farm that is a sanctuary for birds and other animals. As you would expect in a 200-year-old, ivy-covered farmhouse, each guest room is charming and uniquely decorated. Morning brings a relaxed breakfast schedule (served 9:30am–noon) and perhaps a walk to Mount Brandon or the nearby cairn (prehistoric burial mound)—a trail heads out from the back gate. Dinner—costing €30—begins around 9pm,

announced by the sound of a gong, and guests sometimes don't depart from the candlelit dining room until the wee hours. This place is a good bet if you like good food, candlelight, and cats. *The Rower, Inistioge, County Kilkenny. On R700, 9.7km (6 miles) from New Ross.* ☎ *051/423614. €60–€90 double. Rates include full breakfast. No credit cards. Amenities: Conservatory.*

➜**Danville House** On the outer fringe of historic Kilkenny, this old Georgian (ca. 1735) farmhouse is an affordable, rural haven within walking distance of the city center, tucked down an oak-lined lane. Kitty Stallard is an engaging, unpretentious hostess with a flair for creating old-world comfort. Her quartet of guest rooms is stylish and bright, and there's a walled garden, paddock, and apple orchard out back. *New Ross Rd., Kilkenny, County Kilkenny. On R700, 1.6km (1 mile) from Kilkenny.* ☎ *056/77772. €60–€70 double. Rates include full breakfast. No credit cards. Closed Nov to mid-Mar. In room: Hair dryer.*

➜**Lawcus Farm Guesthouse** This fabulously rustic 200-year-old stone cottage at the edge of the King's River near the village of Kells cries out to be photographed. Owner Mark Fisher bought the place years back to be near good fishing waters, and has gradually converted it into a relaxing, modern country lodge, with walls paneled in polished wood, brass bedsteads, and endless green views. He's added on a deck now, so that you can relax outside with a glass of wine and watch the sun set over the fields. Mark knows the best places to hear traditional music, have a pint, or dine, and he's happy to share them. There are no TVs or outside distractions. *Stonyford, County Kilkenny. Off the N10 on the Kells Rd.* ☎ *056/772-8949. www.lawcusfarm guesthouse.com. €100 double. Rates include full breakfast. No credit cards. Amenities: Dining room; lounge.*

SPLURGE

➜ **Butler House** Built in 1770 by the 16th earl of Ormonde as an integral part of Kilkenny Castle, this elegant, castlelike building has a front door facing busy Patrick Street and a backyard overlooking secluded 17th-century-style gardens. Converted into a guesthouse 20 years ago, it has a sweeping staircase, marble fireplaces, and beautifully decorated guest rooms with peaceful views, neutral color schemes, and quality contemporary furnishings. *16 Patrick St., Kilkenny, County Kilkenny.* ☎ *056/776-5707. www.butler. ie. €110–€250 double. Rates include full breakfast. Amenities: Restaurant (international); bar; babysitting. In room: TV/VCR, tea/ coffeemaker, hair dryer.*

DO IT YOURSELF

➜ **Clomantagh Castle** This huge, rambling castle building sleeps 10 and is ideal for a large group traveling together. Around it, the complex of buildings includes the ruins of a 12th-century church and an early-15th-century crenellated tower house attached to an 18th-century farmhouse. There are four large double bedrooms in the farmhouse, with a staircase leading to a fifth medieval double bedroom in the tower. The decor throughout is rustic, with fine period pieces and brass beds. There are several reception rooms and an enormous country kitchen with a flagstone floor, timbered ceiling, and Stanley range. Like all Irish Landmark Trust properties, Clomantagh Castle has no TV. Although the setting is rural, Kilkenny City is only about 20 minutes' drive away. *Freshford, County Kilkenny. Contact the Irish Landmark Trust* ☎ *01/670-4733. www.irishlandmark.com. From €580 for 4 nights in low season, sliding up to €1,360 per week in high season. Amenities: Dishwasher; kitchen; washing machine.*

Eating

Its strong arts community and busy tourist scene ensures there's no shortage of great places to eat in Kilkenny, and the presence of a few gourmet food stores ensures you'll be eating well no matter what. For picnics, try **The Gourmet Store** (56 High St.), in the center of town, which makes delicious hot and cold sandwiches for a few euros. The other option is the funkily named **Shortis Wong's** (75 John St.), which serves a wide variety of well-stuffed sandwiches and baked goods. For dinner, you could cop out and pick up a frozen pizza at Dunnes Stores (St. Kieran's St.) or Superquinn (Second Floor, Market Cross Shopping Centre, off High St.).

All the pubs serve decent food, too, usually for under €10. Try The Pumphouse or Caisleán Uí Cuain; both serve food till around 8pm.

CHEAP

➜ **The Pantry** IRISH/SANDWICHES This place is cheap and convenient, but the food is by no means spectacular. You can get an adequate sandwich and french fries for under €8 or a full Irish breakfast for even less. *St. Kieran's St., Kilkenny, County Kilkenny.* ☎ *056/62250. Main courses €7–€12. Mon-Sat 7am–2pm.*

➜ **Pennefeathers Café** CAFE This cafe above the Book Centre, is a good cheap choice for breakfast or lunch. The fare's standard, with all sorts of sandwiches for only a few euros or a full Irish breakfast in the morning. *10 High St., Second Floor, Kilkenny, County Kilkenny.* ☎ *056/64063. Main courses €7–€12. Daily 7am–2:30pm.*

➜ **Kilkenny Design Restaurant** CAFETERIA Above the Kilkenny Design shop, this spacious self-service restaurant is a classy place, with whitewashed walls, circular windows, beamed ceilings, and fresh, delicious food. The ever-changing menu often includes local salmon, chicken-and-ham platters, salads, and homemade soups. The pastries and breads offer some unique choices, such as cheese and garlic scones. *The Parade, Kilkenny, County Kilkenny.* ☎ *056/772-2118.*

Reservations not accepted. All items €3–€11. Year round Mon–Sat 9am–5pm; May–Dec Sun 10am–5pm. Closed Sun Jan–Apr.

→**The Water Garden** TEAROOM Just outside Thomastown on the road to Kilkenny, this tearoom and small garden is operated by a local group that helps mentally and physically handicapped people. The cafe serves lunch, tea, and baked goods; meals are prepared with organic vegetables and meats raised on the community farm. Lunches include sandwiches made with home-baked bread, soups, and a vegetable or meat pâté. Buy a ticket to the garden (admission €2.50) and you can take a stroll along a trickling stream; there's also a garden shop. *Thomastown, County Kilkenny.* ☎ *056/772-4690. Main courses €4–€7. No credit cards. Tues–Fri 10am–5pm; Sun 12:30–5pm. Closed Sun Christmas through Easter.*

DOABLE

→**Café Sol** SOUTHERN AMERICAN/ MEDITERRANEAN This bright cafe with light streaming in through floor-to-ceiling windows is a cheerful place in both cuisine and appearance. It's open all day, starting with homemade scones and biscuits at breakfast time, moving on to a lunch menu stocked with comfort foods for busy Kilkenny shoppers and business folk—mainly homemade soups, salads, sandwiches, and hot plates. But the place really comes into its own at dinnertime, when the menu comes alive with zestier options, like Louisiana crab cakes with tomato salsa, or chicken and mozzarella wrapped in phyllo. *6 William St. (opposite the Town Hall), Kilkenny, County Kilkenny.* ☎ *056/776-4987. Reservations recommended for dinner. Lunch main courses €4–€10; dinner main courses €9–€21. Mon–Fri 10am–9pm; Sat 10am–5pm.*

SPLURGE

→**Lacken House** MODERN IRISH With a stately Victorian house as its setting, this restaurant is exceptional, offering meals created with local produce. The menu changes daily but starters might include spring onion and red cheddar soup or smoked salmon on a bed of cucumber ribbons with homemade chive dressing, while mains might include roast leg of lamb and breast of chicken with blue cheese and bacon wrapped in phyllo pastry. *Dublin Rd., Kilkenny, County Kilkenny.* ☎ *056/776-1085. Reservations required. Fixed-price 4-course dinner €39. Tues–Sat 7–10:30pm.*

Partying

To find out what's going on around town, pick up a copy of the local weekly paper *Kilkenny People.* Kilkenny is home to the small-but-mighty **Watergate Theatre,** Parliament Street (☎ **056/776-1674**), a 328-seat venue for local talent and visiting troupes in classic and contemporary plays, concerts, and ballets. Ticket prices average €10 to €20.

Across the street from the theater **John Cleere's,** 28 Parliament St. (☎ **056/776-2573**), is a pub theater that's good for music and local productions, including the hugely popular Cat Laughs comedy fest. It is also a venue for the Kilkenny Arts Week. Tickets average €6 to €10.

PUBS

Kilkenny makes pub crawls just too easy. Some of the best are lined up in a row on Parliament Street across from the Watergate Theatre and the Kilkenny Tourist Hostel. Could they have made it any more convenient for us immoderate world-traveling hooligans?

If you're in a medieval mood, check out **Kyteler's Inn** (27 St. Kieran's St.; ☎ **056/21064**). It's one of the oldest buildings in the city, dating to 1324, and was once the home of Dame Alice Kyteler, the "Witch of Kilkenny." You can cozy up to a large open fire on a chilly night, or take your pint out into the courtyard when it's sunny (which isn't too often).

Bursting at the seams every night of the week, **Caisleán Uí Cuain** (2 High St.; ☎ 056/65406) is a bit tiny, but it's a comfortable enough place to have your pint. This is the pub-bastion of the Irish language in Kilkenny, so you can hear it spoken liberally here. When there's not a trad session going on, the Corrs serve as ear candy.

Hear the bodhran at its best at **Maggie's** (60 High St.; ☎ 056/61017), which is, at least unofficially, the coolest pub in the city due to its old-style pub atmosphere and excellent live trad. Kilkenny lads and lasses showcase some of the best vocal chords on the island 4 nights a week, along with the bodhran, lute, guitar, and tin flute. On Wednesdays and Thursdays live bands shake the floorboards with some lively folk and traditional music. The musicians sing the old ballads so passionately you'd swear they were the ones who wrote them. It's no surprise that this place is hopping like a jackrabbit on steroids. Good luck finding a seat. *FYI:* Just to confuse you, there are two separate facades—one for Jim Holland's and one for Maggie's—but they both lead to the same pub.

Across St. John's Bridge on the east side of the Nore River, is **Edward Langton's** (69 John St.; ☎ 056/65133). Decked out with a sleek horseshoe-shaped bar, posh booths, sofas, and an elegant, modern ambience, it's not your typical pub.

Nobody's grieving at **Widow McGrath's** (29 Parliament St.; ☎ 056/52520), a popular hangout for Kilkenny youth, especially on the weekends. The Widow's much more spacious and modern than Caisleán Uí Cuain or Maggie's. The beer garden out back makes a nice place to enjoy an especially good lunch menu with a nice lukewarm pint on sunny days.

If you want to linger awhile at any one pub on the Parliament strip, let it be The **Pumphouse** (26 Parliament St.; ☎ 056/63924; no credit cards). The pool table, dartboard, cheap sandwiches, and lively vibe make it a popular spot for rowdy young Irishmen. The Pumphouse has one of the best pub grub menus, and the live rock, blues, and folk sessions on Sunday nights make a nice change from the ubiquitous trad. It's definitely one of the coolest places for meeting people and hanging out.

Set on a side street off the southern edge of High Street, **Andrew Ryan's** (3 Friary St.; ☎ 056/62281) is your quintessential Irish pub, with live trad Thursday and Friday nights year-round, a young local crowd, and a beer garden out back. The music isn't quite as typical as the atmosphere, though: Sessions have been known to include Australian aboriginal sounds. If you're up for it, bring your own guitar or violin—all musicians are welcome.

On the northwest periphery of the old town, the **Cat Laughs** (Dean St.; ☎ 056/64398), as you might guess, is run by the organizers of Kilkenny's annual **Murphy's Cat Laughs Comedy Festival** (see "Festivals," above). The bar's got a cool cosmopolitan feel, although the place is best known for its theater, the Mouse Trap, with comedy acts several nights a week. You can usually find a live band playing here on a Saturday night as well.

Want less drink and more laid-back conversation? **Tynan's Bridge Bar** (2 Horseleap Slip, at St. John's Bridge; ☎ 056/21921), a well-preserved Victorian pub, is the perfect place. Red oil lamps and watercolors adorn the walls, and Sinatra songs play softly on the stereo. You could spend all night drinking Bailey's at the classy horseshoe-shaped bar while discussing the meaning of life with your travel buddy, if that's your thing. Tynan's won't be jamming, maybe because it's a bit off the beaten path, but that's why it's so darn likeable. Upcoming renovations will provide more space that'll be used for live music sessions; it's a little too small to accommodate musicians as is.

Pop in at least for a second at **Marble City Bar** (66 High St., Kilkenny, County Kilkenny; ☎ **056/776-2091**) just to see its marvelous facade of carved wood, wrought iron, polished brass, with flower boxes overhead—and the interior is equally inviting. Even if you don't stop for a drink here, you'll certainly want to take a picture.

MUSIC SCENE

You won't be hard-pressed to find music in Kilkenny—most nights of the week trad spills from the pubs. Music usually begins between 9 and 9:30pm in the pubs, although some musicians take their sweet time setting up, especially at Caisleán Uí Cuain—you might have to wait awhile before hearing any music other than what's coming out of the CD player.

The best places in town for trad are Maggie's (Mon–Thurs) and Ryan's (Thurs–Fri); see "Pubs," above, for both. **John Cleere's** (28 Parliament St.; ☎ **056/62573**), in addition to an entertaining open mic night on Wednesdays, has the longest-running trad session in Kilkenny on Monday nights.

You can also find live trad at the Widow McGrath's on Wednesdays; Langton's on Mondays, Fridays, and Saturdays; and at Caisleán Uí Cuain on Mondays and Tuesdays (see "Pubs," above, for all). Kyteler's (see "Pubs," above) also has trad on Thursday and Sunday nights. Sometimes the music schedules vary, but there's definitely live music at a few places at least every night of the week.

There's also a super-popular live rock, blues, and folk happenin' at The Pumphouse (see "Pubs," above) on Sundays beginning at 9:30pm.

CLUBS

There are only a few nightclubs here in Kilkenny, but with such a fabulous pub scene, nobody notices. Times are 11pm to 2am across the board. Expect to pay more here for drinks than you would in the pubs.

Nero's (St. Kieran's St.; ☎ **056/21064; 11pm–2am Thurs–Sat)** is part of Kyteler's Inn. The setup is pretty traditional for a disco: top-40 and cheesy '70s hits on two floors, full bar, and a relatively strict dress code— no "runners" or "trainers" allowed (that's sweatpants and sneakers to you). Nero's gets packed, especially on weekends, so be prepared for crowds.

Locals consider **Langton's** (69 John St.; ☎ **056/65133;** Tues, Thurs–Sun) to be the nicest club in town, probably because it's situated in the posh reception hall in Langton's Hotel. The music's pretty much the same as at Nero's, with the same dress code. The bar and seating area is separate from the dance floor, which is nice if you'd actually like to hear what your partner is saying to you.

The **Flagstone Winebar** (Parliament St.; 11:30pm–2am Thurs–Sun, Wed–Sun in summer) is the coziest club in town. You can dress down here, but there's no beer, so skip it if you've just gotta have that Kilkenny brew. The bar serves wine, cider, and alcoholic soft drinks. There's none of that hokey disco stuff here; the music of choice is techno, and live bands play on Thursday nights.

Sightseeing

Because Kilkenny is Ireland's major medieval city, the city and surrounding area are filled with impressive old structures bearing histories richer than chocolate mousse.

The main business district sits on the west bank of the River Nore. High Street runs the length of the city north to south, changing its name to Parliament Street at midpoint. It starts at the Parade, on the south end near Kilkenny Castle, and continues through the city to St. Canice's Cathedral at the northern end. Most of the city's attractions are along this route or on cross-streets such as Patrick, Rose Inn, Kieran, and John. The tourist office can supply you with a good street map.

FREE → **Black Abbey** Nobody is sure why this Dominican church, founded in 1225, is named Black Abbey. It may be because the Dominicans wore black capes over their white habits, or perhaps because the Black Plague claimed the lives of eight priests in 1348. The Black Abbey's darkest days came in 1650, when Oliver Cromwell used it as a courthouse before destroying it; by the time he left, all that remained were the walls. The abbey was rebuilt, and opened in 1816 as a church, a new nave was completed in 1866, and the entire building was fully restored in 1979. Among the elements remaining from the original abbey are an alabaster sculpture of the Holy Trinity that dates to 1400, and a pre-Reformation statue of St. Dominic carved in Irish oak, which is believed to be the oldest such piece in the world. The huge Rosary Window, a stained-glass work of nearly 45 sq. m (484 sq. ft.) that represents the 15 mysteries of the rosary was created in 1892 by Mayers of Munich. *Abbey St. (off Parliament St.), Kilkenny, County Kilkenny.* ☎ *056/772-1279. Free admission; donations welcome. Apr–Sept Mon–Sat 7:30am–7pm, Sun 9am–7pm; Oct–Mar Mon–Sat7:30am–5:30pm. No visits during worship.*

Best → **Kilkenny Castle** Standing majestically beside the River Nore on the south side of the city, this landmark medieval castle—built in the 12th century and remodeled in Victorian times—was the principal seat of the Butler family, who were the earls, marquises, and dukes of Ormonde. In 1967 the castle was given to the Irish government to be restored to period splendor as an enduring national monument. From its sturdy corner towers to its battlements, Kilkenny Castle retains the imposing lines of an authentic fortress and sets the tone for the city. The exquisitely restored interior includes a fine collection of Butler family portraits, some from as far back as the 14th century. The old castle kitchen operates as a tearoom in the summer. The 20-hectare (49-acre) grounds include a riverside walk, extensive gardens, and a well-equipped children's playground. Access to the main body of the castle is by guided tour only, prefaced by an informative video on the rise, demise, and restoration of the structure. This is a very busy site, so arrive early (or quite late) to avoid waiting. *The Parade, Kilkenny, County Kilkenny.* ☎ *056/772-1450. Admission €5 adults, €2 students. Apr–May daily 10:30am–5pm; June–Sept daily 10am–7pm; Oct–Mar Tues–Sat 10:30am–12:45pm and 2–5pm, Sun 10am–7pm.*

→ **Rothe House** This is a typical middle-class house from the Tudor period. Originally a merchant's home, built in 1594, it consists of three stone buildings divided by cobbled courtyards. It has an arcaded shop front and a remarkable timber ceiling. Purchased in 1961 by the Kilkenny Archeological Society, it was restored and opened to the public. Inside is a museum of sorts, filled with artifacts and period costumes. A family history research service for Kilkenny city and county has its offices here. *Parliament St., Kilkenny, County Kilkenny.* ☎ *056/772-2893. Admission €3, €2 students. Jan–Mar and Nov–Dec Mon–Sat 1–5pm; Apr–June and Sept–Oct Mon–Sat 10:30am–5pm, Sun 3–5pm; July–Aug Mon–Sat 10am–6pm, Sun 3–5pm.*

→ **St. Canice Cathedral** At the northern end of the city, this is the church that gave Kilkenny its name, although the current structure is a relative newcomer—it was built in the 13th century on the site of a 6th-century church. The cathedral was built in early Gothic style, but has been much restored and altered over the years, not least after Cromwell's gang defaced the building—using it as a stable for their horses. Restoration after that took more than a century to complete. It is noteworthy for its rich interior timber and stone carvings, its colorful glasswork, and the structure itself. Its roof dates from 1863, and its marble floor is composed of the four marbles of Ireland. On the grounds, amid the tombstones in the church-yard, is a massive round tower, 30m (98 ft.) high and 14m (46 ft.) in circumference, believed to be a relic of the ancient church (although its original conical top has been replaced by a slightly domed roof). If you want to climb to the tip of the tower, it will cost you €1.30 and more calories than you can count (it's a steep and very narrow climb that is not for the faint of heart or the unfit). The steps that lead to the cathedral were constructed in 1614, and the carvings on the wall at the top of the stairs date to medieval times. *Coach Rd., Irishtown, Kilkenny, County Kilkenny.* ☎ *056/776-4971. Free admission; suggested donation €1.30, €1 students. Easter–Sept Mon–Sat 9am–1pm, daily 2–6pm; Oct–Easter Mon–Sat 10am–1pm, daily 2–4pm.*

Best ➔**St. Francis Abbey Brewery** Established in 1710 by John Smithwick, the brewery occupies a site that originally belonged to the 12th-century Abbey of St. Francis. A popular local beer called Smithwick's is produced here, as are Budweiser and Land Kilkenny Irish beer. A video presentation and free samples are offered in the summer. *Parliament St., Kilkenny, County Kilkenny.* ☎ *056/772-1014. Free admission. June–Aug Mon–Fri at 3pm.*

Sightseeing Beyond Kilkenny City

FREE ➔**Duiske Abbey** Duiske Abbey (1204) is a fine example of an early Cistercian abbey. It was suppressed in 1536, but its monks continued to occupy the site for many years. In 1774 the tower of the abbey church collapsed. In 1813 the roof was replaced and religious services returned to the church, but the abbey didn't approach its former glory until the 1970s, when a group of local people mounted a reconstruction effort. Now, with its fine lancet windows and a large effigy of a Norman knight, the abbey is the pride of Graiguenamanagh. The adjacent visitor center has an exhibit of Christian art and

artifacts. *Graiguenamanagh, County Kilkenny.* ☎ *0503/24238. Free admission; donations welcome. Daily 8am–7:30pm.*

➔**Dunmore Cave** This gloomy series of chambers, formed over millions of years, contains some fine calcite formations. Known to humans for many centuries, the cave may have been the site of a Viking massacre in A.D. 928. Exhibits at the visitor center tell the story of the cave. It's about 11km (7 miles) from Kilkenny City. *Off Castlecomer Rd. (N78), Ballyfoyle, County Kilkenny.* ☎ *056/776-7726. Admission €2.75, €1.25 students. Mid-Mar to mid-June and mid-Sept to Oct daily 9:30am–5:30pm; mid-June to mid-Sept daily 9:30am–6:30pm; winter Fri–Sun and holidays 9:30am–5:30pm.*

➔**Jerpoint Abbey** About 18km (11 miles) southeast of Kilkenny, this is an outstanding Cistercian monastery, founded in the latter half of the 12th century. Preserved in a peaceful country setting, one of the abbey's highlights is a sculptured cloister arcade. There is a splendid array of artifacts from medieval times, including unique stone carvings on ancient tombs and Romanesque architecture in the north nave. A tasteful interpretive center with an adjoining picnic garden makes this a perfect midday stop. Sheila Walsh, who runs the front desk, is as friendly and knowledgeable as they come. She's also a font of information about the area. *On the N9, 2.4km (1½ miles) south of Thomastown, Thomastown, County Kilkenny.* ☎ *056/772-4623. Admission €2.75. Mar–May and mid-Sept to mid-Nov daily 9:30am–5pm; June to mid-Sept daily 9:30am–6pm; late Nov daily 10am–4pm.*

➔**Kells Priory** With its encompassing fortification walls and towers, as well as complex monastic ruins enfolded into the sloping south bank of the King's River, Kells is a glorious ruin. In 1193 Baron Geoffrey FitzRobert founded the priory and established a Norman-style town beside it. The current ruins date from the 13th to 15th centuries. The priory's wall has been carefully restored, and it connects seven towers, the remains of an abbey, and foundations of chapels and houses. You can tell by the thick walls that this monastery was well fortified, and those walls were built for a reason—it was frequently attacked. In the 13th century it was the subject of two battles, and was burned to the ground. The priory is less than a half-mile from the village of Kells. If you have some time to spare, there's a footbridge behind it, which takes you across the river and intersects a riverside walk leading to a picturesque old mill. *Kells, County Kilkenny. Off N76 or N10. From N76 south of Kilkenny, follow signs for R699/Callan and stay on R699 until you see signs for Kells.*

→ **Kilfane Glen and Waterfall** The main place of interest in this small garden is the glen, created in true picturesque style, with an artificial waterfall and a rustic cottage. Views of the cottage and waterfall have been carefully composed, and the sound of water creates a counterpoint to the visual delights of the garden. An installation by the American artist James Turrell, *Air Mass*, is open to visitors, although the time of day it was intended to be seen—dusk—unfortunately doesn't correspond with the garden's hours in summer (the sun's still shining when they close at 6pm). *Thomastown, County Kilkenny.* ☎ *056/772-4558. Admission €4, €2.50 students. Apr–June and Sept Sun 2–6pm; July–Aug daily 11am–6pm. Other times by appointment. Closed Oct–Mar.*

Playing Outside

BICYCLING For complete 1- or 2-week cycling holidays in the Southeast, contact Don Smith at **Celtic Cycling,** Lorum Old Rectory, Bagenalstown, County Carlow (☎/fax **059/977-5282;** www.celticcycling.com).

FISHING The River Nore, southeast of Kilkenny, is known for salmon and trout. For advice, permits, and supplies, visit the **Sports Shop,** 82 High St., Kilkenny (☎ **056/772-1517**).

Shopping

If you like Irish crafts, Kilkenny City is well worth the trip. Its crafts scene is famously happening, and it's hard to leave empty-handed. The local tourist office provides a free Craft Trail map and information on local artisans.

Kilkenny shopping hours are normally Monday to Saturday 9am to 6pm; many shops stay open until 9pm on Thursday and Friday.

Kilkenny Design Centre (Castle Yard, The Parade, Kilkenny, County Kilkenny; ☎ **056/772-2118**) is in an 18th-century coach house and stables of Kilkenny Castle that have been converted into shops and workshops for craftspeople. The center and the smaller shops collected nearby provide a showcase for handcrafted products—jewelry, glassware, pottery, clothing, linens, and furniture. There's also an excellent coffee shop and restaurant upstairs. Open year-round Monday to Saturday from 9am to 6pm, and summer Sundays from 11am to 5pm.

Liam Costigan (Colliers Lane, off High St., Kilkenny, County Kilkenny; ☎ **056/776-2408**) is an alumnus of the Kilkenny Design Centre who produces fine handcrafted jewelry in gold and silver in this tiny studio. You can watch him work as you browse. Open Monday to Saturday 9am to 6pm.

P. T. Murphy (85 High St., Kilkenny, County Kilkenny; ☎ **056/772-1127**) is Kilkenny's master jeweler. The shop is a very good source for Irish Claddagh and heraldic jewelry.

Just outside of Kilkenny town in Bennettsbridge, even more artists have their studios. At **Bridge Pottery** (Chapel St., Bennettsbridge, County Kilkenny; ☎ **056/772-7077;** www.bridgepottery.com) Mary O'Gorman and Mark Campden's shared studio is filled with their mugs, bowls, tiles,

THE SOUTHEAST

plates, even drawer handles—there's something here for every taste and budget, with prices from €4 to €400. Open year-round Monday to Saturday from 10am to 5pm.

Jerpoint Glass Studio (signposted from the N9 just south of Jerpoint Abbey, Stoneyford, County Kilkenny; ☎ 056/772-4350) is the last stop on the "Craft Trail" from Kilkenny to Stoneyford. Here you can watch the creation of Jerpoint Glass, which you've probably been admiring in shops all across Ireland. The lines of the glasses, goblets, and pitchers are simple and fluid, highlighted with swirls of color. You can watch the glass being blown and then blow your budget next door at the shop, which includes an entire room of discounted seconds. Open Monday to Friday from 9am to 6pm and Saturday from 11am to 5pm.

The studios of **Nicholas Mosse Pottery** (The Mill, Bennettsbridge, County Kilkenny; ☎ 056/772-7105; www.nicholasmosse.com) are in a former flour mill on the banks of the River Nore. Using hydropower from the river to fire the kilns, he produces colorful country-style earthenware from Irish clay, including jugs, mugs, bowls, vases, and plates. All are hand-slipped and hand-turned, then decorated by hand with cut sponges and brushes. An on-site museum displays antique Irish earthenware. Open year-round Monday to Saturday from 9am to 6pm, July and August also Sunday from noon to 5pm.

Stoneware Jackson (Bennettsbridge, County Kilkenny; ☎ 056/772-7175; www.stonewarejackson.com) is another fine pottery studio in Bennettsbridge, fast becoming a one-stop village for some of Ireland's most beautiful earthenware. The pieces are hand-thrown, featuring two-color glazing and Celtic motifs. Open Monday to Saturday from 10am to 6pm.

Back in Kilkenny Town, the **Book Centre** (10 High St., Kilkenny, County Kilkenny; ☎ 056/776-2117) offers a fine selection of books about Kilkenny and the area, as well as books of Irish interest. You can grab a quick daytime snack at the Pennefeather Cafe, upstairs.

If you still haven't got that Irish wool sweater, the **Fallers Sweater Shop** (75 High St., Kilkenny, County Kilkenny; ☎ 056/777-0599) will fill the gap. As its name implies, this shop specializes in Aran hand-knit sweaters (of which it carries a large selection) and mohair, cotton, and linen knits.

Kilkenny Crystal (19 Rose Inn St., Kilkenny, County Kilkenny; ☎ 056/772-1090) is the best shop in town for hand-cut local crystal. The factory is on Callan Road (☎ 056/772-5132), 16km (10 miles) outside of town, and it welcomes visitors.

Cork City

Cork City has always played second fiddle to Dublin, its larger and more tourist-friendly cousin to the north. However, Cork was the 2005 European Capital of Culture, meaning the Rebel City now boasts a calendar of cultural events to rival Ireland's capital. Native Corkonians will tell you Cork has always been superior to Dublin. They're fiercely proud of their city, especially its sports teams.

One thing's for certain: Cork is second to none in Ireland when it comes to food. It's packed with fabulous restaurants and is a food-lover's paradise. The nightlife is pretty lively, too. The university scene is thriving so expect bars, pubs, and clubs to be packed most nights of the week with 20-somethings watching "Corcaigh" play football or downing pints of Murphy's (forget Guinness, locals here drink Cork's own brew and you should, too).

But Cork isn't all about knocking back the booze. There are also top-class art galleries like the Crawford and theatre venues like the Cork Opera House, which sell out nightly. If you're not tempted by Cork's cultural offerings, don't miss The English Market, its name a throw-back to days of English rule. Chances are you'll be more fascinated than revolted by the bizarre local food offerings in each stall (innards and the like).

Don't be surprised if you're slightly confused by the lingo in Cork; there's a distinct accent and slang here compared to other parts of the Emerald Isle—even native Irishmen from other parts of the country get lost trying to understand.

If you're a history buff, you'll love all the ancient buildings and churches in Cork, and will want to learn all about the rebel Michael Collins at the Cork Public Museum—he's the area's most famous son. There's a lot to do on the outskirts of Cork too, like visiting the Blarney Castle and kissing its stone. Yes, it's cheesy, but would a visit to Cork and its environs be complete without a quick smooch? You decide.

Best of Cork City

○ **Exploring Seaside Kinsale:** Kinsale's narrow streets all lead to the sea, dropping steeply from the hills around the harbor, although the crowds of visitors teeming on the sidewalks every summer attest to the fact that the Kinsale secret is out. The walk from Kinsale through Scilly to Charles Fort and Frower Point is breathtaking. Kinsale has the added benefit of being a foodie town, with no shortage of good restaurants. See p. 251.

○ **Kissing the Blarney Stone:** Despite the mobs of tourists who besiege it daily, this majestic tower house is worth a visit. While you're there, check out the Badger Cave and dungeons at the tower's base, as well as the serpentine paths that wind through the castle gardens. Need we mention the stone? You sidle in under the upper wall with your head hanging over a 10-story drop. You kiss it. It's a thing people do. See p. 249.

○ **Checking Out Charles Fort:** On a promontory in Kinsale Harbor, this fortress's massive walls enclose a complex of buildings in varying states of repair. At the entrance you're handed a map and left to explore, discover, and almost certainly get lost in the maze of courtyards, passages, walls, and barracks. See p. 257.

○ **Bicycling near the Sea:** The peninsulas and islands of Cork are perfect for cycling, with an abundance of stunning places to visit. Roycroft's Stores in Skibbereen rent bikes that are a notch above the usual rental equipment. See p. 271.

○ **Sea Kayaking Your Heart Out:** I said it in the "Best of" chapter at the beginning of the book, and I'll say it again: GO SEA KAYAKING! It will probably be the highlight of your trip. In Castletownbere on the dramatic, rugged Beara Peninsula, Beara Outdoor Pursuits specializes in accompanied trips out and around Bere Island and as far as Glengariff. You can play it as safe or as rough as you want. See p. 265.

Getting There

BY PLANE There are no transatlantic flights directly into Cork Airport, but this could all change soon, as the airport is currently expanding its services. **Aer Arann** (☎ 0818/210-210 in Ireland or 011-353/617-04428 from the U.S.; www.aerarann.com) flies from Dublin and Belfast to **Cork Airport,** Kinsale Road (☎ 021/413131; www.cork-airport.com), 13km (8 miles) south of the city. Other airlines serving the city include **Aer Lingus** (☎ 800/474-7424 in the U.S. or 0818/365-000 in Ireland; www.aerlingus.ie) with flights from London and Europe. **British Airways** (☎ 800/247-9297 in the U.S. or 087/085-9850 in Britain; www.ba.com) with flights to Manchester and the north of England. **Ryanair** (☎ 01/609-7800 in Ireland or 0906/270-5656 in Britain; www.ryanair.com) serves Cork from London Stansted and Liverpool, while **easyjet** (☎ 1890/923-922;

www.easyjet.com) runs a daily service to London Gatwick, and **bmi baby** (☎ **800/ 788-0555** in the U.S. or 01/242-0794 in Ireland; www.bmibaby.com) serves Cork from Manchester and Birmingham in the north of England.

BY TAXI There are **taxi** ranks outside the arrivals hall of the airport. A journey to the city center should cost from €10 to €13.

BY BUS **Bus Eireann** (☎ **021/450-8188;** www.buseireann.ie) provides bus service from the airport to Parnell Place Bus Station in the city center; the fare is €3.50 one-way, €5.70 round-trip. The trip takes between 18 and 24 minutes, depending on what time you jump aboard. Buses from all parts of Ireland arrive at **Bus Eireann's Passenger Depot,** Parnell Place, in the downtown area, 3 blocks from Patrick Street.

BY TRAIN **Iarnrod Eireann/Irish Rail** (toll-free ☎ **1850/366222** or 01/836-6222; www.irishrail.ie) operates the train services in Ireland. Trains from Dublin, Limerick, and everywhere else in Ireland arrive at **Kent Station,** Lower Glanmire Road, Cork (☎ **021/ 450-4777**), on the city's eastern edge.

BY FERRY Ferry routes into Cork from Britain include service from Swansea on **Swansea/Cork Ferries** (☎ **021/427-1166;** www.swansea-cork.ie), and from Roscoff on **Brittany Ferries** (☎ **021/427-7801;** www. brittany-ferries.com). All ferries arrive at Cork's Ringaskiddy Ferryport. If you're approaching Cork from the east, take the Carrigaloe-Glenbrook ferry from Cobh across Cork Harbour. This ferry can save you an hour's driving time around the edge of Cork Harbour, and you'll save yourself getting caught in Cork's notoriously heavy traffic. The ferry runs from 7:15am to 12:30am. Cars cost €3.50 one-way, €5.50 round-trip, plus €.65 for each additional passenger. For cyclists, the fare is €.75 one-way, €1.30 round-trip. The trip lasts less than 5 minutes. For more information, contact **Cross River Ferries Ltd.,** Westland House, Rushbrooke, Cobh (☎ **021/481-1485**).

BY CAR Many main national roads lead into Cork, including N8 from Dublin, N25 from Waterford, N20 from Limerick, N22 from Killarney, and N71 from West Cork.

Getting Around

BY PUBLIC TRANSPORT **Bus Eireann** operates bus service from Parnell Place Bus Station (☎ **021/450-8188;** www.buseireann. ie) to all parts of the city and its suburbs, including Blarney and Kinsale. The flat fare is €1.10. Buses run frequently from 7am to 11pm Monday to Saturday, with slightly shorter hours on Sunday.

BY TAXI We know you're not going to be swanning around in taxis all the time. But if you need one, taxis are easy to find throughout Cork. The main taxi ranks are along St. Patrick's Street, along the South Mall, and outside major hotels. To call for a

taxi, try **ABC Cabs** (☎ **021/496-1961**), **Cork Taxi Co-Op** (☎ **021/427-2222**), or **Shandon Cabs** (☎ **021/450-2255**).

BY CAR Finding a parking spot in the busy city center can be a bit of a nightmare. You're better off parking at your hotel (if possible) and exploring the city on foot or perhaps by bus. If you just can't be separated from your motor, you'll have to park in public areas; it costs €1.80 per hour, whether you park in one of the city's two multistory parking lots, at Lavitt's Quay and Merchant's Quay, or on the street. There are plenty of ground-level parking lots throughout the city.

CORK CITY

Sleeping & Eating in Cork City

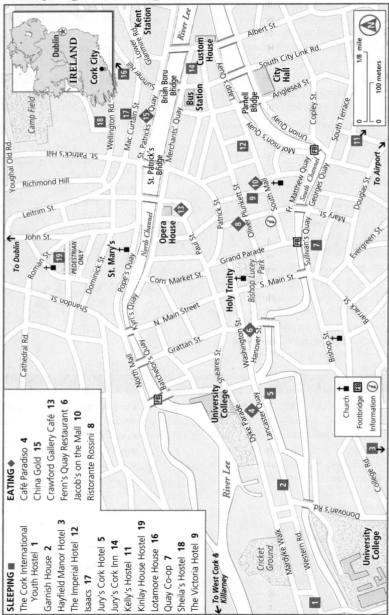

SLEEPING ■

The Cork International Youth Hostel **1**
Garnish House **2**
Hayfield Manor Hotel **3**
The Imperial Hotel **12**
Isaacs **17**
Jury's Cork Hotel **5**
Jury's Cork Inn **14**
Kelly's Hostel **11**
Kinlay House Hostel **19**
Lotamore House **16**
Quay Co-op **7**
Sheila's Hostel **18**
The Victoria Hotel **9**

EATING ◆

Café Paradiso **4**
China Gold **15**
Crawford Gallery Café **13**
Fenn's Quay Restaurant **6**
Jacob's on the Mall **10**
Ristorante Rossini **8**

If you're flying into Cork Airport and want wheels, rent a car there. Rental agents include **Alamo** (☎ 021/431-8636), **Budget** (☎ 021/431-4000), **Hertz** (☎ 021/496-5849), and **Murray's Europcar** (☎ 021/491-7300). **Avis** also has a large depot in Cork City at Emmet Place (☎ 021/428-1111).

ON FOOT This is the best way to see Cork. Lucky for you, there's a signposted Tourist Trail to help you navigate Cork on foot. Give yourself 2 days if you want to see the whole city without a car. Start with the central Flat and the South Bank and then head to the North Bank and the hilly outskirts.

BY BICYCLE Although it's probably a lot easier to walk around Cork, you can rent a bicycle at **Cyclescene** (396 Blarney St.; ☎ 0214301183). It will set you back €15 per day or €80 for a whole week. The office is open Monday through Saturday, 8:30am to 5:45pm.

Orientation

Okay. Let's stamp out any confusion here and now. The first thing you have to realize about Cork is the city center is basically an island in the River Lee. The city is then divided into three main sections: South Bank, North Bank, and the Flat. The South Bank contains the old city walls from the 17th century and remains of what used to be the most important government buildings in the city. This area is now best known for St. Finbarr's Cathedral. The Flat is the core of today's Cork. The main thoroughfare is St. Patrick Street, although locals just call it Patrick Street. It's a street full of shops, cafes, and throngs of people. The South Mall, also on the Flat of the city, is lined almost exclusively with realtors' offices, banks, and law firms. In 1986 Bishop Lucey park was added, bringing a welcome green patch to the grey city center. The North Bank is somewhat reminiscent of San Francisco, with steep streets and great views. MacCurtain Street is the busiest commercial area on this side of the River Lee.

CORK CITY

Basics

TOURIST INFORMATION The **Cork Tourist Office** is located at Tourist House, 42 Grand Parade (☎ 021/427-3251; www.corkkerry.ie). There you'll find maps, brochures, and any other information you might need. Check out the website for an idea of what to expect.

RECOMMENDED WEBSITES The Cork Guide at www.cork-guide.ie is pretty comprehensive. Make sure to check out www.cork2005.ie, the site dedicated to the European Capital of Culture. If you need to book a hotel room, you can't beat www.book-a-hotel-in-cork.com. Of course, there's also the official tourist website mentioned above, www.corkkerry.ie.

Nuts & Bolts

Cellphone Providers It is likely that if your cellphone is less than a couple years old, it will automatically switch over to an Irish network upon your arrival. If this doesn't happen, don't panic; just buy a SIM card from a mobile phone retailer on Patrick Street. **Vodafone** is located at 97 St. Patrick St. (☎ 021/278808); O_2 is at 39 St. Patrick St. These two networks serve over 90% of Cork residents.

Crisis Centers   The **Cork Sexual Violence Centre** (5 Camden Place; ☎ 021/450-5736) can be phoned if you need to talk to someone about something that has happened to you or someone you know. Surprisingly homosexuality was only decriminalized in Ireland in 1993. If you need to speak to someone about LGBT issues, call the **Gay Information Line** (☎ 021/427-1087).

Currency   In Cork, as in all of Ireland, the euro is the recognized currency. To change your money into euros, go to any bank or find a bureau de change. There's one at Cork Airport (☎ 021/496-6487) and one at the large Dunnes department store on Patrick Street (☎ 021/427-0705).

Embassies   There is no American Embassy in Cork. The nearest one is in Dublin (42 Elgin Rd. Ballsbridge; ☎ 01/668-8777).

Emergencies   As in England and Scotland, dial ☎ 999 in an emergency. Note the police here are called Garda. A visit to the A&E (that's Brit-speak for the ER) will set you back about €45. Try **Cork University Hospital,** Wilton Road (☎ 021/454-6400), or **Bon Secours Hospital,** College Road (☎ 021/454-2807). The local Garda Headquarters is on Anglesea Street (☎ 021/452-2000).

Internet/Wireless Hot Spots   **Cork City Library,** 57 Grand Parade (☎ 021/427-7110), has a bank of public Internet workstations available. You can also try **Wired to the World,** 12A Washington St. (☎ 021/427-8584; www.wiredtotheworld.ie). In addition to Internet access for 5 eurocents a minute, it also offers cheap international phone calls. The entire city center of Cork is covered by a Wi-Fi (Wireless Fidelity) network called the MeshHopper. All you need to log on is a credit card.

Laundromats   If you've been wearing the same shirt for 3 days, it's time to go to **Duds'n'Suds** (Douglas St.; ☎ 021/4314-7999; from €4). You can also get clothes dry-cleaned here.

Luggage Storage   Your best bet for dumping your bags while you sightsee is the Cork Bus Station. Their Left Luggage area is open 7 days a week and costs €3.60 per bag per day. Don't bother looking at the train station as their Left Luggage office closed down.

Post Offices   The **General Post Office** is located on Oliver Plunkett Street (☎ 021/485-1012) and is open Monday through Saturday from 9am to 5:30pm.

Safety   The best safety tip for any American across the pond is to remember that the Irish drive on the LEFT. That means you need to look RIGHT when you're crossing the road. Otherwise, Cork City is fairly safe—it's not teaming with pickpockets like other European cities but don't go leaving your hotel door open or anything.

Telephone Tips   The country code for America is 1, so dial ☎ 011 to call anywhere in the United States.

A really reliable service for Directory Assistance is ☎ 11811, although it can be expensive.

Some telephone booths in Cork now have Internet access available so look carefully when you pass them.

Tipping   Don't tip bartenders or waitstaff. It will invariably lead to an awkward exchange and your €2 will be handed back to you.

Sleeping

Hostels

→ The Cork International Youth Hostel
Although the location is nothing to write home about, the hostel itself is far nicer than others you might find closer to the action. The Victorian building is particularly grand and, unusually, the hostel offers two-bed rooms for couples seeking privacy. These rooms go first so call ahead. There's a communal TV room if you're inclined to socialize and a bureau de change for converting dollars to euros. *1–2 Redclyffe, Western Road.* ☎ *021/454-3289. €14 for a dorm; €38 for a double room. Amenities: Coin-operated laundry machines; TV room; kitchen; luggage storage. Bus: 8.*

→ Kelly's Hostel With walls covered in Celtic artwork and rooms themed after famous Irish poets, this small hostel radiates eccentricity and color. All the rooms, except the Seamus Heaney, are nonsmoking. You'll find young travelers lounging in front of the fireplace in the TV room on Sunday mornings. *25 Summerhill South.* ☎ *021/431-5612. Dorms from €14. Amenities: Laundry service; kitchen.*

→ Kinlay House Hostel One of three Kinlay House hostels in Ireland, the Cork branch is clean, comfortable, and provides every amenity you could need, from Internet access to a bureau de change. Some rooms have private bathrooms, and the hostel, located in peaceful Shandon, offers free breakfast if you can make it up before 9:30am. Breakfast included. *Bob and Joan's Walk, Shandon.* ☎ *021/450-8966. Dorms from €13. Amenities: Bureau de change; Internet; laundry service.*

→ Sheila's Hostel While the rooms here are small, most backpackers would consider this fun, friendly place the best hostel in Cork City. Snacks are sold at the front desk, and

you can rent videos and check your e-mail in-house. The sauna is a huge draw, even though you have to pay a couple euros for the privilege. *3 Belgrave Place, Wellington Rd.* ☎ *021/450-5562. Dorms from €10. Amenities: Laundry service; sauna room.*

Cheap

→ Garnish House This B&B is the favorite of travelers in the know, and for good reason. Proprietor Hansi Lucey is one of the friendliest Corkonians you're likely to find—you'll feel like family. The rooms are nicely decorated and exceedingly comfortable for the price. Try the champagne breakfast recently added to the menu. *Western Rd.* ☎ *021/427-5111. €80–€110 double. Amenities: Hair dryer; lounge; nonsmoking rooms; TV.*

→ Jury's Cork Inn Overlooking the River Lee, the Jury's is part of a successful chain and is particularly well suited if you're traveling with younger siblings as there are special prices for kids. The rooms have a bright, contemporary feel and there's a passable European restaurant in-house. *Anderson's Quay.* ☎ *021/427-6444. €80–€89. Amenities: Restaurant; bar; coffee/tea facilities; hair dryer; laundry service; TV.*

→ The Victoria Hotel You might remember the 19th-century Victoria as the place Stephen Dedalus stayed in Joyce's *A Portrait of the Artist as a Young Man.* Then again, you might not. Nowadays the Victoria still feels old-fashioned, with its mahogany cocktail bar, but the rooms have been recently modernized with multi-channel TVs and en-suite bathrooms. ☎ *021/427-6444. €75. Amenities: Restaurant; bar; hair dryer; laundry service; TV.*

Doable

→ Lotamore House Located in Tivoli—a few minutes outside central Cork by taxi or bus—Lotamore House benefits from beautiful, green grounds and individually decorated bedrooms. The staff, many of whom are French, are friendly and accommodating. The breakfast is truly delicious so forget counting calories and order the full Irish fry-up. *Dublin-Waterford Road, Tivoli.* ☎ *021/482-2344. €120 double. Full breakfast included. In room: TV, coffee/tea facilities, hairdryer, trouser press.*

➔**The Imperial Hotel** There's loads of lore associated with this local favorite—for instance, Michael Collins, the revolutionary negotiator of the Free State Treaty, spent his last night here, and Charles Dickens was a guest. Right in the city center, this hotel has the best modern amenities in this price range, like DVD players and fax machines in the executive suites. The decor is full of old-school charm, like Waterford crystal chandeliers. *South Mall.* ☎ *021/427-4040. €125 double. Amenities: 2 restaurants; 2 bars; coffee/tea facilities; concierge; iron; laundry service; radio; room service; trouser press; TV; voice mail.*

Splurge

➔**Hayfield Manor Hotel** If money's no object, check in here without a second thought. This is by far the most luxurious hotel in Cork City, from its marble entrance foyer to the beautiful orchard you can see from your window; it's all just divine. It's slightly off the beaten track near the university campus, but you'll welcome the seclusion as the hotel is just so comfortable and your every whim will be catered to, whether you fancy a day spent lolling in the Jacuzzi or an afternoon sipping tea in the conservatory. *Perrott Ave., College Rd.* ☎ *021/431-5600. €365 double; €420 junior suite; €565 executive suite; €990 master suite. Amenities: Restaurant, bar, indoor pool, health club with treatments, steam room, Jacuzzi, room service, concierge, laundry service, babysitting, trouser press. In room: A/C, TV, hair dryer.*

➔**Jury's Cork Hotel** Jury's is in a perfect location, a few minutes from the University and the banks of the River Lee. The public areas of the hotel are bright and airy, and it's a health nut's paradise with a gym, squash court, and indoor pool. It's naturally a real hit with business people, but the modern amenities and well-designed rooms make it perfect for young tourists, too. *Western Rd.* ☎ *021/427622. €140–€210 double. Amenities: Restaurant, 2 bars, gym, indoor pool, sauna, concierge, laundry service, dry cleaning, non-smoking rooms, squash court. In Room: TV, trouser press, hair dryer, radio.*

Eating

Cheap

➔**Crawford Gallery Café** TRADITIONAL Owned by the same family that runs the famed Ballymaloe House hotel, this cafe, on the ground floor of the Crawford Art Gallery, makes a mean smoked salmon sandwich, made with fresh fish from Ballycotton Bay. All the delicious, light breads and baked goods are courtesy of the Ballymaloe House kitchens. *Emmet Place.* ☎ *021/427-4415. Main courses €4–€12. Mon–Sat for lunch.*

Best ➔**Quay Co-op** VEGETARIAN On the second floor of a whole foods market, this hidden gem is a favorite for Cork's vegetarian and vegan community, who gather for the creamy lentil and coconut soup and the homemade breads and cakes. The restaurant is self-service but don't let that put you off; the food is worth queuing for. *24 Sullivan's Quay.* ☎ *021/431-7026. Main courses €7–€9. Daily for breakfast, lunch, and dinner.*

Doable

→ **Fenn's Quay Restaurant** INTERNA-
TIONAL The O'Learys' restored 18th-
century terrace house attracts Cork's trendsetters and ladies who lunch, making midday
quite crowded at Fenn's. The food is unpretentious, although you may be surprised at
some of the inventive combinations, like a
spinach and cream cheese strudel covered in
black olive sauce. Come for dinner if you
don't want to wait for ages for a table. *5 Fenn's
Quay.* ☎ *021/427-9527. Main courses €16–
€24. Mon–Sat for breakfast, lunch, and
dinner.*

→ **Isaacs** INTERNATIONAL   It's likely that
your hotel concierge or taxi driver—if you're
fancy enough to have one—will recommend
Isaacs above anywhere else for dinner in
Cork. It's very trendy, but the staff aren't
show-offs and the menu is understated, with
classic dishes like Caesar salad and pasta

dishes. The decor is contemporary and all the
diners seem to be having such a great time.
Join in the fun, if you've got a large enough
wallet. *48 MacCurtain St.* ☎ *021/450-3805.
Main courses €14–€25. Mon–Sat for lunch
and dinner; Sun for dinner.*

→ **Jacob's on the Mall** INTERNATIONAL
You're sure to hear all about Jacob's before
you even make a reservation. It's housed in a
grand old Turkish bathhouse, with tall windows letting the sunlight flood in. Chef Mercy
Fenton is a master of mix and match, adding
a hint of unexpected flavor to every dish, like
mackerel with fennel. *30A South Mall.* ☎ *021/
425-1539. Main courses €16–€30. Mon–Sat for
lunch and dinner.*

→ **Ristorante Rossini** ITALIAN   This
place is old-school Italian, from the candle
wax dripping down Chianti bottles in the
center of each table to the deliciously creamy
homemade pasta. If you love Italian food you

What's That on My Plate?

Cork is a good place to get acquainted with the traditional Irish dishes. You'll
probably see some unfamiliar terms on menus in Cork, or you might spot an
interesting meatlike item on sale at the English Market and wonder what on
earth it is. Here's an easy guide to Cork food. What? Did you think they only
ate potatoes?

→ **Crubeens:** Pigs' trotters (feet).

→ **Drisheen:** Main intestine of animals, usually sheep or goats.

→ **Tripe:** Muscular stomach lining, usually from a cow. Often paired with
drisheen.

→ **Black and White Pudding:** Meat dish, often served as part of Irish breakfast. Black pudding is made with pig's blood and suet (fat). White pudding
is made from minced liver, without blood.

→ **Champ:** Potato and onion dish with a coin hidden inside; often made for
Hallowe'en.

→ **Barmbrack:** Traditional bread made with fruit.

→ **Corned beef:** Brisket pickled in brine overnight.

→ **Dulse:** Edible purple seaweed.

→ **Yellowman:** Sticky honeycomb toffee.

→ **Boxty:** Potato and egg dish.

→ **Colcannon:** Mashed potato and cabbage meal.

MTV 🍵 Cafes, Coffeehouses & Late-Night Bites

You'll find a whole host of cafes and tearooms filled with students and hipsters on Patrick Street. If you want something slightly different, head to the English Market and stop by at the **Farmgate Café** (English Market, ☎ 021/463-2771). Have a drink on the balcony and watch the bustling crowd browse the stalls below. You can order up traditional Irish fare like blood sausages if you get hungry. If you want a faster caffeine fix, try the **Gingerbread House** at St. Paul Plaza in the city center (☎ 021/427-6411). You can grab a cup of tea on the go or stay for one of their popular pizzas or sandwiches.

The best coffee house for sipping a latte and reading the paper is **Gloria Jean's** (84 Patrick St.; ☎ 021/427-0555). They sell freshly baked breakfast goodies and make a mean banana mocha. If you're a coffee aficionado, you'll love **Café Gusto** (3 Washington St., ☎ 021/425-4446). Their perfectly roasted espresso is complemented by really good food, like the goat's cheese and roasted red pepper wrap.

For those who prefer hot chocolate to cold beer—or those who are too young to drink—**Tribes** (8 Tuckey St.; ☎ 021/427-6070) is the place to spend your night. Tribes plays funky music and serves herbal tea to caffeine junkies 'til 4am on the weekends. For tasty food when most restaurants are shut, head to **Café Mexicana** (1 Carey's Lane; ☎ 021/427-6433). It bills itself as open "'til late" so it's up to you what time they close. Their traditional Mexican dishes are sizzling and piled with cheese and vegetables. If you find yourself craving noodles after a few drinks, head over to **Star Vast** (17 Princes St.; ☎ 021/425-4969). They stay open late for hungry partygoers and serve tasty fusion cuisine, with special emphasis on vegetarian options.

really can't go wrong. *34 Princes St. ☎ 021/427-5818. Main courses €16–€23. Mon–Sat for lunch and dinner.*

Splurge

→**Café Paradiso** VEGETARIAN This restaurant is one of the best in Ireland, regardless of the fact that meat is not served. Chef Denis Cotter uses organic local produce and Irish cheeses to create mouthwatering concoctions like his signature beetroot, sugar snap, pesto, and goat's cheese salad. The desserts are to die for, and include a killer baked Alaska, so save some room. The Café Paradiso Cookbook makes a great gift. *16 Lancaster Quay, Western Rd. ☎ 021/427-7939. Main courses €20–€30. Tues–Sat for lunch and dinner.*

→**China Gold** CHINESE China Gold is busy and popular with a laid-back atmosphere and a huge menu, including lots of shellfish and dishes from Thailand and Malaysia as well as China. The staff is on the ball and you won't wait long for your sweet and sour pork. *43 St. Patrick St. ☎ 021/427-3535. Main courses €20–€30. Daily for lunch and dinner.*

Partying

Cork nightlife is lively for such a small city, mostly due to university students and a young, cool art crowd. You'll find events going on at bars and clubs every night of the week, and concerts or plays being staged at venues all over the city. Pick up a copy of *The Event Guide* magazine at a newsagent or bookstore to see listings. Of course, for tourists of a certain age, traditional Gaelic music is a huge draw, but if you find that eye-rollingly dull, there's all sorts of other fun to be had after dark.

Bars/Lounges

You can't turn a corner in Cork without discovering a new bar or pub, usually heaving with students and professionals alike all nights of the week. While there are the usual touristy pubs with fiddlers playing traditional, or "trad," music, there are a handful of very sophisticated, stylish wine bars and lounges that attract good looking young people. Just remember when ordering a drink: Here in Cork they drink Murphy's and Beamish, brewed locally, not Guinness. Also remember a Cork native's accent becomes far harder to understand when they've had 4 or 5 pints.

➜ **Billy Morgan's**   Centrally located and full of professional types, Billy Morgan's is always comfortable and friendly due to the stringent door policy—no troublemakers allowed. Popular sports matches are broadcast on the big screen by day, but by night the music is turned up and patrons relax with a beer or five. *Marlboro St. No phone.*

➜ **The Black Stuff**   By day, the relatively new Black Stuff is a cafe, with 30-something customers drinking coffee and reading the papers. At night, DJs spin music of all kinds, with Friday being '60s night. The Black Stuff attracts older partygoers than most other bars but there's something to be said for a civilized night out. *17 Devonshire St. ☎ 021/450-7116.*

Best ➜ **Bodega**   This place just oozes cool with its two-story mirrors and random car parts chained to the walls. The patrons are the very hippest of university students dressed as if they just raided a vintage boutique. The drinks are somewhat expensive but the vibe is very young and fun. *46–49 Cornmarket St. ☎ 021/427-2878.*

➜ **The Exchange**   If you love wine, you'll love The Exchange. You'd be hard pressed to find a more comprehensive wine list anywhere in the country. Luckily for those without a trust fund, the pricier wines are sold by the glass as well as the bottle, so you can have your own wine tasting session without breaking the bank. *George's Quay. ☎ 021/431-1786.*

➜ **Le Cheile**   If you're headed to the Gate Cinema to see a movie, definitely pop into Le Cheile before or after for a drink—it's right next door. The bar is new and stylish and the staff eager to assist. The atmosphere is buzzing, with customers sipping white wine and discussing the latest Jude Law film. If you're there around noon, stop in for lunch; their sandwiches and salads are above average. *104 N. Main St. ☎ 021/425-1571.*

➜ **LV**   For beer-lovers, this bar is paradise, with a long list of imported brews. The LV is a popular spot for pre-club boozing, and even on Sunday nights, when DJ Miss Ken D spins funk and soul, it's pretty crowded. The wine list is comprehensive and there's a pool table if you'd rather play than chat. *55 MacCurtain St. ☎ 021/455-1241.*

➜ **Maguire's Warehouse Bar**   There's a really lively, excited vibe at Maguire's, a large central bar popular with Cork's young 9-to-5 workers looking for a good time at the end of a long day. The good looking staff show off their cocktail shaking skills while DJs spin chart dance music. Come at 10, when the night really gets going. *Daunt Sq. ☎ 021/427-7825.*

➜ **The Roundy**   This sleek, small round lounge is the favorite watering hole of Cork's stylish artsy set. The music is at the perfect volume, allowing you to chat to the hipper-than-thou musician or sculptor next to you but still functioning as a soundtrack to your night. Drinks are pricey but the scene makes it worth it. *1 Castle St. ☎ 021/427-7682.*

The Talk of the Town

3 Ways to Start a Conversation with a Local

1. Cork was named the 2005 European Capital of Culture. Just mention this and you're sure to get a lecture from any local about the reasons why.

2. Every Irish county has its own football team and locals are fiercely loyal. If you start a convo based around the Cork team, you'll have plenty to talk about.

3. If you want unbiased info on what attractions to see—especially those outside the city itself, perhaps without much publicity—ask a native. They will have no qualms about sharing their opinions, trust us.

➔**Scotts**   Scotts is an odd mixture of traditional pub and chic, sleek bar—it serves a carvery lunch in the daytime, but at night the whole place pulsates as DJs spin an assortment of happy dance tunes. On Fridays there's a jazz night to ring in the weekend. The crowd consists of lots of regulars—a testament to the friendly atmosphere at Scotts. *Caroline St.* ☎ *021/422-2779.*

Pubs

➔**An Brog**   This pub is a real hit with students, mostly due to its close proximity to a handful of really good clubs. The music is decidedly indie and metal, with favorite local bands like Semi playing gigs to a packed house. Get to happy hour at 5 on the dot if you want a seat—students will flock here after lectures end. *74 Oliver Plunkett St.* ☎ *021/427-1392.*

➔**Clancy's**   Clancy's is just beside the city's financial district, so expect lots of business types with suits and loosened ties sipping lager and nibbling at delicious food from the bar menu, which features vegetarian cuisine. At night, music takes over, both traditional Irish and modern. *15–16 Princes St.* ☎ *021/427-6097.*

➔**Gallagher's**   Where else in Cork can you get a 3-pint pitcher of beer for less than 10€? Or at all? This is a pretty run-of-the mill student and traveler's pub, with the requisite Black Eyed Peas song barely audible over the booming voices of patrons. Get there early if you want a seat as it's crowded most nights. *MacCurtain St.* ☎ *021/455-1526.*

➔**The Goat Broke Loose**   Once you get over the humorous name, you'll realize this pub—known simply as "the Goat"—is a fun place to spend an evening. It's definitely aimed at a young crowd, and most of the patrons seem to be under 21, drawn in by the big screen, DJs, and happy hour specials from 3pm 'til 8pm every day. The cocktail list is especially good. *51 Grand Parade.* ☎ *021/427-9186.*

MTV **Best** ➔**The Old Oak**   If you're even slightly claustrophobic, steer clear of the Old Oak on weekends, as seemingly every student and young professional from miles around flocks here for a beer while U2 blasts from the speakers. You'd be forgiven for thinking the Old Oak's a bit of a meat market; all those girls aren't wearing skintight jeans for nothing. *113 Oliver Plunkett St.* ☎ *021/427-6165.*

➔**Rearden's**   Popular with the football and rugby crowds, Rearden's is the only place to watch a sporting event on the big flatscreen TVs while downing pints of Beamish or Murphy's. Occasionally there are silly promotional events involving staff wearing costumes, but usually this is a well-regarded pub with an impressive roster of music gigs and big sandwiches at lunch time. *26 Washington St.* ☎ *021/427-1969.*

Run That by Me Again

The Cork lingo can take a little while to master. Words have filtered into the everyday vernacular of Cork natives from languages as diverse as Hindustani and Shelta (the language of Gypsies). You'll get brownie points from locals you meet at pubs if you know a few of these indigenous terms:

Aish: person/character: He's a great aish.
Baytur: fool: You're being a stupid bayter.
Chaw: castigate: She really chawed me out.
Flah-bag: woman of loose morals: Your mom's a huge flah-bag.
Gutty: uncouth/vulgar: Ew, he's such a gutty boy.
Ire, touch of: To be sexually aroused: I met this hot girl and had a touch of ire.
Joulter: derogatory name: Hey, you dumb joulter!
Ledder: to beat someone up: I leddered him with a lamp.
Nooks: money.
Ownshuck: a really simple person: Leave him, he's an old ownshuck.
Queer-hawk: weird individual: She only eats foods that are blue—what a queer-hawk.
Smack: to hold someone in high regard: I have a great smack for my teacher.
Vamp: to walk.
Whacker: a measure of alcohol: I'd like a whacker of whiskey, please.

➜ **Sin E**   Gaelic for "That's it," the Sin E is a real favorite with locals, particularly the artsy crowd. Old movie posters cover the red walls, and the landlord plays selections from his own somewhat eclectic music collection. It's perfect in the winter time with its roaring fireplace and little fairy lights glowing in the darkness. *Coburg St.* ☎ *021/450-2266.*

Clubs

Whether you like sake-bombing at a sleek Japanese club or sweating to the newest Usher song on a crowded dance floor, there's something for you in Cork. The busiest nights of the week, as you would imagine, are Friday and Saturday but there are certain nights during the week that bring in the crowds, like Tuesdays at the Red Room. You'll want to turn up at clubs before 11:30pm as you'll usually get in for a reduced rate. The night usually dies down at about 2am, when clubs stop serving booze. As for dress code, don't fret: Cork might be a City of Culture, but her natives aren't exactly straight off the catwalk. You can get away with

being less than totally trendy at Cork night-clubs, as guys favor sportswear and girls dress in simple, preppy gear. Nice jeans or basic black will pass the test.

➜ **Club FX**   You have to be over 21 to get into Club FX, which means you'll avoid binge-drinking "freshers" or first-year students but will have to dress up slightly. The theme is sub-aqua, so you'll find underwater creatures and plants adorning the walls. The music is perhaps a bit dated, with '70s and '80s hits getting a fair amount of air time. You can sneak in through the Mardyke Tavern before 11pm and avoid cover charge. Cover €6. *Lynch's St.* ☎ *021/427-1120.*

➜ **Cubin's**   This club caters for everyone, whether you want to dance 'til the early hours or chat with friends, as the dance floor is huge and packed, but there's a quiet bar with a chill-out room off to the side. Cubin's closes at 2:30am, slightly later than other local clubs, so many a great night ends here. Cover €7. *Hanover St.* ☎ *021/427-9251.*

→**Mangan's** If you like the sorts of clubs where every surface is covered in chrome and metal, people pose sexily at the bar, and the latest top-20 tunes blast from a state-of-the-art sound system, then Mangan's is for you. Nothing here is low-key, but there are some perks that you won't enjoy anywhere else like a free drink on Sundays and free entry for women before midnight. Cover €6. *Carey's Lane.* ☎ 021/427-5530.

→**The Pavilion** Known as "the Pav," this former movie theater is tucked away up Carey's Lane but has hosted some famous DJs despite its diminutive size. The decor is stylish and the patrons seem to be having a great time sipping reasonably priced cocktails to a mix of house, funk, and dance music. Cover approx €7. *Carey's Lane.* ☎ 021/427-6288.

→**Rafterz** Situated on Hanover Street and recently refurbished, Rafterz bills itself as a student nightclub so expect lots of overexcited, drunk kids buying cheap beer at this popular haunt. The DJs spin everything from classic house to chart hip-hop. Cover €6. *Hanover St.* ☎ 021/427-1969. *Tues, Wed, Thurs only.*

→**The Red Room** This club only admits people aged 23 and over, so you won't find any drunk students puking on themselves in the corner. A favorite with clean-cut rugby-playing types, the Red Room isn't particularly raucous, but if all you want is a stiff drink and a dance then this is the club for you. Cover €5. *17 Liberty St.* ☎ 021/425-1855.

MTV Best →**Savoy Theatre** Savoy Theatre is one of Cork's newest and coolest nightclubs, and its central location on Patrick Street makes it a huge draw for locals and tourists alike. They've already hosted some big-name music acts like Fun Loving Criminals and drum 'n' bass king DJ Hype. The club used to be a cinema, and vestiges like red velvet curtains still remain. Cover approx €10. *Patrick St.* ☎ 021/425-3000.

→**The Yumi-Yuki Club** A fabulous Japanese restaurant by day, Yumi-Yuki comes alive at night with roots and reggae or jazz music and the occasional karaoke night on Wednesdays or Thursdays. Revelers come from all walks of life, from musicians to professors. You have to try their signature drink, the saketini. *Tobin St.* ☎ 021/427-5777.

Gay Scene

Okay, so neither Cork nor Ireland as a whole is exactly flying the Pride flag from every building. In fact, homosexuality was outlawed until 1993, horrifyingly enough. However, these days the Rebel City is making an effort to include partiers of all orientations. There aren't many venues specifically for the LGBT crowd, but some clubs and pubs offer gay nights once or twice a week. There are a couple of guesthouses that cater specifically to the gay crowd; see "Guesthouses Catering to the Gay & Lesbian Community," below.

Culture Tips 101

Cork is known as the Rebel City so expect all sorts of controversial, cutting-edge arts exhibitions and a vibrant theater scene. The arts are part of Cork's heritage, and the locals will be well versed in the goings on in their galleries and performance spaces. Cork is in some ways a bizarre blend of no-nonsense, old-fashioned, working class Irishness and modern European cosmopolitan cafe lifestyle. The former dates back to Cork's roots as a shipping town, and the latter is due to the huge university scene and the thriving arts sector. Corkonians are especially proud of their city—they've even named it the People's Republic of Cork. Compare it to Dublin and expect a barrage of negativity about the larger, more touristy city to the north.

Guesthouses Catering to the Gay & Lesbian Community

The following guesthouses are geared to the gay and lesbian community:

Located in Cork's historic district, **Roman House** (3 St. Johns Terrace; ☎ **021/450-3606;** €50 for a double room; www.interglobal.ie/romanhouse) is a cozy guesthouse with large, colorful bedrooms and lots of parking. If you can't bear to leave Tinkerbell behind, not to worry: The owners allow small dogs! Try the vegetarian breakfast and head out to explore the city from this ideal base. **Emerson House's** (2 Clarence Terrace; ☎ **021/450-3647;** €35 for a double room. www.emersonhousecork.com) friendly gay owner Cyril really makes every effort to make guests feel comfortable at this well-appointed Edwardian guesthouse. The clientele is overwhelmingly comprised of male couples—many of whom are repeat guests, a testament to the pretty rooms, delicious breakfast, and relaxing surroundings.

Best ➜ **Loafers** This gay bar is relaxed and friendly, with a beer garden for sunny days and a pool table for restless revelers. Often Loafers hosts charity functions like bingo nights, but don't expect to see anyone with blue-tinted hair filling in their cards—it's usually 30 and under here. On the weekends, DJs get the party-loving crowd on their feet. *26–27 Douglas St.* ☎ *021/431-1612.*

➜ **The Other Place** Cork's only gay nightclub, The Other Place welcomes regulars and visitors alike, so don't be shy about turning up on the weekend. Spread over two floors, the club offers a large bar, often with free food up for grabs. The DJs here are better than at most other local clubs, spinning exclusive dance remixes. *8 Main St.* ☎ *021/427-8470.*

➜ **Half Moon Theatre** A performance space best known for staging concerts and plays, the Half Moon doubles as a hot nightspot, with two gay-friendly nights per week: Yo! Latino on Thursdays and Soulsides on Sundays. When the Half Moon returns to a normal theatre on other nights of the week, the drama and music on show is worth a look—for instance, a great production of King Lear was on recently. *Emmet Place.* ☎ *021/ 427-0022.*

Live Music

Cork's music scene is very lively, and you'll find all genres represented, from traditional Irish to blues and jazz. The best venue is undoubtedly **The Lobby** (1 Union Quay; ☎ **021/431-9307**)—the upper floor of a rather ordinary bar. Every single night you'll find a different sort of music being played here, whether it's bluegrass or New Age. If you feel at home in a crowd of middle-aged men with tie-dyed T-shirts and Grateful Dead obsessions, head to **Charlie's** (2 Union Quay, ☎ **021/496-5272**). The artwork on the walls is slightly bizarre and it can get busy, but if you want to hear some favorite local bands jamming, this is the place to go. The biggest live music venues for nontraditional, chart-topping acts are actually outside Cork City as the centre itself is too small to support stadium-filling gigs. If you check out www.corkgigs.com, you'll see who's lined up to play while you're visiting. The best arena is probably **Green Glens** (☎ **029/70707;** www.ticket master.ie/venue/196829) in Millstreet, about 40 miles from the city itself. Popular crooner James Blunt, '90s bad boys Prodigy, and Red Red Winers UB40 have all performed recently. For more details on the Green Glens venue, see www.ticketmaster.ie.

CORK CITY

A Miniguide to Irish Music (and, for Once, We're Not Talking about Fiddling)

You might be forgiven in thinking the only Irish musical talent of the last few decades has been U2, what with all the coverage lead singer Bono gets for his good deeds. However, while in Cork, it would be worth your while to download some of these Irish acts to get you in the mood for fun in the Rebel City. Here are the top 10 songs by Irish bands (not including lame grand-mother-friendly acts like Enya):

10. Thin Lizzy: "Whiskey in the Jar." The lyrics don't make much sense ("whack for my daddy-o"? What?) but the boys from Dublin rocked the big-hair-and-bellbottom look with the best of them.

9. The Pogues: "A Fairytale of New York." The kings of Irish Folk wrote this ballad of two Irish immigrants in a drunk tank over Christmas. Full of awesome swear words.

8. Shane MacGowan: "That Woman's Got Me Drinking." The title of the former Pogues singer's 1994 single is interesting seeing that he's a complete drunk.

7. Boyzone: "I Love the Way You Love Me." The now-defunct boy band's cheesy love ballad may turn your stomach now, but after a few listens you'll be singing along.

6. The Thrills: "Big Sur." The hippest band to come out of the Emerald Isle in years, The Thrills write melancholy songs like this one that asks if you'll "dance to the end."

5. Ronan Keating: "Life Is a Rollercoaster." Once the grinning blonde lead singer of Boyzone, Ronan made this rather sweet, positive song a big hit with teenyboppers a few years back.

4. Westlife: "You Raise Me Up." This ballad from today's top Irish boy band is the stuff of love stories and . . . reality TV background music. If you're feeling moody anyway, it will make you cry.

3. Sinéad O'Connor: "Nothing Compares 2 U." Chances are you know all the words anyway, so why not have this on your iPod while touring the bald rebel's home country.

2. U2: "With or Without You." Bono's smooth voice and The Edge's cool guitar riffs make U2 arguably the biggest rock group on the planet.

1. Van Morrison: "Moondance." The mainstay of frat parties and parents' CD mixes alike, this is a true Irish anthem.

Of course, some small, cool nontraditional acts play live in Cork. DJ Sammy Jo of the Scissor Sisters just played the Savoy Theatre (see "Clubs," above), as did old-school '90s rapper Jazzy Jeff.

Comedy Clubs

The comedy scene in Cork is really small, with most local comedians doing one-off acts every so often at various venues. The best purpose-built comedy club is the **City Limits Comedy Club** (Coburg St.; ☎ 021/450-1206; www.thecomedyclub.ie), where famous acts like Jo Brand and Johnny Vegas have graced the stage. After the show, stay for a drink as City Limits turns into a night club with DJs spinning everything from indie to dancehall.

Performance Halls/ Stadium Shows

The **Cork Opera House** (Emmet Place; ☎ **021/427-4308;** www.corkoperahouse. ie) is Southern Ireland's major venue for concerts, musicals, opera, and drama. Its 1,000-person capacity means there are the occasional big names performing, like favorite son comedian Patrick Kielty and popular jazz acts from America. Across the river from the opera house is the **Cork Arts Theatre** (7 Knapps Sq.; ☎ **021/450-8398**), which presents contemporary plays and musical comedies to packed-out houses.

Sightseeing

There's quite a variety of places to see in Cork despite its size. Because it's such a cultural haven for Ireland, there are some great galleries and museums worth a visit. As it's very old—dating from the 7th century or before—there are many magnificent ancient structures like St. Finbarr's Cathedral to see. Cork, being a foodie's paradise, is also home to the Old English Market, Ireland's best food market, dating from the 18th century and brimming with stalls of local delicacies that might turn an American's stomach: tripe (animal stomach) and drisheens (blood sausage), for instance. For those alone, it must be seen.

Where to Find Out What's On/ Where to Get Tickets

The Event Guide magazine will contain all the information you could possibly need regarding exhibitions and special events all over Cork. Find it at the nearest newsagent or bookstore and plan accordingly. To learn all about attractions in Cork, you could simply go to the Cork Tourist Office (see "Tourist Information," p. 232) and grab all the brochures you can get your hands on. It's worth taking a look at the websites listed in the Cork "Basics" section (see p. 232) before you decide what you'd like to see.

Festivals

March: In Cork City, celebrate Celtfest (www.celtfest.org), paying homage to Celtic art, music, song, dance, language, and culture. Of course, the 17th is St. Patrick's Day, and the parade in Cork is like no other.

May: This month marks the 27th annual Cork Youth International Video, Film and Arts Festival (☎ **021/430-6019**), encouraging young people to experiment with filmmaking.

June: During the last 2 weeks of the month is the Cork Midsummer Festival (www.cork festival.com), a fun celebration staged at unusual locations and including events from all sorts of artistic disciplines.

July: Cork celebrates Pride (www.corkpride. com) this month. Expect everything from parades and discos to workshops on flirting and dressing in drag!

Hanging Out

The ultimate people-watching, picnic-eating spot in Cork is Bishop Lucey Park (see "Gardens & Parks," below). You'll of course find a gaggle of cellphone-toting teenagers but you'll also come across uni students relaxing or reading. If you like to pass your time with a lager glued to your hand, then try the Bodega, the Roundy, or one of the almost official college student hangouts like Rearden's on Washington Street (see "Partying," earlier, for all these bars), which is the largest and probably the best watering hole of its kind. You can while away the hours watching Cork's football team on the big screen while nursing a pint.

MTV The Local University Scene

Much of Cork's late-night scene is dominated by the thriving student culture, mostly thanks to students from **University College Cork** (☎ 021/490-3000; www.ucc.ie), Ireland's leading university. When not downing cheap pints at the Student Union on their campus, which sits on the banks of the River Lee, they can be found drinking coffee at Tribes, dancing the night away at The Red Room, or coolly sipping a vodka at The Roundy or Bodega (see "Partying," earlier). Uni students here are chatty and eager to meet new people, so pull up a stool.

September: The Cork Folk Festival (www.corkfestival.com) has been going strong since 1979. Famous folk and traditional music groups perform all over the city.

October: Cork Film Festival (www.corkfilmfest.org) is highly regarded internationally, and presents a program ranging from big-budget films to independent shorts. The Oscar-winning documentary *Chernobyl Heart* about Irish volunteers in Russia was first screened here.

November: Murphy's UnCorked (☎ 021/450-1673), sponsored by local brewery Murphy's, is a fairly new annual festival of roots and blues music and promises to improve each year.

MUSEUMS/ART GALLERIES

→**Cork Public Museum** If you want to learn about the history of Cork, look no further. There are exhibits detailing what life would have been like in medieval times and some excavated artifacts that are over 4,000 years old. There's a wealth of information about famous Corkonians like the patriot Michael Collins. *Fitzgerald Park.* ☎ *021/427-0679. Admission free weekdays; €1.50 Sun. Mon–Fri 11am–1pm and 2:15–5pm; Sun 3–5pm (until 6pm July–Aug). Bus: 8.*

FREE →**Crawford Municipal Art Gallery** Housed in Cork's 18th-century former customs house, this is a truly excellent gallery featuring works by the likes of James Barry and Daniel Maclise in the permanent collection. Recent exhibitions have included the art of the Dutch masters and a

collection of rare gold and silver from abroad. *Emmet Place.* ☎ *021/427-3377. www.crawfordartgallery.com. Admission free. Mon–Sat 9am–5pm.*

FREE →**The Fenton Gallery** The Fenton is considered by many to be the best contemporary arts gallery in Cork, exhibiting the best in Irish painting, sculpture, and ceramics. Recent exhibits include the works of Basil Blackshaw, Ireland's greatest living painter. The sculpture courtyard is a real highlight. *Wandesford Quay.* ☎ *021/431-5294. Tues–Sat 10:30am–6pm.*

FREE →**Lavitts Quay Gallery** This gallery is operated by the Cork Arts Society and is intended to promote visual arts in the area. The building itself is beautiful—a Georgian mansion overlooking the River Lee. Go upstairs for works by young, unknown artists; you can say you knew them before they were famous. *5 Father Matthew Street.* ☎ *021/427-7749. Admission free. Tues–Sat 10:30am–6pm.*

→**Triskel Arts Centre** As well as being a space for avant-garde performing arts productions, the Triskel houses two galleries devoted to visual arts. However, don't expect run-of-the-mill still life paintings: For instance, a recent exhibitor created chandeliers out of household waste. *Tobin St.* ☎ *021/427-2022. €2–€10. Mon–Sat 10am–5:30pm.*

HISTORIC BUILDINGS

→**Cork City Gaol** This jail housed some of Cork's most notorious prisoners over the course of the last 200 years. Now when you

Cork City Attractions

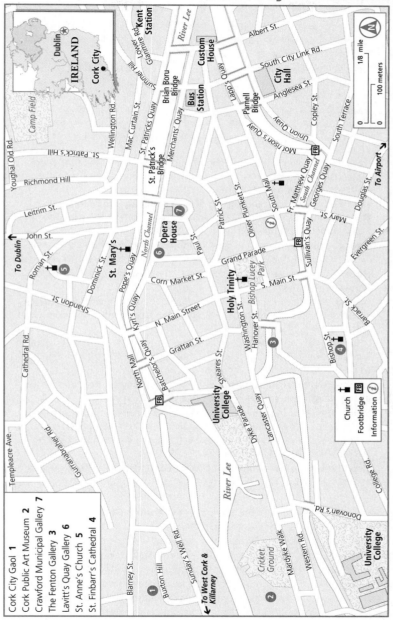

Cork City Gaol 1
Cork Public Art Museum 2
Crawford Municipal Gallery 7
The Fenton Gallery 3
Lavitt's Quay Gallery 6
St. Anne's Church 5
St. Finbarr's Cathedral 4

IRELAND
Dublin
Cork City

Camp Field

Kent Station

River Lee

Custom House

Albert St.

South City Link Rd.

City Hall

Anglesea St.

Copley St.

South Terrace

To Airport

1/8 mile
100 meters

Summer Hill
Lower Glanmire Rd.
Wellington Rd.
Mac Curtain St.
St. Patricks Quay
Merchants' Quay
St. Patrick's Bridge

Brian Boru Bridge

Bus Station

Lapp's Quay

Parnell Bridge

Union Quay

Morrison's Quay

Fr. Matthew Quay

South Channel
Georges Quay
Douglas St.
Mary St.
Evergreen St.

Youghal Old Rd.
St. Patrick's Hill

Richmond Hill

Leitrim St.

John St.

Roman St.

To Dublin

St. Mary's

Dominick St.
Pope's Quay
North Channel

Opera House

Paul St.

Patrick St.
Oliver Plunkett St.
South Mall
Sullivan's Quay
Barrack St.

Cathedral Rd.

Shandon St.

Kyrl's Quay

Corn Market St.

N. Main Street

Grattan St.

Grand Parade
Bishop Lucey Park

Holy Trinity

Washington St.
Hanover St.
S. Main St.

Bishop St.

Templeacre Ave.

Gurranabraher Rd.

North Mall

Batchelor's Quay

University College

S'eares St.

Dyke Parade
Lancaster Quay

River Lee

Donovan's Rd.

Blarney St.

Buxton Hill

Sunday's Well Rd.

To West Cork & Killarney

Cricket Ground

Mardyke Walk

Western Rd.

College Rd.

University College

Church
Footbridge
Information

12 Hours in . . . (Walking Tour)

→ **Hour 1:** Stop into the **Gingerbread Café** (St. Paul Plaza; ☎ **021/427-6411**) for the best breakfast in town, whether you want a heart-attack-inducing Full Irish or pancakes and maple syrup.

→ **Hour 2:** Visit **St. Anne's Church** (Church St.; ☎ **021/450-4906**), also known as Shandon Church, and ring the famous bells. The whole city will be able to hear you so don't screw up.

→ **Hour 3:** Take a look at the delicious produce for sale at the **English Market,** a real Cork landmark. If you're even slightly hungover, give it a miss: Your stomach won't be able to handle local delicacies like crubeens (pig's feet).

→ **Hour 4:** While you're in the neighborhood, take a walk through **Bishop Lucey Park.** It's really very pretty if you ignore the groups of teenagers sneaking a cigarette and playing with their cellphones.

→ **Hour 5:** Spend some time looking around the **Crawford Municipal Gallery** (Emmet Place; ☎ **021/427-3377;** www.crawfordartgallery.com) to see the best art on offer in Cork.

→ **Hour 6:** Have some lunch at the **Crawford Gallery Café** (Emmet Place; ☎ **021/427-4415**) while you're there. The fresh fish is really amazing.

→ **Hour 7:** Take a walk down Patrick Street, the main thoroughfare in Cork, for some retail therapy.

→ **Hour 8:** Just so you know some fascinating facts to impress the parents, check out the history of the Rebel City at the **Cork Public Museum** (Fitzgerald Park; ☎ **021/427-0679**).

→ **Hour 9:** Take a walk from the museum down the banks of the Lee through the university campus. Maybe you'll meet a hot date for tonight. End up back in the city center.

→ **Hour 10:** Try to take in a play at one of Cork's many theatres and performance spaces. It is, after all, the European City of Culture.

→ **Hour 11:** If you can part with a few euros, have dinner somewhere trendy and fabulous like **Isaac's** (48 MacCurtain St.; ☎ **021/450-3805**). If not, no big deal: There are plenty of good cheap places like the **Quay Co-op** (24 Sullivan's Quay; ☎ **021/431-7026**).

→ **Hour 12:** Have a few pints at the **Old Oak** or a cocktail at the **Vineyard** and mingle.

wander through the rows of cells you'll hear sound effects and see very realistic figures dressed in period costume. Exhibitions attempt to give a picture of life in the gaol and surrounding area from the famine era onwards. *Convent Ave., Sunday's Well.* ☎ *021/430-5022. Admission €6. Mar–Oct daily 9:30am–5pm; Nov–Feb Sat–Sun 10am–5pm.*

→ **St. Anne's Church**   Also known as Shandon Church, this is Cork's number-one attraction and most famous landmark. You might hear the famous Shandon bells—all eight of them—ringing at all hours of the day since anyone who climbs the belfry is allowed to play a tune. The Church is so famous that its sand and limestone colors have been adopted by the Cork football and curling teams. *Church St.* ☎ *021/450-4906. Admission €3. Mon–Sat 8:30am–6pm.*

→ **St. Finbarr's Cathedral**   Back in A.D. 600, St. Finbarr chose this spot in Cork for his church. Today, the Cathedral, dating from 1880, is an example of Gothic architecture with its ornate spires and colorful interior. The church bells are older than the Cathedral itself, dating from the church that previously stood here. *Bishop St.* ☎ *021/496-8744. Admission €3. Apr–Sept Mon–Sat 10am–5:30pm; Oct–Mar Mon–Sat 2–5:30pm.*

Ⅳ Best →**Blarney Castle and Stone** While Blarney Castle is extremely touristy, it is still one of the most impressive castles in Ireland. The endlessly famous Blarney Stone

itself is wedged far underneath the battlements, but not far enough that countless tourists don't bend over backwards, hang upside down in a parapet, and kiss it in hopes of increased loquaciousness. It's customary to tip the attendant who holds your legs. *R617, 8km (5 miles) northwest of Cork City, Blarney, County Cork.* ☎ *021/438-5252. www.blarney castle.ie. Admission €7 adults, €5 students. May and Sept Mon–Sat 9am–6:30pm, Sun 9:30am–5:30pm; June–Aug Mon–Sat 9am–7pm, Sun 9:30am–5:30pm; Oct–Apr Mon–Sat 9am–sundown, Sun 9:30am–5:30pm. Bus: Marked* BLARNEY *or* TOWER *from bus station on Parnell Place, Cork City.*

Playing Outside

Cork, being a university town, is full of outdoorsy adventure enthusiasts. The first skate park in Ireland was built in Cork. Called Prime Skate Park, it's open on Sundays for skating and often holds special events. Find it opposite the train station at Patricks Quay. For more information head to **Primetime Skateshop** (Washington St.; ☎ **021/427-5922**). If you want to try your hand at catching your own salmon, head to either the central River Lee or the nearby Blackwater River. You'll find the required permits, tackle, and equipment at **T. W. Murray** at (87 Patrick St; ☎ **021/427-1089**). Golf is responsible for

much of Ireland's roaring tourist trade; give it a go at one of Cork's local clubs. Try the **Cork Golf Club at Little Island** (☎ **021/435-3451**), just 5 miles away. Greens fees are €80 on weekdays and €90 on weekends. If you want to hit the open waters, head to Kinsale, only about 25 minutes outside the city. At **Sovereign Sailing** (42 Haven Hill, Summercove, Kinsale; ☎ **021/477-4145**), you can take courses guaranteed by the Irish Sailing Association. In two days, for example, you can learn to competently crew a boat, spinnaker and all. For other outdoor adventures, see "Top 10 Sporty Things to Do in Cork" (p. 250).

Shopping

The main shopping area in Cork is St. Patrick Street, known simply as Patrick Street. The most stylish of these shops is **Brown Thomas** (18 Patrick St.; ☎ **021/480-5555**), a department store and part of a four-strong Irish chain. If you have money to burn, it's the best shop to visit for expensive clothes and accessories. Most of the shops on Patrick Street are run of the mill, and to be found on main streets all over the U.K. and Ireland. If you like your shopping under one roof, try the

Merchant Quay Shopping Centre, on Patrick Street and Merchant Quay. It's the biggest mall in the city centre, with flagship stores Marks and Spencer and Dunnes—the Irish version of Sears. On the ground floor there are stalls selling unique gifts and used books; these change from week to week. The newest mall in Cork is the Grafton Mall on Oliver Plunkett Street. You'll find sleek furniture shops, a cool salon, and a stylish cafe. If you like the idea of browsing market stalls, you

CORK CITY

Top 10 Sporty Things to Do in Cork

10. Let's face it, sports are really only appreciated when viewed through the bottom of a glass. Head to **Reardens** (26 Washington St.; ☎ **021/ 4271969**), the most popular sports bar in the city, open 7 days a week and heaving with big rugby-playing uni students downing pints and cheering for the Rebel City.

9. There's a well-signposted walking tour of Cork City. You can pick up an accompanying booklet at the Cork Tourist Office at 42 Grand Parade (see Tourist Information above for contact details).

8. Fly-fishing is the new snowboarding when it comes to "It" sports, so rent equipment from the **Tackle Shop** at Lavitt's Quay (☎ **021/427-2842**) and head to the River Lee to find some salmon.

7. If you're bored on a Sunday, head down to **Kennedy Park** to watch the Cork Admirals trounce their opponents in American football.

6. Watching a Cork Constitution rugby match is really exciting, if only to hear the abuse screamed at rival teams by rabid fans. Their home grounds are in **Ballintemple** (Temple Hill, Ballintemple, Cork; ☎ **021/ 4292563**) and you can see a fixtures list at www.corkcon.ie.

5. Can't handle a full round of golf? Yeah, neither can we. Try golf on a smaller scale at **Douglas Pitch & Putt** (Carr's Hill, Carrigaline Rd.; ☎ **021/436-2310**) for €3 to €5.

4. Play a round of golf at nearby **Water Rock Golf Course** (Midletown; ☎ **021/461-3499**). It costs about €20, and even less if you get there very early in the day.

3. Take a short trip to the **Oysterhaven Centre** (☎ **021/477-0738**; www. oysterhaven.com), just outside Cork City, where you can rent any sort of watersports equipment you'd like, whether you feel like kayaking or windsurfing.

2. If football's not your bag, go and see a hurling match. Hurling is an ancient Gaelic game and looks somewhat ridiculous at first, but it grows on you. The Cork Rebels were the 2005 All-Ireland Champions so there's no better place to take it in. Buy tickets for a home game at Croke Park at www.gaa.ie.

1. Get a ticket to watch Cork City, the local Premier Division club, play a home game at Turners Cross stadium. Bonus points if it's against rivals Kerry. Go to www.corkcityfc.ie/tickets.htm for up-to-date ticket details and expect to pay €13 to €20. Reserve tickets and pick them up at the box office by calling ☎ **021/432-1958.**

absolutely must try the **English Market** (☎ **021/492-4334**) on the Grand Parade. It's a unique sensory experience and you'll want to buy and devour all the French cheeses and fresh fruits for sale. On Saturdays, head to the **Coal Quay Market** (☎ **021/427-3251**). Don't expect it to be a treasure trove of antiques—the vibe is more that of a flea market. Find it on Cornmarket Street. While in Ireland it'll be all too tempting to buy tacky souvenirs for family members at home, especially if your surname happens to be "O'Brien" or "Murphy," in which case there will be coasters and doormats with your

family crest at every turn. Instead, pick up gifts they'll actually appreciate at **Crafts of Ireland**
(11 Winthrop St.; ☎ 021/427-5864), like handmade stationery or candles made locally.

Road Trips from Cork

The largest of Ireland's 32 counties, the Rebel County of Cork once had the reputation of being inaccessible and untamed. Today, Cork boasts some of the most beautiful landscape in the country, with remote coastal areas and windblown islands to explore. If you like to travel off the beaten track, you'll love the Cork coastline, dotted with bays and harbors and lined with mountains covered in heather. For sports enthusiasts, Cork is the ideal location for sailing—in fact, the oldest yacht club in the world can be found at Crosshaven. Gourmet noshers will love Kinsale, known for its posh food, and whiskey lovers—or those who just like the words "free alcohol samples"—should check out the small town of Midleton, where the Jameson distillery can be found. If you like nothing more than a day lying on the sand listening to the waves, then head to Youghal (pronounced "y'all" for all you Southerners), known somewhat ambitiously as the Irish Riviera. For a pretty-as-a-picture town with flower boxes on every window and great pubs and restaurants, look no further than Clonakilty. Throughout the area are local pubs only too eager to welcome you into the affray. In fact, County Cork has it all—if you're willing to brave bus journeys over empty, inhospitable roads to get there.

Kinsale

Kinsale is considered the gateway to western Cork. While it has only 2,000 year-round residents, it's considered the "gourmet capital of Ireland." Its population quadruples in the summer months, so expect traffic on the tiny roads and crowds exploring the historic buildings. While only a small fishing village, Kinsale boasts multiple awards for its restaurants and pubs. Don't come here looking for cheap little cafes—food here is serious business, and you might need Dad's credit card to sample the

delights at Chez Jean-Marc or The Blue Haven. Kinsale has more to offer than fabulous seaside bistros, however. If you're a history buff, don't miss Desmond Castle, occupied by the Spanish during the famous battle of Kinsale in the 17th century. But unless you are completely bored, Charles Fort, star-shaped and uninviting, is not really worth the few euro to explore. Because the town was a designated "wine port" for centuries, there's now an International Museum of Wine in Kinsale. Go for a free wine tasting after a day of walking down the peninsula and around the harbor. Kinsale is also a perfect place to experience the great outdoors—you can canoe, bike, or go horseback riding on one of the scenic paths.

GETTING THERE & GETTING AROUND

Once in the town, it's so tiny your feet will probably do you; but if you need to catch a cab somewhere, call **Kinsale Cabs** (☎ 021/477-2642), **O'Dea & Sons** (☎ 021/477-4900), or **Allied Cabs** (☎ 021/477-3600).

BY BUS **Bus Éireann** (☎ 021/450-8188; www.buseireann.ie) runs the Parnell Bus Station in Cork City to Kinsale, stopping at the gas station opposite the tourist information office on the pier. There are nine buses a day during the week and three on Sundays.

BY CAR Kinsale is 29km (18 miles) south of Cork City on the Airport Road; if you're coming by car from the west, use the N71.

BY FERRY From East Cork, **Cross River Ferries Ltd.,** Atlantic Quay, Cobh (☎ 021/481-1485), provides regular service across Cork Harbour.

BASICS

TOURIST OFFICES The **Kinsale Tourist Office,** Pier Road, Kinsale (☎ 021/477-2234;

www.kinsale.ie), is open March through November.

RECOMMENDED WEBSITES Get an idea of what Kinsale has to offer before your feet hit the ground: www.kinsale.ie.

INTERNET ACCESS **Finishing Services Internet Bureau** (71 Main St.; ☎ 021/477-3571) offers Internet and e-mail access, plus post box and package services. They're also open late in the peak summer season. **Curtin Electrical** (Pearse St.; ☎ 021/477-2059) also offers Internet service along with 1-hour film processing for anyone out there not yet gone digital.

FESTIVALS

Ride into town in October and you could find it swinging. It's when Kinsale holds the Kinsale Fringe Jazz Festival (www.kinsale.ie/kinsjazz.htm).

SLEEPING

Hostels

➜**Dempsey's Hostel** Tucked behind the Texaco station about 5 minutes outside Kinsale town proper, Dempsey's is simple and clean. If you need anything or have questions during your stay, you're lucky: The friendly manager lives in the attic, which he's converted into a flat, so he's always on hand.

Hanging Out

In the summer, the best place to hang out in Kinsale is the hillside by James Fort facing the harbor. It's the perfect place for a picnic with lots of wine and a stack of postcards to write. In the evening or the winter, definitely head to The Spaniard (see "Partying," below), hands down the best pub in town. According to local lore, this popular hangout spot was where the real-life model for Robinson Crusoe had his last drink before setting sail and getting shipwrecked.

The kitchen is usable and the games room is popular for table tennis, and there's a small TV lounge. There's no curfew but you'll need a security code to get into the hostel at night. *Eastern Rd.* ☎ *021/477-2124. Year round €13–€16 dorm; €17–€20 double. Amenities: Games room; kitchen, security; TV.*

➜**Guardwell House** Located in the heart of Kinsale's historic quarter, Guardwell lodge is both a guesthouse and a hostel, with everything from four-person dorms to large single rooms. With a self-catering kitchen and a common room with a TV and Internet access, Guardwell has all the modern conveniences to make you feel at home. *Guardwell, Kinsale, County Cork.* ☎ *021/477-4686. www.kinsalehostel.com. €17, 4-person dorm; €19 2-person dorm; €29 single room. Amenities: Internet; kitchen; TV.*

Cheap

➜**The Lighthouse** Charming and eccentric, Carmel Kelly-O'Gorman presides over this friendly little B&B, which has won rave reviews and various accolades from travel writers and associations over the years. Rooms are lovingly decorated with trinkets from Carmel's travels around Asia and Africa, and many contain homemade quilts. A delicious full Irish breakfast is included; if you're feeling adventurous, order a mimosa with your smoked salmon and scrambled eggs. *The Rock, Kinsale, County Cork.* ☎ *021/477-2734. www.lighthouse-kinsale.com. €27–€70 double. Rates include full Irish breakfast. In room: TV, coffee/tea facility, hair dryer.*

➜**Walyunga B&B** With views of the Atlantic and set in a lush garden, Walyunga is the perfect place to relax after a long day of sightseeing. Owner Myrtle Levis's home is filled with exotic plants, and each room contains an orthopedic bed and mahogany furniture. All rooms look out over the water or the garden, so you'll have a great view no matter what. *Sandycove, Kinsale, County Cork.* ☎ *021/477-4126. www.walyunga.com.*

Road Trips from Cork City

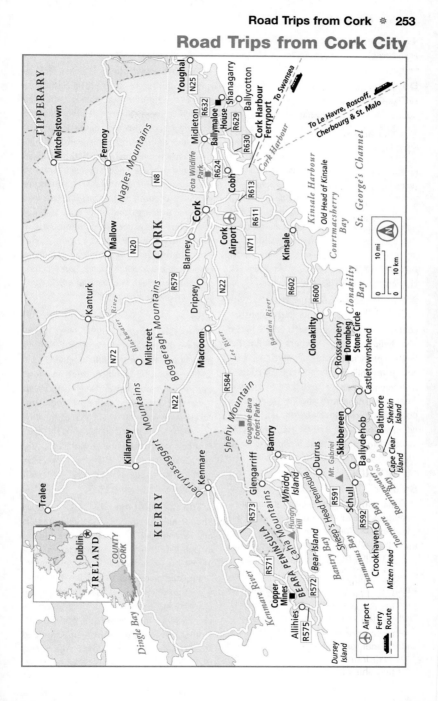

TIPPERARY

Mitchelstown

Fermoy

Nagles Mountains

Youghal
N25

Shanagarry
R632
Ballymaloe House
Ballycotton
R629
Cork Harbour Ferryport
R630
To Swansea

To Le Havre, Roscoff, Cherbourg & St. Malo

Cork Harbour

Midleton

N8

Mallow
N20

Kanturk

Blackwater River

Millstreet

N72

Boggeragh Mountains

R579

Fota Wildlife Park
R624

Cobh
R613

Cork
Cork Airport
N71
R611

Kinsale Harbour
Old Head of Kinsale

Kinsale

Kinsale Bay

St. George's Channel

CORK

Blarney

Dripsey
N22

Lee River

Macroom

Bandon River

R602

R600

Courtmacsherry Bay

10 mi

10 km

N

R584

Shehy Mountain
Gougane Bara Forest Park

N22

Clonakilty

Rosscarbery
Drombeg Stone Circle

Clonakilty Bay

Castletownshend

Killarney

Kenmare

Bantry

Durrus
Mt. Gabriel

Skibbereen

Ballydehob

Baltimore
Sherkin Island

KERRY

Derrynasaggart Mountains

Glengarriff
R573

Whiddy Island

Schull
R591

Cape Clear Island

R592

Tralee

Kenmare River

BEARA PENINSULA
R571

Hungry Hill

Sheep's Head Peninsula
Bantry Bay

Roaringwater Bay

Toormore Bay

Dunmanus Bay

Copper Mines
R572

Bear Island

Crookhaven

Mizen Head

Allihies
R575

IRELAND
Dublin
COUNTY CORK

Dursey Island

Dingle Bay

Airport
Ferry Route

€22–€30 double/triple. Rates include full Irish breakfast. In room: Coffee/tea facility, hair dryer.

Doable

→ **The Gallery**   You can't miss this guest house run by jazz musician and artist Tom and Carole O'Hare—it's canary yellow and violet on the outside, perfect for finding your way home after a few too many drinks. The en suite bedrooms are decorated with pine furniture and Carole's collages adorn the walls. The amicable hosts provide a delicious "Atkins friendly" breakfast—although guests have been known to indulge in ice cream in the mornings. The Glen, Kinsale, County Cork. ☎ 021/477-4558. €45–€55 double. Rates include full Irish breakfast. In room: TV, coffee/tea facilities, hair dryer.

→ **Pier House Boutique Hotel**   With views of the harbor, a sauna, and private balconies, Pier House is the perfect place to rest your head in Kinsale. Owners Ann and Pat Hegarty provide a warm Irish welcome, and a recent refurbishment means each room is tastefully decorated in muted tones and dark wood. The rooms have satellite TV and dataports so you can hook up your laptop. Pier Rd., Kinsale, County Cork. ☎ 021/477-4475. All units en suite. €50–€70 double. In room: Satellite TV, coffee/tea facilities, dataport, hair dryer.

Splurge

→ **O'Connor's**   Des O'Connor has obviously paid lots of attention to detail in this popular B&B in the peaceful Scilly district of Kinsale. You can see the harbor from each room, and if you want to be truly pampered, shell out a few more euro for one of the suites, which have large spa bathtubs and sunrooms where you are served a sumptuous breakfast. There are only four rooms here and two of them have a shower en suite. Scilly, Kinsale, County Cork. ☎ 021/477-3222. €90–€130

double. Rates include service charge and full Irish breakfast. In room: TV, hair dryer.

→ **The Old Presbytery**   Noreen McEvoy runs this downright darling little guesthouse with an eye for detail and a passion for hospitality. Set on a calm street away from the bustling part of town, the house is a charming labyrinth of half-staircases and landings, giving each room a private feel (though it can be tricky to trace your way back down to breakfast in the morning). Guest rooms are winningly decorated with brass and cast-iron beds, old armoires, and other auction finds. Breakfasts are especially fabulous. All 10 rooms have a shower inside. 43 Cork St., Kinsale, County Cork. ☎ 021/477-2027. www. oldpres.com. €80–€140 double. Rates include full Irish breakfast. In room: Hair dryer.

EATING

Cheap

→ **The Greyhound** IRISH   Most of the food on the menu at this cozy, pretty little pub is fairly run of the mill: shepherd's pie and beef stew, for instance. There are, however, a few really tasty and slightly different items to choose from, such as seafood pancakes made with the local catch of the day. You might be surprised at how good this food is at relatively cheap prices. Market Sq., Kinsale, County Cork. ☎ 021/477-2889. No reservations. Main courses €6–€12. No credit cards. Daily 12:30–10pm.

→ **The Spaniard Inn** IRISH   For delicious Bandon salmon and locally caught mussels and oysters, look no further than this popular pub, winner of the prestigious James Joyce award for its authentic Irish atmosphere. While other pubs stick to easy fare like sandwiches and chips, at the Spaniard they serve up a mean farmhouse duckling in cherry brandy sauce for a reasonable price. Go for dinner and stay for drinks—the ales and stouts on tap and, if you know your wines,

Kinsale

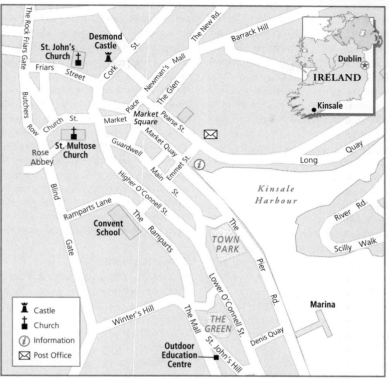

there's a pretty decent selection of those, too. *Scilly, Kinsale, County Cork.* ☎ *021/477-2436. No reservations. Main courses €8–€12. Daily noon–10pm.*

Doable

→ **Fishy Fishy Cafe** SEAFOOD According to the owners of this hip, laid-back little culinary gem, Fishy Fishy is "so good we named it twice." If you love seafood, you'll be in heaven, as the cafe features local selections like cod, monkfish, haddock, and lobster. The menu changes daily, and the salads and puds are just as good as the yummy fish. Show up early as they don't accept reservations. *Guardwell, Kinsale, County Cork.* ☎ *021/477-4453. Lunch average €16–€20. Year-round daily noon–3:45pm.*

→ **The Little Skillet** IRISH Although this place has been here for over a decade, it still feels as if you've stumbled upon a hidden treasure. The food is trad Irish fare like stew, shepherd's pie, and, of course, champ, a potato dish you won't find outside of Ireland. The owners Richard and Anne make you feel like the place is yours, and if it's packed, you can have a drink in the bar across the road while you wait for a table. Perfect after a cold, stormy day. *Main St., Kinsale, County Cork.* ☎ *021/477-4202. Reservations recommended. Main courses €15–€18. Daily 12:30–2:30pm and 6–10:30pm.*

→ **Max's Wine Bar Restaurant** INTERNATIONAL Max himself may be long gone, but his Wine Bar remains a popular place for tourists and locals alike to munch down on contemporary meals and snacks using fresh ingredients, like goat cheese pasta and vegetable soups. Ask to sit on the outdoor patio or in the conservatory. *Main St., Kinsale, County Cork.* ☎ *021/477-2443. Reservations recommended. Fixed-price early-bird 3-course dinner €18; dinner main courses €18–€26. Daily 12:30–3pm and 6:30–10:30pm. Closed Nov–Feb.*

→ **Savannah Waterfront Restaurant** SEAFOOD   Half the draw of this recently done-up eatery is the location: While you eat, you can enjoy brill views across the harbor. The menu is eclectic but decidedly trendy and international, with *mille feuille* of organic smoked salmon and crabmeat for starters and Irish beef served with warm oysters for a main course. Don't worry if you're thinking, *mille* what? It's still a great place to treat yourself, and the traditional roast lunch served on a Sunday is the best in town. *Trident Hotel, Kinsale, County Cork.* ☎ *021/477-2301. Reservations recommended. Main courses €14–€24. Daily 12:30–2:30pm and 6–10:30pm.*

Splurge

→ **The Blue Haven** SEAFOOD   At first glance the prices at The Blue Haven may have you fighting an urge to run off gripping tightly to your wallet. But there are options here. You can choose the upscale restaurant with its skylight and fab full a la carte menu. Or you can eat in the old-world pub. In the latter you'll get the most delicious, flavorful lamb stew you'll find anywhere in Kinsale. If you really want to impress someone, eat at the restaurant, where fresh local seafood is served, alongside duck and venison dishes. *3 Pearse St., Kinsale, County Cork.* ☎ *021/477-2209. Reservations recommended. Main courses at the bar €10–€20; fixed 3-course dinner €35; dinner main courses €20–€37. Bar daily 12:15–3pm and 6:30–10pm; restaurant daily 7–10pm.*

→ **The Vintage** SEAFOOD/CONTINENTAL Eat here and you won't just be feeding yourself but also the families of local Cork farmers, as owners Diana and Frank do their best to support local businesses in West Cork. Fresh is the big word round here. The restaurant is popular for locals popping in for a pint of Murphy's and some oysters, as well as in-the-know travelers hungry for grilled whole lobster or Irish salmon. The chefs are believers in "slow food," so sit back and prepare to spend rather a lot of money on one of the best meals to be had in Kinsale. *50–51 Main St., Kinsale, County Cork.* ☎ *021/477-2502. www.vintagerestaurant.ie. Reservations recommended. Main courses €28–€33. Mid-Feb to Apr and mid-Oct to Dec Tues–Sat 6:30–10pm; May to mid-Oct daily 6:30–10:30pm. Closed Jan to mid-Feb.*

Cafes/Tearooms

Cucina Café (9 Market St., Kinsale; ☎ **021/ 470-0707;** www.cucina.ie) is a stylish, Mediterranean little place with a bright blue exterior and a fresh, modern interior. Stop by for breakfast or a cappuccino, or sample their light, healthy lunch options, like roasted field mushrooms on toasted country bread with thyme and talleggo cheese with a smoothie. More traditional is **Mother Hubbard's Café** (Market St., Kinsale; ☎ **021/477-2440**), serving up groaning plates of full Irish breakfasts and coffees to locals and tourists alike.

PARTYING

Kinsale isn't exactly known for its vibrant nightlife—you might want to check out nearby Cork if you're in search of clubs and lounge bars. In the summer months, the pubs can get very crowded, especially for traditional music sessions. If you absolutely must hit the dance floor, head to the White Lady; but there's a better night to be had by chilling with a pint at the Spaniard or the Shanakee.

Bars/Clubs/Live Music

With its nautical theme, sawdust-covered floor, and lively traditional music nights, **The Spaniard** (Scilly, Kinsale, County Cork; ☎ 021/477-2436) is possibly the best pub in Kinsale, attracting a loyal following as well as some famous Irish singers on occasion. In the summer months, you can sit outside on a picnic table overlooking the harbor where Don Juan de Aguila, for whom the pub was named, rallied his fleet in 1601. Another fun pub is the Shanakee, with a vintage feel and a full menu. Like the Spaniard, **the Shanakee** (6 Market St., Kinsale; ☎ 021/477-7077) is popular for its traditional tunes and ballads nightly. About a mile along the quay towards Fort Charles, you'll find **the Bulman** (Summercove, Kinsale; ☎ 021/477-2131), where fishermen and yachtsmen in their work garb down pints alongside students, artists, foreign expats, and anyone else who's in the mood for some *craic* in a lovely location. Be there to watch the sun set over the wharf and you're in for a treat. If sports bars are more your scene, head to **the White Lady** (O'Connell St., Kinsale, County Cork; ☎ 021/477-2200), a hotel with a restaurant, bar, and nightclub on-site. The bar has a widescreen TV so you can catch up on sports fixtures, plus a selection of good beers on tap and a bar menu. The nightclub is admittedly fairly cheesy, with neon lights and a "disco" ambience, but after a few vodkas you'll want to be out on the dance floor rubbing shoulders with other tourists. The most cosmopolitan bar in town is the bizarrely named **Hole in the Wall** (The Glen, Kinsale, County Cork; ☎ 021/477-2939). With atmospheric lighting and a pretty outdoor area for smokers, the Hole in the Wall wouldn't look out of place in a much larger town or city. The menu is filled with tasty foreign nosh like ciabatta sandwiches, and there's always a DJ spinning or a guest band playing at night. Definitely sit in the unique cliff-facing beer garden if you visit during the summer.

SIGHTSEEING

It's all about eating, not looking, in Kinsale, but there are a couple of sights to see while you work up an appetite.

Best → Charles Fort This fort had armed soldiers in it as recently as 1921. They were stuck there to watch who came in and out and to guard the town of Kinsale behind. Soldiers of some description had been doing the same thing since it was originally built in the 17th century. That other fort you can see across the river is St. James Fort (1602). There's an exhibition inside and, more importantly, a cafe. *Off the Scilly Rd., Summer Cove, County Cork. ☎ 021/477-2263. Admission €3.50 adults, €2.50 students. Tours available on request. Apr 15–Jun 15 and Sept 15–Oct 15 Mon, Sat, Sun 9am–5pm; Jun 16–Sept 14 daily 9am–6pm; closed Oct 16–Apr 14; last admission 45 min. before closing.*

→ Desmond Castle This may sound like a rather pleasant place owned by a nice chap called Desmond, Des to his friends, but it has a dark history. Built around 1500 as a customhouse for the Earl of Desmond, Spanish troops got their hands on it in 1601 and the Brits later used it as a place to keep captured American soldiers during the War of Independence. Around these parts, it's known as the "French Prison" because French prisoners were kept here during the 1700s and 54 died in a nasty fire in 1747. And the awfulness doesn't stop there. During the Great Famine the building was used as a workhouse for some of the starving. Now finally, it's just back to benign stones. It also houses the **International Museum of Wine,** celebrating the Irish emigrants who colonized the wine trade throughout the world after being forced to leave their own shores. Yes, you do get a free sample. *Cork St., Kinsale, County Cork. ☎ 021/477-4855. Admission €2.75 adults, €2 students. Mid-Apr to mid-June Tues–Sun 10am–6pm; mid-June to Oct daily 10am–6pm. Last admission 45 min. before closing. Closed Nov to mid-Apr.*

CORK CITY

(FREE) ➔ **Kent Gallery** Let the light shine forth. Opened in 1997, this gallery is split into three distinct spaces, all flooded with daylight. There's lots of stuff here ranging from serigraphs to paintings and sculptures. Yes, there are the usual local landscapes too, but they've been given a twist by Irish artists in bright oils and on silk screens. Gallery operator Jennifer Goldstone is always on the hunt for new talent to install upstairs for a one-man shows. *Quayside, Kinsale, County Cork.* ☎ *021/477-4956. Admission free. Open year-round.*

(FREE) ➔ **Kinsale Art Gallery** Really for posh Irish people looking to kit out their mansions, this is also worth a quick stroll around to see paintings and sculptures, including oils depicting life in rural Cork and female torsos in cast bronze. The art here is not going to set the world on fire, but if it's raining it's interesting to see some work by Irish artists. *Pier Head, Kinsale, County Cork.* ☎ *021/477-3622. Free admission. Open year-round.*

➔ **Kinsale Regional Museum** Can't get enough Kinsale tales? There's always this small but enthusiastic museum in the historic Market House (1600) telling the town's story from its earliest days, with paintings and photos. Only for hardcore Kinsale fans. *Market Sq., Kinsale, County Cork.* ☎ *021/477-2044. Admission €2.50 adults, €1.50 students. Apr–Sept daily 10am–6pm; Oct–Mar Mon–Fri 11am–1pm and 3–5pm. Closed Jan.*

PLAYING OUTSIDE

BICYCLING Kinsale Harbour is perfectly designed for biking. To rent a bike, contact **The Hire Shop,** 18 Main St. (☎ **021/477-4884**). Rentals average €10 a day, €60 per week; it all depends on what you want to hire. The shop is open weekdays from 8:30am to 6pm. In summertime it's also open Saturday from 9am to Sunday from 10:30am to 5:30pm.

FISHING Fishing might not usually be your bag, but if you've ever thought you'd like to swing a big old timer onto the back of your boat, this is the place to do it. Kinsale is one of the southern Irish coast's sea-angling centers. There are numerous shipwrecks in the area for wreck fishing (not the least of them the *Lusitania,* near the Old Head of Kinsale). As many as 22 species of fish have been caught off Kinsale in a single day. **Sporting Tours Ireland,** 71 Main St. (☎ **021/477-4727**), arranges sea fishing from Kinsale Harbor or game fishing for salmon and trout in nearby rivers. The fee for sea fishing averages €160 per day with a six-person maximum. This may sound mighty steep, but round up six friends and it's not bad for a day out on the high seas. It's open year-round Monday to Friday 9am to 5:30pm. For fishing tackle or to rent a rod and other equipment, try The Hire Shop (see above).

HIKING The Scilly Walk is a signposted pedestrian path along the sea running from Scilly, the community across the harbor from Kinsale, all the way to Charles Fort. Continue to walk south along the sea from Charles Fort, and you'll find another path that follows the headland to the tip of Frower Point, offering fabuloso views across the harbor to the Old Head of Kinsale. The complete walk from Kinsale to Frower Point is 8km (5 miles) each way, and it's all pretty good. If you prefer a guided walk, there are 1-hour walking tours of Kinsale every day in the summertime. The tours are run by **Herlihy's Guided Tour** (☎ **021/477-2873;** €4.50) and leave from in front of the tourist office at 11:15am. Ask in the tourist office for details.

SHOOTING Ever fancied a spot of ferret racing? A few miles from Kinsale is the town of Nohoval, where you can try a variety of rather odd "sports" like clay-pigeon shooting, falconry, and . . . 📺 (Best) **ferret racing.** For 3 hours, shoot simulated pheasants, woodcocks, partridges, and even rabbits for €85. If guns aren't your bag, place bets and watch cute ferrets Max, Champ, and their friends

I See Fairies

Fairies, it is said, are really fallen angels. At the beginning of time, or so the legend goes, during the battle between God and Satan, some angels remained neutral, willing to go along with whomever won. When it was all over, Satan and his followers were banished to Hell and God cast the neutral angels, who had committed a sin of omission, to the Earth as fairies. They occasionally accompany departed souls to heaven, but they can never enter through the gates.

Fairies are supposed to live in old ruined castles and churches, deserted graveyards, and secluded mountain glens, lakes, and caves, especially on the west coast. Translucent and usually the size of a human finger, they can assume any conceivable form or become invisible at whim. The question of whether or not they have wings is still open to debate—witnesses are usually too schnockered to tell for sure. Sociable and mischievous, fairies are known to be as helpful as they can be nasty; it all depends on how they're treated. A few pointers, should you ever come across one:

1. Don't talk about Yeats. Fairies despise all academic pursuits and cannot be found anywhere near a school.

2. Be respectful. Even if they drink your last bottle of whiskey, don't complain—it's not worth the trouble they'd cause you afterwards.

3. If you're ever invited to a fairy ball, count your lucky stars. Their music and dancing far surpass anything you'll see in the human realm. Don't speak, though, or the scene will immediately vanish and you'll wake up lying in the middle of the road in the morning with a headache the size of Montana.

4. Hold onto your baby. Fairies are known baby-snatchers—they can't help it, they just love those cute, pudgy, googly-eyed little things so much.

5. Don't speak of the fairies to anyone. They do not like being talked about, and besides, silence is your best bet for preserving your illusion of perfect sanity.

CORK CITY

race. €45. Claybird Ltd. The Turrets, Nohoval, County Cork. ☎ 021/4887149.

TENNIS   Court time can be had at the **Oysterhaven Activity Centre** (☎ 021/477-0738), 8km (5 miles) from Kinsale, for €10 per hour. Racket rental is an additional €2. It's open Monday to Thursday 10am to 9pm, Friday and Saturday 10am to 6pm, and Sunday 1 to 6pm.

WATERSPORTS   At **Sporting Tours Ireland,** 71 Main St. (☎ 021/477-4727; www. sportingtoursireland.ie), prices for scuba diving start at roughly €40 per dive (minimum group of three). Canoeing, windsurfing, and dinghy sailing cost at least €15 per hour. Or

hire a yacht from a minimum of €200 per half-day. Hours are daily 9am to 5:30pm. The **Oysterhaven Activity Centre** (☎021/477-0738), 8km (5 miles) from Kinsale, rents Windsurfers, dinghies, and kayaks. It's open Monday to Thursday 10am to 9pm, Friday and Saturday 10am to 6pm, and Sunday 1 to 6pm.

SHOPPING

For one-of-a-kind gifts that don't have shamrocks all over them, there are lots of choices in Kinsale. Check out the Dolan family's silversmith workshop, **Kinsale Silver** (Pearse St.; ☎ 021/477-4359). Watch as Pat Dolan forges pieces by hand using old-fashioned tools. For a gift of a completely different kind, go to **Roots Records** (1 Short Quay, Kinsale, County Cork; ☎ 021/477-4963). A store with a distinctly Caribbean, laid-back feel to it, Roots Records has the most comprehensive collection of Jamaican music in Ireland, and music lovers come from miles around to buy vintage vinyl and rare reggae cuts. If you've ever wanted to own a Victorian muff or an Edwardian ring, look no further than **Linda's Antiques** (Main St., Kinsale, County Cork; ☎ 021/477-4754), filled with a whole host of wonderful knickknacks. If you want to take some of the gourmet food Kinsale is famous for home with you, go to the **Kinsale Gourmet Store** (Guardwell, Kinsale, County Cork; ☎ 021/477-4453). Owners Martin and Marie Shanahan sell amazing cheeses, breads, and snacks, which you can sample in the store with a cup of coffee.

East Cork County

This part of Cork County may not visually be as drop-dead-gorgeous as the West, but it has some world-famous stop-offs like the Ballymaloe House and the world's top yacht club, the Royal Cork Yacht Club at Crosshaven. The major towns in East Cork are Youghal (pronounced "y'all") and Cobh (pronounced "cove")—fairly attractive coastal towns drawing some tourists away from the better-known western part of the county.

GETTING THERE

BY TRAIN On **Irish Rail** (toll-free ☎ 1850/366222 or 01/836-6222; www.irishrail.ie), take the suburban service from Cork or Cobh to Fota Island. The train runs every hour from Cork and takes 13 minutes.

BY CAR Take the N25 east from Cork City then turn off on the R624 to Cobh/Carringtwohill.

EATING

At the top-notch Fota Island Golf Club, twice the venue for the Murphy's Irish Open golf tournament, you'll find **Niblicks Restaurant** (☎ 021/4883710), overlooking the 18th green. The upscale eatery is a popular choice for golfers and visitors alike with its traditional Irish cuisine.

SIGHTSEEING

Some 16km (10 miles) east of Cork city on N25, look for signposts pointing to **Barryscourt Castle** (☎ 021/488-2218; www.heritage ireland.ie) in the small town of Carrigtwohill. This place is well worth a stop. From the 12th to the 17th centuries, the castle was the principal residence of the lords of Barrymore. The present castle houses an exhibition on the history of the Barrys and the castle, and there are guided tours. Admission is €2.75 for adults, €1.25 for students. The castle is open daily from June to September from 10am to 5:45pm, and Friday to Wednesday October through May from 11am to 5pm. Also popular with visitors to the area is the **FOTA Wildlife Park** (Carrigtwohill; ☎ 021/4812678; www. fotawildlife.ie), which isn't a zoo but a conservation project where endangered species like the red panda and the European bison live together in a free-range environment. There is a Direct Rail Service to FOTA Wildlife Park Station, or the park is accessible via the Cobh Road from Cork City, just off the N25. Admission is €11 for adults, €6.50 for students. The park is open Monday through Saturday from 10am to 4:30pm and on Sundays from 11am to 4:30pm.

Midleton

GETTING THERE

BY RAIL **Irish Rail** (toll-free ☎ 1850/366222 or 01/836-6222; www.irishrail.ie) operates service from Cork City and other locations.

BY CAR If you're driving from Cork City take the N25 and look for the signposted exit.

TOURIST OFFICES **Midleton Tourist Office** is seasonal, so check it out for information during the summer months on Distillery Road (☎ 021/4613702).

SLEEPING

If you decide Midleton is worth more than a day trip, stay the night at **An Stor Hostel** (Connelly St., Midleton, County Cork; ☎ 021/633106; €10 for a dorm; €14 per person double/single). Its name translates as "the treasure," and it could be considered a real find with its smiley staff and welcoming atmosphere.

SIGHTSEEING

The main draw in Midleton is the ⭐ Best Old Midleton Distillery and the Jameson Heritage Centre (Distillery Rd., Midleton, County Cork; ☎ 021/4613594), where you'll learn everything there is to know about Irish whiskey. You get to see the largest pot still in the world—it holds 30,000 gallons of booze. Many of the original buildings from 1825 remain, having been meticulously preserved, including mills, corn houses, and a water wheel. The Jameson Heritage Centre offers photographs and models showing the history of whiskey production and, yes, you get a glass of the old firewater at the end of your tour. Admission €7 adults, €5.75 students. Daily 10am–6pm; 30-minute tours on request; last tour at 4:45pm.

PLAYING OUTSIDE

Ballynamona Beach attracts swimmers to its safe shores in the summer, with its clean sands and gentle waters. It's also a popular place to fish and bird-watch as the area has an internationally renowned bird sanctuary. If you want to top up your tan, this is the place to do it.

Cobh

Pronounced "cove," this small port town was the last port of call of the doomed *Titanic* before she sunk in 1912. There is still an exhibit devoted to the *Titanic* disaster, and one for the *Lusitania*—when it was sunk by Germans in 1915 the survivors were brought to Cobh. Cobh is also where 19th-century Irish emigrants fleeing the famine departed from, so the town draws tourists with Irish roots who want to see the last bit of land their ancestors saw before leaving.

GETTING THERE

BY RAIL **Irish Rail** (toll-free ☎ 1850/366222 or 01/836-6222; www.irishrail.ie) operates a service from Cork City.

BY BUS **Bus Eirann** (☎ 021/450-8188; www.buseireann.ie) will run you direct from Cork City to Cobh and back.

BY CAR From Cork City take the N25 east and exit at R624 for Cobh. Alternatively take the train from Cork.

TOURIST OFFICES The tourist office is open daily 9:30am to 5:30pm weekdays and 1 to 5pm weekends at the Old Yacht Club in Cobh lower harbor (☎ 021/481-3301).

SLEEPING

→ **Amberleigh House** You're not going to find this level of luxury in Cobh for this price anywhere else. Unlike many other B&Bs in rural Ireland, the interior of Amberleigh doesn't feel like the home of an old woman who only speaks to her cats. The bedrooms are decorated entirely in white, so they feel clean and modern, and you get unparalleled ocean views from the huge bay windows downstairs in the palm-tree dotted sitting room. *West End Terrace, Cobh, County Cork.* ☎ *021/481-4069. www.amberleigh.ie. All units en suite. €35–€65 double. In room: TV, coffee/tea facilities, hair dryer.*

EATING

→ **Napoleon's** SEAFOOD This eatery sits in a house once owned by Napoleon Bonaparte's private doctor. Don't worry; he's cleared out all his things now and this small, family-run restaurant offers top-notch views of Cork harbor and St. Coleman's Cathedral. The menu changes depending on what the local fishermen catch each day, but you could find creamy seafood chowder and stuffed filet of plaice, among other delish treats.

CORK CITY

Get in. *Bella Vista House, Bishop's Rd., Cobh.* ☎ *021/821-450. Reservations recommended. Average cost of a meal €29; Mon–Sat noon–3pm and 6–9:30pm.*

SIGHTSEEING

→ **Cobh: The Queenstown Story** Housed in a restored Victorian railway station, "Cobh: The Queenstown Story" is a permanent exhibit commemorating Cobh's history as the last bit of Ireland emigrants saw on their way to new lives, whether as convicts in Australia or workers in America. The exhibit also re-creates the sinking of the *Titanic* and that of the *Lusitania*—both of which departed from Cobh (once called Queenstown)—with audiovisual presentations. The heritage center also has a new genealogical referral service for those seeking their Irish roots. *Cobh Railway Station, Cobh, County Cork.* ☎ *021/481-3591. Admission €5 for adults, €4 students. Feb–Dec daily 10am–6pm. Last admission 5pm. Closed Jan.*

Youghal

Texans will have no problem pronouncing Youghal—that's "y'all," y'all. The town's got a nice, if overcrowded, beach, and pretty coastal views that are spoiled somewhat by the unsightly sprawl of parked vacation caravans and RVs. The beach is blue-flagged, meaning the EU has dubbed it safe for swimming. It can be a decent place to spend the night if you're traveling between Cork City and Waterford and want to get some use out of that bathing suit. And the city's medieval charm (with Norman walls dating from 1275 surrounding the city) adds to the lure. If Youghal can't quite compare to the amazingly beautiful—and surprisingly untouristed—towns of West Cork like Union Hall, it has a couple of claims to fame: *Moby-Dick,* with Gregory Peck, was filmed in Youghal in 1954. And, there's more: It's said that Sir Walter Raleigh used to stroll these beaches (though probably not in his swimwear).

May God Go with You

The Irish have endless little phrases for greetings and goodbyes. Here's a quintessentially Irish blessing to keep you or your mates safe on your travels.

"May the road rise up to meet you.

May the wind always be at your back.

May the sun shine warm upon your face, and rains fall soft upon your fields.

And until we meet again,

May God hold you in the palm of His hand."

GETTING THERE

BY BUS & RAIL **Irish rail** (toll-free ☎ 1850/366222 or 01/836-6222; www.irishrail.ie) and **Bus Eirann** (☎ 021/450-8188; www.buseireann.ie) operates multiple services daily from Cork City and elsewhere.

BY CAR Take the Waterford road from Cork City (N25) east and follow signs to Youghal.

TOURIST OFFICES The tourist office is seasonal, and operates at Market Square from May/June through September. Hours are 9:30am to 5:30pm. ☎ 024/92390.

SLEEPING

The cheapest place to sleep in Youghal is in its hostel, **the Stella Mara** (☎ 024/91820; €10 for a dorm; €12 for an en suite double or twin; no credit cards). It's not going to win any awards for comfort, but try for a room with an ocean view and it might be worth a night's stay. Otherwise, if you have a bit more money to spend, try the charming and family-run **Devon View** (Pearse St.; ☎ 024/92298; www.devonviewbb.com; en suite rooms €25 euro per person sharing), a Georgian B&B in central Youghal.

Youghal

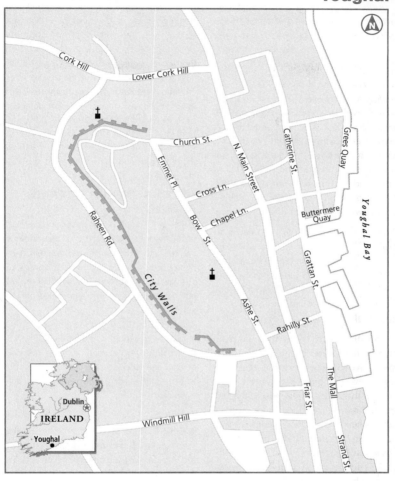

EATING

➔ Aherne's Seafood Restaurant
SEAFOOD The favorite restaurant for tourists and restaurant critics from far and wide is Aherne's Seafood Restaurant, located in a small luxury hotel. The seafood is fresh and locally caught, and the menu changes constantly. For instance, try cod and prawn risotto for starters and then order grilled turbot with lemon butter for an entree. If the price here is a tad steep, you can eat at the bar instead, where seafood pie will set you back only 13€. *163 N. Main St., Youghal, County Cork.* ☎ *024/92424. www.ahernes.com. Bar lunch from €10; dinner main courses €24–€30.*

➔ Tides SEAFOOD Tides is an excellent choice for any budget as there's a bar menu with tempting pasta and burgers as well as a main restaurant menu, concentrating on seafood but offering juicy sirloin steaks and

Barbary duck among other dishes for meat lovers. Order anything with goat cheese, which is especially good and creamy. *Upper Strand Youghal, County Cork.* ☎ *024/93127.* *www.tidesrestaurant.ie. Bar lunch from €13; dinner main courses €22–€28.*

PARTYING

Youghal isn't the place to come for wild nights out, but there are some traditional pubs that are worth visiting. A favorite local pub is the **Cotton Ball Lounge** (18 Old Youghal Rd., ☎ **021/450-3096**), established in 1874 and recently lovingly refurbished. Its large lounge is perfect for sitting with a pint after a day at the beach, and the staff is very personable.

SIGHTSEEING

Tynte's Castle is really the lone item of cultural interest in Youghal. Owned by the McCarthy family and the reason Youghal is a heritage town, Tynte's Castle can be found off North Main Street, although its interior is not open to the general public.

PLAYING OUTSIDE

Youghal is a **beach** town, with a few really clean, pretty strips of sand and clear blue water. **Youghal Strand** is the best beach for swimming, with lifeguards on duty during the peak season. More sheltered is Youghal's **Green Park beach,** popular for its proximity to holiday accommodation. The best sunbathing spot isn't a beach per se but an area of rocks, steps, and sandy coves by the lighthouse called the **49 Steps**. It catches the sun for most of the day. If you want to try something a bit more adventurous than tanning, the nearby town of Ardmore is home to **Ardmore Deep Sea Diving** (☎ **058/46577**), who will happily take you to local dive sites, including several wrecks. They offer PADI courses for €50 and will rent you equipment for €35 for the day.

West Cork: Castletownbere

This small town is worth visiting for one very un-Irish attraction: a secluded Tibetan Buddhist retreat overlooking the ocean along the Beara Peninsula. While the scenery on this rugged part of the coastline is beautiful in itself, Castletownbere is tiny and only really on the map thanks to the Dzogchen Beara centre, led by renowned spiritualist Sogyal Rinpoche. However, the town itself is charming and has in the last few years been given some press thanks to the late humorist Pete McCarthy's bestselling Ireland travel book *McCarthy's Bar*—the eponymous bar in the cover photo is in Castletownbere, in all its old-fashioned glory, adjacent grocery store and all.

GETTING THERE & GETTING AROUND

From Cork and all points east, take the N22. From the west, take the N71. **Bus Eirann** (☎ **021/450-8188;** www.buseireann.ie) runs from Cork to Castletownbere on routes 46 and 236, but be warned: The Buddhist retreat and hostel are a 5-mile walk or cycle from the bus stop.

It can be really difficult to get around this coastal area without your own car. The town of Castletownbere itself is easy to walk around, but to access the retreat you might want to phone and ask for pickup from the town centre.

BASICS

TOURIST OFFICES Go to the **Beara Tourism and Development Association** in the Square, Castletownbere, which is open during the summer (☎ **027/70045;** www.bearatourism.com).

RECOMMENDED WEBSITES To learn more about the town and its surrounding countryside, go to www.bearatourism.com. For a comprehensive look at the Dzongchenbeara Buddhist retreat, see www.dzogchenbeara.org.

SLEEPING

If you can't afford a stay in one of the Buddhist retreat's cottages, stay next door at

Garranes Farmhouse Hostel (Cahermore, Castletownbere; ☎ **027/73147;** dorms €14; family rooms €35), open year-round with separate dormitories for men and women. You'll need to book well ahead, especially in the summer months.

EATING

The best inexpensive choice is the **Old Bakery** in the West End of Castletownbere (☎ **027/70790**). Their homemade Irish food is delicious, as are their fresh baked goods like breads and cakes. More expensive but worth the trip for its eclectic menu of inspired Continental cuisine is the **Mariner,** also in the West End (☎ **027/71111**).

PARTYING

Okay, so it's very touristy thanks to Pete McCarthy's bestseller in which it's featured on the cover, but **McCarthy's Bar** is really a great place for a drink. The owner Adrienne is really friendly, and the layout is the way bars used to be—half pub and half convenience store. Play a game of darts with the locals—mostly fishermen—to get a real taste for the town (☎ **021/434-7717**).

SIGHTSEEING

MTV ⚫ **Best** → **Dzogchen Beara Retreat Centre** (Garranes, Allihies; ☎ **027/73032**; www.dzogchenbeara.org; rates vary greatly— call for details; free admission for meditation classes only). This Tibetan Buddhist retreat is the main draw in Castletownbere, and visitors come from all over the world to learn under the supervision of Sogyal Rinpoche and other masters. The atmosphere here is one of peace and serenity, which is helped by the stunning views over the Beara peninsula. You can enroll in a number of seminars and special events, all aimed at attaining *rigpa,* or intelligence and awareness. For example, spend a week learning to meditate. If you can't handle—or afford—a whole week at the retreat, you're welcome to stay at their

hostel (€14 per night) next door and visit for the day.

PLAYING OUTSIDE

Beara Outdoor Pursuits (Castletownbere, Beara; ☎ **027/70692;** www.seakayaking westcork.com) specializes in accompanied kayaking trips out and around Bere Island and as far as Glengariff. Frank Conroy is a terrific guide and can lead you to waters that are as protected or as rough as you want them. Eamonn Orpen's company, **Ireland Sea Fishing,** offers a really fun day out in his new boat the *Silver Dawn* for €450, for up to 12 people. He also conducts sightseeing tours of the area—you'll see lighthouses, wrecks, a castle, and of course sea life. That costs only €25 per adult. Bring your own wine and snacks and make it a date (☎ 027/70979; www.irelandseafishing.com).

Dursey Island

A mere 250 meters off the coast of the Beara Peninsula is Dursey Island, which takes 10 minutes to reach via Cork's famous cable car. You might find the ride unsettling and the ways of island residents old-fashioned—for instance, cows get precedence over people on the cable car, and it's used on Sundays to shuttle locals to church services. There are only a handful (literally, 12 at last count) full-time Dursey residents, but don't let that stop you from taking a few hours to look around, especially for you amateur photographers— the view is truly fabulous.

GETTING THERE

The only way to get to Dursey Island is by Ireland's only **cable car,** which you can board by driving past Cahermore on the R571 to its terminus. You can't cross by boat as the journey is often too dangerous. You can read Psalm 91 while swaying precariously in mid-air, as the owners have posted it up to comfort nervous travelers. To find out the schedules for the cable car, call ☎ **027/73017.**

Girls & Boys, Raise Your Glasses, Please

There's no harm in saying a few words before downing a pint. Here are a couple of real good toasts. Stand up and say one after you've got a round in—the locals will love you for it.

"Here's to a long life and a merry one.
A quick death and an easy one.
A pretty girl and an honest one.
A cold pint—and another one!"

"May you have the hindsight to know where you've been,
The foresight to know where you are going,
And the insight to know when you have gone too far."

SLEEPING

Beware if you miss the last cable car that there isn't a single place to stay on the island itself, but there is one right by the cable car station in Allihies. Paddy Sheehan operates the cable car to Dursey; he and his wife Agnes run the **Windy Point House B&B** (Beara Peninsula, County Cork; ☎ 027/73017; www. windypointhouse.com; €30 double en suite with breakfast) overlooking the sound. The rooms are simple yet comfortable and there is a TV in the residents' lounge. All the rooms have a view over the sound, which can't be beat.

EATING

Bring a packed lunch as there is no restaurant on the island. You can, however, get a light meal and a drink at Windy Point House (see "Sleeping," above) while waiting for the cable car.

SIGHTSEEING

Dursey Island is home to an awful lot of sheep, cows, and birds—in fact, it's a bird sanctuary, so many of its visitors are "birders," that is, bird-watchers with more than a casual interest in the subject. Take that as you will. Luckily there's more to see on Dursey than the hooded crow or the pied wagtail. The scenery is stunning—think crumbling stone towers and houses from centuries ago, plus sweeping views of the entire peninsula from its lush green hilltops.

Glengarriff

GETTING THERE Glengarriff is situated on the N71 between Bantry and Kenmare. **Bus Eireann** (☎ 021/450-8188; www.buseireann. ie) operates a daily service from Cork and Killarney all year round.

SIGHTSEEING

➔ **Drombeg Stone Circle** This ring of 17 standing stones is the best megalithic stone circle in all of County Cork. Sitting on a little hill overlooking the sea, the builders couldn't have found a better location. The circle dates from sometime between 153 B.C. and A.D. 127, but little is known about what went on here and why it was built. Just west of the circle are the remains of two huts and an ancient outdoor kitchen; it is thought heated stones were placed in a water trough (which can be seen next to the huts), and the hot water was used for cooking. The kitchen dates from between A.D. 368 and 608. *Off R597 between Rosscarbery and Glandore, County Cork.*

Union Hall

Union Hall is a sleepy but pretty little town on the road to Skibbereen. The town sits around a natural lagoon, its colorful houses and shops resembling a ribbon around the water. Watersports are popular here—you can do anything from kayaking and waterskiing to diving and deep-sea fishing. The pubs are lively and you can always expect good *craic* from Union Hall, a town admired by Jonathan Swift and more recently Lord David Puttnam, who set his cutesy film *War of the Buttons* here. Also, though not a festival as such, on February 1 every year, pilgrims come to Union Hall from far and wide to pray at a Holy Well dedicated to St Brigid, patron saint of boatmen.

GETTING THERE

BY BUS   Bus Eireann doesn't stop in Union Hall, but if you plan to stay at Maria's Schoolhouse Hostel (and you should; see "Sleeping & Eating," below), the kind folks there will pick you up from the bus station in Skibbereen if you call ahead.

TOURIST INFORMATION   The **Tourist Information Office** operates out of the Town Hall and is open October to March from 9:15am to 5:30pm Monday to Friday, from April to June 9am to 6pm, and from July to September 9am to 7pm (☎ **028/21766**).

SLEEPING & EATING

➜ **Maria's Schoolhouse Hostel**   As the name suggests, Maria's is housed in a Victorian schoolhouse, closed for good in 1987 and now consistently appearing on top hostel lists. The decor inside is eclectic, but the bedrooms are neat and the hostel attracts repeat visitors. Maria's breakfast is famous and costs €5. The Schoolhouse overlooks Lake Cluhir, and the ruins of Cahergal Fort still preside over the valley from the hill above. Maria's Schoolhouse is also unsurprisingly the favorite place to eat for travelers. Where else can you eat a three-course gourmet meal for about €15? *Cahergal, Union Hall, County Cork.* ☎ *028/33002. Mar–Dec. €65 per room for a 5-person dorm; €35 for a bunk-bedded twin. Amenities: Kitchen; laundry; TV room.*

PLAYING OUTSIDE

A great way to explore Union Hall is with 📺 **Best** **Atlantic Sea Kayaking** (Union Hall, Cork County; ☎ **028/33002;** www.atlanticsea kayaking.com). You'll be paddling around lots of craggy deserted islands, tiny secluded coves, and fish of all kinds. Try their Moonlight Adventure trip, where you set off at dusk and explore under the stars and amid the phosphorescent lights. The company welcomes all levels of experience and also

groups. A half-day sea kayaking trip is their most popular package, and sells for €45 including equipment. Another great way to spend a day? West Cork is known for the sheer number of whales and dolphins swimming in its waters. A 4-to-5-hour tour with well-known outfit **Whale Watch West Cork** (Union Hall, County Cork; ☎ **086/120-0027;** www.whalewatchwestcork.com) will cost you €40, and you'll hear commentary from skipper and zoologist Nic.

Schull

Schull, pronounced "skull," is the jewel of the Mizen Head Peninsula, which may not be saying much as it's the only town of any size there. For outdoor enthusiasts, there's no better place for biking, walking, golf, tennis, horseback riding, and watersports. *Be warned:* In July and August the tour buses descend on this town in herds, so you'll be sharing the pubs and beaches with loads of middle-aged Americans in search of the real Ireland. Schull makes an ideal base to explore nearby Cape Clear Island and Sherkin, and unlike most small towns around this area, there is a fairly lively pub scene, with traditional music sessions and a blend of locals and backpackers. If it happens to rain, check out the Planetarium (see "Sightseeing," below), rumored to be the best in Ireland.

GETTING THERE

Schull lies 107km from Cork City. Take the N71 out of Cork and drive on through Bandon, Clonakilty, Skibbereen, Ballydehob, and into Schull. Be careful if you're relying on **Bus Eireann** (☎ **021/508188;** www.buseireann. ie) to get you to and from Schull—there are only three buses from Monday to Saturday and one on Sunday, and only from June through September.

GETTING AROUND

There's only one street in Schull—Main Street, of course—so it won't kill you to walk.

CORK CITY

However, you can rent a bicycle from **Free-wheelin'** (Cotter's Yard; ☎ 028/28165; Mon–Sat 10am–noon)—if you don't mind paying the €11 per day rental fee.

RECOMMENDED WEBSITES Get information on Schull and the surrounding area at www.schull.ie—it includes helpful links and phone numbers for every possible amenity in the area.

FESTIVALS

If you're in Ireland in the summer, try to be in Schull for the impressive **Calves Week Sailing Regatta** (☎ 021/434-2855), usually held over the last week of July and first week of August. The event includes an Olympic course, a race to Cape Clear Island, and a trophy race around the coast.

SLEEPING

→ **Schull Backpacker's Lodge** A pristine wooden lodge with high-quality amenities, the Schull Backpacker's Lodge is often in the top three on hostel lists worldwide. The owners have obviously gone out of their way to give pricier local B&Bs a run for their money. You can book sea kayaking tours and horseback riding days through the front desk, and should you want to use the hostel's kitchen and bathroom facilities for a fraction of the price, you can camp on the grounds for only €7.50. *Colla Rd., Schull, County Cork.* ☎ *028/28681. www.schullbackpackers.com. €15 for a dorm; €40 for a double room. Amenities: Basketball; private car park; Internet access; kitchen; laundry; TV room.*

EATING

→ **Adele's** CAFE Adele Connor's little bakery and coffee shop is so damn popular you may have find yourself waiting for a seat, especially at breakfast time. If you're not tempted by the homemade baked goodies (scones and biscuits made on the premises, for instance), then how about Tuscan bean stew (€12) or an omelet made with smoked ham and local Gubeeen cheese, plus apple and sage? *Main St.* ☎ *028/28459. Main courses about €11. Tues–Sat 9:30am–6pm; Sun 11am–6pm.*

→ **TJ Newman's** CAFE/PUB The owners here, John and Bridie, are obviously doing something right, as this place is packed out. While half of TJ Newman's is still a pub attracting local fishermen, the D'Alton's new cafe and wine bar next door offers lovely grub in an art gallery setting, with free newspapers to browse and wireless Internet. The Newman's West Gourmet Choice is a real favorite, and includes West Cork salamis, gravalax, Irish cheeses, and thick brown bread. Dig in. *Main St., Schull, County Cork.* ☎ *028/27776. Main courses about €13. Daily 9am–11:30pm.*

PARTYING

There are 10 pubs in Schull, the two best probably being **An Tigin** (Main St.; ☎ 028/28830) and the **Bunratty Inn** (West End; ☎ 028/28341). An Tigin is frequented by both locals and backpackers, who enjoy the live music sessions twice a week at around 9:30pm. The Bunratty Inn is a small, classy little place with its own music sessions weekly.

SIGHTSEEING

→ **Mizen Vision** One sight you just have to see in Schull—in fact, the sole reason some travelers come here—is to see the Mizen Vision lighthouse. At Mizen Head, the southernmost point in Ireland, the land plummets down into the Atlantic breakers in a row of spectacular 700-foot sea cliffs. A suspension bridge will get you to the old signal station, now a visitor center, on a small rock promontory, the southernmost point on the Irish mainland. It affords pinch-yourself-it-can't-be-real views of the surrounding cliffs, open sea, and nearby Three Castle Head. Whales, seals, dolphins, porpoises, and daredevil seabirds contribute to the spectacle. No matter what the weather, it's worth a trip. On

And This One You Can Make at Home

Irish Soda Bread is really easy to make at home. It's best made with simple fresh ingredients and eaten within hours of baking. And the bonus is it's really cheap, so perfect when you're stuck in a hostel with no food and no dosh. To make it yourself, preheat the oven to 450°F (230°C) and sift four cups of flour, one teaspoon of salt, and one teaspoon of baking soda into a bowl. Pour in one and two-thirds cups of buttermilk or sour milk (to sour fresh milk, add a few teaspoons of lemon juice—don't use fresh milk, or the bread won't rise) and mix the ingredients together by hand. Put the dough on a floured board and knead lightly for a minute until the dough is smooth, then shape it into a mound about an inch-and-a-half high. Cut a deep cross into the dough and place on a floured cookie sheet. Bake at 450°F (230°C) for 15 minutes, then at 400°F (204°C) for another half-hour. Let cool before enjoying with a generous dollop of creamy butter and a nice hot sweet cup of tea. Lovely.

wild days, tremendous Atlantic waves assault the cliffs. On a clear day, seals bask on the rocks and gannets wheel over the sea and dive into the tranquil waters. Brilliant. On the way out to Mizen Head, you'll pass Barleycove Beach, one of the most beautiful beaches in southwest Ireland, and a great place to explore. *Mizen Head, County Cork.* ☎ *028/35115. Admission €4.50 adults, €3.50 students. Apr–May and Oct daily 10:30am–5pm; June–Sept daily 10am–6:30pm; Nov–Mar Sat–Sun noon–6pm. Closed weekdays Nov–Mar. Take R591 to Goleen and follow signs for Mizen Head.*

→ **Planetarium** Rainy day? Never fear! Schull also offers what a lot of folks say is Ireland's best planetarium. It's part of the Schull Community College and it's right down the road from the Schull Backpacker's Lodge. The price of admission includes a 55-minute "star show" which begins at 4pm or 8pm. *Colla Rd.* ☎ *028/28552. Admission €3. Apr–May 3–5pm Sun; June 3–5pm Tues, Thurs, Sat; Jul–Aug 2–5pm Tues–Sat, 7–9pm Mon, Thurs.*

PLAYING OUTSIDE

You can rent a dinghy, windsurf, or dive from **the Schull Water Sports Centre** (by the pier; ☎ **028/28554**). It's open 9:30am to 8:30pm

from Monday to Saturday. Windsurfing costs €10 for a half-day and dinghy rental €25; call for diving prices. The water's fine, and, as in Baltimore, there are plenty of old shipwrecks just waiting to be explored.

For those with wheels, you could take the R592 (which later becomes the R594) southwest to Crookhaven, a teeny little town located on a peninsula on the peninsula, and savor the gorgeous **Barleycove Beach,** which has been hailed as one of the finest in the region. The water might be just a tad chilly (okay, try totally freezing), but it makes a nice romantic spot for a picnic lunch.

Skibbereen

The biggest town in West Cork with a whopping 2,000 residents, Skibbereen can get really congested in the summer months as it's really popular on the tourist trail. Everyone from Tony Blair to members of Oasis have vacationed here, and its historical significance draws a lot of interested visitors. Skibbereen was one of the towns hit hardest during the famine—indeed, there are around 10,000 victims buried locally at Abbeystrewery Cemetery. Today there are 26 pubs—a shocking number considering the population—mostly serving pints to the town's inbound travelers.

GETTING THERE & GETTING AROUND

From the north and south, take the N71. From Cork and points east, take the N22. You may also travel via Drimoleague (R593). Skibbereen is a main hub for bus service to West Cork. Contact **Bus Eireann** (☎ **021/450-8188;** www.buseireann.ie) for up-to-date timetables and fares. There is an online booking facility.

Your feet will do you fine in Skibbereen. Alternatively, the following taxis are available if need be: **Alwyn Harris** (Cork Rd.; ☎ **086/250-4255**), **Dolphin Cabs** (☎ **086/606-7037**), and **Skibbereen Cabs** (Bridge St.; ☎ **086/834-6396**).

BASICS

TOURIST INFORMATION **The Skibbereen Tourist Office** is located on North Street (☎ **028/21766**). It's open year-round Monday to Friday 9:15am to 5:30pm, with weekend and extended hours May through September.

RECOMMENDED WEBSITES The official website for Skibbereen is www.skibbereen.ie. It's full of useful information on hotels, restaurants, and things to do in the town and surrounding area. Also helpful is www.westcork.ie, a site about the entire region but centered on Skibbereen.

FESTIVALS

There's always something going on in Skibbereen or in West Cork—literally, you'll find something festive happening every weekend. For an up-to-date events calendar, check out www.westcorkweek.com. It's updated regularly and will take you through events day by day.

SLEEPING

➔ **Eldon Hotel** Right across from the bus stop and with an award-winning in-house restaurant, the Eldon is the perfect place for an overnight stop in Skibbereen. The rooms are tastefully decorated, and the beds are orthopedic and extra-large. The caring staff will happily arrange sea kayaking or scuba diving days out for you. Make sure you stop in at the hotel's bar for the traditional music sessions. *Bridge St.* ☎ *028/21300. Double room €44 low season, €80 high season. Amenities: Internet access; library. In room: TV.*

➔ **Russagh Mill Hostel and Adventure Centre** If you love sports and outdoor activities, this is the hostel for you. Mick Murphy's establishment, housed in a 200-year-old corn mill, boasts dorm rooms plus eight private rooms, but the main draw is the itinerary. Spend the day canoeing, biking, kayaking, hitting the archery range, or whatever else Mick has on offer. *Castletownshend Rd., Skibbereen, County Cork;* ☎ *028/21256. Mid-Mar to Oct. Dorm €11; double room €30. No credit cards. Amenities: Kitchen; laundry; free parking; TV room.*

EATING

➔ **Mary Ann's** PUB This adorable little place has a real West Cork feel to it, with a non-cheesy nautical theme (ship's wheels decorate the interior) and fabulous local seafood fare. In sunny weather, sit outside in the courtyard and eat deep-fried prawns or sirloin steak with garlic butter. *Castletownshend.* ☎ *028/36146. Reservations recommended for dinner. Main courses €15–€20. Daily 12:30–2pm and 6–9pm. Closed holidays.*

➔ **Thai @ Ty Ar Mor** THAI The upstairs of an award-winning Breton restaurant, Thai @ Ty Ar Mor is known for mixing up fresh seafood with tasty, spicy dishes. If you're not a fish fan, order the beef with ginger and spring onions or red roast pork. If you want to feel like you've left Ireland for Bangkok for the night, check out the new Khantok room, complete with traditional low tables and cushions. The service, from mostly French and Thai staff, is first-rate. *48 Bridge St.* ☎ *028/22100. Reservations recommended for dinner. Main courses about €15. Daily 12:30–2:30pm and 6–9pm. Closed Sun and Mon in winter, end Sept to mid-Oct, Feb.*

PARTYING

The best pub in Skibbereen, packed with 20-somethings and those in search of the perfect pizza, is undoubtedly **The Wine Vaults** (73 Bridge St.; ☎ **028/22110**). If you want a glass of wine and some good live music, this is the place to come. Another solid pub is **Sean Og's** (Market St.; ☎ **028/21573**). There are either traditional, folk, or blues sessions most nights, and you can have your Guinness outside in the beer garden in the summer. If you're up for some dancing and the usual crooners with their fiddles aren't doing it for you, check out **The Cellar Bar** (Main St.; ☎ **028/21329**). It's Skibbereen's only nightclub on Friday and Saturday nights, open 'til 2am with a €7 cover charge. Otherwise, it's known for its pool table and crowd of regulars on other nights.

SIGHTSEEING

→**Skibbereen Heritage Centre** It might be a morbid way to spend the day, but learning about the famine and its local victims can be fascinating. Go to this centre, where the famine is commemorated with artifacts and informational screens and panels. After you visit the Centre, you could walk the Famine Trail, which starts at Skibbereen Town Square—just follow the numbered plaques and visit sites with direct links to the Great Famine. For something slightly more cheerful, visit the beautiful, temperate Lough Hyne, 5km (3 miles) southwest of Skibbereen. This seawater lake is a complete anomaly—scientists have never been able to figure out why it's 86°F (30°C) warmer than the sea or why marine life usually found in the Mediterranean can be found here. Before you go, visit the Lough Hyne Interpretive Centre, also found at the Skibbereen Heritage Centre. *Old Gas Works, Upper Bridge St.* ☎ *028/40900. Mar 15–May 24 and Sept 25–end of Oct Tues–Sat 10am–6pm; all of Nov and Mar 1–Mar 15 Mon–Fri 9.30am–5.30pm; May 27–Sept 24*

daily 10am–6pm; adults €4.50; students €3.50.

PLAYING OUTSIDE

BICYCLING If you want to rent a bicycle, try **Roycroft's Stores** (☎ **028/21235;** roycroft@iol.ie); prices run €60 to €80 per week, depending on the season. If you call ahead, you can reserve a lightweight mountain bike with toe clips at no extra cost—an enormous advantage over the leaden, battleship-like bicycles rented at most stores. One-way riding from Skibbereen to Killarney or Kenmare can be arranged for an additional €30.

HIKING One of the most beautiful coastal walks in West Cork begins along the banks of Lough Hyne, the largest saltwater lake in Europe. Connected to the sea by a narrow strip of land, the lake is in a lush valley of stunning beauty. To get there, follow signs for Lough Hyne along R595 between Skibbereen and Baltimore. You can park at the northwest corner. The wide trail proceeds gradually upward from the parking lot through the woods on the west slope of the valley, with several viewpoints toward the lake and the sea beyond. Once you reach the hilltop, there is a sweeping view of the coast from Mizen Head to Galley Head. Walking time to the top and back is about 1½ hours.

Baltimore

Baltimore is absolutely tiny, with a mere 200 year-round residents, although the population grows in the summer. If you're into watersports, Baltimore is the perfect place to spend a couple of days, as it's known for sailing and diving. The underwater scene is ghostly, with shipwrecks dotting the ocean floor. Baltimore is also a haven for foodlovers with its popular seafood festival in May. You'll hear a lot about the O'Driscoll family—you can't escape them round here; they've got their names on everything including the Dun Na Sead castle, which you can see from just about everywhere in town.

CORK CITY

GETTING THERE

The drive from Cork is painless; take the N22. Cork Airport is about 100km (62 miles) away if you plan on flying in, then hiring a car from there. If you plan on taking the bus, you'll have to go via Skibbereen, the main hub for the area (☎ 021/450-8188; www.buseireann.ie).

GETTING AROUND

Baltimore is a small town and definitely walkable from end to end. If you need a lift while you're there, get a taxi. Try Declan Croke at the **Dolphin Taxi Service** (☎ 028/23323) or **Tom O'Brien** at ☎ 086/810990.

BASICS

TOURIST INFORMATION The **Baltimore Tourist Office** is located by the pier and open 'til 5:30pm every day from July through September. Call ☎ 028/21766.

RECOMMENDED WEBSITES The semi-official website for Baltimore, which is fairly helpful, is www.baltimore-ireland.com. There's information on local accommodation and links, plus all you need to know about festivals and travel.

FESTIVALS

The **Baltimore Seafood Festival** (☎ 028/21766), presented in conjunction with Guinness, is held annually over a 3-day weekend in late May. Expect to eat lots of fresh mussels while listening to live jazz music. This festival is held in conjunction with the **Baltimore Wooden Boats Festival** (www.baltimore woodenboatfestival.com), which includes competitions for building wooden boats. On the last weekend in June each year since 1986, there's been a festival to celebrate the large O'Driscoll clan so prominent in the area. Hosted by Heineken Ireland, it's a chance to hear music and see dancing in the square plus hear about the family's heritage in addresses by clan chieftains.

SLEEPING

→ **Casey's of Baltimore** This family-run hotel occupies an enviable piece of land overlooking the natural harbor and the Ilen river estuary. Recently renovated, all the rooms have large king-size beds, satellite TV, and sea view. Casey's boasts a pub, a restaurant, and a beer garden in good weather. The staff seems to genuinely want to make sure you have a great stay. The legendary breakfasts—warm brown bread, farmhouse cheeses, seafood, and more—are included in the tariff. *Baltimore, County Cork. ☎ 028/20197. www.caseysofbaltimore.com. Double €70–€85. In room: Coffee/tea facilities, hair dryer, satellite TV, trouser press.*

→ **Rolf's Holiday Hostel** Every dorm at this cool backpacker favorite is a separate 300-year old stone cottage. The rooms are clean and tastefully decorated, with stunning views across the water. Café Art, the in-house restaurant, is well regarded not just with guests but with Baltimore locals (see "Eating," below). Have a drink at the Wine Bar, do your laundry, or relax in the large gardens. Just book in advance because the merits of this friendly place are known far and wide. *Baltimore Hill. ☎ 028/20289. www.rolfsholidays. com. Dorm €13–€15; double room €40–€70. Amenities: Kitchen; laundry; TV room.*

EATING

→ **Café Art** CONTINENTAL The in-house restaurant at Rolf's Holiday Hostel earns rave reviews from locals by staying open long after the summer tourists have left Baltimore. Chef Johannes Haffner uses as much home-grown, organic produce as he can, serving up delish spins on classic dishes to keep both veggies and meat-eaters happy. I suggest my favorite: the beef stroganoff, cooked the authentic way with vodka, followed up with the apple tart. *Baltimore Hill, Baltimore, County Cork. ☎ 028/ 20289. Reservations recommended. Main courses €15–€20. Daily 12:30–3pm and 6–9:30pm (9pm off season). Closed Mon and Tues off season.*

→ **The Customs House** IRISH Run by a couple of Aussies, this clean, contemporary restaurant feels like it's been kitted out according to the laws of feng shui. The menu is simple and changes daily according to the season, so stop by, and you're guaranteed the freshest ingredients. You could go for the three-course Tourist Menu for €28 if you want a taste of Baltimore, or try the seafood tapas plate with Dublin Bay prawns if you've got someone to share with. *Baltimore Hill.* ☎ *028/20200. Reservations recommended. Main courses €15–€20. Dinner Thurs–Sun; daily July–Aug. Closed mid-Sept through Easter.*

PARTYING

Baltimore is small and not exactly happening at night time, but you could do worse than **Declan McCarthy's** (above the pier; ☎ **028/20159**). There's sometimes a €7 cover charge in the summer for the trad music sessions, but if you want to be in the center of the action, then it's worth the money. You'll meet all your fellow hostellers plus some chilled out locals. Another favorite is **Bushe's Bar** (town centre; ☎ **028/20125**), where the Bushe family, including their three children, have presided since 1973. The maritime artifacts reflect the patronage at Bushe's—sailors come here so much that showers have been installed for their benefit. You can also order food here—the homemade soups are popular.

SIGHTSEEING

Walk out to **The Beacon,** a lighthouse perched dramatically on a cliff overlooking the ocean and with amazing views of Sherkin Island. Just follow the main road. Alternatively, you could check out **Dun Na Sead,** overlooking the harbor. It's free to get in, although the jewels kept in this old fort were lost long ago and are now somewhere on the sea floor.

PLAYING OUTSIDE

BOATING   The **Atlantic Boating Service** (tel **028/23420**) is a fun way to get wet, with boat rental by the hour and water-skiing for €27. If you find yourself in Baltimore but don't fancy getting wet, you could rent a bike

from **Rolf's Holiday Hostel** (☎ **028/20289**) for around €10 a day and cycle eastward out of town to Lough Hyne (more info under "Sightseeing" in the "Skibbereen" section, earlier), the only saltwater lake in Ireland. You might have to push yourself on the steeper trails but the views are fantastic—bring a camera.

DIVING   The **Baltimore Diving & Watersports Centre** (☎ **028/20300**) provides equipment and boats to certified divers for exploring the many shipwrecks, reefs, and caves in this region. The cost is €40 per dive with equipment. Various 2-hour to 15-day certified PADI courses are available for all levels of experience. For example, beginners can take a 2-hour snorkeling course for €30 or a scuba-diving course for €45 to €450, depending on duration; experienced divers can take the 2-week PADI instructor course. The **Glenans Irish Sailing Club** (www.glenans-ireland.com) was founded in France and has two centers in Ireland, one of which is in Baltimore Harbor. The centers provide weeklong courses at all levels, using dinghies, cruisers, catamarans, or windsurfers; prices are €369 to €529. The living facilities are pretty basic, with dorm-style accommodations and you cook for yourself. Weekend sailing courses are available in Baltimore in May, June, September, and October for €175 per person; call ☎ **01/661-1481** for advance booking. The center also offers weeklong windsurfing lessons and hire.

Cape Clear Island

Cape Clear, only 3 miles by 1 mile, is Ireland's last frontier, 8 miles off the coast of West Cork. It is probably best known for its presence within the Gaelic-speaking region—teenage students flock here in the summer for lessons in the national language. The scenery is wild and romantic, with flora of all kinds and medieval structures like the ruins of a 12th-century church. The island draws

CORK CITY

lots of middle-aged bird-watchers, but for those in search of adventure, there are watersports like sea kayaking. There's also no better place for whale-watching, so get out those binoculars.

GETTING THERE

First you've got to get there. The *Naomh Ciarán II* offers ferry service (no cars, passengers only) year-round, leaving the harbor at Baltimore daily in July and August at 11am (noon on Sun), 2:15, 5, and 7pm, and leaving Cape Clear Monday to Saturday at 9am, noon, and 6pm (Sun 11am, 1, 4, and 6pm). Service is always subject to the seas and is somewhat more limited off season. The passage takes 45 minutes and costs €12 round-trip. If you've got questions, contact Captain Conchúr O'Driscoll (☎ 028/39135 or 086/266-2197). For the same price, there's also the *Karycraft* (☎ 028/28278), departing Schull daily in June, July, and August at 10:30am, 2:30, and 4:30pm; and departing Cape Clear at 11:30am, 3:30, and 5:30pm. In September, service is limited to one crossing daily, departing Schull at 2:30pm and Cape Clear at 5:30pm.

GETTING AROUND

Cape Clear Island is definitely small enough to walk, but if you'd like, you can bring a bike rented from Baltimore on the ferry.

BASICS

TOURIST OFFICES   There's a tourist information booth on the pier in the summer, where the ferry docks (☎ 028/3919).

RECOMMENDED WEBSITES   Cape Clear has a really helpful, comprehensive website at www.oilean-chleire.ie.

FESTIVALS

For something out of the ordinary, there's the **Cape Clear Island International Storytelling Festival,** an annual event drawing eccentric performers from all over the world spinning tall tales and singing in English, Irish, and French (☎ 028/39116; stories@indigo.ie).

SLEEPING

The island's **An Óige Youth Hostel** (☎ 028/39198) at the Cape Clear Adventure Centre is open March through October. Most B&Bs are open year-round. They include **Fáilte** (contact Eleanór Uí Drisceoil, ☎ 028/39135); and **Ard na Gaoith** (contact Eileen Leonard, ☎ 028/39160). For self-catering cottages by the day or week, contact **Ciarán O'Driscoll** (☎ 028/39135).

EATING & PARTYING

You can't really miss the island's three pubs and two restaurants. Try **Cistin Chleire** (no phone) on North Harbour for homemade fruit scones or stop in for a beer at **The Southernmost House** (☎ 028/39157), the best place for good *craic* on the island.

SIGHTSEEING

Once you've arrived on Cape Clear, there are a number of things to see, including birds galore, seals, dolphins, the occasional whale, ancient "marriage stones," and a goat farm offering courses on everything you ever wanted to know about goats—and don't miss the hauntingly spectacular ruins of the O'Driscoll Castle on the island's western shore.

PLAYING OUTSIDE

Cléire Lasmuigh, Cape Clear Island Adventure Centre (☎ 028/39198), offers an array of outdoor programs, from snorkeling and sea kayaking to hill walking and orienteering. Instruction or accompanied sessions are available by the hour, day, or week. For example, prices for a 5-day sea-kayaking package (including meals, housing, instruction, and equipment rental) start at €250. **Coastal cruises** for sea angling, scuba diving, or bird-watching are the specialty of Ciarán O'Driscoll (☎ 028/39153).

SHOPPING

Fortunately, there are no plans for a shopping mall, but you enjoy some retail therapy and buy local crafts and books for family in

A Deep & Meaningful Leaf

Shamrocks are everywhere in Ireland and seem to have become the international symbol of Ireland and Irishness. But why?

Unless you've never left your house, you'll know a shamrock is a three-leaved green clover (yes, we know; there are some four-leaved ones but we'll get into those later). But why all the fuss? The Druids worshipped it as sacred plant because of its mystical three-pronged form. The best-known legend surrounding the shamrock, however, involves Irish superstar, Saint Patrick. It is said that ol' Patty used the leaf as a metaphor for the theory behind Christianity, no doubt banking on past fascinations with the shamrock.

As the first purveyor of "the word of the Lord" in Ireland, Saint Patrick used the shamrock to explain the idea of the inter-relationship of the Father, the Son, and the Holy Ghost: As each leaf of the clover is separate, so are the divisions of the holy trinity. However, all are connected as one. In the shamrock it is through the stem; in the trinity, it is through God. Don't ask us what he would have made of those "lucky" four-leafed clovers . . . .

Harpercraft and The Back Room in **Cotter's Yard,** in the village of North Harbour, as well as the nearby pottery shop. While you're at it, pick up a copy of Chuck Kruger's *Cape Clear Island Magic,* a good introduction to the beautiful island.

Sherkin Island

There are more cows than tourists in Sherkin Island, population 70. Visitors flock here from all over Ireland for the clean, quiet sandy beaches, which can be found opposite the pier. Only 10 minutes by boat from Baltimore, the island is home to a 15th-century Franciscan friary and yet another ruined O'Driscoll castle. The scenery here is beautiful, but if you get bored exploring, there are two very quaint old pubs with lots of charm where you can happily spend a few hours.

GETTING THERE

A licensed ferry makes the trip from Baltimore to Sherkin Island seven times daily. For a schedule of these trips, go to www.sherkin island.ie (☎ 028/20125).

TOURIST OFFICES   The best place to get information on the island is at the local **Post Office** (☎ 028/20181), open 9am to 6pm Monday through Friday June through August,

and closing for lunch between 1pm and 2pm at all other times of the year.

RECOMMENDED WEBSITES   For such a small place, Sherkin Island has a really useful website, found at www.sherkinisland.ie. There's info on everything you could possibly need to know, from accommodation to books on the island, plus links.

SLEEPING

Horseshoe Cottage ([tel] **028/20598**) and **Cuinne House** (☎ **028/20384**) are your two best bets if you'd rather stay the night than return to Baltimore or if you miss the last ferry. Both are B&Bs (€30–€60 for doubles), whose owners pride themselves in a warm welcome and a huge breakfast.

EATING & PARTYING

Okay, with 70 residents, Sherkin isn't a clubbing hotspot, but if you want a drink, try the **Jolly Roger** (☎ **028/20379**) or the **Islanders Rest** (☎ **028/20116**), directly opposite from each other on the only road and open year-round.

SIGHTSEEING

Sherkin Island is the ideal spot for history buffs—you can explore the ruins of the 15th-century Franciscan friary or the O'Driscoll castle. If it's nice weather the best places to visit are the beaches—long, white, and peaceful. Check out Silver Strand, Cow Strand, and Tra Ban, which are safe and sheltered.

Clonakilty

Well known for its pretty beach and lively pub scene, Clonakilty has yet to go the way of Kinsale, although more tourists descend on this flower-box-covered little town every summer. It's a perfect place to spend a night on the way to or from Cork City as it's only about 45km (28 miles) away. In August the Clonakilty Festival offers street entertainment and live music late into the night. You'll find more Gaelic speakers here than any nearby town and you'll see rows of old-fashioned shops surrounding perfectly manicured squares. Make sure you check out the famous pub De Barra's, whatever you do—Paul McCartney and David Bowie love it there.

GETTING THERE & GETTING AROUND

The easiest way to get to Clonality is from Cork on **Bus Eireann** (☎ 021/450-8188; www.buseireann.ie)—there are about four buses daily. There are two or three buses daily from Skibbereen, too. The bus stop is in front of the Spar supermarket on Pearse Street.

With its narrow streets and nearby beach, Clonakilty is the perfect place to stroll or to rent a bike. If the latter is your thing, head to **MTM Cycles** (Ashe St.; ☎ 023/33584; €12 per day).

BASICS

TOURIST INFORMATION The **Clonakilty Tourist Office** is on Wolfe Tone Street and is open from 9am to 6pm daily from May through December (☎ 023/33226).

RECOMMENDED WEBSITES There are two major websites about the town: www. clonakilty.ie is somewhat helpful, with an events calendar and a facility for booking a hotel room; www.clon.ie has a more budget look about it but functions almost like the

U.S. Yellow Pages, with phone numbers for watersports companies and schedules of church services.

INTERNET ACCESS If you have a laptop, you can access a wireless network at the **Kilty Stone** pub on Pearse Street, right in the center of town (☎ 028/34129). If you want run-of-the-mill Internet access for a flat hourly fee (€4), try **Clonakilty Cyber Centre,** 10/12 Astna St. (☎ 023/34557).

FESTIVALS

In August, Clonakilty attracts tourists and locals from nearby towns for the Clonakilty Festival, complete with daily entertainment, music sessions, and the obligatory fireworks. Call ☎ 023/33226 for more information and dates. More out of the ordinary is the **Black and White Festival** (☎ 023/33226) in the second week of July. It offers a contest to see who can consume the most black and white pudding—and no, that doesn't mean Jell-O; that's blood sausage. Don't go if you don't have a stomach of steel or if you had too many pints the night before.

SLEEPING

Cheap

➜**Old Brewery Hostel** If you're planning on staying here during the August festival, definitely call well ahead—there are only 26 beds and they'll be full. The Old Brewery is clean, social, and convenient for the pubs as you're within stumbling distance from the best ones. You can rent a bike or cook for yourself in their well-stocked kitchen. Just beware as they have some strange rules about check-in times and are liable to give away your room without notice. Keep calling before you arrive and make sure there are no mix-ups. *Emmet Sq., Clonakilty, County Cork.* ☎ 023/33525. Dorms €12; doubles €22. Amenities: Cycle rental; kitchen; TV room.

Doable

➜**O'Donovan's Hotel** A fifth-generation family-run hotel, O'Donovan's is somewhat of a Clonakilty institution, with three bars

Clonakilty

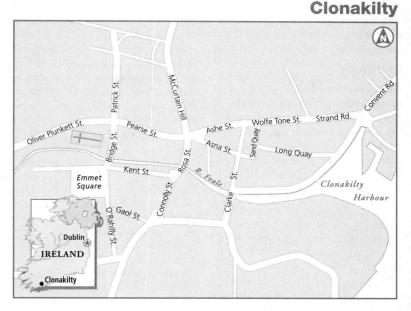

and a restaurant of its own. The hotel is located right on Pearse Street so you won't be far from the action. The rooms are basic but bright with lots of light coming in, and the staff will be happy to help you find some outdoor activities to keep you entertained or plan a route for a cycling trip. *Pearse St., Clonakilty, County Cork.* ☎ *023/33250. www. odonovanshotel.com. Singles and doubles €60 per person. In room: TV, coffee/tea facility, hair dryer.*

Splurge

→ **Randles Clonakilty Hotel**   Part of a small family-owned chain, Randles is comfortable, well-decorated, and staffed by friendly, helpful English-speakers—more than can be said for other hotels of its type. The real draw here is the location—right in the town center and a short walk from every local attraction. The Randles makes a good base for travel around West Cork. There are really cheap deals if you head there in the off season. Otherwise, expect to pay for the three

stars on the door. *Wolfe Tone St.* ☎ *023/34749. Doubles from €100. Rate includes Irish breakfast. In room: TV, coffee/tea facility, hair dryer.*

EATING

→ **An Sugan** PUB   The seafood on the menu at An Sugan wouldn't be out of place in a much fancier eatery; you might just forget this is an ordinary pub in a small Irish town. Those in the know order the fish pie or the salmon and potato cakes, while the fresh oysters, scampi, and seafood chowder win rave reviews. Splash out on some wine or get a pint; the stouts on tap are better. Come for lunch/dinner and stay for the rest of the day/evening. A fab place to warm your toes on a cold Clonakilty day. *41 Wolfe Tone St.* ☎ *023/ 33498. www.ansugan.com. Average meal €15. Year-round daily lunch and dinner.*

→ **Richy's Bar and Bistro** INTERNATIONAL   The lights are dim, the music is Thievery Corporation, and there are stacks of design magazines on the table. Hang out with friends on the big orange couches or have a quiet dinner alone—Richy's might be a little overpriced but the ambience is pretty cool for old-fashioned Clonakilty. Their tapas plates for sharing are the perfect way to start a night out, although if you're hungry go for the Mauritian beef cashew-nut curry or the monkfish tandoori. The waitstaff need to be hurried along as they can often be found chatting with young local regulars. *Pearse St., Clonakilty, County Cork.* ☎ *023/21852. www. richysbarandbistro.com. Average meal €18. Year-round daily lunch and dinner.*

PARTYING

There isn't really a bad pub in Clonakilty so you could turn up anywhere and have a really fun night, especially in the summer when the town is heaving with travelers. Make **De Barra's** (55 Pearse St.; ☎ 023/33381; www. debarra.ie) your first stop—and get there early as it gets packed. Famous musicians like Paul McCartney, Bowie, Springsteen, and Sting have all stopped by here, and there are photos lining the walls to prove it. This place is traditional meets kitsch, with kooky masks hanging above a stage where a 200-year-old harp is still played during nightly folk sessions. Contemporary artists like Ken Cotter have been known to play gigs, so check the website for details on who's playing during your stay. If De Barra's is far too crowded, try any other pub on the street, like Mick Finns or the Kilty Stone.

SIGHTSEEING

The ancient stone ring fort Lios na gCon is located 3 miles east of Clonakilty. Follow the main Bandon-Clonakilty road to the campus of the agricultural college; you'll have to pay about €4 to see the ring. On a clear day the mouth of Clonakilty Bay can be seen from the site. It is one of three circular earthworks in the land known as Darrara and one of 48 circular earthworks or possible ring fort sites recorded by the Cork Archaeological Survey in the Clonakilty area. If you're a medieval buff, you might also want to check out the Templebryan Stone Circle a mile or so up MacCurtain Street past the tourist office. The circle comprises five huge megaliths, although once there were nine. Slightly closer to the town center is Inchydoney Beach, a great place to meet young locals before they hit the pubs in the evening. Sandy and set at the foot of a rolling hill, Inchydoney is the ideal spot to spend a day in the summer.

SHOPPING

Like many other towns of its size in the area, Clonakilty is lined with arts and crafts and gift shops where you can buy any sort of touristy trinket to take home and gather dust. However, there are also cute traditional wool and cashmere shops, and some "confectioners" and "victuallers" (candy shops and grocery stores). Simply walk up Pearse Street for the best selection of shops.

County Kerry

Kerry might just be the Ireland you imagined with your eyes closed: Rolling green hills, rugged cliffs overlooking perfect harbors, vibrant towns with pastel colored houses, and country pubs filled with amiable locals.

Yes, it's true, there are parts of Kerry that could pass for a huge Irish-themed Disneyland crawling with obnoxious tour groups, but you can easily skip these places and head to the Iveragh or Dingle Peninsula for a taste for the real Kerry.

History buffs will love the Skellig Islands—windswept and steep—home to crumbling monastic residences and thousands of birds. Sun worshippers and watersport lovers should head to Dingle, a postcard-perfect town far removed from the world of shamrock-filled shops, with miles of beaches and quiet lagoons for sailing or diving.

And then there's Killarney. On one hand, Killarney National Park—and the surrounding area—is beautiful and tranquil. On the other, Killarney Town is best seen through your rear view mirror. Sporting a manufactured "heritage" and all the atmosphere of an amusement park, it is undoubtedly the tourist center of Ireland.

If you really feel the need to go, try to stay outside the town itself and visit Muckross Estate and Ross Castle, two impressive sites that won't leave you feeling sick.

The Best of County Kerry

○ **Chilling Out and Exploring Kenmare:** This is the best base you could wish for at the mouth of the River Roughty on Kenmare Bay. The town is picture perfect with stone cottages, colorful gardens, and

flowers overflowing from window boxes. See p 302.

○ **Exploring MacGillycuddy's Reeks:** An awesome mountain range on the Iveragh Peninsula, MacGillycuddy's Reeks not

County Kerry

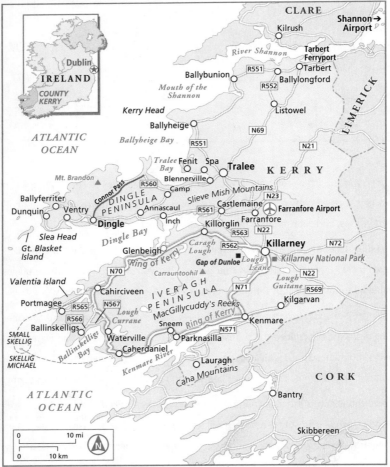

only has the coolest name of any mountain range in Ireland, but also boasts the highest mountain on the island, Carrantuohill (1,041m/3,414 ft.). The Reeks are among Ireland's greatest spectacles. See p. 288.

○ **Hiking Up Skellig Michael:** Thirteen kilometers (8 miles) offshore of the Iveragh Peninsula, rising sharply 214m (702 ft.) out of the Atlantic, this is a remote, rocky crag dedicated to the

Archangel Michael. In flight from the world, early Irish monks in pursuit of "white martyrdom" chose this spot to build their austere hermitage. Today the journey to Skellig, across choppy seas, and the arduous climb to its summit are challenging and unforgettable. See p. 293.

○ **Checking Out Fungie:** Every day, fishing boats from Dingle ferry visitors out into the nearby waters to see Fungie, the friendliest dolphin you're ever likely to meet. Fungie swims right up to the boat, and the boatmen stay out long enough for ample sightings. You can also arrange an early-morning dolphin swim. See p. 308.

○ **Splurging for Dinner at The Chart House:** In this inviting Dingle bistro,

everyone comes for Laura Boyce's confident, simple cooking. Think wonderful comfort food with a flair—the kind of food you never tire of. And the service is, as the Irish would say, "spot on." See p. 308.

Killarney Town

The first thing you'll notice about Killarney natives is they're pros when it comes to dolling out the Irish charm. It's not surprising; they get plenty of practice. This place draws millions of visitors a year. It can feel as if the whole town is devoted to the pursuit of the almighty euro, and downtown Killarney is to be avoided altogether unless you're desperate for a pair of overpriced Celtic cross earrings or something similar. But the valley surrounding the town is gorgeous, with three lakes, scenic islands, and 25 miles of woodlands.

Getting There

BY PLANE   **Aer Arann** (☎ 061/704428; www.aerarann.ie) regularly zips from Dublin into Kerry County Airport, Farranfore, County Kerry (☎ 066/976-4644; www.kerry airport.ie), about 16km (10 miles) north of Killarney. **Ryanair** (www.ryanair.com) flies direct from London (Stansted) to Kerry.

BY TRAIN   **Irish Rail** trains from Dublin, Limerick, Cork, and Galway arrive daily at the **Killarney Railway Station** (☎ 064/31067; www.irishrail.ie), Railway Road, off East Avenue Road.

BY BUS   **Bus Éireann** operates regularly scheduled service into Killarney from all parts of Ireland. The bus depot (☎ 064/34777; www.buseireann.ie) is adjacent to the train station at Railway Road, off East Avenue Road.

BY CAR   Kerry folk like to say all roads lead to Killarney; thankfully there is some escape, but at least a half-dozen major national roads do. They include N21 and N23 from Limerick,

N22 from Tralee, N22 from Cork, N72 from Mallow, and N70 from the Ring of Kerry and West Cork.

Orientation

With only 7,000 full-time residents, Killarney only has one main thoroughfare, simply called Main Street. Halfway through town it becomes High Street. The big roads to look out for off Main Street are Plunkett Street, which becomes College Street, and New Street. The Deenagh River edges the western side of town, and East Avenue Road the eastern side. Things get really busy at the southern tip of Main Street, where it meets East Avenue Road. Here the road curves and heads southward out to the Muckross road and the entrance to Killarney National Park.

Getting Around

BY FOOT   Killarney is so weeny it doesn't have a bus service. It's not a problem; the place is so compact your feet will do you just fine. Want a quick and easy tour? Follow the signposted "Tourist Trail" for the highlights of the main streets. It shouldn't take you more than 2 hours. Pick up a booklet about what's what along the way, from the tourist office.

BY TAXI   If you find yourself needing a cab, taxis line up at the rank on **College Square** (☎ 064/31331). You can also phone for a taxi from **Killarney Taxi** (☎ 064/30444), **Dero's Taxi Service** (☎ 064/31251), or **O'Connell Taxi** (☎ 064/31654).

BY CAR   If you need somewhere to park your car, head to the large public parking lot near the town center, where parking costs

Hanging Out

Young travelers have been known to hang out in the front room of the Sugan Hostel (see "Hostels," below), especially when the sun goes down and it gets cold. You'll find European and American kids strumming their guitars and sipping hot chocolate in front of the fire. While the sun's out, head to Killarney National Park where there are acres and acres of land to explore and a couple of pubs, like Molly Darcy's and Kate Kearney's, catering to tourists.

€1 per hour. If you want to rent one here, try **Avis,** the Glebe Arcade (☎ **064/35544;** www. avis.ie); **Budget,** c/o International Hotel, Kenmare Place (☎ **064/34341;** www.budget. ie); **Hertz,** 28 Plunkett St. (☎ **064/34126;** www.hertz.ie); or **Randles Bros.,** Muckross Road (☎ **064-31237**).

BY BUGGY   Alternatively you can leave your reputation on the sidewalk and jump aboard a horse-drawn **buggy** or "jarvey" lined up at Kenmare Place in Killarney Town. If you can stand the shame, they'll take you to Killarney National Park sites or another pretty place nearby. The price depends on how far you want to go, ranging from €16 to €40 per ride (up to four persons). To arrange a tour in advance, contact **Tangney Tours,** Kinvara House, Muckross Road, Killarney (☎ **064/33358**).

Basics

EMERGENCIES   In an **emergency,** dial ☎ **999.** The **Killarney District Hospital** is on St. Margaret's Road (☎ **064/31076**). The **Killarney Garda Station** is on New Road (☎ **064/31222**).

INTERNET ACCESS   Killarney has a handful of places to check your e-mail thanks to the large number of visitors each summer. Try

Café Internet (New St.; ☎ **064/36741**), where you can order some food while surfing the net with their lunch'n'surf specials: A sandwich, a drink, and half an hour access for €10. You could also head to **Web-Talk** (Main St.), open 10am until 10pm Monday through Saturday, although there's no food here and the surroundings aren't quite as comfortable.

LAUNDRY   If you need to do your laundry, head for the **Gleeson Launderette,** Brewery Lane, off College Square (☎ **064/33877**).

LIBRARY   The **Killarney Public Library,** on Rock Road (☎ **064/32972**), provides free Internet access from its bank of computers.

PHARMACY   If you need a drugstore, try **O'Sullivans Pharmacy,** 81 New St. (☎ **064/ 35866**), or **Donal Sheahan,** 34 Main St. (☎ **064/31113**).

POST OFFICE   The **Killarney Post Office,** New Street (☎ **064/31051**), is open Monday and Wednesday to Saturday 9am to 5:30pm, Tuesday 9:30am to 5:30pm.

TOURIST OFFICE   The **Killarney Tourist Office,** Aras Fáilte, is at the town center on Beech Road (☎ **064/31633**). It's open October to May, Monday to Saturday 9:15am to 5:15pm; June and September daily 9am to 6pm; July to August daily 9am to 8pm. During low season, the office sometimes closes for lunch from 1 to 2pm. There's plenty inside including the *Tourist Trail* walking-tour guide and the *Killarney Area Guide,* with maps. Another useful publication to get the low-down on mainstream tours, activities, events, and entertainment is **Where: Killarney,** a quarterly magazine distributed free at hotels and guesthouses.

FESTIVALS

This ain't the place for hip urban festivals bursting with cutting-edge talent, but if you're around in February, look out for the **Éigse na Brídeoige** (☎ **094/74123**). It's an annual spring festival based in Waterville, outside of

Killarney Town

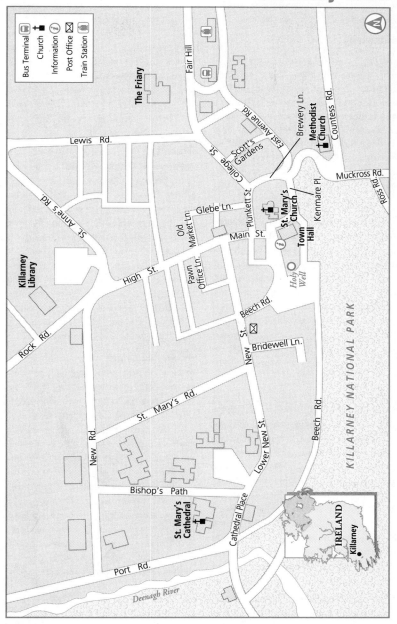

Legend
- Bus Terminal
- Church
- Information
- Post Office
- Train Station

Lewis Rd.

The Friary

Fair Hill

East Avenue Rd.

Scott's Gardens

College St.

Brewery Ln.

Methodist Church

Countess Rd.

Muckross Rd.

Ross Rd.

St. Anne's Rd.

Glebe Ln.

Old Market Ln.

Plunkett St.

St. Mary's Church

Kenmare Pl.

Main St.

Town Hall

Killarney Library

High St.

Pawn Office Ln.

Holy Well

Rock Rd.

Beech Rd.

New St.

Bridewell Ln.

Beech Rd.

KILLARNEY NATIONAL PARK

St. Mary's Rd.

New Rd.

Lower New St.

Bishop's Path

St. Mary's Cathedral

Cathedral Place

Port Rd.

IRELAND

Killarney

Deenagh River

Killarney, with events held all over South West Kerry. There's plenty of music and theater, plus lectures and discussions.

Sleeping

Killarney has as many hotels as towns many times its size, with every type of establishment from four-star luxury palaces to little hippie hostels. Expect to pay a small fortune for the best suites. Killarney is far more expensive than its neighboring towns—up to €720 nightly for the crème de la crème. Even if you're just after a hostel bed, book well in advance as Killarney fills up fast in the summer months.

HOSTELS

➜ **Neptune's Town Hostel** This large, comfortable hostel offers all kinds of rooms, from dorms to en suite singles. Travelers and families from Naples to New Zealand flock here in the peak season for the excellent self-catering facilities and the helpful staff, who are all too happy to help you plan day trips to Dingle or the Ring of Kerry. *Bishop's Lane, off New St.* ☎ *064/35255. www.neptuneshostel. com. Dorm €14 per person; double €19 per person. Discount with IHH/Student cards. Amenities: Bureau de change; Internet; kitchen; laundry.*

➜ **Railway Hostel** This clean, bright hostel is certainly your most attractive option if you arrive at the train station totally exhausted in the pouring rain. Completely renovated in 2005, the hostel provides dorm accommodation and en suite rooms. Unlike some other establishments in the town, the Railway Hostel is staffed 24 hours a day 365 days a year. If you want to rent a bike, this is the place to do it. *Park Rd., across from the train station.* ☎ *064/35299. Dorm €12 per person; double €16 per person. Amenities: Internet.*

➜ **The Sugan Hostel** You just can't say enough about The Súgan Hostel. It has atmosphere, a manager who seriously resembles a leprechaun, and the most comfortable beds around. Sure, the rooms are on their last legs, but you won't notice or care. Pa, the manager, will tell you about absolutely everything there is to do in town, yet when nightfall arrives you won't want to leave the hostel. There is no curfew or lockout, and there is a large modern kitchen for guests. *Lewis Rd.* ☎ *064/33104. www.killarneysuganhostel. com. Dorms €15 per person; double €18 per person. Amenities: Kitchen.*

DOABLE

➜ **Fairview Guest House** You won't find a better hotel in this price range in Killarney. The rooms are sleek and elegantly decorated, with king-size beds and satellite TV. The guesthouse is close to the town center, but you'll get sleep as it's out of the noisy area near all the pubs. Everything you could want is here, whether that be Jacuzzi baths (in the better suites) or wireless Internet. Hosts James and Shelley are young and clued up. *College St.* ☎ *064/34164. Double €40–€75. Amenities: TV, Wi-Fi Internet.*

SPLURGE

➜ **Randles Court** This former old rectory glistens with gold and marble. The reception area may look a tad old-fashioned, but the rooms are kitted out with wide screen satellite TVs, DVD players, and some even have Jacuzzis. The in-house restaurant, Checkers, is pretty expensive but exudes old-school glamour even if you're in jeans and sneakers. The staff is helpful and the hotel is only a 5-minute walk from downtown Killarney. *Muckross Rd.* ☎ *064/353333. www.randlescourt.com. Double €140–€190. Full Irish breakfast included. Amenities: Restaurant (international); bar; fitness center; laundry service; limited room service; swimming pool. In room: TV, hair dryer.*

Eating

➜ **Cooperage** CONTINENTAL Highly recommended by food bible *Le Routiers*, the

Cooperage is riotously popular so you'll need to book in advance. Order the steak or some fresh local seafood. You won't make a mistake; everything is spot on. With its unique view of the old terraced stone cottages in the area and a deli shop on the premises, the Cooperage ain't your usual run of the mill eatery. *Old Market Lane.* ☎ *064/37716. Average meal €32. Noon–10pm daily.*

➜ **Foley's Seafood and Steak** SEAFOOD A huge fave with visitors and locals alike, Foley's is known for fresh seafood and juicy steaks (if you didn't guess from the name). If you're feeling adventurous, pluck a live lobster from the tank in the front of the dining room. Family run with fantastic service, it's not a surprise to find Foley's has won heaps of awards. Book in advance or you won't get a table. *23 High St.* ☎ *064/31217. Average meal €32. 12:30–3pm and 5–11pm daily.*

➜ **Mac's Restaurant and Ice Cream Parlour** CAFE   If you've only ever eaten ice cream at boring chains like Dairy Queen, check out this traditional ice-cream parlour, and their delicious, indulgent sundaes—topped with colorful umbrellas. Ice cream is only the beginning; Mac's boasts a full lunch and dinner menu including meat, fish, and vegetarian dishes. Their lasagna gets rave reviews. *6 Main St.* ☎ *064/35213. Average meal €15. 9am–10pm daily.*

➜ **Panis Angelicus** CAFE   This charming, hip little cafe has a very continental feel, with terra-cotta walls and the smell of homemade bread wafting through the room. The menu features sandwiches, salads, and soups—try the warm goat's cheese on crostini. If you're up early, go for breakfast and enjoy the fresh juice and croissants. If you want to eat outside in the sun, Panis Angelicus offers a convenient takeaway service. *15 New St.* ☎ *064/39648. Average meal €13. No credit cards. 9:30am–5:30pm daily.*

➜ **Rozzers** CONTINENTAL   Located in the Killeen House Hotel, Rozzers has won prizes for its delish fixed-price menu, prepared by chef Paul O'Gorman. For starters, go for the saltwater oysters or the unusual crispy spiced lamb cakes. For an entree, order the Dingle Bay lobster or the supreme of chicken with red pepper and chorizo mousse. All the Rozzers dishes are served up with a twist and it certainly doesn't feel like a hotel restaurant. Leave room for dessert—you won't be disappointed. *Aghadoe.* ☎ *064/31711. Fixed-price 4-course dinner €50. Open for dinner daily.*

PARTYING

There are more cheesy "ye olde"–style Irish pubs in Killarney than you can count on a millipedes toes, but there are some decent places to get a drink and/or get raucously drunk. First, to highlight ***pubs and bars to be avoided:*** American theme bar **Mustang Sally's** (Main St.; ☎ **064/35790**) is a no-go zone, unless you have a penchant for big sugary cocktails and greasy burgers. The **Gleneagle** (Muckross Rd.; ☎ **064/31870**) is also pretty hideous. A polite one-word description would be "megapub": It's massive, cavernous, and geared toward the tour bus groups with a Summer—cringe—Cabaret.

With those out of the way, consider heading toward **Kelly's Korner** (Michael Collins Place; no phone). It is tiny, but packed with 20-year-old travelers from the hostel next door. The sign outside the door advertises Kelly's as "Drinking Consultants" and, true to their word, the staff make every effort to get booze down your throat. If you want something a bit quieter, try the **Acorn** (Muckross Rd.; ☎ **064/37600**), just toward the outskirts of town. The bar feels luxurious with lots of space and comfortable seats. Bar food like stir-fries is served alongside pints and cocktails. The best gastro-pub in town is **Buckley's** (College St.; ☎ **064/31037**) next to the Arbutus Hotel. The interior is oak-paneled and traditional, but the food is mostly Mediterranean, with ciabatta and panini served at lunch. If you can't possibly fathom a night out without your Louboutin heels and Marc Jacobs skirt, then head to **The Kube** (Killarney Towers Hotel; ☎ 064/31038), where trendy Killarney natives go to see and be seen. The whole place feels slick and modern, with the ubiquitous black and chrome accessories. There's an outdoor seating area for good weather—just don't expect to get into the Kube in jeans and sneakers. For guys who prefer lively banter and large men with big necks, there's always **Tatler Jack's** (Plunkett St.; ☎ 064/32361), Killarney's most raucous sports bar and the home haunt of Dr. Crokes, a local Gaelic football team. Conversation focuses on the national sport, and the crowd swills beer and eats generous portions of local fare. The best wine bar in town is **Jordie's** (Inishfallen Mall; ☎ 064/30832), usually packed out with a lively crowd of 20-something locals and visitors; open until 10pm at the weekends. The food is great, with lots of vegetarian options and really juicy steaks, plus the wine list is a winner. For post-pub options, Killarney is pretty shocking—there's nothing much going on, and you might end up going to bed by midnight. There's **Alchemy** (New St.; ☎ 064/31640), one of the only nightclubs around, open until 1:30am on weekends and nightly during the summer. Every Wednesday ladies get in free before 11pm. Don't come here expecting Boujis, Lotus, or Marquee—Alchemy is fun but it's really provincial with a distinct lack of beautiful people. If you're over 23, head to the **Crypt** (College Sq.; ☎ 064/31038), with a dark Gothic interior befitting its name but, luckily, up-to-date dance music from the charts.

SIGHTSEEING

The main reason to visit Killarny is to set up lodging here and use it as a base to explore **Killarney National Park** (see p. 287 for details).

FREE → **St. Mary's Cathedral** St. Mary's is free, so if you're in town you may as well wander by. It's the town's most impressive building. Designed in the Gothic Revival style by Augustus Pugin, it's cruciform in shape and made out of limestone. Building work began in 1842, was halted during the famine years when people had more pressing matters to attend to, and finished off in 1855. The stunner spire was added in 1912. It's at the edge of town, on the far end of New Street. *Cathedral Place, off Port Rd., Killarney, County Kerry. ☎ 064/31014. Free admission; donations welcome. Daily 10:30am–6pm.*

SPECTATOR SPORTS

The people of Killarney are completely obsessed with the national sports of hurling and Gaelic football. Games are played almost every Sunday afternoon during the summer at **Fitzgerald Stadium,** Lewis Road (☎ 064/31700; www.gaa.ie). If you're lucky enough to be there in the summer, you'll notice every shop window, pub entrance, and wall decked with the team's colors and words of encouragement for favorite players. For complete details, consult the local *Kerryman* newspaper or the Killarney Tourist Office (see "Basics," above). In addition, Killarney has two annual horse-racing meets, in early May and mid-July. Each event lasts for 3 or 4 days and draws large crowds. For more information, contact the **Killarney Racecourse,** Ross Road (☎ 064/31125), or the tourist office (see "Basics," above).

Shopping

Admittedly, most of Killarney's shops are of the Guinness-shot-glass-and-shamrock-keychain variety. *From experience:* Don't go in search of a hot black cocktail dress for a party or you'll be bitterly disappointed. There are some boutiques with semi-trendy clothes, including **Suburbia** (College St.; ☎ 064/37822), which targets women under 25 with its boho skirts and skimpy tops, and **Weardrobe** (New St.; ☎ 064/39933), where the friendly staff are dying to help you find an outfit to match your new Jimmy Choos.

For really casual women's clothes like fleeces and jeans, **Trigger Happy** (9 Main St.; ☎ 064/37917) has the best selection, although it gets crowded with teenyboppers after school and on weekends. For the guys, **Celsius** (10 New St.; ☎ 064/32938) stocks a great range of informal menswear like jeans and jackets. If you're feeling brave or stupid, **Steelworx** (☎ 064/37811) provides the coolest service in Killarney: Mobile body piercing. Surprisingly it's not too expensive to get a bar shoved through your septum.

Killarney National Park

This is the real reason you're in Killarney. Ten thousand hectares of natural beauty right on the town's doorstep. Prepare to be wowed by three storied lakes—the **Lower Lake** (or **Lough Leane**), the **Middle Lake** (or **Muckross Lake**), and the **Upper Lake**—a myriad of waterfalls, rivers, islands, valleys, mountains, bogs, woodlands, and lush foliage. Among this lushness look out for the rhododendron bush. It's an alien invader rampantly taking over the park and killing the local plant life. More benignly, there's also a large variety of wildlife, including a rare herd of red deer. You can't get your car in here, so plan on hiking, biking, or hiring a horse-drawn jaunting car. There are four nature trails along the lake shore and plenty of other places to wander.

Getting There

There's access to **Killarney National Park** from several points along the Kenmare road (N71). The main entrance is at Muckross House, where you'll also find a visitor center dishing out maps for walking or driving, as well as a good rundown on what to expect. There's also a handy cafe. Call ☎ 064/31440 for more information on the park. Admission is free, and it's open in all daylight hours year-round.

Getting Around

Grab a bike from Killarney if you want to get farther into the park. Various vehicles are available for rent, from 21-speed touring bikes and mountain bikes to tandems. Rental charges average €13 per day, €70 per week. Bicycles can be rented from **O'Sullivan Cycle Hire,** Bishop Lane, New Street, Killarney (☎ 064/31282).

Sleeping

No camping is permitted in Killarney National Park so you'd better book a room at a local B&B or hostel.

What a Load of Blarney

Wondering just where the old "gift of gab" lore stems from? Well, we've all heard some blarney in our lives, but the person who did it best (and first) was the charismatic Lord of Blarney, Cormac McDermot McCarthy. When Queen Elizabeth asked all Irish Lords to effectively sign over their land to the crown, McCarthy was determined not to. For every demand the queen made, he responded with eloquent letters that claimed undying loyalty and dripped with flattery, although he had no intention of giving in to her demands. After receiving yet another crafty letter, the queen, exasperated, proclaimed, "This is all Blarney. What he says, he rarely means." So today, anyone who uses a lot of eloquence and empty phrases and playfully deceives or exaggerates is said to be talking blarney.

Macgillycuddy's Reeks

These marvelously named mountains just west of Killarney is beautiful to look at—they were formed of red sandstone that was gradually shaved down by glaciers until they reached the gentle shape they hold today. The name, though, is a bit baffling. It turns out the mountains were named after an ancient clan once predominate in this area—the Mac Gilla Machudas. The word "reek" is an old Irish term for a peaked hill. So these are the mountains of the Mac Gilla Machudas. Just in case you were wondering.

Located just above the Upper Lake, **Aghadoe House Hostel** (Killarney, 3 miles west of town on the Killorglin Rd.; ☎ 064/31240; dorms €10) offers free pickup service from the train or bus station in Killarney. It's a real gem. Not only will you be staying at a huge, gorgeous old stone mansion in the middle of the forest, but you can enjoy barbecues, live music, history lectures, and cheap cafe food on the premises. You can also rent a bike there.

Highly recommended by all who pass through its doors, **Peacock Farm Hostel** (Gortdromakerry, Muckross, Killarney; ☎ 064/33557; dorms €10; Apr–Sept) offers excellent sky-lit rooms and comfortable facilities. To reach the hostel, take Muckross Road out of Killarney and turn left just before the Muckross Post Office. Follow the signposts along that road for 2 miles. If you can't handle the walk, call the hostel and arrange a pickup. Your dorm views encompass Lough Guitane, which you'll pass on the way to Muckross and the Middle Lake, and the surrounding hills, not to mention the family of peacocks who lent the hostel their name.

Not quite as cool, but still adequate, **Black Valley Hostel** (Beaufort, Killarney; ☎ 064/34712; dorms €9; Mar–Nov) is located about a kilometer or two from the Upper Lake in the National Park. Meals are provided, for an extra charge, of course. Basic meals are €6 and €8, four courses around €12. There's a small store, so luckily there's no need for you to venture the 10 miles back into town to stock up on food. Considering that there's no public transportation from here into Killarney, this isn't your best bet if you don't have wheels or the legs for pedaling. Black Valley is, however, situated a mere mile from the Gap of Dunloe and within (serious) hiking distance of Macgillycuddy's Reeks.

Eating & Partying

The pubs in Killarney National Park unfortunately cater to the masses of summer tourists. Still, if you want a drink at the end of the day, you could do worse than **Molly Darcy's** (Muckross Village; ☎ 064/34973) at the park entrance. The food is pretty good, so stay for dinner if there's any breathing room. **Kate Kearney's** (Gap of Dunloe; ☎ 064/44146) is another fairly standard watering hole—touristy and old-fashioned with dancing sessions every night during the summer.

Sightseeing

→ **Crag Cave** Believed to be more than a million years old, these limestone caves were only discovered and first explored in 1983. Guides now accompany you 3,753m (12,510 ft.) into the passage on a well-lit tour revealing some of the largest stalactites in Europe. You'll find a shop and restaurant on-site. 24km (15 miles) north of Killarney. *Off Limerick Rd. (N21), Castleisland, County Kerry.* ☎ 066/7141244. *www.cragcave.com. Admission €6.50 adults, €5.50 students. Mid-Mar to June and Sept–Oct daily 10am–6pm; July–Aug 10am–7pm.*

Killarney National Park

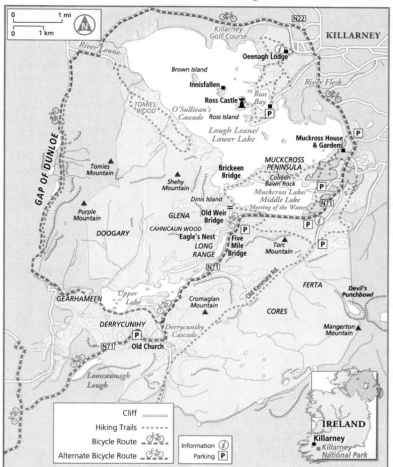

Gap of Dunloe The Gap is technically outside Killarney National Park, but it still gets a flow of Killarney-bound tourists, who gape at the high cliffs, low valleys, and burbling little streams through their viewfinders. The Gap is located 9.7km (6 miles) southwest of Killarney. You can reach it by taking a path that begins at the Upper Lake within the Park and leads right through the Gap. The best way to take in this scenery is by bike (see above), although you'll have to dodge the herds of horse-drawn buggies. In the summer, no cars or motorized vehicles of any kind are allowed in the Gap. If you're biking here and back from Killarney, set aside an entire day.

Muckross House & Gardens This is the park's big pad, a huge ivy-covered Victorian mansion dating from 1843. It's now a strange old mix of locally carved furniture, paintings, and crafts, mixed up with imported treasures like Oriental screens, Venetian mirrors, and Turkish carpets, but it's still quite

Iveragh Peninsula & the Ring of Kerry

For the majority of tourists who descend on County Kerry yearly, the Iveragh Peninsula is synonymous with the Ring of Kerry. This couldn't be further from the truth as the Ring is a touristy two-lane strip of road measuring 110 miles and clogged with tour buses while the Iveragh is nearly 700 miles of untamed beauty and jagged coastline. Once you get off the tourist trail of the Ring you can explore the peninsula, which is great for biking and hiking. The most amazing part of the Iveragh has to be its central mountain range, the evocatively named Macgillycuddy's Reeks, its tallest peak covered in snow.

If you encounter any middle-aged American tourists on your travels, which you undoubtedly will, chances are they're doing the Ring of Kerry on their tour bus or in their rented car. Although many stops on this well-traveled 110 mile circuit are very beautiful, you can't escape the seething packs of baseball-capped grandparents with their digital cameras at the ready. If you must tour the Ring, there are a few must-see spots. For starters, it's best to begin and end the Ring at Kenmare rather than Killarney, which is the favorite base for the tour bus crowds. It's smaller and less commercial than Killarney, and because the hordes clear out at the end of the day, you're likely to get a seat in a pub and order a pint without spending your inheritance. From Kenmare, travel counter-clockwise through the scenic mountain range Moll's Gap. Bypass Killarney Town and head straight to the **Killarney National Park** (p. 287), known for its spectacular scenery. From there, move on to Killorglin, a cute little town known for its mid-August Puck Fair, where general debauchery ensues. Continue on the N70 and the vistas of Dingle Bay will appear, as will Carrantuohill, Ireland's tallest mountain at 3,414 ft. Drive

interesting to meander around. The ruin of the 15th-century **Muckross Abbey,** founded about 1448 and burned by Cromwell's troops in 1652, is also near the house. Its top feature is a vaulted cloister around a courtyard containing a huge yew tree, said to be as old as the abbey itself. *Kenmare Rd. (N71), Killarney.* ☎ *064/31440. www.muckross-house. ie. Admission €5.50 adults, €2.25 students. July–Aug daily 9am–7pm; mid-Mar to June and Sept–Oct daily 9am–6pm; Nov to mid-Mar daily 9am–6pm.*

➔ Ross Castle A 15th-century fortress sitting on the edge of the Lower Lake, 3.2km (2 miles) outside Killarney Town. Built by the O'Donoghue chieftains, the castle showed what it was made of in 1652 when it became the last stronghold in Munster to surrender to Cromwell's forces. Today, just a tower house surrounded by a fortified walled

garden is left. Nip up top for a fab view of the surrounding lakes and islands. Access is by guided tour only. There's a great lakeshore walk stretching a measly 3.2km (2 miles) between Killarney and the castle. *Ross Rd., off Kenmare Rd. (N71), Killarney, County Kerry.* ☎ *064/35851. Admission €5 adults, €2 students. Mar–May daily 9:30am–4:45pm; June–Sept daily 10am–6pm; Oct Tues–Sun 10am–5pm. Last admission 45 min. before closing. Closed Nov–Feb.*

PLAYING OUTSIDE

FISHING   Fishing for salmon and brown trout in Killarney's unpolluted lakes and rivers is a popular pastime round these parts. Brown-trout fishing is free on the lakes, but a permit is necessary for the rivers Flesk and Laune. A trout permit costs €4 to €14 per day.

cautiously along the cliffs and ridges of the Ring as you'll notice there's not much between your car and the crashing waves. The next town to visit is Glenbeigh, but only for its gorgeous beach, the palm-tree-lined Rossbeigh Strand, warm thanks to the presence of the Gulf Stream. From there go to Cahirciveen, where you can take a detour to Valentia island, connected to the mainland by a bridge at Portmagee. In the 18th century, the pretty harbor at Valentia was famous as a refuge for pirates and smugglers; now it's a popular vacation spot. Next on the route is Waterville, where Charlie Chaplin used to spend the summer. An idyllic spot wedged between Lough Currane and Ballinskelligs Bay, Waterville is home to the only Irish branch of the rather vile Club Med. If you want to get a feel for Gaelic language and culture, head to the Irish-speaking village of Ballinskelligs, and from there go to Caherdaniel, the home of Irish hero Daniel "the Liberator" O'Connell, who freed Irish Catholics from the English Penal Laws in 1829. At Caherdaniel is Derrynane, a national monument, park, and major center of Gaelic culture. If you want to see the Ireland represented in glossy calendars, make Sneem the penultimate stop on your tour of the Ring of Kerry. Its buildings are candy-colored—little pink, orange, and blue boxes in a row. On the way back to Kenmare, drive through Parknasilla, with its lush subtropical vegetation thanks to the Gulf Stream. **Be warned:** If you choose to drive—or even cycle—the Ring in July or August, you'll be at the mercy of the packs of American and European tourists who descend on the area annually. If you want to see the area without queues, go in June or September when the weather is still somewhat cooperative.

Salmon fishing anywhere in Ireland requires a license; the cost is €10 per day, €20 for 21 days. In addition, some rivers also require a salmon permit, which costs €10 to €14 per day. Permits and licenses can be obtained at the Fishery Office at the **Knockreer Estate Office,** New Street (☎ 064/31246).

For fishing tackle, bait, rod rental, and other fishing gear, as well as permits and licenses, try **O'Neill's,** 6 Plunkett St. (☎ 064/31970). The shop also arranges the hire of boats and *ghillies* (fishing guides) for €80 per day on the Killarney Lakes, leaving from Ross Castle. Go get supper.

HORSEBACK RIDING Many trails in the Killarney area are suitable for horseback riding. Hiring a horse costs about €20 per hour at **Killarney Riding Stables,** N72, Ballydowney (☎ 064/31686), and **Rocklands**

Stables, Rockfield, Tralee Road (☎ 064/32592). Lessons and weeklong trail rides can also be arranged.

Horse lovers may also fancy booking themselves on one of the tours offered by **Castlelough Tours,** 7 High St. (☎ 064/31115); **Corcoran's Tours,** Kilcummin (☎ 064/36666); **Dero's Tours,** 22 Main St. (☎ 064/31251 or 064/31567); or **Tangney Tours,** Kinvara House, Muckross Road (☎ 064/33358). Combination horse/boat tours cost €20 per person.

WALKING If you want to keep things simple, there are four signposted nature trails in the **Killarney National Park.** The **Mossy Woods Nature Trail** starts near Muckross House, by Muckross Lake, and rambles 2.4km (1.5 miles) through yew woods along low cliffs. The **Old Boat House Nature Trail** begins at the old boathouse below Muckross Gardens

The Iveragh Peninsula & the Ring of Kerry

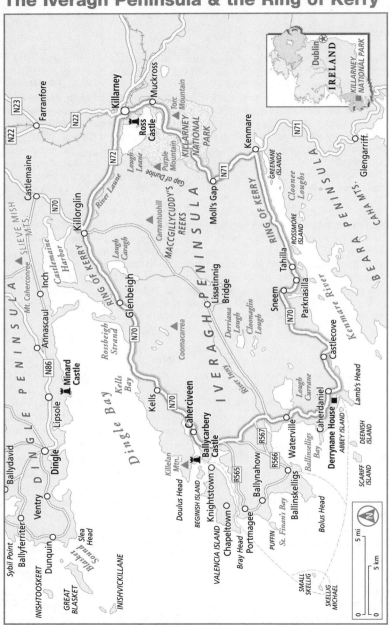

and heads .8km (half a mile) around a small peninsula by Muckross Lake. **Arthur Young's Walk** (4.8km/3 miles) starts on the road to Dinis, crosses natural yew woods, and then follows a 200-year-old road on the Muckross Peninsula. The **Blue Pool Nature Trail** (2.4km/1.5 miles) travels from Muckross village via woodlands and an itsy lake known as the Blue Pool. Maps of the four trails are available at the park's visitor center.

Rearing up from the south shore of Muckross Lake, **Torc Mountain** provides spectacular views of the Killarney Lakes and nearby ⅋ Best **MacGillycuddy's Reeks** (see box p. 288), a moody mountain range. Start at the **Torc Waterfall** parking lot, about 6km (3³/₄ miles) south of Killarney, and follow the trail to the top of the falls. At a T-intersection, turn left toward the top parking lot, and almost immediately turn right on the Old Kenmare Road, which follows a small stream along the south slopes of Torc Mountain. After leaving the woods, you will see Torc Mountain on your right. Look for a crescent-shaped gouge in the side of the road, about 9m (30 ft.) across, with a small cairn at its far edge. This is the beginning of the path to the ridge top, marked on and off by cairns along the way. Go back the way you came; the whole trip is just under 10km (6¹/₄ miles), and takes about 4 hours. It's quite taxing but not impossible, even for the unfit.

If you prefer a little guidance, what about a guided walk? **SouthWest Walks Ireland Ltd.,** 40 Ashe St., Tralee, County Kerry (☎ **066/712-8733;** www.southwestwalks ireland.com) offers up tours ranging from a day to a week. Or you can arrange in advance to meet up with the **Wayfarers,** an international organization of passionate pedestrians, who schedule 5-week-long footloose circuits of the Ring of Kerry each spring, summer, and fall. To receive a schedule, contact the **Wayfarers,** 172 Bellevue Ave., Newport, RI 02840 (☎ **800/249-4620;** www.thewayfarers.com).

Long-distance walkers might like to know about the 202km (125-mile) **Kerry Way,** a signposted walking route heading out from Killarney around the Ring of Kerry. Hardy types will first find themselves walking inland from Killarney National Park to Glenbeigh over rolling hills. Next it's off around the Iveragh Peninsula via the towns of Cahirciveen, Waterville, Caherdaniel, Sneem, and Kenmare with another inland walk along the old Kenmare Road back to Killarney. The route is largely traffic-free on paths and "green roads" (old, unused roads converted into walking paths). Grab a map and find out how to do it at the Killarney and Kenmare tourist offices or keep your eyes peeled for one of the walking guides in the local shops.

The Skellig Islands

If you visit the Iveragh Peninsula you absolutely must see the Skellig Islands—two crags jutting out of the violent sea, acting as an eerie home to monastery ruins and thousands of gannets. George Bernard Shaw of Pygmalion fame perhaps described the Skelligs as "an incredible, impossible, mad place," and "part of our dream world." ⅋ Best **Skellig Michael,** the larger of the two islands, seems ridiculously steep—the whole land mass is one sloping cliff face, with disused buildings

perched precariously on its sides. Small Skellig seems to be hosting one huge pillow fight with all the feathers flying thanks to its only inhabitants—birds.

Getting There

Ferries from Valentia Island are run by Des Lavelle (☎ **066/947-6124**) while those from Portmagee are run by O'Keefe's (☎ **066/ 947-7103**). The average cost is €35 per person.

Basics

TOURIST OFFICE   The Skellig Experience Centre is located on the waterfront of Valentia Island, off the western sector of Ring of Kerry. Head there for all the info you'll ever need before you head to the Skelligs, or call them at ☎ **066/947-6306.**

RECOMMENDED WEBSITES   The website for the Skellig Experience is the best you'll find about the islands. Go to www.skellig experience.com. Other websites about the islands have a budget feel about them and mostly contain photos.

Orientation

Skellig Michael, the larger of the Skellig islands, is to the southwest of Small Skellig. They lie approximately 8 miles off the coast of the Iveragh Peninsula. Small Skellig is slightly closer to the mainland than Skellig Michael. It covers some 7 hectares (17 acres), whereas Skellig Michael covers 18 hectares (44 acres) and rises some 218m (715 ft.) above sea level.

Sightseeing

Once you dock at Skellig Michael, climb the (many) steps up to the old monastery, which consists of six "beehive" huts used as sleeping and living quarters, two oratories, a small graveyard, and a high cross. Only a dozen monks called this place home a thousand

Yeah Man

If you tour around Ireland for a while, you'll probably hear people referring to *yer man* (as in, "I was talking to *yer man* the other day . . . "). You may well wonder who this incredibly popular person is. Well, he's the fella Americans call *this guy* (for example, "I was talking to this guy the other day . . . " and British call "this bloke." You may also hear yer man's feminine counterpart, *yer won.*

years ago, but today approximately 15,000 people visit yearly. This area is one of the best preserved examples of Early Christian architecture left, and as such is designated a World Heritage Site. The smaller Skellig has never been inhabited by humans but does provide a home for almost 50,000 gannets.

Playing Outside

Depending on weather, you can sign up for the **Skellig Experience Cruise** at the center of Valentia Island. This 2-hour tour will allow you to see all the wildlife on and around the islands. En route to the islands you will meet the seabirds of Skellig—gannets all season long, puffins in the spring and summer, as well as kittiwakes, razorbills, guillemots, Manx shearwaters, and fulmars. In later season keep an eye out for interesting migrants from outside the area, like skuas. If you're lucky you'll see some bottlenose and common dolphins, and maybe even a minke whale or a basking shark. When you sail past Small Skellig, make sure you check out the rock ledges at sea level to see the island's family of grey seals. They're especially likely to be visible on sunny days. Of course, you'll also have a great view of the monastery as you travel past Skellig Michael. To book a cruise, call ☎ **066/947-6306.** The Skelligs are also really popular with divers. You can see the dolphins, porpoise, killer whales, turtles, seals, large fish, lobsters, and crayfish in the water around the Skelligs with **Activity Ireland** (☎ **066/947-5277;** www.activity-ireland.com)—Ireland's longest-established PADI dive center. Dive near Skellig Rock and Bull Rock, and rent all your equipment from Activity Ireland. The company also specializes in fishing trips by shipwrecks and reefs in the area, plus boat trips on the very fun ▐MTV ▐Best▌ zapcat—an incredibly fast power boat with a Ferrari-style engine that can jump 8m (26 ft.) in the air. For adrenaline junkies, it doesn't get any better than a high-speed tour of the harbor.

Killorglin

For most of the year, Killorglin isn't somewhere you'd voluntarily spend a night. However, for 3 days in August every year, Ireland's oldest street fair turns Killorglin into the place to be, with a bacchanalia unlike any other involving the winning combination of Guinness and goats. The Puck Fair turns a small, unexciting village into New Orleans for a weekend—making more than €6 million in the process.

Getting There

Killorglin is located on the Ring of Kerry Road. From Killarney take the N72 and from Tralee take the N70. **Bus Éireann** (☎ 01/830-2222; www.buseireann.ie) runs one bus from Killarney to Killorglin each day and another twice daily through Killorglin to other towns farther out on the Iveragh, like Waterville and Sneem.

Getting Around

If you want to test your fitness up and down the rolling hills, rent a bicycle from **O'Shea's Cycle Centre** (Lower Bridge St.; ☎ 066/976-1919; €11 daily).

Basics

TOURIST OFFICE   **The Killorglin Tourist Office** is open Monday to Friday 9:30am to 5:30pm, Saturday 9am to 6pm and Sunday 10am to 3pm from May to September. It's located on Main Street (☎ 066/976-1451).

Festivals

Let's face it, the ☒ Best **Puck Fair** is the only real reason to come to Killorglin. The 3-day festival celebrates the Celtic god Pan with drinking, dancing, and carousing. The highlight of the festival is the crowning of King Puck—the most eligible male goat in town. Go to www.puckfair.ie for a very comprehensive rundown of the events.

Sleeping

➜**Bianconi**   If you're looking for a lively place to stay, try Bianconi, a restaurant and bar with guest rooms upstairs run by the amiable Ray and Rick Sheehy. The rooms are basic but comfortable, and you can see the whole town from your window. If you want to enjoy a pint of Guinness in one of Killorglin's most popular European restaurants then crawl up to bed, this is the best spot to do it. *Annadale Rd., Killorglin.* ☎ *066/976-1146. Double €100. Amenities: Restaurant, bar.*

➜**Carrig Country House**   If you have a bit of money to spend, definitely spend a night at Carrig Country House, especially if you're a lover of the great outdoors. It's right on Carrig Lake and the garden is even home to its own waterfall. You'll feel like you've stepped into some sort of Kate Winslet costume drama in the elegant house, overlooking 2 hectares (4 acres) of beautiful green backed by the lake and mountains. The restaurant features delicious Irish favorites like lamb with a port and raspberry glaze. *Carrig Lake, near Killorglin.* ☎ *066/976-9100. Double €65– €150.*

➜**Laune Valley Farm Hostel**   A mile and a half outside Killorglin on the Tralee Road is this working Irish farm, where you'll wake to chickens, pigs, and cows poking around outside your dorm window. The owners will not only sell you produce from their farm but also cook you delicious breakfasts with their fresh eggs. A thoroughly pleasant experience. *Bansagh, near Killorglin.* ☎ *066/976-1488. Dorms €14–€16, double €19–€22. Amenities: Laundry; satellite TV.*

➜**Riverside House**   A family-run B&B with gardens and a patio, Riverside House makes a good base for exploring the Ring of Kerry, plus it's only 20 minutes from central Killarney. Eat breakfast in their dining room overlooking the river and ask for help if you want to plan a fishing or hiking trip. *Killarney Rd., Killorglin.* ☎ *066/976-1184. Double €26–€32.*

Eating

→ **The Asian Garden** INDIAN   Located above a pub in the center of Killorglin, the Asian Garden will satisfy your craving for spice. The menu features a wide range of delicious favorites like tikka masala, dansak, pasanda, and rogan josh. Although plain or pilau rice accompanies all main courses, there are several tandoori breads available as side dishes. Curries can be adjusted to individual palates if you can't handle the heat. *The Square, Killorglin. Average meal €32. Daily 5–11pm.*

→ **Broadbery's Irish Food Hall** IRISH Local foodies love this eatery serving up posh organic grub. Order a platter to share and you could get a farmhouse chicken with vegetables, salads, and blue cheese, for instance. Elsewhere on the menu, the Puck Platter features goat's cheese, pesto, salad, bread, and relish, raising a cheer for the town's infamous Puck Fair. If you can't get through lunch or dinner without a slurp, the wine list is full of organic bottles from all over the world. *The Square, Killorglin County Kerry.* ☎ *064/976-2888. Average meal €20. Daily 9am–10pm.*

→ **Da Vinci** ITALIAN   A popular Italian with a top atmosphere and even better pizzas. Prepare to chow down on some thin, crisp crust discs with very creative toppings. The Atlantic seafood, Parma ham, and Pizza Hell all come especially recommended. Of course, if you're not a pizza fan, there are the usual pasta and meat dishes like lasagna and penne. If you're feeling lazy, virtually all of Da Vinci's dishes are available for delivery. *Old School Rd., Killorglin.* ☎ *064/976-8552. Average meal €19. Daily 6–9:30pm.*

→ **Natterjack's** CAFE   Open for all three meals, Natterjacks is a great, friendly place

to grab a croissant and coffee in the morning, a salad at lunch, or a steak for dinner. The menu changes throughout the day, with all items reasonably priced. Service is quick and there's lots of choice but, be warned, if you like a cocktail or glass of wine at dinner (or breakfast . . .) look elsewhere as Natterjacks has no liquor license. *Mill Rd., Killorglin. Average meal €18. Daily 9am–5pm and 6:30–9pm.*

Partying

The only place you're likely to see people standing on each other's shoulders to order a pint is in the **Old Forge pub** on Main Street (☎ **066/976-1231**) during the Puck Fair, where tourists and visitors spill onto the streets with their Guinness, chatting and generally having a good time. The atmospheric old stone bar attracts a wide range of clientele, from energetic backpackers to older music lovers (there are trad sessions Mon–Wed and normal chart music on other nights). If you want a testosterone injection, head to **Falvey's** (Lower Bridge St.; ☎ **066/ 976-1254**), Killorglin's favorite sports bar. The enthusiastic crowd mostly consists of people in their twenties screaming at the TV and spilling their beer. For a more civilized night, try the **Railway Bar** at the Manor Inn (Sunhill Rd.; ☎ **066/976-1317**), where you can order some bar food with your wine or go next door to the restaurant for a real meal, like a roast with fresh vegetables.

Playing Outside

Four miles out of Killorglin is Caragh Lake, surrounded by mountains and serenely beautiful. The best way to check it out is to rent a bike from **O'Shea's** (p. 295). Near Caragh Lake just north of Killorglin is the **Cappanalea Outdoor Education Centre** (☎ **066/976-9244**), where you can try canoeing, kayaking, and climbing. To get there, turn left off the main street onto Lower Bridge Street and follow signs to the adventure center.

Cahirseveen

The first thing you'll notice about this small Ring of Kerry town is that no one can agree on a spelling—you'll see it spelled as Cahirsiveen, Cahersiveen, Caherciveen, and so on. Regardless, the town is tiny—one main road, unsurprisingly called Main Street, but well known as the birthplace of Daniel O'Connell, the Liberator, a household name if you're Irish Catholic. In Cahirseveen you'll find great pubs, the popular Sive Hostel, and the 15th-century Ballycarbery castle, the ancestral home of Daniel O'Connell. In a nutshell, Cahirseveen is well worth a night's stay on your way to Dingle or on your travels around Kerry.

Getting There

Bus Éireann (☎ 01/830-2222; www.bus eireann.ie) runs one or two daily buses to and from Killarney. The bus stop is outside the Cahirseveen Library on Main Street. From Killarney by car, take the N70 through Killorglin.

Getting Around

You can rent a bike at **Casey's** (Main St.; ☎ 066/947-2474) for about €10 per day and cycle around Cahirseveen and the surrounding area.

Basics

TOURIST OFFICE   At the **Cahirseveen Tourist Office** (The Barracks, Main St.; ☎ 066/947-2580; Mon–Sat 10am–6pm, Sun 1–6pm, May–Sept) you can learn all about Daniel O'Connell, the Ring, and local trails.

INTERNET ACCESS   Tucked away on the second floor of the Old Oratory and decorated in bright jungle decor is **Javasite.ie** (W. Main St.; ☎ 066/947-2116), outrageously expensive at €7 per hour, but with the fast computers, coffee, candy, TVs, plus PlayStation, this Internet cafe is so comfortable you'll want to stay here all day. If you're feeling broke, you can check your e-mail for free at **Cahirseveen Library** (Church St.; ☎ 066/947-2287; 10am–5pm daily).

RECOMMENDED WEBSITES   For a pretty good overview of the town, go to www. cahersiveen.com, where you'll find info on local accommodation, places to visit, and links to sites for other nearby areas if you're planning to hang around Kerry for a while

Festivals

Over a long weekend every summer, Cahirseveen hosts the **Celtic Festival of Music and the Arts** (www.celticmusicfestival.com), established in 1995 and growing in popularity yearly. In the morning there are educational endeavors like workshops in art and music and guided walks through the countryside. There are also lectures on music and the history of the area given by visiting professors. The art exhibition, held in the old library on Church Street, is a must-see, with paintings and sculptures by artists both local and foreign. At around 4pm on each day of the festival, entertainment begins onstage. Then, when darkness falls partying begins with excellent bands on stage followed by sessions in all the pubs around town that go on into the early hours of the morning.

Sleeping

→**Ocean View**   Claire O'Donoghue's cheerful B&B actually overlooks the ocean, unlike many conspicuous Irish hotels with "view" in the title. You can see Valentia Harbour from this pretty house, which backs onto the rolling green hills of the region. The rooms do look like they may have been decorated by a blind nun, but Claire and her staff will set up a trip to Skellig Michael for you, and the palm tree—lined garden is second to none for an afternoon sitting in the sun by the Gulf Stream—warmed waters. The B&B is also close to the town's best restaurants. *Renard Rd.* ☎ *066/947-2261. Double €50–€60.*

COUNTY KERRY

➔ **Sive Hostel**   Although it won't cost you your trust fund to stay here, the beds are about the most comfortable you'll find anywhere. The whole hostel is clean and the staff friendly, and you'll find all the amenities you'll need, like laundry facilities and a kitchen to cook your Pot Noodles. Patrick Casey, one of the Skellig ferry operators, has an arrangement with the Sive whereby he'll come by each night to ask who needs a ride to the islands. Mr. Casey will even pick you up from the hostel at 9:30am. *15 East End, Main St. ☎ 066/947-2717. Dorm €12; private €14. Amenities: Kitchen, laundry.*

Eating

➔ **The Seahorse** VEGETARIAN   You'll never leave Cahirseveen's favorite restaurant still feeling hungry—alongside the delicious pine nut roast or vegetarian meatloaf, you get a salad, bread, and vegetables. If you're a fish lover, look no further—each seafood dish is fresh and lovingly prepared. Leave room for dessert if you can, and go for the banana boozy: an ice cream sundae with whipped cream, almonds, bananas, raisins, and a dash of rum. *Main St. ☎ 066/947-2153. Mains €11. Daily 5–10pm.*

➔ **QC's** BASQUE   Okay, how often do you get to eat at a Basque restaurant? For those of you not in-the-know, Basque country straddles the French-Spanish border along the western Pyrenees; its three million inhabitants have their own language and food, like the delicious grilled fish you'll find here, cooked on a traditional *assador*. The Basque salads are fresh and tasty, and if you're not feeling too adventurous, order a Spanish omelet. Lots of wines, too—imported from Spanish *bodegas*, or vineyards. *3 Main St., Cahirseveen. ☎ 066/947-2244. Reservations recommended. Average main €15; 12:30–2:30pm and 6:30–9:30pm.*

➔ **Cupan Eile** ★ CAFE   The owner, Aoife, once owned a cafe with her ex-girlfriend called An Cupan—"the cup"—so it makes sense that her post-breakup enterprise is called "the other cup." Cupan Eile has a cheerful yellow and blue interior with pine furnishings and a steady stream of loyal customers. There's nowhere better to eat a traditional Irish fry-up for breakfast—vegetarians even have their own fried option. For lunch, there are the usual comfort foods like shepherd's pie and quiche, and the dessert case is very enticing indeed. You'll feel so welcome here you won't want to leave. *Main St. No phone. Average meal €10. No cards. Mon–Sat 9am–6pm.*

Partying

There are loads of pubs in Cahirseveen, but most aren't really happening 'til the weekend, when they're full of fun-loving locals and young travelers until last call. For something out of the ordinary, head to **The Fertha** (W. Main St.; ☎ **066/947-2023**), where you'll see a natural spring flowing in the corner behind a little glass window. At the **Skellig Rock Bar** (W. Main St.; ☎ **066/947-2305**), the music is live, alternating between traditional fiddle-and-guitar stuff and regular pop. At **An Bodhran** (E. Main St.; ☎ **066/947-3023**), you'll find good pub grub and a pool table, plus live music on the weekends—watch out, you'll be encouraged to join in. To get a real feel for the area, you could have a drink at **Mike Murts** (East End; ☎ **066/947-2396**), an exclusively local spot that doubles as a farming equipment store.

Sightseeing

All the sights in Cahirseveen are connected to local hero Daniel O'Connell, the first Irish Catholic to win a seat in the British House of Commons (no mean feat), where he served from 1829 to 1847, when he died. He pushed the Catholic Emancipation Act successfully through in 1829, which gave Catholic men the right to hold public office in Great Britain, then subsequently the Reform Act of 1832, which gave the vote to middle-class men. He

Valentia Island

A short walk across the bridge from Portmagee is Valentia Island. Here you'll be treated to amazing views of Dingle Bay and the Skellig Islands, especially if you go to the lookout tower at Bray Head. Valentia is the gateway to the Skelligs, so if you're interested, check out **The Skellig Experience** (Skellig Heritage Centre, Valentia, County Kerry; ☎ **066/947-6306;** Apr–Oct 10am–6pm; €5), where you can learn about the history of the islands and book yourself a boat tour. Valentia isn't particularly easy to reach, however, as Bus Éireann doesn't provide service to Portmagee, so you'll either have to stay overnight after seeing the Skelligs or catch a ferry (☎ **066/947-6141**) back to Reenard Point near Cahirseveen—they run all day til 10:30pm and cost about €5. Otherwise, you can probably get a lift back to Cahirseveen or Waterville with one of the ferry operators. If you do end up staying the night on Valentia, you could do worse than **Coombe Bank House** (☎ **066/76111;** www.coombe.20m.com), a hostel and B&B. Dorm rooms cost €12, while a double room with breakfast will set you back €22. Across the bridge in Portmagee is **Moorings B&B** (☎ **066/77108**), attached to The Bridge Bar, where you can get good fresh seafood for lunch. Valentia probably isn't worth a whole night's stay, although, for such a small place, it has a lot of interesting history. For instance, did you know TVs wouldn't have been invented if Joseph May hadn't found selenium on the island in 1873? Or that Valentia was also the first piece of land sighted by Charles Lindbergh on his round-the-world flight in 1927?

was jailed for a few months in 1844 for plotting against the government by supporting a campaign for freeing Ireland from English rule. Today, O'Connell is a tourist draw in Cahirseveen—check out the **Old Barracks Heritage Centre** (Main St.; ☎ **066/947-2589;** Mon–Sat 10am–6pm; Sun 1–6pm; €5), celebrating every facet of the man's life. Left off the bridge by the Barracks is **Ballycarbery Castle,** the 15th-century home of O'Connell's ancestors. Admission is free and it's about a half-hour walk out of town. The well-preserved forts of **Cahergall** and **Leacanabuaile** are located 200 yards down the road from the castle turnoff.

Playing Outside

Past the two forts near Ballycarbery Castle is **Cuas Crom beach,** an ideal spot for swimming or sun-worshipping in the summer. If you want to explore the evocative countryside around Cahirseveen a different way, check out **The Final Furlong Riding Stables** (Glenbeigh Rd.; ☎ **066/947-3300**), about a mile out of town. Gallop along the sand and get a taste for what it felt like hundreds of years ago when the local cavalry was protecting the nearby castle and fortifications.

Caherdaniel & Derrynane

Caherdaniel is one of the Ring of Kerry's best-kept secrets, with an incredible beach and easy access to watersports equipment. As in Cahirseveen, Daniel O'Connell features prominently here—the Derrynane House National Historic Park, where he lived for most of his life, is now a monument. Caherdaniel is a welcome respite from the overwhelming tourist trail that is the Ring of Kerry, so get here before the other visitors figure it out.

Getting There

Caherdaniel is south of Waterville and southwest of Sneem on the Ring of Kerry. To get there, take the N71 from Killarney and then the N571 from Kenmare. You can get **Bus Éireann** (☎ 01/830-2222; www.buseireann. ie) from Killarney on the Waterville route.

Basics

TOURIST OFFICE The **Caherdaniel Tourist Office** (no phone; 8am–10pm daily May–Sept) is located a mile east of town. If you have trouble getting there, you can just pop into **Mathius Adams Junk Shop** (☎ 066/947-5167) in the center of town and ask the owner, a veritable wealth of knowledge.

Sleeping

There are a handful of particularly good hostels in Caherdaniel. For large dorm rooms, try the **Traveler's Rest Hostel** (☎ 066/947-5175; dorm €11) in the town center, where the common room is above average. **The Carribeg Hostel** (Derrynane, Caherdaniel; ☎ 066/947-5229; dorm €8–€9, double €16–€17) has a totally unbelievable location next to the Derrynane House and the sea. The owners will cook for you and pick you up from the bus stop 2 miles out of town. There's also **Caherdaniel Village Hostel** (☎ 066/947-5227; dorm €10; Mar–Oct) where staff organize diving excursions and trips out into the Iveragh countryside. Make sure to call ahead, as it gets busy in the summer months.

Eating

You can buy your own groceries at **Freddy's Bar** (☎ 066/947-5400), or you can get a takeaway at **Courthouse Café** (☎ 066/947-5005; most meals under €7; 5–11:30pm daily). You can take your sandwich and soda to the Derrynane Strand. Otherwise, have a cup of tea and a pastry at Anne's Tea Room in Derrynane National Park—they also have fresh soup and salads.

Partying

Okay, Caherdaniel isn't Dublin, but there is fun to be had at night, mostly thanks to the notable absence of middle-aged American tour bus passengers. **The Blind Piper** (☎ 066/947-5126) in the town center is the very definition of "quaint," with its outdoor tables and stream running through the garden, but a good time can be had here with the right company (and amount of Guinness). There are trad music sessions here in the summer months. Freddy's Bar (see above) is a bar as well as a grocery store.

Sightseeing

The two main points of interest in town are Staigue Fort and the Derrynane House National Historic Park. **Staigue Fort** (no telephone; free admission) is pre-Christian, and the largest fort in Ireland, requiring a bracing uphill climb to reach. Once you get there, though, the views down to the sea are amazing. The walls are an astounding 4m (13 ft.) thick and the diameter is 27m (90 ft.). The fort is 10km (6 miles) west of the town of Caherdaniel. **Derrynane House** (☎ 066/947-5113; admission €2.75 adults; Nov–Mar Sat–Sun 1–5pm; Apr and Oct Tues–Sun 1–5pm; May–Sept Mon–Sat 9am–6pm, Sun 11am–7pm) is signposted from Derrynane Beach. Set on a 128-hectare (320-acre) site between Waterville and Caherdaniel, the house has been turned into a museum. Expect lots of Daniel O'Connell memorabilia, and don't go unless you have a genuine interest in the history of the area or you're liable to get really bored and wish you'd spent the admission fee on a beer at a pub.

Playing Outside

Caherdaniel's known for its excellent diving possibilities. Try **Skellig Aquatics Dive**

School (across from the Caherdaniel Village Hostel; ☎ 066/947-5227), where you can dive for half a day for €38. There's also the **Derrynane Watersports Centre** (☎ 066/947-5266), where you can windsurf, sail, or water-ski. A water-skiing lesson will cost you

€20, three 2-hour sailing lessons will set you back €65, and a 2-hour intro to windsurfing course is €20. The Derrynane Strand beach is divinely free of tourists. Bring a bottle of wine and stay for the sunset.

Sneem

Ahh, Sneem. The ideal picture-postcard Irish village, with its pastel colored houses and cute harbor. Unfortunately, Sneem is selling out—by selling too many postcards of itself. It's still worth a visit before it becomes Six Flags Ireland. Anyway, admittedly, the little yellow, pink, purple, and blue houses make a great photo op.

Getting There

Sneem is east of Waterville and southwest of Killarney on the Ring of Kerry. To get there, take the N71 from Killarney and then the N571 from Kenmare. You can get **Bus Éireann** (☎ 01/830-2222; www.buseireann.ie) from Killarney on the Waterville route.

Basics

TOURIST OFFICE   The Sneem Tourist Office is essentially run out of a local woman's home so she opens and closes it at whim. Stop by **Joli Coeur Shop** (☎ 064/45270) between March and November, 10:30am to 5:30pm, and you should find her there.

Sleeping

For its size, Sneem is home to an absolute ton of B&Bs, some better than others. If you can't afford B&B living, try the **Harbour View Hostel** (Kenmare Rd.; ☎ 064/45276), although what mysterious "view" they're referring to I have no idea. It's only €10 for a bed in a dorm, but the whole place lacks character. If you can spend a bit more money, try **Bank House** (North Sq.; ☎ 064/45226), a cozy B&B painted the color of a bluebird egg.

The Harringtons are extremely welcoming and will feed you until you need to lie down.

Eating

In the center of Sneem is the vegetarian **Riverain** (☎ 064/5245), a favorite with locals and passersby. The interior is warm and inviting and the pasta, soups, and salads are well prepared and tasty. Main dishes cost around €13. If you're looking for the only beach bar in Ireland, you're at the right place: **Carroll's Cove** (☎ 066/57171), in between Sneem and Caherdaniel, is the one restaurant where you can enjoy a New York style pizza and a beer with your toes in the water. The beach is intensely beautiful, and feels Floridaesque thanks to the Gulf Stream. For those of you in a great hurry, you can always grab fish and chips at **The Hungry Knight** (☎ 064/45727) in the town center.

Sightseeing

There really isn't a whole lot to see in Sneem; it's a good town to stop for a few hours and take photos but it's slightly lacking in attractions. One bizarre if amusing sight in Sneem is **The Way the Fairies Went,** a curious collection of sculptures ranging from Charles de Gaulle (dead French president) to "Crusher" Casey (wrestler). Down by the water is a group of old stone huts to explore. The whole series of artworks is strange but interesting and can be found in South Square. The only other point of interest in Sneem is Bull Rock, near Derrynane, a sacred spot for the Gaels. They believed Bull Rock was the entrance to the Kingdom of Donn, God of the Dead. According to Gaelic legend, when the sun shines through a hole in the rock, it becomes a gate into the afterlife. If you sit at Bull Rock at sunset and watch what the sun does, you'll almost believe it's true.

Kenmare

Kenmare is by far the most attractive town on the Ring of Kerry—a good place to start your travels, finish, or both. The town is beautiful, clean, and easy to navigate, with above average restaurants, pubs, and shops. Tucked between the River Roughdy and Kenmare Bay, Kenmare's location is perfect and the whole landscape is enchanting. There's something for everyone here, whether you want to explore druid stone circles or go seal-watching on an eco-cruise. And you won't have to move on right away, as there are some brill B&Bs to be found in Kenmare.

Getting There

Bus Éireann (☎ 01/830-2222; www.bus eireann.ie) runs from Killarney to Kenmare twice daily, three times in the summer months. The bus stop is outside Brennan's Pub on Main Street. Call or check their online schedule for times. If you're driving, the N71 goes directly from Killarney to Kenmare.

Getting Around

The town is easy to get around as it's laid out as a big X, with The Square intersecting Henry and Main streets in the middle; this junction and nearby is where you'll find most of the pubs, restaurants, and shops.

TOURIST OFFICE   If you're starting your tour of the Ring of Kerry here, be sure to go to the **Kenmare Tourist Office** (The Square; ☎ 064/41233; 9am–5:30pm Mon–Sat Apr–June, Sept–Oct; 9am–7pm daily July–Aug).

INTERNET ACCESS   Check your e-mail at the **Bean and Leaf** (Rock St., off Main St.; ☎ 064/42019; €9 per hour; 9:30am–6:30pm Mon–Fri, 10am–6:30pm Sat–Sun, Mar–Nov) where the expense is justified by the excellent coffee and cake.

RECOMMENDED WEBSITES   The official website for Kenmare is www.kenmare.com, and contains all the info you'd expect, like little blurbs on each hotel plus the history of the town. There are some other websites on the town but they're all very budget, although www.kenmare-exclusive.com has some useful links at the bottom of the page.

Festivals

The only festival that doesn't involve sheep or little girls in costume is the annual **Walking Festival** (www.kenmarewalking. com). In 2006 it's from May 27 until June 4 and culminates in the ascent of Carrantuo-hill, Ireland's highest mountain at 1,039m (3,408 ft.). There are different walks for various fitness levels: "A" if you've pretty much hiked up Everest, "B" if you hit the gym regularly, and "C" if your idea of exercise is lifting a glass to your lips.

Sleeping

→ **Dromquinna Manor**   This is possibly the coolest hotel in Kenmare for one reason alone: You can stay in a tree house. If getting back to nature doesn't really appeal, then the hotel itself is stylish and comfortable, with four-poster beds and an excellent restaurant full of fresh local cuisine. The coach house contains the largest bedrooms and the hotel will happily organize outings like watersports trips. Even if you don't stay in the tree house, you'll have great views—of the sea, islands, and mountains instead of branches and leaves. *Blackwater Bridge.* ☎ *064/41657. Double €102. In room: TV, coffee/tea facilities, hair dryer.*

➜**Failte Hostel** There aren't that many hostels in Ireland where you can see palm trees from your window. Failte isn't the most luxe or stylish place to stay—the accommodation is basic and all the curtains and tablecloths look like they've been ripped from a 1970s trailer home. But the location is good—right across from Seafari Ireland and near Reenagross Park—and you can use their kitchen, complete with old-school Aga cooker. *Shelbourne St.* ☎ *064/42333. Dorm €14 per person; double €18 per person. Amenities: Laundry; Internet.*

➜**Kenmare Lodge Hostel** With its modern furnishings and fully equipped kitchen, Kenmare Lodge is the ideal base for traveling around Kenmare and the Ring of Kerry. The hostel also benefits from its courtyard, where backpackers eat their breakfast or read in the sun. But don't check in here if you're on a bachelor or bachelorette party (stag or hen night as they're called on this side of the pond); you won't be allowed to stay for fear of the chaos you'll cause. *27 Main St.* ☎ *064/40662. Dorm €15 per person. Amenities: Laundry.*

➜**Sea Shore Farm** Situated right above Kenmare Bay, this handsome guesthouse has winning views and many of the rooms have their own patios. If you like fishing, you may have found a haven: The Sea Shore owns a private stretch of the River Roughdy, where salmon and trout await. Even non-fish lovers will enjoy the unspoiled walk from the farm to the seashore. *Tubrid, Kenmare.* ☎ *064/41270. Double €102. In room: TV, coffee/tea facilities, hair dryer.*

➜**The Wander Inn** Cringe-inducing punny name aside, The Wander Inn is a charming little family-run place—and the Keanes will treat you like a long lost relative. The 11 rooms are individually decorated with cool antiques, and the restaurant is better than you might expect from a small B&B. The

two bars are perfect if you're looking for good *craic* and smooth lager. The staff will help you figure out an itinerary, whether you want to go horseback riding or hiking. *Henry St.* ☎ *064/41038. Double €63. Amenities: Restaurant. In room: TV, coffee/tea facilities.*

Eating

➜**Café Indigo** CONTINENTAL Café Indigo is stacking up awards and it's quite obvious why. The eye-catching exterior is bright violet and covered with hanging baskets of flowers, while the interior is Art Deco chic. Try the corn-fed chicken on a cake of roast garlic bubble and squeak (a classic potato and cabbage dish). If you like seafood, definitely go for the roast sea scallops in an asparagus risotto. The wine list is sort-of expensive—stick to the ones nearest the top! Reservations recommended. *The Square.* ☎ *064/42356. Average meal €32. 7–10:30pm daily.*

➜**Casey's** IRISH This Irish restaurant offers up trad faves with a contemporary twist like Guinness beef stew and salmon with leek and pepper sauce. Sunday roast lunch is particularly delicious and highly recommended. It's not all one big meat-fest; vegetarians are catered for, too. Stay for the night-time music sessions, when there are special deals offering discounts on a three-course meal plus Irish coffee and entertainment. *Gortamullen, Kenmare.* ☎ *064/42077. Average meal €19. noon–10pm daily.*

➜**Jam** CAFE Bright, well decorated and filled to the door during lunchtime hours, Jam has an enticing menu of sandwiches, salads, soups, and hot entrees—favorites include bacon cheese quiche or olive flatbread stuffed with Mediterranean fillings. The display case of cakes and sweets is so tempting you can't help leaving Jam with something for later. Don't come expecting an afternoon bevvie as Jam doesn't have a liquor license. *6 Henry St.* ☎ *064/41591. Average meal €13. 8am–6pm Mon–Sat.*

Partying

There are a handful of really lively, fun pubs in Kenmare, not least of which is the neon pink **Moeran's** (Main St.; ☎ 064/41368), named after a composer of Irish descent. The ceiling has exposed beams and the stone hearth houses a roaring fire on cold nights. It all screams "old country pub" but don't let that put you off; the atmosphere is light-hearted and the music sessions get really loud. For something more modern and hip, head to **Mulcahy's Wine Bar** (16 Henry St.; ☎ 064/42383). Here, younger Kenmare residents quaff Pinot Noir while decked out in their trendiest summer outfits. The food here is top-notch and you can't go wrong ordering some wild Irish duck to go with your drinks. For hot days, there's nowhere more relaxed then the **Square Pint** (The Square; ☎ 064/42357), where the beer garden behind the vibrant blue building acts as a real oasis. At night music hums out into the starry night beyond.

Sightseeing

On a small hill near the center of town is the **Kenmare Druid Circle,** a large Bronze Age druid stone circle that is magnificently intact, with 15 standing stones surrounding a dolmen tomb. Other than this, Kenmare is somewhat lacking in sites of interest—there aren't any castles or forts or natural wonders around here. To learn more about the delightful town itself, the Ring of Kerry's "little nest," step inside the **Kenmare Heritage Centre** (The Square; ☎ 064/41491; free admission; Mon–Sat 10am–5pm, with extended summer hours). Exhibits explain how Kenmare began life as a planned estate town built around the mine works started in 1670 by Sir William Petty, ancestor of the Lansdownes, the local landlords. There are also displays of locally made lace and info about the woman who started off the lace-making craze.

Playing Outside

As Kenmare is right on the water, there are some fun ways to spend an afternoon here. The very best way to see the sights and splendors of Kenmare Bay is on board a 15m (50-ft.) covered boat with **Seafari Eco-nature Cruises and Seal-Watching Trips** (Kenmare Pier; ☎ 064/83171; www.seafari ireland.com; tickets €20 adults, €15 students; May–Oct four cruises daily). The 2-hour cruises cover 16km (10 miles) while well-versed guides chat about local history, geography, and geology. Follow their pointing fingers to spot dolphins, sea otters, gray seals, herons, oystercatchers, and kingfishers. Boats depart from the pier next to the Kenmare suspension bridge. Reservations are recommended. If you're looking for a little more action, try the **Kenmare Bay Sea Sports Centre** (3 miles west on Sneem Rd. at the Dromquinna Manor Hotel; ☎ 064/42255; €8–€14 per person), where you can windsurf, kayak, water-ski, or go tubing.

Shopping

The best shopping on the Ring of Kerry can be found in Kenmare, where shops are often open until 9 or 10pm in the summer and many on Sunday 'til 5 or 6pm. Check out the Kenmare branch of the fashionable Dublin-based women's wear shop **Cleo** (2 Shelbourne St., Kenmare; ☎ 064/41410). Pick up trendy versions of classic wardrobe staples, like cool little capes and blazers to wear over jeans. If you want to learn more about Ireland, stop at the **Kenmare Bookshop** (Shelbourne St., Kenmare; ☎ 064/41578; Mar–Dec), which specializes in books about—you guessed it—the Emerald Isle itself. You'll find biographies, books by Irish writers, maps and guides on the Ring of Kerry and surrounding areas, plus cards and gifts.

Dingle

Dingle is a charming, authentic Irish seaside town located on a stunning peninsula—think traditional architecture and little colorful shops set against a backdrop of awe-inspiring cliffs, mountains, and the ocean. The most famous resident isn't a celebrity—although they do flock here in the off season—it's Fungie the dolphin, and if you're lucky you'll get to swim with him. Dingle is a compact and perfectly manicured fishing village that's done well for itself thanks to tourism, but hasn't yet tipped into the nauseating territory of Killarney.

Getting There & Getting Around

Bus Éireann (☎ 01/830-2222; www.bus eireann.ie) provides daily coach service to Dingle from all parts of Ireland to Upper Main Street. If you're driving from the east, take the R559.

There's no local bus service in Dingle although Bus Éireann will get you from the bus stop in town to other parts of the peninsula. For local taxi or minibus service, call John Sheehy at ☎ 066/905-1301. The town of Dingle itself is small, so you can get around the narrow, winding streets by walking.

Basics

TOURIST OFFICE   The **Dingle Tourist Office** is on Main Street (☎ 066/915-1188). It's open from mid-April to October to accommodate the influx of seasonal tourists. Its regular hours are Monday to Saturday 9am to 5pm although in the summer you'll often find it open on Sundays.

INTERNET ACCESS   **DingleWeb** (Lower Main St.; ☎ 066/915-2477) is open late during the summer and 'til 6pm in the winter, and boasts of being the most westerly Internet cafe in Europe. If you get there before noon, you get "early-bird" rates. It costs about €7 per hour, so if you're feeling broke, you can have a half-hour for free at the **Dingle Library** on Green Street (☎ 066/915-1499).

RECOMMENDED WEBSITES   For detailed visitor information check out www.kerry-tourism.com, www.dodingle.com, and www.dingle-peninsula.ie.

Festivals

For some really good Euro-rock and famous acts from every musical genre, check out the **Dingle Music Festival** (☎ 066/915-2477)

Five Ways to Start a Conversation with a Local

1. Talk about Fungie. Yes, he's a dolphin, and yes, they've heard it all before, but it's a harmless conversation and it'll make you look interested in the town.
2. Where do I get the best seafood in town? There are so many good restaurants, this question is sure to spark a debate.
3. Dick Mack's or McCarthy's? Any young local has their opinion on the best place for a beer and some *craic*.
4. The best beach in town . . . Inch? Brandon Bay? There are lots around here and they're all really beautiful, but the locals are sure to point you in the right direction.
5. Celebrity spotting. Someone famous is always here for to make a film or grab a quiet pint. Did you see Pierce Brosnan that time?

Hanging Out

There are a bunch of small, friendly cafes in Dingle where you can chat with locals and other travelers. The best is **The Loft Café** (Green Street Lane; ☎ **066/915-2431**), where you can draw on the walls with colored chalk while you wait for your coffee and Bailey's cheesecake. Definitely check out **An Café Liteartha** on Dykegate Street (☎ **066/915-2204**), where you can browse the book-store in the front room, order a light lunch, and practice your Irish on the owner. If you want to exercise your brain cells a little, try one of Dingle's many artsy establishments like the **Greenlane Gallery** (Green St.; ☎ **066/915-2018**), filled with contemporary Irish art in many mediums, from still life to sculpture. Of course you'll find the expected landscapes of Dingle and the sur-rounding area, but there are also some offbeat abstracts and bronze works.

in September. The town fills up for the fes-tival so if you plan on going, book a hotel room a couple months in advance. For 4 days, you'll get to hear up-and-coming performers against the beautiful backdrop of this still-unspoiled town. What's more, ticket prices are, for the most part, under €20. Get in.

Sleeping

→ **The Captain's House** Jim and Mary Milhench run this cute, friendly B&B right in the center of Dingle. You're really made to feel welcome—offered tea and scones as you check in and an amazing breakfast (every-thing's homemade from the muesli to the marmalade) before you leave. Because the building is rather old, the rooms are small, but you won't feel cramped as the furnishings and decor are arranged well. Try to book Room 10, under the gables and with a sloped ceiling. *The Mall.* ☎ *066/915-1531. Double €90–€100.*

→ **Grapevine Hostel** Open all year except from December 24 through 26, the Grapevine is a home away from home for 30 travelers at a time. Right in the center of town, the Grapevine is seriously comfortable, with a big sitting room and fireplace and a fully equipped kitchen, where you can make beans on toast (or a four-course meal, what-ever). There's no curfew and the Grapevine is near all Dingle's pubs and restaurants. The hostel's size means it's a great place to meet fellow backpackers. *Dykegate Lane.* ☎ *066/915-1434. Dorm €15. Amenities: Laundry; Internet.*

→ **Greenmount House** Perched on a hill overlooking the bay and town itself, Green-mount House is a small bungalow B&B owned by the highly professional John and May Curran. You'll feel like you've checked into somewhere far more swish—the rooms are really spacious for the price, and each has its own sitting area. The "superior rooms" have newer furnishings and look over the sea. Breakfasts are yummytastic, with unusual items like ham and pineapple toasted sand-wiches. *John St.* ☎ *066/915-1414. Double €75–€150.*

→ **Mill Town House** This is definitely the best Dingle hotel in its price range. Mark and Anne Kerry are superfriendly—expect offers of a ride to the pub and tips on where to eat. The rooms are cozy with harbor views and the bathrooms are nicer than you'll find in most B&Bs, with big tubs to relax in after a day of sailing or hiking. To get you in an Irish state of mind, each TV has an in-house movie channel playing Ireland-related films like *Far and Away* and *Ryan's Daughter*—the cast of the latter stayed here for a year during filming. The breakfast is unlike any other you'll see, so hopefully you'll wake up hungry. *Milltown, Dingle.* ☎ *066/915-1372. Double €45–€75.*

Dingle Peninsula

IRELAND
Dublin

area of detail

Mouth of the Shannon
Ballybunnion

Kerry Head

Ballyheigue
Ballyheigue Bay
Banna

MAHAREES
ISLANDS

Rough Point
Kilshannig
Ardfert

*ATLANTIC
OCEAN*

Brandon
Head

Brandon
Creek

Brandon

*Tralee
Bay*
Fenit
N86

Ballydavid Head
▲ Mt. Brandon
Kilcummin
Castlegregory
Tralee

Dún an Oir
Fort
Cloghane
Connor
Pass
▲ Mt. Beenoskee
Camp Mt. Baurtregaum

Sybil Point
Ballydavid
D I N G L E   P E N I N S U L A
SLIEVE MISH
MTS.

Ballyferriter
Ventry
Mt. Caherconree
Castlemaine

INISHTOOSKERT
Dingle
Lipsole
N86 Annascaul
Inch
*Castlemaine
Harbor*
N70

Dunquin
▲ Minard
Castle

GREAT
BLASKET
Slea
Head
Dunbeg
Fort

Dingle Bay
*Kells
Bay*
Glenbeigh
*Lough
Caragh*

INISHVICKILLANE
N70
Killorglin

Kells
I V E R A G H   P E N I N S U L A
▲ Mt.
Carrantuohill

Doulus Head
N70
0   10 mi

VALENCIA ISLAND
Caherciveen
0   10 km

→ **Old Mill House B&B** The Old Mill House is full of contradictions. Housed in a crumbling yellow building complete with a big old fireplace and creaky wooden floors, it also has some modern elements including a bizarre infra-red therapeutic sauna. The rooms are well kitted out, with orthopedic beds, TVs, and power showers. Make sure to stay for breakfast—pancakes are a house specialty. *3 Avondale St. ☎ 066/915-2349. Double €60–€90.*

→ **Rainbow Hostel** For the whole hippie backpacker experience, stay at the Rainbow Hostel, where the laid-back vibe will transport you back to the '70s—as will the sight of their multicolored van, which will pick you up from the bus stop. The hostel itself is small

and surrounded by farm land, so expect to share the garden with animals. Hospitality in the Irish sense of the word abounds, and the motto at the Rainbow Hostel is "nobody is a number." If you're traveling with friends, reserve a dorm room, which sleeps between four and six. *Strand Rd. ☎ 066/915-1044. Dorm €14; double €20. Amenities: Internet.*

Eating

→ **Beginish** SEAFOOD You might have to save up to eat here, or forget about that diving trip you wanted to take, but the food here is so outstanding it's worth the sacrifice. Chef and owner Pat Moore runs this small, elegant restaurant, renowned for the best seafood in Dingle. Although you can order beef or lamb, the emphasis is definitely on fish, with dishes like monkfish with Provencal sauce and old-fashioned creamy fish chowder. If you don't eat fish or meat, the goat's cheese and tomato mousse is absolutely delicious. If you can manage dessert, Pat's rhubarb soufflé is legendary. *Green St., Dingle, County Kerry.* ☎ *066/915-1588. Reservations recommended. Average entree €16–€28. 12:30–2:15pm and 6–10pm Tues–Sun; closed Dec–Feb.*

MTV Best →The Chart House IRISH Definitely book ahead if you want to have dinner here—folks come from all around to eat at this destination bistro. The atmosphere is buzzing, and the staff are chatty and—let's be honest—highly attractive. Owner/chef Jim McCarthy's cooking is simple and confident; sample menu items include filet of beef with garlic mashed potato, or pork with brandied apricots and blue cheese. It's gourmet comfort food, and the Chart House is the kind of place you'll want to dine at every night—that is, if you can hear yourself think above the din of the American families sitting at the next table. *The Mall.* ☎ *066/915-2255. Reservations required. Average entree €20. 6:30–10pm Wed–Mon.*

→Lord Bakers SEAFOOD For pub fare, the food at Dingle's oldest pub is pretty good, and as a nod to the town's seaside location, the menu contains a ton of seafood cooked every way imaginable. Try crab claws or prawns in garlic butter, or lobster Thermidor if your budget allows. If you're not a huge fish fan, this might not be the place for you, although they do a killer steak and a juicy rack of lamb. *Main St.* ☎ *066/915-1277. Bar food €10–€13; dinner entrees €16–€28. 12:30–2pm and 6–9:30pm Fri–Wed.*

Partying

There are a few good pubs in Dingle, the most eccentric of which is **Dick Mack's** (Green St.; ☎ **066/915-1070**), which doubles as a boot repair shop. A favorite with locals and visitors, Dick Mack's has been frequented by

celebrities who stop by Dingle—look for their names on stars on the sidewalk outside. **An Droichead Beag** on Lower Main Street (☎ **066/915-1723**) is the most popular pub in Dingle, where friendly Irishmen mingle with travelers amid a fun atmosphere with nightly live music sessions. If you crave the sort of camaraderie only found when jostling between sweaty football-crazy young men, head to **McCarthy's** (Main St.; ☎ **066/915-1205**), where the crowd is loud and lively and you'll find loads of 20-somethings packed onto beat-up leather couches and waiting in line to play darts. Dingle certainly isn't the place to visit if you need to go clubbing every night—there's only one place to dance, and it's in a hotel (Hillgrove Hotel, Spa Rd.; ☎ **066/915-1131;** 11pm–2am Fri–Sun; cover €6). Local teenyboppers don their best countrified clubbing gear and head here after the pubs close, then dance like robots on Red Bull 'til it closes. Afterwards, it's on to the kabob stand 'til someone starts a fight and the cops show up.

Sightseeing

There's a lot to see and do on the Dingle Peninsula, but the most high-profile attraction is oddly enough a 600-pound mammal—Fungie the dolphin. Every day fishing boats ferry tourists to the waters off the coast of the town to see the village's famous mascot. **MTV Best Fungie the Dolphin Tours** leave about every 2 hours in the off season and every half-hour during the summer, and tours last an hour. Fungie swims up to the boat and flips around for your entertainment. You'll also get unparalleled views of beautiful Dingle Bay. If you're up for an early morning adventure, try swimming with Fungie. Fungie can actually swim about 25 mph but will slow down for you, as well as playing, jumping, and interacting. To arrange your swim, call John Brosnan (☎ **066/915-1967**), who will rent you a semi-dry suit, mask, snorkel, fins, and boots for €20 per person. If you want an escorted swim for a full 2 hours, it will cost you an extra €25, but you're welcome to swim on your own if you'd like. If you had a big night out and you're not feeling particularly adventurous but would like to take advantage of your gorgeous seaside location, go to **Slea Head** for the day. It's at the most southwestern point of the peninsula and boasts some pristine beaches, pretty walks, and archaeology to explore. If you have a real interest in historical buildings, check out **Sciuird Archaeological Adventures** (Holy Ground; ☎ 066/915-1937). A local expert leads these tours, which last 2¹/₂ hours and involve a bus journey and some easy walking. You'll see four or five monuments dating from the Stone Age en route. The groups are small—8 or 10 people—and you meet at the top of the pier. It costs €15 per person and runs daily from 10:30am to 2:00pm from May through September.

Playing Outside

The Dingle Peninsula is one of the best spots for walking, cycling, swimming, sailing, and diving. The nicest 📺 (Best) **beaches** are at Brandon Bay on the northern part of the peninsula and Tralee Bay on the western side. Check the Bus Éireann timetables outside Garvey's Supervalu for times to the beaches. If you're looking to stay closer to Dingle, the beach at Ventry and the beaches at Inch are pretty good too. If you're into hiking, you'll want to check out Mount Brandon, all 937m (3,123 ft.) of it. The easiest climb is the western side, but the better views are from the eastern side, so if you're up for some serious legwork, start at Cloghane. The tourist office will help you out with directions, maps, and tips. If you want to really see Dingle's landscape, try cycling Slea Head Drive, which takes you from Dingle town center through Ventry and out to Dunquin. You'll pass the beehive huts of the Fahan Group and you'll see Dunbeg Fort on the way to Slea Head. In fact, if you want to cover a lot of the tourist sites on your way,

ask for the Dingle Way Map Guide at the tourist office. You can rent a bike from **Paddy's Bike Shop** on Dykegate Street (☎ 066/915-2311) for €10 per day, or less if you have a student ID. If you're too lazy to pedal, you can let a horse do the work at **Dingle Horse Riding** (The Stables, Baile na Buaile; ☎ 066/915-2199), a luxury stable facility. They'll organize a day trip for you— picture yourself galloping down a beach into the sunset. Or just trying not to fall off. If you prefer activities that don't involve possibly breaking bones, Dingle is a great place to explore the ocean floor. **Dive Dingle** (Dingle Marina, Dingle, County Kerry; ☎ 066/915-2422) is your best bet for PADI courses, snorkeling, cave diving, or diving with seals. Look out for Saska, a bottlenose dolphin who has recently taken up residence and, of course, you'll see Fungie. The staff is totally professional and really helpful. Dingle Harbour is an excellent place for sailing, and the **Dingle Sailing Club** (The Wood, Strand St.; ☎ 066/915-1984) will hook you up with boats and equipment. If you want to try windsurfing, check out the highly professional **Jamie Knox Watersports** (The Maharees, Castlegregory, County Kerry; ☎ 066/713-9411), located at Brandon Bay, just outside Dingle Town. It's well loved by wind freaks and you can rent a wetsuit as well as any equipment you need.

Shopping

As you would probably expect, the shops in Dingle stock the sort of items that might appeal to middle-aged tour bus passengers, like woolen sweaters, Celtic jewelry, and handmade pottery. There are a couple of decent shops, like the **Music House** (6 Orchard Lane; ☎ 066/915-2633), which is the self-proclaimed "largest record store" in Dingle (not difficult). They stock Irish music as well as contemporary stuff. If you need to get kitted out for hiking or cycling or any other endeavor you might take on in Dingle, try the **Mountain Man** (Strand St.; ☎ o66/915-2400) where you'll find clothes and footwear by brands like Columbia and Patagonia.

Tralee

Tralee is best known for two very different reasons: The Rose of Tralee Festival and the Ballybunion Golf Course. If you're not a huge fan of roses (who is?) or a champion golfer, there isn't a whole lot to see or do in Tralee, which functions as the economic hub of Kerry. With a whopping 20,000 residents, Tralee feels like a "real" town, with industry rather than simply lots of quaint tourist pubs. However, it's a necessary stopping point on the way from Killarney out to the smaller towns on the peninsula and there are some decent pubs to be tried. **Warning:** You won't want to spend more than a day and night here for fear of dying of boredom.

Getting There & Getting Around

Tralee's downtown area is easily walkable, but if you need a cab, call **Kingdom Cabs** at ☎ o66/712-7828 or **Tralee Radio Cabs** at ☎ o66/712-5421. Everything you'll need is to be found along the Mall, Castle Street, and Denny Street. They are a 10-minute walk from the bus and train station.

You can get to Tralee pretty easily, with bus services by **Bus Éireann** from all parts of Ireland (☎ o1/830-2222; www.buseireann. ie). You can also get a train to Tralee from all major cities, arriving at the station on John Joe Sheehy Road (☎ o66/712-3522; www. irishrail.ie). If you're driving, take the N69 and N21 from Limerick and the north, the N70 from the Ring of Kerry and the south, and the N22 from Killarney and the east.

Basics

TOURIST OFFICE The **Tralee Tourist Office** (☎ o66/712-1288) is located at Ashe Memorial Hall on Denny Street. They're open 9am to 1pm and 2 to 5pm on weekdays, but it's open on weekends in the summer months.

INTERNET ACCESS Check your e-mail at **Cyberpost** (26 Castle St.; ☎ o66/718-1284), for €6 per hour. During the summer months it's open from 10am to 10pm so surf to your heart's content.

RECOMMENDED WEBSITES To find out more about Tralee, check out www.tralee.ie and www.tralee-insight.com.

Festivals

You might have heard of the Rose of Tralee Festival in August, the only time when the number of visitors outnumbers the population of locals. Tralee is celebrated for its roses, but there are other aspects to the Festival, like a beauty pageant. Call ☎ o66/712-1288 and ask for info about it.

Sleeping

→ **Abbey Gate Hotel** Easily the best hotel in its price range in Tralee, Abbey Gate has two restaurants, a bar, and room service if you're looking to really relax on your way to the coast or to another part of the country. The guest rooms are newly decorated with art prints and fresh fabrics, and the hotel is located within walking distance of all the decent pubs and shops in town. *Maine St.* ☎ *o66/712-9988. www.abbeygate-hotel.com. Double €130–€170. Amenities: Restaurant; bar. In room: TV, coffee/tea facilities, hair dryer.*

→ **Finnegan's Holiday Hostel** Right across from the tourist office, Finnegan's benefits from its location, plus has a comfortable, lived-in feel without being seedy or dirty. It's also a stone's throw from the action (well, you know . . .) in Tralee's pubs. The dorm accommodation is very cheap but the

Where Did I Come From?

If you're on the hunt for your long-lost Irish relatives, it can be helpful to know where to start looking. Below are just a few popular Irish surnames and the counties where they originated. May of these families later spread throughout the island and beyond. Each name has plenty of variations; for instance, FitzGerald has derivations of Fitzpatrick, Flanagan, Flynn, Fogarty, Foley, and Gaffney.

- **Abearne:** Clare, Limerick
- **Butler:** Kilkenny
- **Donoghue:** Cork, Kerry
- **Fitzgerald:** Cork, Kerry, Kildare
- **MacCarthy:** Munster
- **Maguire:** Ulster
- **Martin:** Connaught
- **Murphy:** Sligo, Tyrone, Wexford
- **O'Brien:** Clare, Limerick

- **O'Donnell:** Donegal
- **O'Keeffe:** Cork
- **O'Kelly:** Galway
- **O'Neill:** Ulster
- **O'Sullivan:** Tipperary
- **Power:** Waterford, Wicklow
- **Regan:** Dublin, Meath
- **Ryan:** Limerick, Tipperary
- **Walsh:** Dublin, Kilkenny, Leitrim, Waterford, Wicklow

What's in a name? Ages ago, the prefixes of Irish last names signified a great deal. *Mc* or *Fitz* meant "bastard son of," and *O* before a name meant "grandson of" or "from the family of." So the name O'Brien means "ancestors of the Brien family" (in this case the ancestors of Brian Boru, the most famous of the high kings of Ireland). You also occasionally see a name with an *Ni* prefix (such as Ni Dhomhnaill) but not often as it's a bit old-fashioned. It literally means "formerly of" as in Triona Briain Ni Dhomnaill, the name Triona might go by if she were a proud Dhomnaill who married a Briain.

COUNTY KERRY

beds will do for a night. *17 Denny St.* ☎ *066/712-7610. Dorm €8–€10; double €13 per person. Amenities: Internet.*

Eating

→ **Restaurant David Norris** CONTINENTAL Comfort cooking with a modern spin. Lift your knives and forks for dishes like pineapple and duck confit and Kerry beef with colcannon. The look is understated and the restaurant's location in the center of town is supreme. The service is as good as the desserts. If you want to be part of the in crowd, make reservations, because everyone wants to be seen here. *Ivy House, Ivy Terrace.* ☎ *066/718-5654. Reservations necessary. Entrees €15–€25; Tues–Fri 5–9:30pm; Sat 7–9:30pm.*

→ **The Tankard** SEAFOOD The Tankard has sweeping views across Tralee Bay, huge windows, and a wow position on the edge of the sea. The menu features fresh local seafood like lobster, scallops, and sole, while for carnivores there's lots to choose from, like steak and duck. If you find the main restaurant a little on the pricey side, there's bar food, too. *Kilfenora, Kenit, County Kerry.* ☎ *066/713-6164. Mains €15–€30. Restaurant daily 6–9:30pm; bar food daily 12:30-10pm.*

Partying

None of the pubs in Tralee are really anything to write home about, although some of them are pleasant enough for a night of drinking while in town. **Harty's Lounge Bar** (30 Lower Castle St.; ☎ **066/712-5385**) is celebrated as the original meeting place of the founders of the Tralee Rose Festival. The pub grub, like Irish stew, is really tasty. **The Oyster Tavern** (Fenit Rd.; ☎ 066/713-6102) has the best location of any watering hole—it's right west of downtown, overlooking Tralee Bay. There's nowhere better to sink a few pints and watch the sunset. **Kirby's Olde Brogue Inn** (Rock St.; ☎ 066/712-3221) feels like a big barn, with farm equipment everywhere and rowdy music sessions.

Sightseeing

There's a selection of rather random sights in Tralee, like the **Blennerville Windmill** (R559, Blennerville, Tralee; ☎ 066/712-1064), the largest working windmill anywhere in Britain. Tourists with Irish blood check it out for the emigration exhibition center as, to be honest, other than that, it's just a building producing ground whole meal flour. It costs €5 for adults and €4 for students. The biggest tourist attraction in Tralee is the **Kerry the Kingdom** exhibit (Ashe Memorial Hall, Denny St.; ☎ 066/712-7777), where you can examine 7,000 years of life in the county of Kerry. There's info on Gaelic football and traditional music, plus an endearingly budget theme-park ride called the Geraldine Tralee, taking you through a re-creation of Tralee during the middle ages.

Playing Outside

Golf is a big deal around Tralee. One favorite Irish course is **Ballybunion** (☎ 066/27146; www.ballybuniongolfclub.ie). The club offers two challenging 18-hole courses, both with views overlooking the Shannon estuary and the ocean. Playing here could burn a hole in your pocket—it costs between €80 and €125—but it's worth it to play one of the best courses in the world. If you want to see the sights of Tralee on horseback, hire a horse from **Eagle Lodge Equestrian Centre** in Gortatlea (☎ 066/37266). Prices start at €20 per hour for 1 or 2 hour rides on the Slieve Mish Mountains and Queen Scotia's Glen. If you prefer spectator sports to actual participation, go to the dogs—that is, watch the greyhound racing at the **Kingdom Greyhound Racing Track** on Brewery Road (☎ 066/712-4033). Admission is €6, which includes a program. There's also a horse-racing track if you want to get some gambling out of your system. **Tralee Racecourse** is at Ballybeggan Park (☎ 066/713-6148; admission is €6 for students and €11 for adults) and the races usually take place in June and August; phone ahead for details.

Dunquin

If you find yourself in Dunquin, chances are you're here to see the seven Blasket Islands, which lie off the tip of Dunmore Head. With Gaelic language speakers, native poets, and an old-fashioned lifestyle, this area has been hailed as one of the last remaining hotbeds of real Irish culture. The rest of the country believes the tip of Great Blasket, rising 300m (1,000 ft.) above the Atlantic, is where the last surviving Kerryman stood when he was trying to get a ride on Noah's Ark after the flood.

Getting There & Getting Around

Dunquin Ferries (☎ 066/915-6455) leave for the Blaskets from Dunquin daily, weather permitting (and weather can be severe, so call and check). **Bus Éireann** (☎ 066/712-3566; www.buseireann.ie) leaves from Dingle on Mondays and Thursdays. Call for the schedule or stop at the tourist office (see below).

The ferry will deposit you on the eastern shore of Great Blasket and pick you up later in the day. The island is definitely walkable within a few minutes.

Orientation

Great Blasket is 440 hectares (1,100 acres) of unspoiled mountainous terrain measuring 4 miles by half a mile. The village of Tra Ban (White Strand in English) is located on the northeast of the island, and it faces the mainland and Slea Head.

Basics

TOURIST OFFICE   Check out the **Blasket Centre** in Dunquin (☎ **066/915-6444**). It costs €.50 for students to get in, but has a wealth of information, including presentations on the lost lifestyle of the Blasket Islanders and the history of the Irish language, as well as info on its current status.

RECOMMENDED WEBSITES   To read up on these interesting islands, go to www.great blasketislandcom or www.dingle-peninsula. ie/blaskets.html. To find out about the literary heritage of the islands, go to www. blasketislands.com.

Sleeping & Eating

In the last few years, the **Great Blasket Island Hostel** (Great Blasket; ☎ **066/848-6687**; dorm €12; open Apr–Oct) opened outside the old village of Tra Ban. All the facilities you take for granted become luxuries out here: Showers, toilets, and a kitchen. There's no curfew but, come on, you're not going clubbing here anyway. If you don't fancy a bed for the night, you can camp for free but, beware, the weather in this most westerly part of Europe can get really horrendous. If you can't get to the Blaskets due to the storms, stay at Dunquin for the night. **Kruger's Guest House and Bar** (Ballinahara, Dunquin; ☎ **066/915-6127**; double approx €45) is steeped in history and mystery, mostly surrounding its thoroughly unorthodox owner—ask the patrons and you

shall be told. Every major Hollywood film made in the area has touched Kruger's—Tom Cruise and Nicole Kidman drank here while making *Far and Away,* just for starters. The place feels stuck in another decade, so expect to hear *sean nos*—old Irish traditional singing—every other night.

When you get hungry, head to **Kruger's** (see above), which also doubles as a bar and restaurant. Seriously, it's all there is in Dunquin. The interior is covered in artwork and feels cozy and comfortable. Order their specialty, fish and chips, before sleeping in one of their simple but clean bedrooms. An average meal will set you back about €8.

Sightseeing

You can spend an afternoon exploring Great Blasket, walking its perimeter, swimming off Blasket Beach, or visiting the restored houses of famous native authors. The island had to be permanently abandoned in 1953 due to the extreme weather conditions, so be warned: Tourists have been known to be stranded here for weeks at a time. There is nothing in particular to look out for except a handful of historic ruins and a large amount of sea and wildlife. The whole island seems like a time capsule of Ireland in earlier times. Across the water, Dunquin is absolutely tiny—population less than 200—and there is very little to see, although a few kilometers away there is a strand of sandy beaches. The views from the rugged cliffs making up the coastline are quite spectacular, though, and the pier is the best place to watch the magnificent summer sunset over the North Atlantic. Dunquin natives are very proud their first language is Gaelic and their village, known to them as Dun Chaoin, seems like something out of the past—they hope to have Internet installed in 2006.

➔**Ionad An Bhlascaoid Mhoir/The Blasket Centre**   On the westerly tip of the Dingle Peninsula, this visitor center is dedicated to the remote Blasket Islands. The largest of the islands, Great Blasket was once an outpost of Irish civilization and a nurturing ground for Irish-language writers, but its inhabitants abandoned the island in 1953. The center explains in interesting style the cultural and literary traditions of the Blaskets and the history of Corca Dhuibhne, the *gaeltacht* area. There's a bookshop specializing in local literature, and a handy cafe with views of the Blaskets. *Dunquin, County Kerry.* ☎ *066/915-6444. www.heritageireland. ie. Admission €3.50 adults; €8.25 students. Apr–June and Sept–Oct daily 10am–6pm; July–Aug daily 10am–7pm. Closed Nov– Mar.*

County
Limerick &
County Clare

L imerick and Clare in the Midwest of Ireland are known for their natural beauty, from the unparalleled, enigmatic Burren region of Clare to the stunning green land surrounding the Shannon estuary in Limerick. Limerick City has suffered for years with a bad reputation—it was known as "Stab City" for years—but its residents have been working hard to shed its *Angela's Ashes* image. Today, Limerick is cleaner and brighter than ever, with an up-and-coming music scene and some hot clubs. Clare, meanwhile, benefits from some quirky tourist towns like Doolin, which is breathtakingly beautiful and a mecca for Irish music. You'll find much of this region very desolate and often startlingly antiquated—there are towns near the Burren without cash machines or taxi services, so having your own car and carrying piles of cash is a must. However, for all the provincial, primitive aspects of this windswept, desolate area, there's something very appealing about being so far from the intense tourist-oriented towns of the Southwest.

The Best of Counties Limerick & Clare

○ **The Burren:** We can guarantee this: The Burren is one of the strangest landscapes you're likely to see. Its vast limestone grassland is spread with a quilt of wildflowers from as far afield as the Alps, all softening the stark stones jutting out of the ground. Its inhabitants include nearly every species of butterfly found in Ireland. See p. 335.

○ **Cliffs of Moher:** Rising from Hag's Head to the south, these magnificent sea cliffs reach their full height of 214m (702 ft.) just north of O'Brien's Tower. The views of the open sea, of the Aran Islands, and of the Twelve Bens mountains of Connemara are spectacular. A walk south along the cliff edge at sunset makes a perfect end to any day. See p. 334.

Counties Limerick & Clare

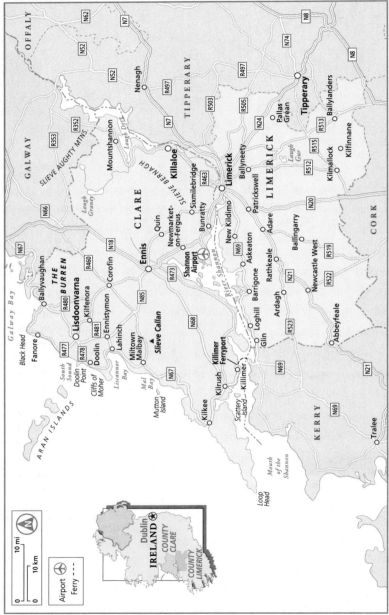

○ **Going Spelunking:** County Clare is one of the best places in Ireland to go spelunking—you know, putting on an unfashionable jumpsuit and squirming your way through underground caves. It sounds insane, but it is a load of fun, and you might get hooked. Go on, give it a try. Travel is all about new experiences, right? See p. 332.

Limerick City

In the past, Limerick has been seen as dangerous, dirty, and generally to be avoided. While it would still not be advisable to wander the streets at 2am drunk, wearing bling, and carrying 500€, modern-day Limerick has excellent museums and art galleries, a fun-loving college crowd, and a fascinating history (you'll leave the town with an encyclopedic knowledge of Eamon de Valera, for instance). There's also a wide spread of ways to fill your day from gay bars to greyhound tracks. Add Limerick to your must-see list right now.

Getting There

BY PLANE   From the U.S., Aer Lingus, Continental, and Delta Airlines run regular scheduled flights into **Shannon Airport,** off the Limerick-Ennis Road (N18), County Clare (☎ 061/712000; www.shannonairport. com), 24km (15 miles) west of Limerick. Domestic flights from Dublin and overseas flights from Britain and the Continent are also available with a range of airlines. (See "Basics" chapter, p. 28 for all the airlines' toll-free numbers and websites.) A taxi from the airport to the city center costs about €25.

BY BUS   **Bus Éireann** (☎ 061/313333; www.buseireann.ie) provides bus service from Shannon Airport to Limerick's Railway Station. The fare is €5.20. Bus services from all parts of Ireland come into Limerick's Colbert Station, Parnell Street.

BY TRAIN   **Irish Rail** chugs directly from Dublin, Cork, and Killarney, with connections from other parts of Ireland. They arrive at Limerick's Colbert Station, Parnell Street (☎ 061/315555; www.irishrail.ie).

BY CAR   Limerick City can be reached on N7 from the east and north; N20, N21, N24, and N69 from the south; and N18 from the west and north.

Getting Around

BY BUS   **Bus Éireann** (☎ 061/313333) operates local bus service in Limerick and roundabouts; the flat fare is €1.50. Buses depart from Colbert Station, Parnell Street.

BY TAXI   If you need a cab, grab one from outside Colbert Station, at hotels, and along Thomas and Cecil streets, off O'Connell Street. To reserve a taxi, call **Economy Taxis** (☎ 061/411422), **Fixed Price Taxis** (☎ 061/417777), or **Top Cabs** (☎ 061/417417).

BY CAR   Driving around Limerick can be a bit of a nightmare thanks to all the one-way streets—do yourself a favor, park up and walk. If you must park downtown, head for the lot at Arthur's Quay, in the center of daytime activities and well signposted. Parking is €1.30 per hour. If you need to rent a car in Limerick, contact **Alamo/Treaty Rent-A-Car** (☎ 061/363663; www.carhire.ie) or **Irish Car Rental** (☎ 061/328328; www. irishcarrentals.com).

BY FOOT   The best way to get around Limerick is on your own two legs. To get a flavor of the city follow the signposted "Tourist Trail" around the main sights; a booklet available at the tourist office and in bookshops will point you in the right direction.

Orientation

Limerick straddles the River Shannon, spreading out across the estuary with its unsightly factories and industrial districts. The river has split the town so it appears quite

Tips to Start a Conversation with a Local

If you must drink too many pints and slur into the ear of a local, whatever you do don't mention Limerick rhymes or try making up your own . . . they've heard it all before and you'll seem like the most lame first-time-traveler ever. You'll seem pretty cool if you talk about something relevant for their newly cool city, like the music scene; you could ask if they know which bands are playing at the Warehouse or Doc's this weekend (see "Live Music," below). You could also talk about their ultra high profile book-club-fave famous son Frank McCourt, who wrote *Angela's Ashes* and its sequel *'Tis;* do they think the portrayal of Limerick was fair? Did they even read the books? Opinions are divided. If you're a shopaholic, you could talk style with a Limerick native; after all, the Limerick School of Art and Design is beginning to churn out hip designers, and college kids are finally starting to ditch the hoodies for drainpipes and statement hats. Into sports? Learn those Limerick football and hurling songs ("Limerick, you're a lady, your Shannon Water, tears of joy that flow") and get down to the next match. Really stuck for a conversation topic? Limerick natives, and the Irish in general, love to chat about their beautiful country, the best pubs in each town, where to find the really good *craic,* sports and teams, and if all else fails the crappy weather. You really can't lose!

orderly—the downtown area is to the east while the residential areas are to the north and west. To the north are historic sights like Saint Mary's Cathedral, City Hall, and King John's Castle. The main street where all the action takes place is called O'Connell Street, and runs north to south. Other streets with lots of pubs and restaurants include William Street, which intersects O'Connell; everything is incredibly easy to find as the streets form a grid reminiscent of central Glasgow—it's very un-Irish indeed. Nearby is People's Park, a popular place for dog-walking and bench-sitting. Limerick University, a huge Irish center of learning, is 3km (5 miles) outside the city itself on the banks of the Shannon.

Basics

TOURIST OFFICE **The Limerick Tourism Centre** is on Arthur's Quay, Limerick (☎ 061/317522). It is open Monday to Friday 9:30am to 5:30pm, Saturday 9:30am to 1pm, with expanded and weekend hours in summer. Ask for a free copy of the *Shannon*

Region Visitors Guide, which is packed with helpful information about activities and events in Limerick and the surrounding areas. A seasonal tourist office is open March to November in the **Adare Heritage Centre,** Main Street, Adare (☎ 061/396666).

INTERNET There are a handful of decent Internet cafes in Limerick. The best is **Javas** (5 Catherine St.; ☎ 061/418-077; 9am–8pm Mon–Sat; Sun 11am–8pm; €3 per hour), a cafe which is pretty much a Limerick institution, full of hungover students trying to read thick novels and professional types madly typing into Blackberries or reading the paper. They've recently added a bank of Internet-ready computers upstairs. There's also **Surfers Internet Café** on Upper William St. (☎ 061/440-122), where the main draw is the 40% student discount, so bring a college ID if you have one. There are snacks and coffee on offer, plus you can make cheap international calls. Internet use costs €5 per hour.

RECOMMENDED WEBSITES For good all-around visitor information on the Web,

Limerick City

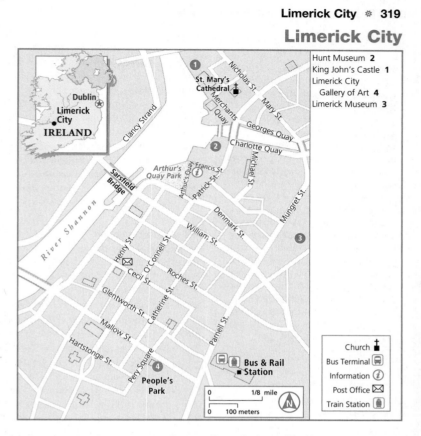

Hunt Museum **2**
King John's Castle **1**
Limerick City
   Gallery of Art **4**
Limerick Museum **3**

Dublin
Limerick
City
IRELAND

St. Mary's
Cathedral

Nicholas St.
Mary St.
Merchants Quay
Georges Quay
Charlotte Quay
Clancy Strand

Arthur's
Quay Park
Francis St.
Michael St.
Arthur's Quay
Patrick St.
Sarsfield
Bridge

River Shannon

Denmark St.
William St.
Mungret St.

Henry St.
O'Connell St.
Cecil St.
Roches St.
Glentworth St.
Catherine St.
Mallow St.
Parnell St.
Hartstonge St.
Pery Square

People's
Park

Bus & Rail
Station

Church ✝
Bus Terminal
Information ⓘ
Post Office ✉
Train Station

0   1/8 mile
0   100 meters

see **www.visitlimerick.com** or **www.limerick.com**.

Sleeping

→ **Broad Street Hostel** If security is important to you, then stay at Broad Street—it's locked up tighter than Fort Knox. You'll be fed at breakfast time and the kitchen is clean and large, plus the bedrooms are spacious and have desks for the all-important writing of postcards. The downside? The social vibe is about as buzzing as an Amish convention. *Broad St.* ☎ *061/317-222. Dorms €15; singles €22; doubles €22 per person. Amenities: Internet.*

→ **Courtbrack Accommodation** The name of this place doesn't exactly scream "luxury"—they call it like it is. A short walk from the downtown area, Courtbrack is meticulously clean and the amenities are modern. The exterior does however resemble a retirement home, but you'll get your money's worth and you're provided with a continental breakfast. *Courtbrack Ave.* ☎ *061/302-500. Dorms €18; doubles €28. Amenities: Laundry.*

DOABLE

→ **Alexandra Guest House** Guests here will give you mixed reviews about this place: Some say it's charming and relaxing, while some say they couldn't get a good night's sleep due to the thin walls. Regardless, this elegant Victorian house is only a 5-minute

Hanging Out

For just hanging out and not getting ridiculously drunk, the locale of choice is the **Locke Bar** (see "Partying," below). If it's even vaguely warm, you won't find a seat in the packed outdoor area. One of the oldest and most atmospheric joints in the city, the Locke is popular with jocks, fashionable college kids, and older professionals alike—the owner, a former rugby star, is jocular and attracts a following from all walks of life. The food is also above par so it's no wonder people come for a drink and stay for lunch . . . and dinner. Like American kids, Limerick locals love some retail therapy, so a logical hangout for them is the mall—in this case, **Arthur's Quay Shopping Centre** (see "Shopping," below) with its high-end stores selling the usual clothes and sporting goods.

walk from the station and the staff will do their best to help you plan an itinerary or explore the area. *5–6 O'Connell Ave.* ☎ *061/318472. Double €40–€50. In room: Coffee/tea facilities.*

→ **Hanratty's Hotel** Anyone important who has passed through Limerick has stayed at the town's oldest hotel, from Irish hero Eamon de Valera to the infamous Che Guevara, whose grandmother was a Lynch (no joke) and who liked a rowdy St. Patrick's Day celebration here with his Cuban comrades. Hanratty's has kept its old-world feel over the years but has managed to introduce all the modern amenities. *5 Glentworth St.* ☎ *061/410999. Double €30–€80. In room: TV, hair dryer, coffee/tea facilities.*

→ **O'Grady's Iroko House** Deirdre and Jack O'Grady put their hearts and souls into the running of Iroko—just check out their

website and see photos of Deirdre laying the table herself. The grounds are manicured and the bedrooms wouldn't look out of place in a doll's house—think perfectly made beds with crisp white linens and plush red headboards. Iroko House is a bit out of Limerick City proper, but don't let that put you off, as there's lots more to see around here, like Bunratty Castle. Breakfasts range from the healthy (yogurt and cheese) to the indulgent (sausage, egg, and bacon). *Cloughkeating, Patrickswell.* ☎ *061/227861. www.irokohouse. com. Double €32. In room: TV, coffee/tea facilities, hair dryer.*

→ **Old Quarter Lodge** Limerick's largest guesthouse, Old Quarter calls itself a "boutique hotel," although it has a rather eclectic B&B-type feel. It is definitely the best accommodation you'll find for this price. It's near all the best pubs, shops, and restaurants and if you find yourself with some extra money, splurge on a suite—they all have widescreen TVs, velvet couches, and DVD players. The in-house pub is genuinely cool, with Art Deco design elements and drinks like a "Hollywood-tini." The coffee menu in the cafe is just as good if you're laying off the booze. *Little Ellen St.* ☎ *061/317095. Double €80–€90. Main hotel facilities? In room: TV, coffee/tea facilities.*

SPLURGE

→ **Adare Manor and Golf Club** This hotel should really have its own category as the word *splurge* doesn't really do justice to the price. You could stay in a cheap hostel for a month for the price of a night in this stunning, luxurious manor. If you have the bank account of an Olsen twin or very generous parents, by all means check into this massive castlelike hotel in the middle of acres of woodlands and gardens. *Condé Nast Traveler* named it their top European resort and you can see why: Eating breakfast overlooking a tranquil river, getting a massage at a renowned in-house spa, and sleeping in rooms that seem worthy of royalty? Yes, sign us up. *Adare.* ☎ *061/396-566. www.adare manor.com. Double €305. Amenities: Restaurant; horseback-riding; spa. In room: TV, dataport, hair dryer, minibar, safe.*

→ **Castleroy Park Hotel** The Castleroy is definitely one of the finest hotels in the area, offering the latest in modern amenities: Free wireless broadband throughout and a low GI (Glycemic Index) menu—a faddy eating program that has its fair share of celeb followers. The health and fitness center is a real draw, with a particularly inviting pool and a well-equipped gym. The rooms are decorated in subtle, stylish muted browns and creams. The Merry Pedlar bar and bistro and McLaughlins restaurant definitely don't feel like your typical sub-par hotel establishments, so book ahead. *Dublin Rd.* ☎ *061/335566. www.castleroy-park.ie. Double €155. Amenities: Bar; bistro; gym; pool; Wi-Fi broadband. In room: TV, dataport, hair dryer, minibar.*

Eating

There are loads of hip new dining establishments in Limerick as it's a university town with lots of young blood. Expect lots of fusion-y places and little cafes with cool decor and slick waitstaff. Thankfully it's a far cry from the cheesy "ye olde" restaurant scene in Killarney or similar Disneyland Ireland towns. Just save some money to eat and don't be boring and buy your own food from the grocery store, *please;* you're on vacay.

CHEAP

→ **Café Vienna** CAFE This large self-service restaurant just off Limerick's main drag attracts a young, health-conscious crowd after their fresh, filling sandwiches and fruit juices. However, just as popular is a full Irish breakfast—a sinful, heaving plateful for €5. You can get a smaller version for a little cheaper if all those sausages and bacon

rashers are intimidating. *67 William St.* ☎ *061/411-720. Average meal €5. No cards. Mon–Sat 8am–6pm.*

→ **DuCartes at the Hunt Museum** CAFE The setting of this museum cafe is what makes it worth a visit—sit on the terrace in good weather as it overlooks the river. You can order coffee or a light lunch, like a crisp salad with the best local ingredients. They also serve up a mean goat's cheese bruschetta. *Hunt Museum, Old Custom House, Rutland St.* ☎ *061/312-662. Average entree €12. Mon–Sat 10am–5pm, Sun 2–5pm.*

→ **O'Brien's Irish Sandwich Bar** CAFE Okay, O'Brien's is a chain, now to be found all over Ireland, Scotland, and England, but you can't beat them for cheap lunches, especially if you're avoiding fattier fast food places. You can get a really tasty low calorie, low fat wrap and some quality coffee. This particular O'Brien's has outdoor seating for warm weather and the location is perfect for watching the world go by. *73 William St.* ☎ *061/313-699. Sandwiches about €6. Mon–Sat 8:30am–6pm.*

→ **Wild Onion Café** CAFE For something a little different from the usual croissant-and-latte cafe experience, head to the American-style Wild Onion, a bakery serving up stateside specialties like French toast with Vermont maple syrup and hash browns or a Tex-Mex grilled chicken breast with their own salsa. Owners Bob and Ruth DiGirolamo have a huge local following, and punters come in from miles around, so orders for favorites like the chocolate truffle tart have to be placed in advance. Of course, you could always just order a coffee—but go for the Americano. *Cornmarket Row on High St.* ☎ *061/440055. Average entree €10. Tues–Fri 8am–4pm; Sat 9am–3pm.*

DOABLE

→ **Copper and Spice** INDIAN/THAI This is the best Indian restaurant in Ireland. The mod dining room sets a brilliant backdrop for

Seema Conroy's superb cooking: Terrific breads, tantalizing curries, wonderful veggie pakoras. Whatever your favorite Indian dish, she does it better than you've ever had it. A fabulous addition to Limerick's food scene, with excellent service and a friendly staff to boot. *2 Cornmarket Row.* ☎ *061/313620. Reservations recommended. Main courses €9–€16. Wed–Fri 12:30–2pm; daily 5–10:30pm.*

➜ **Texas Steak Out** AMERICAN   Try not to cringe at the punny title and the steer horns on the front of the building—Limerick's Wild West saloon–themed restaurant has above average food for reasonable prices, and serves up everything from the Tex-Mex burgers you'd expect to pasta and curry dishes. If you want something light, go for the warm Cajun chicken and bean salad. If you have a Texas-size appetite, order a BBQ sirloin topped with mushrooms and onions—don't forget the Jack Daniels sauce on top! *116 O'Connell St.* ☎ *061/410350. Average entree €13. Mon–Sat 10:30am–11pm; Sun noon–11pm.*

SPLURGE

➜ **Aubars** MODERN IRISH   Padraic Frawley returned home to Limerick full of ideas after culinary school, and he has indeed turned this former pub into a mecca of city cool. The setting is contemporary without being pretentious, and you can eat in the bar or the separate restaurant, depending on what you fancy eating. Vegetables are integrated into every meal so you can at least attempt to be healthy, while vegetarians are well looked after. Try the smoked venison starter with celeriac rémoulade—delish. After dinner, have a drink at the mod black and white bar and then head to the in-house club, Opus, with its underwater feel. This place has it all. *49–50 Thomas St.* ☎ *061/317-799. Reservations required. Restaurant entrees €15–€30. Tues–Sat from 8am.*

➜ **Green Onion Caffé** MODERN CONTINENTAL   This is a restaurant of the moment

in Limerick City, and a shining light in the still-working-on-it renaissance of this culinary landscape. Jeff Gloux is an extremely talented chef and his down-to-earth cooking is all about letting the wonderful flavors of natural ingredients shine through. His wild-mushroom-and-garlic soup packs a tremendous punch of flavor—but then, nothing is bland here. For a main course, go for comfort food—perhaps beef-and-Guinness stew (again with loads of mushrooms) or a perfect pasta with pesto. Add a great wine list, a terrific staff, fun background music, and you'll see why Limerick folks just can't get enough of the Green Onion. Come for lunch before or after visiting the Hunt Museum, just across the street. Or better yet, book for dinner, when the place is buzzing. *Old Town Hall Building, Rutland St.* ☎ *061/400710. Reservations recommended for dinner. Main courses €12–€23. Tues–Sat noon–10pm.*

➜ **The Mustard Seed** IRISH   Although this excellent restaurant is located a few miles outside the Limerick city center in Ballingary, it has to be included in any roundup of the city's best eateries for its beautiful surroundings (the building housing the Mustard Seed is an old convent) and its flawless cuisine—think creamy, heavenly soups and meat dishes garnished with fresh local produce. The house itself perches atop a hill and is surrounded by herb gardens, from which thyme and rosemary are picked daily to flavor that delicious salmon you're eating. The price, however, might give you heartburn. *Echo Lodge, Ballingary, County Limerick* ☎ *069/68508. Reservations recommended. Average meal €38. Mon–Sat 6–10pm.*

➜ **River Bar & Restaurant** FRENCH   It's not necessarily the food that makes this place such a favorite with discerning hipsters. The menu is definitely full of good, classic bistro fare like French onion soup and salmon in white wine sauce, but it's the atmosphere that makes River Bar special. The place is always

Sorry Son, You Can't Do That Here

First let us say, obviously the general rule when traveling abroad is **don't break the law.** Going to jail in any foreign country is such a buzz killer. There you are one minute meeting Irish people and hanging out in bars, and next thing you know you're meeting Irish police, and Irish lawyers, and Irish jailors—majorly uncool.

Given that, you should know that the official government attitude toward illegal drug use or purchase in Ireland is pretty hardcore. "Soft" drugs, such as marijuana, are illegal, and "hard" drugs, such as cocaine and heroin, are definitely absolutely illegal.

In cities like Dublin the police can be laid-back about small amounts of drugs, but that does not apply elsewhere, and, as a foreigner, you cannot expect the kind of friendly treatment they might offer to a local.

Laws forbidding importation of drugs are severe, and the country enthusiastically prosecutes to the fullest extent of the law—in other words, expect to do time in an Irish jail if you get caught.

For possession of drugs, punishment depends on the kind of drugs possessed. You can be fined hundreds of euros for possession of marijuana, or thousands for possession of a small amount of cocaine. If you have more than a small amount on you, expect to spend time in prison.

Be aware that the Irish police (the *Garda*) can detain you for up to 7 days without charge if you're arrested. There's no Miranda Law here either. So whatever you decide to do, we highly recommend you don't get caught.

humming with friendly chit chat and the staff seem to really enjoy serving you, unlike the surly waiters you might expect at such a place. *4 Georges Quay.* ☎ *061/401-883. Reservations recommended. Average entree €15. Dinner daily 6:30pm–midnight.*

Partying

Limerick is not the best place for a night out, although it has earned mixed reviews from locals willing to dispense their opinion, ranging from "great fun" to "absolutely brutal." It's a far cry from Dublin, but thanks to the university crowd, there are some pubs and bars with a young, fun feel—if you don't mind a sort of meat-market atmosphere on weekends, when University of Limerick guys attempt to pick up jailbait girls. The club scene is limited—and the gay scene is practically nonexistent—but the few we list are well-worth a visit, and there's always a good night to be had if you know where to go.

BARS

There are loads of fairly decent pubs and bars in Limerick, whether you want to watch the big game or just soak up the atmosphere and the *craic*. For sports fans, there's the **Brazen Head Sports Bar** (103 O'Connell St.; ☎ **061/417412**), a so-called "super pub" incorporating the Carlsberg Sports Bar and the Brazen Head Lounge—the former for watching football and rugby thanks to big screens and surround sound, and the latter for relaxing with a beer and some food. For a very lively, fun Happy Hour head to the **Dog House** (19 Thomas St.; ☎ **061/401905**), where the bartenders like to put on a show (think Tom Cruise in *Cocktail*) and the crowd dances to the DJs disco tunes. While the pub itself may look antique, there's nothing elderly about the scene at the Dog House. If you're looking for some variety, try **Riddler's** (9 Sarsfield St.; ☎ **061/414149**), which has three different bars, with one serving as a rugby shrine, covered in memorabilia. There's music, either live or DJ'd, Thursday through Monday, so expect to feel the floorboards shaking. For a young crowd, head to the **Old Quarter** (Little Ellen St.; ☎ **061/401190**), where you can sit outside in the summer and a DJ spins most nights of the week. The marble topped bar is always heaving with college students having a few drinks after a long day of lectures. If it's warm out and not raining (that is, once in a blue moon), you won't find a seat outside at the **Locke Bar** (3 Georges Quay; ☎ **061/413773**). Probably the most popular watering hole in the city for the scenester crowd, the Locke Bar is one of the oldest pubs in Limerick, owned by a former rugby star and buzzing with business every night of the week. There's nowhere better to sink a few pints of lager and make some friends. If you go for the whole old-world, atmospheric look in a pub—without being cheesy or themed, that is—head to **Nancy Blake's** (19 Upper Denmark St.; ☎ **061/416443**), with dim lighting, roaring open fires, great pub food, and a pretty beer garden. As its name suggests, **The Thirsty Scholar** (46 Roches St.; no phone) attracts a student clientele, who fill this dark, moody bar. The music is heavily top-40 and played at an extremely loud volume. For an artsy crowd, head to **The Gate** (☎ **061/411423**), where students from the nearby Art College regularly hold parties or just prop up the bar. With its convenient location at the top of the only pedestrian street in Limerick, **Charlie Chaplin's** (Chapel Lane, Cruises St.; ☎ **061/419885**) is a cafe-bar, serving sandwiches at lunchtime but also drawing heaving crowds of young people at night. It's definitely a good place to spend a few hours. Looking for something a little classier? Try **Ruben's Café and Wine Bar** (17 Denmark St.), a delicious spot for a vegetarian meal during the day and a wine bar popular with students at night. Ruben's is housed in a beautiful, old high-ceilinged building so the atmosphere is second to none.

CLUBS

Thanks to the university scene, there is a handful of good clubs in Limerick. Generally students and other partiers head there after the pubs close at 11 and stay 'til they get thrown out at about 1. The best, most exclusive club is 📺 Best **The Globe** (Cecil St.; ☎ **061/313533**), but don't be fooled by the reasonable cover charge (about €8)—the drinks are so expensive you'll have to eBay your belongings the next day. Famous acts like U2 and the Cranberries have been known to pop some champagne in the top floor member's only bar—you'll have to know someone or—ahem—get to know someone if you want to get in. Downstairs in the regular section, Limerick's hottest young things dance 'til the wee hours (okay, 2am, when it closes) and order ridiculous colorful cocktails. Open every night from 10pm to 2am during the college term but quieter during the summer, student club **The Lodge** (Dublin Rd., Castleroy; ☎ **061/331133**) teems with drunken university kids who've paid €7 to get in. The music is definitely chart-based, with the occasional old-school dance classic. The emphasis here is on downing as many drinks as possible before the lights go up. The most mainstream choice is **The Market** (Robert St.; ☎ **061/316-996**), a sprawling complex with a huge dance floor and a very loud sound system. The cover charge varies by the night but you won't pay more than €10. The DJ spins typical dance music and you'll find yourself on the dance floor 'til they boot you out at 3am. Part of Aubars (see "Eating," above), **Opus** (50 Thomas St.; ☎ **061/317799**; €8–€10) is exclusive bordering on pretentious—you won't get in if you don't look like a cool, well-dressed yuppie. If you do, the atmosphere is busy and fun, with chart music being played and fashionistas shaking their thing on the cramped dance floor.

Late-Night Bites & Coffee Shops

There isn't much in the way of proper late-night dining in Limerick, although, like in most U.K. and Irish cities, there is an array of kabob shops on every street corner, the best of which is chain restaurant **Abrakebabra** (119 O'Connell St.; ☎ **061/316900;** Mon–Sun noon–"late"), an American-style diner serving all sorts of fast food, while focusing on kabobs and also serving falafel, hot dogs, and fries. The food is better quality than other nonfranchise kabob shops, but Abrakebabra gets really busy after the pubs shut when drunk uni students jostle for a position in the line. If you're not in the mood for meat, check out **Apache Pizza** (4 Henry St.; ☎ **061/209888),** open 'til 1am on weekdays and 'til 2am on Fridays, Saturdays, and Sundays. Try the Cajun Apache—Cajun chicken, tomatoes, and jalapeño peppers. If you just want to relax in a coffeehouse instead of going out for a big night of boozing, check out the sleek, tranquil **Pier One Bar,** housed in the Sarsfield Bridge Hotel (Sarsfield Bridge; ☎ **061/317179)** but free from all chintzy hotel-cafe associations. Pier One is somewhat of a destination spot, where stylish Limerick locals head for an espresso and a session of people-watching. Another great destination for late-night coffee is the cafe at **Aubars** (see "Eating," above). You can order a decadent dessert with your latte and check out all the teenyboppers attempting to get into the Opus club housed in the complex.

LIVE MUSIC

Although there are some good live sessions at pubs around Limerick, there is a purpose-built facility just outside the city called **The Stroller** (Ballyneety; ☎ **061/351062),** with arguably the best live music in the region, plus a good lounge and dancing area. In the summer, the music is mostly Irish, but if you get sick of it, you can always head to the well-equipped games room next door. Housed in an old Irish farmhouse, **An Sibin** (O'Connell St.; ☎ **061/414566)** certainly looks the part, setting the scene for its nightly traditional music sessions with antique furniture and Victorian memorabilia. Arguably the best pub for live music that doesn't involve a fiddle, **Dolan's** (Dock Rd.; ☎ **061/314483)** has seen acts like The Proclaimers and Mel C grace their stage—okay, not exactly Coldplay, but not bad for a family-run joint in Limerick. On Tuesday, Thursday, and Sunday nights, **Doc's** (The Granary, Michael St.; ☎ **061/318466),** is heavily populated by University of Limerick and College of Art and Design students and is the place to be if you like live rock, reggae, and acoustic sets. And who doesn't?

GAY SCENE

Like most Irish towns, Limerick leaves a lot to be desired when it comes to gay culture. However, the top floor of the old Savoy complex (Bedford Rd.; no phone), a well-known building where the live music scene used to flourish, now plays host to **Bubblicious,** a popular gay night. Twice weekly, on Fridays and Sundays, gay and lesbian Limerick residents dance to disco tunes and gay anthems—think lots of sweaty 20-somethings jumping around to ABBA and Madonna. Otherwise, there's not much on offer, although the first weekend of every month is **Club Wilde,** held in the basement of the Best Western (Glentworth St.; ☎ **061/413822).** It's not as tacky as it sounds—this Best Western is a boutique hotel and used to be privately owned, so it's a nicely furnished Georgian town house rather than a cheesy motel, and the monthly parties feature lots of flirting and schmoozing.

Sweeping Up

Born in New York and raised in Limerick, Frank McCourt returned to the Big Apple at age 19, attended New York University, and taught in the New York City school system for 30 years. His childhood memoir, *Angela's Ashes*, sent readers clamoring to the bookstores in search of one of the most popular and fantastically successful volumes in history, an achievement that culminated in the Pulitzer Prize (and probably more money than he knows what to do with). It was also made into a movie of the same name, starring Emily Watson. Citizens of Limerick have grumbled about the city's less-than-sparkling depiction in the book, but in reality the miserably negative role belonged to McCourt's drunken and reckless father. McCourt writes, "When I look back on my childhood I wonder how I survived at all. It was, of course, a miserable childhood: the happy childhood is hardly worth your while. Worse than the ordinary miserable childhood is the miserable Irish childhood, and worse yet is the miserable Irish Catholic childhood." And there are tons more who would agree with whole hearts and big mouths.

At any rate, the city's grousing hasn't kept it from making tons of money off bus and walking tours catering to American readers eager to see the locations in Limerick that were mentioned in the book. Bottom line: *Angela's Ashes* is depressing and emotionally gut-wrenching, but it's extremely well-written, proving that the old Irish storytellers do indeed have their contemporary counterparts. Required reading.

Sightseeing

FREE → **Angela Woulfe Gallery** Open year-round and celebrating its 20th year, the gallery is full of paintings by the artist and various guest painters (all European and usually Irish). Woulfe's work largely focuses in on the play of light in Limerick landscapes. Some of it is really quite good and genuinely beautiful. *16 Pery Sq.* ☎ *061/310-164. 11am–5pm Mon–Thurs, Fri–Sat by appointment. Free admission.*

FREE → **Chris Doswell's** Non-naff prints by Irish craftsmen, including etchings, engravings, and lithographs. If you have a stack of leftover euros, these would certainly be a good investment. *Nicholas St., King's Island.* ☎ *061/318-2992. 9am–5:30pm Mon–Fri, 10:30am–2:30pm Sat. Free admission.*

→ **Hunt Museum** Two thousand ancient, medieval, and modern treasures stuffed inside an Old Custom House with a facade made to look just like the Petit Trianon at the Palace of Versailles in France. Those in the know say this is the finest collection of antiquities and art objects in Ireland, outside the Dublin National Museum. When you've reached cultural saturation point, pop into the incorporated shop and restaurant to relax. *The Custom House, Rutland St.* ☎ *061/312833. www.ul.ie/-hunt. Admission €6.50 adults, €5.50 students. Mon–Sat 10am–5pm; Sun 2–5pm.*

→ **King John's Castle** When King John of England visited Limerick in 1210 he was so taken with the place he immediately ordered his minions to build a "strong castle." King John's is the result. Today it's one of the oldest examples of medieval architecture in Ireland, with stand-out rounded gate towers and curtain walls. Thanks to a recent €7-million ($9.5-million) restoration, visitors can now also treat their peepers to an authentic archaeological excavation dating to Hiberno-Norse times. But take a stroll along the castle battlements and climb the towers for the best views. *Nicholas St., Limerick, County Limerick.* ☎ *061/411201. Admission €7.50 adults, €6 students. Apr–Oct daily 9:30am–5:30pm (last admission 4:30pm).*

FREE ➔ **Limerick City Gallery of Art** Hadn't yet had your fill of Yeats? How about checking out the painting talents of his bro, Jack B. Yeats This gallery is home to some of his output together with other works from the 18th to 20th century. There's usually a traveling contemporary art exhibition here, often touring from the Irish Museum of Modern Art. Some evenings there are literary readings or traditional- or classical-music concerts. Check local listings to see what's happening during your stay. *Pery Sq., on the corner of Mallow St. in the People's Park.* ☎ *061/310633. Free admission. Mon–Wed and Fri 10am–6pm; Thurs 10am–7pm; Sat 11am–6pm; Sun 2–6pm.*

FREE ➔ **Limerick Museum** This small museum may not be as info-packed as the Hunt (above) but it's free and interesting. History buffs can look forward to displays on Limerick's archaeology and natural history, together with old paintings, maps, prints, and photos. Definitely worth a look are the city's original charter, signed by Oliver Cromwell and King Charles II, and the civic sword presented by Queen Elizabeth I. *Castle Lane, at Nicholas St., Limerick, County Limerick.* ☎ *061/417826. Free admission. Tues–Sat 10am–1pm and 2:15–5pm.*

FREE ➔ **The '75' Gallery** Okay, so you'll need to hold your breath to navigate this tiny space, but Limerick's smallest gallery makes up for a lack of room with a ton of enthusiasm. You won't find any scenic landscapes featuring cliffs or sheep here so don't bring grandma, but you will find some edgy works by new, young artists. *75 O'Connell St.* ☎ *061/315650. 10am–5:30pm Mon–Fri. Free admission.*

Performing Arts

The **Belltable Arts Centre** (69 O'Connell St.; ☎ **061/319866**) is Limerick's cultural hub, with a theater, cinema, and exhibition area for a variety of artistic endeavors. You can see anything from opera to dance to poetry recitals—not to mention screenings of international films, lectures, and art exhibitions. You can have a drink in their coffee shop or a drink in their bar; all in all the Belltable is a great place to spend an evening. Check out www.belltable.ie for scheduling details. Recent events have included a screening of the award-winning film *Me and You and Everyone We Know* and a stage adaptation of Sue Townsend's beloved Adrian Mole diaries.

Playing Outside

BICYCLING   Outside Limerick city is Ireland's most important archaeological site, Lough Gur, occupied continuously since Neolithic times. Excavated and studied by John Hunt of **Hunt Museum** (p. 326) fame, Lough Gur is home to Ireland's own Stonehenge—the Grange Stone Circle, plus ruins of homes over a thousand years old and a 4,500-year-old tomb serving as a communal grave. In the middle of all this history is a beautiful lake amid hectares of green. It makes a perfect day trip out of Limerick, but you'll have to be in good shape—Lough Gur is 11km (7 miles) away and it's not all flat terrain. Rent a bike from **Emerald Cycles** (1 Patrick St.; ☎ **061/416983**) for around €15 per day. It is usually a bit cheaper at **McMahon's Cycle World** (25 Roches St.; ☎ **061/415202**). If you're not keen on bicycling all the way to Lough Gur, there are plenty of country roads nearer to the city. Pick up a map of bicycling routes at the **Limerick Tourism Centre** (p. 318).

GO-KARTING   The **Kilcornan Karting Racetrack** is opened Monday to Sunday all year and features a floodlit track, so the weather never need stop you indulging in some serious fun. In Limerick for a bachelor party or birthday? The track loves catering to large groups; just call them ahead of time to check if there's room. (Kilcornan, County Limerick; ☎ **061/393728.**)

HORSEBACK RIDING County Limerick's fertile fields provide good turf for horseback riding. Rates run about €22 per hour. The Clonshire Equestrian Centre (Adare, County Limerick; ☎ 061/396770; www.clonshire.com) does the works including treks into the forest and lessons in cross-country riding, dressage, and jumping.

SAILING The nearest place to make use of the River Shannon is actually across the border in Killaloe at the **University of Limerick Activity and Sailing Centre** (Killaloe, County Clare; ☎ **061/376622**). Catch Bus Éireann route 323 or 345 from Limerick to Killaloe for sailing, windsurfing, or canoeing (see "The Midlands," p. 391, for more details).

Shopping

Limerick is far, far better for shopping than some other towns of its size, mostly thanks to the sizeable university crowd. For cool street wear that isn't overly slavish to of-the-minute fashion, try **A-Wear** (13 Bedford Rd.; ☎ **061/416117**), chock-full of wearable and well-cut clothes by the likes of Irish designer John Rocha among others. Their shoe collection is good, too. Need something that screams "teenybopper" for a fun night out? Try **Swamp** (9A Williams St.; ☎ **061/410904**), where you'll find an abundance of little tank tops and colorful combats for that pre-baby

Britney Spears look. For one-stop shopping, look no further than **Arthur's Quay** (City Centre; ☎ **061/419888**), Limerick's very own Americanized shopping mall where you'll find specialty stores like **Golden Discs** (Unit 5, Arthur's Quay; ☎ **061/418877**). Here, they stock the latest chart hits and the most obscure classical music, and they're happy to fulfill special requests. Other autonomous shops you should check out include the aptly named **Wacky Shoes** (O'Connell St.; ☎ **061/318660**), where you'll want to buy all the weird and wonderful stilettos and sneakers on offer, like those from the Argentine range Spiral (think pink and yellow chunky skater shoes—hot!). For all your stationery, newspaper, and related needs, the most friendly little bookstore in Limerick is the **Paper Mill** (Patrick St.; no phone), where you can buy postcards, guide books, and gifts. As a bonus, the staff is so great and willing to answer any questions you might have about the city. For a really authentic Irish experience, check out the **Milk Market** (Market Quarter; ☎ **061/317522**) on a Saturday (although it's open weekdays, too). Originally formed in the 1830s, the Milk Market functioned as a place to sell produce from nearby farms, plus fresh cheese and milk (hence the name). The market still thrives as a place to bargain for great local food, but today you can buy homemade beauty products, clothes, and maybe a little something to take home to mom/dad/boyfriend/girlfriend. Plus, it's unbeatable for gossip and banter.

Ennis

Ennis is best known as a gateway to the coast—most buses and trains going to the Burren or out to Doolin pass through this vaguely dreary town. Ennis is Clare's principal town, with a whopping 16,000 residents, but it's unfortunately landlocked and there's not really much of interest compared to nearby towns. No one's ever accused Ennis

of being a cultural hub or a town with great restaurants or nightlife. Really, Ennis is a pit stop on the way to more exciting places in Clare and beyond. If you have to stay more than 1 night, there are a couple of decent pubs, but you'll find mostly locals and few travelers as all the backpackers have moved on to the Cliffs of Moher.

Getting There

Lucky for you, Ennis is one of the most reachable towns in Ireland thanks to its central location. **Bus Éireann** (☎ 061/313333; www.buseireann.ie) runs from Doolin, Limerick, the Shannon Airport, and even Dublin if you're up for a long journey. If you're near the station all the times are clearly posted, but otherwise you can call or go online. **Irish Rail** (www.irishrail.ie; ☎ 061/315-555) runs trains to Limerick, Waterford, Killarney, Tralee, and elsewhere.

Getting Around

Ennis was not built around a grid; in fact, the town is quite confusing, with narrow, winding streets. To get to the town center from the bus and train station, walk down Station Road making a right on O'Connell Street. You'll come to the town square and its statue of hero Daniel O'Connell. From here, streets like High Street and Abbey Street jut out—this is where you'll find pubs and eateries. If you're feeling lazy or lost, call a taxi, like **James Moylan Taxi Service** (2 Orchard Lane; ☎ 065/20441) or **Michael Casey Cabs** (2 Tulla Rd.; ☎ 065/22230).

Basics

TOURIST OFFICE The **Ennis Tourist Office** can be found at O'Connell Square (☎ 065/28366). Opening hours are 9am to 9pm during the summer. From October to May, it's open 9am to 6pm Monday to Friday and 10am to 6pm Sunday.

INTERNET In the late 1990s, Ennis won a $21-million prize from eircom, Ireland's chief telecom provider, to invest in technology to update the town. Almost every home has free broadband access, and children as young as 4 are learning to be proficient computer users. As a result of this tech boom, there are a few really good Internet cafes in Ennis. Try **Dimension X** (4 Lower Market St.; ☎ 065/689-3767), where you can get online for

under €5 per hour, plus indulge in some competitive Xbox play if that's your sort of thing. The seats are luxurious leather and the whole place seems modern and cutting edge. Cozier is the cutely named **Coffee and Bytes** (37 Lower Market St.; ☎ 065/686-8359), which charges €1.50 per half-hour and offers refreshments.

RECOMMENDED WEBSITES For anything you could want to know about Ennis, from walking tours of the town to a What's On guide, go to www.ennis.ie.

Festivals

The only festival of note is the annual Fleadh Nua (www.fleadhnua.com), which happens over the last weekend of May and features traditional music, dancing, and storytelling. The festival celebrates Irish traditions and promotes use of the Gaelic language—its organizer Domhnall Ó Loingsigh has won awards for his efforts to preserve the native tongue in County Clare.

Sleeping

→ **Abbey Tourist Hostel** The location of the Abbey hostel is ideal: Slap bang in the town center, with the River Fergus running right past the windows. The building itself is mightily swish as it used to be the so-called "County Club" in the 18th century. For a hostel, it seems pretty luxe, especially as it's just been renovated. For the price, you get breakfast thrown in and use of the roomy self-catering facilities. *Harmony Row. ☎ 065/682-2620. www.abbeytouristhostel.com. Dorm €14–€16, double €20 per person. Kitchen, luggage storage*

→ **Lakeside Country Lodge** Just 5 minutes outside Ennis, Lakeside looks like something out of a children's picture book: From the front windows of this little yellow gingerbread house you can see horses grazing in a field, and from the back, oh-so-cute views of Killone Lake. George and Joan Quinn run

Lakeside and offer a taxi service to and from the airport or a tour of the area. *Barntick, Clarecastle.* ☎ *065/683-8488. Double* €*62. In room: Coffee/tea facilities, hair dryer.*

Eating

→ **Hal Pino's** IRISH   Derek Halpin's jam-packed eatery is located above a bar in the centre of town, so you can have a drink while perusing the compact menu. It's all about local and regional cuisine here, so everything is fresh, like the Clare potatoes that come with the roast rack of Burren lamb. Try one of the special house dishes, like the seafood platter. The set menu is pretty good bang for your buck... well, euro. *7 High St.* ☎ *065/684-0011. www.halpinos.com. Average entree* €*14. Daily 5–10:30pm (Sun to 9:30pm).*

→ **Town Hall Café** CAFE   This modern bistro may be next to the Old Ground Hotel, but don't go thinking it's nothing more than a dull hotel eatery. The decor is hip, with big colorful paintings and oversize potted plants. You can stop in for morning coffee, lunch, tea, or dinner, where the menu tends toward continental fare like goat's cheese or steak in a mustard sauce. The desserts are luxe and stuffed full of calories. *O'Connell St.* ☎ *065/682-8127. www.flynnhotels.com. Reservations recommended for lunch and dinner. Open from 10am daily.*

Partying

Ennis is not party central. For a trad pub where the occasional sing-song breaks out, try **Tailor Quigley's** (Auburn Lodge, Galway Rd.; ☎ **065/682-1247**), named after a famous tailor immortalized in the song "Spancill Hill." It's a good place to stop for a carvery lunch on the way to Galway on the N18. Probably the oldest pub in Ennis, the **Usual Place** (Market St.; ☎ **065/682-0515**) is beautiful to look at, its exterior crafted from hand-cut stone and rustic brick, and its interior filled with black-and-white photos. The Usual Place is popular with tourists and natives alike; you

can usually spot a few local "characters" propping up the bar.

Sightseeing

The only real spot worth checking out here is the **Ennis Friary** (Abbey St.; ☎ **065/682-9100**), dating from the 13th century and featuring cool sculptures of Catholic figures like St. Francis, the Virgin Mary, and Jesus. At one time, there were 1,000 people living here, both monks and students, flagellating themselves and generally living ascetic lives. Make sure to take a look at the McMahon tomb, which is beautifully carved.

Playing Outside

BICYCLING   Want to do something really different this vacay? Ennis is the starting point for the **ExperiencePlus** bicycling tour of the west coast of Ireland. Over the course of 10 days, you get use of a cycle, hotel rooms, breakfasts and most dinners, plus any ferry trips or incidentals. You cycle from Ennis to Galway, seeing sights like the Cliffs of Moher and the Aran Islands on the way. Sounds amazing, right? Well, yes, because it costs €2,310, but if your parents are feeling generous, it's probably the best way to see Ireland. See www.experienceplus.com for details of the itinerary.

Shopping

If you want to buy something out of the ordinary to take home for your brother or sister that isn't in a can marked "Guinness," check out **Custy's Traditional Music Shop** (Francis St.; ☎ **065/682-1727**). You know those fiddles, concertinas, flutes, banjos, bodhrans, and whistles you've been hearing almost nightly in pubs around the country? You can buy your own instruments and make your own Celtic music. Plus, the staff at Custy's is comprised of cool, weird hippies who know about all the concerts going on around Clare, so you might as well stop in and say hello. If only for its name, head to

Celtic Pzazz (3 Parnell St.; ☎ 065/682-1791), where you can buy sterling silver rings plus jewelry made from semi-precious stones. There are a few cute, small boutiques in Ennis, like Nozomi (71a O'Connell St.; ☎ 065/682-8655) where Mary Ryan sells shoes and accessories like funky gold stilettos with a purse to match. Not that you'd have anywhere in Ennis to wear them!

Doolin

Tiny Doolin is renowned worldwide as the traditional music capital of Ireland. It's therefore a major tourist draw, both with middle-aged couples in buses and European hippies wearing hemp and thumbing rides. Situated on a popular tourist trail that includes the Burren and the Cliffs of Moher, Doolin is in essence a one-horse fishing village. Most of the year it is fairly quiet but in the summer the pubs gets packed out with Americans guzzling gifts from the few local shops. *Warning:* Don't get stuck in Doolin without cash. The nearest ATM is in Lisdoonvarna, 6km (3³/₄ miles) away, which feels like 100km (62 miles) when you're breaking in new shoes. If you do make this fatal error and you're starving, go to O'Connor's pub, the only place in town that accepts credit cards.

Getting There

It's not easy getting to Doolin—most people exploring this part of Ireland do so on a tour bus or in a rented car. Bus Éireann (☎ 061/313333; www.buseireann.ie) stops on the only road running through Doolin a couple times a day, taking you to Galway, Ennis, and nearby towns like Lisdoonvarna. Don't leave it 'til the last minute to check the schedule or you might find yourself waiting for 4 long hours when you've finished exploring the town.

Getting Around

You can rent a bike at Doolin Bike Store (Fisherstreet, next to Aille River Hostel; ☎ 065/707-4282) for €10 per day. They're open daily from 9am to 8pm. If you need a taxi, call Dial A Cab on ☎ 086/812-7049, and Mick, Noel, or John will do short- or long-distance drops.

Orientation

Doolin only has one street, Fisherstreet, running east to west through the Upper and Lower villages. The Upper Village is slightly inland, where you'll find two pubs and a hostel. The Lower Village contains a couple more hostels, including Paddy Moloney's, as well as a few shops and pubs.

TOURIST OFFICE   The nearest tourist office is at the Cliffs of Moher (☎ 065/81171), open April through October from 9:30am to 5:30pm, although most of the hostels have information offices and are good sources for everything you'd need to know.

INTERNET ACCESS   Doolin isn't the most technologically advanced place on earth. You can beg to check your e-mail at the Doolin Activity Lodge and B&B—you can't miss it; it's the biggest building in town and right in the middle of Fisherstreet between Lower and Upper Village. Call them at ☎ 065/707-4888.

RECOMMENDED WEBSITES   Try www.doolin-tourism.com for comprehensive info on everything from accommodation to local artists. While far more budget looking, www.doolinireland.net has the best list of links for other sites, like those of local shops and B&Bs.

Festivals

The Micho Russell Festival (☎ 065/707-4595; www.michorussellweekend.ie) of traditional music is annual, and held over the last weekend in February. Micho himself was a famous Irish musician who died in 1994 after a car crash. Expect concerts, food, and wine

Get Spelunking

Ireland is so riddled with caves that in some parts of the country you can hardly swing a flashlight without shining a light into some deep, subterranean cavern. This means little to most people except to watch where they're going, but for cavers it's heavenly. If you're one of those, here's a quick rundown of good places for caving in Ireland but, we beg of you, use common sense. Don't wander off on your own without appropriate experience or without letting people know where you are. Once you've sorted all that out, well, here's where to go underground.

County Clare is one of the best regions for caving, and, in particular, the quaint area around Doolin is a bit of a cavers haven, riddled with potholes and caverns. The Poll na gColm cave, just northeast of Lisdoonvarna, has caverns wandering for miles through underground passageways, spectacular vaults, and natural wonders. There's also the Aillwee Cave (p. 337). Those who like their caves free of charge but under water will want to explore the Green Holes of Doolin, just north of Doolin's harbour; but if you want to see what awaits you, stop by the area known as "Hell," where the roof of a cave has worn away and you can see the water rushing through the open cavern below.

Before you head out, stop by the Doolin tourist office and pick up brochures from local caving guides, as well as useful maps.

Clare's not the only place to head underground; in County Kerry the Crag Caves are believed to be more than a million years old, not that the locals knew—the caves were only discovered in 1983. Guided tours will take you through the well-lighted caverns for a view of the stalactites and caverns—it's interesting, but, well, there's a gift shop. Which should tell you most of what you need to know about the place.

For something slightly less family-friendly, head to the Dingle Peninsula, where Traberg Beach is a wonder at low-tide, with wave-sculpted sandstone shapes and small sea caves lined with veins of Crystalline quartz. It's a magical place. And there's no gift shop.

In Northern Ireland, County Fermanagh holds the gorgeous Marble Arch Caves about 12 miles from Enniskillen. These extraordinary caves hold underground rivers, winding passageways, enormous stalactites, and hidden chambers. It's all very touristy, though, as electrical boat tours take you underground, while guides give you the Cave 101 spiel. And it's not cheap (£6 adults, £4 students). But it's still pretty cool.

Wherever you decide to cave, check out www.cavingireland.org for information before you go.

receptions and dancing sessions. On the Sunday, an anniversary Mass is held at the Doolin Church in memory of musicians who have passed away. Recent performers have included Coir Cuil Aodh and Liam Og O Flynn. You probably haven't heard of them but their names are fun.

Sleeping

→ **Aille River Hostel**   Situated on a quiet road next to the Aille River, this hostel has three private rooms as well as large dorms that can sleep 30 between them. One huge perk of this hostel is free laundry facilities, which are key after a day bicycling to the Cliffs of Moher. You can check your e-mail but it's a little expensive at €8 per hour. The hostel is open all year except the last half of January and the first half of February, so if you plan on staying during the off season, this is your best bet. *Aille River.* ☎ *065/707-4260. Double €16; dorm €13. Amenities: Internet, laundry.*

➔ **Aran View House Hotel** A huge, sprawling Georgian building surrounded by coarse grasses and perched on a cliff overlooking the rough ocean. It may look forbidding from the outside but once you get in, you'll find the Linnane family's hotel is just waiting to throw its warm arms around you. Yes, the decor could do with updating, but the rooms have sea views and are probably tidier than your room at home. Guests are largely honeymooning Americans or golfers who fill out the restaurant and bar on a nightly basis. *Doolin.* ☎ *065/707-4061. Double €55–€70 per person. Amenities: Restaurant, bar. In room: TV, hair dryer.*

➔ **Churchfield B&B** Open year-round and run by the easygoing Fitzgeralds, the Churchfield is a short walk from the local pubs and provides a decent bed at a decent price. Opened in 1981, but refurbished a couple years ago, Churchfield benefits from large beds, airy bay windows, and good-natured staff. Maeve's breakfast will set you up for the day. *Doolin.* ☎ *065/707-4209. Double €60. In room: TV, coffee/tea facilities, hair dryer.*

➔ **Paddy Moloney's Doolin Hostel** Paddy and Josephine Moloney lovingly run this well-known hostel, which is luckily situated right opposite the local bus stop. The rooms are simple but clean and comfortable, and the hostel shop and bureau de change are a godsend in such a tiny town. The hostel is the closest to the Cliffs of Moher so it makes a good base for exploring. You also have use of a hard tennis court as a guest here. *Fisherstreet.* ☎ *065/707-4421. www.doolinhostel.com. Dorm €14. Amenities: Internet; Bureau de change; shop; tennis court.*

Eating

There are only a few spots in town to get a decent meal. If you've made the mistake of showing up in Doolin armed with a credit card and a prayer, you can eat lunch at **O'Connor's** (see "Partying," below), if you can find a seat. They have all the usual pub staples like fish and chips and lasagna, served up in hearty portions to excitable crowds of tourists. If you're in Doolin in the summer, you might be tempted to sit on the outdoor benches across from O'Connor's to eat your lunch. Don't if you can help it, as the heat makes the river smell extremely vile. Also, you'll get about five American couples coming up to you asking to take a picture of them in front of the O'Connor's sign because their surname happens to be the same. For something a little more exciting, check out **Bruach na hAille** (Fisherstreet; ☎ **065/74120**), open from March through October. Main courses can be pricey, around €15, but try the excellent vegetarian tortillas. They do a three-course cheap menu before 7pm so get there nice and early. *Remember:* Bring cash as they won't take your Visa card. For a really reasonably priced sandwich, head to **Doolin Café** (Fisherstreet; ☎ **065/707-4795**). It's kind of hit or miss as to when they'll be open as they keep fairly irregular hours, but if you get lucky, you'll find excellent, freshly prepared fish courses for about €12, as well as options for meat-lovers and veggies. If you feel like a short walk—a little bit uphill—head 20 minutes out of the main town to the **Doolin Craft Gallery and Restaurant** (next to the cemetery; ☎ **065/74309**). In the summer you can sit in the garden out back, and order a salad or sandwich and a delicious pastry for dessert.

Partying

There are three pubs in Doolin, and they're all basically interchangeable, with live music sessions every night at around 9 and on

Sunday afternoons. **O'Connor's** (Lower Village; ☎ 065/74168) is the most crowded of the bunch, and it's hard to find even room to stand in the summer. The decor is kitschy and the staff friendly, while many of the travelers have been known to pull out their own instruments and jam along with the trad bands that show up daily. 🎬 Best **McGann's** (☎ 065/707-4133) and **McDermott's** (☎ 065/707-4328) are both in the Upper Village part of town, and are less frequented by tourists than O'Connor's. They're worth a visit, though, as the music is just as good up here as in the Lower Village. McDermott's is the bar most popular with locals (all 200 of them in Doolin), while McGann's has won national awards for its trad sessions.

Sightseeing

The 🎬 Best **Cliffs of Moher** are totally breathtaking and must be seen. Located in the parish of Liscannor about 8km (5 miles) from Doolin, the cliffs rise 120m (400ft.) above the Atlantic Ocean, extending for 8km (5 miles) to a height of 210m (700 ft.). From O'Brien's Tower, a round stone observation tower at about midpoint of the cliffs, you can see the Aran Islands, Galway Bay, and the distant Maumturk Mountains and the Twelve Bens in Connemara. Living in the Cliffs are 30,000 birds, including Atlantic Puffins, hawks, and gulls. You might recognize the Cliffs of Moher from the 1987 film *The Princess Bride*, in which they were known as the Cliffs of Insanity. Unfortunately, the smog-spewing tour buses arrive at Moher by around 9am, so the best time to see these natural wonders is first thing in the morning. Otherwise, sights to see around Doolin include **Doonagore Castle,** 3km (2 miles) south of town on the coastal road, an atmospheric fortress dating from the 15th century with great views of Doolin and the Aran Islands, especially at sunset. There's also **Ballinalacken Castle,** 5km north of Doolin on the road to Fanore, a tower also built around the 15th century. If you climb to the top you'll see amazing views of the Burren.

Playing Outside

BOAT TRIPS   You can take a cruise on the *Moher Princess,* skippered by PJ Garrihy. Get on the boat at Doolin and view the famous cliffs from the water. You'll also approach Galway Bay and the southern tip of the Burren. Check out the schedule at www.cliffs-of-moher-cruises.com, or call PJ at ☎ 065/707-5949. Prices are about €20–€25 per person.

CAVING   Doolin is a great site for caving and diving enthusiasts. The Doolin Cave System is home to Poll an Ionain, the cave with the largest free hanging stalactite in the world, a sight to behold at 7m (23-ft.) long. Local guides will take first-time cavers down underground, where among other things you'll see bear hibernation chambers and rivers flowing through the limestone. For info on how to get down there, talk to Niall or Deirdre at the **Doolin Activity Lodge** (☎ 065/707-4888).

HIKING   The Burren Way links Doolin with the Cliffs of Moher, and makes a great 8km (5-mile) walk or bike ride. For a map of the entire Way, go to Paddy Moloney's Hostel (see "Sleeping," above).

WATERSPORTS   Diving and snorkeling are also popular around here, especially around Crab Island or the underground caves known as the Green Holes of Doolin, discovered in the 1980s. Again, talk to the staff at the Activity Lodge (see "Caving," above).

Shopping

With an exterior resembling a pink marshmallow and a thatched roof that wouldn't look out of place in Shakespearean times, **The Sweater Shop** on lower Fisherstreet is a total photo op for all the grandparents in baseball caps crowded outside. It sells all sorts of wool clothing, from, of course, sweaters to huge thick socks for hiking and gift items. Next door is **The Village Crafts Shop** (☎ 065/707-4633), where you'll find something for everyone on your list, from your mom (pashmina) to your roommate (cheap Ireland shot glasses). Proprietors Guss and Maeve Fitzgerald also own the Church-field B&B (see "Sleeping," above).

The Burren

This extraordinary landscape of the region looks like something from another world. 📺 Best The **Burren,** from the Irish *bhoireann* meaning a rocky place, combines desolation and beauty in a killer cocktail. Massive sheets of rock jut and undulate through lakes and ponds in a never-ending moonscape and, despite the rocky soil, exotic orchids, ferns, and violets call out to butterflies from the dirt. The Burren animals are also unusual: The pine marten, stoat, and badger, all rare in the rest of Ireland, trot around here.

It got its strange and unforgettable appearance 300 million years ago when layers of shells and sediment were deposited under a tropical sea. Many millions of years later, those subterranean layers were thrust above the surface by erosion and poor pre-historic farming methods, and since then it's been battered by the Irish rain and winds, producing all that you see today. About 7,000 years ago, when this landscape was already very old indeed, humans first began to leave their mark here, in the form of Stone

Hanging Out

The best thing about **Clare's Rock Hostel** (see "Sleeping," p. 336), the best place to stay around here, is the reasonably priced aromatherapy massage you can get after a full day of tiring hiking and exploring. For the price of a few drinks (€15–€25), residents can get a back or full body massage. It's completely worth it, especially as there isn't much to do out here in the wilderness.

Age burial monuments, such as the famed **Poulnabrone Dolmen** and **Gleninsheen wedge tomb.**

Getting There

The only really reliable way to get here from points south and east is by rental car—it's rare that tourists get here any other way. However, **Barratt Coach Tours** (☎ 061/384-800) will drop you at the best hostel in the area (Clare's Rock Hostel, see "Sleeping," below). It departs from the Limerick and Ennis tourist offices on Thursdays and Saturdays. Call ahead to book and find out times. If you're coming to the Burren from Galway, **Bus Éireann** (☎ 061/313333; www.bus eireann.ie) stops at Bellharbour, from where the hostel staff will pick you up if you arrange it. There are usually three scheduled stops here in the summer and one in the winter.

Getting Around

The best way to get around the Burren is on foot, that is, if you want to explore the Burren Way. It runs for 35km (23 miles), but of course you don't have to do it all. Start at the Cliffs of Moher by Doolin and walk to Ballyvaughan if you're up to it, and you'll see some of the most amazing views in Ireland.

If you've got a car, one of the best ways to explore the Burren is to take the R480. The corkscrewlike road leads in a series of curves from **Corofin** through gorgeous scenery to **Ballyvaughan,** a sweet little village overlooking the blue waters of Galway Bay.

Basics

TOURIST OFFICE   Check out the **Burren Centre** in Kilfenora, which is reachable by

Roads to Nowhere

"Green roads" are old highways crisscrossing the Burren landscape in inaccessible areas. Most of them are unpaved roads created during the Famine as make-work projects for starving locals, although some are ancient roads whose origins nobody knows. They all make great hiking routes—look out for the signposts.

bus from Ennis, Galway, or Doolin on route 337. Its hours are 10am to 5pm from March through October and 9:30am to 6pm from June to October. It costs €3 to get in and €2 for students, and you'll find all the info you'll need on the famous rocky landscape.

RECOMMENDED WEBSITES Burren Beo, or the Beautiful Burren, is a very polished website—nay, "interactive interpretive centre"—set up by two creative Irish professionals, one a multimedia journalist and one with a PhD in agriculture. www.burrenbeo. com is really helpful, with all sorts of dates for walks, planned itineraries, and inevitably a shopping section.

Sleeping

→ **Clare's Rock Hostel** Employing half the population of Carron, Clare's Rock Hostel is a great place to base yourself while visiting the Burren. It doesn't take credit cards, but it is welcoming and cozy, providing bike rentals on top of the excellent massage service (see "Hanging Out," above). From your dorm room window you'll get views over a lake. If you call ahead, a staff member will collect you from whatever bus stop you arrive at. *Carron, County Clare. ☎ 065/708-9129. www.clares rock.com. Dorm rooms €12; private rooms €13–€15 per person. Amenities: Bike rental, Internet, massage.*

→ **Gregans Castle Hotel** For the absolute opposite of a hostel experience, and only if you've suddenly cashed in your inheritance, head to the eminently luxurious Gregans Castle in the tiny hamlet of Ballyvaughan. A divine old country house overlooking a lush valley and Galway bay. Definitely eat dinner at the modern Irish restaurant, but don't go expecting a big night out afterwards. Ballyvaughan is miniscule. There's nothing to do after sunset and there are no TVs in the rooms. Your best option is to grab yourself a Guinness in Simon's Corkscrew Bar. *Gregans Castle, Ballyvaughan, County Clare. ☎ 065/707-7005. www.gregans. ie. Doubles €180–€370. Amenities: Restaurant, bar. In room: Coffee/tea facilities, hair dryer.*

Eating

→ **Bofey Quinn's** SEAFOOD/GRILL A chill pub-restaurant in the center of Corofin. Take your pick from lobster, fresh wild salmon, and cod, as well as a whole load of steaks, chops, mixed grills, and also pizza. Pub-grub lunches are available throughout the day. From May to mid-September, Mondays to Thursdays from 7:30 to 9:30pm, there's a harpist to serenade you. *Main St., Corofin, County Clare. ☎ 065/683-7321. Main courses €6–€9; lobster €35. Jan–Mar and Oct–Dec daily noon–9pm; Apr–Sept daily 10:30am– 10pm.*

→ **Trina Cheile** CONTINENTAL A cozy eatery in the middle of Ballyvaughan village offering meals made with the freshest Irish ingredients at affordable prices. On the menu are sirloin; mussels and linguini; whole crab; beef curry; filet of salmon; roast lamb with anchovies, garlic, and rosemary; and roast chicken. Vegetarian options are also available. *Main St., Ballyvaughan, County Clare.*

Lookin' for Love in All the Wrong Places . . .

If this is you, get yourself to Lisdoonvarna. This little County Clare spa town lives for love. There's a Matchmaker Pub on the main street and two towns-folk officially call themselves matchmakers (Willie Daly, a horse dealer, and James White, a hotelier—wink, wink).

Every autumn, the entire town gets involved in the matchmaking business, setting up the monthlong Lisdoonvarna Matchmaking Festival. Thousands of lovelorn singletons stream upon the town looking for "The One." It may sound like a pot of potential partners but, be warned, most would-be lovers are in the 40+ age range. Perfect if you've always dreamed of settling down with an Irish farmer.

To find out more about Lisdoonvarna and its love of love, visit its mar-velously pink website www.matchmakerireland.com.

☎ 065/707-7029. Reservations recommended. Fixed-price 2-course dinner €18, 3-course dinner €23; dinner main courses €13–€21. May–Sept Mon–Sat 6–10:45pm; Sun 12:30–3:30pm

Partying

→ **Vaughn's** This is a music pub with a countrywide reputation for attracting excellent traditional bands and stellar Irish dancing. Summers are the busiest times (things quiet down quite a bit in the off season). There's a barn next door, which hosts dancing on Thursday and Sunday. The trad Irish food ain't bad either. Main St., Kilfenora, County Clare. ☎ 065/708-8004.

Sightseeing

There are some fantastic megalithic ruins in the Burren, the most famous being Poulnabrone, about 6.5km (4 miles) north-west of Carron. You'll find loads of tombs, forts, and other ancient stone formations. Also make sure you visit the Aillwee Cave.

→ **Aillwee Cave** This mysterious cave was literally stumbled upon by a local farmer looking after his sheep 50 years ago. What he found was a huge cavern reaching almost a kilometer into the mountain. Prepare to see astounding sights, including a frozen water-fall and bear pits dug out over time by brown

bears (extinct in Ireland for over 10,000 years). Guided tours, lasting about 30 min-utes, take place all the time. There's also a cafe and shop, a farmhouse cheese-making enterprise, and an apiary where honey is pro-duced. Ballyvaughan, County Clare. ☎ 065/707-7036. www.aillweecave.ie. Admission €10 adults, €8 students. Daily 10am–5:30pm. Closed mid-Nov to Feb.

→ **The Burren Centre** When it's raining large domestic animals, this is a fine place to acquaint yourself with the local geology, flora, and fauna of the Burren without actu-ally having to go outside. Lots of films, land-scape models, and interpretive displays show you what's out the window. There's also a tearoom, and a shop stocked with locally made crafts and products. R476 to Kilfenora, County Clare. ☎ 065/708-8030. Admission €5.50 adults, €4.50 students. Oct and Mar–May daily 10am–5pm; June–Sept daily 9:30am–6pm. Closed Nov–Feb.

→ **Burren Exposure** A compact multi-media exhibition center providing a stunning intro to the Burren. Intelligent and well put together, it's a bit like the Burren Center but better. Time here will be well spent. Galway Rd. (N67), .4km (¼ mile) north of Ballyvaughan, County Clare. ☎ 065/707-7277. Admission €5 adults, €3.50 students. 1 week before Easter to Oct daily 10am–6pm (last admission 5:20pm).

FREE →**Corcomroe Abbey** Set, jewel-like, in a languid, green valley bounded by rolling hills, the jagged ruins of this Cistercian abbey may well make you gasp with pleasure. The abbey was founded in 1194 by Donal Mór O'Brien, and his grandson, a former king of Thomond, is entombed in the abbey's northern wall. Nice. *1.5km (1 mile) walk inland from Bellharbour, County Clare. Free admission.*

FREE → **Glenisheen Wedge Tomb** One of the country's best-known pre-historic gravesites, Glenisheen is over 5,000 years old and thought to have been a grave for many people. In 1930, a local boy found a beautifully preserved beaten gold *torc* (a heavy gold necklace) from 700 B.C. No, he didn't get to keep it. It's now on display in the National Museum in Dublin. But, keep your eyes open. You never know. *R480 just south of the Aillwee Caves, County Clare. Free admission. Daily 10am–6pm.*

FREE →**Poulnabrone Dolmen** Another ancient tomb. This one was excavated in the 1980s, and 16 people were found inside. Don't worry, they'd been dead about 5,000 years. With an absolutely huge dolmen "stone table" surrounded by a pavement of stones, the greatest mystery remains how all these stones were moved and lifted into place—the capstone alone weighs 5 tons. *R480 8km (5 miles) south of the Aillwee Caves, County Clare. Free admission. Daily 10am–6pm.*

FREE → **Spa Wells Centre** Ireland's only working spa is a Victorian complex, featuring a massage room, sauna, and mineral baths, all centered around the stinking sulfur-laced mineral waters, drawn from an illuminated well. Old docs once said these waters were good for rheumatic complaints. Have a glass if you want, but, be warned, this isn't Evian. *Kincora Rd., Lisdoonvarna, County Clare. ☎ 065/707-4023. Free admission. June–Oct daily 10am–6pm. Closed Nov–May.*

Playing Outside

The Burren community has its very own **Outdoor Education Centre** (Bell Harbour, North Clare; **065/78033;** burroec@tinet.ie), purpose built for all sorts of activities and pursuits around the rocky landscape. Think you've done it all? Here they offer canoeing, orienteering, team challenges, hill walking, caving, abseiling, boardsailing, sailing, and environmental studies, so we dare you to get bored. Try some caving or abseiling as the peaks and crevices of the Burren are unlike anywhere else in the world. Want something slightly alternative and un-Irish while in the Burren? Well, there's always the **Burren Yoga and Meditation Centre** (Cappaghmore, Kinvara, County Galway; ☎ **091/637-680;** www.burrenyoga.com), a popular and comfortable yoga retreat in Cappaghmore. What could be better than some yoga and meditation on the warm, flat rocks overlooking the Atlantic? The center is quite remote and definitely a hot spot for Euro hippies, but an unparalleled spot for relaxation. If you catch a bus or train to Gort or Galway, you can get a cheap taxi here. If you're driving, there are all sorts of maps on their website

Fanore

Fanore is completely adorable—a tiny village north of Doolin, it seems untouched by tourism and, well, modern life. There's one local grocery store, which is also the newsagent, post office, and tackle shop; a pretty stretch of beach; and a few vestiges of the Ireland of the past. You can even swim with the few locals off Fanore beach, which is safer than others in the area, but can be dangerous due to the tides. Because it is really such a miniature town, there isn't too much to do or a reason to stay the night, but if you're driving through, Fanore is the perfect place to spend a sunny afternoon.

Getting There

You basically need a rental car to get to Fanore, as **Bus Éireann** (☎ 061/313333; www.buseireann.ie) doesn't regularly stop here, but you can request a stop here on route 423, the Ennis/Doolin/Galway route.

TOURIST OFFICE For the nearest tourist office providing info on the region, you'll need to stop at nearby Lisdoonvarna at the **Burren Smokehouse Visitor Centre** (Doolin Rd.; ☎ 065/707-4432). It is open 10am to 6pm, and even later in the summer.

Sleeping

The Bridge Hostel (☎ 065/76134) is so cute, and its staff so friendly, you'll want to rearrange your schedule so you can crash for a night here. The hostel is right by the river, so you have great views of both the water

and the Burren's rocky scenery. The Bridge Hostel is open from March to October and charges €10 for a night in a dorm, although they don't take credit cards. You can even have a whole meal here for around €6—bargain.

Eating & Partying

It goes without saying that little Fanore is not a culinary hot spot. Unless you want to bring your own sandwich or buy supplies at the local shop, Fitzpatrick's, right on the seaside, you'll be eating at the only pub in town, called **O'Donoghue's** (just outside the town itself; ☎ 065/76104). The food is nothing to write home about but if you eat there, you'll be able to have a pint or two, listen to the trad music, and chat with the other visitors—yes, it gets busy in the summer; it's one of the few places around! There's also the **Admiral's Rest Seafood Restaurant** (☎ 065/707-6105), which won't win a Michelin star but which is decently priced and doubles as a B&B.

Lahinch

If you're a surfer, you may have heard of 📺 (Best) **Lahinch,** which is considered one of the best places to hang ten in Ireland. The water might be cold—okay, freezing—but there are a bunch of shops lining the beachfront that will rent you a wetsuit along with your board. The beaches in Lahinch are scenic and the town offers some cute B&Bs and typical seaside-town-style amusement arcades. Lahinch is definitely a sweet little town to spend a day or two if you don't mind being one of hordes of summertime tourists.

Getting There

Bus Éireann (☎ 061/313333; www.bus eireann.ie) provides service from Doolin to Lahinch via Route 15 twice a day. The trip takes approximately half an hour.

Basics

INTERNET ACCESS You won't find anywhere better than **Raphael's Internet and Ice Cream Café** on Main Street (☎ 065/708-1020) to check your e-mail. Not only can you peruse the Internet for €5 per hour, but you can do it with a chocolate cone in your hand. Heaven.

Sleeping

You could definitely do worse than **Lahinch Hostel** (Church St.; ☎ 065/708-1040; http://homepage.eircom.net/patshostel/hostel/index.htm), with its 55 clean and comfortable rooms. Lahinch Hostel hosts international surf enthusiasts, who clean off their wetsuits at the outside facilities and store them in the secure indoor area. The bedrooms are

Hanging Out

If you tire of the beach and the surf, check out **Lahinch Seaworld Leisure Centre** (The Promenade; ☎ 065/708-1900), where you can swim in a (warm) pool or relax in the steam room or the sauna. There's an aquarium with all kinds of tropical fish on show and an in-house cafe. It costs €10 per person to get in.

spartan, with pine bunk beds, but the location is perfect for playing on the beach by day and exploring the laid-back town by night. It costs €15 for a bed in a dorm and €20 to €45 for a family or private room. If you want some more privacy and luxury for a little more cash while in the area, stay at **Fairy Fort Lodge** (Moymore North; ☎ 065/707-2911), a couple of minutes' drive from the town of Lahinch, surrounded by rolling hills and with views of the Atlantic. Angela and Mark Kerin are excellent hosts, and will ask you five times a day if you want something to drink or if you need more blankets. Luckily, the family owns the local taxi service, so after a relaxing night's stay at this well-decorated B&B, you can easily get to the next town on your list.

Eating

→ **Barrtra Seafood Restaurant** SEAFOOD Award-winning seafood with fab views. Try the mouth-wateringly tangy crab salad with homemade mayonnaise, followed by a perfectly cooked filet of cod with orange and ginger sauce and Clare potatoes. Non-fish fans will be pleased to find meat and veggie meals on the menu, too. If you're feeling broke, eat an early lunch then head to Barrtra for their 5pm special menu. *Barrtra.* ☎ *065/708-1280. www.barrtra.com. 3-course dinner at 5pm for €24; 6-course dinner €37.*

average a la carte entree €20. Mon–Sat 5–10pm; Sun 1–10pm.

→ **Mr. Eamon's** IRISH Nestled between the sea and the golf club is Mr. Eamon's, a modern Irish restaurant concentrating on seafood thanks to its location next to the Atlantic. After a day of surfing, what could be better than a satisfying dinner of hot buttered lobster, roast duckling, or fried goujons of monkfish? Well, nothing—except maybe the desserts, which tend to be of the rich, creamy cake variety. Don't come here expecting health food—even the starter salads are drenched in dressing and croutons. *Kettle St.* ☎ *065/708-1050. Set 3-course dinner €27.*

Partying

The majority of the pubs in Lahinch are located on Main Street and are of the traditional, "ye olde" variety. They're not cheesy and overly touristy, although some have lots of history. **P. Frawley** on Kettle Street, the oldest and friendliest pub in town, is run by Tom Frawley, Lahinch's oldest eligible bachelor at age 87. Also try **Kenny's** on Main Street, **Galvin's** on Church Street, and the **Spinnaker** on the Marine Parade.

Playing Outside

There is one main draw in Lahinch—the ocean. Never surfed before? Then head to ▶️ **Best** **Lahinch Surf School** (Ballyfaudeen, Lahinch; ☎ **087/960-9667**), the only ISA-approved school in town. The head instructor is John McCarthy, current Irish Senior champion and member of the Irish Surf Team; he and his staff will teach anyone between 9 and 90 the ins and outs of the sport. During a 2-hour lesson, you'll first learn the basic three steps to getting up on the board but most likely spend a whole hour and a half in the water. Expect to spend about €30 on one group lesson and €60 for a one-to-one lesson.

Shopping

Other than some tourist schlock shops and old-fashioned general stores, there isn't much to buy here that you haven't seen elsewhere. However, definitely stop in at the **Lahinch Surf Shop** (☎ 070/81543; www. lahinchsurfshop.com), the first surf shop in Ireland. Opened in the 1980s, the shop quickly became so popular for surf info that a daily Surf Report is now published online and recorded as a phone message. You can find everything here from surf-oriented DVDs like *Endless Summer* to accessories like sunglasses. Of course, you can buy boards and body-boards, too.

Kilkay

If you love diving and swimming, head to Kilkay—sometimes spelled Kilkee on signs and in books. Admittedly the majority of tourists are families from Clare and Limerick and the beaches can be quite crowded, but the limestone caverns you'll encounter underwater are worth the nuisance. Situated right on the Atlantic, Kilkay boasts an abundance of seafood restaurants—some quite expensive, but if you love shellfish, chowder, and the like, you'll love Kilkay. Even if you're just in town for a few hours, wander down the Kilkay coastline, with its rocky nooks and crannies and stunning sea views.

Getting There

You can get to Kilkay from the hub town of Ennis on **Bus Éireann** (☎ 061/313333; www. buseireann.ie) on route 15. There are also buses from Galway and Limerick, as well as towns on that route. If you're driving, take the N68 from Ennis through Kilrush.

Basics

TOURIST OFFICE   The tourist information office for Kilkay is located in the town square and run by either Antoinette Murphy or Julie O'Gorman, who will answer the phone at ☎ 065/905-6112. It is open from May through September daily, 9:30am to 5:30pm.

RECOMMENDED WEBSITES   The official website of the town of Kilkay is www.kilkee. ie. The site is definitely geared to small town life—there's a section on who to pray for if someone is dead or dying. Unfortunately, it's not terribly helpful for visitors. Most other websites with information on the town seem cheaply made and unreliable. Better to stick to guidebooks or go to the tourist office.

Sleeping

→ **Bay View B&B**   Right in the heart of Kilkay with views of the bay and cliffs is the Hickie family's beloved B&B, run by Mary and her son John. You might find the decor a little overwhelming—tons of shiny antiques, plus Mary's collection of Victorian dolls—but ignore the chintz and you'll love the Bay View, with its clean, blue-hued bedrooms overlooking the ocean and its cozy sports bar with big screen TVs. The breakfast is as delicious as you might expect, with homemade whole meal bread and whatever else you could want. *O'Connell St. ☎ 065/905-6058. www. westclare.net/bayview. Doubles €53–€60. In room: TV, coffee/tea facilities, hair dryer.*

→ **Nolan's**   This family-run B&B is adorable, clean, and comfortable—everything you'd want in a guesthouse for a decent price. The friendly Nolan family will welcome you in a typical Irish way, with scones and coffee plus advice on what to do in Kilkay. You'll be a quick half-mile walk down the road from the beach, and across the street is Bourke's Tackle Shop in case you want to stock up on fishing supplies. You know it makes sense. The rooms are neat, decorated in green and white, and the breakfasts range from traditional Irish to healthy. *Kilrush Rd.* ☎ *065/906-0100. www.nolanskilkee.westclare. net. Doubles €55–€60. In room: TV, coffee/tea facilities.*

Eating

→ **Keane's Oyster Bar** SEAFOOD   Delish trad dishes served up in a crumbling old yellow house—a meal at Keane's feels like a step into the past. The bar is just part of a mini–business empire including a B&B and general store. Husband Michael harvests the oysters fresh from his own beds on the Shannon estuary, while wife Bridie is in the kitchen baking bread and desserts. Daughters Aisling and Lorraine manage the eatery, where you must order the house specialty: oysters on a bed of salad, served with brown bread. Or there's Cajun cod or a juicy 10 ounce sirloin. It's all good. *Lisdeen, Kilkay.* ☎ *065/ 905-6302. www.keaneskilkee.com. Average entree €18. Open year-round from 5:30pm.*

→ **The Strand** SEAFOOD   This is Kilkay's finest seafood establishment, with its fancy dishes utilizing the best the Atlantic offers up. Every delicious fish dish you can think of will be on the menu at this seaside establishment, and you'll be able to gaze out at the ocean while you dine on their creamy fish chowder. Not a seafood lover for some reason? There are some dishes here aimed at carnivores, too, and a selection of salads. *The Strand.* ☎ *065/905-6177. Average entree €18. Apr–Oct daily 6:30–11pm.*

PLAYING OUTSIDE

The **Kilkay Dive Centre** (East End, Kilkay; ☎ **065/905-6707**), under new management

Hanging Out

The only real reason anyone comes to Kilkay is the beach. In the winter, the town is empty and dreary. In the summer, however, the best place to hang out and meet new people is on the sand, although the natural swimming pools called the Pollock Holes are popular for lazing around, too. They're replenished by fresh seawater at every tide. If you're a fan of the all-over tan you'll love Kilkay Beach, as it's been approved as a nudist or naturist beach.

and as popular as ever, is well equipped to show you the underwater sites off the Clare coast. The waters around Kilkay are known for being deep and clear, with an abundance of flora and fauna and there are over 20 dive sites to visit. Check out the Diamond Rocks, so named because of the quartz that makes them glisten in the sunshine, where you'll see spider crabs and the skeleton of a ship. Not into diving? The center also offers fishing trips, sailing lessons, jet-skiing, and dolphin-watching sessions. For a real authentic Victorian day out like visitors would have experienced when Kilkay first grew in popularity, head to **The Trekking Centre** (Tarmon West, Kilkay; ☎ **065/906-0071**), where you can go on supervised pony treks down country lanes, along the Shannon estuary, or along the waterfront.

The Northwest: Mayo, Sligo & Donegal

Welcome to the wild and woolly Northwest. If it's wilderness you're after, this is it—the rough and rugged Ireland mythologized in songs, movies, and poems. Here you'll find some of the most breathtaking cliffs, majestic mountains, and desolately beautiful stretches of coastline in all of Ireland.

Near the bottom of County Mayo is Westport, a big holiday destination where people come to have a good time. It's a postcard-pretty little town in the Georgian style, but the streets bustle with a surprisingly urban energy for a town of only a few thousand people. Ever wondered what happens to resort towns when they fall out of fashion? Just visit sparsely populated Achill Island, once a major tourist destination and now an eerie ghost of its former self. Although scores of ugly white vacation cottages still dot the landscape, Achill's rugged cliffs, harsh seas, and pristine beaches (not to mention good budget accommodations) make it more than worth a visit.

Northern County Mayo is definitely, with the exception of Ballina, as rural as rural gets. Around the Moy Valley, Killala Bay, and to the west, there are ancient ruins, beautiful cliffs and ocean views, and inviting seaside villages. You can practically hear the strains of traditional Irish music as sweet-smelling blue smoke from burning peat floats from chimneys across the countryside. Bogs and mountains and heather and lakes—this is probably what you imagined Ireland would be like, and this is where you can find it.

Come by car and you'll spend half your time thinking you're lost. You probably are. The road signs round these parts are virtually nonexistent and often just plain wrong. But, if you don't mind being lost, because Ireland is an island, you'll soon find yourself back on track, with plenty of adventures under your belt to brag about later.

As the roads are so windy, fewer tourists make it through to the Northwest. This means the locals aren't so accustomed to throngs of travelers and can seem a bit unfriendly at first. They're not. They're shy. Once they get talking you may have difficulty getting some of them to stop. These are some of the most genuinely warm and hospitable people you're likely to come across in all of your Irish travels.

The Best of the Northwest

- **Croagh Patrick:** Rising steeply 750m (2,460 ft.) above the coast, Croagh Patrick is seen as a holy mountain, where a saint is said to have retreated in penance. Traditionally, barefoot pilgrims climb it on the last Sunday of July, but in recent years, hundreds of Nike-shod tourists have been making the ascent daily. The view from above can be breathtaking or nonexistent—the summit is often wrapped in clouds. See p. 350.

  Exploring the Hairpin Turns of the Donegal Coast: The wild and woolly coast of Donegal offers the perfect scenic backdrop for an awesome drive, and as varied a terrain—beaches, countryside, mountains—as you'll find anywhere. See p. 370.

- **Carrowmore and Carrowkeel:** These two megalithic cities of the dead (Europe's largest) may have once contained more than 200 passage tombs. The two together—one in the valley and the other atop a nearby mountain—convey an unequaled sense of the scale and wonder of the ancient peoples' reverence for the dead.

Carrowmore is well presented and interpreted, while Carrowkeel is left to itself and to those who seek it out. See p. 369.

- **Inishmurray:** This uninhabited island off the Sligo coast holds another striking monastic ruin, this one surrounded by what appear to be the walls of an even more ancient stone fort. Despite its remoteness, the Vikings sought out this outpost of peace-seeking monks for destruction in A.D. 807. Today its circular walls and the surrounding sea create a stunning view. See p. 369.

- **Yeats & County Sligo:** With its many connections to the beloved poet W. B. Yeats, this county is a pilgrimage destination for Yeats fans. The poet's writing was shaped by the landscape and people in this farming region, and many of its monuments—including Lough Gill, Glencar Lake, Ben Bulben Mountain, and Maeve's tomb—appear in his poetry. There are also several museums housing first editions, photographs, and other memorabilia, and Yeats's dark and somber grave is in Drumcliffe. See p. 360.

County Mayo

Westport

Westport is a cute little place. One of the few planned towns in Ireland, designed in the 18th century by James Wyatt. Prepare for Georgian streets, beautiful row houses, a leafy mall, and an octagonal square. Amazingly it has avoided the kitschy excesses of so many other major vacation spots in Ireland, opting for a refreshing tranquillity instead. It's still a resort town, though, and there's a

County Mayo

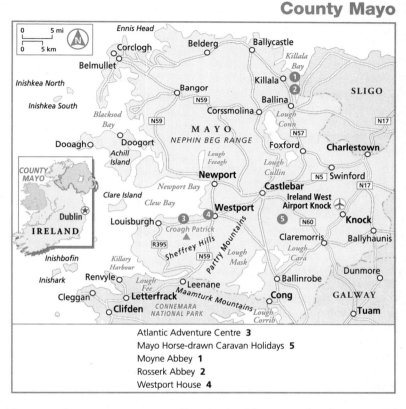

Atlantic Adventure Centre **3**
Mayo Horse-drawn Caravan Holidays **5**
Moyne Abbey **1**
Rosserk Abbey **2**
Westport House **4**

welcome emphasis on enjoying oneself, eating well, and drinking aplenty. The crowd is generally older, although enough young people stop by to find some playmates.

With its proximity to the Atlantic, Westport is a natural destination for watersports lovers. This area has produced some world-class stand-ups (surfers) and spongers (boogie boarders), who honed their craft in the chilly Atlantic at the excellent nearby surfing spots (see "Playing Outside," below).

If getting bashed by waves isn't your thing, don't stay away; the town is worth visiting itself. Spend an afternoon shopping in some of the sweet shops on the main streets or sipping tea and reading a book at a cafe,

then head down to a pub in the evening and sing along to some incredible traditional music.

The trad music here is top-notch. This might be helped by the fact that one of the main music pubs, Matt Malloy's, is owned by the flautist of the internationally renowned group the Chieftains.

GETTING THERE & GETTING AROUND

BY PLANE Several airlines serve **Knock International Airport,** Charlestown, County Mayo (☎ **094/906-7222;** www. knockairport.com). From Dublin and Liverpool you can fly to Knock on **Aer Arann** (☎ **0818/210210** in Ireland; www.aerarann.

com). **Ryanair** (☎ 0818/303-303; www.ryan air.com) serves Knock from London Stansted, while **easyJet** (☎ 1890 923 922; www.easy jet.com) runs a daily service to London Gatwick, and **bmi baby** (☎ 1890/340-122 in Ireland; www.bmibaby.com) serves Knock from Manchester and Birmingham. A shuttle bus service can be caught from the airport to Charlestown where passengers can jump aboard the express service to Westport.

BY TRAIN **Irish Rail** (www.irishrail.ie) and **Bus Éireann** (☎ 096/21011; www.bus eireann.ie) provide daily service from Dublin and other cities into Westport. There is also express service from Galway into Westport.

BY CAR To go on from Mayo and explore the surrounding county, it's best to rent a car. Three firms with outlets at Knock International Airport are **Casey Auto Rentals, Ltd.** (☎ 094/932-4618; www.caseycar.com), **Europcar** (☎ 094/936-7221; www.europ car.ie), and **National Car Rental** (☎ 094/ 936-7252; www.carhire.ie). To get to Westport from Knock airport is just under 64km (40 miles) but takes over an hour on the winding roads. Welcome to the country.

ORIENTATION

Westport is really a tiny town; all of its downtown streets, of which there are about 10, can be walked in under 2 minutes if you're under the age of 90 and have no serious injuries. Westport's gentle sprawl emanates from the Octagon, a roundabout in the town center. At its center stands a statue of a beardless St. Patrick, one of the few depictions of the saint in his youth. From here, dozens of pubs, shops, restaurants, cafes, and more pubs are an easy walk away. Head north on James Street, past St. Mary's Church, and wind up at the west end of The Mall, a handsome tree-lined street on either side of the canal of the Carrowbergh River. Quay Road leads out of town toward the coast.

BASICS

EMERGENCIES In an emergency call ☎ 999. The local **police (Garda)** can be contacted at ☎ 098/25555. The nearest **hospital** is in nearby Castlebar (☎ 094/ 21454).

INTERNET Dunning's **Cyberpub** (inside Dunning's B&B, on the Octagon; ☎ 098/ 25161; www.dunningspub.com; €5 per hour) has full Internet access on iMacs.

LAUNDRY Bring your soiled goods to **The Washeteria** (Mill St.; ☎ 098/25261; €3 wash and dry).

PHARMACY If you've cut your finger surfing, you can pick up bandages and the like at **O'Donnell's** (Bridge St.; ☎ 098/ 25163).

POST OFFICE You can mail your packages and whatnot from the **Westport Post Office** (North Mall; ☎ 098/25475).

TOURIST INFORMATION For year-round information, visit or contact the **Westport Tourist Office,** The Mall (☎ 098/25711; http://westport.mayo-ireland.ie). It's open September through May, Monday to Saturday from 9am to 5:45pm, and June through August, Monday to Friday 9am to 7pm.

If you've come in by plane, the **Knock Airport Tourist Office** (☎ 094/936-8103) is open June to September at times coinciding with flight arrivals.

RECOMMENDED WEBSITES For thoughts on what to do around the county including outdoor adventures, try www.mayo-ireland. com.

FESTIVALS

In late September, Westport celebrates its annual **Arts Festival** (contact the tourist office, ☎ 098/25711), a weeklong orgy of artistic endeavors. Poetry, music, art, drama, and drinking are all well represented. Shunning the coming of the crisp autumn chill, the festival heats up the streets with unbridled *craic.*

Westport

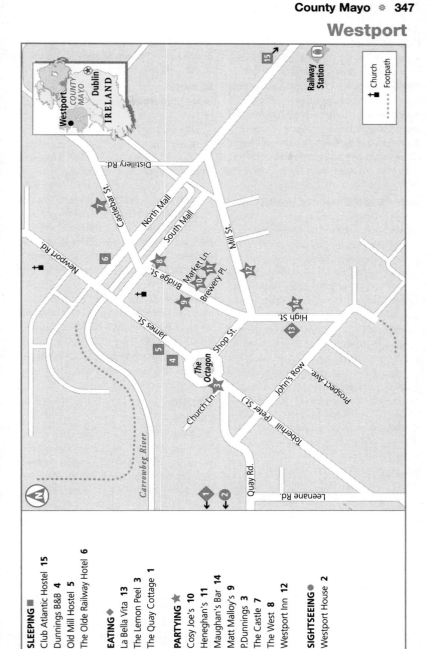

SLEEPING ■
Club Atlantic Hostel **15**
Dunnings B&B **4**
Old Mill Hostel **5**
The Olde Railway Hotel **6**

EATING ◆
La Bella Vita **13**
The Lemon Peel **3**
The Quay Cottage **1**

PARTYING ★
Cosy Joe's **10**
Heneghan's **11**
Maughan's Bar **14**
Matt Malloy's **9**
P.Dunnings **3**
The Castle **7**
The West **8**
Westport Inn **12**

SIGHTSEEING ●
Westport House **2**

SLEEPING

Cheap

If you can't get into the old Mill (see below), try the **Club Atlantic Hostel** (Altamont St.; ☎ 098/26644; €20 dorm) about a 10-minute walk from the center of town. It sports a summer-camp vibe and is often full of school trips. But don't run screaming yet. They've got a handy shop that sells pasta, batteries, and all sorts of travel goodies. And their big rec room—complete with Ping-Pong, pool, and upright piano—really is fun.

→ **The Old Mill Holiday Hostel**   Most budget travelers on their way out of Westport will rave about The Old Mill Holiday Hostel. Whispering excitedly about its old stone building and exposed wooden beams, its proximity to the centre of town, the lack of curfew, and the little outdoor area where everyone gathers in the summer to eat. But if you haven't booked in advance, it's very unlikely you'll find a bed here. There are only 52 and they tend to fill up quickly. Do yourself a favor and phone ahead. If you do get in, expect to sit up talking until the early hours in the huge common room and kitchen, before falling asleep in a comfortable bed topped off with a duvet. *Barrack Yard, James St.* ☎ *098/27045. www.iol.ie/~oldmill. Dorm €14, €1.50 for linen. Breakfast not included. Amenities: Kitchen; laundry.*

Doable

You can't beat the central location of **Dunning's B&B** (The Octagon; ☎ 098/25161; www.dunningspub.com; €60 double), which offers a cozy bed-and-breakfast, with meals served at Dunning's restaurant downstairs and accommodation including six-bed rooms. The Dunning's empire also includes the popular P. Dunning's (see "Bars," below), and Dunning's Cyberpup (see "Internet," above), both attached to the B&B.

You'll also have good luck at a few other moderately priced spots like **Plougatel House** (Distillery Rd.; ☎ 098/25198), right in the town center; **Woodside** (Golf Course Rd.; ☎ 098/26436), a 5-minute walk from downtown; or **The Anchorage** (7A Altamont St.; ☎ 098/25448), in the center of town.

Splurge

→ **The Olde Railway Hotel**   Act like Lord or Lady Muck at The Olde Railway Hotel. It was originally built in 1780 by Lord Sligo to accommodate his "overflow" houseguests, and has now been restored. Old wordman William Thackeray described the hotel as "One of the prettiest, comfortablist inns in Ireland" in 1834. It's still true today. Not a place to party in, perhaps, but a great place to relax and soak up the atmosphere of old Irish charm and elegance. All the rooms are different. Twenty-two rooms face the tree-lined Carrowbeg River. The best-of-the-best rooms are more spacious and include a sitting area with sofa. Bicycles are also available for guests who wish to take a pedal through pretty Westport. *The Mall, Westport, County Mayo.* ☎ *098/25166. www.anu.ie/rail wayhotel. 27 units. €130–€160 double. Rates include full breakfast. AE, DC, MC, V. Amenities: Restaurant; bar. In room: TV.*

EATING

Doable

→ **La Bella Vita** ITALIAN   Its name means "The Beautiful Life" and that just about sums things up. This is a chill, feel-good Italian wine-bar/restaurant serving all you'd expect from your local Italian—pasta, risotto, veal, poultry, and game—with open fires and candlelight to top it all off. Start with the antipasti or bruschetta, and leave room for one of the homemade puds. A great first date location. *High St., Westport, County Mayo.* ☎ *098/29771. Main courses €7–€12. Tues–Sun 6–10pm.*

Splurge

→ **The Lemon Peel** FUSION   A buzzy bistro where chef/owner Robbie McMenamin often pops out to chat about what's on your plate. He only uses local produce to make

Paint Your Wagon

For a completely different take on self-catering, head out of Westport toward Castlebar and then on to Belcarra village. Here you'll find caravans for rent, drawn by horses, at **Mayo Horse-Drawn Caravan Holidays** (☎ **098/903 2054;** www. horsedrawn.mayonet.com). These are not your modern shiny embarrassments but real old-fashioned wagons pulled down winding lanes by an Irish cob. They sleep four and this outfit has teamed up with various guesthouses and farms to provide places to stay along the way. The cost runs between €651 and €784, dependent on time of year, with overnight stays charged at €16. No horse experience necessary.

"modern Irish" fare (code for traditional Irish dishes in smaller portions, with a bit more color, a lot less fat, and perhaps a hint of exotica). His pan-fried loin of pork in black-bean sauce comes on a bed of Chinese noodles, his fish is scrummy—Cajun crusted salmon, or cod served on crab mash (mixed in with spuds) with a sweet basil sauce. Everything comes with fresh veg on the side, and the cheese sauce on the broccoli is a state secret. *The Octagon, Westport, County Mayo.* ☎ *098/26929. www.lemonpeel.ie. Reservations required on weekends. Early-bird menu 5–7pm €18; main courses €13–€19. Tues–Sun 5–11pm.*

➔ **The Quay Cottage** SEAFOOD This place does the best seafood in Westport. But at these prices you better really like your food fishy in order to book a table. Foodies will find it worth the expense. In an old stone building overlooking the harbor, Quay Cottage is decked out entirely in nautical knick-knacks. The menu presents fresh, beautifully

prepared seafood, such as lemon sole beurre blanc or wild local salmon, with loads of daily specials too, often including steaks. *The Quay, Westport, County Mayo.* ☎ *098/26412. Reservations recommended. Main courses €18– €27. May–Oct daily 6–10pm; Nov–Apr Tues– Sat 6–10pm. Closed Christmas.*

PARTYING

For a town of only 4,500 there sure are a lot of places to drink in Westport. Their vibe is celebratory 365 days of the year. Even off season, when there are no tourists around, Westport's pubs are full of life, often full in the middle of the afternoon. Clubs are usually bars with dance floors and DJ booths, and are only marginally less casual than the pubs. Pub hours are generally from early afternoon, around 1 to 3pm, till 11:30pm.

Bars & Clubs

In addition to the choices listed below, you might try **The West** (Bridge St.; ☎ **098/ 25886**). This spot right on the river is dark, smoky, and packed with kids. The average age is 19 but the weekend rock sessions thrill all.

If you're dying to catch a game of Gaelic hurling or football on TV, head to **Maughan's Bar** (High St.; ☎ **098/28494**). They've got a big-screen TV, a pool table, and a dartboard, where you can pit your-self against the thick-necked regulars. **Heneghans** (Bridge St.; ☎ **098/25561**) is a rustic, back-to-basics, check-your-guns-at-the-door type of pub. The crowd varies, depending on time of day and year, but is usually older. There's music throughout the week, and the Sunday night trad sessions are a good way to bid farewell to the weekend.

➔ **Matt Molloy's** By day Matt Molloy's is a cozy pub with a coal fireplace in the back and an enclosed beer garden beyond. At night it's elbow-to-elbow and almost impossible to get served at the ram-packed bar. This is because it is owned by world-renowned,

Mayo-born millionaire/musician Matt Molloy of the Chieftains. Some superlative trad sessions happen here several times a week. As it says on the man himself's website, the music here is "dark, deep and unpasteurised, like its pints." *Bridge St.* ☎ *098/26665. www.matt molloy.com.*

➔ **P. Dunning's** If you can't get in at Matt's try Dunning's where they have music sessions 3 nights a week, at least. An older crowd generally hangs out here, sipping drinks slowly while they talk about old times, although they have been known to break into spontaneous bouts of dancing. By day it's also a great place to sit outside and eye up fellow travelers in the sunshine. There is also a B&B attached (see "Sleeping," above). *The Octagon.* ☎ *098/25161.*

There are no real clubs in Westport. It's just not that sort of place. What counts as a club is simply somewhere that stays open later and you might have to pay to enter.

Shake your booty to live music at **Westport Inn** (Mill St.; ☎ **098/29200**) until 1 or 2am.

Alternatively gyrate amid laser lights and theatrical smoke at **The Castle** (Castlecourt Hotel, Castlebar St; ☎ **098/25444**) until 1am on the weekends. This is one of the few dance venues in town. There is also **Cosy Joe's** (Bridge St.; ☎ **098/28004**), a cheesy disco upstairs from a pub.

SIGHTSEEING

Westport isn't really a sightseeing stop, more a watersports and stroll-around-the-town-stopping-for-numerous-coffees type place. However, Westport House proves a big draw for many.

➔ **Westport House** At the edge of the town of Westport, this late-18th-century residence is the home of Lord Altamont, the marquis of Sligo, and a descendant, so it is rumored, of Grace O'Malley, the "Pirate Queen"—check out the bronze statue of her on the grounds. This really is a stunning pad

featuring a staircase of ornate white Sicilian marble, unusual Art Nouveau glass and carvings, family heirlooms, and silver. The grandeur of the residence is undeniable, but it is tainted by the commercial enterprises on its grounds, including a small children's zoo, and prices are quite high. *Westport.* ☎ *098/ 25430. www.westporthouse.ie. Admission to house and children's animal and bird park €23 adults, €15 students; to house only €12 adults, €7.50 students. Westport House and Gardens only: Mar 1–Oct 1 daily 11:30am–5pm; Open Sat–Sun (same hours) only in Nov. Attractions Apr–Jun Sat–Mon 11:30am–5pm; July–Aug daily 11:30am–5pm.*

PLAYING OUTSIDE

BICYCLING At Westport grab a bike from **Irish Cycle Hire** (☎ **041/685-3772**; www. irishcyclehire.com) for €70 for the week or €15 for the day. You can either ride it in the local area, or for an extra €20 you can ride it on to one of their other depots across Ireland in Dublin, Donegal, Galway, Ennis, Dingle, Killarney, or Cork. They've got the lot: mountain bikes, touring bikes, bikes with comfy saddles—very important—and they're new each season.

HORSEBACK RIDING **Westport Woods Hotel** (☎ **098/25811;** www.westportwoods hotel.com) runs a high-standard riding school 5 miles away in a center overlooking **Best** **Croagh Patrick**—the mount where the saint fasted, which has now become an international pilgrimage center. Head up this way on horseback or onto the beach. Treks last between 1 and 4 hours.

WATERSPORTS The **Atlantic Adventure Centre** (Lecanvey; ☎ **098/64806**) offers courses in kayaking, windsurfing, surfing, boogie boarding, and pier jumping. It is primarily aimed at youngsters but also caters to adults. Courses range from 1 to 5 days; prices range from €15 to €125. On-land activities, including rock-climbing and abseiling, are also offered up for consumption. Most of the

We Are Now Entering the Gaeltacht

Don't dare call it "dead"; Irish may still be a minority language, but this haunt-ingly melodic tongue is becoming more and more popular every day. Thank-fully just about all Irish-speaking men and women, even in the Gaeltacht (areas in which Irish is the primary language spoken), also speak English, but it still definitely scores points if you can speak a few words in Irish. Who knows? You might even get a free pint out of the deal.

Call the old language "Irish" rather than "Gaelic," because the latter term is too vague—there's Scottish Gaelic, too. (Both languages have the same roots but aren't super-similar.) There are three main Irish dialects—an Irish speaker in Donegal will sound significantly different from a Cork speaker—but speak loudly and clearly and they should still be able to understand you. And now for your first language lesson:

- *Go raibh maith agat* ("go row my ah-gut"): Thank you; when spoken to more than one person, replace *agat* with *agaibh* ("ah-give"). You can also use it to mean "please."

- *Dia duit* ("gee-ya ditch"): The traditional greeting, preferable to "hey you." To more than one person, it's *dia daoibh* ("gee-ya yee-iv").

- There isn't a more romantic way to say "I love you" than in Irish; *Tá mo chroí istigh ionat* ("ta mo hree ISS-tee YUH-nat"), literally "My heart is inside you." Aww . . . .

- You've seen *fáilte* ("FALL-cheh") around; it means "welcome." There's a bunch of ways to say good-bye: *Slán* ("slahn"), literally "safe," *sláinte* ("SLAWN-cheh"), literally "health" (it's also used to mean "cheers"), or *slán abhaile* ("slahn ah-wall-eh") for "safe home."

- Technically there are no words for "yes" and "no"; to answer a question you reply with the verb the speaker used to ask you the question. This explains why, instead of saying "yes," a native will say, "I am," "I did," and so on. The closest thing to "yes" and "no" is *sea* ("shah"), meaning "it is," and *ní hea* ("knee ha"), meaning "it is not."

- *Bá mhaith liom pionta eile* ("Bah why lum pyon-ta el-leh"): "I would like another pint."

- Emotions and illnesses are always said to be "on you." *Beidh áthas orainn* ("bay ah-hass or-in"): There will be joy on us. *Bhí imní orthu* ("vee im-knee or-hoo"): There was worry on them. *Tá poit orm* ("tah poych a-rum"): There is a hangover on me. (That one's likely to be the most useful.)

- *Cá bhfuil an seomra folctha?* ("cah will an show-mra fulc-ha?"): Where is the bathroom?

- And if anybody makes an unwanted advance, you can always say, *"Pog mo thoin"* ("pohg mo hoe-in")—that is, "Kiss me arse."

kayaking is done at Old Head, Bertra, and Carramore. Bargain accommodations rates are available for campers.

Many traveling surf freaks base them-selves in the Westport area and head out to Louisburgh, Killary, Easky, and Bundoran, which are all great surf spots, and all within a half-hour drive.

SHOPPING

Because Westport is a major destination for those seeking Irishness, the shops downtown tend to sell goods loaded with Irishness. With tons of shops in town, you'll also find the goods to satisfy almost any shopping urge.

BOOKS   Do you like interesting books? Well, **Young's Interesting Books** (Lime Court off James St; ☎ 098/22914) is, obviously, the place to buy them. Young's has a good collection of secondhand and antiquarian books. Besides being one of the few shops open on Sunday year-round, **The Bookshop** (Bridge St.; ☎ 098/26816) has a fairly comprehensive selection of Irish literature.

CRAFTS   The pieces stocked in the local craft shops are generally authentic, but if you're about to shell out serious money for a cool pot or bodhran (traditional Irish drum), make sure it's really handmade. On the art front, The **Andrew Stone Gallery** (Bridge St.; ☎ 098/25619) is a particularly good gallery and also comes attached to a great cafe serving up homemade quiches and savories.

MUSIC   You'll find mostly Irish trad music and assorted, rather out-of-place pop cheese for sale at Downtown Records (The Octagon; ☎ 098/26841). But you can also buy concert tickets for any venue in Ireland here as well, through the Ticketmaster system.

Achill Island

If you're heading north from Westport or south from Sligo, you owe it to yourself to spend a day on Achill Island. Rugged cliffs, pristine beaches, and friendly pubs dot the island's shores, while bleak bogs blanket its interior creating an almost supernatural emptiness. Tax incentives in the '60s and '70s made Achill a prime resort area for moneyed folk from Ireland and England. It also led people to build ugly white houses everywhere like a crop of sore thumbs, marring the otherwise beautiful landscape. These little

houses look totally out of place, but even they cannot ruin the overwhelming beauty of Achill.

These days, Achill is a seldom-visited place, almost forgotten by the rest of Ireland. This works to your advantage—accommodations are cheap, and beaches and scenic roads aren't cluttered with people. This is true even in the summer. There is plenty of space for quiet contemplation, walking, and relaxation. Achill sees a lot of rain, and it can be miserable when the weather sucks. On a sunny day, though, or during a sunny period on an otherwise dismal day, the island offers stunning views of the sea as the bright sunlight etches detail into all those craggy cliffs and mountains.

GETTING THERE & GETTING AROUND

Achill Island is reached by a bridge that runs over from the mainland to Achill Sound. The only way of getting to and around the island is by road.

BY BUS   Buses run three to five times a day from Westport, Sligo, and Galway to and from the island with **Bus Éireann** (☎ 01/8366111; www.buseireann.com). A bus runs the length of the island and makes many stops along the way (including Dooagh, Dugort, Keel, and Achill Sound). You can pick up the bus outbound at any of the stops. Inbound buses generally go to the end of the island and wind up in Keel. If you want to stop before Keel, ask the driver and he'll gladly let you off.

BY BIKE   Achill Island is a top spot for easy cycling. The roads are quiet and the distances between villages are short enough to schedule in plenty of tea breaks. You can rent a bike in Keel at **O'Malley's Island Sports** (Keel Post Office; ☎ 098/43125).

ORIENTATION

A string of villages stretches along the island's 20km (12-mile) breadth. Because they're all so small, it's better to think of the island as a whole, and each village as a neighborhood. From east to west, you pass through Achill Sound, Cashel, Keel, and Dooagh, finally running out of land and hitting the ocean at Keem Bay.

You'll find a tourist office in Achill Sound where you can grab a map of the island. There is also a post office, gas station, and food shop, making it a good place to stock up on necessities before you head out onto the island for the night.

The most scenic route on the island is the Atlantic Way, a series of roads taking you around the coast. You can join it in Achill Sound, or even before you get on the island in Mulrany. This route gives you maximum views of the ocean and the rugged terrain of Achill. It also takes you through most of the minute villages on the island.

BASICS

MONEY   Go to the post office in Achill Sound. Make sure to get money there, as there are no banks anywhere on the island. Many places still don't take credit cards either, so if you're cashless, you're gonna wind up washing dishes to pay off that tuna melt and lemonade.

PHARMACY   The island's lone pharmacy is in Achill Sound (☎ 098/45248).

POST OFFICE   The lone post office is in Achill Sound (☎ 098/45141). It also has a bureau de change.

TOURIST OFFICES   There is a seasonal tourist office in Achill Sound open during the summer months (☎ 098/45384).

WEBSITES   Surf to www.achill-island.com, www.achilltourism.com, and www.visitachill. com for general information about the island.

FESTIVALS

During the **Soil Acla Na Milaoise** festival (☎ 098/47353), in the first 2 weeks of August, Achill becomes a music and arts retreat, offering performances, workshops, and overflowing *craic.* You can learn to play the

uilleann (elbow) pipes, take a painting course, or learn the jig. Or you can just go to the pubs and listen to music. Trad sessions happen everywhere every night, with all students and teachers participating. The atmosphere is great, and everyone spends all night jamming, talking, and drinking.

SLEEPING

Achill has a wide selection of hostels although not all of them are open year-round. In Achill Sound, **The Wild Haven Hostel** (behind the church; ☎ 098/45392; €15 dorm) is your best bet for its friendly staff, nice furniture, and comfy bar. Also in Achill Sound, **The Railway Hostel** (☎ 098/45187; €15) provides basic accommodations in—you guessed it—a converted railway station.

Arguably the best place to sleep on the island is **The Rich View Hostel** (☎ 098/43264; €16) in Keel. The husband, wife, and cat are all ultrafriendly. Shay, the man of the house, plays trad at The Annexe (see "Bars," below) on Saturdays. There are musical instruments and small brightly painted rooms, as well as a fireplace and Internet access.

The Wayfarer Hostel (☎ 098/43266; mid-Mar to mid-Oct only; €15), also in Keel, is big and cheap and has great views.

For a B&B, head to Dooagh and check in to the **New Verona House** (Dooagh; ☎ 098/43160; €50 double). The rooms are basic but spotless. Some even have a spectacular view of Keem Bay; they say on a good day you can see dolphins.

Groigin Mor (Keel; ☎ 098/43385; €50 double) also does the basic B&B thing but is only open March to November.

If you want a hotel, head for **The Achill Head Hotel** (☎ 098/43108; www.achill head.com; from €70 double) in Keel. The main thing going for it is its bar and Club Zamba, one of the more lively nocturnal spots on the island.

EATING

Many of the eateries on Achill are located within guesthouses or hotels, leading them to have a slightly sanitized atmosphere. The **Achill Sound Hotel** (☎ 098/45245; www. achillsoundhotel.com; from €5) does fairly cheap salads and toasties at the bar, while serving up three course affairs in the restaurant. At the other end of the isle, **The Beehive Handcrafts and Coffee Shop in Keel** (☎ 098/43134; all items €2–€7) is a haven for home-baked cakes and bread, while also selling traditional crafts. Would you like cream with that sweater? There are also chip shops around Achill Sound and Keel, and a supermarket in Achill Sound for getting buys to take back to your hostel.

PARTYING

Achill Island's nightlife is pretty much the same as its day life—laid-back and quiet (make that *really* quiet in the winter). The best pub on the island is **The Annexe** (☎ 098/43268), in Keel, a long, rustic establishment with friendly proprietors and an earthy crowd. Trad music plays every Saturday, and every day in July and August. A great place to sip a whiskey or take pity on a pint of Guinness when the weather closes in—it always does at some point in the day.

Gieltys Clew Bay (Dooagh; ☎ 098/ 43119; www.gieltys.com) is another local favorite with trad sessions nightly in the summer months and during the weekends in the winter. Food is also available year-round. Other decent traditional pubs on the isle include **The George** in Corraun House (Currane; ☎ 098/45858) and the teeny **Lynotts** (no phone; between Bunacurry and Cashel).

SIGHTSEEING

Most of the sightseeing to be done on Achill is about enjoying the outdoors and hiking and cycling to one of their five blue-flag beaches. Beyond that, there is the 16th-century tower at Kildavnet, said to have once been used by Pirate Queen Grace O'Malley. Next door in the graveyard are some medieval gravestones and memorials to the Clew Bay Drowning of 1894 and the Kirkintilloch Fire of 1937. Both were tragedies involving "tatie hoking" or potato picking. The first involved a boatload of young people heading over to Scotland to work for the summer. The boat capsized; thirty-two died. The second involved a similar group of farm workers from the island who burned in a barn in Scotland. Ten people died. More reminders of Ireland's historical poverty can be found at the Deserted Village at Slievemore (take a right onto the road that veers off the main road as you approach Keel from the east). This eerie settlement was home to sheep ranchers until the mid-1800s. No one is really sure why the inhabitants left. Some say the Famine had something to do with it; others say aliens landed and abducted everyone and took them and their sheep into outer space. Get the lowdown at the pub later. The village consists simply of between 80 to 100 stone houses all falling into ruin. More a cycle past than an all-day excursion.

PLAYING OUTSIDE

HIKING   For experienced hikers, Achill offers the daunting challenge of Mount Slievemore. At 661m (2,204 ft.), it takes almost 12 hours to reach the summit and return (not one for the winter then). Begin at the Slievemore Deserted Village car park. Along the way you'll encounter panoramic vistas of Mullet and Blacksod Bay. You can also climb Mount Croaghaun at 655m (2,182 ft.). It lies on the west side of the island. The approach is from Keem Bay where you head north to Corrymore Lough. From here some of the most precipitous cliffs in northern Europe drop down to the sea. Unlike Mount Slievemore, Croaghaun takes about 6 hours for a return journey. Before attempting either of these climbs, always let someone know you are heading out and make sure you are armed with good maps, which can be purchased in town or from the tourist office (see "Tourist Information," above).

SURFING   If you know what you're doing with a surfboard, Keel offers some of the best surfing in Ireland. Still not as well known as other beaches, you'll find the waves aren't crowded and regularly reach 3m (10 ft.) or more. There are, however, some nasty rips so talk to locals before going out. Unlike other surf spots in Ireland, they're surprisingly welcoming.

WATERSPORTS & ADVENTURE ACTIVITIES **McDowell's Hotel and Activity Centre** (Slievemore Rd., Dugort; ☎ **098/43148;** www.achill-leisure.ie) offers courses in sailing, surfing, canoeing, powerboating, and windsurfing with instructors from the Irish Sailing Association. **Achill Outdoor Centre** (Cashel; ☎ **098/47253;** www.achilloutdoor. com) also offers beginners windsurfing as well as mountaineering and navigation courses for serious hikers. To take things to the next level on the water **Windwise** (Keel; ☎ **098/43958**) offers advance windsurfing courses. **Tomas Mai Lochlainn** (☎ **098/45085**)—a native Irish speaker—also offers tastes of adventure in the form of surfboard hire and lessons, as well as mountaineering courses.

Clare Island

The tourist brochure hits this place right on the nose—this really is a "miniature paradise" made up of beaches, hills, and stunning views. Floating a mere 5.6km (3½ miles) off the Mayo coast, just beyond Clew Bay, Clare Island is roughly 104 sq. km (40 sq. miles) of unspoiled splendor. Inhabited for 5,000 years and once quite populous—with 1,700 pre-Famine residents—Clare is now home to 160 year-round islanders, and perhaps as many sheep. Grace O'Malley's castle and the partially restored Cistercian Abbey where she is buried are among the island's few official attractions. The real draw is the island's remote natural beauty—the sea cliffs on the

north side of the island being particularly spectacular.

GETTING THERE & GETTING AROUND

To get out here, you need to jump on the *Pirate Queen* owned by the **Clare Island Ferry Company** (Clare Island Ferry Office, The Tourist Office, James St., Westport; ☎ **098/28288;** www.clareislandferry.com), who have been running services to the island since 1880 (not in the same boats; don't fret). Ferries depart from Roonagh pier several times a day in summer, less often in winter. Buses depart the Westport Tourist Office twice daily to take you to the pier. From there, it's a pleasant 15-minute cruise to the island. The return fare is €22 for adults (€17 for students). Much of the island is walkable, but it's worth hiring a bike in Westport as they are free to take over on the ferry.

BASICS

TOURIST INFORMATION   There's no official tourist information center on the Island. You're best off calling in at the Bay View Hotel (see below), who are usually happy to dish out info on the island. I also recommend the official site for Clare Island (the website includes a tourism section): www.clare island.org/.

FESTIVALS

Twice a year (usually June & Sept) the love hungry of Ireland head here for **Singles Weekend,** hoping to find someone who makes their heart beat louder than the surrounding sea. Don't come expecting handsome surfer boys and girls looking for love. This is for the 25+ age group. With the emphasis on the plus. Find out more from Ireland West (www.irelandwest.ie).

SLEEPING, EATING & PARTYING

The only hotel on the island is **Bay View Hotel** (☎ **098/26307;** €70 double), which also provides hostel-type accommodation and is a good place for tourist information and general happenings on the island, including the island's two "singles" weekends (see "Festivals," above). It's also your best bet for a meal or a pint (drinking tends to continue until the early hours of the morning).

You might also want to try the affordable **Cois Abhainn** (☎ 098/26216; €60 double), in the countryside on the west side of the island or try the eco-friendly, veggie-eating **Clare Retreat Centre** (☎ 098/25412; €60 double; €30 single) that sometimes has B&B rooms or self-catering available, and also runs renowned yoga retreats. Most of the B&Bs around the island also offer dinner. Alternatively there are a couple of grocery stores offering provisions for self-catering. If you've got the gear and the guts—it can get a wee bit chilly out here—Clare Island is a good place to camp, with a dirt-cheap camping area down by the beach with washing facilities available in the nearby community center. Book through **Clare Island Tourism** (☎ 098/26525; cliara@anu.ie).

SIGHTSEEING & PLAYING OUTSIDE

Much of what there is to see on Clare Island focuses on the O'Malley family, particularly daughter Grace. Thelma and Louise were nothing compared to this 16th-century piratess. Clare Island was her home base; from here she would board passing ships to levy heavy duties on them or else wreak havoc on the crew and steal cargo. Fans of Grace, pirating, or debauchery in general can go to the 14th-century Clare Island Cistercian Abbey, where a stone is inscribed with the O'Malley family motto: "Invincible on land and sea"—a philosophy Grace clearly embraced with gusto. Elsewhere is her 15th-century castle, a tower to defend against attack by Napoleon, and lots of prehistoric goodies such as tombs and old cooking devices.

Outdoor lovers can climb the short—but still impressive—Mt. Knockmore, dominating the island with its 461m (1,512-ft.) height, or swim on the sandy beach. Individual B&Bs may also be able to arrange other activities such as sea angling trips, while bicycles can usually be found for hire around the harbor.

Ballina

Most visitors come here for the fishing. If you dip a rod in the water here, it's more likely to come up with a salmon hanging on the end of it than anywhere else in Ireland. Ballina itself has a bustling, urban mentality—quite different from the surrounding rural towns. Its streets are crowded all day long and its pubs are crowded all through the night. It's a perfect base for exploring County Mayo—being close to scenic villages like Killala, Ballycastle, and Enniscrone—and a better example of modern Irish life than Westport. The 9,000 people here are not used to seeing a lot of tourists and for this reason seem to take a genuine interest in outsiders' lives. The youngsters also moan about there being nothing for them to do here and are therefore always eager for entertainment in the form of travelers. Despite a thriving nightlife, there's little to see by day and an afternoon to look around is all you'll really need.

GETTING THERE

BY BUS   Bus lines to and from the town take travelers to Galway, Westport, Donegal, and Sligo one to three times daily with **Bus Éireann** (☎ 096/71800; www.bus eireann.ie).

BY TRAIN   Trains run from Dublin thrice daily except on Sundays (when there are no trains; ☎ 096/71818; www.irishrail.ie).

ORIENTATION

All the commerce and nightlife happens on the west side of the river. Pearse Street is the main street with other streets running perpendicular off it. This is where most of the pubs are. Emmet Street runs along the west bank of the Moy. Cathedral Road runs along the east bank: The tourist office, St.

Muredach's Cathedral, and the ruins of an Augustinian abbey are all found here.

BASICS

TOURIST INFORMATION **Ballina Tourist Information Centre** (Cathedral Rd.; ☎ **096/70848**) is open May Monday to Saturday 10am to 1pm and 2 to 5.30pm; June to August 10am to 5.30pm daily; September Monday to Saturday 10am to 1pm and 2 to 5.30pm.

RECOMMENDED WEBSITES Taking in the larger Moy valley, www.ballina.ie is largely for a golfing/fishing/history-loving audience, but if you can sift through the dull stuff there's also info on places to stay and eat.

FESTIVALS

The Salmon Festival (☎ **096/70905**), a music, fish, arts, theater, parade, fireworks, and fish extravaganza happens here around the second week in July. Then, live music fills the streets, people in crazy costumes walk around entertaining the kids, and the pubs, of course, are packed.

SLEEPING

Further proving the theory that Ballina is not a tourist destination, there's no hostel here (there used to be, but it closed). Budget travelers have to make do with B&Bs. But there are plenty of them and they're generally run by warm women keen to point you in the direction of a friendly pub.

Sycamore View (Cathedral Close, right behind the Cathedral on the east side of the River Moy; ☎ **096/21495**; www.sycamore view.com; €70 double) has a super-friendly proprietor and a bunkhouse in the backyard—the closest thing to a hostel in Ballina. The main house is clean and welcoming, with a bright yellow glass entrance bathed in golden light at dusk. Rooms with a bath are a couple of euros more; otherwise, you shower down the hall. The street is extremely quiet but still close to downtown.

You'll have a similar experience at **Greenhill** (next door to Sycamore View;

☎ **096/22767**; €65 double), minus the golden light. Most of the rooms have TV, and some have their own bath (again for a few more euros).

The **Downhill Inn** (1km/³⁄₄ mile outside of Ballina on the N59 Sligo Rd.; ☎ **096/73444**; www.downhillinn.com; double €98–€130 depending on time of year) is a standard, chain-type hotel. It's clean and relatively cheap for a three-star place, plus you get a bathroom and TV in your room. Not to be confused with the **Downhill House Hotel** (Downhill Rd.; ☎ **096/21033**; doubles from €184) a super-fancy establishment with a pool, Jacuzzi, and sauna all set on a quiet hillside just outside of town. If you're spending this much you might as well stay at the stunning **Belleek Castle** (☎ **096/22400**; www.belleekcastle.com; double €140).

During the summer camping is also an option at the fully equipped **Belleek Caravan and Camping Park** (☎ **096/71533**; www.belleekpark.com; 3km/2 miles) from Ballina off the road to Killala) where you'll find campers' kitchens and tennis courts.

EATING

If you like your meat and veg, you'll like the food in Ballina. If a morsel of meat hasn't passed between your lips for years, you might find your options a little limited, although this is beginning to change as European cafe culture makes its mark around town.

The **Coffee Vine Café** (Tone St.; ☎ **096/21458**; sandwiches from €4) is an example of Ballina's gastronomic move on from pub grub, offering up wraps, open sandwiches, quiches, soups, and salads every day from 9am to 6pm.

If it's pub grub you're after, try **The Broken Jug** (O'Rahilly St.; ☎ **096/72379**; mains from €8) to exchange very little cash for a very huge plateful of food. Alternatively **Tullios** (Pearse St.; ☎ **096/21890**; pizzas from €10) is the locals fave for pizzas and pastas. Murphy Brothers Bar and Restaurant (see "Partying," below) has a bar menu severing everything from fried potato skins to steaks. It's a little bit more expensive than other places in town but then the view from the verandah over the River Moy is a little more appealing. There's also a flash restaurant where mains start from 15€. If you do want to pay that little bit more, the best bet is **Crockets on the Quay** (☎ 096/75930; www.crocketsonthequay.ie; mains from €14) that's had all the Irish papers raving about its trad-with-a-twist dishes.

PARTYING

Ballina's pubs pack a surprising punch for a small town. There are about 50 of them. Not all worth going to (some are strictly reserved for large men to suck alcohol out of cans and smoke high-tar cigarettes out the back). All are generally open till around 11:30pm or midnight every day. Most of them also have pub grub from around noon until 3pm. The worthwhile pubs are on or nearby Pearse Street. On weekends, this is where things start to get crazy as young folk ship in from the surrounding villages, desperate for some urban action.

The Bard (Garden St.; ☎ 096/21894) is a splendid mix of classic pub and contemporary bar. Recessed lighting and backlit stained-glass insets deliver a lounge ambience while a huge copper and brass bar winds around the front room. The crowd is multigenerational, with a lean toward the young pro, and the music is a bubbly mix of the techno-pop variety. It's always guaranteed to have something happening whether during the week or weekend. **The Broken Jug** (see "Eating," above) is a more traditional affair, spread over two levels and filled with all sorts, all friendly, all ages. There's trad music here every now and then. Call ahead to find out what's on when you're in town. **The Loft** (Pearse St.; ☎ 096/21881) mixes Victorian glass with 1950s kitsch and slick

dancing lights. Let's just call it eclectic. It doesn't stop the punters storming in on a Saturday night to get their fill of commercial dance. During the week there's often more rocky live music. **Murphy Brothers** (Clare St.; ☎ 096/22702; www.murphy-brothers.com; past the tourist office on the way out of town) is a huge old-style saloon sporting a healthy range of whiskeys. The crowd is generally older and more touristy than in other places in town, but it's still fun. Murphy's is attached to Longneck's, a crowded club with a top-40 and techno-pop music policy. It's open on weekends only and draws a younger crowd—not all with long necks.

SIGHTSEEING

There isn't much to see in Ballina itself, but there are some minor distractions within a few kilometers. These include the **North Mayo Sculpture Trail** (☎ 098/45107), a route of 14 outdoor sculptures celebrating the 5,000-year history of Mayo. Sculptors from around the world were commissioned to create work for this project. The trail begins in Ballina, off R314, and runs through Killala, Ballycastle, Belderriig, Belmullet, and finally into Blacksod Point. Besides all the cool sculptures, you'll also get to enjoy the views of and from this stretch of rugged coastline. A car is needed.

It seems that the 16th-century English governor of Connacht, Sir Richard Bingham, made it a point to burn just about every Irish religious site he saw, and **Rosserk Abbey** (take R314 north for 6.5km/4 miles, turn right at sign, take first left at the crossroads; continue for 1km/³/₄ mile, then look for signs; no phone; free admission) is no exception. But despite the arson, Rosserk, the finest Franciscan abbey in the country, is remarkably well preserved. There is no public transportation to the abbey, but it's totally bikeable at only 7km/4¹/₃ miles out of town.

Moyne Abbey (follow directions to Rosserk Abbey, above, but continue straight for 1km /³/₄ miles after you see the last sign for Rosserk Abbey; no phone; free admission) is a Franciscan friary founded around 1460 by Mac Uilliam Iochtarach. It grew to be a major learning center in the region until it was burned by (you guessed it) Sir Richard Bingham in 1590. The architecture is late Irish Gothic and the abbey has an impressive six-storied square tower, added on later. Proving that people were just as mischievous back in the day as they are now, you can see 16th-century graffiti on the plaster of the west nave wall.

PLAYING OUTSIDE

CYCLING   If it's a two-wheeler you seek, check out **Gerry's Cycle Centre** (6 Lord Edward St.; ☎ 096/70455) to rent a bike for a day for under a tenner, and even better deals for a week.

FISHING   Ballina is salmon mecca, so between April and September, fishing goes on here all the time. If you're interested in doing some angling but don't know the difference between a salmon and a sardine, contact **Compleat Salmon Holidays** (☎ 096/31011). Whether you're Captain Ahab or Captain Never-fished-before, these guys will take you out and help you catch fish. Of course, you don't necessarily need a guide to catch fish. For fishin' holes around Ballina, go to the tourist office (see "Tourist Information," above) and they can point you in the right direction.

Killala

Wee Killala is one of the wee-est places you've ever been. A 23m (75-ft.) round tower is the dominant feature of the village's minimalist skyline. Nothing really goes on in Killala except now and then, a person will come out of a house, take a look in both directions, and decide to cross the street. A place this tiny and slow-paced may be just what you need to complete your memories of Ireland.

Three intersecting streets make up the village, with a handful of pubs, a post office, and no bank. There is also a waterfront area that's kinda pretty, too. Down the road a bit is the secluded Ross Strand beach, a lovely place to loll about in the sun. Altogether Killala makes for a tranquil vacation from your vacation.

GETTING THERE

BY BUS   **Bus Éireann** (☎ 074/21309; www.buseireann.com) goes from Ballina to Killala once per day, stopping near the post office. You can buy your ticket on the bus.

BASICS

There is no tourist information here. Locals are usually happy to help you out with directions. There is a **post office** (Market St.; ☎ 096/32022).

SLEEPING & EATING

Most of the accommodation surrounding Killala is self-catering. If this appeals and you have enough friends, **Broadlands Holiday Homes** (Ballysakeery, 5km/3 miles out of Killala; ☎ 096/32038; www.broadlands holidays.com; from €199 per week for six) is a good bet. Otherwise a good B&B option is **Avondale House** (Pier Rd.; ☎ 096/32229; double €30), a modern bungalow overlooking the wild Killala bay. If you haven't got a car, Killala really works best as a day trip from Ballina.

The **Country Kitchen Restaurant** (down the street from the Anchor Inn; no phone; mains from €7) besides being one of the only options in town, is rustic and friendly—and even serves up veggie burgers.

PARTYING

A colorful cast of regulars decorates the bar at **The Anchor Inn** (Ballycastle Rd.; no phone), a local favorite. In summer, they have live trad on weekends. It's the kind of place you go for a game of snooker at noon on a Wednesday.

Knock

If it's divine intervention you seek, come to Knock, in the eastern part of County Mayo. Back in August 1879, the Virgin Mary, her hubby Joseph, and St. John the Evangelist were said to have appeared here before two women. More than a dozen others witnessed the apparition, which lasted over 2 hours. It was immediately pronounced a miracle, and Knock's future was assured as a site of pilgrimage, tacky tourist shops and all. Today around 1.5 million people each year make the spiritual journey to Knock.

GETTING THERE

BY BUS   Bus Éireann (☎ 094/88150; www.buseireann.com) runs lines to Galway, Sligo, and Westport daily from Lennon's on Airport Road; buses to Dublin leave from a stop 90m (300 ft.) down the road from Lennon's.

BY PLANE   See "Getting There & Getting Around" section under "Westport."

BASICS

TOURIST INFORMATION   The **Knock Airport Tourist Office** (☎ 094/936-8103) is open June to September at times coinciding with flight arrivals. **Knock Village Tourist Office** (☎ 094/938-8193) opens during the summer months only.

RECOMMENDED WEBSITES   Get the low-down on the where the pope trod in Knock and more at www.knock-shrine.ie.

SLEEPING, EATING & PARTYING

There are no youth hostels here, so B&Bs and hotels are your only options. Staying at **The Knock International Hotel** (Main St.; ☎ 094/88466; double €90) is perhaps not as glam as it sounds, and actually little more than a motel, but it is right next door to the shrine (a plus or minus depending on how your halo fits). A more inexpensive option is **Aisling House** (Ballyhaunis; ☎ 094/88558; double €50) where all rooms have private baths, but it is a short walk (10 minutes) outside the town center. In July and August, you're as unlikely to find a room by turning up on the day as the Virgin Mary was in Bethlehem, so make sure to call ahead.

Camping is also available at the **Knock Caravan and Camping Park** (Claremorris Rd.; ☎ 094/938-8100; tents from €10–€18 per night plus €2 for each adult), a three-star site with all the required washing and cooking facilities. There's little in the way of eateries in Knock and, understandably, it's not party central, but **The Conservatory** (Main St.; ☎ 094/88459) will get you a slap up three-course meal for under €30, or get a plateful of something and chips for under €8 at any one of the caffs on the main street or the **New Thatch Pub** (Main St.; ☎ 094/88153), where you can also get yourself a pint.

SIGHTSEEING

There's really only one thing people come to see in Knock and that's the shrine. This ain't no little figure of the Virgin Mary nestled against a rock; it's a large collection of buildings and sites with a pilgrimage route winding its way around all the chapels. Heathens may like to take a look at the Church of the Apparition (Main St.; free admission) and find out about the apparition in a historical context at The Folk Museum (south of the Basilica; 4€; open May, June, Sept, and Oct 10am–6pm, July and Aug 10am–7pm).

County Sligo

Sligo Town

Bustling and gritty Sligo makes no pretense of being a quaint Irish village. It is what it is, a thriving center of commerce in the west of Ireland. Things are changing though—it's currently in the middle of a major renaissance featuring its "Left Bank" where cafes and restaurants spill over onto the waterfront.

County Sligo

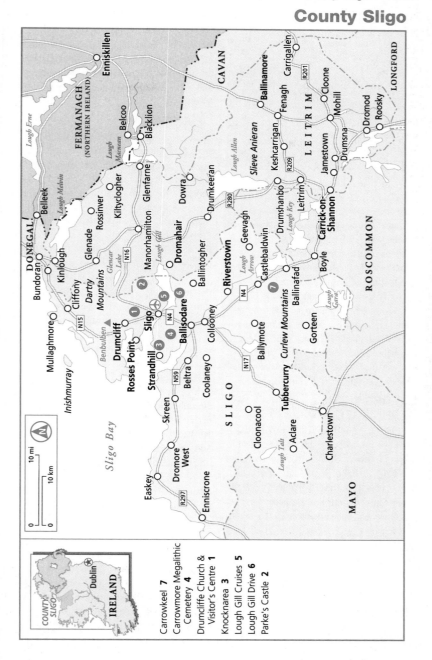

Carrowkeel **7**
Carrowmore Megalithic Cemetery **4**
Drumcliffe Church & Visitor's Centre **1**
Knocknarea **3**
Lough Gill Cruises **5**
Lough Gill Drive **6**
Parke's Castle **2**

But don't come here looking for the sort of tourist attractions offered by Westport or Donegal. What you will get instead is a real sense of modern Irish life.

On top of this Sligo offers a rampant nightlife, holding the crown for best in the northwest, and second only to Galway in the whole of the west. People here take partying seriously: On the weekends, they pull on their fancy clothes and pour on the perfumes ready for the nocturnal festivities erupting in Sligo's pubs, clubs, and restaurants.

When that's all out the way, Sligo is a great place to base yourself to explore the majestic beaches and mountains now known as Yeats' Country. Although the great man himself was born in Dublin, the poet W. B. Yeats spent so much time in County Sligo that it became a part of him, and he a part of it—literally, as he is buried here.

The Yeatsmania can get a bit out of control with every hill, cottage, vale, and lake seemingly bearing a plaque stating exactly when the man was here and which poem he was subsequently inspired to write, but if you can filter it out the countryside is the majestic-yet-quaint Ireland of dreams.

GETTING THERE & GETTING AROUND

BY PLANE   **Aer Arann** (☎ 01/814-5240; www.aerarann.ie) operates daily flights into **Sligo Airport,** Strandhill, County Sligo (☎ 071/916-8280; www.sligoairport.com), 8km (5 miles) southwest of Sligo Town. The bus to Sligo town from the airport will cost you under €3, while you can expect a taxi to cost around €14.

BY TRAIN   **Irish Rail,** with its station on Lord Edward Street (☎ 071/916-9888; www.irishrail.ie), operates daily service into Sligo from Dublin.

BY BUS   **Bus Éireann,** also pulling into Lord Edward Street (☎ 071/916-0066; www.buseireann.ie), operates daily bus service to Sligo from Dublin, Galway, and other points, including Derry in Northern Ireland.

BY ROAD   Four major roads lead to Sligo: N4 from Dublin and the east, N17 from Galway and the south, N15 from Donegal to the north, and N16 from County Fermanagh in Northern Ireland.

ORIENTATION

There are 18,000 people in town, and they all seem to be outside by day and in the pubs by night. Sligo is compact and easy to figure out, with everything of interest in its busy city center, only about a half-mile square. The River Garavogue bisects Sligo with an L-shaped bend. West and south of the river are the bus and train stations (see "Getting There & Around," above), and the busy intersection of Wine Street, O'Connell Street, Hyde Bridge, and Fish Quay. Also south of the river you'll find High Street, a cinema, and a theater (see "Partying," below), The Abbey (see "Sightseeing," below), several restaurants, most of the pubs and shops, and a host of B&Bs. North of the river is the mall. More restaurants and pubs line the bank.

If you head west on Wine Street and drive or bike for 7km (4¹/₃ miles), you will come to Strandhill, a fun little resort village on the ocean. Knocknarea Mountain and the airport are also out here. Head north along the coast and you'll end up in Rosses Point (see "Playing Outside," below), another resort town with its own Coney Island (minus the dilapidated roller coasters and garbage) and a great beach.

BASICS

EMERGENCIES   In an emergency, dial ☎ 999. St. John's Hospital is at Ballytivan, Sligo (☎ 071/914-2606), or you can try **Sligo County Hospital,** the Mall (☎ 071/914-2620). The local **Garda Station** is on Pearse Road (☎ 071/914-2031).

INTERNET   Right in the center of Sligo Town, you'll find the **Cygo Internet Café**

Sligo Town

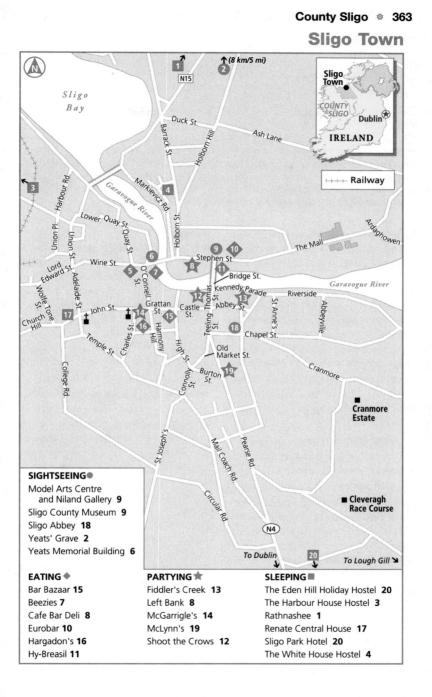

Sligo Town

COUNTY SLIGO

Dublin

IRELAND

Sligo Bay

Garavogue River

Garavogue River

├─┼─┤ Railway

SIGHTSEEING●
Model Arts Centre
  and Niland Gallery **9**
Sligo County Museum **9**
Sligo Abbey **18**
Yeats' Grave **2**
Yeats Memorial Building **6**

EATING ◆
Bar Bazaar **15**
Beezies **7**
Cafe Bar Deli **8**
Eurobar **10**
Hargadon's **16**
Hy-Breasil **11**

PARTYING ★
Fiddler's Creek **13**
Left Bank **8**
McGarrigle's **14**
McLynn's **19**
Shoot the Crows **12**

SLEEPING ■
The Eden Hill Holiday Hostel **20**
The Harbour House Hostel **3**
Rathnashee **1**
Renate Central House **17**
Sligo Park Hotel **20**
The White House Hostel **4**

cool cafes

Bar Bazaar (Market St., at Gratton St.; ☎ **071/9144-749;** all dishes €3–€8; Mon–Fri 9am–6pm, Sat–Sun 10am–6pm) is *the* place to hang with a young boho crowd. Here you can check out fliers on Buddhist meditation, browse through secondhand philosophy books, and encounter unwashed French philosophers, all while sipping a cappuccino.

Another great find *and* one of the few places open on a Sunday is **Eurobar** (Stephen St., north side of the river; ☎ **071/9161-788;** mains from €8), a slicker cafe that lacks the cozy charm of Bar Bazaar but is popular with locals and big on multiculturalism, as is the nearby **Hy-Breasil** (Bridge St., north side of the river; ☎ **071/9161-180;** mains from €7), which offers a more basic and new-agey feel and some scrumptious homemade food.

(19 O'Connell St.; ☎ **071/914-0082;** www.cygo.ie), open Monday to Saturday 9am to 6pm and Sunday 1 to 5pm. Internet access is €1.25 for 10 minutes, €2.50 for 30 minutes, and €4 for an hour. Students get a small bit knocked off the price. There are also Internet-accessible PCs at the **County Sligo Library,** on Stephen Street (☎ **071/914-2212**), which is open Tuesday to Friday 10am to 5pm, Saturday 10am to 1pm and 2 to 5pm.

POST OFFICES   The **Sligo General Post Office,** Wine Street (☎ **071/914-2646**), is open Monday through Saturday 9am to 5:30pm.

RECOMMENDED WEBSITES   The most comprehensive local Internet source for Sligo can be found at **www.sligotourism.ie.**

TOURIST OFFICES   For information about Sligo and the surrounding area, contact the **North West Regional Tourism Office,** Aras Reddan, Temple Street, Sligo (☎ **071/916-1201;** www.northwestireland.travel.ie). It's open year-round, weekdays 9am to 5pm, with weekend and extended hours April to August.

SLEEPING

Sligo is blessed with heaps of hostels, and if they're full there are plenty of good B&Bs too. The welcome is big and honest in Sligo and fellow travelers are usually up for a good time.

Hostels

➔ **Eden Hill Holiday Hostel**   The Eden sits 10 minutes out of town in an imposing Victorian building. There's no curfew and stunning views from the rooms. The same views that Yeats might have looked at when he stayed here. Yes, he's been all over the county and he's been here, too. His cousin once owned the house. *Pearse Rd., Marymount.* ☎ *071/9143-204. €14 dorm. MC, V. Amenities: Camping; kitchen; laundry.*

➔ **The Harbor House Hostel**   A beautiful old 19th-century building hides 50 beds inside. This hostel is so immaculate it almost makes up for the slightly uptight nature of the owners. Almost. The dorms have great beds, some have TVs in the room—a major rarity for hostels—and all have clean bathrooms. The downstairs has a superb kitchen, an adjacent dining area, and a comfortable TV room that's so lovely it seems out of place in a hostel. Avoid making loud noises or using the kitchen late at night. If you're after somewhere quiet to stay, the only real drawback is the 10-minute walk to town. *Finisklin Rd.* ☎ *071/9171547. www.harbourhousehostel.com. €18 dorm; €40 doubles; €25 single. MC, V. Amenities: Kitchen; laundry; TV.*

➔ **The White House Hostel**   On a good night this is the best party hostel in town. On a bad night the crowd tends to be a bit more aloof and in need of a few drinks to get conversation flowing. The other things that don't flow too well are the showers—prepare for that frustrating lukewarm trickle. On the plus side, the kitchen is stocked full of goodies, there's a warming open fire, and a sociable smoking porch. *Markievicz Rd.* ☎ *071/9145160; €13–€14 dorm in 8 12-bedded rooms. Amenities: Kitchen.*

Doable

→ **Rathnashee** Rathnashee (meaning "Fort of the Fairies") is home to Tess and Sean Haughey, experts on their local area and owners of one of the best private libraries in town. They'll arrange tours with archaeologists for you if you like and will chat on and on round the table. Tess dishes out traditional Irish food and homemade preserves. The B&B itself is a modern bungalow and no smoking is allowed anywhere in the building. *Teesan, Donegal Rd., Sligo. On N15, 3km (2 miles) from Sligo Town center.* ☎ *071/43376 or 087/220-4423. €32 single without bathroom, €36 single with bathroom; €50 double without bathroom, €56 double with bathroom. Rates include full breakfast. MC, V. Amenities: Lounge.*

→ **Renate Central House** This small, gabled B&B is surely one of the most conveniently located in Sligo Town, within easy walking distance of the town center. John and Ursula Leyden offer sweet guest rooms, decorated with pine furnishings and crisp Irish linens. *9 Upper John St., Sligo.* ☎ *071/62014. 6 units, 3 with bathroom (shower only). €32 single without bathroom, €36 single with bathroom; €50 double without bathroom, €56 double with bathroom. Rates include full breakfast. No credit cards. In room: TV.*

Splurge

→ **Sligo Park Hotel** With a glass-fronted facade and sky-lit atrium lobby, this is Sligo's most contemporary hotel, set in sprawling parkland, and sporting distant views of Ben

Bulben to the north. The decor in the lobby is modern and creative, with a good use of color, and sleek contemporary furniture. The guest rooms are more generic but inoffensive, with pastel-toned floral fabrics, quilted headboards, and orthopedic beds. The real reason to splash out on this one is the leisure center with a gorgeous indoor pool, and plenty of other facilities to keep you busy. *Pearse Rd. (just over 1.6km/1 mile south of Sligo on the Dublin Rd./N4), Sligo.* ☎ *071/916-0291. www.leehotels.ie. 140 units. €130–€170 double. Rates include service charge and full breakfast. DC, MC, V. Amenities: 2 restaurants (international, cafe); bar; gym; indoor swimming pool; Jacuzzi; nonsmoking rooms; tennis court; sauna/steam room. In room: TV, tea/coffeemaker, hair dryer, radio.*

EATING

Sligo may not be brimming with tourists but gone are the days when the only thing you could get was pub grub. The new Sligo resident is a sophisticated young thing who likes his/her food to match.

Cheap/Doable

→ **Beezies** PUB GRUB   Even if you're not hungry, Beezies is worth a visit, if only for a drink or a look around. The marble counters, bar partitions of Tiffany glass, and lamps with tulip-shaped shades give a real 19th-century look to the place. The bar food is good and filling, with simple lunches of soup and sandwiches. *45 O'Connell St., Sligo, County Sligo* ☎ *071/43031. Lunch under €8. Mon–Sat noon–3:30pm. Closed Good Friday, Christmas Day.*

→ **Cafe Bar Deli** MEDITERRANEAN   Part of a small Irish chain offering a test of the urbane in rural areas and simple yet sophisticated cuisine in relaxed, attractive surrounds. Good salads include the one with goat cheese, beet root, and walnuts, while there's a lengthy menu of stone-baked pizza, and plenty of light, healthy pasta dishes. This is just the place when you're looking for a break from hefty traditional Irish dishes. *15 Rear Stephen's St., Sligo, County Sligo.* ☎ *071/ 914-0100. Main courses €10–€13. Tues–Sat 6–10pm.*

→ **Hargadon's** PUB GRUB This pub is legendary. More than a century old, it's the most atmospheric bar in the center of the downtown area. Although strictly a pub now, it also used to be a grocery shop, as you'll see when you enter if you glance at the shelves on the right. The decor is a mix of dark-wood walls, mahogany counters, flagstone floors, colored glass, old barrels and bottles, a potbellied stove, and alcoves lined with early prints of Sligo. There are four snugs, each with its own special features. Strung together, they are reminiscent of an old-fashioned railway carriage—a bit cramped but it sure gets everyone talking. As for the food, it outshines other bar food by far, with a wide array of dishes such as smoked salmon, country baked mushrooms, ratatouille, and pork Stroganoff. For dessert, try the delish whiskey cake. *4 O'Connell St., Sligo, County Sligo* ☎ *071/70933. Bar food under €10. No credit cards. Food served Mon–Sat 9am–5pm (bar open regular pub hours).*

PARTYING
Bars & Clubs

Sligo's cardinal virtue is its nightlife. The pubs crank especially hard on the weekends but you'll find a great scene any night of the week. Whether you're looking for trad, folk, blues, or techno, hippies, or hipsters, Sligo will find something that suits. High Street and the banks of the River Garavogue have the biggest glut of pubs, but there are finds all over town. Explore and don't settle for one that isn't quite your cup of cocoa. Pubs in Sligo, unless otherwise noted, keep traditional pub hours. Besides the list below don't forget Hargadon's (see "Eating," above) which also does plenty of drink alongside the food. Check the *Sligo Champion* for info about live

music and other nightlife happenings; you can find it at any bookstore, clothing store, or record store, as well as in most pubs.

→ **Fiddler's Creek** A local favorite, Fiddler's Creek is traditional without being stodgy. There's bags of atmosphere soaked up by a mainly 30- and 40-something crowd speckled with youngsters. But the best thing about Fiddler's is the space itself—stone archways, tin ceilings, and a peat fireplace. The attached restaurant offers filling pub grub. *Rockwood Parade.* ☎ *071/9141866.*

→ **Left Bank** Here the polo-shirted crowd mingles over beer and the whole place has a bustling-but-carefree vibe. Drinks are €3 to €5 more expensive than most other places in town, but the space is 30% to 50% more impressive. Live DJs spin soul, funk, and house from Thursday to Saturday for a grungier crowd. The complex also includes the Café Bar Deli (see "Eating," above). *15–16 Stephen's St.* ☎ *071/9140-100.*

→ **McGarrigle's** A fun, smoky, hippie hangout crossbred with a honky-tonk joint. The bar is too brightly lit, and the crowd seems a gently misanthropic set, but they're all friendly. Grab a pint, settle into a booth, and listen to live acoustic blues (or rock on some nights). They also have bargain soup, sandwiches, and coffee by day. BYO patchouli. *O'Connell St.* ☎ *071/9171193.*

→ **McLynn's** A trip to Sligo is not complete without a night at McLynn's. You can count on great live music every evening, but the best nights are when Shane, the wild, white-haired owner, jumps up on the bar with his guitar and leads the whole back room in a singalong. Arrive at about 8 or 8:30pm and grab a table in the back. It may be empty but within the hour you'll have the best seat in the house. *Old Market St., near the courthouse.* ☎ *071/914-2088.*

→ **Shoot the Crows** This long, narrow pub on Castle Street is one of Sligo's favorite haunts, bursting with younger drinkers and music lovers, as bands play here nightly. Decor is a kooky mix of red copper ceilings, African wood objects, and dust. Every square inch of bar, wall, and shelf is covered with cool stuff, and not in a scary TGI Friday's kind of way. Ladies, come here to meet a bohemian intellect. Fellas, order pints of Guinness and ponder the meaning of their goatees. All played out to a soundtrack encompassing Miles Davis, the Velvet Underground, and Tom Waits. Traditional music is played on Tuesday and Thursday nights. *Castle St, Sligo.* ☎ *071/916-2554. www.shootthecrows.ie.*

CINEMA

There's no art house affair here, just the **Gaiety Cinema** (Wine St.; ☎ **071/916-2651;** www.gaietysligo.com), a 12-screen giant playing mostly mainstream American flicks at night, with late-night showings and matinees on the weekend.

PERFORMING ARTS

→ **Blue Raincoat Theatre** This is Sligo's award-winning theater company. It is one of only three professional Irish acting companies (the Abbey in Dublin and the Druid in Galway are the others) that own their own theaters. During July and August, the Blue Raincoat often presents lunchtime performances of Yeats's plays as well as other Sligo-related productions. Evening shows usually start at 8pm. *Lower Quay St., Sligo.* ☎ *071/9170431. Tickets average €10–€12.*

→ **Hawk's Well Theatre** The premier stage of Ireland's northwest region, this modern 350-seat theater presents a varied program of drama, comedy, ballet, opera, and concerts of modern and traditional music. It derives its name from *At the Hawk's Well,* a one-act play by Yeats. The theater occasionally produces shows, but mostly books visiting professional and local companies. *Johnston Court, Sligo.* ☎ *071/916-1526. Tickets average €10. Mon–Sat box office 10am–6pm; most shows at 8pm.*

SIGHTSEEING

→ **Model Arts Centre and Niland Gallery** Housed in a 19th-century Romanesque-style schoolhouse, the M.A.C. has nine rooms for touring shows and local exhibits by artists, sculptors, writers, and musicians. In the summer there are often poetry readings and arts lectures. *The Mall, Sligo, County Sligo.* ☎ *071/914-1405. Free admission. Readings and lectures free–€7, depending on artist. No credit cards. Tues–Sun 11am–6pm; evening events 8pm.*

→ **Sligo Abbey** Founded as a place for Dominican monks to hang out in 1252 by Maurice Fitzgerald, Earl of Kildare, Sligo Abbey was the center of early Sligo Town. It was an important spot during medieval times and the burial place of the chiefs and earls of Sligo. But, as with other affluent religious settlements, the abbey was under constant attack, and it was finally destroyed in 1641. A lot of work has been done in recent years to bring it back up to scratch. The cloisters contain some fancy stone carving and the 15th-century altar is one of few intact medieval altars in Ireland. *Abbey St., Sligo, County Sligo.* ☎ *071/914-6406. Admission €2 adults, €1 students. No credit cards. Daily 10am–6:30pm. Closed Nov–Mar.*

(FREE) → **Sligo County Museum** History, history, history. Housed in a 19th-century church mansion, this museum starts with Sligo's Stone Age history and ends up back at Yeats, with a display of his complete works in first editions, poems on broadsheets, letters, and his Nobel Prize for literature (1923). There's also a collection of oils, watercolors, and drawings by Jack B. Yeats (W. B. Yeats's brother) and John B. Yeats (William and Jack's father). And a permanent collection of 20th-century Irish art, including works by Paul Henry and Evie Hone. *Stephen St., Sligo, County Sligo.* ☎ *071/914-2212. Free admission. Tues–Sat 10am–noon and 2–4:50pm. Closed Oct–May.*

FREE ➜ **Yeats Memorial Building** In a 19th-century redbrick Victorian building, this memorial is really one for hard-core Yeats fans only. However the building is also home to the Sligo Art Gallery, where you'll usually encounter a high standard exhibition by local, national, or international artists. More recently a bustling cafe has been added on to the complex. *Douglas Hyde Bridge, Sligo, County Sligo.* ☎ *071/914-2693. www.yeats-sligo.com. Free admission. Mon–Fri 9:30am–5pm.*

PLAYING OUTSIDE

Sligo lacks a good park, but if you want to get outdoors you only need head to the coast.

BEACHES For walking, jogging, or swimming, there are safe sandy beaches with places to promenade—always important—at Strandhill, Rosses Point, and Enniscrone on the Sligo Bay coast.

BICYCLING With its lakes and woodlands, Yeats Country is particularly good biking territory. To rent a bike, contact **Gary's Cycles Shop** (Quay St., Sligo; ☎ 071/914-5418).

FISHING For fishing gear and tackle, see **Barton Smith** (Hyde Bridge, Sligo; ☎ 071/914-6111). For boat rental, see **Kingfisher Bates** (Pier Rd., Enniscrone; ☎ 096/36733).

HORSEBACK RIDING An hour's or a day's riding on the beach, in the countryside, or over mountain trails, can be arranged at **Sligo Riding Centre** (Carrowmore; ☎ 071/916-1353), or at **Woodlands Equestrian Centre** (Loughill, Lavagh, Tubbercurry, County Sligo; ☎ 071/918-4207). Rates average €20 per hour.

SHOPPING

Most Sligo shops are open Monday to Saturday 9am to 6pm, and some may have extended hours during July and August. There are plenty of bookshops about, less music and clothes shops. The craft shops mentioned below might be a little on the steep side but they still make for good browsing.

In addition to the shops listed below, other places worth popping into include **Addam** (10 Gratton St.; ☎ 071/914-2977) where the trendy boys and girls around town get their clothes, and **The Record Room** (Gratton St.; ☎ 071/914-3748), which sells lots of Irish music and a small selection of vinyl, mostly techno and pop for the local DJs. It's also a good place to find out who's playing around town during your stay.

Crafts

➜ **M. Quirke** Michael Quirke started out as a butcher, but a few years ago he traded his cleaver for woodcarving tools and transformed his butcher shop into a craft studio. Step inside and watch as he transforms chunks of native timbers into Ireland's heroes of mythology, from Sligo's Queen Maeve to Cu Chulainn, Oisin, and other folklore characters. He also carves chess sets and other Irish-themed wood items. The price of an individual carving averages €85. *Wine St.* ☎ 071/914-2624.

➜ **Sligo Craft Pottery** This shop features the work of one of Ireland's foremost ceramic artists, Michael Kennedy, who produces pottery and porcelain with layers of textured markings and drawings that form a maze of intricate patterns. He then applies glazes that reflect the strong tones and shades of the Irish countryside in vases, jars, and dishes. *Market Yard.* ☎ 071/914-2586.

Food

➜ **Kates Kitchen** Splurge picnic supplies. Kates has a fab deli section, with gourmet meats, cheeses, salads, pâtés, and breads baked on the premises. Don't miss the handmade Irish chocolates and preserves. *24 Market St.* ☎ 071/914-3022.

Road Trips from Sligo: The Countryside

County Sligo is one of the best parts of Ireland for spotting ancient settlements and burial grounds, some dating back to the Stone

Age. As you cruise along country lines you'll often spy a dolmen (ancient stone table) in fields where sheep or ponies graze casually around it. Some are open to the public; most are not. And the Irish are pretty fierce when it comes to their property rights, so don't go clambering over a fence for a better pic without permission.

You really need a car to fully explore this area of Ireland as buses don't go to all the sites and are often infrequent. If you have a car, all these trips can be made in a day from Sligo.

To plunge in at the deep end of ancient sites, stop by the vast and strangely beautiful Carrowmore (see listing, below). It's a huge Neolithic cemetery that once contained as many as 200 passage tombs, some of which predate Newgrange by 500 years. From Carrowmore, you can see the hilltop cairn grave of Knocknarea as a lump atop the large hill in the distance. Local legend says this is the grave of the "fairy queen" known as Queen Maeve (Queen Mab in Shakespeare plays). If you have the energy to make the 30-minute climb to the top, the views are stunning. (Knocknarea is on the same road as Carrowmore—follow signs for "Mescan Meadhbha Chambered Cairn.") From Carrowmore and Knocknarea, it's about an hour's drive to the Neolithic mountaintop cemetery of Carrowkeel, which offers an unforgettable experience: After a breathtaking climb on foot, you'll find yourself alone with the past. The tombs face Carrowmore below and are aligned with the summer solstice.

Northwest of Sligo Bay, 6km (3³/₄ miles) offshore, lies the uninhabited island of ⚟ Best **Inishmurray,** where you'll find the spooky ruins of one of Ireland's earliest monastic settlements. Founded in the 6th century and destroyed by the Vikings in 807, the monastery of St. Molaise contains in its circular walls the remains of several churches, beehive cells, altars, and an assemblage of "cursing stones" once used to bring ruin on those who presumably deserved it.

SIGHTSEEING

⚟ Best FREE →**Carrowkeel Passage Tomb Cemetery** On top of a hill overlooking Lough Arrow, this ancient cemetery is gorgeous, isolated, and frequently empty. It's 14 cairns, dolmens, and stone circles date to the Stone Age (3,000 B.C.), and it's easy to feel its history, standing among the cold, ageless rocks. There's about a 20-minute walk to the top from the parking area—you'll need a car to get here—at the bottom. This is one of those undeveloped ancient sites—no visitor center or tea shop here, just ancient beauty. *West off the N4 (signposted on N4), between Sligo Town and Boyle, County Sligo. Free admission.*

⚟ Best → **Carrowmore Megalithic Cemetery** Here, at the dead center of the Coolera Peninsula, sits a massive passage grave that once had a Stonehenge-like stone circle of its own. Encircling it were as many as 100 to 200 stone circles and passage graves. The site predates Newgrange by more than 500 years. Over the years, some of the stones have been moved, but more than 60 circles and passage graves still exist, although the site spreads out so far that many of them are in farmer's properties adjacent to the main site. Look out for your first dolmen in a paddock next to the road about a mile before you reach the site. The dolmens were the actual graves, once covered in stones and earth. Some of these are open to visitors—you can get a map from the visitor center to those that are. On the main site, Tomb 52A, excavated in August 1998, is estimated to be 7,400 years old, making it the earliest known piece of free-standing stone architecture in the world. This is one of the great sacred landscapes of the ancient world. The visitor center offers informative exhibits and tours. *Carrowmore Visitors Centre (signposted on N4 and N15), County Sligo.* ☎ *071/916-1534.*

Admission €2 adults, €1 students. No credit cards. Daily 9:30am–6:30pm. Both visitor center and site closed Oct–Apr.

→ **Drumcliff & Yeats's Grave** Eight kilometers (5 miles) north of Sligo Town, Drumcliff is a small, stone church somehow dominating the valley in which it sits—drawing your eye with its tall steeple, and its ancient Celtic crosses. When Yeats died in 1939 in France, he asked that, "If I die here, bury me up there on the mountain, and then after a year or so, dig me up and bring me privately to Sligo." It happened. In 1948 his body was moved here, to the church where his great-grandfather had been a rector. As you walk into the graveyard, Yeats's grave is marked with a small, dark stone just to the left of the church. He's buried alongside his young wife Georgie Hyde-Lee (when they married in 1917 he was 52 and she was 23). The moving epitaph on the grave comes from his poem "Under Ben Bulben": "Cast a cold eye on life, on death; Horseman, pass by." The high cross in the churchyard is from the 11th century, and its faded eastern side shows Christ, Daniel in the lions' den, Adam and Eve, and Cain murdering Abel. On the simpler west side there's a scene of the crucifixion. There's also a little visitor center and a great tea shop with cakes; good, filling sandwiches; and fresh hot soup. *Drumcliffe Churchyard, Drumcliffe (off N15), County Sligo.*

→ **The Lough Gill Drive** This 42km (26-mile) drive-yourself tour around Lough Gill is well signposted. Head 1.6km (1 mile) south of town and follow the signs for Lough Gill, a beautiful lake that was constantly present in Yeats's writings. Within 3.2km (2 miles) you'll be on the lower edge of the shoreline. Among

the sites are Dooney Rock, with its own nature trail and lakeside walk (inspiration for the poem "Fiddler of Dooney"); the Lake Isle of Innisfree, made famous in Yeats's poetry and in song; and the Hazelwood Sculpture Trail, a cool forest walk along the shores of Lough Gill, with 13 wood sculptures. The storied Innisfree is one of 22 islands in Lough Gill. You can drive the whole lakeside circuit in less than an hour, or you can stop at the east end, if you like and visit Dromahair, a sweet village on the River Bonet, in County Leitrim. The road along Lough Gill's upper shore brings you back to the northern end of Sligo Town. Continue north on the main road (N15), and you'll see the graceful profile of Ben Bulben (519m/1,702 ft.), one of the Dartry Mountains, rising to the right. *County Sligo and County Leitrim.*

→ **Parke's Castle** On the north side of the Lough Gill Drive, on the County Leitrim side of the border, Parke's Castle stands out as a lone outpost in the natural lake and woodland scenery. Named after an English family that gained possession of it during the 1620 plantation of Leitrim (when land was confiscated from the Irish and given to favored English families), this castle was originally the stronghold of the O'Rourke clan, rulers of the kingdom of Breffni. Now restored using Irish oak and traditional craftsmanship, it's a great example of a 17th-century, fortified manor house. Cake lovers might like to know the tearoom has some tasty pastries. *Lough Gill Dr., County Leitrim.* ☎ *071/916-4149. Admission €2.75 adults, €1.25 students. St. Patrick's weekend 10am–5pm; Apr–May Tues–Sun 10am–5pm; June–Sept daily 9:30am–6:30pm; Oct daily 10am–5pm.*

County Donegal

Donegal Town

Set peacefully in Donegal Bay at the edge of the Atlantic, Donegal Town is a little blip of bustle in an otherwise isolated region. It's a

place to stop before you set off for adventures in the wilderness that begins as soon as you step outside the town's borders. There are other reasons to come to Donegal Town

County Donegal

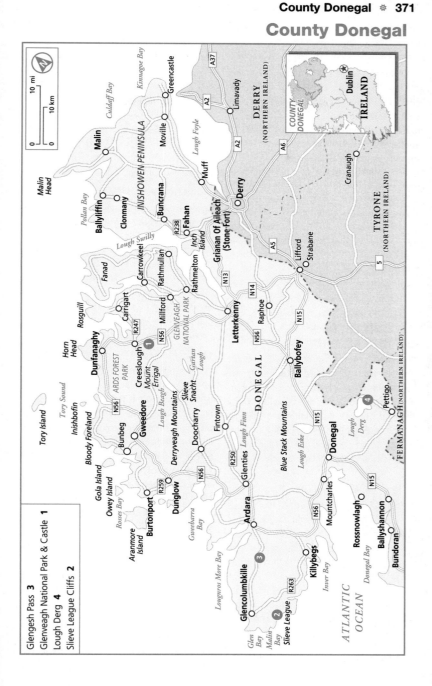

Glengesh Pass **3**

Glenveagh National Park & Castle **1**

Lough Derg **4**

Slieve League Cliffs **2**

besides its proximity to the wilds and woolies of the northern country. The hostels are quirky and extremely social, there are delicious little restaurants like the Blueberry Tea Room (see "Eating," below), and traditional music flourishes, at Murphy's Riverside Pub (see "Partying," below).

The town gets pretty crowded and busy on weekdays, but it's so small—only 3,000 people live here—that it's a pleasant sort of congestion. Donegal is also the transportation hub for the region, so you'll find buses to take you almost anywhere you want to go—if you're willing to wait for them.

After a day or so in Donegal, you'll inevitably want to start heading out into the wilderness. If you don't have a car or bike, and don't want to risk hitching or waiting all day for a bus, there are organized tours you can take to the surrounding areas. Check with the tourist office.

GETTING THERE & GETTING AROUND

BY PLANE   **Aer Arann** (☎ 01/814-5240; www.aerarann.ie) and **Aer Lingus** (☎ 01/886-8888; www.aerlingus.ie) operate regularly scheduled flights from Dublin to tiny **Donegal Airport,** Carrickfinn, Kincasslagh, County Donegal (☎ 074/954-8284; www.donegalairport.ie), about 65km (40 miles) northwest of Donegal Town on the Atlantic coast.

BY BUS   **Bus Éireann** (☎ 074/912-1309; www.buseireann.ie) operates daily bus service to Donegal Town from Dublin, Derry, Sligo, Galway, and other points. All tickets are issued on the bus. The pickup and boarding point is in front of the Abbey Hotel on The Diamond.

There are also a small number of private bus companies serving the northwest region. For example, **McGeehan's Coaches** (☎ 074/954-6150; www.mgbus.com) operates multiple daily buses between Donegal and Dublin. They leave from the Garda Station opposite

the Donegal Tourist Office. Between Galway and Donegal (via Ballyshannon, Bundoran, and Sligo), **Feda O'Donnell** (☎ 074/954-8114; www.fedaodonnell.com) operates at least one daily private coach. Other routes are also available.

BY CAR   If you're driving from the south, Donegal is reached on N15 from Sligo or A46 or A47 from Northern Ireland; from the east and north, it's N15 and N56; from the west, N56 leads to Donegal Town.

GETTING AROUND

Easily walked, Donegal has no local bus service within the town. If you need a taxi ask at your hostel, or call **Jim Johnston** (☎ 074/972-1349) or **Brendan McBrearty** (☎ 074/913-3420). Car drivers can park along the quay beside the tourist office, although you'll have to pay so you may be better off finding a back street. Just turn off Main Street toward the castle and river, and you'll see a space before too long.

ORIENTATION

This town is on the small side, maybe a 10-minute walk from one end to the other, and is centered around The Diamond. This little roundabout is the commercial heart of Donegal. Three main streets branch off the Diamond. Head south and you'll be on Quay Street, which leads you to the very helpful tourist office (see "Tourist Information," below) and then, eventually, to Sligo. East is Main Street, and west is Bridge Street. The River Eske flows north alongside the western edge of Donegal, then takes a sharp bend east and cuts across the top of town.

BASICS

EMERGENCIES   In an emergency, dial ☎ **999. Donegal District Hospital** is on Upper Main Street (☎ 074/972-1019). The local **Garda** Station is on Quay Street (☎ 074/972-1021).

INTERNET   **Donegal County Library,** Mountcharles Road (☎ 074/972-1705), is

Donegal Town

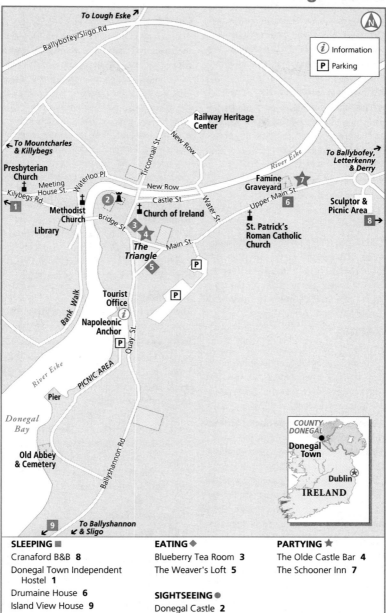

To Lough Eske ↗
Ballybofey/Sligo Rd.

ⓘ Information
P Parking

Railway Heritage Center

New Row
Tirconaill St.

← To Mountcharles & Killybegs

River Eske

To Ballybofey, Letterkenny & Derry

Presbyterian Church
Meeting House St.
Kilybegs Rd.
Waterloo Pl.
New Row
Castle St.
Water St.
Upper Main St.

Famine Graveyard ✩ **7**

6

Sculptor & Picnic Area
8 →

1

Methodist Church
Bridge St.
2
Church of Ireland

Library

3
4

The Triangle
5

Main St.

St. Patrick's Roman Catholic Church

P

P

Bank Walk

Tourist Office ⓘ

Napoleonic Anchor
P
Quay St.

River Eske

PICNIC AREA

Pier

Donegal Bay

Old Abbey & Cemetery

Ballyshannon Rd.

COUNTY DONEGAL
Donegal Town

Dublin ✷

IRELAND

9 ↙
To Ballyshannon ↙ & Sligo

SLEEPING ■
Cranaford B&B **8**
Donegal Town Independent Hostel **1**
Drumaine House **6**
Island View House **9**

EATING ◆
Blueberry Tea Room **3**
The Weaver's Loft **5**

SIGHTSEEING ●
Donegal Castle **2**

PARTYING ★
The Olde Castle Bar **4**
The Schooner Inn **7**

open Monday, Wednesday, and Friday 3 to 6pm, Saturday 11am to 1pm and 2 to 6pm. Internet access is free (for the time being), but there is a limit of 1 hour per session. Book ahead. **The Blueberry Tea Room** (see "Eating," below) also offers Internet access but here you'll have to pay €4 per hour. It's open Monday to Saturday 9am to 7:30pm.

POST OFFICE   The **Donegal Post Office** on Tirconnail Street (☎ **074/972-1024**) is open Monday, Tuesday, and Thursday to Saturday 9am to 5:30pm, Wednesday 9:30am to 5:30pm.

RECOMMENDED WEBSITES   For a wealth of online tourist information, the best websites are www.goireland.com/donegal and www.donegaltown.ie.

TOURIST INFORMATION   The **Donegal Tourist Office,** Quay Street (☎ **074/972-1148**), is open Easter through September, Monday to Friday 9am to 5pm, Saturday 10am to 6pm, and Sunday noon to 4pm, with extended hours in July and August.

SLEEPING
Hostels
Donegal has one of the friendliest hostels in Ireland. It's a ways out of town, but when you get there prepare to receive a very warm welcome. In town are plenty of B&Bs

➔ **Donegal Town Independent Hostel**
Within 10 minutes of arriving at this hostel, you'll have been introduced to everyone else in the place and have a cup of tea in your hand. The owners like to make you feel like part of their family. But what about the bunk rooms? Well, they're decorated with funky murals, and are really clean and spacious. Kitchen? Bit small but it's got everything you need. Showers? Hot and strong. This place gets our highest recommendation. The Paddywagon tour bus rolls through here once a week, filling up half the hostel so make sure to call ahead. *A half-mile out of town on the Killybegs Rd., on the right side and up a little hill.* ☎ *073/9722805. www.donegalhostel.com.*

€12 dorm; €32 double. Amenities: Camping; kitchen; TV; video.

Doable
If all you need is privacy and giant fry-ups in the morning, head to the **Drumaine House** (Upper Main St.; ☎ **073/972-1516**). It's right in the middle of town, allowing easy access after a night at the pubs or a long day out in the wilderness. And all rooms have their own bath. Close to downtown, the **Cranaford B&B** (take Main St. away from the Diamond and make a right past the school, across from the hospital; ☎ **073/972-1455**) is totally unremarkable, but offers a great night's sleep at a good price.

Located a little ways outside of town, the **Island View House** (on the Ballyshannon Rd. outside of Donegal; ☎ **073/972-2411**) does the basic B&B thing. All rooms are clean, plain, and comfortable, with TVs and baths, plus there are views of the ocean.

EATING
There's not a lot of eating options in this small town, but what is there is really rather good.

➔ **Blueberry Tea Room** CAFE   The best budget food in town. You could have a different delicious meal here every day of the week. Fry-ups start off the day while inventive sandwiches and delicious soups with homemade brown bread are served all afternoon. Lastly, oozing puds like sticky toffee should slap on some survival fat to get you ready to head out into the wilds of Donegal County. The Internet cafe upstairs is a bonus (see "Basics," above). *Castle St. right off the Diamond.* ☎ *073/9722933; Mon–Sat 9am–6pm. All items €4–€10.*

➔ **The Weaver's Loft** CAFE   Upstairs from Magee's tweed shop, this 60-seat self-service restaurant with its huge mural of Donegal has a "times-past" vibe. The menu changes daily, but usually includes prawn, cheese, and fruit salads as well as scrumptious sandwiches, soups, cakes, and tarts. *Magee Shop, The Diamond, Donegal, County*

Donegal. ☎ *074/972-2660. Main courses €5– €8. Mon–Sat 9:45am–5pm.*

PARTYING

Donegal isn't about wild nights out until dawn but there's still some fun to be had in the pubs along the main drag. The soundtrack to most nights out is definitely trad music.

Bars

Let's face it, young people here are not in overabundance. Most people who grow up here leave when they graduate from secondary school, so there's a big gulf between 18 and 30. The biggest crowd of 20-somethings you're likely to encounter will be fellow travelers. Donegal draws a different kind of globetrotter than those who flock to Dublin or Galway. More laid-back and earthy, the travelers here will be happy to go out for a pint, listen to some music, and talk the night away. Cocktails are pretty much unheard of in these parts, and Guinness is, as always, the drink of choice. This fits perfectly with Donegal's attitude toward nightlife: relaxed, friendly, and fun. There are plenty of other pubs besides the ones below. Just wander along the main drag until you hear the fiddle.

→ **Biddy O'Barnes** This is a ways out of town, but if you're having a night off the booze and have a car, it's worth it. You have to detour into the Blue Stack Mountains— don't you just love the sound of those already?—and the scenic Barnesmore Gap, 11km (6³/₄ miles) northeast of Donegal Town, to visit this pub, which has been in the same family for four generations. Passing through the front door—with its etched-glass window and iron latch—is like entering a country cottage, with blazing turf fires, stone floors, wooden stools, and benches. On most evenings there's a spontaneous music session. *Donegal Ballybofey Rd. (N15), Barnesmore, County Donegal.* ☎ *0749721402.*

→ **The Olde Castle Bar** There is an old-Donegal aura at this little pub, which has a welcoming open fireplace, etched glass, and whitewashed walls. The bartenders are friendly, and there's a good menu of pub food on offer. *Castle St.* ☎ *074/9721062.*

→ **The Schooner Inn** Given the name, it's somewhat unsurprising that this pub is decorated with model ships and seafaring memorabilia. There is music on most summer evenings, with traditional Irish music on Monday and Saturday, folk on Wednesday, and singing acts on Thursday, Friday, and Sunday. *Upper Main St.* ☎ *074/9721671.*

PERFORMING ARTS

If you're in Donegal during July and August, try to take in a show put on by the Donegal Drama Circle at the **Donegal Town Summer Theatre,** O'Cleary Hall, Tirconnaill Street (no phone). Performances are held on Tuesday, Wednesday, and Thursday at 9pm and usually feature works by Donegal-based playwrights. No reservations are necessary; admission prices start at €5 for adults, €2.50 for students.

SIGHTSEEING

Donegal doesn't have many sights to see but it's a pleasing town to stroll around for a morning or afternoon. The role it fulfills better is a rest stop and a place to find a pub and food after a day in the hills.

Lough Derg and its many islands lie about 16km (10 miles) east of Donegal. Legend says St. Patrick spent 40 days and 40 nights fasting in a cavern at this secluded spot. Ever since, it has been a place of penance and pilgrimage. From June 1 to August 15, thousands of Irish people take turns coming to Lough Derg to do penance for 3 days at a time, remaining awake and eating nothing but tea and toast. It's considered one of the most rigorous pilgrimages in all of Christendom. To reach the lake, take R232 to Pettigo, then R233 for 8km (5 miles).

→ **Donegal Castle** Built in the 15th century on the banks of the River Eske, this magnificent castle was once the chief stronghold for the O'Donnells, a powerful Donegal clan. In the 17th century, during the Plantation period, it ended up with Sir Basil Brook, who added a huge extension. Much of the building has survived the centuries; it was all restored in 1996. Free 25-minute guided tours are available. *Castle St., Donegal, County Donegal.* ☎ *074/972-2405. Admission €3.50 ($4.55) adults, €1.25 ($1.65) students. Mid-Mar to Oct daily 10am–5:15pm. Closed Nov to mid-Mar.*

FREE →**Old Abbey** Sitting in a peaceful spot where the River Eske meets Donegal Bay, this old Franciscan monastery was founded in 1474 by the first Red Hugh O'Donnell and his wife, Nuala O'Brien of Munster. It became an important center of religion and learning. Great gatherings of clergy and lay leaders assembled here in 1539. It was from this friary that some of the scholars undertook to salvage old Gaelic manuscripts and compile *The Annals of the Four Masters* (1632–36). Enough remains of its glory—some impressive ruins of a church and a cloister—to give you an idea of what once was. *The Quay, Donegal, County Donegal. Free admission.*

PLAYING OUTSIDE

BICYCLING The north side of Donegal Bay offers some great cycling roads—scenic but very hilly. One good but arduous route from Donegal Town follows the coast roads west to Glencolumbkille (day 1), continues north to Ardara and Dawros Head (day 2), and then returns to Donegal (day 3). It takes in some of the most spectacular coastal scenery in Ireland along the way. Rental bikes are available from **Pat Boyle** (☎ **074/972-2515**). The cost is roughly €10 a day, €60 a week. Alternatively get a bike from **Irish Cycle Hire** (☎ **041/685-3772;** www.irishcyclehire.com) for €70 for the week or €15 for the day. For €20 extra you can ride it on to one of their other depots across Ireland in Dublin, Drogheda, Westport, Galway, Ennis, Dingle, Killarney, or Cork.

WALKING Crossing Boyce's Bridge on the Killybegs road will bring you to the beginning of the Bank Walk to your left. This 2.5km (1½-mile) walk is delightful, following the west bank of the River Eske as it empties into Donegal Bay. It offers great views of the Old Abbey, Green Island, and Donegal Bay.

SHOPPING

You're not going to find any groovy record shops here, but pack up your funky urbane self in your rucksack and open your mind to traditional Donegal crafts as that's what this town has to offer. Most Donegal shops are open Monday to Saturday from 9am to 6pm, with extended hours in summer and slightly shorter hours in winter.

Books

→**The Four Masters Bookshop** Facing the monument commemorating the Four Masters, this shop is a right royal treasure trove of local knowledge, specializing as in books about Ireland and Donegal. *The Diamond.* ☎ *074/9721526.*

Clothes

→ **Magee of Donegal Ltd** Wanna go home with a bespoke Irish tweed suit? Oh go on, you know you do. Think how your mates would swoon with envy as you swanned into the local 7/11. Established in 1866, this shop is the name for fine Donegal hand-woven tweeds, including beautiful suits, jackets, overcoats, hats, ties. Worth a look if nothing else. Tweed was the original hunters camouflage. *The Diamond.* ☎ *074/9722660.*

Craft

→ **Donegal Craft Village** This cluster of artisans' shops in a rural setting about a mile south of town provides a creative environment for an ever-changing group of craftspeople and a range of ancient and modern trades: porcelain, ceramics, weaving, batik, jewelry, and metalwork. You can meander from shop to shop and see the artists doing their thing. The coffee shop serves baked yummies, snacks, and lunch in the summer.

The studios are open year-round Monday to Saturday 10am to 6pm and Sunday noon to 6pm. *Ballyshannon Rd.* ☎ *074/9722015.*

Food

➔ **Simple Simon Natural Foods** This place is so good it's a challenge to leave without buying something. And, once you've bought it, the challenge is to leave the shop before consuming it. Come for the usual health food store selection of organic grains, vitamins, oils, and handmade soaps; stay for the delicious organic breads and cakes. *The Diamond.* ☎ *073/9722687.*

Music

➔ **Melody Maker Music Shop** If you can't get enough of the traditional and folk music of Donegal, stop in here for tapes, recordings, and posters. This is also the main ticket agency for the southwestern section of County Donegal, handling tickets for most concerts and sports nationwide. *Castle St.* ☎ *074/9722326.*

Around Donegal Bay

The rugged coastline around Donegal Bay is one of the wildest places in Ireland, and the drive around its edges is one of the best road trips in the country. The rocky land careens toward the dark blue Atlantic, with the road just stopping short of the icy water. Roads wind so tightly it will almost make you dizzy, and mean it's difficult to get up speeds of more than 35 mph. This gives you plenty of time to take in the awesome views: rolling hills, jagged mountains, bright green fields, and the sea sparkling down below. On a map, the coast looks like a lobster claw reaching out from Donegal Town to grasp the bay's beautiful waters. There's plenty of mischief to get up to here, whether it's hiking in the mountains, catching waves on some of Ireland's best surf beaches, or simply holing up in a hostelry to listen to some traditional jamming.

Other cool stuff to do around here includes getting your soul blown into life on top of the Slieve League cliffs, watching the fish being unloaded in the very real town of Killybegs and the drive through the Glengesh Pass a narrow, sinuous, scenic roadway that rises to a height of 270m (886 ft.) before plunging, in a tortuously zigzag pattern of hairpin curves, into the valley below. It runs between Glencolumbkille and Adara, both cute stops in their own right.

Bundoran

One particular town on the coast—Bundoran—may not seem like much to look at, but it is the place to go surfing in the area. Nearly 10 years ago an Australian film collective called The Val Dusty Experiment drifted into Bundoran to capture locals and travelers surfing in this—then unknown—town. The result was the trippy cult classic *Litmus.* It left a magical trail and put Bundoran on the world surfing map. Don't leave the area without grabbing yourself a viewing or get your own copy at www.litmus.com.au. More recently Bundoran has played host to the European Surfing Championships and the Quiksilver World Masters. If you know your surfers, you'll be pleased to hear Tom Curren, The Malloy Brothers, Michael and Derek Ho, Gary Elkerton, Mark Richards, Serena Brooke, and Claire Bevacqua are all likely to be catching waves out on the water.

GETTING THERE & GETTING AROUND

Buses with **Bus Éireann (071/916-0066; www.buseireann.ie)** run direct from Bundoran to Sligo, Derry and Galway.

BASICS

TOURIST OFFICES Bundoran is a place to watch tumbleweed drift across Main Street in the winter and consequently only has a seasonal tourist office at The Bridge on Main Street, directly overlooking The Peak bay (☎ **071/984-2539**). Open May to October, daily 10am to 4pm; November to April, Friday and Saturday 11am to 3pm. Bank Holiday weekends 10am to 4pm.

Hang Ten

A few things to know about surfing in Ireland: It's very cold and it's very, very good.

Okay, that's only two things, but they're the ones that really matter. Over the last few years, word has spread through the international surfing community that Ireland offers a few of the things surfers particularly love— uncrowded beaches, powerful waves, and great pubs. That was pretty much all they needed to start coming here for cold-water surfing.

The thundering Irish surf is fed by North Atlantic storm systems that create a surprising swell, but they're all in rather obscure places, so to surf here you need a good wetsuit, a car, and plenty of time to wait for the waves to cooperate.

While there's surfing to be had just about anywhere, the west coast is undeniably better than the east. The hottest surfing beach in the country is Bundoran, on Donegal Bay north of Sligo. It and the Tullan Strand nearby both have consistent and outstanding beach waves (on Tullan the best are at the south end of the beach).

Not quite as good, but still not bad at all, Kilcummin Harbour offers a long left big wave reef break with strong currents and rip tides. If there's a good north wind the swells can be fantastic, but that's a fairly big "if." Here you can escape the crowds by heading past Kilcummin to Lackan Bay, where a secluded beach at the foot of towering cliffs offers peace and quiet at the end of a battered road. It also has a beach break with multiple peaks. Not too shabby.

Another place to head if crowds aren't your scene is Easky, a good 45 minutes south of Sligo. This is a small town favored by good offshore breezes. The best surfing spots here are the reefs near the ruined castle tower.

Down south in County Clare, Doolin is known for consistently good surfing conditions, and you'll find great breaks off Crab Island, at the town beach in tiny Lahinch, and in Doolin itself. Isolationists should know that there are excellent beaches to be found in between those three. With a good map and a car, you can explore the more remote coastal nooks and crannies to find surfing spots where nobody will be out on the water except you and the occasional passing fishing boat.

RECOMMENDED WEBSITES Information for travelers can be found on www.donegal bay.com.

SLEEPING

There's not that much budget accommodation in Bundoran but, then again, it's not that big a town. The best bet is **Homefield Quality Budget Accommodation** (yep, that's really is its name), Bayview Avenue (☎ 071/984-1977; homefield@indigo.ie; dorm €18 including basic breakfast), in a 250-year-old building staffed by an ultrafriendly brigade. If you're planning on staying around a while, try **The Surfers Cove Holiday Village** (Tullan Strand Rd.; ☎ 071/984-2286; www.surferscove.com; four-bed house from €300, six-bed house from €400), its sweet little whitewashed abodes bizarrely mismarketed in the local tourist brochure as "directly behind the Kentucky Fried Chicken Restaurant"—don't be put off.

EATING & PARTYING

Food and drink options are a mixture of tacky seaside pleasures and traditional Irish *craic*.

Thursday nights are probably the liveliest in the week. The bars are usually open until 11.30pm. An hour later on the weekends.

The one place you really need to know about to go is the **Madden's Bridge Bar** (West End Bundoran; ☎ 071/984-2050; www.maddensbridgebar.com), an all-in-one eating-and-drinking establishment where the surfers gather in the evenings. Tuesday, Thursday, and Sunday are trad music nights. Surfing fanatics should make sure to catch the signed world surf team T-shirts down the back of the pub. There's a posh menu serving fish, Tex-Mex, and steaks for €11 to €23 and a bar menu with good warming dishes including bacon and cabbage, Irish stew, and Beef and Guinness Casserole all going from about €9.25 to €13. Upstairs are some great views out over the bay, and they promise their pints "slide down the gullet like a penguin in a wetsuit"—what further recommendation do you need?

Other eating options include **Zaika** (Main St.; ☎ 071/984-1543; dishes €8 to €15), a surprising Indian and Turkish restaurant in an old church, with a welcome BYO wine policy. Farther down is **The Barbecue Restaurant,** Main Street (☎ 071/413-7498; dishes €5–€20), not the friendliest place in town but it does answer the carnivore call with ribs, chicken wings, lamb cutlets, spit roasts, fresh fish. You get the picture.

When you've had your fill of food, you'll find Bundoran drinking can be a pretty crazy affair. **Bootleggers Saloon** (Main St.; ☎ 071/984382) displays a sign on the door stating it's "licensed to sell strong beer and hard licquor." That just about sets the tone for the evening. There's often live music, too. On a good night, this is rowdy, noisy Irish drinking at its best. On a bad night . . . perhaps best find somewhere else to down your pint.

The Chasing Bull (Main St.; ☎ 071/984-1988) usually has some live rock going as its friendly sports-mad landlord is a big Elvis

fan. You'll find a mixed crowd in here ranging from 18 to 88, although later in the night the octogenarians start tottering off home to bed leaving a bar full of lively youngsters.

For a night off the sauce, try the **Bundoran Cineplex** (Station Rd.; ☎ 071/982-9999) showing most of the big U.S. blockbusters throughout the year. Although by the time they get here you've probably already seen them back home.

FESTIVALS

The big, wet, watery event in Bundoran is the annual _MTV_ Best **Ocean Fest** (www.bundoran oceanfest.com) when there are loads of free surf lessons and screenings of extreme sports videos, plus 2005 saw the town's first surfathalon.

PLAYING OUTSIDE

On an average day in Bundoran the waves are 1m (3 ft.). In a storm these rise to 3 to 4.5m (10–15 ft.). Often you'll find 2m (6 ft.) smoothies after just a little inclement weather out to sea. The big wave season is late August to November thanks to the U.S. hurricanes spinning a little of their power out across the Atlantic.

With all these wonderful waves in the area, if you've come to Bundoran it's probably because you surf or want to learn to surf. Either way, go to _MTV_ Best **The Bundoran Surf Company** (Main St.; ☎ 071/984-1968; www.undoransurfcompany). These guys really live the surfing dream and will pump you up with their passion. They'll get beginners out on the water from €30 for a 3-hour session. Most people book in for a few days (sessions running in the morning and afternoon on most days) so they can head out onto the water without shame. If you're an expert, it's still worth swinging by to get the word on good beaches for the current conditions and dangerous rips to watch out for. Their shop on Main Street is a real hang-out, too. Tea and coffee are always being served up to shivering Atlantic returnees, and there's also a copy of the hippy surf film *Litmus* they're usually happy to stick on the TV. They'll also introduce you to the increasingly popular buzz of kitesurfing, best done on the nearby beach of Tullen Strand, which is also where the novice surfers start out. The main town beach is strictly for experts, thanks to its vicious reef.

Another outfit is **Donegal Watersports** at the Donegal Adventure Centre (Bayview Avenue; ☎ **071/984-2277;** www.donegal watersports.com), who also offer climbing, abseiling, and hill walking in the area, if you can find some buddies to go with you.

Alternatively, stay on shore and rent a bike from **Rent-a-Bike** (West End; ☎ **071/984-1526;** mggoodwin@eircom.net; €12 per day, €56 per week) where owner Michael will point you in the direction of some good rides, including those to Mullaghmore, Kinlough, and Ballintrillick; or get in the saddle at **Stracomer Riding School,** off the Sligo-Ballyshannon Road (N15), Bundoran (☎ **071/984-1787**), where they specialize in trail riding across farmlands, beaches, dunes, and mountain trails. An hour's ride averages €18.

Slieve League Cliffs

One of the most beautiful stretches of coast in the country, the 🎬 Best **Slieve League Cliffs** are just a hop and a skip from Donegal town. A bumpy, winding mountain road takes you all the way up to Bunglass, the rock formation making up the lower side of the cliffs. The view is incredible from here, and you'll need to decide whether you want to merely gaze at their 300m (1,000-ft.) splendor as the rough Atlantic pounds away at the cliffs, or get up close and personal on the wind-buffeted walk along the ridge (only the fearless and fit need apply).

You can hike from the Bunglass lookout point all the way to Tramane Strand in Malin Beg, a few miles southwest of Glencolumb-kille. This walk involves crossing the infamous

"One Man's Pass," a narrow ridge with steep drops on both sides that should not be attempted by the acrophobic, nor those wearing high heels. It's a 15km (9-mile) walk, and you'll have to arrange a pickup at the end. The summits of Slieve League are often capped in clouds—think twice about this escapade if there is danger of losing visibility along the way.

GETTING THERE & GETTING AROUND

It's about a 29km (18-mile) stretch of road from Donegal Town to the cliffs, so a car is your best option. To get here, follow Slieve League road signs from Donegal on the R263 Killybegs Road past Kilcar. Here, turn off to Teelin and follow signs for the Bunglass viewing point, about 2km (1 mile) away. There are also various bus tours of Slieve League that leave from Donegal. Check with the tourist office in Donegal for details.

Letterkenny

Letterkenny is Donegal's biggest town. Many people whiz through it on their way to or from the wilder regions of Donegal. Big mistake. Letterkenny is a fab place to base yourself for exploring Donegal or getting reacquainted with civilization after some rural adventures. The town has exploded in the past few years, thanks to U.S. investment and an up-and-thrusting youthful population seasonally expanded with the students from the Letterkenny Institute of Technology. Okay, so it's pretty much a one-street town, but that street is packed full of pubs, many of which are packed full of students or outdoor obsessives. Plus the town's got a fascinating Republican history, a good live music scene, and even an art gallery. What more do you want?

GETTING THERE & GETTING AROUND

Regular buses run to and from Letterkenny from Derry, Sligo, Galway, and Dublin throughout the day with **Bus Éireann**

(☎ 074/912-1309; www.buseireann.ie), with a less frequent service to Donegal. The bus station sits at the corner of Pearce Road and Port Road.

BASICS

TOURIST INFORMATION **Letterkenny Tourist Office** can be found at Derry Road (☎ 074/912-1160) and is open Monday to Saturday 9am to 8pm, Sunday 10am to 2pm in July and August; Monday to Friday 9am to 5pm from January to June; and Monday to Friday 9am to 5pm September to December.

INTERNET In the centre of town **Cyberworld** (underneath The Courtyard Shopping Centre; ☎ 074/912-0440) has the atmosphere of a bus station but is open Monday to Friday 10am to 9.30pm, Saturday 10am to 7pm, Sunday 2 to 7pm, and charges €5 per hour for Internet access with a discount for students. Cyberworld also operates as an international call center. Cash only. Up the other end of town **Onvi** (76 Upper Main St.; ☎ 074/910-3290) is far cleaner and cooler charging only €3 per hour for access to its fab flatscreen machines. Open Monday to Saturday 9am to 9pm, Sunday 1 to 7pm.

RECOMMENDED WEBSITES www.letterkennyguide.com does a fairly decent job of pointing out local places to stay and things to see, or there's always the regional site www.irelandnorthwest.ie.

FESTIVALS

The **Earagail Arts Festival 2006** (www.earagailartsfestival.ie) will run from July 10 to July 23. During this time thought-prodding theatrical and artistic events will happen in the town and spin out across Donegal. The next month, the whole town gets ready for a good old-fashioned knees up with the 2006 All-Ireland Fleadh (www.comhaltas.com), a bacchanalian trad music event where the amount of playing is matched only by the amount of drinking.

SLEEPING

Not being a tourist hotspot, Letterkenny isn't blessed with huge amounts of budget accommodation. If you can, nab yourself a room at the **Port Hostel** (Orchard Crest; ☎ 074/912-5315; dorm €12–€20 dependent on number of beds in dorm and season; double €40–€45; single €25), a surprisingly green and leafy place right near the center of town. Yes, the '70s floral wallpaper might leave a little to be desired, but there's no curfew so you can avoid it all night if you like. Camping is also available during July and August.

Straightforward B&B accommodation can be found at **Ardlee,** Gortlee (☎ 074/912-1943; double €60), within walking distance of the bus station, while a treat sleep awaits at the new **Radisson SAS Hotel,** The Loop Road (☎ 074/919-4444; www.radissonsas.ie; doubles from €120), where you'll get access to the gym and pool thrown in for the night.

EATING

As this town starts to make some serious cash, its eateries have begun to breed. Prepare for some high standard food at fairly grounded prices.

For a pseudo-meal in a cup, check out **Guava** (The Courtyard Shopping Centre; ☎ 074/916-0804; juices and smoothies €2–€4; Mon–Sat 9am–6pm), a mall juice bar popular with locals. Stop by to pick up milkshakes, lattes, juices, and herbal teas. Wilderness returnees can boost their vitamin C intake with a Flu Jab combo juice (pink grapefruit, orange, and strawberry) or cool off in summer with a Guava Goodness smoothie (guava, pear, banana, orange, and yoghurt).

Cheap/Doable

Another spot offering cheap grub includes **The Brewery** (see "Partying," below), where fish and chips and steak baguettes can be had for between €8.50 and €12.

➔ **The Lemon Tree** INTERNATIONAL   The blue-tiled exterior of The Lemon Tree might look a little run-down, but it doesn't stop droves of locals from packing the place out on a nightly basis. They come for the warm interior and modern Irish food, including tasting plates of local seafood and roast tenderloin of lamb with rosemary jus. A reliable treat if you don't need fancy surrounds to enjoy your food. Eat between 5 and 7pm to get a shot at the cheaper early-bird menu. *39 Lower Main St.* ☎ *074/912-5788. Early bird mains €8–€17; a la carte mains €8.95–€35.*

➔ **Simple Simon's** CAFE   One of only three Simple Simon's shops in Ireland providing healthy bites in a tasty format. Take a seat in the wooden-floored, orange-walled cafe and take your pick from lots of organic and gluten-free options including soups, salads, veg dishes, freshly baked soda bread, and local cheeses. There are plenty of cakes for afters and a health food shop next door for takeouts. *Oliver Plunkett Rd.* ☎ *074/912-2382. Cakes 50c–€1, soup and small salad €7.50. Mon–Fri 9am–6:30pm; Sat 9am–6pm.*

➔ **The Yellow Pepper** INTERNATIONAL   Located in an old Victorian shirt factory, this eatery is remarkably contemporary. The floors and walls may be original but the subtle lighting is warm and modern. The pasta and vegetarian dishes make up the doable dishes, but venture into the realms of the splurge with starters such as salmon and ginger rice paper roll or mains like baked cod and chorizo oil and sirloin steak jalfrezi. *36 Lower Main St.* ☎ *074/912-4133. ypepper@indigo.ie. Mains €12 to €20. Mon–Sat noon–10pm; Sun 1–10pm.*

PARTYING

Doing a pub crawl in Letterkenny is so simple. You simply stumble from one end of the Main Street to the other. On your way you'll find lively dance clubs, traditional pubs, and alternative music venues. Most pubs stay open until 11.30pm with an hour extra on one or more nights at the weekend.

➔ **Bar Mono**   Mention Bar Mono and the hipper Letterkenny residents will wrinkle their faces in disgust. Desperate to be a sophisticated urbane bar, Mono somehow missed the mark and has become better known for being on the wrong side of rough. However, if you want to get down to R&B and hip-hop with a lively crowd of 18- to 30-year-olds, and have a choice of three bars to sup at, this isn't a bad place to do it. Especially as it's open until 2.30am on Friday and Saturday nights. *Lower Main St.* ☎ *074/917-7911.*

➔ **The Brewery**   As the manager states, it's "upstairs for live bands and downstairs for a quiet pint." Popular with hen parties and a slightly older crowd, things can get quite lively on the weekends when the appearance of a few men and their instruments has been known to cause spontaneous outbreaks of dancing. Inside are simple stripped floorboards and a huge copper bar but outside is where you want to be in summer, sitting Euro-style on the town square. Open until 1am. *Market Sq.* ☎ *074/912-7330.*

📺 **Best** ➔**The Casbah**   Scuffy. Dirty. Fantastic. This is Letterkenny's equivalent of an underground music club. The minute you walk down the stairs, your ears are attacked by a wild guitar, and a rush of adrenaline pumps right through your soul. The crowd is young and sulky. The staff are pierced. The decor is posters of rock heroes: Lennon, Cobain, and Hendrix. The music is largely alternative. The aim is to make it the best live music venue in the Northwest, providing a stage for Irish and international indie acts. They're very nearly there. Open until 2.30am at the weekend. *Main St. No phone.*

➔ **The Cavern**   This cavern, made of light-wood and plasma screens, provides a nocturnal home to scores of smart, casual 20-somethings. During the summer most of them can be found up on the glam smoking verandah where huge heaters keep the scantily clad from catching a chill. Back down in the main arena, Wednesday ushers in a karaoke night before the weekend brings on the DJs spinning everything from R&B to rock. *46 Lower Main St.* ☎ *074/912-6733. www.the cavern.ie.*

→ **The Cottage** Letterkenny's favorite drinkery, equally beloved by boho students and ageing old farmer types. Inside is a visual cacophony of potted plants, old washboards, and wooden spoons, all scattered above and around the roaring open fire. Here you'll meet some of the coolest characters in town. Impromptu trad sessions are liable to occur at any time and DJs throw out some funky sounds in the back garden now and then. *Main St.* ☎ *074/912-1388.*

→ **McGineley's** A middle-of-the-road option in the middle of town. Cozy up with the locals in this redbrick hostelry filled with nooks, crannies, and a crowd of—mostly older—drinkers. Tuesday sees a funky house DJ shipped in, Wednesday is trad night, and Monday a chance to test your knowledge of obscure Irish history on quiz night. The weekend sees more live gigs in the main bar. *Lower Main St.* ☎ *074/912-1106.*

🎬 Best → **Sister Sara's** Along with Cavern and Mono this bar packs out with younger drinkers all week long. Sporting a cheeky church theme complete with mock stained-glass windows, Sister Sara's draws partygoers in from across the local region. They come for the wild student nights on Tuesday and Thursdays, the constant drinks promotions, and the commercial dance parties on the weekends, spread over three floors. Open until 2.30am except on Mondays and Wednesdays. *Port Rd.* ☎ *074/912-2238.*

🎬 Best → **The Wolfe Tone** Don't leave town without grabbing a pint here. Named after a Republican hero, despite being recently opened, it feels more like a museum than a bar. The interior is filled with gorgeous green and velvet furniture, set against dark wood paneling, while the walls are plastered

The Rebel Yell

Now seen as cute and harmless, traditional Irish music was once highly political and potentially explosive. It was consequently outlawed by the English during several periods in Ireland's troubled history. Elizabeth I once instructed all Irish musicians should be hanged and their instruments burned. Giving new meaning to the phrase "a hot tune."

with Republican memorabilia: photos of Michael Collins, medals from the 1916 rising, and portraits of Bobby Sands. A history of the birth of a nation with drinks on the side. Traditional bands often singing political songs can be heard on the weekends. *Lower Main St.* ☎ *074/912-4472.*

SIGHTSEEING

You don't come to Letterkenny to sightsee, more to indulge before heading out into the country. One place worth poking your nose into is the **Letterkenny Arts Centre,** downstairs from the Central Library (Oliver Plunkett Rd.; ☎ **074/912-9186**), a passionately run venue largely featuring local artists and plenty of contemporary photography. Drop-ins can also hope to catch a comedy show, free talk, musical performance, or art house film screening. Engaging stuff.

PLAYING OUTSIDE

Letterkenny may not have many outdoor options itself, but there's more than enough to do in the surrounding area, including hiking in the Donegal hills or surfing on her beaches.

→ **Gartan Outdoor Education Centre** One of Ireland's top adventure centers, Gartan is run from a restored stone building set in 35 hectares (87 acres) of lush Irish loveliness. As well as hill walking, navigation, climbing, and mountain biking, Gartan also runs a full range of wet courses including kayaking, windsurfing, sailing, and surfing. As much for adults as for kids, this center is a top place to get official certificates in many of the sports on offer under the eye of qualified instructors. These guys know their stuff. There's also some decent hostel accommodation on-site to save popping back to Letterkenny. Prices stretch from €540 to get an experienced sailor qualified as an instructor to €190 for a sea kayaking weekend. *Church Hill, Letterkenny.* ☎ *074/913-7032. www.gartan.com.*

➜ Glenveagh National Park & Castle

Lots of people will tell you this thickly wooded valley is one of the most beautiful places in Ireland. They could well be right. It's a stunner. At its core is the lavish Glenveagh Estate, originally the home of the notorious landlord John George Adair, much despised for his eviction of Irish tenant farmers in the freezing winter of 1861, apparently because their presence ruined his view. Today the mystical-tale setting includes woodlands, herds of red deer, and the highest mountain in Donegal, Mount Errigal. There's a visitor center with some cool interactive machines explaining what all those twittering birds out in the trees are really trying to say. There is also a restaurant in the visitor center, and a tearoom in the castle. *One thing to note:* The national park, especially on humid summer days, is absolutely infested with midge bugs. So small that it's impossible to swat—or see—them; they're an unfortunate but inevitable part of your visit. Avoid wearing perfumes or scented anything when visiting and you'll save yourself a lot of itchiness later on.

Mt. Errigal looks like a squat Mt. Fuji, with its symmetrically pointed peak, rocky surface, and complete dominance of the surrounding landscape. The second-highest peak in Ireland at 752m (2,467 ft.), it's a difficult climb, not for the wimpy outdoorsman.

You'll be rewarded, weather permitting, with great views of this lonesome countryside. Leave yourself at least 4 to 5 hours for the climb, a rest at the top, and the descent. At the top, there are two summits, about 27m (90 ft.) apart; they're connected by the dangerous "One Man's Pass." It's narrow and sheer, so be careful. *Main entrance on R251, Church Hill, County Donegal.* ☎ *074/913-7090. www.heritageireland.ie. Park admission and castle tour €3 adults, €1.25 students. No credit cards. Mid-Mar to 1st Sun in Nov daily 10am–6:30pm. Closed Fri in Oct.*

SHOPPING

➜ Adventure One

Being only half an hour away from Ireland's hottest surf beaches, Letterkenny is a good place to begin preparations. Shop owner Ian Gilmour is a keen surfer from England who fell in love with a local girl and settled in the area. Brands stocked include Billabong, Ripcurl, Quicksilver, and O'Neil. There are also some skateboards and, for those who thought the beaches in Ireland would be warm, plenty of ski wear. Yes, it is that cold. *Oliver Plunkett Rd.* ☎ *074/917-6487. Mon–Sat 10am–6pm.*

➜ The Garage

Despite the very ordinary interior—livened up only with a vague gas station theme—this shop stocks some sound urban brands including Miss Sixty, Diesel, Gas, G-Star, and Old Glory. There are threads for both boys and girls but, compared to the U.S., prices are likely to make both sexes swoon. Jackets start from €200. *The Courtyard Shopping Centre. No phone.*

➜ Universal Records

No, not an outlet for the big U.S. record company, just a small small-town record store. A fine place to pick up music from Irish and international old-timers—including Jimi Hendrix, Foo Fighters, The Pogues, and the Saw Doctors—but not really somewhere to get a trance wh"label 12." *Market Sq.* ☎ *074/912-8899.*

Road Trips in the Atlantic Highlands

This is the most isolated part of Donegal, which is the most isolated county in Ireland, so it doesn't get much more rugged, exhilarating, and, well, isolated than this. There is a point when you're driving through the highlands, where the signs drop all pretence at bilingualism and switch to Gaelic. This is disconcerting because most maps are in English, and the Gaelic names and the English names of places frequently are not even distant relatives. It's disorienting—one minute you know exactly where you are, and the next you haven't a clue. It's as if somebody's stolen your compass. At that moment, which often occurs on a mountainside by a rushing stream amid rocky terrain where there's no space to pull the car over and stare more closely at the useless map, it's just possible that you see Ireland as the locals see it—which is to say, as their own country: a somewhat private, and not always hospitable place. Coming this far would be worth it for that moment of understanding alone, but there is much more to draw you here. There is the breathtaking coastal scenery, the surprising mountain ranges, the lunar landscape of the rocky beaches . . . You will use up all of your film (or fill your memory card) here.

Tory Island

A trip to Tory Island is certainly a weird sociological experience. The mostly Gaelic-speaking locals in this burg of 160 people have created their own little country: They elect a king of the island, pay no Irish taxes, and refer to mainland Ireland as "the country." They're an independent lot but not unfriendly to visitors—just largely oblivious of their presence. Thirteen kilometers (8 miles) across the Atlantic from "the country," tiny Tory Island (5km/3miles long, 2km/miles wide) gets a constant pounding by Mother Nature. With no landmasses around to protect it from the chilling, harsh wind—and but

one lonely tree on the whole island—it's certainly a bleak spot. But a climb up the sloping bird cliffs, high above the pounding sea, is an unforgettable experience. If you've never seen puffins in action, this is your chance.

Tory Island has two tiny villages. West Town has one street and is the center of Tory life. East Town is the other little town and also has one street.

If you see someone walking around with a little plastic baggie full of dirt, it's probably a mainlander bringing some Tory soil back to wherever they came from. Legend has it that St. Colmcille came here 1,400 years ago and drove all the rats away. People gather the earth to take back to their rat-infested towns in hopes of repeating Colmcille's miracle.

GETTING THERE

The only way to get to Tory Island is by boat. If the weather is bad, you could get stuck out here so only come out if your schedule is flexible. Donegal Costal Cruises, aka **Turasmara** (☎ 074/953-1320; www.littleireland.ie), runs ferries between Bunbeg and Tory (take the R258 from Gweedore to Bunbeg Ferry Office; ☎ 074/953-1991) with one ferry per day in spring and summer, fewer in winter. They also offer ferries from Magheraroarty to Tory (off the N56, between Gweedore and Dunfanaghy; look for signs to the **Magheraroaty ferry office; ☎ 074/953-5061**), with two to three per day from June to September only. Most ferries run about €12 round-trip.

SLEEPING, EATING & PARTYING

Club Soisialta Thoraigh (West Town, Tory Social Club; ☎ 074/956-5121; open till 11:30pm daily) is the best pub on the island, often featuring unique Tory trad music sessions here—imagine John Lee Hooker playing trad. A few doors down is **Ostan Thoraigh** (☎ 074/956-5121), the other pub in West Town, serving reasonably priced pub food day and night.

Are you stranded due to the weather, or have you taken a liking to Tory? In either case, you can rest your head at the **Radharc na Mara Hostel** (West Town; ☎ 074/956-5145; Apr–Oct only; double €24) where some of the rooms even have open fires.

Horn Head

Horn Head is a small peninsula with incredible scenery jutting out into the fury of the Atlantic Ocean. It's about a 3- or 4-hour hike from Dunfanaghy to the tip of Horn Head, but it's so worth the trek. From the Head, you can see ocean, cliffs, the village below, and sailing vessels on the horizon. Truly breathtaking. Skip the Horn Head hike if you suffer from vertigo.

GETTING THERE

The **Lough Swilly bus company** (☎ 074/912-2863) links Letterkenny with Dunfanaghy. At the western edge of Dunfanaghy, there is a turnoff marked with a sign for "Horn Head Drive." This is the only way to get to the Head. Continue past the sign and it will take you all the way to the head. Those with cars can drive up.

Malin Head

The farthest point north on the Ireland map, Malin Head tops off the beautiful Inishowen Peninsula made up of rugged land and seascapes, punctuated by giant sand dunes. Although it's slowly becoming a popular backpacker destination, few travelers currently make it this far and the Head remains pristine. Check out the fantastic graffiti at the end of the head, made of piles of stones. This was inspired by the still-visible EIRE sign built here during the Second World War to let American bomber pilots know they were back over friendly territory.

GETTING THERE & GETTING AROUND

The easiest way to get here by bus is from Derry on **Lough Swilly Buses** (Derry

☎ 028/7126-2017; or Letterkenny ☎ 074/912-2863), running one to four times each day from Monday to Saturday, with no bus on Sunday. If you're behind the wheel, head up the R238/242 from Carndonagh. In a car it's also possible to skip across to the Inishowen Peninsula from County Derry on the Lough Foyle ferry (☎ 074/938-1901; www.lough foyleferry.com) running from Maglligan Point to Greencastle Harbor.

Once there, if you've got a bike—or if you rent one at the Malin Head Hostel (see "Sleeping, Eating & Partying," below)—you can spend a day pedaling up the coast. From Malin village, head north out of town on Inish Eoghin 100 (this is a road name) and you'll hit Malin Head proper after about 13km (8 miles; after you've passed Ireland's mostly northerly B&B and crafts shop). The scenery is terrific, replete with rocky coast and rough ocean all the way up. Between are isolated churches, colorful little villages, tumbledown farms, and ever-winding roads. Looking out to sea, sharp eyes may spy whales, dolphins, sharks, and even a surprised turtle or two washed down from the tropics.

SLEEPING, EATING & PARTYING

Prepare yourself for a treat. The ⚑ Best Malin Head Hostel (Inishowen; ☎ 074/937-0309; €13 dorm, €36 double; closed Nov–Feb) is a budget travelers' paradise—this tranquil hostel even includes a lovely garden, a kitchen, and a cozy lounge. Run by the rosy-cheeked Mary Reynolds—whose great-grandfather originally lived in the same building before her grandmother ran the post office here until 1939—it's a selection of pine beds dotted around a pretty cottage with a quiet room up top pasted with reading material. Sustenance comes in the form of local produce—including crab—prepared by guests in the friendly kitchen accompanied by Mary's organic eggs and vegetables from her garden, including strawberries in season. Bikes can be hired from €10 per day. If that gets your legs aching, there are reflexology and aromatherapy treatments available, also provided by the multi-tasking Mary.

A triangle-shaped green is the center of Malin Village. Trad and tackle are available—in addition to plenty of beer and whiskey—at **Farren's Bar** (☎ 074/937-0128), the northernmost watering hole in the land.

The
Midlands

Ahh, the middle lands, a land of gentle rolling hills and boredom. The story of the
center of so many countries is seemingly retold in Ireland. And, yes, it is true,
Ireland's Midlands don't possess the dramatic scenery of Sligo, the crazy nightlife of
Galway, or the raw wild appeal of Donegal, but don't go crossing it off your must-see
list just yet; there is still some bang in The Midlands' gun.

For starters The Midlands does have the mighty Shannon River. At 386km (240
miles) long this huge greeny-blue snake is the longest river in Ireland, and tops anything Great Britain has on offer, too. Starting up at the Shannon Pot in the Cuilcagh
Mountains in County Cavan it slips down past nine other counties: Leitrim,
Roscommon, Longford, Westmeath, Offaly, Galway, Tipperary, Clare, and Limerick,
before gushing out into the ocean—just after Limerick city—between Counties Clare
and Kerry.

Along the way, the slinky creature shifts from lakes to streams, sometimes
stretching to 16km (10 miles) wide, sometimes slimming down to a few hundred
yards. What this means for the adventure-seeking independent traveler is a plethora
of watersporting opportunities, especially on—"pleasure lake"—Lough Derg, a large
wet playground measuring 39km/24 miles long and 10km/6 miles wide. These range
from canoeing, kayaking, sailing, swimming, windsurfing, water-skiing, and diving to
the more laid-back "sport" of renting a luxe cruiser and steaming down the river in
your own pad.

If this is your bag, supper can be caught from the water as The Shannon is crammed full of fish. Alternatively there are some cute little towns and villages to stop in at along the way, Athlone being particularly worth an overnighter to experience Sean's Bar (p. 404), the world's oldest according to the Guinness book of Records, complete with sawdust on the floor. There's also a trendy Parisianesque Left Bank filled with groovy shops, cafes, and—for the boatless—one of the coolest B&Bs in Ireland, The Bastion (p. 402).

This chapter divides the river up into three handy chunks: Lower Shannon (from Killaloe, County Clare to Portumna, County Galway) and Lough Derg, Middle Shannon (a small passage from the Birr/Banagher area in County Offaly to Athlone, County Westmeath), and Upper Shannon (from Lough Ree in Westmeath to Lough Allen in County Leitrim). Few will follow the river the whole way but, as The Midlands is largely defined by The Shannon, even for those on the road it still acts as a guide to top spots in the region.

The Best of The Midlands

○ **Exploring Athlone:** Sitting at the edge of the River Shannon, its streets curving around a sturdy, fortresslike castle, Athlone is a charmer. Houses are painted in bright hues, and with its small, funky boutiques and spirit of fun, it has the feel of a busy university town. Good restaurants and lively pubs add to its charms. See p. 401.

○ **Horseback Riding along the Slieve Bloom Trail:** Slieve Bloom, Ireland's largest and most unspoiled blanket bog, rises gently above the peat fields. Its beauty—gentle slopes, glens, rivers, waterfalls, and bog lands—is subtle but persistent, and it is comparatively untouched. You can have it more or less to yourself, apart from its deer and foxes, and an occasional frolicking otter. See p. 397.

○ **Be Serene in Clonmacnois:** This was once one of Ireland's most important religious, artistic, and literary centers, a place of pilgrimage and culture. Founded in the mid–5th century at the axis of the River Shannon and the medieval east-west thoroughfare known as the Eiscir Riada, Clonmacnois thrived for centuries until its prime riverfront location brought repeated violent raids that proved its undoing. Even in ruins, Clonmacnois remains a place of peculiar tranquility. See p. 398.

Lower Shannon: The Lough Derg Road Trip

To really explore the Lough Derg region you need a car, as public transport does not stray far from the beaten track. For a quick overview of all that Lough Derg has to offer, take a motor for a quick spin around the outside of the lake. A road runs the entire 153km

The Midlands: The River Shannon's Shores

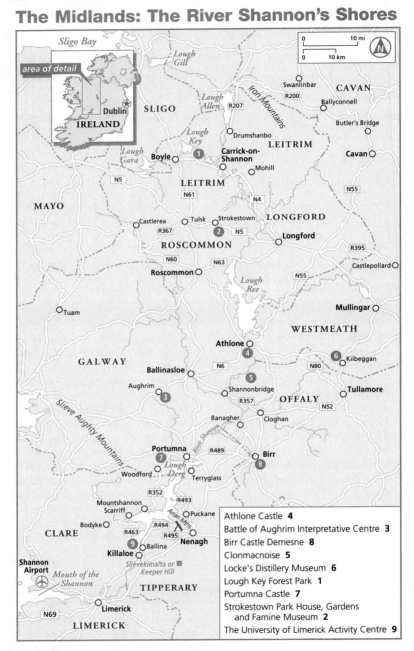

Athlone Castle **4**
Battle of Aughrim Interpretative Centre **3**
Birr Castle Demesne **8**
Clonmacnoise **5**
Locke's Distillery Museum **6**
Lough Key Forest Park **1**
Portumna Castle **7**
Strokestown Park House, Gardens
    and Famine Museum **2**
The University of Limerick Activity Centre **9**

(95 mile) distance through forests and farmland, over rolling hills and alongside the sparkly lake, passing through cutesy harborside villages and towns including Killaloe and Portumna at either end, Mountshannon and Dromineer and the villages of Terryglass and Woodford where it is impossible to predict in which character-laden pub the next spontaneous outburst of traditional Irish music will occur. Fiddle, fiddlers, fiddle.

Killaloe

Killaloe is a small riverside town linked to the community of Ballina on the other bank by a 13-arch bridge. Sweet as they are neither is likely to set adrenaline levels racing. But, between them—with a few decent pubs and eateries—they do make a good stopping-off point for road and river travelers exploring The Midlands and a jumping-off point for Lough Derg itself.

GETTING THERE

BY CAR   The N7, the main Dublin to Limerick road passes just a couple of miles from Killaloe and Ballina. Keep an eye out for a right turn, just after the Nenagh turning, marked Killaloe/Ballina. Coming the other way look out for a left turn just after Birdhill, signposted Killaloe/Ballina again.

BY BUS   **Bus Éireann** (☎ 061/313333; www.buseireann.ie) runs a service from Limerick bus station seven times a day from 8.20am to 5.45pm

BY TRAIN   Trains run from Dublin Heuston station to Ballybrophy and then on to Birdhill (about 2km/1^1/$_4$miles from Killaloe) at 8.30am and 5.30pm Mon–Sat and 6.30pm on Sunday, taking between 2^1/$_2$ and 3 hours, costing €35 one-way. (☎ 1850/366222; www.irish rail.ie).

BY TAXI   **Josey Reddan** (☎ 061/376-146) is a local taxi driver based in Killaloe.

BASICS

RECOMMENDED WEBSITES   With news of recent deaths and lost dogs, www.killaloe.ie

is more of a community website than a travelers' website, but it does have a smattering of info on places to stay, eat, and see.

TOURIST OFFICE   **Killaloe Tourist Information Office** (The Lough House; ☎ 061/376886) is almost in the river, accessed via a bridge. There's very little here, but the staff will try to help. Open May to September, Monday to Saturday 10am to 6pm and Sunday noon to 5pm.

FESTIVALS

Mid-July sees the village of Killaloe celebrating "Feile Brian Boru"—a crazy weekend of family fun with lots of singing, dancing, and drinking. Brian Boru may sound like a dull man but he was actually the highest of the High Kings of Ireland, born near Killaloe in the 10th century. *Word of warning:* It is almost impossible to squeeze a car into the village during the festivities.

SLEEPING

Killaloe, like the rest of the Lough Derg region, suffers from a lack of cheap places to stay, or places to stay at all for that matter. For this reason renting a cottage in the area can be a great way to go (see "A Pad of Your Own," p. 409).

Kincora House (Church St.; ☎ 061/376149; www.kincorahouse.com; €70 double) is a lovely old B&B with charming-old-grandma appeal. The building is over 300 years old and painted canary yellow on the outside. Indoors there are roaring fires, antique furniture, and cozy red walls. Ooh, yes, a cup of cocoa before bed would be lovely.

EATING

There's not much about on the eating front in Killaloe, but it's only a tiny wee town.

Café Latte (Convent Hill, next to Supervalu; ☎ 061/376888; sandwiches €4–€8) is a modern coffee shop with an outdoor seating area serving good Italian coffee. There are also sandwiches, paninis,

THE MIDLANDS

cakes, and the odd alcoholic beverage. It is lacking a soul but fills a hole. **Derg House—Coffee Pot and Deli** (opposite the Tourist Office; ☎ 0161/375559; sandwiches €6, meals €4.50–€8.50) is far more appetizing if you can find a table inside—it fills up quickly during the summer months. Cozy and traditional without toppling over into tweedom, it's all natural wood and neutral walls inside. All-day breakfasts dominate the menu, with a few main meals such as curry and lasagna, plus various sandwiches including a "weight watchers helper" of tuna fish with a low calorie dressing in pita bread. **Molly's Bar and Restaurant** (next to the bridge; ☎ 061/376632; all food €6–€20) is in another brightly colored building looking out over the harbor. The interior is all very cottagey, stacked with old plates, vintage clocks, period prints, and an old stove fireplace. On the menu are snacks and full slap-up dinner suggestions including baked Limerick ham with Madeira sauce, Atlantic salmon Hibernian, and chargrilled steaks. Open-faced fresh crab sandwiches on brown bread make for a lunch treat sitting outside on the picnic benches. There's live music, traditional and modern, Thursday to Sunday evening, and a disco and sports bar in the basement.

Other than that it's a question of scoffing pub grub in one of Killaloe's hostelries (see "Partying," below).

PARTYING

Partying may be a slightly over-optimistic description of what goes down in Killaloe. There are no all-night raves here. This is strictly a one-slow-pony town. There are, however, a handful of warm, friendly pubs where drinking, talking, and toe-tapping to trad Irish music can make for a surprisingly wild night out.

Brendan Grace's Bar (Main St.; ☎ 061/374-066; www.brendangracesbar.com) looks like just another sweet, sleepy, brightly

Going…Going…Gone

The Irish, renowned for their love of spirits, consider drinking a fine art and drunkenness a matter of opinion. The Irish language, in fact, has many phrases to distinguish between specific degrees of inebriation. Here are five, one for each finger of your sober hand:

➤ *súgach* (soo-gakh): tipsy
➤ *ar meisce* (air maysh-ka): drunk
➤ *ar deargmheisce* (air jar-egg-vaysh-ka): quite drunk
➤ *ólta* (awlta): very drunk indeed
➤ *caoch ólta* (kay-oakh awlta): blind drunk

painted Irish pub from the outside. Don't be fooled. This place gets raucous. Owned by the traditional Irish comedian and musician Brendan Grace, it is filled with showbiz snapshots and knickknacks picked up on his travels. Despite being built in 1863 it's not brimming with tourist-luring character; drinking is the main priority here. And smoking. A sign in the window promotes the pub's private room as the "best lil smoke house in the west." Don't expect to meet bearded Brendan himself. He now lives it up in Florida but the music goes on regardless—traditional and blues music most weekend nights. Not somewhere to get a meal. A perfect place to get a pint of Guinness.

The first thing that catches your eye at **Crotty's Bar** (Bridge St.; ☎ 061/376965) is the outdoor drinking area hidden behind an archway, a glorious mishmash of wooden benches up against ivy-clad walls, decorated with old advertising signs and brimming over with flowers. Perfect for afternoon drinking after a lazy day on the river. Inside is dark and cozy, if a bit scruffy, in a good way, with lots of old wooden ordinary prices ranging from sandwiches at €5.50 to sirloin steaks at

€13. Packed between are burgers, fish pies, and chicken goujons, plus the odd curry, pasta, and Tex-Mex dish.

Other pubs worth a pint or two include **The Anchor** (opposite the Tourist Information Centre; ☎ **061/376-108**), a down-at-heel affair (read: could do with a clean) offering live music on the weekends and Irish line-dancing on Wednesdays; and **Josie Reddan's** (next to Brendan Grace's Bar on Main St.; ☎ **061/376-146**), a traditional purple-fronted pub catering mainly to locals and an older crowd.

SIGHTSEEING

There's little to see in Killaloe and most independent travelers are eager to get stuck into the watersports available on Lough Derg; but if you are washed up in the area for a day, Killaloe Irish Heritage Centre (the same building as the Tourist Information Centre, see above; admission free) gives a lowdown on Celtic Ireland during the time when Brian Boru was king and Killaloe was the capital of the country. There is no escaping Brian in Killaloe—elsewhere **St. Flannan's Cathedral** (Limerick Rd.; ☎ **061/76687;** free admission) was built upon the site where King Boru originally built his own church.

PLAYING OUTSIDE AROUND KILLALOE & LOUGH DERG

BICYCLING   The Lough Derg cycleway leads pedalers on a 132km (70mile) route around the lake. Most people start in Killaloe/Ballina, but you can pick it up anywhere en route as it is signposted both clockwise and counterclockwise. It is generally easygoing and flat, with the occasional steep hill paying back with interest in the form of fab views across the Lough and surrounding forests. Chill for most of the year, the roads do get crazy, and a little hairy, during the summer and holiday seasons. Bicycles can be hired in Killaloe (Killaloe; ☎ **061/376866;** rates €12–€20 per day).

CRUISING   Cast aside images of steering a quaint little wooden boat up into a deserted lakeside bay; most of Lough Derg's cruisers are big and plastic but they can be quite luxe, and they do enable groups to throw off all ties and set out on a weeklong boat party. Companies renting cabin cruisers from two to eight berths in size and €150 to €300 per week include **Emerald Star Line** (The Marina, Portumna; ☎ **090/974-1120;** www. emeraldstar.ie), **Shannon Castle Line** (The Marina, Williamstown; ☎ **061/927-042;** www.shannoncruisers.com), and **Shannon Sailing** (New Harbour; ☎ **067/24499;** www.shannonsailing.com).

HIKING   The **Lough Derg Way** (☎ **061/ 317-522**) is a walk divided into two parts. The first stretches between Limerick City and Killaloe, measuring 26km (16 miles); the second part links up Killaloe and Dromineer on the eastern bank of Lough Derg. It is 32km (20 miles) in length. From Limerick to Killaloe it follows the old Shannon canal, while from Killaloe to Dromineer it is uphill—most of the way—for a top view of the Lough. There are plans to push the walk all the way up to Portumna, so call the number above to find out what the score is.

HORSEBACK RIDING   **Clonlara Equestrian Centre** (Clonlara; ☎ **061/354172;** www. clonlaraequestrian.com) is the biggest horse-riding center in the area with around 15 horses and 10 ponies. Situated about 10km from Killaloe, in the countryside, it has both indoor and outdoor arenas and offers lessons for beginners or country hacks for the more experienced rider. There is also a cafe on-site.

SWIMMING   Lough Derg has a rep for clear, unpolluted waters. It is also relatively shallow and shelves gently, making it ideal for swimming. Hot spots (of a type) are to be found at Castle Lough, Dromineer, and Portumna Bay. The latter has changing rooms and showers.

WATER-SKIING For water-skiing or variations on this theme, get in touch with Mark Dunne at **Watermark Ski Club** (☎ 087/ 257-3661; www.irishwaterski.com), based between Terryglass and Portumna. Besides trad water-skiing he offers wake boarding, wake skating, wake surfing, bare-footing, trick-skiing, and body-boarding, as well as the opportunity to take a zapcat for a spin—the new craze for mini-RIBs mixing sweety appeal with high speeds. Prices range from €50 for a beginner's "crash-course" to €38 for a 20-minute set. For ladies wanting to learn together there is a special girls-only wake-boarding clinic, plus plenty of other mixed courses all taught by national champions in their field.

WATERSPORTS **The University of Limerick Activity Centre** (3km/2 miles north of Killaloe on the Scariff road running alongside the lake; ☎ 061/376622; www.ulac.ie) is a superb outfit with constantly updated equipment offering a whole heap of adventurous activities and courses without a high price tag. Ways to get warm include hot showers, heated changing rooms, and a sauna. Ways to get cold include sailing, windsurfing, powerboating, kayaking, canoeing, and dragon boating on the lake, plus archery, orienteering, and a high-ropes course on shore. Wannabe sailors can take their pick from Wayfarers, Topazes, and 420s to Lasers, Laser 2s, and Hobie Cats, while kings can zoom around in 5.5m (18-ft.) RIBs. Learn-to-windsurf-or-sail weekends start from €185; canoeists get a weekend "Intro to Whitewater" for €190. Instructor courses are also available. Sunday afternoons are set aside for non-course rentals to people who have already completed a course at the center or have relevant certification. Time to get wet.

To get out on the water for a quick burst of activity, **Lakeside Watersports Centre** (1km/¹/₂ mile north of Mountshannon on the Portumna Road; ☎ 061/927225) has rowing

So Tired, Tired of Waiting

Always expect an Irishperson at least an hour later than the time you've agreed upon. It's "Irish time": Nobody thinks anything of telling you they'll be there at 2pm and then showing up at 3:30pm (that's "half-three" in Irish/Anglo-speak, by the way). It's just the way things are done. Oh, and don't bank on that bus arriving on time, either; many a tired and cranky traveler has waited for a half-hour or more after its scheduled stop, wondering if the bus would ever come.

boats, windsurfers, and sailing dinghies available for rent by the day or week.

Portumna

Portumna—meaning the landing place of the oak—is a sweet historical town, sitting on the top of Lough Derg, besides the River Shannon. As with Killaloe, most people are here to access the bounty of the Lough, but it does also offer up some nocturnal fun in the form of nearby trad music pubs and a great outdoors package in the form of the green and lush Portumna Forest Park, just outside the town.

GETTING THERE

BY CAR Head down the N7, the main Dublin to Limerick road turning off for Roscrea. Go through Roscrea and Birr, take the N52 towards Nenagh, then keep your eyes peeled for signs to Portumna as you enter Riverstown. Coming the other way, turn off the N7 at signs to Nenagh, Borrisokane. Go all the way to Borrisokane and then follow signs to Portumna.

BY BUS Direct buses (☎ 01/8366111; www.buseireann.ie) leave from Dublin Store

Street at 4pm every day, taking approximately 2¹/₂ hours to make the journey.

BY TAXI   **Mr. Ambrose Sheehy** runs a local taxi service (Brendan St.; ☎ **0509/41140**) in Portumna.

BASICS

TOURIST OFFICE   There is a tourist information office at the entrance to the castle grounds in Portumna (☎ **0509/41644**), open from June to Sept, daily from 9am to 9pm. Further information about the surrounding area can be picked up from the **Ireland West Tourism office** (Victoria Place, Eyre Square, Galway, County Galway; ☎ **091/537700**; www.westirelandtravel.ie), open May through September daily 9am to 5.45pm, October to April Monday to Friday 9am to 5.45pm, and Saturday 9am to 12.45pm.

SLEEPING

Portumna's hostel **Galway Shannonside Hostel** (St. Brigid's Rd.; ☎ 0509/41032; €33 dorm, €41 double) is really rather gorgeous. Situated on a lake inside an old schoolhouse, it's a little like staying in a country house. There are showers in many of the dorm rooms and a scrumptious breakfast of juice, coffee, cereal, and toast.

There are a few B&Bs but many are situated outside the main town. To be in the midst of the limited action, check into **Clonwyn House** (Brendan St.; ☎ **090/974-1420**; www.clonwynhouse.com; €70 double), a trad historical inn painted pink on the outside. Inside the fluffy theme continues with an overdose of flowery curtains and bedspreads. Don't be frightened; the bar is good. Prepare for a pool table, live music on the weekends, and Irish music sessions nearly every night in the summer. Plus there's late-night disco dancing in the club upstairs at weekends. See? We knew you'd come round.

EATING

Popular with the water-going folk and locals is **An Bialann** (Main St.; ☎ **0509/41929**; mains €7–€18), a warm and friendly restaurant serving Irish homemade classics and delicious freshly baked bread. For a change the **Oriental City Chinese** restaurant (Main St.; ☎ **090/9759917**; €6.50–€8.50) serves bargain Chinese food in clean, new surroundings.

PARTYING

Portumna may not be party central, but the surrounding countryside is renowned for its rollicking traditional music sessions. Grab a cab or hop in your car and head out there. Woodford in County Galway on the west shore of Lough Derg and Terryglass in County Tipperary on the east shore are both known for particularly lively music nights. Top fiddle and tin-whistle player Anthony Coen was born in Woodford, part of a musical tribe from which six out of nine kids became traditional musicians. Catch him and his daughters at J. Walsh's Forest Bar or Moran's (see below).

The Derg Inn (Terryglass; ☎ **067/22037**) is as sweet as they come with three cozy little rooms and a beer garden in the courtyard. Inside is filled with pictures of the county's horses, old plates, books, beer posters, vintage bottles, hanging tankards, and lanterns. A real Irish pub. Locals and travelers alike gather for the free traditional music on Wednesday and Sunday evenings.

Catching a session at **J. Walsh's Forest Bar** (Woodford; ☎ **090/974-9063**) is less easy. The sessions are spontaneous and can seemingly spring out of nowhere. If you do catch one, hometown favorite Mr. Coen is likely to be in the midst of things.

In the same village, **Moran's** (Woodford; ☎ **090/974-9063**) overlooks the river. But that's not why people come here. Besides the music, this is probably the only pub in Ireland where clerics dole out the devil water in the summer months. Prepare to be surprised by a pair of Carmelite Order priests. They are the owner's sons and, being nice chaps, return to help out the family business during their summer vacation.

Just a short stumble up a winding lane finds you at **Paddy's Pub** (Terryglass; ☎ 067/22147), a tiny, dark pub stocked full of atmosphere and antiques, with spirit-stirring traditional music sessions in the summer months.

SIGHTSEEING

The best—and almost only—sight to see in Portumna is **Portumna Castle** (no phone; admission to castle €1.90 adults; free admission to gardens). Built in 1609 by the grand old Earl Richard Burke, this huge house was considered to be one of the finest 17th-century manor houses in Ireland. Fire put an end to that, ripping through the castle in 1826. Restorers are now at work, limiting the public to the ground floor only. Doesn't stop anyone from wandering around the walled organic kitchen gardens, though. And, out back, the castle's estates are home to a huge herd of wild deer.

PLAYING OUTSIDE

BICYCLING   Rent a bike from **Tony Cunningham's** (Dominic St.; ☎ 0509/41070; rates €10–€16 per day).

GO-KARTING   Had enough of all that fresh air and nonsense? Petrol-heads can get their fix at **Pallas Karting** (Tynagh, Loughrea; ☎ 0509/45147; www.pallaskarting.com; €20 for 15 minutes on the big track), one of the largest karting centers in Europe. There are over 1,500m (almost 1 mile) of tarmac track, 11m (36 ft.) wide at points—meaning there are no excuses for not overtaking—and the 13hp single engine karts can reach speeds of 113kmph (70 mph). First-time drivers can practice their skills on a 500m (1,640-ft.) beginners/family track. There are arrive and drive sessions available, but do phone in advance to check what's going down on your chosen day to visit.

HIKING   The **Portumna Forest Park** (☎ 0905/42365; free admission) on the shores of Lough Derg is situated east of the town, off the main road. It offers 560 hectares

(1,400 acres) of lush greenery run through with trails and signposted walks, plus some brilliant wow-look-at-the-view points. Even solo travelers won't be alone here; there are 16 species of animals—including otter, pine martins, and deer—and more than 85 species of birds living within the forests.

Slieve Bloom Mountains

The forests and boglands of the fantastically named Slieve Bloom Mountains in Counties Offaly and Laois are perfect for taking an isolated hike into the middle of nowhere. You are unlikely to spot another traveler, meaning you'll have the wooded hills, top-notch views, and sleepy villages all to yourself.

GETTING THERE

BY BUS   Bus Éireann (☎ 01/836-6111; www.buseireann.ie) service number 12 travels to the entry point at Portlaoise (where you'll also find the tourist office; see below) every day, hourly, from Dublin.

BASICS

TOURIST OFFICE   The **Portlaoise Tourist Office** (James Fintlan Lawlor Ave., Portlaoise, County Laois; ☎ 0502/21178), open from 10am to 6pm Monday to Saturday, can help plan a route and find the perfect farmhouse to stay in.

WEBSITES   Check out the fantastic and comprehensive www.slievebloom.ie for myriad ideas on where to stay and eat, and what to do afterward.

FESTIVALS

The unmissable World Sheep Dog Trials (www.worldsheepdogtrials) invite over 200 sheepdogs from 21 different countries to do their doggy thing in Tullamore annually around July.

SLEEPING

At the southeastern end of the Slieve Bloom Way (see below), the **Pine House Farm**

(Annaghmore; ☎ **0509/37029;** €65 double) is a comfy farmhouse that takes in boarders. Farther into the just-doable section is **Ardmore House Bed and Breakfast** (Kinnitty; ☎ **0509/37009;** www.kinnitty.net; €70–€76 double). The rooms are filled with antique wooden furniture and—fairly tasteful—flowery wallpaper, while the cherry on the cake is homemade soda bread for breakfast, and a few other treats besides.

EATING

The have-to-visit for the Slieve Bloom area is the **Monks Kitchen in Kinnitty Castle** (☎ **0509/37318;** www.kinnittycastle.net), where eating is done in a medieval style with old-fashioned crockery, drinking is done from huge metal goblets, and a monk hands out the daily feast. Okay, it is a bit naff but for €20 for an all-you-can-eat menu—consisting of spit-roast leg of lamb, marinated rolled beef prepared with red wine and thyme sauce, wild Irish mushrooms, seafood chowder, Bailey's profiteroles, and various other barbecued meats, salads, and potatoes—who's complaining.

PARTYING

Even the smallest village seems to have a cozy pub in this area. One of the best is a classic pub in Cadamstown called **Dempsey's** (☎ **0509/37103**), run by the same Dempsey family for over 200 years and now a huge favorite with hill walkers. Traditional Irish singing takes place here on the last Monday of each month.

PLAYING OUTSIDE

WALKING/DRIVING   Find a walk by following the Slieve Bloom Way, a 50km (31-mile) circular drive through the area, accessed from Mountmellick via R422. Start at the northern end of the route, at Glen Barrow's Car Park, and meander through ancient hills and valleys to Cadamstown, featuring Dempsey's, the pub (see "Partying," above)

HORSEBACK RIDING   _MV_ **Best**   **Slieve Bloom Trail** (☎ **0506/53046;** www.slievebloomtrail.com) organizes 3- to 6-day treks for hard-core riders capable of taking 4 to 5 hours in the saddle each day in return for magnificent access to usually hidden areas of Ireland. Expect to travel high into the mountains along old unused pre-Famine roads, across bogs, and through forests. Sound good? The trips are not cheap costing between €650 and €1,250 but they do receive rave reviews from previous participants.

Middle Shannon: From Birr to Athlone

The middle chunk of the Shannon is home to Clonmacnoise, one of Ireland's prime historic sites. Far from boring, this early Christian settlement has been a honey pot for visitors since the 6th century, thanks to its ruined cathedral, six temples, numerous high crosses, two round towers, and even a magic whispering arch. There are also vast areas of bogland along this stretch of the river—a chance to check out how peat is farmed—and the towns of Birr and Banagher are useful stop-off points for road and river travelers. But by far the best town around these parts is Athlone, a dual-natured beast balancing astride the River Shannon, with an ordinary commercial town on one side and a cool Left Bank on the other, filled with streets winding up past old Irish pubs and artsy shops and cafes. Public transport does service the main towns of this area and a railway runs into Athlone, but to really explore along the river banks a car or boat is needed.

Middle Shannon Basics

TOURIST INFORMATION

Information on this area can be obtained from the **Ireland West Tourism Office** (Foster St., Galway; ☎ **091/537700;** www.westireland.travel.ie), and the **East Coast & Midlands Tourism Office** (Clonard House,

CRUISING IN THE MIDDLE SHANNON REGION

Carrick Craft (The Marina, Banagher, County Offaly; ☎ **01/278-1666;** www. cruise-ireland.com) rent out big white motor cruisers James Bond would be proud of at prices ranging from €540 to €1,650 for 7 days (depending on time of year and the number of berths in the boat). Boats range from two to eight berths. Other possibilities include **Athlone Cruisers** (Jolly Mariner Marina, Athlone, County Westmeath; ☎ **090/647-2892;** www.acl.ie), **Silverline Cruisers** (The Marina, Banagher, County Offaly; ☎ **090/975-1112**), and **Tara Cruiser Ltd.** (Kilfaughna, Knockvicar, County Roscommon; ☎ **071/966-7777**). Crafts range from four to six berths; rates average €1,000 to €1,700 per week in high season.

Dublin Rd., Mullingar, County Westmeath; ☎ **044/48650**). Both are open Monday to Friday 9am to 5:45pm, plus Saturday during peak season. Seasonal tourist information points are open from May or June to September at signposted sites in **Ballinasloe** (☎ **090/964-2131**), **Birr** (☎ **090/972-0110**), and **Clonmacnoise** (☎ **090/967-4134**).

MIDDLE SHANNON WEBSITES

Useful websites covering this area include www.offalytourism.net, www.shannonregion tourism.ie, www.galwaytourist.com,www.ely ocarroll.com, and www.eastcoastmidlands.ie.

Middle Shannon Festivals

Those on the road in this region in early October might want to keep an ear out for **The Ballinasloe Horse Fair,** when farmers from across the region still gather to trade horses, and cattle on the village green. Since the introduction of the tractor into Irish farming, trading hasn't been quite as brisk but a huge fair has grown up to keep the carnival atmosphere alive (www.ballinasloe. com).

Clonmacnoise

GETTING THERE

BY CAR   Unfortunately, a car is the only convenient way to get to Clonmacnoise, taking Route 457 north out of Shannonbridge for 6km (4 miles).

BY RAIL   The closest rail station is in Athlone, about 97km (60 miles) east of Galway and a stop on the Dublin-Galway **Irish Rail** (☎ **1850/366222;** www.irishrail. ie) route; from Athlone Castle, Paddy Kavanagh runs a daily bus to Clonmacnoise (☎ **0902/74839**), departing at 11am and returning at 4pm.

SLEEPING

The nearest hostel is in Banagher, where you'll find **Crank House** (Main St.; ☎ **0509/ 51798;** abguinan@eircom.net; dorms from €12, doubles €24), an imposing 17th-century Georgian town house with 40 beds available in rooms from doubles to six-bed dorms. They are not huge but they are clean, and the shared kitchen makes up for things size-wise. Staff are very friendly, even if they don't always know what they are doing. Downstairs is a coffee shop and tourist information center. Laundry service and bike hire are also available. Alternatively **Kajon House** (Crevagh; ☎ **090/967-4191;** kajonhouse@eircom.net; doubles €63, triples €86) is a modern bungalow on the shores of the Shannon river offering basic B&B accommodation very near Clonmacnoise. The minute you've stepped through their doors they'll have you lounging on the sofas feeding you homemade scones and cups of tea. There are seven bedrooms (five with their own bathrooms) including doubles, twins, and triples. Prices include a

The Battle of Aughrim Interpretative Centre

The Battle of Aughrim Interpretative Centre is an unforgettable lesson in Irish history and goes a long way to explaining why the Orange men still cause so much trouble. And adds a few more reasons why the Irish don't like the English. Using a high-tech three-dimensional audiovisual presentation, the center invites visitors to relive the Battle of Aughrim, which took place on July 12, 1691. On that day, the army of James II of England confronted the forces of his son-in-law, William of Orange, and staged the bloodiest battle in Irish history. The confrontation involved 45,000 soldiers from eight European countries and cost 9,000 lives, changing the course of Irish and European history. The center, which also houses a bookshop, craft shop, and cafe, is in Aughrim village, adjacent to the actual Aughrim battlefield. Galway-Dublin Rd. (N6), Aughrim, near Ballinasloe, County Galway. ☎ 090/967-3939. Admission €4 adults, €3 students. June–Aug Tues–Sat 10am–6pm; Sun 2–6pm. The easiest way to get to the center is by car; it is signposted off the main Galway-Dublin Road, near Ballinasloe. You can also get there by bus: Catch the Dublin airport bus (☎ **091/797144;** www.busnestor.galway.net) from outside Galway Tourist Office (the bus takes just over 40 min., costing €5 one-way).

There is also a hostel on the actual battle site in Aughrim, **Hynes Hostel** (☎ **090/967-3734;** hynes@infowing.ie; dorm €30) run by Mr. and Mrs. Hynes who treat you like their own children, in a good way. The hostel also houses a bar filled with battle memorabilia—trad musicians often stop by to entertain guests with a tune or 10.

full Irish breakfast, or pancakes if that's your fancy. But, be warned, if you can't handle kiddies, this place is very family-friendly. If you can, come on in and make yourself at home.

SIGHTSEEING

➔ **Clonmacnoise** Lying quietly on the east bank of the Shannon, Clonmacnoise is one of Ireland's most profound ancient sites. St Ciaran—look out for his mug shot around the ruins—started up a community of monks here in 548. Although the grounds might look dozy now, he chose this spot because it was on a busy crossroad between the Shannon and the main Dublin-Galway Road. Soon it became one of Europe's great centers of learning and culture. It bloomed for nearly 1,000 years thanks to the sponsorship of numerous Irish kings. The last high king, Rory O'Conor, was buried here in 1198. After that things went downhill. Clonmacnoise was raided repeatedly by native chiefs, Danes, and Anglo-Normans, finally being abandoned in 1552. What's left are a ruined cathedral, some fantastic Celtic crosses, two round towers, over 200 monumental slabs, and eight churches, some still in use. One that isn't is St Ciaran's, where the walls are collapsing inwards. Why? Because rumor got around a few hundred years back that grabbing some earth from inside the church and spreading it to all four corners of your fields would result in amazing crops. Farmers through the years thought this sounded like a fine idea and helped themselves to this unusual fertilizer resulting in some very wobbly walls. Elsewhere, as you enter the cathedral, is an arch; this is the Whispering Arch where monks would gather to have their naughty confessions heard. And it still works. Tell your darkest secrets into one side of the arch and get a friend to listen on the other side. They should be the only one to hear.

THE MIDLANDS

Hopefully. Guided tours can be arranged in advance, lasting 45 minutes. There is also an audiovisual display and various exhibits in the visitor center to explain what all the stones mean, plus a teashop and toilets. This place heaves in summer so expect long queues. *On R357, 6.5km (4 miles) north of Shannonbridge, County Offaly.* ☎ *090/967-4195. Admission €5 adults, €2 students. Nov to mid-Mar daily 10am–5:30pm; mid-Mar to mid-May and mid-Sept to Oct daily 10am–6pm; mid-May to mid-Sept daily 9am–7pm.*

Birr

GETTING THERE

BY CAR   To reach the castle by car, take the Birr turn off the main Dublin-Limerick Road (N7) when Birr (N62) is signposted. Alternatively come off the Dublin-Galway Road (N6) when Tullamore/Birr is signposted.

BY BUS   Bus Éireann (090/648-4406; www.buseirann.ie) buses run between Athlone and Birr taking approximately 45 minutes, four times a day Monday to Saturday, twice a day on Sunday.

SLEEPING

There is no hostel in Birr. Accommodations in the splurge price range include:

Dooly's Hotel (Emmet Sq.; ☎ **090/972-0032;** www.doolyshotel.com; double €75–€135), a three-story Georgian hotel dating from 1747, is one of Ireland's oldest former coach houses. Right in the middle of Birr, it has 18 rooms, all with a private bathroom, phone, and TV, plus views of the town or backyard. There are two restaurants on-site (one being an affordable cafe serving mixed grills and homemade scones) and three bars (the traditional Coach House Lounge, Nebula Bar specializing in world beers and cocktails, and The Latin Quarter where things get more lively); all have a suitably historic atmosphere, including Melba's, the establishment's nightclub, open Thursday to Sunday. Come on the weekend to see double rooms

drop as low as €75, making the hotel suddenly seem a far more tasty option.

Nuzzling up beside the castle is **The Maltings Hotel/Leisure Centre** (☎ **0509/21345;** singles €40, doubles €68), with 10 rooms all with private bathrooms. These Georgian-style buildings date from 1820 when they were used to store malt for Guinness stout. Sitting on the banks of the River Camcor, this is a great place for watching wildlife and chilling out to the sound of water as it gushes over the weir outside. Not a place to go wild but a place to recover. What really puts it into the treat category is the fitness suite and sauna. All rooms have phones and TVs.

EATING

In town, much of what Birr has to offer is fine dining. On the road, the **Enroute Bistro** (Fivealley; ☎ **0509/33976;** www.guesthouse. ie; mains €11–€19, plus a cheaper bar menu), sitting on the N52 between Birr and Kilkormac, makes a surprisingly good refueling station. Built in old stone in 2003, it serves up a wide range of main meals from Offaly lamb cutlets served on herb and garlic potatoes with a red wine and shallot sauce, to supreme of chicken wrapped in salmon. Not your usual roadside caff then. There is a cheaper bar menu, however, doing good versions of steaks, sandwiches, omelets, and pasta dishes, making it a worthwhile lunch stop. It is also possible to stay here, in clean rooms decorated with cool wooden furniture, for rates from €25 per person including breakfast.

PARTYING

The town's younger folk tend to hang out in **The Market House Tavern** (Market Sq.; ☎ **0509/20180**), a modern bar that is light and bright and hits like an ice-cold glass of water after all the dark cozy pubs in the area. Otherwise **Craughwell's Bar and Lounge** (Castle St.; ☎ **0509/21839**) is a traditional family-run affair, where drinkers can expect to be entertained with Irish music on Friday and run the risk of getting caught up in a singalong on Saturday. Go on, show them what you can do with a few pints of Guinness inside you.

SIGHTSEEING

→ **Birr Castle Demense** Don't go putting on your chain mail just yet; Birr castle *itself* is not open to the general public as it is home to Lord and Lady Rosse. But they don't mind you looking around their garden, hence the word Demense in the title, meaning estate. Over 40 hectares (100 acres) in size, it is laid out around a lake and along the banks of the two side-by-side rivers. It contains more than 1,000 species of trees and shrubs, including magnolias, cherry trees, chestnut, and weeping beech. The box hedges are featured in the *Guinness Book of Records* as the tallest in the world, while the most recent and present Lord Rosses have been plant-hunters extraordinaire capturing seeds in Nepal, Tibet, and Western China before releasing them into the garden. Farther along the path you may come across the most enormous telescope, measuring 1.8m (6-ft.) and built in the 1840s when it was the largest in the world, for over 75 years. It is now part of the Historic Science Centre and operates twice daily, at noon and 3pm. *Birr, County Offaly.* ☎ *0509/20336. www.birrcastle.com. Admission €9 adults, €7 students. Daily 9am–6pm. Within walking distance of the center of Birr.*

PLAYING OUTSIDE

The **Birr Outdoor Education Centre** (Roscrea Rd.; ☎ **0509/20029;** birroec@ eircom.net) isn't just for kids. It arranges rock-climbing, abseiling, canoeing, kayaking, orienteering, hill walking, gorge walking, and raft building through courses lasting from 1 to 5 days. They'll also put you up for a little bit extra.

Athlone

Athlone is the biggest town in the Shannon region and, if you prefer to be somewhere semi-urban, the best place to base yourself while in the area. There are plenty of shops, bars, cafes, a theatre and a cinema, plus a castle and, of course, the river. The Left Bank is where it's at in terms of a groovy bohemian vibe while "the other side" has all the normal chain stores and restaurants.

GETTING THERE

BY CAR Athlone is about 1 hour and 40 minutes from Dublin on the N6 Dublin-Galway Road.

BY BUS **Bus Éireann** (☎ **01/836-6111;** www.buseireann.ie) runs the number 20 bus service that leaves from Busárus Bus station in Dublin 15 times each day from 7am hourly, going to Galway, stopping at Athlone just over 2 hours into the journey. The 21 going to Westport also stops at Athlone. Other services run to Athlone from Waterford, Belfast, Cork, and Limerick.

BY TRAIN **Irish Rail** (☎ **1850 366222;** www.irishrail.ie) trains leave Dublin Heuston station 14 times each day, Monday to Saturday, taking between 1 hour and 1 hour 30 minutes. Only six trains run on Sunday. Ticket price is €28.

BASICS

TOURIST INFORMATION The **Athlone Tourist Office** (☎ **090/649-4630**) is situated up in a stone building just inside the castle entrance, open Monday to Friday from 9.45am to 5.30pm with an hour off for lunch between 1 and 2pm. It is closed on Saturday and Sunday

INTERNET **The Lost Highway** (Castle Court, O'Connell St.; ☎ **090/649-2696;** www. thelosthighway.org) offers Internet access for €4 per hour in an eco-hippy den also housing a shop/cafe with a good line in all things alternative, from eco-friendly paints

Who Lived in a House Like This?

Castles are everywhere in Ireland. They may look romantic now but at one time they were fear-inducing fortresses and often homes, too. During your time in the Emerald Isle, you'll probably visit a few and, if you're lucky, may even get to sleep in one.

Listen carefully and you'll hear the stones whispering secrets about the people who once lived here. Okay, you won't really; it's a metaphor, but everything in a castle was built for a purpose, and once you know the signs you can read a castle and work out the daily actions and needs of the people who lived here centuries ago.

First off, take a look at where it's been built. Castle-builders were a canny lot. There top concern was to keep out the enemy. Consequently, you'll find, wherever possible, castles were built on rock to prevent invaders from digging tunnels under the walls, which would then have collapsed.

But what were they all fighting over? This can usually be determined from the position of a castle—perhaps built over a harbor mouth, a vital pass, or a river, all of which would have given the occupier power over transport, communications, and consequently trade. The location of other castles—for instance, the crannógs (fortified lake dwellings) built on tiny islands in the centers of lakes—shows their previous dwellers were simply a bunch of wimps more interested in hiding than in domination.

Whether occupied by wimps or warriors, once inside a castle, the first things to look for are signs of the wooden features that once were there before they rotted away. A pair of vertical slots opposite each other in the entrance corridor of the castle often indicates a portcullis, or heavy sliding

to hemp clothing and a unique vegetarian slow-food bar.

PHARMACY **McSharry's Pharmacy** (5/6 Belhavel; ☎ **090/647-6767**) also sells alternative health products.

RECOMMENDED WEBSITES   www.athlone. ie covers the basics.

SLEEPING

Possibly the coolest B&B in Ireland, MTV Best **The Bastion** (4 Bastion St.; ☎ **090/ 649-4954;** www.thebastion.net; single €36, doubles €65, Long Room €70) is a manifestation of all the dreams you've ever had of buying up a guesthouse and doing it up just as you'd like it. Completely boho, it has been decorated over 10 years by the owner and his brother. Now there are seven rooms scattered higgledy-piggledy over the house, all with stripped wooden floorboards and white walls. Mute green plants fill the window

spaces and, elsewhere, exotic paraphernalia such as stuffed animals stare out at you from the hallway. Groovy. There is also a small studio available to rent opposite. There are seven rooms altogether giving 14 or 15 spaces. If there are three of you, grab the Long Room, a stupendous room with two beds over two levels and a balcony. The price includes a buffet breakfast served in a sociable lounge-cum-kitchen. Packs up like a sardine can in the summer so book ahead by at least a week.

For bargain basement rooms that don't skimp on atmosphere, try **Athlone Holiday Hostel** (The Crescent; ☎ **0902/73399;** athhostl@iol.ie; dorm €30) just 50m (15 ft.) from the railway station. Smothered in Celtic murals, inside are 85 beds in bright dorms with wooden floors. Add in a big kitchen-cum-dining room, an adjoining restaurant, bike hire, and sky TV, and you have yourself a rather fine place to stay.

barricade. This would have been used as part of the entrance fortifications. Doors often rested on donut-shaped rings carved from stone; if you can find these rings you'll know where the doors were and which way they opened.

You can also see where the wooden floors would have been by looking for stone blocks protruding at regular intervals from the walls. The floor would have rested on timbers on these blocks, so imagine the floor 30cm to 60cm (1 ft.–2 ft.) above these stone blocks. You can also get an idea of the room layout within the castle by looking for slots or a row of holes in a stone floor. These are where the wooden partitions dividing rooms would have been.

The windows of the castle can also tell a tale. In the central tower or keep, defense was top priority, so the windows of the lower floors only have slits for firing arrows, making them horribly dark and stuffy inside.

The most important rooms for the life of the castle dwellers were on the upper floors, where windows could be somewhat larger, allowing light and air to enter the room. The brightest room of the castle, on the top floor, was often the kitchen and dining area, where all the parties and feasts took place. Signs of a former kitchen might be an especially large fireplace or a slop-stone, a drain of sorts that passes through the outer wall at floor level.

Of course, most of Ireland's castles are records of the lives not only of their original inhabitants, but of everyone who has lived in them, shaped them, and reshaped them during centuries of living. Ireland's people are experts in creatively mixing up the past and the present, and this skill is definitely visible in their castles.

EATING

Most of the best restaurants are on the Left Bank. Particular favorites are picked out below:

Cheap

→ **A Slice of Life** You'll be lucky to find a seat in here. If you can, grab a window stool and watch Left Bank life go by while feasting on paninis and wraps, or daily-changing specials such as pies and lasagnas served at a price of €6.95 or €7.95 for a huge, mounded plateful with vegetables and potatoes, or whatever you fancy from various made-that-morning salads. *High St.* ☎ *090/649-3970. Sandwiches €3.50–€5.25; breakfast €4–€6. Daily 8:30am–6pm.*

📺 Best → **Foodies** An unrivalled lunch stop that really understands the word *simple.* The walls are exposed stone, the floors are bare wood, and the food is fantastic. With magazines and newspapers scattered everywhere, it is also the perfect place for a weekend lounge about. On top of breakfasts, Foodies does some yummy sandwiches such as turkey breast with herb and onion stuffing and cranberry relish, or brie with sun-blushed tomatoes and green salad. For even hungrier lunchers there are specials like beef lasagna and smoked salmon with cream cheese. Oooh, and the owner is cute, too. *6 Bastion St.* ☎ *090/649-8576. Breakfast €4–€5.90; sandwiches €3.50–€4. Mon–Sat 9am–5:30pm.*

→ **Korma** A contemporary Indian restaurant situated on the waterfront in a big dark-saffron colored building right by the castle. It's not just mild dishes here; there are also spicy and hot options, plus a range of veggie options, which also make for a good budget dinner. *The Docks.* ☎ *090/649-8658. Mains €5.95–€14. Tues–Sun 5–11:30pm.*

Doable

➜ **Di Bella** In contrast to Pizza Mama (see below), Di Bella is a trendy Italian where the colors are kept strictly neutral. The staff are handsome as are the dishes—a range of pizzas and pastas done with flair. At lunchtime all the meals are a bit cheaper and often a bit smaller, too. Perfecto. *High St.* ☎ *090/644-4830. Mains €7.95–€19. Daily 10am–10pm.*

➜ **Pizza Mama** Your classic Italian restaurant with a squadron of tables decked out in the obligatory red-and-white check. The food doesn't disappoint either. There are pizzas, pastas, wraps, and paninis, plus risotto, steaks, chicken cordon bleu, and chicken Siciliano. Just what you'd expect. Pastas go for €9.75, as do pizzas with three toppings. *Pauper tip:* You can bring your own wine here. *4 Pearce St.* ☎ *090/624-4009. Mains €9.50–€16, slightly cheaper at lunch. Mon–Fri 11am–3pm, 5–11pm; Sat 1pm–late; Sun 1–11pm.*

Splurge

➜ **Kin Khao** The Irish media go mad about this restaurant. And it is good, but it's also quite pricey. Set in a traditional Irish building painted bright red and yellow, it is run by an Irish/Thai couple who dish out lots of bizarre-but-delish curries ranging from fruity duck to sour orange curry prawns. The express lunch makes eating here more affordable, offering a starter, main, and side salad for €9.95. Scoffers can choose from plates including satay chicken, crispy prawn won tons, various colored curries, or a pad Thai of stir-fried spring lamb. *Abbey Lane, just off High St.* ☎ *090/649-8805. Mains €17–€24. Tues–Sun for lunch and dinner.*

➜ **The Left Bank Bistro** Adding to the cosmopolitan atmosphere, The Left Bank Bistro couldn't be more like a Parisian eatery, with its traditional wooden exterior, huge windows, and cool bright interior where cakes sit in rows and flowers decorate tables. This is a place for weekend indulgence amidst the bustling composure of its ever-efficient staff. Food includes salads, focaccia sandwiches, spring rolls, and creamy pastas for lunch. Dinner sees steaks, Thai chicken breast, and Asian-marinated half-roast duck paraded past. *Fry Place.* ☎ *090/649-4446. www.leftbankbistro.com. Mains at lunch €5.50–€12, dinner €19–€23. Tues–Sat 10:30am–10pm.*

PARTYING

🎖 Best **Sean's Bar** (Main St.; ☎ **090/649-2358**) can't be beat for atmosphere—it's so thick here you could drink it. The old locals spend all day pondering around the bar, the fires are stocked with peat, the furniture is all old and wooden, there's even sawdust on the floor. Built in A.D. 900, The Guinness Book of Records has officially said this is the oldest pub in Ireland. It could even be the oldest in the world—nothing older has been found yet. Out back is where the young people hang, smoking on the beer terrace looking out over the river. Everyone is kept warm by a nifty collection of outdoor heaters. Expect raucous live music sessions on a nightly basis, and even during the day on the weekends. Mostly traditional, occasionally blues.

The place of the moment is **Palace Bar** (1–2 Castle St.; ☎ **090/649-2229**), a faux-colonial building looking mighty refined decked out in cream slatted wood. There are three levels with wooden floors and black-and-white photography decorating the walls. This is not a place to be scruffy. The crowd are young professionals sipping cocktails and bottled beers. Late bars take place every Thursday, Friday, and Saturday. There is also plenty of sport action, with football and hurling matches being shown on big screens.

SIGHTSEEING

➜ **Athlone Castle** This mighty fortress, lording it over the River Shannon, was built in 1210 for King John of England. It played a starring role in Athlone's history, first as the seat of the presidents of Connaught and later as the headquarters of the governor of Athlone during the first Siege of Athlone in 1690 and the second in 1691. Declared a national monument in 1970, it was recently restored and adapted for use as a visitor center, museum, gallery, and tearoom. The exhibition area offers an audiovisual presentation on the Siege of Athlone. It also contains displays on the castle, the town, the flora and fauna of the Shannon region, and the top Irish tenor John McCormack, himself a much-loved child of Athlone. The castle's original medieval walls have been preserved, as have two large cannons dating from the reign of George II and a pair of 10-inch mortars that were cast in 1856. *On the riverbank, signposted from all directions.* ☎ *0902/92912. Admission €5 adults, €3 students, €1.50. May to mid-Oct daily 9:30am–5pm.*

PERFORMING ARTS

Once a church, the recently opened **Dean Crowe Theatre and Arts Centre** (Chapel St.; ☎ **090/649-2129;** www.deancrowetheatre.com; tickets €10–€22) now hosts a mixture of Irish and international touring shows ranging from the avant-garde to the widely popular. Consequently one night will see a comic-tragedy in two acts featuring a soldier forced to exist on a diet of peas, while another will feature circus acts, gospel music, or jazz. Then there are Irish comediennes and heaps of tribute nights. Upstairs is an art gallery exhibiting the work of fairly well-known artists from Ireland and abroad. Open Monday to Friday 10am to 5pm, Saturday 1 to 4pm, and on show nights.

MEDITATION CENTRES

For those who've had enough of exploring outside and want to remind themselves what's on the inside, Athlone's **Tibetan Buddhist Meditation Centre** (1 Bastion St.; ☎ **087/749-6498;** athlone@rigpa.ie) offers meditation on Wednesday evenings from 7:30 to 9pm, with advanced practice sessions taking place on Tuesdays.

PLAYING OUTSIDE

BICYCLING   Dermot at **DB cycles** (Unit 3, Magazine Rd.; ☎ **090/649-2280;** dbcyclesandbabyland@eircom.net) hires out bikes at €15 per day (open to haggling for groups and weekly rents) with mountain, hybrid, and racer bikes all available in a variety of frame sizes. A popular day trip is across to the ancient monastic site of Clonmacnoise (see "Clonmacnoise," earlier), approximately 26km (16 miles) away; but why follow the herd, when Dermot has plenty of other suggestions, too.

SPECTATOR SPORTS

HORSE RACING   Horse racing takes place in July, August, and September at the **Kilbeggan Racecourse** (Loughnagore, Kilbeggan, County Westmeath; ☎ **0506/32176);** admission €12 adults, €7 students). Find the racecourse off the main Mullingar Road (N52), 1.6km (1 mile) from town.

SHOPPING

The **Liturgical Book Restorers** (17 Main St., Left Bank; ☎ **0906/493442;** Mon–Thurs 8am–5pm; Fri 8am–2pm [lunch 1–2pm]) may not be the place to pick up pressies for all the family back home, but it is worth a peek just to see the old tiled floor and antique printing presses. It's more like a minimuseum than a shop. If you do happen to be carrying around a valuable antique book that has perhaps gotten a bit battered on the journey, this is the place to get it "rebound, restored, repaired."

Run by the same people as the sacred Bastion B&B, **The Bastion Gallery** (6 Bastion St.; ☎ **090/649-4948;** bastiongallery@eircom.net) worships at the goddess of alternative. Filled with mythological guides to Ireland, Celtic jewelry, hippy clothes, bach flower remedies, embroidered bags, and health food, it is a definite must for browsing. The things calling out "buy me" the loudest are the mounted examples of ancient Ogham script, Ireland's first language.

Sightseeing Side Trips from Athlone

Whiskey fans might like to take a trip out to **Locke's Distillery Museum** (On N6, east of Athlone, Kilbeggan; ☎ **0506/32134;** admission €5 adults, €4 students; Apr–Oct daily 10am–6pm; Nov–Mar daily 10am–4pm) to get a lesson in making the stuff. Established in 1757, this 18th- and 19th-century enterprise was one of the oldest licensed pot-still whiskey distilleries in the world. After producing whiskey for almost 200 years, it closed in 1953. Over the past 15 years, a local group has restored it as a museum. In 1998, a major exhibition space opened in the restored front grain loft to display a host of distilling artifacts. A 35-minute tour will not only tell you how whiskey was distilled using old techniques and machinery, but also inform you about the area's social history. If you're not staying in Athlone or Kilbeggan particularly, it's almost midway between Dublin and Galway, making it a good stop-off point while you're on a cross-country journey or touring in the area. On the premises, you'll find a restaurant, coffee shop, and craft shop.

Next door **Garbz** (Bastion St.; ☎ **090/649-4954)** sells clothes and clobber perfect for a cool Irish road trip or visit to one of Ireland's top musical festivals. There are sunglasses, bags, and jeans plus some more urban wear: puffas and mod coats, with some great sale bargains, too. Dotted among the outerwear are rock-tastic rings and dream catchers hanging from the ceiling.

Upper Shannon: From Lough Ree to Lough Allen

The Upper Shannon River region is home to Lough Ree, the second-largest of Shannon's lakes where the wet 'n' wild theme continues. Powerboating, sailing, and wakeboarding are all available here at various spots across the lough.

Farther inland this area is splattered with museums and castles. Exerting one of the biggest pulls is the Irish Famine Museum, Strokestown, County Roscommon. Not exactly packed full of laughs, it does a good job of explaining what went on. The Famine changed both Irish and world history forever as millions of Irish people fled to America, Canada, Australia, and England. Find out why.

Above Lough Ree, the river skinnies in as it rushes down from Carrick-on-Shannon, a boating town that also houses Ireland's smallest chapel, built as a symbol of romantic love. Farther up still, Lough Key partners up with the Lough Key Forest Park, 336 hectares (840 acres) of forest, lake, and islands where powerboats or rowboats can be commandeered for explorations.

From this end of the river, it is possible to follow the water to Lough Erne in Northern Ireland, using a stretch of water known as the Ballinamore-Ballyconnell Canal or Shannon-Erne Waterway. Opened in 1994, after 125 years of restoration, it stands as a symbol of new cross-border cooperation.

Upper Shannon Basics

TOURIST INFORMATION FOR THE UPPER SHANNON REGION

Information on County Roscommon is available from the **Ireland West Tourism Office** (Foster St., Galway; ☎ **091/537700;** www.westireland.travel.ie). Hours are May, June, and September daily 9am to 5:45pm; July and August daily 9am to 7:45pm; October to April Monday to Friday 9am to 5:45pm and Saturday 9am to 12:45pm. Information on County

Longford is available from the **East Coast & Midlands Tourism Office** (Clonard House, Dublin Rd., Mullingar, County Westmeath; ☎ **044/48761**), open Easter through September, Monday to Friday 9:30am to 5:30pm, with extended hours in July and August; on County Cavan from the **Cavan Tourist Office** (Farnham St., Cavan, County Cavan; ☎ **049/433-1942**), open May through September, Monday to Friday 9am to 6pm, Saturday 10am to 2pm; on County Leitrim from the **North-West Tourism Office** (Aras Reddan, Temple St., Sligo; ☎ **071/916-1201**), open Easter through September, Monday to Friday 9am to 6pm, Saturday 9am to 5pm, and Sunday 9am to 3pm, with extended hours in July and August; and from the **tourist office at Carrick-on-Shannon** (☎ **071/962-0170**), open May through September, Monday to Saturday 9:15am to 5:30pm, Sunday 10am to 2pm. **Seasonal information points,** operating from June to August, are signposted in **Boyle** (☎ **071/966-2145**), Longford (☎ **043/46566**), and **Roscommon** (☎ **090/662-6342**).

Lough Ree

GETTING THERE

The N6 Dublin-Galway Road zips right underneath Lough Ree, almost grazing the bottom of the lake as it goes through Athlone (see "Getting There" under "Athlone").

SLEEPING

The aptly named **Lough Ree Lodge** (Dublin Rd.; ☎ **0902/76738**; www.athlonehostel.ie; dorm €30) is a purpose-built hostel on the main Dublin-Athlone Road. No, it's not brimming with character but it does provide somewhere cheap to stay near the lake. Rooms range from singles to quadruples, all with en suite shower, cable TV, and continental breakfast included. Meet other outdoor-loving budget travelers in the large kitchen-cum-dining room or playing pool.

PLAYING OUTSIDE

POWERBOATING   **Lough Ree Powerboat School** (Hodson Bay, Athlone; ☎ **049/952-9750;** www.hodsonbay.com) is one of Ireland's top powerboating schools, promising high-adrenaline days out such as their 1-day introduction to powerboating for €275, including a three-course lunch and free après-course drinks at a nearby hotel. These guys know their stuff, which is why they teach military and government officials how to handle boats. Want to get your hair all messed up for less? Try their eco tours for €25 per person, and spend a day with a personal guide exploring the history and ecology of the lake by boat. A sailing school caters for those who like to go with the breeze. The craft are Backman 21s, simple, backless, three-man dinghies with a focus on speed.

WAKEBOARDING   **Lough Ree Wakeboarders** (☎ **087/819-8038**) does exactly what it says on the tin and offers water surfing, boarding, and skating. For excitement without effort try the doughnut and banana boat rides.

SHOPPING

Puffers driving round the lake can stop in at Knockcroghery and get something to smoke, a *didn,* or clay pipe, made from the original Victorian moulds. This wee village was pipe-making central for over 300 years until it was burned down in 1921 during the War of Independence. Ethel Kelly now uses the old ways to make new pipes. There are heaps of trad Celtic designs and prices start from €7 for a *duidin* (half pipe) which was a particular fave with old ladies who had lost their teeth. She puts the finished pieces up for sale in the **ClayPipe Visitor Centre** (Knockcroghery; ☎ **090/666-1923;** ethelkelly@eircom.net; free admission; open June–Sept only, 10am–6pm).

THE MIDLANDS

Strokestown

Strokestown is actually a small town built up around the 18th-century Strokestown Park House, but most travelers swing this way to visit the Famine Museum.

GETTING THERE

BY CAR   Strokestown is situated on the main Dublin-Castlebar Road, the N5, 14 miles (23km) from Longford.

BY BUS   Seven **Bus Éireann** (☎ 01/836-6111; www.buseireann.ie) buses travel daily (service no. 22) from Dublin Busárus station to Strokestown, taking between 2 and 3 hours. Services also run to and from Sligo, Ballina, Longford, Athlone, and Westport.

SLEEPING

There is no hostel in Strokestown. The best bet is to stay in Lough Ree Lodge (see "Sleeping" under "Lough Ree," above) or Athlone (see "Sleeping" under "Athlone," above). If you get stuck, the **Percy French Hotel** (Bridge St., Strokestown; ☎ 071/963-3300; www.percyfrenchhotel.com; doubles €80) has 11 en suite rooms, all with TVs, and an affordable restaurant attached serving up chargrilled meat and bistro specials (€20 gets you two courses and a drink).

EATING

Strokestown Restaurant (Strokestown Famine Museum; ☎ 071/963-3013; mains 9.50€, baked potatoes 7€, soup 3.50€) is usually cram-packed with tourists. Elbow through the crowds to enjoy not-bad-at-all food at not-bad-at-all prices. Specials have included baked salmon in soy, honey, and sesame sauce. Ordinary offerings include topped baked potatoes served with salad or a daily choice of two homemade soups.

SIGHTSEEING

➔ **Strokestown Park House, Gardens and Famine Museum**   One of the

Lough Allen

Lough Allen is visually one of the most exciting lakes in the Midlands. Here the hills begin to grow in size, peaking in the dramatic scenery of County Sligo. The village of Drumshanbo acts as an access point to Lough Allen with the Iron Mountains rising up beyond, in the far northeast of the lake.

defining events of Ireland's history, the Great Potato Famine of the 1840s is the focus of this museum. Housed in the stable yards of Strokestown Park House, this museum illustrates how and why the Famine started, how English colonial officials failed to prevent its spread, and how it reduced the Irish population of 8.1 million by nearly 3 million through death and mass emigration. This museum is particularly interesting for Irish Americans, tens of millions of whom trace their ancestry to those who left the country during and after the Famine. The museum also seeks to relate the events of the Irish Famine to contemporary world hunger and poverty. The house is also worth a peek, a 45-room Palladian beauty, home to the Pakenham-Mahon family from 1600 to 1979. The north wing houses Ireland's last existing galleried kitchen (where the lady of the house could check how dinner was coming on without getting covered in gravy). The south wing is an elaborate vaulted stable, often described as an equine cathedral. *Strokestown Park, Strokestown. ☎ 071/963-3013. www.strokestownpark.ie. Admission to house or gardens or museum €5.50 adults, €4.50 students; admission to any 2 of 3 (house, gardens, museum) €9.50 adults, €8 students; admission to all 3 attractions €14 adults, €11 students. Mar–Oct daily 10am–5:30pm.*

A Pad of Your Own—Rent an Irish Cottage

Places to Stay around the Lough

Despite being beautiful and filled with activities, the Lough Derg region lacks myriad cheap places to stay. In many ways this is good, meaning the wide open spaces can be enjoyed without Maccy-D and motel signs spoiling the view but, however great the great outdoors is, coming indoors at the end of the day can often be better. Enter the "Rent an Irish Cottage" program. Pioneered in the area over 30 years ago, the idea was simple: Build small rental cottages in the traditional one-story style, with whitewashed walls, thatched roofs, stable doors, and turf fires. Add modern plumbing, heating, and kitchens. The result? Fab, reasonably priced accommodation enabling everyone from independent travelers to small groups a place to stay and party in the area. Most of the cottages are built in groups of 8 to 12, in remote, oh-so-sweet villages such as Puckane, Terryglass, and Whitegate, often over-looking—or at least near to—Lough Derg's shores. As there are no bars or restaurants on-site, you shop in the local store, cook your own meals, get chatting with the locals over a pint of the black stuff at night. Before you know it you'll feel like one of the villagers. Rates stretch from €230 to €1,300 per cottage per week, depending on the size (one to six bedrooms) and time of year, making it as cheap as or cheaper than shelling out for a hostel or B&B. And you get to decide what's for breakfast. Rental rates include bed linens and color TV; towels and metered electricity are extra.

Recently individual owners have got in on the game, building modern cottages with slate or tile roofs. They still do the trick. One of the best collections can be found in Mountshannon, County Clare, where there is a herd of 12 pastel-colored one- and two-story cottages on the shores of Lough Derg at Mountshannon Harbour. Grouped like a little village, the three-bedroom cottages cost €230 to €610 per week, depending on the time of year. Elsewhere on the shores of Lough Derg are 12 cottages in the rural village of Puckane, County Tipperary, costing €230 to €610 per week, for a two- to three-bedroom cottage, depending on season and number of bedrooms.

Find out more from **Rent an Irish Cottage** (51 O'Connell St., Limerick, County Limerick; ☎ **061/411109**; www.rentacottage.ie).

Lough Key Forest Park

GETTING THERE

BY CAR   Taking a car to Lough Key is the easiest way to get there, entering from the main Dublin-Sligo Road (N4), 3.2km (2 miles) east of Boyle.

BY BUS   **Bus Éireann** (☎ **01/836-6111**; www.buseireann.ie) buses go into Boyle from Sligo and Dublin. The Dublin bus leaves Busárus station seven times a day (five on Sundays and bank holidays) taking between 3 and 4 hours.

SLEEPING

A caravan park in the forest park's ground offers space for tents at a cost of €12. The facilities include toilets, showers, and a launderette. Alternatively **Cesh Corran** (Sligo Rd., Boyle; ☎ **071/966-2265**; www.marycooney.com; double €69, single €45) is an Edwardian B&B in nearby Boyle with a friendly owner, TVs in rooms, heaps of homemade foods, and even a special fridge for fishermen to keep their maggots in. Always important. Save cash by ordering a

THE MIDLANDS

continental breakfast in the morning, making rates per person €5 cheaper.

SIGHTSEEING/PLAYING OUTSIDE

Spanning 336 hectares (840 acres) along the shores of Lough Key and made up of mixed woodlands, a lake, and more than a dozen islands, **Lough Key Forest Park** (☎ **071/966-2363;** admission to park €5 per car charged Apr–Sept only; open year-round daily dawn–dusk) is one of Ireland's top lakeside parks. The grounds include nature walks, ancient monuments, ring forts, a central viewing tower, picnic grounds, a cafe, and a shop (open Apr–Sept). Deer, otters, hedgehogs, birds, pheasants, and many other forms of wildlife roam the park. The lake is navigable from the Shannon on the Boyle River. Powerboats and rowboats are available to rent, and there are pony and cart rides through the park.

If you are up for a bit of horseback riding, **Moorlands Equestrian & Leisure Centre,** Drumshanbo, County Leitrim (☎ **071/964-1500**), offers lessons as well as trail rides along Lough Allen and the nearby hills. During the off season, courses in equestrian science are offered. Book lessons or trail rides at least a day in advance. You can get mountain walking, watersports, and somewhere to sleep here, too.

Northern Ireland

From the Belfast club scene to the surfer's hangout in Portrush, Northern Ireland is buzzing into life. Walk down any street and you can feel the excitement bristling in the air. Nobody is apathetic. Everyone seems saturated with passion. It's rare, in fact, to meet a person without an opinion.

The Troubles

In the past, opinions caused trouble. For years the country was scored off the traveler's map thanks to what is referred to as "the Troubles," a feud caused by the English invasion of Ireland over 800 years ago.

We don't want to dwell on Northern Ireland's history, but it's impossible to go anywhere without being reminded of local politics, from the Irish or British flags flying above cities to politically charged student graffiti in country towns. So before you visit, you need a quick rundown of the history of it all, if only so you can tell your UFFs from your IRAs.

Why Did They Fight?

It all started when the British waged a largely futile effort to make Ireland, and the Irish, British. Their tactics included outlawing the Gaelic language, banning Catholicism, barring Catholics from land ownership, and, finally, Oliver Cromwell's New Model Army simply killed them in droves. British families were imported to take Irish land (essentially, physically replacing Irish Catholics with British Protestants). The descendants of those British settlers, generally speaking, form the Protestant population of Northern Ireland today.

Ireland finally won independence of a sort from Britain in 1921, in the aftermath of the 1916 rebellion. After much arguing, it was decided that the island would be divided. Twenty-six Irish counties would form an independent, free state (now the Republic of Ireland, or simply "the Republic"), while six counties in the Ulster province with predominately Protestant populations would become Northern Ireland and remain a part of the United Kingdom.

After the division, the British police and government in Ulster (as well as the *Ulster Freedom Fighters,* or the *UFFs*) were quite brutal toward the Catholic minority. Things got even worse in the 1960s when the Catholics started protesting against their treatment. The authorities came down hard. The *Irish Republican Army,* aka the *IRA,* reemerged in response and 3 decades of sectarian violence began, involving kidnappings, bombings, and the loss of many innocent lives.

Peace, Sort of

With the hands-on involvement of former United States President Bill Clinton urging them to find a peaceful solution to their disagreements, the Belfast agreement, universally known as the "Good Friday Agreement," was signed on May 22, 1998. It rejected the claims of both Ireland and Britain to the North, giving Northern Ireland its own government.

It's still been a rocky road to peace, with sporadic outbreaks of violence—although nothing on a scale of the previous carnage—and endless political bickering, but every day the country moves closer to a lasting peace. It's what nearly every single person in Northern Ireland wants, especially the young folk.

From a visitor's perspective, the violence has always been remarkably contained. Like diplomats, foreigners enjoy a kind of immunity. Derry and Belfast at their worst have always been safer for visitors than almost any comparable American city, and the Ulster countryside was and is as idyllic and serene as Vermont. When I've marveled at this, more than one Northern Irish person has told me gently, "No matter how much you care, it isn't your fight. Everybody knows that. Outsiders have always been safe here."

What this means for you is that you'll land in a dynamic, evolving country just waiting to be discovered. You'll fall in love with the place. You won't be alone. It has something to do with the straight-talking honesty of the Northern Irish. Their lust for a good night out. Their ability to look effortlessly hip. And the fierce intelligence and conviction that seems to run through everything they do.

You can feel it in the über-trendy bars, clubs, and hotels springing up in Belfast; in the art galleries in Derry; and in the thrusting indie music scene visible in virtually every town.

When you've finished with the urban entertainment, head out into the countryside to chill out, hike, wander, and grab a dose of fresh air. Top dazzlers are the Antrim coast with its cobalt seas, high rugged cliffs, and lush hills, or the wild and desolate Mourne mountains.

As peace settles into Northern Ireland, it will find itself overrun with travelers like the Republic. Already herds of hedonistic Dubliners are making a weekly pilgrimage to Belfast's clubs. Soon the secret will be out. Get here quick and enjoy it before the rest of the world finds out.

The Best of Northern Ireland

Belfast

○ **Black Taxi Tour:** Essential homework. Tours with attitude around the Republican and Loyalist areas of Belfast including the political murals and the "peace" wall. Guaranteed to explain why Belfast hasn't always been one big happy-skippity family. Find out who got shot where and why. See p. 441.

○ **Best Night Out: The Cathedral Quarter:** The hip, up-and-coming, artsy quarter of the city. Ignore the odd burnt-out building. In a few years you won't be able to move for private members clubs and chi-chi hotels. Right now it's for those in the know. Don't miss The Spaniard (see p. 433) for ultimate boho drinking and The Potthouse (see p. 435) bar-eatery-club to mingle with the city's über-trendy elite.

- **Best Lazy Day: The Botanic Gardens:** On a sunny day—yes, it does happen occasionally—bliss out in Belfast's best park, along with the youth of the city. When you're done rolling around on the grass, stroll through The Palm House—a beautiful old greenhouse—to get a feel for what Belfast must have looked like in ye olde days. See p. 441.

- **Best Gig: Limelight:** It's down. It's dirty. And it's damn-blast fantastic. One of the three adjoined bars that make up the city's live music holy trinity, this is *the* place to get sweaty while listening to up-and-coming bands. They've all passed through here: Oasis, Manic Street Preachers, Primal Scream, and so many more. There's no pretension here, just a scruffy crowd hungry for very loud music. See p. 438.

- **Best Splurge on a Bed:** If it's good enough for Franz Ferdinand and The Scissor Sisters, it's good enough for you. This is the ultimate Belfast splurge. The **Malmaison Hotel** knows how to do decadent, and their Rock 'n' Roll suites are where they do it best. Picture beds as big as your backyard, a shower for two, and your own private billiards table. Borrow a credit card or 10 and live the high-as-a-kite life. See p. 425.

- **Best Stroll: The Public Art Trails:** Public art is big in Belfast. Not just popular, some of it is huge. Art trails link up the most stunning examples and what better way to spend a hungover Sunday. To top it all off it's free, unless you grab an audio tour from the Lagan lookout. See p. 444.

- **Best Meal: Benedicts** has become a Belfast institution in less than a decade. Join the city's locals—from babies to grannies—as they pile into this awesome restaurant kitted out with bits of old French villas. Music is served up to the sound of good-time tunes or live bands.

And—this is the best bit—if you go between 5 and 7:30pm your meal costs the time you ordered it at. Way cool. See p. 426.

Derry

- **Strolling around Derry's City Walls:** A wander around the walls—hundreds of years old and still standing—is the best way to get acquainted with the city. It only takes 30 minutes and it's free. Where's the reason not to? See p. 474.

- **Taking a Free Derry Tour:** Derry has long been a focus point for Northern Ireland's republican struggle. Find out why on a Free Derry tour lead by a Catholic republican. There's no doubt it's one-sided but it's also a terrific insight. See p. 472.

- **Having a Night Out on Waterloo Street:** These old pubs are where Ulster natives got drunk before they set sail for America in the 19th century. Now they are a hub for rowdy music nights—trad, rock, and blues. Start in Peadar O'Donnell's and follow your ears. See p. 469.

- **Visiting the Void Gallery:** Just opened in 2005, this is a gallery fuelled by passion, bringing the best of thought-provoking international art to Derry. Expect poetic video installations and images strong enough to incite a revolution. See p. 473.

- **Having a Drink in Sandino's:** Derry's coolest bar, by far. A chill shoebox ruled over by Che Guevara. The music policy is funky and all embracing. The staff is hip and unbothered. It's where to find Derry's artsy crowd. See p. 470.

- **Taking in a Cultural Event at the Nerve Centre:** A cultural factory for new music, film, video, animation, and digital media churning out pure brilliance. There's always something happening here, be it art house cinema or punk rock mayhem. See p. 471.

NORTHERN IRELAND

Northern Ireland

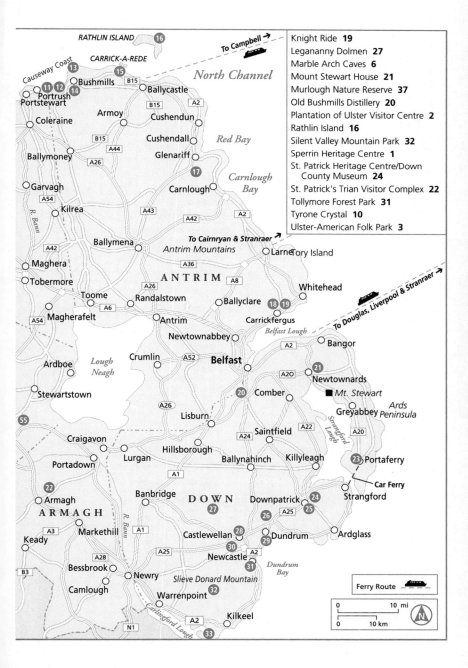

Knight Ride **19**
Legananny Dolmen **27**
Marble Arch Caves **6**
Mount Stewart House **21**
Murlough Nature Reserve **37**
Old Bushmills Distillery **20**
Plantation of Ulster Visitor Centre **2**
Rathlin Island **16**
Silent Valley Mountain Park **32**
Sperrin Heritage Centre **1**
St. Patrick Heritage Centre/Down
   County Museum **24**
St. Patrick's Trian Visitor Complex **22**
Tollymore Forest Park **31**
Tyrone Crystal **10**
Ulster-American Folk Park **3**

Getting Around in the North

BY TRAIN   Belfast is the hub for **Northern Ireland Railways** (also known as Translink) ☎ **028/9066-6630,** with two principal rail stations: **Great Victoria Street Station,** on Great Victoria Street, and **Belfast Central Station,** on East Bridge Street. Most trains depart from Belfast Central. The three main routes in the North's rail system are north and west from Belfast to Derry via Ballymena; east to Bangor, along the shore of Belfast Lough; and south to Dublin via Newry. See "The Basics" chapter for all-Ireland deals.

BY BUS   Ulsterbus (☎ **028/9033-3000;** www.translink.co.uk) runs daily services from Belfast to major cities and towns throughout Northern Ireland. From the **Laganside Bus Centre,** Donegall Quay, Belfast (☎ **028/9032-0011),** buses leave for destinations in the North, including Belfast International Airport and the Larne ferries, as well as the Republic. Bus services in the North are good and will get you to the most remote destinations. See chapter 2 for all-Ireland deals.

BY CAR   The best way to travel around rural Northern Ireland. Mostly, distances between towns and villages here are quite small. If you want to rent a car, **Avis** (☎ **028/ 9024-0404), Budget** (☎ **028/9023-0700), Europcar** (☎ **028/9031-3500),** and **Hertz** (☎ **028/9073-2451)** have offices in Belfast, and most have branches at the airports. If you rent a car in the Republic, you can drive it in the North as long as you arrange the proper insurance. You will need to check this.

Nuts & Bolts

Area Code   The area code for all of Northern Ireland is 028. Drop the "0" when dialing from within Northern Ireland.

Currency   Since Northern Ireland is a part of the United Kingdom, it uses the pound sterling and not the euro.

Embassies & Consulates   The U.S. Consulate General is at Queen's House, 14 Queen's St., Belfast BT1 6EQ (☎ **028/9032-8239).** Other foreign offices are across the water including the Australian High Commission, Australia House, Strand, London WC2 B4L (☎ **020/7379-4334);** Canadian High Commission, Macdonald House, Grosvenor Square, London W1X 0AB (☎ **020/7499-9000);** New Zealand High Commission, New Zealand House, 80 Haymarket Sq., London SW1Y 4TQ (☎ **020/7930-8422).**

Emergencies   Dial ☎ **999** for fire, police, and ambulance.

Mail   United Kingdom postal rates apply, and mailboxes are painted red. Most post offices are open weekdays 9am to 5pm, Saturday 9am to 1pm.

Parking   Because of the Troubles, parking attendants can understandably get a twitchy about an illegally parked car. You will get fined. Consider yourself warned.

Petrol (Gas)   Fill her (or him) up in the Republic, as gas is much cheaper up there. In the North, the approximate price of 1 liter of unleaded gas is 90p sterling. There are 4 liters to the U.S. gallon, which makes the price of a gallon of unleaded gas a whopping £3.60.

Safety   Forget what you've seen on the news, the North has one of the lowest levels of crime in western Europe. Historically, the high rate of serious crime such as homicide and robbery was almost all due to terrorism and the Troubles. But don't be stupid, look out for pickpockets in crowded areas and don't wander into known sectarian areas at night. For details on neighborhoods/areas to avoid, see the "Safety" sections listed for each town in this chapter

Telephone To reach Northern Ireland from anywhere but the Republic of Ireland or Great Britain, dial the country code (44) and then 28 (the area code minus the initial 0) and finally the local eight-digit number. From the Republic of Ireland, omit the country code; dial 048 and then the local eight-digit number. From Great Britain, dial 028 and the eight-digit number. For local calls within Northern Ireland, just dial the eight-digit local number.

Belfast

Belfast has stormed back onto the world travel map like a hero returning from battle. Sure he might be looking a bit run-down, and there's the odd scar here or there, but underneath all that stubble you can see he's a mighty fine looking man. And what does every soldier returning from the front want to do? That's right, they want to party. Hard.

Cast out of your mind every piece of news footage you've ever seen on Belfast's troubles. That was then. This is now. With its gorgeous old buildings and beautiful young people, Belfast is busy re-creating itself as one of the hippest cities in Europe. Whether you're after hard house nights, velveteen lounge bars, artsy bohemian conversation or sweat-splattering live rock, Belfast has what you want. Guaranteed.

Getting There

BY PLANE Fly direct from Newark (New York) to **Belfast International Airport** (☎ 028/9448-4848; www.belfast airport.com) on scheduled flights with **Continental Airlines** (☎ 800/231-0856; www.continental.com) now departing daily during the summer months, four times each week in the winter. Flights take between 6½ and 7½ hours. Otherwise, **Aer Lingus** (☎ 800/474-7424; www.aerlingus.com) offers scheduled flights from Boston, New York, LA, and Chicago via Shannon or Dublin.

It's the same story with **Delta Airlines** (☎ 800/241-4141; www.delta.com) who fly via Shannon and Dublin from Atlanta and **US Airways** (☎ 800/622-1015; www.us airways.com) from Philadelphia. **American Airlines** (☎ 800/433-7300; www.aa.com) also fly from Boston via Shannon or Chicago via Dublin. Other big airlines offer connecting flights from the United States and Canada via London/Heathrow, Glasgow, or Manchester.

With the explosion in budget airlines, there are now a myriad of companies flying to the island of Ireland from England, Scotland, and Wales. **British Airways** (☎ 800/403-0882; www.britishairways. com) flies from Birmingham, Edinburgh, and London/Heathrow into Belfast International Airport and into **Belfast City Airport** (☎ 028/9093-9093; www.belfastcityairport. com) from Glasgow and Manchester, but why fly with them when there are so many cheaper options available. The super-friendly and clean **BMI baby** (☎ 08702/642229 in Britain; www.bmibaby.com) flies to both Belfast City Airport and Belfast International Airport from various destinations in the U.K. as do **Flybe** (☎ 0871/700-0535 in Britain; www.flybe.com), with **Easyjet** (☎ 0871/750-0100 from the U.K.; www.easyjet.com) only flying into Belfast International Airport. Although **Ryanair** (☎ 0871/246-0000 in Britain; www.ryanair.ie) doesn't fly directly to Belfast but, with flights from as little as one English penny, it can be worth flying into the Republic and catching a bus or checking out their service to Derry. To see all the airline routes from the U.K., the U.S., and elsewhere, check out www.tourismireland.com.

GETTING INTO TOWN FROM THE AIRPORT
Belfast International Airport is nearly 31km (19 miles) north of the city in the lush green Antrim hills. The best bet is to catch a **Translink Airbus** (☎ 028/9066-6630; www.translink.co.uk) into the city center. It operates daily from 5:35am to 11:20pm (from 6:20am on Sat and 6:50am on Sun) leaving every half-hour (up to hourly on a Sunday), takes 30 minutes, and costs £6 for a single or £9 for a return. Taxis will be £25 to £30.

From Belfast City Airport, less than 6.4km (4 miles) from the city center, it's easiest to grab a cab for about £6 to get into the city. You can also take 600 bus service (leaving from 6am until 10pm Monday to Saturday, 7:30am to 9:50pm on Sunday and costing £1 from the airport terminal to the Europa Bus Station). Or catch the air shuttle bus to the Sydenham Halt train station. From here trains leave every 30 minutes (until 6pm when they go hourly) from 6am until 11pm. From Sydenham to Central Station it's £1.05 and takes 8 minutes. All timetables are available on www.translink.co.uk.

BY FERRY The quickest sea crossing from Britain to Northern Ireland is from Scotland aboard a fast craft from Cairnyan to Larne (30 min. from Belfast) taking just 1 hour, with **P&O European Ferries** (☎ 0870/242-4777 in Britain; www.poferries.com). Then it's a close-run race between the Troon to Larne fast craft service offered by P&O again coming in at 1 hour 50 minutes or the slightly faster Stranraer to Belfast crossing from **Stena Line** (☎ 08705/707070 in Britain; www.stenaline.com) coming in 5 minutes faster at 1 hour and 45 minutes. There's also an 8-hour crossing

from Liverpool with **Norse Merchant Ferries** (☎ 0870/6004321 in Britain or 01/819-2904 in Ireland; www.norsemerchant.com), but the Irish Sea can be fairly rough and you might not want to be feeling seasick for that long.

BY TRAIN Trains on the **Irish Rail** (☎ 1850/366222; www.irishrail.ie) and **Northern Ireland Railways** (☎ 028/9024-6485) systems travel into Northern Ireland from Dublin's Connolly Station daily. They arrive at Belfast's **Central Station,** East Bridge Street (☎ 028/9089-9411). Monday to Saturday, eight trains a day connect Dublin and Belfast; on Sunday, five. The trip takes about 2 hours.

BY BUS **Ulsterbus** (☎ 028/9033-3000; www.translink.co.uk) runs buses from the Republic to Belfast and nearly all the bus services within Northern Ireland. The express bus from Dublin to Belfast takes under 3 hours and runs eight times daily Monday to Saturday, three times on Sunday. All the timetables can be found online. **Aircoach** (☎ 0870/225-7555; www.aircoach.ie) offers some bargain fares from Dublin airport to Belfast, often making it cheaper than the bus from Belfast airport to Belfast and consequently opening up more flight options. The service starts up from Dublin airport at 6am and the last run is at 9pm. You can also ride from Dublin city to Belfast, transferring at the airport.

BY CAR It's easy to speed into Belfast from the Republic of Ireland, and you might well be glad to exchange the pot-holed roads of the Republic for the smoother ride in Northern Ireland. You may encounter checkpoints on the border but it's unlikely. Often you won't even notice you've crossed, apart from the change in road signs from kilometers to miles. Main roads leading to Northern Ireland from the Republic include N1 from Dublin, N2 from Monaghan, N3 from Cavan, N14 and N15 from Donegal, and N16 from Sligo.

If you're renting a car and doing a border crossing, make sure your insurance is valid in both the North and the Republic.

Orientation

It's incredibly easy to work out where everything is in Belfast. The City Hall in Donegall Square is essentially the center of the city and all roads radiate out from there. Walk north to find the main shopping drag on Royal Avenue. All the chain shops are located here. Keeping on walking and turn right at the top, where the shops start to peter out, to find The Cathedral Quarter, a bohemian district with many artist studios. West of Donegall Place is the West Belfast, the rather dodgy part of town where you'll find the Republican Falls area and Loyalist Shankill area. East of the square is the River Lagan with its fab views down to the industrialized harbor farther north (set to become Titanic Quarter, a hugely ambitious development mixing a marina with all-day-all-night living). On the way is St. George's Market and more gorgeous Georgian houses. Across the river there's very little to explore apart from the Odyssey Centre. Amble south from Donegall Square to find The Golden Mile, a city center area containing The Grand Opera House and upscale hotels together with a number of traditional pubs. This area tends to become extremely quiet at night as people party closer to home. Farther along Bedford Street and on down Dublin Road are a myriad of contemporary eateries. Then it's on to the student zone at the end of the road: the Queens Quarter. This is where the nightlife heats up and many of the music bars are to be found. It's also where the über-chill Botanical Gardens are located. The whole area is serenely quiet in the day during the student summer holidays. Farther out is Lisburn road: a rather refined, almost suburban area dotted with cafes, outrageously priced fashion shops, and the occasional ultraglam bar.

Getting Around

BY CAR   It seems crazy to bring a car into Belfast. The city is so compact it's a breeze to walk from one side to the other. But if you must drive here, leave your car near your hotel or hostel and explore the city on foot. Look for the universal blue P signs designating parking areas. Don't park where there is a pink-and-yellow sign. These are "control zones" where there is no parking. The easiest places to find a space are behind City Hall (south side), St Anne's Cathedral (north side), and around Queen's University and Ulster Museum.

CAR RENTAL   Need a car to get out into the greenery and explore? **Avis** (☎ **028/9024-0404;** www.avis.com), **Budget** (☎ **028/9023-0700;** www.budget.com), **Europcar** (☎ **028/9031-3500;** www.europcar.com), **Hertz** (☎ **028/9073-2451;** www.hertz.com) and **Easycar** (☎ **0906/333-3333** [be warned this is a 6op per minute phone number]; www.easycar.com) have offices in either Belfast city, or at least one of the Belfast airports, sometimes both. You generally need to be over 25 to hire a car in Northern Ireland. Some companies will rent to people over 21 but this is unusual.

BY BUS   **Metro** (☎ **028/9066-6630**) is the new name for Belfast's city buses. All their info including map routes can be found on www.translink.co.uk, the organization bringing together all Northern Ireland's bus and train services. Twelve color-coded buses and routes now cross the city center with departure points centering around Donegall Square. Fares are £1 to £1.50 within Belfast. A Smartlink card makes it even more of a bargain for travelers taking more than 10 journeys. Hop aboard the party bus—night buses shift revelers out from the city center for a cost of £3.50 to various outlying districts—leaving Donegall Square West at 1 and 2am.

BY TAXI   Taxis are available at all main rail stations, ports, and airports, and in front of City Hall. Most metered taxis look like London black cabs with a yellow disc on the window. These can be hailed. Other taxis are usually pre-booked and may not have meters so check the fare before you get in. They should still have a green license disc; if they don't they are probably illegal and potentially unsafe. Even if they do have a meter you can haggle a price if you like. Some taxi services will ask if you mind sharing. Each departing customer then pays a little less than the current meter fee. This normally works out a bit better value for the passengers and a lot better value for the driver. **Value cabs** (☎ **028/9080-9080;** www.valuecabs.co. uk) are honest, clean, a big company, and open 24/7. Like most services in Belfast they are quite pricey (minimum charge of £2.50 and £1.05 per mile). Prices are slightly cheaper up and down the Shankhill and Falls roads.

BY BICYCLE   The city is a good place to cycle around. The traffic is not too heavy and the city center is flat, with some more challenging rides available just beyond the city limits. Hire a bike from **McConvey** (☎ **028/ 9033-0322;** www.mcconveycycles.com) from £10 per day or **Life Cycles** (☎ **028/9043-9959;** www.lifecycles.co.uk) from £9 per day. Take a peek at www.belfastandbeyond.com for route ideas including the Giant's ring to a "huge megalithic henge" and a trip along the Lagan towpath—40km (25 miles) of hangover-friendly, hill-free cycling.

ON FOOT   Belfast is a winning city for walking. The Belfast Welcome Centre has walks in leaflets but really it's best just to meander. Along the river to the port area, the Cathedral Quarter and university area are all particularly smile-making. Most places are safe around town but check with locals if you are visiting in **Marching Season** (a series of Loyalist and Unionist parades between Easter Monday and September; see box on p. 457 for details) if there is anywhere they would currently consider a no-go zone. It is usually safe to walk up into the Shankill and Falls area during the day (although once again check the news and with locals) but it is better to use taxis at night. As with most U.K. cities after 10pm things start to get a little dodgy in the center as some residents and visitors become booze-fuelled.

Belfast Basics

TOURIST OFFICES   All sorts of info, including maps and leaflets about Belfast and the rest of Northern Ireland, is waiting for you the **Belfast Welcome Centre,** up the escalator at 47 Donegall Place (☎ **028/9024-6609;** www.gotobelfast.com). It's open June through September, Monday to Saturday 9am to 7pm and Sunday noon to 5pm; October through May, Monday to Saturday 9am to 5:30pm. There is also a TI desk at **Belfast City Airport** (☎ **028/9045-7745**) open year-round Monday to Friday 5:30am to 10pm, Saturday 5:30am to 9pm, and Sunday 5:30am to 10pm. The desk at **Belfast International Airport** (☎ **028/9442-2888**) is open March to September daily 24 hours, October to February daily 6:30am to 11pm.

RECOMMENDED WEBSITES   The official tourism website for Belfast is www.goto belfast.com but it's not very inspiring. Better check out www.belfast.net, a cover-all guide to the city with news for travelers, events, and nightlife info. For an insider look at Belfast life, plus entertainment listings, try www.belfasttelegraph.co.uk or "Belfast in Your Pocket," http://www.inyourpocket.com/ ni/en; the latter also contains short, downloadable PDF city guides. Also, print copies of In Your Pocket Belfast web content are distributed in local hotels, car-rental offices, and visitor centers.

Nuts & Bolts

Cellphone Providers/Servicers   **Rentaphone-Ireland** (☎ 011/3538-7683-4563; www.rentaphone-ireland.com) can arrange to have a phone waiting for you in Ireland at a post office or your accommodation. It's all done online. Rates start at €75 per week. *Tip:* If you are American, remember this—unlike in the U.S., text messaging is MUCH cheaper than making a phone call. But if you receive a phone call, the caller pays, not you.

Emergencies   In an emergency dial **999** for the fire, police, and ambulance services. The most central hospital is **Shaftesbury Square Hospital,** 116–120 Great Victoria St. (☎ **028/9032-9808**). **Belfast City Hospital** (☎ **028/9032-9241**) is south on Lisburn Road. West of the city center on Grosvenor Road is the **Royal Victoria Hospital** (☎ **028/9024-0503**), great experts in gun wounds thanks to the positioning in West Belfast during the Troubles.

Doctors   Dial the free-phone number **0800/665544** for advice on medical and dental emergencies.

Embassies   The **U.S. consulate general** is at Queen's House, 14 Queen's St., Belfast BT1 (☎ **028/9032-8239**).

Internet/Wireless Revelations   The Internet Cafe, 27 Shaftesbury Sq., Belfast (☎ **028/9032-0337**), is on the way to the uni area. Inside you'll find friendly staff serving good snacks and coffee. It's £4 per hour to surf. The **ITXP,** The Kennedy Centre, Falls Road, Belfast (☎ **028/9096-2222**), is cheaper at £3 per hour but a little way out. Wi-Fi around Belfast starts from £2 per hour and can be found at approximately 50-plus places around town. Largely the big hotels, but also **Europa bus station, Burger King** (18 Dublin Rd.; ☎ **028/9032-4292;** www.burgerking.co.uk) and the **Virgin Megastore** (Royal Ave.; ☎ **028/9023-6623**). Check out www.totalhotspots.com for a directory of paid-for hotspots and www.consume.net for places where it is free to surf.

Laundromats   Unless you have a particular penchant for hanging around washing machines, scoop up your dirty socks and give them to **Belfast Laundry** (96 Sunnyside St.; ☎ **028/9064-2080;** www.belfastlaundry.com) who will pick up your washing and return it to you for prices ranging from £4 for up to 16lb

Lost Property   Call the police lost property line (☎ **028/9065-0222**) to be put in touch with the local station.

Luggage Storage   Due to the city's turbulent past there are NO left luggage facilities at the major bus and train stations in Belfast, but most hostels and hotels will be happy to provide this service if you are staying with them.

Newspapers   Belfast is spoilt for print with three dailies, *The Belfast Telegraph, Irish News and Newsletter,* plus the *Sunday Life*—all with info of what's going on about town.

Pharmacies   For prescriptions, toiletries, and first-aid kits there are a number of **Boots** (www.boots.co.uk) chain stores around town including one at 35-47 Donegall Place; ☎ 028/9024-2332. Late-night chemists work on a rotating basis, details of which can be found in the local papers.

Photography Stores   There are two **Jessops** (19-21 High St., ☎ **0845/458-7031;** 7 Arthur Sq., ☎ **0845/458-7032;** www.jessops.com) in Belfast, part of a chain where the staff are normally amateur photographers. Employees tend to know their stuff.

Post Office   The **Belfast GPO** (General Post Office) at Castle Place is the main post office at the intersection of Royal Avenue and Donegall Place. It's open Monday to Friday 9am to 5:30pm, Saturday 9am to 7pm. If you miss this post, slightly later collections are taken from Tomb Street sorting office.

Restrooms   Most public restrooms do not charge a fee. In town, look for facilities on the corner of Great Victoria Street and Hope Street (just down from the Europa Hotel), in the Castle Court Centre, next to the big cinema on Dublin Road, east of Donegall Square on Montgomery Street, and just off, Ann Street in the edge of the Cathedral Quarter.

Safety   Belfast has a very low crime for an industrialized nation BUT ask the locals which areas travelers should not stray into at night. These are mainly in West Belfast, but there are some other sketchy areas near hostels and bars (see neighborhood info, above). As with any UK city, drunkenness can be a problem and lead to scuffles after 10pm. Simply try to avoid confrontation.

Telephone Tips   Belfast numbers are made up of 02890 followed by six digits. Inside Belfast you only need dial from the 9. If someone is phoning in or you are using a mobile you need to use the whole number, unless it is an international call in which case the international access code from the country you are dialing from is followed by 44 2890 followed by the last six digits of the number.

Tipping   This is generally left up to the customer in restaurants, although big groups may be charged on their bill. 10% to 15% is the usual amount for good service. People don't generally tip in bars but instead buy the barmen (or gal) a drink.

Sleeping

Considering its size, Belfast does not have a lot of hostels. Only six. Consequently, beds tend to fill up quick so it pays to book ahead. That said, outside of the summer months and due to its slightly out-of-the-way location, you can usually turn up and find a room at the Farset International Hostel (see below). Most hostels are clean and decent but few are wildly fun. Due to the compact nature of the city, there is no need to trek way out of town for budget accommodation and affordable B&B's exist near the city center, too. Thanks to Belfast's reincarnation as one of the hippest cities in Europe, if you deserve a treat—and you know you do—you'll find plenty of fab boutique hotels dotted around town. Most of them cater to men in suits, so if you want to snag yourself a cheap(er) room, the best time to hit them is on the weekends when prices drop, to sometimes as much as half.

HOSTELS

📺 **Best** → **Arnie's Backpackers**
Entering Arnie's is a bit like coming home—to a mad, crazy, family. There's a cup of tea, a log fire, a garden, and two welcoming Jack Russell pups (Snowy and Rosy). It may not be tidy but it has bags of character and really is the quintessential independent hostel. And there's no curfew—way hey. The atmosphere is relaxed, the guests are fun-loving, and the owner is more than friendly. Arnie's gets very crowded and cramped in the summer so you will need to book ahead. If you like lots of quiet solitude this may not be your scene. *63 Fitzwilliam St.* ☎ *028/9024-2867. www.arnies-backpackers.co.uk. £7.50 dorm. Amenities: Garden; kitchen.*

→ **Farset International Hostel**   A long way away from Arnie's both in terms of location and atmosphere, the Farset International offers stunning views over the city from a position almost in the Antrim Hills.

Sleeping & Sightseeing in Belfast

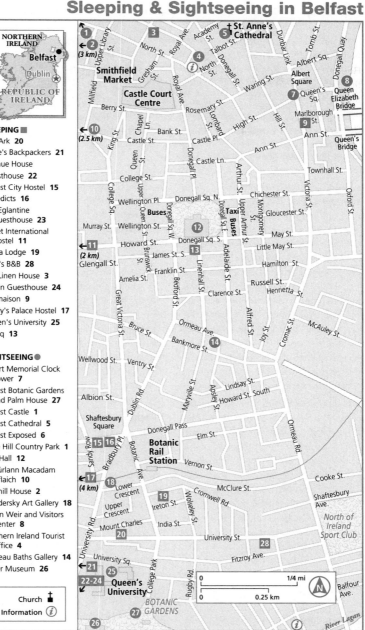

SLEEPING ▧

The Ark **20**

Arnie's Backpackers **21**

Avenue House
Guesthouse **22**

Belfast City Hostel **15**

Benedicts **16**

The Eglantine
Guesthouse **23**

Farset International
Hostel **11**

Helga Lodge **19**

Kate's B&B **28**

The Linen House **3**

Liserin Guesthouse **24**

Malmaison **9**

Paddy's Palace Hostel **17**

Queen's University **25**

TENsq **13**

SIGHTSEEING ●

Albert Memorial Clock
Tower **7**

Belfast Botanic Gardens
and Palm House **27**

Belfast Castle **1**

Belfast Cathedral **5**

Belfast Exposed **6**

Cave Hill Country Park **1**

City Hall **12**

Cultúrlann Macadam
Óflaich **10**

Fernhill House **2**

Frendersky Art Gallery **18**

Lagan Weir and Visitors
Center **8**

Northern Ireland Tourist
Office **4**

Ormeau Baths Gallery **14**

Ulster Museum **26**

Church ✝

Information ⓘ

Finding Great-Great-Grandma

Think you have a bit of Irish in you? Contact the **Ulster Historical Foundation,** Balmoral Buildings, 12 College Sq. E., Belfast BTI 6DD (☎ **028/9033-2288;** www.uhf.org.uk) to find out for certain. They'll help you track down Irish ancestors, particularly in Belfast, County Antrim, and County Down. The staff will fling useful publications in your direction and help you out in the research process. A brilliant new online resource covering all 32 counties of Ireland is the **Irish Family History Foundation's** Internet site at www.irishroots.net. Heaps of the info is free for you to browse through, and you can also rent researchers to do the tough stuff for you. Initial searches cost from €75 and full-on family searches cost from €250.

The downside is walking up the Springfield Road (not the safest street) to get here, right through the center of West Belfast. During daylight hours, don't fret, but be sure to get a taxi home at night (£2.50–£3 from the city center). Most rooms are en suite twins with a modern college dorm feel. During the summer this place fills with international (often outdoor-loving due to the hostel's location) travelers. Past September it can feel a bit like you're the only nut left rattling around in a huge concrete larder. *466 Springfield Rd.* ☎ *028/9089-9833. www.þarsetinternational. com. £20 single, £30 double, £4 extra þor break-þast. Amenities: Restaurant; Internet.*

➔ **The Ark** The Ark is slap-bang in the middle of the university area inside a beautiful old red brick town house. If you are looking for work in the city, this is a good place to base yourself. The job bulletin board has sound advice about where to go for jobs and the 2am curfew will stop you missing any early morning interviews. Roomy, clean dorms and firm beds also make it conducive to a good night's rest. *44 University St.* ☎ *02890/329626. www.arkhostel.com. £11 þor dorms (6–12 beds), long-term stays can be negotiated. Amenities: Broadband Internet (£1.20 per hour); central heating; DVD; kitchen; TV.*

➔ **Belfast City Hostel** Seeking a wild, crazy, time in Belfast? Don't check in here.

The Belfast City Hostel is a huge, austere building that somehow manages to make you feel naughty the moment you walk in the door. Due to the lack of a common room, there is little interaction between travelers. But the on-site Causeway Café serves bagels, toasted sarnies, or griddled soda bread from £1, or a lunch-to-go for £4. Showers are powerful and hot, and staff members are reliable. Make sure to check with them to determine where it is safe to wander at night. The hostel is situated on the west of the Sandy Row neighborhood, a dodgy Loyalist enclave. *22 Donegal Rd.* ☎ *02890/324733. Dorms £7.50–£11 (4–6 beds); £36 doubles. Amenities: Bicycle store; Internet; kitchen; laundry; TV.*

➔ **Paddy's Palace Hostel** Thank whoever-is-up-above for Paddy's Palace Hostel. The "party people" make a beeline for punch and Irish stew nights in the hostel's posh Georgian dining room. Prepare for raucous nights of much drinking and occasional outbursts of singing. Peppering the hedonism are lectures by local university professors and a staff keen to tell you about their city. Black taxi (see p. 441) and walking tours set off from here daily. There is no curfew and the communal kitchen is huge and full of fancy new appliances. When the Paddywagon rolls into town—no, not a police van, it's the outrageous party tours who use the six Paddy Palaces around Ireland as their stop-off points—the Palace fills up quickly, so be sure to book ahead. *68 Lisburn Rd.* ☎ *028/9033–3367. www.paddyspalace.com. 12 2-bed dorms £8.50–£15, doubles £37. Amenities: Internet; kitchen; laundry.*

➔ **The Linen House** The largest independent hostel in Ireland is the best bargain in town for a single room. Housed in a beautiful old linen factory, its location in the north of the city takes you away from the uni action but instead gives you access to the up-and-coming Boho district, Cathedral Quarter, and they city's main shopping street, Royal Avenue. This also puts it quite close to the sketchy Falls/Shankill neighborhoods meaning don't walk home alone at night. The basement common room lures you in with couches and a snooker table. The beds and rooms are okay, but the showers can be a little stingy on the hot water front. Internet access is cheap at 50p/10 minutes. *18-20 Kent St.* ☎ *028/9058-6400. www.belfasthostel.com. Beds £6.50–£10 dorm; £30 double; £20 single. Amenities: Bike storage; Internet; kitchen; TV.*

UNIVERSITY ACCOMMODATIONS

➔ **Queen's University** These halls house travelers from June to September and on Christmas and Easter breaks. The setting is institutional and sterile, but you get a big, clean room cheap in a secluded parkland setting. From the Opera House, follow directions to Arnie's until you get to University Road. Continue on University until it turns into Malone Road. About a 30-minute walk from the Opera House or take the bus. *78 Malone Rd.* ☎ *02890/381608. qehor@qub.ac.uk. £9.40 (student rate) or £11.75 (nonstudent rate) rooms. Singles and doubles only. AE, MC, V. Amenities: Kitchen; TV.*

DOABLE

Many redbrick guesthouses in the University area all serving up big breakfasts and a friendly welcomes. The **Liserin Guest House** (17 Eglantine Ave.; ☎ **028/9066-0769; £40 double, £23 single) has showers and TVs in all**

the rooms, and you can even bring along your dog—if you ask nicely first. The **Avenue House Guest House** (23 Eglantine Ave; ☎ 028/9066-5904; £50 double; £40 single) is less old grandma and more cool aunt. All the rooms have baths and the whole place is a Wi-Fi hotspot. For the ultimate breakfast though, it has to either be Jacqui's fry-up at **The Eglantine Guesthouse** (21 Eglantine Ave.; ☎ **028/9066-7584; £40 double, £40** single) or the homesick might try **Kate's B&B** (127 University St.; ☎ **028/9028-2091; £50** double) for a real family feel and to try her "heart attack on a plate" in the morning. "Go on, kill yourself!" as she likes to say.

➔ **Helga Lodge** Staying here is a bit like going to visit your granny. The furniture forces you to sit up straight and everything, including the walls, is floral. If you can overlook the chintz, Helga Lodge is a decent Victorian-style redbrick town house, right near all the goings-on in the Queen's student zone. All 31 rooms have their own TV and 8 have showers. *7 Cromwell Rd.* ☎ *028/9032-4820. £50 double with private bathroom; £40 double with shared bathroom. MC, V. Free parking. Bus: 83 or 85. In room: TV, phone.*

SPLURGE

📺 (**Best**) ➔ **Malmaison** Imagine an ornate Victorian warehouse decorated with dark, decadent colors and oodles of velvet. Filled with beds so enormous that sleeping alone feels, well, just plain wrong. This is Malmaison Hotel in Belfast, *the* place where visiting rock stars and artists lay their coiffured heads. It's not cheap, but people like the Fun Loving Criminals, Paul van Dyke, and Ian Brown seem to think it's worth it. Staying for a night is a little like starring in your own version of *Moulin Rouge*—without the tragedy. Staff is so friendly and cool it is difficult to know whether to tip them or tag along when they go out raving. Before you do either, seat yourself in their restaurant for some of the best food in Belfast (see p. 430). Or pop into the bar, perfect for pre-dinner Black Velvets (Guinness with expensive champagne) and early-hours nightcaps. Give them a ring to find out about weekend deals starting from £90 including breakfast. *34-38 Victoria St.* ☎ *028/9022-0200. www.malmaison.com. Double/single £135 (room only), breakfast £9.95. AE, MC, V. Amenities: A/C; bar; broadband Wi-Fi; gym; restaurant. In room: TV, iPod docking stations.*

➜ **TENsq**   If you can't afford Malmaison, don't even think about Ten Square. Inspired by the sky-stroking hotels of Shanghai's Pudong district, this is celeb central. U2's Bono, Meatloaf, Duran Duran, and Westlife have all stayed here, while Moby even ran his fingers over the ivories in the bar. Go barefoot in the bedrooms to appreciate toe-loving rugs and real-wood floors. It's almost as hip as Malmaison but a little less decadent. Cream and beige decor is spiced up Chinese style with low-level beds, wooden shutters, dim lighting, and glowing lanterns. The crowd is cool business people during the week and creative young couples on the weekends (when the prices drop as low as 2 nights for the price of 1). Downstairs is The Bar Room and Grill, where breakfast is served up alongside laid-back reggae. Groovy. *10 Donegall Sq.* ☎ *028/9024-1001. www.ten-sq.com. £160-£240 double (including breakfast). Check the Web for weekend specials. AE, MC, V. Amenities: AC; bar; restaurant; Wi-Fi. In room: TV, broadband.*

MTV **Best** ➜ **Benedicts**   Picture a posh bed-and- breakfast and you'll be near the mark with this self-titled "boutique hotel." A mainstream rock 'n' roll soundtrack fills the commons spaces—think Oasis and U2—and the staff is refreshingly genuine, no-nonsense, hard-working, and fun. There's free Wi-Fi access throughout. All rooms are en suite, the beds are supersize with crisp white sheets and—this is the best bit—the most expensive rooms come with a Jacuzzi bath

and one of those reclining leather chairs Joey was forever sitting on in *Friends*. It also incorporates an institution: Benedicts restaurant and bar (open to 3am and featuring remarkably great food deals; see below for full review). This hotel is perfectly positioned for wild nights out in the city's young party zone. Go play. *7-21 Bradbury Place.* ☎ *028/9059-1999. www.benedictshotel.co.uk. £70-£80 double; £60 single. AE, MC, V. Amenities: A/C; Internet access; TV.*

Eating

Belfast is now a cosmopolitan metropolis with a restaurant scene to prove it. Everything from builders' caffs to fine-dining establishments can be found in the city center, and it's hard to walk more than a few blocks without getting a whiff of freshly ground coffee. For cheap eats, head to the university area: Dublin Road offers up plenty of the U.K.'s finest—fish and chips—as well as cheap Chinese offerings, although nothing can beat Benedicts for sheer volume of food per pound spent.

CAFES & TEA ROOMS

➜ **Bewley's**   Bewley's big mama in Dublin is 150 years old. In the last few years she has been breeding, sending her offspring out across Ireland. This one shares the same family characteristics: lots of roasted coffees, blended teas, home-baked pastries, salads, and hot dishes all served up in an ordinary Irish-style cafe. Bewley's is not everyone's cup of cocoa, being pretty standard, but they do the job. *Donegall Arcade.* ☎ *028/9023-4955. Lunch £6. Mon–Fri 8am–5:30pm; Sat 8:30am–5:30pm. Bus: Any city center bus.*

➜ **Maggie May's**   Hang with students and independent travelers at Maggie May's, a wooden-boothed, open-fronted cafe serving up home-style cooking, stir-fry, veggie options, and paninis. Beefsteak stew, burger and chips and all-day breakfasts are all under

The Talk of the Town

Four Ways to Start a Conversation with a Local . . . & One Tip

Older Belfasters may not be as straight-off chatty as Dubliners—sometimes they can seem downright unfriendly—but don't be put off. Remember where you are. These people have good reason to be suspicious of outsiders. Spend a bit of time getting to know them and you'll discover some of the most raucous, honest people on the planet. **Ask . . .**

1. . . . how much their home has changed. Belfast never used to be this achingly cool and the city's residents are proud of the transformation. Let them show-off. They love it.

2. . . . which bands are playing in the city while you're here. Belfast is a haven for live music. Most of the big European tours stop off here, as do all the hot indie acts.

3. . . . what the giant sculpture of the tasty lady with the hula-hoop by the Lagan River is actually doing. Everyone has his or her own interpretation. They're usually entertaining.

4. . . . any of the sassy young things where the latest bar is. Belfast is exploding with hip bars and eateries. Those in touch with the scene are proud to point you in the right direction.

You might not want to ask about . . .

5. . . . religion and politics. Unsurprisingly, these can be touchy subjects in Belfast. Those hoping for insider insights will find Belfast locals are usually happy to talk about "the Troubles," but it may be best to let them do it in their own time, and let them do most of the talking. Especially if they are drunk, male, have a shaved head, and covered in DIY tattoos.

a fiver. The staff is no-nonsense, the soundtrack is rock, and there are more than enough newspapers and magazines to while away a rainy afternoon—although with a BYO wine policy (£1.50 corkage), why wait until the weather's bad. *50 Botanic Ave.* ☎ *028/9032-2662. Mains £3–£7. No credit cards. Mon–Sat 8am–10:30pm, Sun 10am–10:30pm.*

CHEAP

➜ **Bittles** Proper Irish grub at down-to-earth prices. We're talking steaming Irish stews and champ (a scrumptious old school Irish dish that mixes mashed spuds with spring onions). There will also probably be some pasta concoction, at least one veggie option, as well as steak, ham, and, chicken dishes—all brought to the table with potatoes and vegetables. The homemade soups are particular winners. Bittles is also a fine place to grab a drink (see "Bars," below). *70 Upper Church Lane.* ☎ *028/9031-1088. £3–£7. Mon– Fri 11:30am–2pm. Bus: Any city center bus.*

Best ➜ **Flour Crepe Room 46** A yummy-tastic pancake place just off Donegall Square, with decor representative of the new Belfast. A lush mint-green serving counter balances out just a handful of Scandinavian dark-wood tables. The mirror may make this wee place look long but it is tiny, so be sure to come early—everyone is vying for a bite of their sweet and savory crepes. Lovely fillings include cottage cheese, pineapple, and tomato; Parmesan, sun-dried tomato, and green olives; and Mars bars and

Late-Night Bite

Kebab shops and take-away joints cater to the club-and-pub-spillers around the University area. **Temps** (Botanic Ave.; no phone) is one such place. A TV in one corner and meal deals scrawled all over its white boards. Get chicken curry and chips for £2.50 or fish and chips for £2.60 or even just curry and rice for £1.80. It's also open in the day for a seven-item breakfast for just £2.50. Cheap and scruffy food for cheap and scruffy people.

Baileys, all served up on gorgeous little black plates. Plenty of juices and smoothies too. Not to be missed. *46 Upper Queen St.* ☎ *028/ 9033-9966. Main courses £3.25–£4.65. No credit cards. Mon–Sat 8am–6pm. Bus: Any city center bus.*

→**Far East** A recent addition to the Dublin Road scene, this is a minimalist, wood-floored, Zen spot with four different types of food—Chinese, Japanese, Korean, and Thai—and an international staff to match. The atmosphere is intimate and hushed in the evening, making lunch the top time for a visit when you can nab yourself a two-course Asian feast for £4.90. Or make that a Sunday and get three courses for £4.50. *85 Dublin Rd.* ☎ *028/9023-5557. Main dishes £3–£8. Mon–Thurs noon–2pm and 5–11:30pm; Fri 5–12:30am; Sunday 5–11pm, Sat 5pm–12:30am. Bus: Any city center bus.*

→**Fookin Noodle Bar** A Cantonese canteen with a super all-day-all-night-all-you-can-eat deal. The decor is funky, the atmosphere noisy, and the staff smiley. At the back sit rows of steaming metal containers cooking up meats, dumplings, rice, noodles, and dim sum. An easy place to come on your own and sit mesmerized by the overhead screens blasting out chart hits. *30*

Bradbury Place. ☎ *028/9023-2889. All-you-can-eat £6 at lunchtime, £9 in the evening (a quid less for students). Mon–Fri noon–2pm and 5–10pm; Sat–Sun 3–10pm. Bus: Any city center bus.*

→**Benedicts** Strictly speaking Benedicts should be in the doable section, but its Beat-the-Clock deal is so fantastic you'd be a fool to miss it. Every night between 5:30 and 7:30pm, diners pay a sum connected to the time and quarters of £/quarters of the hour at which they order their meal. Confused? Here's the scoop: Order the normally priced £12 Grilled Irish Salmon with spring onion mash and sweet pimento cream at 5:30pm and pay £5.50 (as in 5 plus one-half-hour, or 5 and one-half £), or the normally £11 Roast Garlic and Mushroom Pasta with white wine cream and glazed Parma at 6.45pm and pay £6.75. Or sirloin steak. Or chicken breast. Or pork kebab. Portions are HUGE, as is the 140-seater restaurant, an ornate wooden dining hall constructed by the owner using reclaimed pieces of antique French villas. A great place to start an evening. After 7:30pm, prices double and the place fills with courting couples. *7-21 Bradbury Place.* ☎ *028/9059-1998. Mains £11–£16. Breakfast Mon–Fri 7–10am, Sat–Sun 7–10:30am; lunch Mon–Sat noon–2:30pm, Sun noon–3:30pm; dinner Mon–Sat 5:30–10:30pm, Sun 5:30–9:30pm. Bus: Any city center bus.*

DOABLE

→**Café Renoir** Café Renoir is about as far from a trad Italian pizza parlor as you can get. There are no checked tablecloths, no fake vines, and no straw-covered bottles of wine. Instead, prepare for fields of light wood, glass balconies, and earthy moss-hued walls. Booking is essential on the weekend when the place heaves. Consequently the staff is brusque albeit bouncy. But eaters come for the posh pizzas—cooked in an Australian wood-fired oven—and they are divine.

Eating & Partying in Belfast

EATING ◆

Archana **29**
Benedicts **31**
Bewley's **9**
Bittles **16**
Café Renoir **42**
Far East **30**
Fookin Noodle Bar **35**
Flour Crepe Room **17**
James Street South **22**
Maggie May's **41**
Malmaison Bistro **14**
Nick's Warehouse **5**

PARTYING ★

Apartment **18**
Auntie Annie's **26**
Bar Bacca **23**
Bar Twelve **39**
Bittles **16**
The Botanic Bar **44**
Club Kia **28**
The Crown Liquor
   Saloon **21**
The Crow's Nest **13**
The Eglantine Bar **45**
The Empire **40**
The Fly **38**
The Front Page Bar **1**
The John Hewitt **4**
Irene and Nan's **24**
Katy Daly's **27**
Kremlin **3**
La Lea **23**
Lavery's Gin Palace **32**
Limelight **27**
M-Club **33**
The Menagerie **46**
Milk **8**
Mono **15**
Morrison's **34**
Mynt **7**
New Moon Showcase **37**
The Northern Whig **11**
The Potthouse **6**
Robinson's **20**
Shine **43**
Skye's **19**
The Spaniard **12**
Spring and Airbrake **27**
Tatu **36**
Thompson's **25**
Union Street **2**
White's Tavern **10**

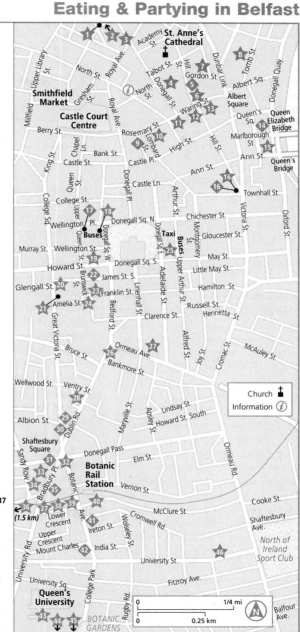

Just take—if you are inclined to—the Sierra: mozzarella, crispy bacon, garlic, and roast potatoes topped with herbed sour cream, onion jam, paprika, and chives. Need I go on? *95 Botanic Ave.* ☎ *028/9024-4244. Pizzas £6.95–£11. Daily 9–11pm. Bus: Any city center bus.*

➔ **Archana** This used to be one of Ireland's few completely vegetarian restaurants. It has now added meat to its menu but still has heaps of veggie and vegan options. The friendly vibe attracts all types from students to business people drawn by the Baltis—a particular type of Indian curry served up in a cast-iron wok in a straw basket—and their freshly made nan breads. *53 Dublin Rd.* ☎ *028/9032-3713. Generally open daily 4–11pm but hours vary. Mains £8–£10. No credit cards. Bus: Any city center bus.*

➔ **Nick's Warehouse** Over in the cathedral quarter, Nick's Warehouse is, well, situated in an old warehouse. Inside is an open kitchen and acres of redbrick walls. It's not all about image. "We're trendy and tasty," the chef assured us on our visit, "You'll be convinced after trying our cuisine prepared with seasonal, local—and often organic—ingredients." Dishes can be Scandinavian, American, or Mediterranean but we think they are all *dee*-lish. We started with fried spiced squid on Thai cabbage salad before moving on to duck breast on mash with a port and green peppercorn sauce and a butternut squash and puff pastry parcel with roasted nuts and seeds. The wine list is long but unpretentious and knowledgeable staff is happy to help out. This is Belfast's original wine-bar-cum-eatery and many would still say the best. *35 Hill St.* ☎ *028/9043-9690. www.nickswarehouse.co.uk. Reservations recommended. Main courses £7–£17. Mon–Fri noon–2:30pm; Mon–Sat 6–9:30pm (drinks until midnight).*

SPLURGE

➔ **James Street South** This place is *so* now and it flies in the face of the common pile-it-high-and-cook-it-with-as-much-butter-as-you-can approach to Irish cuisine. Here it is all about lightness—in the food, in the daylight streaming into the restaurant. But not in the amount of cash you'll have to hand over to eat here. Rich Belfasters can't get enough of it. Try starting with fennel soup with Pernod cream, followed by blackened duck or seared scallops with sautéed prawns, and finish off with lime meringue and gin and tonic sorbet. Vegetables are extra, but while you're spending this much surely you can't say no to a tomato and shallot salad with a 21-year-old balsamic vinegar for £2.50. *21 James St. S.* ☎ *028/9043-4310. www.jamesstreetsouth.co.uk. Reservations required. Mains £15–£20. Mon–Fri noon–2:45pm; Mon–Sat 5:45–10:45pm.*

➔ **Malmaison Bistro** Spending over £20 on a piece of meat might appear insane but after just one bite of a succulent, chargrilled steak in Malmaison's velveteen restaurant, it suddenly seems very sensible. They're from the Duke of Buccleuch's Scottish estate, don't you know. The staff meanwhile are superb cool urbanites and everything is cooked just so, including the crunchy just-picked-from-the-fields-this-morning veg. There are also let-the-juice-run-down-your-chin-who-cares burgers, peppered tuna, lamb cutlets, and, to end, a chocolate fondue—to share—topped off with exotic fruits and marshmallows. *Mmmmmalmaison! 34–38 Victoria St.* ☎ *028/9022-0200. www.malmaison.com. Mains £11–£24. Mon–Sun noon–10:30pm.*

Partying

Oh, yes sir-*eeh*. This city knows how to party. There are enough bars, pubs, and clubs in central Belfast to keep even the craziest hedonist entertained. Most of the wild, cheap nights take place at the far end of Dublin Road where it hits the University Quarter. Meanwhile, more and more ultracool bars and clubs are opening up in the Cathedral Quarter—*the* place to watch in the next few years. Other very trendy bars such as Tatu,

Culture Tips 101

....

Belfast drinking is a caring, sharing affair. If you're out with a group you don't just buy a drink for yourself, you buy "a round" for the whole group.

Apartment, and Irene and Nan's are scattered throughout the city.

Many bars are open late, until 1am or beyond. City center pubs often close before 11pm. Otherwise, you can expect things to shut down around 11:30pm to 12:30am. Drinking venues are often divided up into various areas with entrance to the main bar free, but a couple of pounds extra to get you into the venue's nightclub section.

Find out what's happening where in the bars and clubs by keeping an eye out for flyer postings along the Dublin Road and down into the university area, plus clothes shops such as Cult and Pulse (see Shopping below) or record stores like Hectors and Backbeat Music Exchange (see Shopping below).

BARS

➔ **The Crown Liquor Saloon** The big daddy of all Belfast pubs is a veritable city treasure. Actually owned by the National Trust, it whisks you back to Victorian times with its gas lighting (yes, that's right, good old-fashioned gas), ornate tiled floor, stained-glass windows, glass and marble bar, etched mirrors, and wooden drinking booths. Yes, it's gaudy and, yes, some of its slurpers are pretty old, but it's still got to be experienced for that back, back, back in the day vibe. *46 Great Victoria St.* ☎ *028/9027-9901.*

➔ **Robinson's** Adjacent to The Crown (above), Robinson's is less of a show-off and more of an old-fashioned boozer—picture tiled floors and lots of wood. The front room fills up on the weekends with ordinary blokes out for a pint or 10 while the back room is the

place to catch trad and rock nights almost every other weeknight. There's no need to get dressed up here. Jeans will do, as it's all about the banter. But don't be surprised if there's a spontaneous outburst of dancing later in the night. *38-40 Great Victoria St.* ☎ *028/3902-4477.*

➔ **White's Tavern** One of the oldest pubs in the world with atmosphere to burn. Ancient wood juts out at every angle creating enticing nooks and crannies, crammed with chunky wood tables and cozy lighting. During the day White's is full of people grabbing a quick pint and something wholesome to eat on their lunch break. Like most city center pubs, it may close early or be dead on weeknights, but Wednesdays—aimed at a gay audience—attracts a mixed, laid-back crowd. Most other evenings, the crowd is surprisingly young and punk-bohemian. *Wine Cellar Entry.* ☎ *028/9024-3080.*

➔ **The Front Page Bar** This one's a bit of a dark horse; it looks like a traditional family-owned pub. And it is. As well as being one of the coolest music hubs in town. Primal Scream, Death in Vegas, Asian Dub Foundation, and Lo Fidelity Allstars have all played DJ sets here. Weekends are all about underground dance music—electronica, breaks, beats and/or techno—while Wednesday nights are given over to new bands. *106-110 Donegall St.* ☎ *028/9032-4269. www.thefront pagebar.com.*

MTV Best ➔ **The Empire** Set in a big old historical building, the Empire stands as a gatehouse to the student quarter of the city. Here nightlife throws off any pretence of sophistication and is all about one big party. Don't come here if you want gentle wine-sipping; this is all about drink specials, cover bands, and crazy student nights. Fridays is Glamorama and Salsa and the easy, cheesy music tends to go on until 1am. *40-42 Botanic Ave.* ☎ *028/9032-8110.*

▶ Top Local Student Favorites: Bars

M T V

- **Mynt**—for oh-so-stylish gay glamour. See p. 437.
- **The Spaniard**—for chilled-out Sunday afternoons. See p. 433.
- **Robinson's**—for good old fashioned pint drinking. See p. 431.
- **Shine**—just to say you were at Belfast's hippest club night. See p. 436.
- **Milk**—for pure hedonism and big-name DJs. See p. 434.
- **The Empire**—for cover bands and outrageous dance-on-the bar nights. See p. 431.
- **Morrison's**—for fun nights out with your mates. See p. 432.
- **The Fly**—for finding someone to go home with at the end of the night. See p. 432.
- **The Potthouse**—for mingling with the celebs. See p. 435.

→ The Botanic Bar The Botanic Bar, or "The Bot" to its mates, draws a big student crowd eager to learn exactly how many pints they can down in a night. Rarely a night passes without a drinks promotion of some sort. A big screen in the main bar plays all the top sports events while The Record Club—upstairs on Wednesdays through Saturdays—is a fabulously popular and cheesy disco spinning hits from the '60s, '70s, '80, '90s, and today. Still not enough? Well, there's a quiz night on Tuesday, a folk night on Wednesday, and a Sunday carvery where you can grab a roast and a pint for less than six squiddlies. *20–27 Malone Rd.* ☎ *028/9050-9740. Open late.*

→ The Eglantine Bar Right across from "The Bot," "The Egg" offers the same mix of discos, drinks promos, screened sports, and quiz nights but in slightly classier surrounding—lots of bare brick walls and chrome and wood tables. *32 Malone Rd.* ☎ *028/9038-1944. www.egbar.co.uk.*

📺 **Best** **→ The Fly** Fancy a cheap, trashy night out with hoards of other 20-somethings eager to let their tongues explore more than just the inside of a beer glass? There's no need to be embarrassed. Stroll on into The Fly, a great place for flirting and possibly fondling. The music is cheesy R&B

and the crowd is mainly made up of young, fun-lovin' professionals. Happily, the bouncers on the door are excellent hard nuts who keep out all the dross. *Lower Crescent St.* ☎ *028/9023-5666. www.theflybar.com. Open late.*

→ Morrison's For good times surrounded by tasteful decor try this trad pub sporting a modern makeover. It attracts a down-to-earth but stylish mixture of students and young urban professionals who may be cool but ain't yet cold. Quiet like so many places during the week, but expect some rollicking rock sessions on Friday and Saturday nights and cool dance tunes upstairs. Acts as a club warm-up on the weekends. *21 Bedford St.* ☎ *028/9024-8454.*

→ Lavery's Gin Palace Some might call this place grubby; others adore its low-fi appeal. More a saloon than a pub, it fills up with bikers, students, businessmen, and anyone else attracted by the demon drink. Upstairs in "the attic" are twenty pool tables, retro arcade games, and pinball and air hockey. The "back bar" is devoted to all things alternative in the music world. Nights range from "Hemp—a joint effort" (where it's reggae and ska all the way) to Big Bobby's Retro Rock Disco. You know you love it. *12 Bradbury Place.* ☎ *028/9032-7159.*

→ **Bar 12** More chardonnay and cigars than cigarettes and alcohol, Bar 12 is where thirty-something professionals chat politely over a glass or two as they lounge back on red velvet sofas and survey the light airy room with its cool, creamy walls, dark-wood paneling, and stripped wooden floorboards. The staff are lovely and there are many delightful wines from around the globe . . . Bored? Thought so. Trek across town to the Spaniard (below) for some boho-chilling. *13 Lower Crescent.* ☎ *028/9059-1999. www. belfastpubs-n-clubs.com.*

Best → **The Spaniard** This is the ultimate in artsy urban relaxation. The wallpaper is flock, the tablecloths are a kitsch flowery riot, and the decorations are china dolls, old 45 records, and dripping candles. The bar boys and women are grounded but hip, which is good because they choose the tunes. Expect a lazy Sunday compilation of Billie Holiday, Kaiser Chiefs, Jimi Hendrix, and the likes. And perhaps some live jazz. There's no dress code, no security—so no misbehaving—and great nibble deals such as four tapas and a bottle of wine for a tenner on Thursday, Friday, and Saturday. Other staple pub dishes—road dinners, burgers, Thai curries—are £6.95—£7.95. EAT, DRINK AND THINK says the sign. *3 Skipper St.* ☎ *028/9023-2448.*

→ **Irene and Nan's** Named after two old birds at a nearby regular, there's nothing shabby here now. Smooth dark wood and soft lighting are quirkified with original Bakelite clocks and other vintage paraphernalia. All in all, this place is a gloriously kitsch style bar serving truly sophisticated cocktails such as White Cosmopolitans, Polish Apple Martinis, and Apricot Caipirnhas for upwards of £2.95. Once the *it* girl of Belfast's bars, opinion is now divided on the venue. Regardless, the queues remain longer than the list of complaints. Tagging along is a 30-seater bistro-cafe doling out contemporary European plates from crab, pea, and potato chowder to turmeric risotto with smoked bacon and Parmesan (mains from £10—£16). *12 Brunswick St.* ☎ *028/9023-9123. www.ireneandnans. com. Open late.*

→ **Bar Bacca** A sumptuous, exotic getaway with more than a little Shanghai chic. Dark reds and woods create that luxurious opium den atmosphere, a huge Buddha smiles down at you from above the doorway, and various other Far Eastern artifacts can be found scattered around inside the bar. The crowd is chill. The music is groovy and the cocktails include pink mojitos and a delish sorbet champagne (£3.95—£6.75). *48 Franklin St.* ☎ *028/9023-0200. www.barbacca.com. Open late.*

→ **Apartment** Apartment's creators decided to go with the airport lounge vibe complete with soul-free men in suits. But don't hurry away just yet. The waitstaff do bring you samples of the week's latest cocktail and their leather sofas are rather comfortable. The views over City Hall are also stunning but somehow this place just doesn't swing. Worth stopping by for a quick swig but really that's about it. Warning: Staff can turn unfriendly if they don't think your threads cut the mustard. *Donegall Sq. W.* ☎ *028/9050-9777. www.apartmentbelfast.com. Open late.*

→ **Bittles** A gem run by a true gent called John, who welcomes all sorts into his long dark-green bar. Lightening things up are bright oil paintings, under which groups of friends sit chatting over beers or listening to the DJs play on until the wee hours. A no-nonsense find. Don't tell everyone. Also does food (see "Eating," above). *70 Upper Church Lane.* ☎ *028/9031-1088. Open late.*

→ **Mono** As small as Bittles (see above) but with more attitude, this is a gay-friendly, Japanese-style bar with sofas so divine it is difficult to stay vertical. The attractive crowd—lots of luverly ladies and gents—add to the lure of lying down. Stay upright and enjoy fab Saturday nights where bongos cut it up with sultry saxophone sounds. Don't expect to get in if you're wasted or stinky. A red rope guards this haven most nights. *100 Ann St.* ☎ *028/9027-8886.*

→ **The Northern Whig** From the man behind The Bot, The Fly, and Apartment comes—what was once—one of the coolest bars in town. Set in the old offices of the *Northern Whig* newspaper it is a vast three-level hall filled with old wooden barrels and huge Communist statues imported from the Czech Republic. Fittingly the staff is adept at pouring Eastern European vodkas and house cocktails including Lenins and Tatankas, plus all the usual suspects (£3.75–£4.50). Dour door staff can dampen the atmosphere but a dressed-up crowd still goes wild on the weekends to a mix of R&B and house. *2-10 Bridge St.* ☎ *028/9050-9888. www.thenorthern whig.com.*

→ **Shu Bar** A run-of-the-mill elitist basement bar wearing beige like everyone else. Some appreciate the rarefied atmosphere and expense but most don't. And what sort of bar still sells Deep Throat cocktails? And the Shu bramble (gin, blackberries, chambord, and lime) and apple crumble (apple Schnapps, crème de cacao, and cream) are rather blah. Weekends can offer up an easy-listening mix of funk and soul. For Free. But it really is more of a bar tacked onto their restaurant than a destination in itself. Being out on the Lisburn Road it isn't worth the cab fare, unless of course you're going to Tatu (see below). *253 Lisburn Rd.* ☎ *028/9038-1655. www.shu restaurant.com.*

📺 **Best** → **Tatu** A huge minimalist cavern with a glass front to enable all the beautiful people to be seen. And my-oh-my are they beautiful. A long steel bar keeps them all lubricated with woo woos and bubble gum—house cocktails don't you know—while a 30-foot DVD screen provides visual stimulation. Do pop in but if you're after wild partying rather than posing you

may be disappointed. Expect queues on the weekend. *701 Lisburn Rd.* ☎ *028/9038-0818. www.ta-tu.com.*

→ **The John Hewitt** A haven for traditional music and comfort food (tummy-bursting puddings being a specialty). Run by a non-profit-making community group, the JH is all about local arts, with endless jazz and folk nights plus a singer/songwriter open mike on Mondays—don't be shy. Most events are free but when there is a particularly good band playing expect to pay a few pounds. Check the website for special arts events. A place to escape fellow travelers and chat with the locals. *51 Donegall St.* ☎ *028/9023-3768. www.thejohnhewitt.com.*

CLUBS

Belfast used to be a stag and hen party heaven with various big clubs offering cheesy music; now these big bros have been joined by some cooler, slinkier clubs and it's attracting the well-off creative set. For the latter, dress up. For all clubs, be on your best behavior to get through the door. Bouncers in Belfast don't want any trouble on their turf and will turn away anyone who appears rowdy or drunk. Football shirts and baseball caps are no-nos at many front doors.

Along with the rest of the world, Saturday night is when the city really comes out to play but also when the music goes more mainstream. If that's not your bag, pick a weekday evening to pick up some more alternative sounds. Or hunt down those nights frequented by the cooler uni crowd: Shine and New Moon Showcase.

Many clubs put up the lights at around 1am. To party on until 3am try Thompson's, Milk, Shine, New Moon Showcase, or Lea. After that you need to be in the know or you could try Event Horizon.

📺 **Best** → **Milk** Letting the cat out of the bag is not something anyone need worry about at Milk. Word is definitely out on this one. All the top international DJs play here, and it is considered by many to be *the* hottest place in town to dress up and play. You'll need to look as good as the building does: a converted warehouse in a damp, dark alley that hides its goodies inside. Lots of dark wood, exposed brick, and nifty little orange bar seats. Residents conspire on a wide musical policy ranging from pure R&B to pleasing, teasing, camp house. *13–15 Tomb St.* ☎ *028/9027-8876. www.clubmilk.com. Open late. Cover fee £10.*

→ **La Lea** La Lea wears a look dreamed up by Bill Wolsey and his team of architects; the brief was to create the most beautiful bar in Ireland. They didn't do badly but cheesy handbag music on Saturday nights consistently disappoints the ever-slimming crowds. Somewhere for grown-ups (i.e. over 30) to lounge about and look beautiful—if a little bored. *43 Franklin St.* ☎ *028/9023-0200. www.lalea.com. Cover varies.*

🎵 **Best** → **The Potthouse** Currently being touted as one of western Europe's hottest new venues The Potthouse, dressed from head-to-toe in frosted glass, stands out like an ice queen in this old industrial district. Built on the site of a 17th-century pottery factory, her underwear is all exposed brick and plywood with glass floors allowing a peek at the action on other floors. Luxuriate in the flattering golden glow from hanging yellow lights or cuddle up by the fire in leather-seated snugs. Music alternates between funky vocal house, pure R&B, and classic disco. *1 Hill St.* ☎ *028/9024-4044. www. potthouse.co.uk. Cover varies £3–£10.*

🎵 **Best** → **Bambu Beach Club** The Beach Club isn't known for it's beautiful crowd but just keep drinking 'cos the booze is cheap and those beer goggles can work wonders. Everyone's a winner at the Beach Club—even the ugly ones—and nobody need go home alone. The music is pure cheese and some of your fellow dancers should surely be wheeled back to the old people's home but

rarely is a crowd so relentlessly mad for it. *Odyssey Pavilion. 2 Queen's Quay.* ☎ *028/ 9046-0011. Cover varies.*

→ **M-Club** An ordinary city nightclub with some great crowd-drawing nights such as The Groovy Train, on a Friday, when all the hits are retro. Or Wild Thursdays, probably Belfast's biggest student night—perhaps due largely to the fact that all drinks are £2. All night. Yes, others like the sound of that too. Saturdays are also pretty popular when the DJs churn out commercial house to a warm and friendly herd of limbs. *23/31 Bradbury Place.* ☎ *028/9023-3131. Cover varies.*

→ **Club Kia** Club Kia pleases the masses by dolling out the best in alcopops (at little more than city bar prices) and chart classics. Almost a Belfast institution, it served the city as Dempsey's for over a decade. Now joined by the loft and blue room, there are six bars playing R&B, hip-hop, and house. This ain't a place for posing but for hard, drunken partying. *43 Dublin Rd.* ☎ *028/028/9023-4000. www.club-kia.tk. Cover £5.*

→ **Thompson's** A young crowed delights in commercial music and the odd treat from big names like LTJ Bukem, Dirty Vegas, and various other international acts. For over 9 years this club has been bursting eardrums and dosing guests with euphoria. Don't expect to find any quiet corners on either of the two floors. Throw your hands in the air and go wild for the weekend. *3 Patterson Place.* ☎ *028/9032-3762. www.clubthompsons. com. Cover varies £3–£10.*

→ **Skye's** A ground floor bar welcomes barely legal customers with pool tables and beers before whisking them off upstairs to the space-vibe club. Here ravers are dazzled with plasma screens and aurally serviced with the usual chart, R&B, hip-hop, house, and occasional big name DJ. *21 Howard St.* ☎ *028/ 9032-3313. www.skyebarclub.com. cover varies £5–£10.*

NORTHERN IRELAND

Play That Funky Music, DJ

We've got a surprise for you.

You know how everybody just sort of knows that Dublin is the best place in the country to go clubbing? It's not true. Those in the know prefer Belfast. You wouldn't think it, would you? But the North is increasingly hip, and its underground DJ scene is jumping.

We would like to say that, wherever you are in the country you'll find cool clubs and amazing sounds, but that would be a lie. Out in the countryside you'll find sheep. And jangly folk bands. In Dublin, Belfast, and Galway, though, they get *down.*

Wherever you're staying, look out for these names—these are the DJs who people have been talking about lately. Of course, by the time this is printed, there will be a whole new slate of spinners, but this will give you a rough idea of names to check out in club listings.

In Belfast, and around the country, keep an eye out for Chris Cargo—he's been described by Irish music magazines as one of Northern Ireland's most talented and productive DJs. If you're lucky you might run across Spree, a Belfast-based DJ collective that includes among its members producers, vocalists, and instrumentalists. It has been making waves around the country for a few years now.

Another northern DJ to look out for is DJ Dandelion, whose happy-clappy sets have a devoted following across the island, and in the U.K.

One southerner who moved North is Paul Hamill, who has been DJing around the country for more than a decade. He can be found at regular Belfast club nights like Shine, Deep Fried Funk, and Spirit & Mode.

Among the hottest names at the moment is DJ Tu-ki, who was the Irish DJ Battle Champion in 2005. He always spins a funky set, and can frequently be found in Dublin at Ri-Ra.

Other top DJs you're likely to come across in Dublin and Galway include DJ Scope, and Morgan Geist, who was half of the hugely popular DJ duo known as Metro Area. Look for them, and other top DJs, in Dublin at Ri-Ra and Spy, two of the city's hottest dance clubs.

→ Precious Just want to go where the "in" crowd goes? Check yourself in to Precious, which thinks it's far fancier than it is but does attract the pro-footballers and c-list celebs as they fly by. Lots of different rooms and plenty of drinks offers keep things perky. Wednesday night is student night. And remember, on the weekend, if you can't pull here, the Bambu Beach Club is just across the way. *Odyssey Pavilion, 2 Queen's Quay. 028/9046-7080. www.preciousbelfast.com. Cover £3–£7 (less for students).*

📺 **Best** **→ Shine** Are most of the clubs above too naff for your hot hip pants? Get yourself to Shine, the university's own Saturday club night. Justifiably popular—for over 10 years—it still feels thrillingly edgy and underground. Prepare for sweating herds pulsating to hard house and techno or separate yourself and gaze down knowingly from the balcony above. Nobody looks this ecstatic without some help but the music is good enough to go without. Just a glance at previous lineups sends shivers to all the right places: X-Press 2, Soulwax, Deepdish, Felix da Housecat. And the list goes on. *Queen's Students Union, University Rd.* ☎ *028/9032-3313. www.shine.net. Cover £10 (£8 students).*

➔ **New Moon Showcase** Just as cool as Shine but less crowded is the nearby New Moon Showcase held on the first Saturday of every month. Attracting Belfast's hippest set, this is currently being touted as one of the coolest DJ nights in town. Pay your money and look forward to a funky, laid-back atmosphere livened up with unusual live acts. *Crescent Arts Centre, 2 University Rd.* ☎ *028/9024-2338. www.crescentarts.org. Cover £5.*

GAY SCENE

Belfast's gay scene is definitely there but you might not notice it walking down the street. Walking hand in hand down the streets of Belfast may still lead to some funny looks and the odd verbal slag. Many pubs, clubs, and bars around the University and Cathedral Quarters are likely to be gay-friendly, and as the city gets more stylish ever more über-cool gay and gay-friendly bars are springing up around town.

For help and information on all things gay and lesbian, contact the Rainbow Project N.I. (33 Church St.; ☎ 028/9031-9030; Mon–Fri 10am–4pm) or the Lesbian Line (☎ 028/9023-8668; Thurs 7:30–10pm). To find out what is going on around town, take a peek at www.gaybelfast.net.

➔ **Kremlin** This is the queen mother of Belfast's gay scene, guarded over by a huge statue of Lenin. Different bars offer up the option of getting loved up on the dance floor or simply lounging about on sofas. 2005 saw the place receive some plastic surgery to emerge with a glam new look and a cocktail lounge. Various theme nights while away the week: Twanda spins the Wheel of Misfortune on Tuesdays, and Thursdays welcomes all aboard—gay or wannabe—for a night of Passion. Everyone wants to come in on the weekend and unless you are gay or have a

Kremlin regular as a friend you're not getting in. *96 Donegall St.* ☎ *028/9080-9700. www.kremlin-belfast.com. Cover varies.*

🎬 Best ➔ **Mynt** Mynt makes it clear on the door: "This place is a gay venue—feel free to use it, just don't abuse it." Once Kube bar it has returned to the scene after a fabulous makeover looking divine. The main room is a lounge bar named Establishmynt with two club rooms Movemynt and Excitemynt up above, plus a chill-out area called Coolmynt. The dress code is funky and the vibe code is outrageous. Expect nights like Titti von Tramp's Wankety Wank on Fridays and Gay Bingo on Sundays. Saturdays is the only night when charges are made (£6) and you gotta look good to get in. *2 Dunbar St.* ☎ *028/9023-4520. www.myntbelfast.com.*

➔ **The Crow's Nest** A pub catering to a welcoming crowd whooping it up with a weekly cycle of karaoke and DJs, while currently reinventing itself as a pre-club warm-up for The Potthouse and Milk (see "Clubs," above). *26 Skipper St.* ☎ *028/9032-5491. www.thenestbar.com.*

➔ **Union Street** A stylish city bar that embraces the gay scene in the evenings with bingo, DJs, and karaoke. Once a 19th-century factory the exposed brick has been kept to play off against muted greens and stainless steel for a stunning modern look. Event Horizon club night takes things through 'til dawn on Saturdays. Expect to queue. *14 Union St.* ☎ *028/9031-6060. www.unionstreetpub.com.*

🎬 Best ➔ **Garage** Rubbing up beside Union Street is Belfast's one and only gay sauna offering the usual sauna, Jacuzzi, and steam room plus a video lounge and coffee bar. It is popular with out-of-towners and gets very busy on the weekends. As they say, "Prepare to have your nuts tightened." *2 Union St.; 028/9023-3441. www.garage-belfast. com. Cover £10. Noon–1am except Thurs and Sun until 3am, Fri until 6am; Sat 11am–7am.*

You want more? Howsabout 📺 (Best) **Howl** (www.howlclub.com), an all-girl collective organizing a welcome-all alternative music night on a monthly basis at the **Pavilion** (296–298 Ormeau Rd.; ☎ **028/9028-3283**). They're strictly anti any phobias whether homo or hetero. Other gay/gay-friendly nights around town include **Forbidden Fruit** at Milk on Mondays, **Liquorice** at The Potthouse on Thursdays, and **Camp Out** at Thompsons (see "Clubs," above, for all three) on Thursdays, though these are liable to change so check out www.gaybelfast.net/scene for the latest.

Live Music

Belfast does brilliantly on the live music front, picking up the cream of indie talent on European tours and many a stadium artist too. Plus it really excels is in providing come-as-you-are music venues for Irish talent. And being such a walkable city going to gig can be a spur-of-the-moment decision and doesn't have to be planned at breakfast.

Empire (p. 431) eases visitors in nicely to the music scene with endless cover acts—Stereotonics, The Complete Stone Roses, Cavern Beatles, Stipe, The Paul Weller Experience, Bad Obsession (a Guns N' Roses cover band in case you were wondering)—plus some very cool indie acts ranging from Alabama 3 (the ones who provided the hipster music for *The Sopranos*) to folkie singer/songwriters and the odd '80s leftover such as The Damned. Tickets range from free to about £15 and can usually be bought through www.ticketmaster.ie, Virgin Megastore, or at the door for certain performances. Call in advance to avoid crying on the pavement outside.

→ **Auntie Annie's** A great little dive with two floors, showcasing live music lapped up by a grungy crowd. Revelers often spill out onto streetside tables in the summer months. Inside, open your mind to everything from tender singer/songwriters to furious goth, punk, and metal bands, not forgetting the frisky disco on a Thursday. There's usually something happening every night of the week. *44 Dublin Rd.* ☎ *028/9050-1660. Tickets £3–£5.*

→ **The Menagerie** A torn-n-tattered former paint store where you'll find home-grown MCs and DJs dishing a pick-and-mix of reggae, dub, hip-hop, house, broken beat, and drum and bass. And that's just for starters. Other nights will see acoustic sets, punk, and even some jazz and blues, no two nights ever being the same. One evening may see punters leaving with bleeding eardrums while the next night is quiet as, well, a deserted paint store. The dress code is refreshingly scruffy and the staff refreshingly real. *130 University St.* ☎ *028/9023-5678. Tickets £3–£5.*

These are just the warm-up for Belfast's holy trinity of live music: **Katy Daly's** (16 Ormeau Ave.; ☎ **028/9032-5942;** www.the-limelight-co.uk; tickets £3–£5), 📺 (Best) **The Limelight** (17 Ormeau Ave; ☎ **028/9032-5942;** www.the-limelight-co.uk; tickets £7–£14), and 📺 (Best) **Spring and Airbrake** (17 Ormeau Ave.; ☎ **028/9032-5942;** www.the-limelight-co.uk; tickets £7–£14). All sit together in a row near the city center. Katy's gets a quiz night—not your usual eyes down affair but a riotous event not for the easily shocked—out of the way on a Monday before offering up three nights of—mostly guitar—music from local bands and singer/songwriters.

The Limelight is Northern Ireland's top live music venue, a dark, moody son of a gun where you can catch bands on the brink of mega-success. Oasis, Blur, Primal Scream, Manic Street Preachers, and David Gray have all played here plus The Streets, The Kaiser Chiefs, and The Libertines before Pete shambled off. There are clubs nights too—student night Shag on Tuesdays and Disco-a-go-go

Hanging Around

Ever wanted to fly through the air like a trapeze artist? Or would you like to impress your friends back home with your newfound plate-spinning skills. **The Belfast Community Circus** (23-25 Gordon St.; ☎ **028/9023 6007**; www.belfastcircus.org) may well be the crazy, zany place for you. Situated in a building in the Cathedral Quarter it has been churning out juggling clowns for over 20 years and regularly puts on shows around town. On Wednesday nights they run a come-along session in acrobatics, trapezing, and juggling. For professionals and hobbyists it is a chance to come together and improve or practice your skills. A warm-up is followed by one hour's tuition and the session is finished off with juice and biscuits. Bring on the big top.

on Friday's. It's all alternative. It's all good. Spring and Airbrake is the little baby of the group. Here the music's more diverse and the live acts have included Gomez, the Zutons, and James Blunt. Dave Holmes'—genius Belfast musician, producer, and composer responsible for the music to *Ocean's Eleven* and *Code 46*—also has a monthly residency. Other club nights here include Silver Surfers—real music played by real people—and Guilty Pleasures—air your love of Karen Carpenter and 10cc without shame.

For more sedate acts such as Jools Holland, Jamie Cullum, James Blunt, David Gray, and KT Tunstall take a look at the listings for **The Waterfront** (2 Lanyon Place; ☎ **028/9033-4455**; www.waterfront.co.uk). For big name stadium acts the **Odyssey** arena (2 Queen's Quay; ☎ **028/9045-1055**; www.odysseyarena.com) seats up to 10,000 and has hosted acts such as Oasis, Christina Aguilera, and Destiny's Child, as well as Coldplay, the Prodigy, and Franz Ferdinand. Also see Ulster Hall and Kings Hall Exhibition and Conference Centre in Performing Arts (below).

Comedy Clubs

Belfast is notoriously one of the toughest stops on the U.K. circuit. It doesn't stop them from trying. Political comedy no longer prevails and there are plenty of up-and-coming

young entertainers offering more accessible subjects for outsiders. **The Empire Music Hall** (see "Bars," above) has a Tuesday night comedy club through the summer months and the **Kings Head** (829 Lisburn Rd; ☎ **028/9066-7805**; www.kingsheadbelfast.com) hosts Irish names from 9pm onward on Wednesday nights; otherwise, the **Waterfront Hall** (see "Live Music," above) welcomes in some bigger names and the **Old Museum Arts Centre** (7 College Sq.; ☎ **028/9023-5053**; www.oldmuseumartscentre.org) and **Ulster Hall** (see "Performing Arts," below) are worth checking for more quirky offerings.

Performing Arts

Belfast is experiencing a cultural rebirth right now. On top of the mainstream opera and theatre there are also a myriad of smaller venues offering interesting one-off shows and even a fab circus school where you can pick up some tricks yourself.

Tickets, which cost £8 to £30 for most events, can be purchased in advance from the **Virgin Ticket Shop** (Castle Court; ☎ **028/9032-3744**), or online at www.ticketmaster.ie.

Find out what's going on at www.gotobelfast.com and www.belfast.net or *That's Entertainment*, the *Big List*, and *Artslink* (usually found floating about in pubs or tourist information centers). *The Belfast*

Daily Telegraph and *Irish News* also have events sections are although most is aimed at the older, mainstream crowd.

Starting from the top the **Grand Opera House** (Great Victoria St.; ☎ **028/9024-1919; www.goh.co.uk**) is a stunning old Victorian building, showing everything from modern Irish dramas to cult screenings of *The Sound of Music*. Plus the odd opera. The house first opened in 1895 as a diversion for city folk both rich and poor. It was just as much about looking at the audience as the stage, which was why the boxes to the left and right of the stage attracted a premium of what would be £500 for a seat in today's money. The designs were supposed to evoke the "east" and to 19th-century audiences that meant anything east of the Lagan, so the decor is a truly eclectic mix: a Star of David, several elephants, and a pineapple—a very rare commodity in those days. The architect was only asked for advice twice during the project, once at the beginning of building and once on opening night. It shows.

Elsewhere the design may not be so outrageous but the shows can be just as good. And often cheaper. **Ulster Hall** (Bedford St.; ☎ **028/9032-3900; www.ulsterhall.co.uk**) stages major concerts from rock to classical performances from local orchestras; and **Kings Hall Exhibition and Conference Centre** (Balmoral; ☎ **028/9066-5225; www.kingshall.co.uk**) puts on superstar concerts as well as other musical happenings.

Theaters include the **Lyric Theatre** (Ridgeway St.; ☎ **028/9038-1081; www.lyric theatre.co.uk**), for new plays by Irish and international playwrights (mostly serious stuff but don't knock it, Liam Neeson got his big breaks here); and the **Group Theatre,** found inside the Ulster Hall on Bedford Street (☎ **028/9032-9685; www.ulster hall.co.uk**), for a dose of amateur dramatics or avant-garde shows from local production companies. Near the University is the **Arts Theatre** (41 Botanic Ave.; Inquiries ☎ **028/**

9031-6900, box office ☎ **028/9031-6900**) the resident company generally holds court here, but the theater also hosts other acts from one man or woman shows to stuff from out of town. Call the inquiry line to find out what's on.

Cinemas

The Queen's Film Theatre (Off Botanic Ave. near the college; ☎ **0800/328-2811; www. queensfilmtheatre**) is the art house cinema in town, screening a mix of classics and fresh artsy films throughout the day, every day. For Hollywood blockbusters try **Virgin Cinemas** (14 Dublin Rd.; ☎ **028/9024-5700**), while a completely different experience can be found at the IMAX cinema in the **Odyssey Pavilion** (2 Queens Quay; ☎ **028/9046-7000; www.belfastimax.com**) where 2- and 3-D films are shown on a screen over four times the height of a double-decker bus. 3-D film is still a limited market so prepare for lots of films starring dinosaurs, natural wonders, and strange unearthly planets.

Festivals

Over 100 events including heaps of arty movies and documentaries plus a drive-in make up the **Belfast Film Festival** (www. belfastfilmfestival.org) in April. Just as cool is the [Best] **Cathedral Quarter Arts Festival** (www.cqaf.com) mixing up all sorts from Japanese punk rock to Canadian trip hop in April or May. Lightening things up is the **Festival of Fools** (www.foolsfestival. com), a celebration of all things circus and magic in April. **Belfast Pride** (www.belfast pride.com) gives a big up to the city's gay scene in July or August while **Feile an Phobail** (www.feilebelfast.com) welcomes all in a huge across-the-sectarian-divides community celebration. [Best] **Tennent's Vital** (www.vital05.com) is *the* big summer music festival taking place in August and welcoming bands like the Scissor Sisters, Franz Ferdinand, and Faithless to the Botanic

MTV 🎧 Hanging Out

Belfast is bristling with new life. You can feel it on the streets. Hang out with office workers and skater chicks and chaps in the gardens of the **City Hall** or lounge about with students, freelancers, and out-of-towners in the Botanic Gardens during the summer months. Alternatively, any of the cafes in the **University Quarter** are a good place to get with the boho vibe as is The Spanish Bar (see "Bars," above) in the Cathedral Quarter.

Gardens. Let me hear you scream. The big international event is **Belfast Festival** (www.belfastfestival.com) in October or November encompassing well-known names in comedy, film, theater, and music; while **BelFEST** (www.belfest.com) points a finger or two at the local music scene. To wash it all done the **Belfast Beer Festival** takes place in the Ulster Hall in November (www.ulster hall.co.uk).

Tours

While organized tours are probably not on a to-do list of most self-respecting under-30s, a few in Belfast really are worth shelling out for. These include the 📺 **Best** **Black Taxi tours** taking travelers into the West Belfast area, explaining the history of sectarian violence in the area while pointing out the peace wall and murals in both the loyalist and republican areas. A real education. Various providers offer the service from £8 to £10 per person if you can get a group of three together, or ask to be put with another couple. Ask your local hostel for a recommendation or try **The Original Tour** (☎ 07751/565-359), **Belfast City Black Taxi Tours** (☎ 028/9030-1832; www.belfast cityblacktaxitours.com) or **Belfast Black Cab Tours** (☎ 07990/955-227).

Alternatively enter West Belfast on foot with a member of the Republican community who has spent time locked away as a political prisoner (☎ 028/9020-0770; www. coiste.ie). Or explore the urban jungle on a **Belfast Safari** (☎ 028/9022-2925; www. belfastsafaris.com), a team of local guides keen to introduce you to the "real" Belfast, whether that be the sectarian areas of West Belfast, Van Morrison's Belfast, or various other historical strolls taking in wars and famines, asylums and poorhouses. Tours cost £8 per person or a bespoke service can be arranged for £21.

Another must-do is the Titanic Boat Tour. The mighty sinker was built here. It took one year to design and another year to build. 📺 **Best** **Lagan Boat Company** (☎ 028/ 9033-0844; www.laganboatcompany.com) takes passengers on a boat tour right up to the original slipways that launched Titanic into the River Lagan passing the giant yellow cranes of the Harland and Wolff shipyard, known to locals as Samson and Goliath. Sailings take place all through the year (except January and February) and cost £6.

Sightseeing

When the partying comes to a temporary standstill Belfast is a great place to explore in the day. Most of what there is to see is within walking distance and simply ambling about the streets is an activity in itself. A good place to find out what events or exhibitions are happening around during your stay is at the Welcome Centre (see "Belfast Basics," above). 📺 **Best** **FREE** ➜ **Belfast Botanic Gardens & Palm House** Surprisingly stylish, the Belfast Botanic Gardens & Palm House date from 1828. A decade later the Palm House was added. Now it is filled with rare tropical flora such as sugar cane, coffee, cinnamon, banana, aloe, ivory nut, rubber, bamboo, guava, and the striking bird-of-paradise flower. Nearby The Tropical Ravine, also

The Troubles

West Belfast, home to murals depicting the Troubles, is a neighborhood that's been through hell and is, unfortunately, Belfast's most famous "attraction." Although the mural tradition dates back almost 100 years, most of the murals started appearing in the '60s, when conflict in Belfast and Derry heated up. Although a tour of West Belfast will probably not make you feel good about the world, make sure you do make it here—you'll leave a changed person. It's not particularly dangerous to walk around here during the day, but you may get funny looks or mildly offensive comments made in your direction from the locals if you're snapping pictures at every turn. At night, don't even think of coming here. While the peace process continuously moves forward and the area is significantly safer than it was in past years, assorted violent crimes still happen here.

By far the best way to experience this incredible neighborhood is in a Black Taxi Tour (arrange at any youth hostel in town, or see "Tours," above). Black Taxi provides safe transportation, and excellent commentary. They take you to these disturbingly beautiful expressions of sectarian conflict, and offer insights into the history of the neighborhoods and the Troubles. Any time you want to take a picture of a mural, just ask and they'll stop for you.

West Belfast's two neighborhoods surround Catholic Falls Road and the Protestant Shankill Road. Dividing them is the ironically named Peace Wall, an ugly slab of industrial metal that attempts to keep both sides to themselves. Originally installed to deter troublemakers from starting trouble and then running back to their neighborhood, it's now become more of a Berlin Wall, a symbolic reminder of the differences on both sides. There are several gates in the wall that close at night to deter would-be hooligans.

known as the fernery, provides a setting for plants to grow in a sunken glen. Look the part with a bikini and some shades. *Signposted from M1/M2 (Balmoral exit), Stranmillis Rd., County Antrim.* ☎ *028/9032-4902. Free admission. Palm House and Tropical Ravine Apr–Sept Mon–Fri 10am–noon, daily 1–5pm; Oct–Mar Mon–Fri 10am–noon, daily 1–4pm. Gardens daily 8am–sunset. Bus: 61, 71, 84, or 85.*

FREE ➔ **Belfast Castle** Just out of town is Belfast Castle, perching 120m (400 ft.) above sea level in a 80-hectare (200-acre) estate spreading down to the slopes of Cave Hill (see below). The castle—completed in 1870—gives gasp-inducing views of Belfast Lough and the city. It was the family residence of the third marquis of Donegall, and

was given to the city of Belfast in 1934 for the people to enjoy. And they do. According to legend, a white cat was meant to bring the castle residents luck. Look around for carvings featuring the creature. *Signposted off the Antrim Rd., 4km (2½ miles) north of the city center, County Antrim.* ☎ *028/9077-6925. Free admission and parking. Castle Mon–Sat 9am–10pm; Sun 9am–6pm. Take buses 40 and 41 from Donegall Square.*

FREE ➔ **Belfast Exposed** This isn't a dodgy peep show but an exciting ongoing photography project promoting photographers, both in Ireland and abroad, who have something to say about society. Quite a lot do around Belfast, and there are over 3,000 photos online commenting on the city's

The murals incorporate several recurrent themes of either Nationalist/ Republican (Catholic) or Loyalist/Unionist (Protestant) sentiment. In neighborhoods, martyrdom, militancy, and vigilance are the main themes. On the Falls Road, one recurring icon is Bobby Sands. Sands, a leader of the Nationalist resistance movement, led more than 300 prisoners in a hunger strike in 1981. Sands and many others had been thrown in jail and held without trial, as was the procedure of Britain then. They were not given political prisoner status and so starved themselves in protest. While in prison, Sands was elected as an MP (member of Parliament). He died 66 days later. By the end of the strike, 10 were dead. This act, combined with the hard-line attitude of Margaret Thatcher's government, solidified support for the resistance movement and the IRA.

In both the Protestant and Catholic neighborhoods, murals depict fallen leaders of the "struggle," innocent victims of its violence, and depictions of various paramilitary/terrorist groups. On the Falls Road, the IRA, the Real IRA, and the Provisional IRA are all represented. On Shankill Road, the UVF (Ulster Volunteer Force) and numerous other splinter factions are represented. On both sides of the Peace Wall, these "heroes" are represented in a surprisingly similar way. Men clad in black suits and masks tote automatic rifles, depicting both Catholic and Protestant paramilitary/terrorist groups.

In viewing the often-glorified depictions of these paramilitary groups, it is important to not let the romantic portrayals of the "struggle" of either side obscure the fact that innumerable lives have been destroyed by parties on all sides of the conflict. Talk to most Belfast residents, especially the young ones, and they'll agree that they're sick of the violence and want peace more than anything else.

social and political history. Various exhibitions also take place throughout the year. Often thought-provoking. Usually serious. *The Exchange Place, 23 Donegall St. ☎ 028/ 9023-0965. www.belfastexposed.com. Free admission. Tues–Sat 11am–5pm.*

→ **Cave Hill Country Park** This park lounges about on top of a 360m (1,200-ft.) basalt cliff called Napoleon's Nose by the locals. It has wowzer views, walking trails, and is scattered with interested archaeological and historical sites, such as the Neolithic caves that gave the hill its name, and MacArt's Fort, an ancient earthwork built against the Vikings. The park was opened in 1887 but had to be closed almost straight away due to the "misconduct of youths." Now wildlife rather than wild boys are the main attraction. Also in this direction is the Lagan Valley Regional Park (Citybus 69 or 71 out of the city; ☎ 028/9049-1922; free admission), straddling the River Lagan for 21km (13 miles) and offering lazy-day walks through splendid parks and beside canals, with trees, birds, bees, and people all in their natural habitats. *Off the Antrim Rd., 6.5km (4 miles) north of city center, County Antrim. Parking at Belfast Castle. Bus routes 2-6, 45, 61, 64, 70.*

→ **City Hall** Unmissable at the center of town is City Hall, the hub around which the city spins. It was built after Queen Vic granted Belfast city status back in 1888. A grim-faced statue of the woman herself now stands in front of it, looking as if she wishes she wasn't there. Bronze figures around her represent Belfast's super-powerful textile and ship-building industries. There's also a memorial to the victims of the *Titanic* disaster. When there's no exhibition in the city hall, there's a free guided tour available to fill you in on all the tiny details. *Donegall Sq., Belfast, County Antrim.* ☎ *028/9027-0456. Free admission. Guided tours June–Sept Mon–Fri 11am, 2pm, and 3pm, Sat 2:30pm; Oct–May Mon–Sat 11am and 2:30pm. Otherwise by arrangement. Reservations required.*

FREE ➜ **Cultúrlann Macadam Óflaich** A warm and cozy center for Irish language and culture, housed inside a red brick former church. It holds a tourist information desk and a shop selling books about Ireland, as well as Irish crafts and CDs of Irish music, and has a cafe, too. *216 Falls Rd., Belfast, County Antrim.* ☎ *028/9023-9303. Free admission. Mon–Fri 9am–5:30pm; Sat 10am–5:30pm.*

➜ **Fernhill House: The People's Museum** An educational—if a little biased—museum on Glencairn Road, beyond the end of Shankill Road. It's a re-creation of a Protestant Belfast house as it would have been in the 1930s. Follow the history of the area through Home Rule, war, and the continuing tensions. It may answer some questions you have on Irish divisions. *Glencairn Rd., Belfast, County Antrim.* ☎ *028/9071-5599. Admission £2. Daily 10am–4pm.*

FREE ➜ **Frendersky Art Gallery** Located at the cool and groovy Crescent Arts Centre, this gallery displays—as well as sells—modern art. Exhibitions change frequently, and lean more toward the avant-garde. *2–4 University Rd.* ☎ *028/9024-2338. Free admission. Mon–Sat 10am–5pm.*

FREE ➜ **Lagan Weir & Visitors Center** This center provides an intro into the dockside region with a 2-meter replica of the *Titanic* and ace views down to where she

was once built. Besides the view a top reason to drop in here is to pick up one of the leaflets (free) or headsets (£2.50) to take you on one of three guided tours around the public art scattered across the city. The nearby Bigfish statue celebrates the transformation of the river from a polluted mess in the 1980s to a fish-filled delight in the 1990s. Nearby is the **Albert Memorial Clock Tower** in Queen's Square, tipping a scary 4 feet to one side having been built on reclaimed land over 100 years ago. Not far away is the strange spireless **Belfast Cathedral** (Donegall St.; www.belfastcathedral.org; free admission; Mon-Sat 10am–4pm) that gives the Cathedral Quarter its name. *1 Donegall Quay, Belfast, County Antrim.* ☎ *028/9031-5444. Free admission. Apr–Sept Mon–Fri 11am–5pm, Sat noon–5pm, Sun 2–5pm; Oct–-Mar Tues–Fri 11am–3:30pm, Sat 1–4:30pm, Sun 2–4:30pm.*

FREE ➜ **Ormeau Baths Gallery** Set on the site of the old Victorian swimming baths the Ormeau Baths Gallery opened in 1995 as the city's main space for contemporary visual art exhibitions. Stop by any time to see various exhibitions utilizing this striking and versatile space. This place has become the top show-off spot for all that's hot in Northern Irish contemporary art. *18A Ormeau Ave., Belfast, County Antrim.* ☎ *028/9032-1402. Free admission. Tues–Sat 10am–6pm.*

➜ **Queen's University** This is one of the oldest and most beautiful unis in the UK and currently educates over 17,000 students in a sprawl of over 250 buildings. If you think it looks a bit like England's Oxford University, you're not wrong. The design was based on the Founder's Tower at Magdalen College. Pop in to the visitors' center to pick up a free walking tour leaflet and find out what exhibitions are currently taking place in the various departments. There's usually something on, ranging from Contemporary Chinese Art to

Siqhtseeinq near Belfast

There are a few sights just beyond Belfast worth visiting, including The Giant's Ring and Ulster Folk and Transportation Museum. For more extensive road trips from Belfast, see p. 447.

The name of the **Ulster Folk and Transportation Museum** (153 Bangor Rd.; 11km/7 miles northeast of Belfast on the A2), Cultra, Holywood, County Down (☎ **028/9042-8428** or 028/9042-1444 for 24-hr information; www.nidex.com/uftm; take Ulsterbus 1 from the Laganside Bus Center), may not immediately grab you but it is worth a visit. Sixty acres have been set aside to house old 19th-century buildings, saved from demolition and moved piece by piece to this site and rebuilt. Consequently you can stroll among farmhouses, mills, and churches, climb up to some terraces of houses and explore country schools, a forge, a bank, and a print shop. All the while actors dressed the part wander around playing out olden-day scenes such as spinning and lace making or cooking over an open fire. The transport museum is not quite as exciting but does have donkey carts and one of Europe's top railway exhibitions. Enough said.

The **Giant's Ring,** Ballynahatty, County Down, 8km (5 miles) southwest of Belfast center, west off A24; or 1.6km (1 mile) south of Shaw's Bridge, off B23, is a massive prehistoric earthwork 180m (600 ft.) in width with a megalithic tomb in the middle. Thought to be an important focus of activity for local cults since 3,000 B.C., it is now equally popular with dog walkers and marauding children. Few tourists make it out here. Those who do discover a great place to take artsy black-and-white photos.

exhibitions detailing the student exhibitions to the Arctic. *Visitor Centre, University Rd., Belfast, County Antrim.* ☎ *028/9033-5252. www.qub.ac.uk/vcentre. Free admission. May–Sept Mon–Sat 10am–4pm; Oct–Apr Mon–Fri 10am–4pm. Bus: 61, 71, 84, or 85.*

FREE → **Ulster Museum** The Ulster Museum sums up 9,000 years of Irish history with exhibits on art, furniture, ceramics, costume, and industry. The real gem, however, is its collection of gold and silver jewelry found by treasure-hunting divers in 1968 off the Antrim coast on the 1588 wreck of the Spanish Armada ship *Girona. Signposted from M1/M2 (Balmoral exit); next to the Botanic Gardens, Stranmillis Rd., Belfast, County Antrim.* ☎ *028/9038-3000. Free admission, except to major special exhibitions. Mon–Fri 10am–5pm; Sat 1–5pm; Sun 2–5pm. Bus: 61, 71, 84, or 85.*

→ **Van Morrison's House** *Have I told you lately that I love you?* Don't get nervous, it's not a cheesy chat-up line, just a reminder that Van Morrison was born in Belfast and fans can go and visit 125 Hyndford St., the teeny two-up, two-down terrace he used to live in before he became so famous and miserable. George Ivan Morrison was born in the city in 1945, later fleeing when he made piles of cash from songs such as *Brown Eyed Girl* and even a song called *On Hyndford Street.* The house is now privately owned but a little brass plaque marks his spot. *125 Hyndford St.*

Playing Outside

Belfast is a walkable city with little pollution and the parks (above) perfect for longer hikes or kicking a football about. For something more energetic bikes can be hired from various outlets (see "Getting Around," above) that can point you in the direction of a good ride—whether flat or hilly.

Notching up the stakes the **Lagan Watersports Centre** (Rivers Edge, 13 Ravenhill Rd.; ☎ 028/9046-1711; www.laganwatersports.co.uk) makes full use of the freshly cleaned river—so clean the salmon have returned—with sailing, rowing, canoeing, power boating, and even Chinese dragon boating all available for an hour or longer lesson sessions.

Taking things to new heights the **Belfast Activity Centre** (Barnett's Stable Yard, Malone Rd.; ☎ **028/9060-0132;** www.belfastactivitycentre.co.uk) offers charity abseils down either the BT Tower or the Europa Hotel on a number of dates throughout the year. With 10,000 abseils already under their harnesses your behind will be in good hands. Contact well in advance.

Shopping

The main shopping area is north of Donegall Square on Royal Avenue. All the chains—Boots, Waterstones, Virgin—are situated here plus a few more interesting stores as you head up toward the Cathedral Quarter, with many other names such as French Connection and River Island found along the cross-streets. At the far end of this drag is The CastleCourt Shopping Centre, the main shopping mall with over 70 stores including The Gap, a Virgin Megastore, and a Discovery Store. Lisburn Road is where the city's celebs splash out on the designer togs available in a scattering of exclusive boutiques. Toward the university the more unique bookshops and curiosity/bong shops are to be found, while the gorgeous St. George's Market (east of Donegall Square on May St.) hosts a City Food and Garden Market (10am–4pm) on Saturday with over 100 stalls selling organic and local goodies perfect for cooking up back in the hostel when money is running low. The Friday Variety Market (6am–2pm) also does food and secondhand books, clothes, and antiques. Other shops are generally open 9am–5:30pm with late opening on Thursdays keeping many shops open until 8 or 9pm, and a noticeable increase in Sunday openings.

BOOKS

The Bookfinder's Café (47 University Rd.; ☎ **028/9032-8269**) may look closed from the outside but inside it is a hive of boho activity. There is a decent selection of used books here and a great little cafe in the back serving up homemade cakes and sandwiches. Vegetarians are also provided for.

Making money from mystery and murder is the university quarter's **No Alibis Bookstore** (83 Botanic Ave.; ☎ **028/9031-9607**). Owner David stocks a good range of crime and mystery writing as well as local authors and a broad range of contemporary fiction plus some classics.

CRAFTS

Craftworks Gallery (Bedford House, Bedford St.; ☎ **028/9024-4465**) sells the best of Northern Irish crafts including pottery, wood, and metalwork, plus jewelry inspired by ancient Celtic designs. It can be found just behind the City Hall.

CLOTHES

Moving on to what really matters, **Apache Clothing** (60 Wellington Place; ☎ 028/9032-905; www.apache-tribe.com) sells club wear, has live DJ's, and is one of the best places to find out what's happening around town. **Pulse** (4 Arthur St.; ☎ **028/9033-3595**) also sells club duds—of the bright variety here—and offers an events info service.

For retro styles, check out **Liberty Blue** (9 Lombard St.; ☎ **028/9059-7555**). Groovy tunes play as you pile through jeans, cords, tees, and hats. No vintage, but the new stuff is a bargain anyway. It's also another place to put your ear to the ground for the night's activities.

One shop does offer up some thrift shop style, **Rusty Zip** (28 Botanic Ave.; ☎ **028/9024-9700**). Here you'll find battered cowboy boots, outrageous wigs, screaming '70s glamour frocks, leather jackets, and a whole heap of other kitsch outfits.

If you're looking for something superswanky, head to **The Bureau** (1–4 Wellington St.; ☎ 028/9031-1110). Staffed by well-groomed young men for names such as Paul Smith, Rogan, and Stone Island or for something slightly cheaper The Big B's little B, **Grand Magasin** (46-50 Howard St.; 028/9031-1110), a denim fusion store where it's all about the clothes. Brands stocked include Retro Adidas, Stussy, and Nude.

Alternatively, **Cult** (75 Royal Ave; ☎ 028/ 9024 0116) is a huge two floor bargain-hunters paradise taking the catwalk's edgier urban looks and churning them straight out onto the shop floor at hugely loveable prices. More flyers on what's going on about town to be found here too, plus apparel by Boxfresh, Penguin, Hooch, Embargo, and Skunkfunk.

MUSIC

Backbeat Music Exchange (121 Great Victoria St.; ☎ 028/9020-0397) is the coolest record shop on the block, with a laid-back proprietor eager to guide you through his delicious vinyl and CD collection. It's also a good place for finding out about gigs on while you're in town.

Up in the Cathedral Quarter Hector of **Hector's Records** (5 North St.; ☎ 028/ 9023-4040) is from a far older school of rock. Prepare for a lot of that as well as folk, blues, indie, metal, soul, and country. There are also some secondhand CDs and new releases from local bands. A good place to find out about rocky and folksy gigs taking place in the city. A great deal livelier is **Mixmaster Records** (31 Queen St.; ☎ 028/ 9043-9159; www.mixmasterrecords.com), an underground dance emporium dishing out the goods for over a decade. The music is dance but the style is wide with 300 new releases in house, hip-hop, garage, trance, tribal, hardcore, and breaks—at the very least—each week. Don't be surprised if you end up shuffling through vinyl next to a DJ hero. Nick Warren, DJ Quicksilver, CJ Bolland, Paul Van Dyk, and Layo & Bushwacka have all shopped here.

Road Trips from Belfast

You didn't just want to see Belfast, did you? You wouldn't be doing Northern Ireland justice if you didn't venture out from Belfast for a few days. Below, I've listed some of my favorite road trips from Belfast. And for details on the rest of Northern Ireland, see p. 450.

Carrickfergus

Carrickfergus is a posh medieval harbor town, just 12 miles Northeast of Belfast. Its 38,000 residents seem to like nothing better than puttering around the shops and sipping at lattes. Joining them makes for a chill day out. An amble along the promenade, or up to the lighthouse, adds in a whiff of sea air. In short, this is a top spot for resting your bones after partying hard in Belfast.

GETTING THERE

If you're traveling by car, take the A5 north from Belfast. Otherwise **Ulsterbus** (☎ 028/9033-3000; www.ulsterbus.co.uk) provides regular daily services from Belfast and **Northern Ireland Railways** (☎ 028/9089-9411) also sets off frequently throughout the day from Belfast Central Station to Carrickfergus.

BASICS

The Carrickfergus Tourist Information Office (Heritage Plaza, Antrim St.; ☎ 028/ 9336-6455) is open all year, Monday to Saturday from 9am to 5pm.

EATING

The Dobbins Inn Hotel (6–8 High St.; ☎ 028/9335-1905; www.dobbinsinnhotel.

co.uk; mains £5–£13) does trad Irish food in trad Irish surrounds. Visually you'll get old stone floors with exposed beams on the side. Orally it's steaks, roasts, burgers, sausages, and champ. If you fancy getting the whole restaurant staring, there are also some sizzling platters filled with munch material like shredded duck breast and calamari.

SIGHTSEEING

You can't miss **Carrickfergus Castle** (Marine Hwy.; ☎ 028/9335-1273; admission £3 adults; Apr–Sept Mon–Sat 10am–6pm, Sun noon–6pm; Oct–Mar Mon–Sat 10am–4pm, Sun 2–4pm) so you might as well pop in and see what it's all about. The castle is amazingly well preserved and still gives off an air of menace as you approach. Guides and exhibits color in the past while, in the summer, old-world banquets and fairs show how life might have looked back then, thankfully without the medieval aroma.

Less threatening, but equally interesting, is the **Andrew Jackson centre** (Boneybefore; ☎ 028/9336-6455; admission £1.20 adults; June–Sept Mon–Fri 10am–1pm, daily 2–6pm; reduced hours in Apr–May and Oct, closed Nov–Mar), once the humble home of Andrew Jackson, the seventh president of the United States. Check out how he lived in this tiny one-story cottage, replete with earth floor and open fire, before his parents emigrated to the U.S. in 1765. There's more: The house has a display on the big man's life and illustrious career and, in July and August, all sorts of folksy happenings—lace making, basket weaving, griddle making, quilting—take place outside on the weekend. If even these sound too much, the **Knight Ride** (The Heritage Plaza, Antrim St; ☎ 028/9336-6455; www.carrickfergus.org; admission £2.70 adults; Apr–Sept Mon–Sat 10am–6pm, Sun noon–6pm; Oct–Mar Mon–Sat 10am–5pm, Sun noon–5pm) is perfect for people too monged to do anything but sit still and let a show go on around them. Sadly

David Hasselhoff is nowhere inside but instead you get an action-packed monorail floating riders through 8 centuries of the story of Carrickfergus, from invasions to sailing ships and haunted houses. Buy a ticket to the castle *and* the ride for a discount.

PLAYING OUTSIDE

SAILING   Carrickfergus is above all a sailing town. It has a fab marina and is a perfect place to shake off your land-lubbin' legs. **Ulster Cruising School** (☎ 028/9336-8818; www.ulstercruising.com) offers 5- to 7-day trips aimed at teaching beginners how to sail solo in the Irish Sea—or indeed any sea—and can even arrange to take you out for just a few hours. Call for the latest prices.

WALKING   If you prefer to stay ashore, a good walk takes you down to the cutesy seaside village of Whitehead and around the Blackhead lighthouse on the most eastern edge of Antrim. It is about 12 miles as a circular route or you can always start from Whitehead to make things easier.

Ards Peninsula & Strangford Lough

The Ards Peninsula starts about 16km (10 miles) east of Belfast before curling around the western shore of Strangford Lough. At 29km (18 miles) long this huge sea inlet is one of the largest in the British Isles. It's a real stunner with a wild, raw quality especially noticeable when the wind races in from the sea.

Traveling down the Ards Peninsula from Belfast you'll hit water at Portaferry, a sleepy little village set on the lough, only a short stretch of water from Strangford village on the other side. Take the ferry across to appreciate the full beauty of the lough (and the chill of the sea winds).

Portaferry really perks up in the last week of June for **The Galway Hooker Festival and Boat Regatta** (☎ 076/245-0146). Then yachties and their yachts gather for a week of drinking, singing, and misbehaving. Rowing competitions are also held. The mood is rowdy and festive, with Ferris wheels set up, pubs overflowing, and the village full to bursting. Leave early to get here in a day.

GETTING THERE & GETTING AROUND

The 510 **Ulsterbus** (☎ 028/9033-3000; www.translink.co.uk) leaves the Laganside Bus Centre in Belfast 18 times on Monday to Saturday, 8 times on Sunday. It takes 90 minutes to reach Portaferry. A single is £4.

A ferry (☎ 028/4488-1687) runs between The Strand, Portaferry, and The Square, Strangford every 30 minutes (7:45am–10:45pm Mon–Fri, 8:15am–11:15pm Sat, 9:45–10:45pm Sun). The cost is £1 for people, £5 for cars.

BASICS

The **Portaferry Tourist Information Office** (Shore St., near the Strangford ferry departure point; ☎ 028/4272-9882), is open Monday to Saturday 10am to 5:30pm, Sunday 1 to 6pm.

EATING

There's little in the way of non-greasy cheap food in Portaferry apart from **The Shambles** (Castle St.; ☎ 028/4272-9675; sandwiches £2.20; no credit cards) with its healthy lunches and soups for a bottom dollar price, or the overly pricey **The Narrows** (8 Shore Rd.; ☎ 028/4272-8148; www.narrows.co.uk; mains £16–£21) where you can dine on frogs legs and the like along with the fur-coated bourgeoisie of the Peninsula.

SIGHTSEEING

→ **Exploris Aquarium** This is Portaferry's biggest draw and the only aquarium in Northern Ireland. It's a wonderful way to see all the wildlife swimming in the lough, and farther out in the Irish sea, without actually getting cold and wet. "Touching tanks" allow visitors to get up close and personal with the little fishies and a new seal sanctuary has just been added. Next door is Portaferry Castle, now little more than ruins. A must-do in Portaferry is climbing up to the nearby windmill for a jaw-dropping view of the lough—perfect first date fodder. *Castle Lane.* ☎ 028/4272-8062. *www.exploris.org.uk. Admission £5.40. Apr–Aug Mon–Fri 10am–6pm, Sat 11am–6pm, Sun 1–6pm; Sept–Mar Mon–Fri 10am–5pm, Sat 11am–5pm, Sun 1–5pm.*

→ **Mount Stewart House** If you're into 18th-century art, this house has what is considered to be one of the top 10 paintings in the U.K. and one of the top 100 in the world. What is it? *Hambletonian.* A picture of a great, big, sweaty racehorse getting a rubdown after finishing a race. It was painted by George Stubbs, the legendary British horse painter, who died only a few years after finishing off this work. Outside things lighten up with tropical plants so good they've been nominated as a World Heritage Site. It makes a groovy venue for the free jazz concerts that take place here on some Sundays during the summer months. The romantic-sounding Temple of the Winds, a banqueting house built in 1785, is also on the estate, but it's only open on public holidays. Head up that way regardless to check out the gasp-inducing views over the lough. *On the east shore of Strangford Lough, southeast of Newtownards, 24km (15 miles) southeast of Belfast, on A20, Newtownards, County Down.* ☎ 028/4278-8387. *www.nationaltrust.org.uk. House and garden admission £5.45 adults; garden only £4.40 adults. House Mar–Apr and Oct Sat–Sun 1–6pm; May–Aug daily 1–6pm; Sept Mon and Wed–Sun 1–6pm. Bus: 9, 9A, or 10 from Laganside Bus Centre (Mon–Sat).*

PLAYING OUTSIDE

BICYCLING If you want to explore the Aards Peninsula area on your own two wheels, you can rent bicycles for roughly £10 a day. **Mike the Bike** (53 Frances St., Newtownards; ☎ 028/9181-1311) does daily or weekly cycle rental and delivery/pickup in

NORTHERN IRELAND

the North Down/Ards area. If you don't want to go it alone call Tony Boyd at **The Emerald Trail Bicycle Tours** (15 Ballyknocken Rd., Saintfield; ☎ **028/9081-3200;** www. emeraldtrail.com). From here, 📺 **Best** **Irish Cycle Hire** (☎ **041/685-3772;** www.irish cyclehire.com) do a fantastic weeklong tour encompassing the legends and myths of both Northern Ireland and the Republic, taking in the Mournes and Cooley mountains, as well as Newgrange and the Hill of Tara, before finishing off in Drogheda. It's a great way to get a taste of the North and the South and an insight into all that divides and unites them. It ain't cheap at €1,200 all-in, but if you can't fork out for this they also hire bikes at €70 for the week or €15 for the day and can deliver and pick up bikes from wherever you need them for a bit extra.

DIVING   The waters in this area are a soggy dream for divers—very clear, brimming with untouched first-rate marine life, and scattered with wrecks. Novices can arrange diving lessons leading to qualifications with **DV Diving** (☎ **028/9186-1686;** www.dvdiving.co.uk) from £25 for the scuba swimming pool experience to £225 for a Padi Open Water qualification. Those put off by the chilly water can do their theory here—for £295—before heading to warmer climes for the sea dives. To charter a diving expedition in Strangford Lough, contact **Des Rogers** (200a Shore St.; (☎ **028/4272-8297**). This isn't all Des does. He also offers sea fishing and bird-watching tours. Prices start from around £70 for a half-day (3½ hr.) and £120 for a full day.

HORSEBACK RIDING   To saddle up and ride along the beach on a horse try **Ardminnan Equestrian Centre** (15A Ardminnan Rd., Portaferry; ☎ **028/4277-1321**). They cater to beginners and experts, with horses to suit all human girths. Small groups are welcome. Prices go from £9 an hour.

The Rest of Northern Ireland

Downpatrick

When St Patrick's boat washed up in this area he began spreading the Christian word at Downpatrick. After converting the local chieftain Dichu and his gang to Christianity, he roamed throughout Ireland, returning here to die. A large stone supposedly marks the spot where he is buried in the cathedral grounds.

Beyond the big P memorabilia, there is little else to see in Downpatrick, and few places to really let loose. During the day, the pace is definitely bustling, but it's not nearly as feisty as Belfast. At night, the pub scene seems almost inadequate for a town of around 10,000, although there are a few good spots to hang out if you end up liking the Downpatrick vibe.

GETTING THERE

Ulsterbus (☎ **028/9033-3000;** www.ulster bus.co.uk) provides frequently scheduled daily service from Belfast to Downpatrick. If you're traveling by car, take A7 south from Belfast.

GETTING AROUND

Downpatrick is small and mostly walkable. Buses aren't really a practical way to get around. Catch a cab from **Downpatrick Taxis** (Market St.; ☎ **028/4461-4515**) or **Call-a-cab** (61 Irish Street; ☎ **028/ 4461-3329**). To get in and out of Downpatrick by bus or train, you'll need to pass through at **Ulsterbus Depot** (Market St.; ☎ **028/4461-2384**).

BASICS

EMERGENCIES   The **police station** can be found on Irish Street (☎ **028/4461-5011**).

Downpatrick

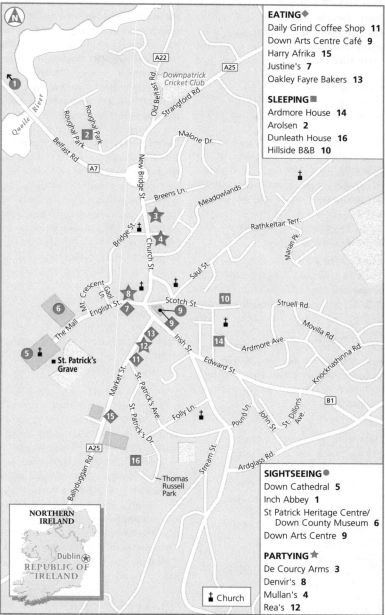

EATING◆
Daily Grind Coffee Shop **11**
Down Arts Centre Café **9**
Harry Afrika **15**
Justine's **7**
Oakley Fayre Bakers **13**

SLEEPING■
Ardmore House **14**
Arolsen **2**
Dunleath House **16**
Hillside B&B **10**

SIGHTSEEING●
Down Cathedral **5**
Inch Abbey **1**
St Patrick Heritage Centre/
    Down County Museum **6**
Down Arts Centre **9**

PARTYING★
De Courcy Arms **3**
Denvir's **8**
Mullan's **4**
Rea's **12**

✝ Church

NORTHERN
IRELAND

Dublin ✪
REPUBLIC OF
IRELAND

Downpatrick Hospital (Irish St. and circular road; ☎ **028/4461-3311**) is centrally located.

PHARMACIES **Deeny Pharmacist** (30a St. Patrick's Ave.; ☎ **028/4461-3794;** Mon–Fri 9am–1pm, 2–5:30pm) is centrally located.

POST OFFICE Postal envelopes come and go via the main **post office** (65 Lower Market St.; ☎ **028/4461-2061;** 9am–5:30pm Mon–Fri, 9am–12:30pm Sat).

TOURIST INFORMATION For information in the Down District, stop into the **St. Patrick Visitor Centre** (53A Market St., Downpatrick; ☎ **028/4461-2233**). It's open October to mid-June Monday to Friday 9am to 5pm, Saturday 9am to 1pm and 2 to 5pm; mid-June to September Monday to Saturday 9:30am to 6pm and Sunday 2 to 6pm.

SLEEPING

If you want to stay, there are a few B&B's around town. One of the best is the **Hillside B&B** (62 Scotch St.; ☎ **028/4461-3134;** doubles £66), set in a grand Georgian building with a rather fancy TV room and a decent bar and restaurant on-site. Others include **Ardmore House** (1 Ardmore Ave.; ☎ **028/4461-3028;** doubles £40) and **Arolsen** (47 Roughal Park; ☎ **028/4461-2656;** doubles £40, singles £22).

EATING

The number of eateries in Downpatrick is growing. Slowly. Most of what is up for grabs is pub grub and coffee shop fodder with the odd posh restaurant here or there. **Justine's** (19 English St.; ☎ **028/4461-7191;** lunch £1.95–£6.95, dinner £7.95–£12) is a rather prim place where paper napkins sprout out of the wine glasses. Situated in the town's old assembly rooms—once home to the 200 year-old Irish Hunt club—it makes the grade by serving up restaurant food at cafe prices during the lunch sessions. Go lightly with soups or dig into a main feature such as pan-fried breast of chicken with peppercorn sauce, deep-fried crispy cod, or sirloin steak. Dinner is pricier but sees all sorts from chicken Italiana (with mushrooms and a creamy garlic sauce) to Barbary duck breast with a honey, ginger, and soy sauce. It's all fresh and bashed together from local Northern Irish produce.

A hearty lunch at an even leaner price can be found at **Harry Afrika** (102 Market St.; **028/4461-7161;** lunch £4), a little diner across from the bus station serving cheap lunches and breakfasts, or the cool **Daily Grind Coffee Shop** (21a St. Patrick's Ave.; ☎ **028/4461-5949**) for the most savory sandwiches in town. You can also find outstanding sandwiches, pies, and soda bread for under £4 at the **Oakley Fayre Bakers** (52 Market St.; ☎ **028/4461-2500**).

You won't have any difficulty finding the **Down Arts Centre Café** (Irish St.; ☎ **028/4461-5283;** all items £2–£6; no credit cards). Look for the clock tower on top of a Victorian redbrick building in the very center of Downpatrick. Enter below. Its soups, salads, sandwiches, and pastries provide a satisfying snack or lunch break on a day's outing from Belfast.

PARTYING

Downpatrick doesn't really have a "scene," but if you want to go have a pint with the locals, **Denvir's Pub** (14 English St.; ☎ **028/4461-2012**) is a really atmospheric old pub dating back to the 17th century. It's got a colorful story too: the United Irishmen, great-great-great-great-grandparents of the IRA, held meetings here prior to the Rebellion of 1798 against Britain. The Denvir clan made it to America by the skin of their teeth and eventually became prominent citizens and the namesakes of Denver, Colorado.

Mullan's (48 Church St.; ☎ **028/4461-2227**) is another good spot for a friendly pint. Trad sessions happen here several nights a week, usually around 10pm. Other pubs known for adequate to above-average *craic* include the **De Courcy Arm**s (Church St.; ☎ **028/4461-2522**) where live music happens some nights, and **Rea's** (78 Market St.; ☎ **028/4461-2017**), with an enticing peat fireplace, perfect for warming cold, wet selves on cold, wet nights.

SIGHTSEEING

FREE → **Down Cathedral** Completed in 1818, Down Cathedral stands on the Hill Of Down. Hardly awe-inspiring, it wins points for its great thundering organ and "Judge's Box," previously used for legal trials (a reminder of the close historical links between the Irish church and state). People usually come here to look at the stone slab in the graveyard commemorating St. Patrick. He's said to be buried under the cathedral itself. The tradition identifying this site as Patrick's grave seems to go back no farther than the 12th century. At that time John de Courcy is said to have shipped the bones of saints Bridgit and Columbanus here to lie beside those of St. Patrick. The Mound of Down, a large lump of grassy earth in the shadow of the larger Hill of Down, was once a round hill fort of the Normans. Over the centuries, everything decayed, leaving just the mound behind. Stonehenge it's not, but it's got a pretty view of the town and makes for a good strolling ground. *The Mall.* ☎ *028/4461-4922. Free admission. Mon–Fri 9:30am–5pm, Sat–Sun 2–5pm.*

→ **Inch Abbey** Perched up on the side of the River Quoile, Inch Abbey was founded in 1180 by John de Courcy, a Norman invader (and bone mover, see "Down Cathedral," above). This former Cistercian abbey gives a taster of how deeply rooted the Anglo-Irish conflict actually is. Operational until the mid-16th century, it refused to admit the native Irish all the time it was open, preferring to import monks from Lancashire to keep a strong English presence in the area. *Admission to abbey 75p adults. No credit cards.*

Abbey open Apr–Sept Tues–Sat 10am–7pm, Sun 2–4pm, Oct–Mar Sat 10am–4pm, Sun 2–4pm.

FREE → **St. Patrick Heritage Centre/Down County Museum** Cuddled up next to the cathedral, the St. Patrick Centre and County Museum provide some intriguing glimpses into how life was once lived in this area. There's a bizarre range of exhibitions including a wax St. Patrick and some old computer equipment and adding machines. The most interesting part is the audio-enhanced exhibit in the original 18th-century jail. Here wax convicts pose with fixed expressions of agony, starvation, and general annoyance. Walking through the exhibit, you'll hear their sad stories emanating from hidden speakers. *The Mall.* ☎ *028/4461-5218. Free admission, except for some special events. June–Aug Mon–Fri 10am–5pm, Sat–Sun 1–5pm, Sept–May Tues–Fri 10am–5pm, Sat 1–5pm.*

FREE → **Down Arts Centre** A beacon of culture in Downpatrick providing a temporary home for shows ranging from contemporary jazz to theater and comedy. It's definitely worth checking out to see what's playing while you're in town. Much of what travels here originates in Belfast or Dublin but the ticket prices are less. Attached is a gallery exhibiting contemporary Irish art and a cool cafe (see "Eating," above) where all the profits go to charity. *2–6 Irish St.* ☎ *028/4461-5283. www.downartcentre.com. Free admission (except to performances). Open Mon–Fri 10am–4:30pm, Sat 9am–4pm.*

SIGHTSEEING AROUND DOWNPATRICK

→ **Legananny Dolmen** Northern Ireland's top dolmen (Neolithic tomb). Over 5,000 years old it was the portal to a chieftain's grave. The huge stones are thought to have been dragged quite some way. Urns were originally found underneath and the remains of a nearby cairn (pile of stones used to mark a significant spot or a path) can still be seen. Now it acts as a flytrap for photographers. They have to find it first, hidden between a farmer's stonewall and a small back road. *Slieve Croob, County Down. Take A24 from Belfast to Ballynahinch, B7 to Dromara, then ask for directions. Free access.*

Lough Neagh

Lough Neagh is the largest lake in the British Isles. Its vital statistics are 396 sq. km (153 sq. miles) coverage, it being 32km (20 miles) long, 16km (10 miles) wide, with a 105km (65-mile) shoreline, for those who are interested. Supposedly the lough was created by the mighty Fionn MacCumhail (anglicized to Finn McCool) when he flung a sod into the sea to create the Isle of Man. But before you think about taking a dip, consider this: The lake's claim to fame is its eels. Yep, the waters are positively infested with the slippery suckers. Hundreds of tons of eels are taken from Lough Neagh and exported each year, mainly to Germany and Holland. This extraction has been going on since the Bronze Age, and shows no sign of letting up. The age-old method involves the use of a "long line," baited with up to 100 hooks. There are often as many as 200 boats trailing a few of these lines each on the lake each night (the best time to go fishing for these slimy things), with a nightly catch of up to 10 tons of eels. If you're not entirely creeped out by that Lough Neagh has plenty of watersporting activities on offer.

GETTING THERE

Ulsterbus (☎ 028/9043-4424; www.trans link.co.uk) runs from Belfast to various villages and towns around Lough Neagh including Randalstown and Craigavon.

SLEEPING

Drumard Cottage (66 Drumhubbert Rd., Dungannon; ☎ 028/8773-8657; www. drumardcottage.com; per week £200–£295, per weekend £115–£150) is your quintessential Irish cottage with whitewashed walls, a thatched roof, bright doors, and roses climbing up the exterior. Inside is a mixture of stripped wooden floorboards and tile floors, with two fires to keep things cozy on winter nights and a BBQ outside to do the same on summer evenings. Kitted out with DVD players and TVs this place can be a lotta fun. Sleeping four at prices ranging from £200 for a week it becomes a seriously viable option if you're thinking of hanging around for some time. All heating (including coal for the fire) is included.

Want somewhere to stay for under a fiver? If you've got a tent the **Ballyronan Marina and Caravan Park** (99 Shore Rd., 8km/5 miles southeast of Magherafelt on the B190 or 12 miles northeast of Cookstown on the A23/B18; ☎ **028/7941-8399;** opservices @cookstown.gov.uk; tents £5; open Apr–Sep) is a seriously good option. There are only three spaces so it's best to ring ahead; those who claim a place will find hot showers, a cafe, and a launderette.

Alternatively, not far away, put a roof over your head at **Hostel 56** (Rainey St., Magherafelt; ☎ **028/7963-2096;** www. hostel56.club24.co.uk; dorm £9) where, despite the name of the street, there's warm, dry rooms and pumping hot showers. On the roof is a made-for-BBQs terrace while inside is a large TV lounge. The staff are eager to point you in the direction of outdoor activities in the area. And—let that smile spread across your face—there's no curfew.

EATING

The local delicacy round these parts is Lough Neagh eel—surprisingly tasty when it's chargrilled. Hundreds of pounds of the stuff will worm its way to chic eateries in Belfast, London, and the rest of Europe, but there will still be plenty left for sale in the pubs around the lake. Alternatively **Gardiners** (7 Garden St.; ☎ **028/7930-0333;** www.gardeners.net;

Bowl Me Over

If, on a Sunday in County Armagh, you happen to see two guys hurling heavy balls of steel down a rural road surrounded by cheering onlookers, you aren't witnessing a group of mental patients on a weekend furlough. What you're watching is probably a road-bowling match. A local favorite, this sport is a true oddity. The object is to get the heavy metal ball to the end of a stretch of road in the least amount of tosses. Matches take place largely in the springtime and rarely make it to the events listings of the local paper, so ask around to find out if there's one happening in the area while you're there. The only other place to see these matches is down south in County Cork.

mains £4.95–£8.95) does a take on Asian fusion. The results are unusual: vegetable tempura served with chili and onion jam together with mash and salad, or Thai curry burger with Irish fries. Don't knock it. It tastes just fine for the price.

SIGHTSEEING

Boat Trips
The best way to experience Lough Neagh is to take a **boat trip,** departing regularly from the nearby Kinnego Marina (☎ 0374/811248 mobile), signposted from the main road. They last about 45 minutes and cost £5.

PLAYING OUTSIDE

CYCLING   A 206km (128 mile) cycle route spins around the edge of Lough Neagh. Officially number 94 on the national cycle route (that's the red number you need to look out for on the signs), it whizzes past old churches, castles, and the odd hide (perfect for ogling at the wildlife). Right next to Belfast International Airport, it makes a great aerobic

activity for a flying visit. Take a look at the excellent website for what to see and places to stay (www.loughshoretrail.com).

WATERSPORTS   **Craigavon Watersports Centre,** 1 Lake Rd. (☎ 028/3834-2669) offers instruction in water-skiing, canoeing, sailing, and windsurfing, plus banana boat rides.

Armagh

The town of Armagh feels a bit pensive, as if it's waiting for a tourist onslaught that never quite arrives. County Armagh was among the hardest hit by the Troubles and now suffers from the lingering effects of all the bad press. Nevertheless, Armagh has emerged like a phoenix from the ashes as a beautiful and engaging town. You'd be hard pressed to find a place as significant to Irish religious history, or one quite as pretty on a spring day.

In a couple years, as word spreads, Armagh could become a hot destination for travelers but, for now, it remains unadulterated.

Legend has it Armagh was founded by the mythical Queen Macha, 600 years after Noah raised anchor in the Flood. It's the "Christian capital" of Ireland. Here, on Árd Macha (Macha's Hill), St. Patrick built a church in A.D. 445. One has stood there ever since. Over the next few centuries, the town flourished as a center of culture and learning. It also excelled at attracting invaders, from Vikings to the English.

The modern city of Armagh embraces its complex and important history—some would say to the detriment of its present. Young people in town will tell you, in much the same vein as kids from American suburbia, there's just "nothing to do." Indeed, a none-too-vibrant youth culture and nightlife may be the only remaining obstacles to this beautiful town becoming a truly incredible place to visit.

The best time to come here is in May, during apple blossom season, when the countryside is in full bloom and everything is

Armagh

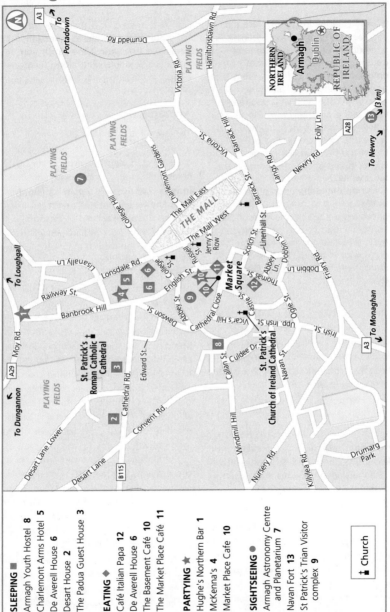

SLEEPING ■
Armagh Youth Hostel **8**
Charlemont Arms Hotel **5**
De Averell House **6**
Desart House **2**
The Padua Guest House **3**

EATING ◆
Café Italian Papa **12**
De Averell House **6**
The Basement Café **10**
The Market Place Café **11**

PARTYING ★
Hughe's Northern Bar **1**
McKenna's **4**
Market Place Cafe **10**

SIGHTSEEING ●
Armagh Astronomy Centre
and Planetarium **7**
Navan Fort **13**
St Patrick's Trian Visitor
complex **9**

☩ Church

Get Off My Land

Generally speaking, things are calmer in Northern Ireland now than they've ever been in most of our lifetimes. In fact, if you could manage to ignore the sectarian graffiti that decorates towns and villages throughout the North you could almost kid yourself that everybody up there is just getting along these days. Except late in the summer that is, when the "marching season" is underway, and the squabbles and violence flare up once again.

As with most things around here, the marching season is a tradition dating back 200 years. And, as with most things around here, it's been a source of tension between Catholics and Protestants throughout its history.

Here's the back story: In 1690 the Protestant English King, William of Orange, defeated the Catholic King he'd already deposed, James II, at the Battle of the Boyne, thus confirming Protestant supremacy in Ireland, at least for a while.

During that same war, a famous incident occurred in Derry, when 13 young apprentice boys closed the gates of that walled city against James II's oncoming forces, thus protecting the town from a Catholic invasion.

Ever since, groups of Protestants in the North have held parades on days related to those events.

Most of the marches are organized by a Protestant group called the Orange Order, and the marchers are called "Orangemen." The group was founded in the Drumcree area of Portadown in 1795, and the first march was held shortly thereafter. While most Orange marches are peaceful, the Portadown march often turns violent. Other contentious marches are held in Derry, Armagh and on Ormeau Road in Belfast.

The problem is that in these towns the neighborhoods changed but the march routes didn't. The Protestant groups still march along the same paths their grandfathers and great-grandfathers followed, but now many of the neighborhoods through which they parade are predominately Catholic.

As you might imagine, this leads to friction.

In Derry the marchers are called the Apprentice Boys, and their parades are the biggest in the region, attracting tens of thousands of Protestant partisans. Like those in Portadown, Derry's marches have been known to get completely out of control. An Apprentice Boys march in Derry in 1969 led to the notoriously violent "Battle of the Bogside," which then led to the mobilization of British troops in the North and 35 years of grief and anger.

For the most part, the marches are contained in neighborhoods out of the tourist areas, so it's unlikely that they will affect you. Still, you never know—in recent years there have been sporadic outbreaks of widespread rioting, particularly in Portadown.

If you're headed to any of those areas in late summer, keep an eye on the Irish press. If it looks like trouble is brewing, change your travel plans.

covered in white blossoms. The worst time to be in Armagh is any Sunday of the year, when everything except the plumbing shuts down.

GETTING THERE

BY BUS **Ulsterbus** (☎ 028/9033-3000; www.translink.co.uk) provides hourly coach services to Armagh from Belfast taking 90 minutes. **Bus Éireann** (☎ 01/836-6111;

www.buseireann.ie) offers daily service from Dublin. If you're driving, Armagh is easily reached from Belfast on the A3. From Derry, take the A5 south. From Dublin, take the N1 north to Newry and then follow the A28 to Armagh.

BASICS

EMERGENCIES   **Police** (Newry Rd.; ☎ **028/ 3752-3311**). **Armagh Community Hospital** (Tower Hill; ☎ **028/3752-2341**) offers medical attention.

INTERNET ACCESS   The computer retail store **Armagh Computer World** (43 Scotch St., the second floor of Wisebuys; ☎ **028/ 3751-0002;** armaghcw@aol.com Mon–Sat 9am–5:30pm; £4 per hour) offers basic Internet services.

POST OFFICE   The main **post office** (31 Upper English St.; ☎ **028/3751-0313;** Mon–Fri 9am–5:30pm, Sat 9am–12:30pm) is in the center of town.

TOURIST INFORMATION   Stop into the **Armagh Tourist Information Centre** (Old Bank Building, 40 English St.; (☎ **028/3752-1800**). It's open all year, Monday to Saturday 9am to 5pm, Sunday 2 to 5pm. For a host of tourist information on County Armagh, take a look at www.armagh-visit.com.

ORIENTATION

Armagh is a small city or large town, depending on whom you ask. There are 14,000 people here. At the center of town stands the impressive St. Patrick's Roman Catholic Cathedral and, up on Ard Macha, the big hill north of the center, is the St. Patrick's Church of Ireland Cathedral (see "Sightseeing," below). These are the major landmarks in town; if you don't know where you are, look up for their spires to get your bearings. The grounds outside the Roman Catholic cathedral are an excellent place to get a panoramic view of town and set the layout in your head.

During the day, people tend to congregate on Market Square, south of Protestant St.

Patrick's. On the square you'll find some cool haunts: bars, cultural centers, and a number of pubs.

From Market Square, head north on English Street, take the first right onto Russell Street, and you'll hit The Mall, a beautiful patch of green ringed with trees and surrounded by Georgian houses. You're likely to see sunbathing cuties, picnicking families, and cricket matches.

Head south from the Mall toward the edge of the city proper and you'll run into the Palace Demesne, an enormous stretch of green that holds the ruins of a Franciscan friary, the beautiful palace stables, and a golf course on its acres of land.

SLEEPING

In the past couple of years, Armagh has done a lot to welcome the budget traveler. Even if you don't want to stay at a hostel, there are other relatively inexpensive options that'll give you more privacy and/or luxury. Overall, accommodations at any price here are excellent: clean, welcoming, and friendly.

Neat freaks who spend most of their travels cringing about the grime coating so many hostels can rest easy at the **Armagh Youth Hostel** (39 Abbey St.; ☎ **028/3751-1801;** dorm £13), possibly the cleanest hostel you'll ever come across. Rooms are all relatively new, all are en suite, and many of the doubles have TV and tea facilities. That said, it doesn't have a tremendous amount of character and feels a little impersonal, like a Motel 6. Still, it's great for the money, has a large, full kitchen, a TV room—and did we mention how clean it is?

The Padua Guest House (63 Cathedral Rd., near the Catholic Cathedral; ☎ **028/ 3752-2039;** doubles £40) is a good B&B option, if you don't mind being surrounded by glassy-eyed toys—the owners have a thing for dolls, which perch all over the place. They're kind of charming in a "Twilight Zone" sort of way. Rooms are clean and comfy. Breakfast is enormous and delicious.

Desart House (99 Cathedral Rd., past the cathedral heading out of town; ☎ **028/3752-2387;** doubles £40) is similar—but minus the doll collection.

The friendly and funky **De Averell House** (47 Upper English St.; ☎ **028/3751-1213;** doubles £60) is a five-minute walk from most pubs, restaurants, and attractions in Armagh. Bright, unique color schemes and new bathrooms are standard in each room, giving this elegant 18th-century house a fresh feeling. All rooms have private baths, and the price includes a full Irish breakfast, with sumptuous fresh fruit, at the downstairs restaurant (see "Eating," below). There is an ultracomfy living room on the first floor where you may get to take a crack at the Playstation belonging to the owners' kids.

The more traditional—and more pricey— **Charlemont Arms Hotel** (57–65 English St.; ☎ **028/3752-2028;** doubles from £80) has an old-time family feeling as moms, daughters, aunts, and uncles all seem to help out. The reception has lots of wood paneling and sit-up-like-your-mother-told-you armchairs. The rooms are nothing too special, but they are comfortable. The restaurant downstairs is a local favorite and offers delicious and filling variations on the cooked animal theme.

EATING

Armagh eats are definitely on the yummy end of the food-quality spectrum, but unfortunately they are not wonderfully diverse. That being said, if you like rich meat and fowl dishes, you'll love it here. Vegetarians, be prepared to eat a cheese sandwich or two.

Tucked underneath the Armagh City Film House (see "Partying," below), **The Basement Café** (Market St.; ☎ **028/3752-4311;** mains £5, soup £2) is a cool hideaway for an afternoon coffee, sandwich, or pre-movie snack. 1950s American ads and pop-culture paraphernalia adorn the walls of this popular youth hangout.

Easily identifiable by its red awning, the cozy little **Italian Café Papa** (15 Thomas St.; ☎ **028/3751-1205;** lunch £4.50) serves up a mean espresso. You can get a great little homemade soup and sandwich lunch, or skip straight to dessert and dig into their fresh-baked and majorly delicious cakes.

The cafe at **The Market Place Arts** (see "Sightseeing," below) compound is swanky and modern—you'll feel like an Armagh high roller as you rub elbows with prominent citizens, patrons of the arts, and ordinary folk gussied up in their weekend best. Lunch is around £5; dinner will set you back £8 to £10.

The De Averell House (47 Upper English St.; ☎ **028/3751-1213;** entrees £8–£10) is, hands down, the best bet for dinner in town. Tony, the head chef and owner of the hotel, serves up a marvelous fusion of Indian, Mexican, Italian, and traditional Irish meat and fowl dishes. As much as possible is organic and locally sourced. There's no getting in here on a Friday or Saturday night if you don't hook yourself a table in advance.

PARTYING

Pub life in Armagh is not extremely swinging. Many of Armagh's local young folk feel pretty alienated by the town's interest in promoting its past and unwillingness to liven up its present, but it is possible to have a fun night out here. The biggest concentration of pubs is on English Street and the surrounding blocks.

The top pub in town is **Hughes' Northern Bar** (100 Railway St.; ☎ **028/3752-7315**) a few blocks north from English Street. Pronounced "Hughe-zes," this is the best place to meet cool, young people. The bar is full of traditional pub elements—a fireplace, wooden booths, stained glass in the windows—yet it manages to feel very now. Upstairs they have live rock music on Friday and Saturday; Sunday features local trad.

McKenna's (21 English St.; ☎ **028/3756-8437**) exudes a lively, fun feeling and, on weekends, it's possible to have a great time. The setting is basic if not a little rustic. There isn't much to look at here, but the people—everyone from old codgers at the bar to 18-year-olds giggling in the booths—seem intent on conversing with anyone and everyone they can throw an arm round.

The chic bar/cafe—actually two bars and a restaurant—at the modernist **Market Place Café** (Market Square; ☎ **028/3752-1820;** coffee house opens at noon for lunch; the cocktail bar opens for performances, usually in the evening from around 7pm till around 11pm), buzzes on theater nights. It's worth a look in the daytime for a snack, a burger, or a glass of wine. The crowd is older, moneyed folk and their young offspring. It's a good place to schmooze with the upper crust of Armagh society; expect people in blazers and long dresses.

PERFORMING ARTS

Armagh's arts scene is small but growing, and is centered at Market Square. **The Market Place Arts Center** (Market Square; ☎ **028/3752-1820;**www.themarketplacearmagh.com; tickets £4–£20; performances usually start at 8pm) has a spacious gallery, spread out over two levels, of modern white walls and glass floors. Most of the work is contemporary Irish: lots of earth tones on minimalist milieus. You can also catch plays, opera, and dance here. The large theater hosts big-name acts like The Chieftains and the Irish Tenors; the smaller studio sees more intimate gigs including stand-up comedy acts. There is also a late-night bar on Friday and Saturday nights attracting groovy art-loving types (see "Partying," above).

CINEMA

The **Armagh City Film House** (Market St.; ☎ **028/3752-4311;** www.armaghfilmhouse. com; tickets £4), down the hill from Market Square, is a decent theater with four screens playing mostly mainstream American films (albeit with the odd, more interesting art house offering thrown in the schedule here and there). Catching a show here is one of the few things to do in town after dark besides drinking.

FESTIVALS

In May, the town gets hoppin' for the Apple Blossom Festival, which features everything from blues music to tours of blossom country to the Apple Blossom Fashion Show. Stop by the tourist office (see "Tourist Information," above) and pick up a brochure for all the happenings.

SIGHTSEEING

→ **Armagh Astronomy Centre and Planetarium** A trip here will probably remind you of a planetarium you visited on a 6th grade field trip, right down to the Atari 520st interactive media display and the 1980's space documentary playing on one of the monitors. The planetarium looks a little run-down, like one too many kids has spun the solar wheel and fondled the fossils. Various exhibits take you through our universe, culminating in the show in the Star Theater (currently closed for renovations although the show is taking place in the Lyndsay Hall of Astronomy in the meantime). Get whisked through a few billion years of cosmic history in only a half-hour. It's majorly trippy stuff. On the same grounds is the Observatory, unfortunately closed to the public. The Planetarium also has a huge telescope, opened up to the public twice a month from September to April. Call ahead for details. There's also a little cafe on-site, and a cheesy gift shop too. *College Hill, Armagh.* ☎ *028/3752-3689. www. armaghplanet.com. Admission to show and exhibition area £3 adults. Mon–Fri 1–4:45pm.*

→ **Navan Fort** Many, many years ago—in pre-Christian Ireland—Navan Fort (in Irish, *Emain Macha*) was a place where powerful people hung out and strange rituals took place. It was, in fact, the royal and religious capital of Ulster. Much like the Hill of Tara, very little remains—only mounds that seem mute and unimpressive. The nearby interpretive center tells their stories. And does it very well. Through a series of exhibits and two multimedia presentations, the history and prehistory of Emain Macha, its mysteries and legends, unfold. A book and gift shop and cafe are also on hand. The center is also the focus of educational and artistic programs and events year-round. *The Navan Centre, 81 Killylea Rd., Armagh.* ☎ *028/3752-5550. Admission £4.50 adults, £3 students. Open year-round Mon–Sat 10am–5pm, Sun 11am–5pm. 3.2km (2 miles) from Armagh on A28, signposted from Armagh town center.*

→ **St. Patrick's Trian Visitor Complex** This modern visitor complex housed inside a church gives a good lively intro to Armagh, the "motherhouse" of Irish Christianity. The presentations are dramatic making this a good first stop to get your bearings in local history and culture. On-site are a craft courtyard and a cafe, as well as a visitor genealogical service, to hunt down the long lost relies. If you're really set on understanding the history of Christianity in Ireland this is a good place to start. If you're not, skip this place as it's usually filled with noisy children. *40 English St. (off Friary Rd., a 10-min. walk from town), Armagh.* ☎ *028/3752-1801. Admission*

(includes 3 multimedia exhibitions) £4 adults, £3 students. July–Aug Mon–Sat 10am–5pm Sun 2–6pm, Sept–June Mon–Sat 10am–5pm Sun 2–5pm.

SHOPPING

As with so many other things in Armagh there are few really cutting-edge shops here but **Sounds Good** (4a Upper St.; ☎ 028/3752-7031) does provide some decent tunes. It may attract some rap from locals for its bountiful country collection but head on up the stairs to find rock and dance, together with CDs from local bands including Ignition (who can also be found playing at Hughes' (see "Partying," above).

Derry

Derry is one of the coolest places to visit in Northern Ireland. It's saturated with history but completely up for having a good time in the present. Due to The Troubles it was once way off the tourist map. But things are changing. Walk through the Walled City at the heart of this 400-year-old city and you'll see slick bars, cafes, and galleries, none of

NORTHERN IRELAND

Talk of the Town

5 Ways to Start a Conversation with a Derry Local

Derry locals are a talkative passionate bunch, once you get them going, but they don't put up with any nonsense.

1. Find out where the best DJs are spinning tonight. Derry has more DJs than it knows what to do with. Meaning whatever you're into you should be able to find a night to match.

2. The Bloody Sunday Enquiry. It's out in 2006 and everyone's got an opinion on it. Rightly so. Don't wait to read the news in the papers. Find out what the locals really think here.

3. Plans and dreams. Every youngster in Derry has one. Most involve getting out of the town. Hopefully tourism will put it on the world map and produce reasons to hang around.

4. Labels. Derry kids are a fabulously stylish bunch. They don't go in for the very commercial big names, tending to pick out a more eclectic look. Either way they love to chat about clothes.

5. Where everyone's going out tonight. It doesn't matter if it's a school night, they'll be something going on, usually involving live music. Hedonism is spelt with capital letters in Derry. Join in the mayhem.

Sunday Bloody Sunday

On January 30, 1972, 20,000 civil rights protesters marched through Derry to oppose discrimination in housing, and employment, and demand an end to the British policy of internment without trial for political prisoners. As the crowd moved through town, small scuffles developed before the First Battalion of the Parachute Regiment opened fire on the crowd. At the end of the day, 14 unarmed men, mostly teenagers, were dead and many were wounded. The army's position was that they were fired upon, even though there was no hard evidence and none of the dead or wounded were found with guns or bombs. The Widgery Commission, created to investigate the incident, was seen by many as a whitewash to cover up the army's irresponsible actions toward the protesters. Many citizens saw this as a call to arms against a government that had fired on its own people, membership in the IRA rose dramatically, and the real Troubles soon began.

These days, the peace process seems to be approaching some semblance of stability. Efforts like the Bloody Sunday Tribunals, an ongoing series of investigations happening right downtown in the Guild Hall, are set to release their findings in 2006. But Derry knows what it wants to hear and is afraid it's just going to be another series of excuses.

which would look out of place on the European mainland. And with 40% of the population under 30, the resulting hot nightlife is drawing in more and more younger visitors.

As is the political tourism. The city was the center of much of the sectarian strife. If you've ever seen any coverage on TV news about violence in Northern Ireland, chances are you've seen pictures of this place. The biggest flashpoint of it all was 1972's Bloody Sunday (see "Sunday Bloody Sunday," above), which left 14 dead and substantially boosted IRA membership. Now Republicans will take you on a tour of the city and tell you what really happened.

GETTING THERE

BY PLANE   Airlines jetting into the **City of Derry Airport** (☎ 028/7181-0784; www. cityofderryairport.com) include **British Airways** (☎ 0345/222111; www.british-airways.com) from Glasgow and Manchester, and **Ryanair** (☎ 0541/569569 in Britain; www.ryanair.com) from London Stansted. The no. 43 Limavady bus stops at the airport. A taxi for the 13km (8-mile) journey to the city

center costs about £10. If you're landing in either of the Belfast airports, without a connection to Derry, the **Airporter** coach can take you straight to Derry. Call ☎ 028/7126-9996 for information and reservations.

BY TRAIN   **Northern Ireland Railways** (☎ 888/BRITRAIL or 028/9089-9411) operate frequent trains from Belfast and Portrush, which arrive at the **Northern Ireland Railways Station** (☎ 028/7134-2228), on the east side of the Foyle River. A free Linkline bus brings passengers from the train station to the city center.

BY BUS   The fastest bus between Belfast and Derry, the no. 212 Maiden City Flyer, operated by **Ulsterbus** (☎ 028/7126-2261 in Derry; www.translink.co.uk), is about twice as fast as the train; it takes a little over 90 minutes. Ulsterbus also has service from Portrush and Portstewart. From the Republic, Bus Éireann offers three buses a day from Galway's **Bus Éireann Travel Centre** (Ceannt Station, Galway; ☎ 091/562000; www.buseireann.ie), via Sligo and Donegal; and there's one bus daily to and from Cork.

Derry

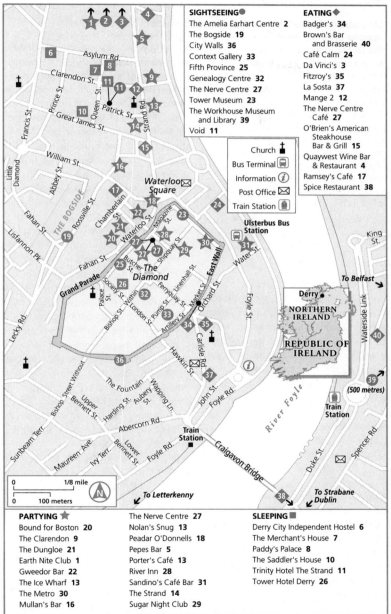

SIGHTSEEING ●
The Amelia Earhart Centre **2**
The Bogside **19**
City Walls **36**
Context Gallery **33**
Fifth Province **25**
Genealogy Centre **32**
The Nerve Centre **27**
Tower Museum **23**
The Workhouse Museum
and Library **39**
Void **11**

EATING ◆
Badger's **34**
Brown's Bar
and Brasserie **40**
Café Calm **24**
Da Vinci's **3**
Fitzroy's **35**
La Sosta **37**
Mange 2 **12**
The Nerve Centre
Café **27**
O'Brien's American
Steakhouse
Bar & Grill **15**
Quaywest Wine Bar
& Restaurant **4**
Ramsey's Café **17**
Spice Restaurant **38**

Church ✝
Bus Terminal 🚌
Information ℹ
Post Office ✉
Train Station 🚆

Ulsterbus Bus
Station

To Belfast

Derry ●

**NORTHERN
IRELAND**

**REPUBLIC OF
IRELAND**

River Foyle

(500 metres)

Train
Station

To Strabane
Dublin

0 —— 1/8 mile
0 —— 100 meters

To Letterkenny

PARTYING ⭐
Bound for Boston **20**
The Clarendon **9**
The Dungloe **21**
Earth Nite Club **1**
Gweedor Bar **22**
The Ice Wharf **13**
The Metro **30**
Mullan's Bar **16**

The Nerve Centre **27**
Nolan's Snug **13**
Peadar O'Donnells **18**
Pepes Bar **5**
Porter's Café **13**
River Inn **28**
Sandino's Café Bar **31**
The Strand **14**
Sugar Night Club **29**

SLEEPING ■
Derry City Independent Hostel **6**
The Merchant's House **7**
Paddy's Palace **8**
The Saddler's House **10**
Trinity Hotel The Strand **11**
Tower Hotel Derry **26**

Culture Tips 🔟

Derry has had more than its fair share of "The Troubles" over the last 40 years. With the new "Bloody Sunday Enquiry" coming out in 2006, this is a hot topic of conversation. It's easy to think Northern Irish politics can be divided up into the good guys and the bad guys, but before you start mouthing off like an Irish Freedom Fighter, remember you could be talking to a Loyalist. It's best to listen and ask lots of questions; you'll learn far more and offend far less.

Lough Swilly Bus Service (☎ 028/7126-2017) serves Derry from a number of towns in County Donegal, including Dunfanaghy and Letterkenny.

GETTING AROUND

Derry is extremely compact, very walkable, and can be reached in minutes from the bus and train stations. If you want to get farther out, Ulsterbus, **Foyle Street Depot,** Derry (☎ 028/7126-2261; www.translink.co.uk), operates local bus service to the suburbs. There is no bus service within the walls of the small, easily walkable city. The black London-style taxis you'll see are known in Derry and Belfast as "people's taxis." These taxis primarily serve nationalist areas outside the walls and will not go to most areas of interest to tourists. Use any of the other taxis available throughout the city, which are plentiful and reasonably priced. There are **taxi stands** at the Ulsterbus Depot, Foyle Street (☎ 028/7126-2262), and at the Northern Ireland Railways Station, Duke Street, Waterside (☎ 028/7134-2228). To call a cab, contact **Co-Op Taxis** (☎ 028/7137-1666), **Derry Taxi Association** (☎ 028/7126-0247), or **Foyle Taxis** (☎ 028/7126-3905).

ORIENTATION

Derry has three major areas, each geographically separated. The most important one is the Walled City and the areas immediately to the north, east, and south. This is the cultural and commercial center of the city. Here you'll find trendy cafes, beautiful old buildings, bookstores, and pubs. At the middle of the Walled City is The Diamond and at the center of the Diamond is the War Memorial. From the Diamond, four streets—Bishop, Butcher, Shipquay, and Ferryquay—go outward in roughly the four cardinal directions. Each of these streets leads to a gate in the wall of the same name, such as Shipquay Gate. These are the city's old valves, once controlling the flow of traffic into its heart.

West of the walled city area is the Bogside, still a Catholic stronghold and the location for much of the city's violent past. Free Derry, nearly autonomous and rife with firepower, was set up by the IRA in this neighborhood in the 1970s. A huge, ominous security tower rises from behind a wall to preside over Bogside, loaded with dozens of cameras and microphones. Free Derry folk say that the police can see and hear for up to 2 miles with the high-tech equipment. Even vibrations coming off windshield glass are enough for them to hear what you're saying. Unsurprisingly they are keen to have the cameras taken it down and it looks like they will be in the very near future.

Directly opposite Bogside, on the other side of the walled city is a Protestant enclave, easily spotted by the red, white, and blue color painted on the roadside curbs. Take the double-decker Craigavon Bridge across the River Foyle and you're in the Waterside, a predominantly Protestant and residential area that makes up the western half of town. The train station is here, as are some loyalist murals and the Workhouse Museum (see "Sightseeing," below).

BASICS

TOURIST OFFICE   The **Derry Visitor and Convention Bureau and Tourist Information Centre** is at 44 Foyle St., Derry (☎ 028/7126-7284). It's open October to March, Monday to Friday 9am to 5pm; April to June, Monday Friday 9am to 5pm, Saturday 10am to 5pm; July to September, Monday to Friday 9am to 7pm, Saturday 10am to 7pm, Sunday 10am to 5pm. As well as the usual booking service for B&Bs and hotels, there are a number of tuned-in younger people working in the office who can recommend good pubs, tours, and activities.

RECOMMENDED WEBSITES   One site, linked to the tourist information office, www.derryvistitor.com, gives good straightforward info about what's going on around town.

Nuts & Bolts

Car Rental   Local car-rental offices include **Europcar** (☎ 028/7135-2777) and **Argus Car Rentals** (☎ 353-1/490-4444) at the City of Derry Airport.

Emergencies   Call ☎ **999** for fire, police, and ambulance. The best choice of hospital is the **Altnagevin Hospital** (Glenshane Rd.; ☎ 028/7134-5171). The main RUC, or police station, is on Strand Road (☎ 028/7136-7337).

Gay & Lesbian Resources   **Foyle Friend** (32 Great James St.; ☎ 028/7126-3120; www.iol.ie/nwgay), operates a drop-in center and coffee bar; check the website for other information and services. Call the **Foyle LGB Line** (☎ 028/7136-0420), Thursday 7:30 to 10pm, or drop in at 37 Clarendon St., Thursday 8 to 10pm.

Internet   You can surf the Web at the **Central Library** (35 Foyle St. in the city center; ☎ 028/7127-2300), for £3 per hour, and at the **Nerve Centre Café** (see "Eating," below) for free when you stop in for something to eat or drink.

Pharmacy   For a centrally located drug store, try **Lloyd's Pharmacy** (25 Strand Rd.; ☎ 028/7126-3376), or **McKenna** (48 Great James St.; ☎ 028/7136-3519). Both are open Monday to Saturday 9:30am to 6pm.

Post Office   Main **post office**, at 3 Custom House St. (☎ 028/7136-2563), is open Monday 8:30am to 5:30pm, Tuesday through Friday 9am to 5:30pm, and Saturday 9am to 12:30pm.

Radio Stations   Local Derry radio stations are **Q102** (FM 102.9) and **Radio Foyle** (FM 93.1).

SLEEPING

Derry's accommodations are cheap and excellent, including one of the coolest hostels in Ireland. There are several inexpensive and excellent B&B's, and beautiful hotels that cost a fraction of what they would in other regions, all the more reason to stay an extra day or two.

Hostels

Most of the hostels are in the same area up to the north of the city in the rows of old Georgian houses. Derry looks set to become a hot spot for 20-something travelers and the number of hostels in the city is on the rise.

Original player, **Derry City Independent Hostel** (4 Asylum Rd., take Strand Rd. past the Tesco and turn left; ☎ 028/7128-0542; www.derry-hostel.co.uk; £10 dorm 5–10 beds, £11 dorm 3–4 beds, £34 double/twin, fifth night free in all rooms) is where you should go first, though it's a bit out of the center, a 10-minute walk north of the Walled

City. Like a college apartment but way cleaner. Be warned you may get caught in the "Derry Vortex" and never want to leave. The lounge is decked out Indian style with TV, VCR, and chill-out couches. The cool dining/social room comes complete with a stereo and CDs. Every night there's a pub crawl. In the summer all-you-can-eat BBQs are arranged for just 2 quid. It's also information central—find out what to do, where to go, and how to have great *craic* Derry-style. It also has a kitchen and laundry (£3 for a wash and dry). If 4 Asylum Rd. is full up, they have an overflow hostel at 44 St James St.

Equally high in the fun stakes is **Paddy's Palace Hostel** (1 Woodleigh Terrace; ☎ **028/7130-9051;** www.paddyspalace.com; £10 dorm four to six beds, £20 single, £30 twin) a stopping-off point for the notorious Paddywaggon. Above the orange door is a quote from Mark Twain, "Travel is fatal to hatred, bigotry and prejudice." You certainly won't find any one of those evil triplets inside. Just 40 beds and a staff eager to acquaint you with all the best drinking establishments in town. Book a long way ahead as this gaff is usually filled out with kids on the Paddywaggon tours. Not for the early-to-bed-early-to-rise brigade.

Doable

MTV Best → **Saddler's House and the Merchant's House** Damn the expense—it's not too much anyway—and stay in one of these two 19th-century houses. They are decked out just as they should be—stripped floorboards, old wooden furniture, and even an English bulldog called Bertie. Whether you're lounging about in the Merchant House's stupendous lounge or sitting up to one of Northern Ireland's best breakfasts—homemade marmalade and bread, luxury muesli, creamy fresh yogurt, locally sourced bacon—in the dining room, you'll feel incredibly grand. Big, old checked

dressing gowns hang up on the back of doorways and Peter Pyne, one half of the husband-and-wife team who run these joints—is an old history teacher from the local university and filled to the brim with knowledge. He may even show you the window of bedroom five in Merchant's House, once used by a sniper to attack a nearby police station. *Saddler's House, 36 Great James St.* ☎ *028/7126-9691. www.thesaddlershouse.com (for both houses). All rooms in Saddler's have private bathrooms. £50 double/twin; £30 single. Merchant's House, 16 Queen St.* ☎ *028/7126-4223. £50 double with private bathroom; £30 single with private bathroom; £45 double/twin with shared bathroom; £25 single with shared bathroom. Rates include full breakfast. MC, V. Amenities: Both houses: Sitting room. In room: TV, tea/coffeemaker.*

→ **Trinity Hotel** One of the city's newer hotels, the Travel Lodge—owned Trinity is clean and modern but not entirely soul-free. Rooms are the usual neutral tones with veneer furniture. Some might say soothing. Others might say naff. What you can't argue about is the price. With special-offer rooms going from as little as £35 (for three people), if you turn up last minute and can't get a room in a hostel, this hotel becomes a serious contender. Still not convinced? The bathrooms are plush with heated towel racks. *2–24 Strand Rd., Derry, County Derry.* ☎ *028/7127-1271. 40 rooms all en suite. £49 double. Continental breakfast £4.50. AE, DC, MC, V. Free parking. Amenities: Two restaurants; bar; free access to nearby fitness center; currency exchange. In room: Phone, TV, hair dryer.*

Splurge

→ **Tower Hotel Derry** Slap-bang in the middle of things is the brand-new Tower Hotel Derry. Okay, so she's not a real beauty from the outside, and you might wonder why the local authorities allowed this to be the only hotel within the gorgeous walled city. Maybe it's because they fancied a go in the hotel sauna or perhaps they wanted access to its leisure complex featuring top views over the surrounding historical buildings. Regardless, guests now enjoy sleeping in light, bright contemporary bedrooms and mingling in the urbane bar and Med-flavored bistro. *The Diamond, Butcher St.* ☎ *028/7137-1000. £70–£110 double. Rates include full breakfast. MC, V. Free parking. Amenities: Restaurant (Mediterranean); cafe/bar. In room: TV, tea/coffeemaker, garment press.*

EATING

Cheap

➔ **Badger's** PUB GRUB This is a local's fave dishing out some of the best pub grub in Derry. Outside it looks like an end-of-row Victorian pub. Inside is light and bright with plenty of trad touches including stained glass and wood panels. Take a comfy pew at lunchtime and prepare for plates of fish and chips; savory steak, vegetable, and Guinness casserole with a crisp puff-pastry lid; or flavor-bursting hot sandwiches known as "damper melts." Dinner is much of the same. Service is friendly and easygoing. Follow the regulars and wash down the dishes with a drink or two. *16–18 Orchard St.* ☎ *028/7136-0763. Dinner main courses £5–£10. Mon noon–3pm; Tues–Thurs noon–7pm; Fri–Sat noon–9:30pm.*

Doable

➔ **Spice Restaurant** INTERNATIONAL Outside is bright purple. Inside is packed. Every night of the week. That's got to say something. It does—this place is damn good. Their bistrolike menu is vast, starring Thai, Portuguese, Caribbean, Indian, and traditional Irish mains. Selections of exotica include coconut-crusted chicken with coriander and tiger prawns, or seared salmon with mango and chili sauce with fresh linguine. Don't even think about not booking ahead on the weekend. *Spencer Rd., Waterside.* ☎ *028/7134-4875. Dinner main courses £8–£14. Tues–Sat 5:30–10:30pm; Sun 5–9pm.*

➔ **Fitzroy's** BRASSERIE This laid-back, brightly colored bistro is open all day, and is a great option for a quick, easy meal at reasonable prices. It tends to have a buzzing crowd of regulars, and it's easy to see why. Food is a casual mix of cultures, from chicken and bacon ciabatta sandwiches to chicken curry or lamb cutlets in red wine jus, along with plenty of vegetarian options. *2–4 Bridge St., Derry, County Derry.* ☎ *028/7126-6211. www.fitzroysrestaurant.com. Lunch main courses £5–£6. Dinner main courses £7–£10. Mon–Tues 10am–8pm; Thurs–Sat 9:30am–10pm; Wed 10am–10pm; Sun noon–8pm.*

➔ **La Sosta** ITALIAN This family-run Italian restaurant is an excellent choice when you have spaghetti on your mind. The menu carries all the usual pasta suspects, and there are also fresh salads and good meat dishes. The sauces here are particularly tasty, and betray the chef's Italian roots. Service is absurdly friendly and the atmosphere is relaxed. *45A Carlisle Rd., Derry, County Derry.* ☎ *028/7137-4817. www.lasostarestaurant.com Dinner main courses £7–£12. Mon–Sat 5:30–9:30pm; Sun noon–2:30pm and 5:30–9pm.*

➔ **Mange 2** FUSION This family-owned restaurant is both romantic and relaxed. Bright by day and candlelit at night, the service is friendly but not intrusive. Its mixed-bag menu of Continental cuisine changes regularly but is reliably good, and made with fresh local produce. This is one of the best restaurants in Derry. *2 Clarendon St., Derry, County Derry.* ☎ *028/7136-1222. Dinner main courses £11–£14. Mon–Sat 11:30am–3pm and 5:30–10pm; Sun 10:30am–3pm and 5:30–10pm.*

➔ **O'Brien's American Steakhouse & Grill** STEAKS This is a loud, bright, extroverted piece of Americana in the middle of central Derry. Big TVs blast music videos or sports, staff are young and cheerful, clientele are known to drink a bit, and the food is

Derry Cafes

→ **Ramsey's Cafe** CAFE   At this great budget-minded eatery in the heart of the city, Anne Ramsey dishes up heaped plates of hot meals, fresh salads, fish and chips, and a variety of bakery items. It's self-service and very busy all day every day. (10 William St. ☎ 028/7126-9236. Main courses £3–£6. No credit cards. Mon–Sat 8am–3am; Sun 6pm–3am.)

→ 🎬 Best   **Nerve Centre Café** CAFE   Many musical gods have eaten in the Nerve Centre Cafe including David Gray and Gomez. Did they go for the vegetable quiche with chips and salad, the nut cutlets, or the stuffed turkey and ham served with pots and veg? Who knows. They were definitely taken care of by the lovely Celia who runs this place, serving up main meals, sandwiches, baked potatoes, and plenty of gluten-free, veggie and vegan options to a motley collection of artsy and traveler types. Behind the cloud of cigarette smoke rising from the diners are three computers offering free Internet access—Celia's cunning ploy to lure in more under 30s. (7/8 Magazine St. ☎ 028/7126-0562. Mains £3.75–£3.95. No credit cards. Mon–Sat 9am–5pm.)

→ **Café Calm** CAFE   Ironically the Café Calm is seriously into its caffeine and it's a good place to get your fix. Along with the drug are soups, paninis, bagels, quiches, scones, and that adopted Irish dish, the lasagna, all served in neutral-tone surrounds. It's no smoking here, as Café Calm doesn't like anything getting between patrons and the taste of their coffee. (4 Shipquay Place. Mains £3–£6, breakfasts £3.50. No credit cards. Mon–Sat 10am–5pm.)

cheap and very good. Considering what you get—huge steaks served on sizzling platters with equally large salads and gigantic mounds of potatoes—prices are beyond reasonable. This place is a steal. *59 Strand Rd., Derry, County Derry. ☎ 028/7136-1527. Dinner main courses £7–£15. Mon–Fri noon–10pm; Sat 4–11pm; Sun 2–10pm.*

→ **Quaywest Wine Bar & Restaurant** INTERNATIONAL   This is one of the trendier options in Derry—you might want to wear your high heels to head out here. The mix of bar and restaurant leans more heavily toward bar as the night goes on, but the food is always excellent, and the international menu travels from Morocco to Mexico and back again. *28 Boating Club Lane, Derry, County Derry. ☎ 028/7137-0977. www.quaywestrestaurant.com Dinner main courses £6–£10. Mon–Sat 5–11pm; Sun noon–10:30pm.*

Splurge

→ **Brown's Bar and Brasserie** INTERNATIONAL   A perfect first date location—provided you've got the cash. The decor is warm, streamlined, and minimalist—conducive to intimate conversation. The innovative menu should impress too, blending as it does the best of modern Irish, Italian, and Thai influences with an emphasis on fresh and, when possible, organic ingredients. Dishes include marinated loin of lamb on a warm noodle salad, or supreme of chicken with parsnip purée and tiger prawn—coconut sauce. Likely to impress. Unlikely to frighten. *1–2 Bond's Hill, Waterside, Derry, County Derry. ☎ 028/7134-5180. www.brownsrestaurant.com. Reservations recommended. Main courses £10–£15. Tues–Fri noon–2:30pm; Tues–Thurs 5:30–10pm; Fri–Sat 5:30–10:30pm.*

➔ **Da Vinci's Bar and Restaurant** INTER-
NATIONAL   If you really want to make a
mark on that girl/guy of your dreams you
could try whisking them off in a cab to Da
Vinci's Bar and Restaurant (It's about 5 min.
out of town). You'll look far more appealing
in the soft candlelight. And if you exchanged
numbers when you were rather the worse for
wear perhaps they will too. The surroundings
are sumptuous: lots of renaissance reds,
stone walls, arched doorways, and dramatic
wrought-iron fittings. The food is top draw:
lots of dishes like grilled sea bass with tikka
crust and lime-cherry relish, or pesto cream
over tender chicken breast stuffed with sun-
dried tomatoes. Stop in at the mahogany bar
for pre-dinner drinks or an after-dinner
coffee. Guaranteed to impress. *15 Culmore Rd.*
☎ *028/7127-9111. Reservations recommended.*
Dinner main courses £9–£16. AE, MC, V.
Mon–Sat 5:30–9:30pm; Sun noon–2:30pm and
5:30–9pm.

PARTYING

Derry locals will tell you to go to Belfast or
Portrush for a proper night out. Don't listen.
They do more than okay on home turf. The
city is heaving with drinking establishments
and ram-packed with locally grown DJs and
musicians. Nights start late, usually around
11pm. Most bars and clubs shut down at
around 1am or 2am.

If you want to tag along, begin with
live music and DJ sets on *TV* (Best) **Waterloo
Street** and follow the crowd on from there.
Popular stop-offs include The Strand and
Metro with nights often ending in Earth.

The nocturnal look is very similar to
the day's: Diesel jeans with a retro Adidas
sports top. Many opt for flashier (for
boy's)/tighter (for girl's) outfits to enter
Derry's trendier establishments. Not to be
missed is Sandino's, a fabulous bohemian
bar where the uniform is strictly come-as-
you-are.

Bars

➔ **The Strand**   The mainstay of all young
partying in Derry, The Strand is packed every
night of the week. The decor is traditional pub
meets colored lights and booming speakers.
The punters are pulled in by everything from
disco to karaoke nights. Don't be fooled if the
place seems dead—everyone's downstairs
rocking out to a live band. During the summer
months look out for the stormingly popular
Bondi Beach Club playing a decade of Ibiza
anthems—dress to get wet. *35–38 Strand St.*
☎ *028/7126-0494.*

➔ **The Metro**   Sitting in the shadow of the
city's historic walls, The Metro is where those
in the know frequent post–Waterloo Street
and pre-Earth. It's a traditional pub with a
contemporary vibe, attracting a lively good-
looking crowd. *3–4 Bank Pl.* ☎ *028/7126-7401.*

➔ **Mullan's Bar**   This is not only a good
place to down a pint, it's also a great place to
hear local music. Bands play most nights, and
the music varies from jazz to blues and traditional Irish sessions during the week. There's
often a DJ on weekends. The interior is all
traditional pub, with stained glass, brass, and
wood polished to a sparkle. The whole place
was rebuilt after being bombed during the
Troubles. *13 Little James St.* ☎ *028/7126-5300.*

➔ **River Inn**   These two adjoining bars
make up the oldest pub in Derry. The downstairs River Inn inhabits cellars opened to the
thirsty public in 1684. Thursday is cocktail
night. *Shipquay St.* ☎ *028/7136-7463.*

➔ **The Ice Wharf**   The Ice Wharf is a huge
cavern of chrome and veneer. At first glance
the appeal of this Wetherspoons chain pub
may not be obvious. Order a round at the bar,
however, and everything becomes clear.
The Ice Wharf is all about drinks promotions.
The best place in Derry to get tanked up on
cheap booze. *Strand Rd.* ☎ *028/7127-6610.*
www.lloydsno1.co.uk.

📺 (Best) → **Sandino's Cafe Bar** This tiny place is definitely Derry's hippest bar, attracting the city's art-loving intelligentsia and embracing everything non-mainstream including the gay community. Its "South of the Border" theme refers to the States' Mexican border, not to the North's border on the Republic. By day sip on fair-trade coffee, by night European beers. A band will be playing by then. Or a DJ. Robdabank, Roots Manuva, and Lemon Jelly have all spread their funky love here, together with folk and trad faves. Come early if you want a seat, this place now has two floors but still fills up fast when the clock strikes five. *Water St.* ☎ *028/7130-9297. www.sandinos.com.*

→ **Porter's Café** One of two pubs in the Trinity Hotel (see "Sleeping," above). Men in suits dot the place by day, while a younger crowd launches an offensive at night. It's an elegant affair: leather-upholstered booths, brownstone pillars, and a slinky dark-wood bar. On weekends DJs bring in the hordes. Nolan's Snug, next door, is somewhere to come over all grown up and sip a Bushmills and soda. *22–24 Strand Rd.* ☎ *028/7127-1272.*

→ **The Clarendon** Occasionally you might find yourself wanting a conversation in the evening. Most of Derry's bars and clubs are not geared up for this hobby. The Clarendon is an easygoing pub for those who are a little older and want a break from the sonic boom. Enjoy the chance to chatter while you sup. *48 Strand Rd.* ☎ *028/7126-3705.*

→ **Peadar O'Donnel's** The beating, bloody heart of traditional music in Derry. Every night sees local lads churning out tunes amidst the old hams and stuffed animal heads decorating the walls. The bands specialize in wistful, bittersweet tunes about leaving home, lost love, and drinking (with the odd Neil Young cover chucked into the mix). The crowd are local pint-swillers interspersed with travelers from across the globe. Don't bother turning up early; the sessions don't

start until 11pm. *53 Waterloo St.* ☎ *028/7137-2318.*

→ **Gweedor Bar** Peadar O'Donnel's brother in arms. The atmosphere is just as cozy and traditional. The drinkers are just a little younger and the music a little livelier. A top spot for watching local rock and blues bands. If you find you want more of the old tunes you can pop back to Pedar's through an interjoining door. *53 Waterloo St.* ☎ *02871/372-318.*

→ **Bound for Boston** Known locally as "The Bound For," this is a grungy little place where the decor is standard-issue Irish pub, the drinkers are young, and the music is rollicking rock 'n' roll. During the Famine exodus, the Bound for Boston was the stopover for a last Irish pint before boarding the boats for America. Originally called the Rosses, the pub drew people from the Rosses region of Ireland, a wild, Gaelic-speaking region in the northwest. Their spirit lives on most nights of the week. Boisterous but fun. *27–31 Waterloo St.* ☎ *028/7137-4343.*

Clubs

→ **Sugar Night Club** A dominant force in Derry nightlife. Spend an evening here and you'll still not see the half of it. It's a giant funhouse for post-adolescent partying, boasting half-a-dozen bars and endless hideaways. The crowd is older than Earth but still largely early twenties. The music is a little bit of everything. Mostly R&B on weekends, when it packs out. Seek refuge in the VIP section or prepare to get moist with over 1,000 other partygoers. Wednesday, Friday, Saturday, and Sunday are the big nights. *33 Shipquay St.* ☎ *028/7126-6017. Cover £4–£5.*

📺 (Best) → **Earth Nite Club** After a recent refurbishment Earth has reclaimed Derry's club crown. Hugely popular with students from the nearby college, Tuesday is dedicated to their needs with an across-the-board music policy. Thursdays bears them in mind too with drinks at £1.50. Saturday is a

where to Find out what's on

Derry has two local papers, each of which has a current "What's On" section: the *Derry Journal* and the *Londonderry Sentinel.* Additionally, the Derry Visitors and Convention Bureau publishes a free quarterly publication called *What's On?* Alternatively simply stroll along to the Nerve Centre, The Void Gallery or The Context Gallery (see below) as there's always something happening at one of these three venues.

mix of R&B and hip-hop. The clientele are notoriously youthful and up for whatever the DJ throws their way. Cover up your tattoos to get in and come early to avoid the queues. *1 College Terrace.* ☎ *028/7136-0556. Cover £5–£6.*

Gay Scene

With its art-loving soul, Derry is generally an all-embracing city although pockets of intolerance do exist in the more traditional bars. **Pepes Bar** (64 Strand Rd.; ☎ **028/7137-4002;** www.pepes-zebar.com) is dedicated to man-on-man action fertilized with a fine mixture of weeklong drinks promos, Sunday strippers, and karaoke nights. Gay women are made very welcome too. Hand-holding and general gay loving is also run-of-the-mill behavior at the **Nerve Centre** (see "Performance Halls," below) and **Sandino's** (see "Bars," above).

PERFORMANCE HALLS

Derry has long been big on the arts, especially theater, poetry, and music. Despite limited cash, it's always been fiercely committed to new work and the pushing back of boundaries. 📺 **Best** The Nerve Centre (7–8 Magazine St.; ☎ **028/7126-0562;** www.nervecentre.org.uk) definitely tops the bill. Alongside DJ and animation workshops, run superb

dance nights from the likes of Tall Paul and John Kelly, and delicious bands and singer-songwriters including Damien Dempsey, The Editors, Idlewild, Ash, and Sinéad O'Connor. The recent addition of the **Millennium Forum** (Newmarket St.; box office ☎ **028/7126-4455**), inside the city walls, added a cultural meeting place and top theater space to the local mix. **The Waterside Theatre** (Glendermott Rd.; ☎ **028/7131-4000**) presents a cocktail of crowd-pleasers and classic Irish theatre. Other venues for concerts, plays, and poetry readings are the **Guild Hall** (Shipquay Place; ☎ **028/7136-5151**); and the **Playhouse,** 5–7 Artillery St. (☎ **028/7126-8027**). Rarely scared to go too far, it puts on plenty of relevant contemporary plays and is also where you'll find the homegrown Echo dance company. There are no swans and tutus here; this is down-and-dirty physical theatre and impressive stuff. **The Verbal Arts Centre** (Stable Lane and Mall Wall, Bishop St. Within; ☎ **028/7126-6946;** www.verbalartscentre.co.uk) is all about promoting reading through spoken-word events. Ticket prices for most performances range from £5 to £15.

CINEMA

The Nerve Centre (see "Performance Halls," above) is the Derry altar at which alternative film can be worshipped, through a brilliant ever-changing program.

COMEDY CLUBS

Sunday nights see professional English and Irish comedians attempt to impress the growing audience at Earth Nite Club (see "Clubs," above) with the search for a comedy star running alongside the main program. **The Millienium Forum** (see "Performance Halls," above) often has comedy nights with everyone from the charming Irish Patrick Kielty to the revolting Roy Chubby Brown. The **Playhouse** (see "Performance Halls," above) also has the odd comedy night from the likes of intelligent alternative comedian Stewart Lee.

SIGHTSEEING

There's a great mix of political history and contemporary art in Derry, all scattered among stunning historical buildings. More than anything it feels as though people have really got something to say and, even better, that it actually matters. Exciting stuff.

FESTIVALS

Derry has a genuinely exciting events calendar that doesn't just include the ubiquitous "Drink Guinness and Listen to Traditional Music" festivals. Spring sees the **Drama Festival** (☎ 028/7126-4455) at the Millennium Forum along with the **Big Tickle Comedy Festival** at boundary-demolishing Nerve Centre (☎ 028/7126-0562), and also **The Playhouse** (☎ 028/7126-8027). The **Feis Doire Cholmcille** is that Guinness-drinking, trad-listening festival but a good, big one (☎ 028/7126-4455). With the advent of summer comes the **City of Derry Jazz Festival** (☎ 028/7137-6545; www.cityofderry jazzfestival.com) and the pure-dynamo **MTV Best** **Celtronic Festival** (☎ 0781/4918-452; www.celtronic.co.uk), one of Ireland's biggest dance music parties. The **Maiden Festival** (☎ 028/7134-9250) coaxes out Derry's Protestant culture and the year is topped off with the mighty **Foyle Film Festival** (☎ 028/7126-7432), Northern Ireland's biggest act of devotion to all things made immortal through celluloid.

TOURS

Ruari O Heara runs the **MTV Best** **Free Derry tours** (☎ 0781-2084-903; www.freederry. net), community-based tours of the city from a Republican perspective—the low-down on the IRA, Bloody Sunday, and the city's moves towards peace. He believes the tours go some way to undoing the propaganda churned out to the world by the British media for the past 30 years. Decide for yourself. Departing daily from Pilot's Row Community Centre (Rossville St., Bogside) at 10am, lasting 1.5 hours costing £4. Highly recommended.

Hanging Out

By day, The Diamond is the center of all action: School kids window-shop on their lunch breaks, shop girls smoke cigarettes outside of boutiques, and businesspeople talk frantically on their cell phones.

Derry lacks a nice park, but if you're looking to walk on a grassy patch, cross the Craigavon Bridge and walk south along the Foyle; there's a scenic river walk trail there. Any of the cafes and many of the pubs around the Diamond teem with activity around lunchtime, while nearer the river **Sandino's** (see "Partying," above) is always a good place to be.

By night, clubgoers gather outside the city walls forming modern plans of attack for entering the city streets. Around 1am the youth of Derry gather in Waterloo Place to figure out where to go next, and who to take with them. Fights, laughter, declarations of love, public displays of affection, and binge drinking can all be witnessed here any night of the week. **Vinyl Junkie** (see "Shopping," below) is favored by dance music fiends who can talk beats with the owner Darren and try-before-they-buy on an impressive sound system.

Far less controversial, the Derry Visitor and Convention Bureau sponsors **Inner City Walking Tours,** June to September Monday to Friday. They depart at 10:30am and 2:30pm from the Tourist Information Centre, 44 Foyle St. The price is £4 adults. Alternatively, Martin McCrossan's colorful **City Tours** (☎ 028/7127-1996/7) group offers informative walking tours all year-round. Tours set out from 11 Carlisle Rd. daily at 10am, noon, and 2pm, but call ahead to book a place. The cost is £4 adults.

The Local University Scene

M T V🞄

The **Northwest Institute of Further Education** (☎ 028/7127-6000; www. nwifhe.ac.uk) has 22,000 students. Many are from Derry itself; others are from the surrounding region and even further afield. Wherever they're from they keep the Waterfront area—where the institute is located—nice and lively. Student hangouts include Earth club (see "Clubs," above), Sandino's (see "Bars," above) and The Nerve Centre (see "Performance Halls," above). A degree-level art school is planned for the near future, which should inject a shot of adrenaline into the local art scene and sprinkle a few more boho faces around town.

MUSEUMS & ART GALLERIES

FREE → **Context Gallery** One of the two most exciting galleries in Derry, Context celebrates what it's already got at home, whereas Void ships in outsider artists to Derry. It showcases emerging local artists who are usually highly ratable. Now also home to the Maiden City Festival celebrating the oft-forgotten Protestant culture of the city. *5-7 Artillery St.* ☎ *028/7137-3538. context gallery@yahoo.co.uk. Free Admission. Tues–Sat 11am–5:30pm.*

MTV Best FREE → **Void** Oooh this place is exciting. It really sums up the spirit of all that's good about Derry—deadly serious but incredibly inspiring. English artist Colin Darke runs what is essentially an artist-led space committed to shipping in the best of international art. There's nothing fluffy here, just a range of ever-shifting video installations, multi-media pieces, and the usual sculpture and imagery. Sometimes hard hitting. Sometimes hilarious. Nearly always astounding. *Patrick St.* ☎ *028/7130-8080. Free admission. Tues–Sat 11am–5pm.*

FREE → **Amelia Earhart Centre** Located 4.8km (3 miles) north of Derry off the A2 road, this cottage commemorates Amelia Earhart's landing here in 1932, as the first woman to fly the Atlantic solo. The grounds encompass the Ballyarnett Community Farm and Wildlife Centre, with a range of farmyard animals and wildlife. *Ballyarnett, County Derry.* ☎ *028/7135-4040. Free admission. Cottage Mon–Thurs 10am–4pm, Fri 10am–1pm; farm and sanctuary daily 10am–dusk.*

→ **Tower Museum** Set in a medieval-style fort, this museum tells the history of Derry in a surprisingly entertaining way. Take a trip through time from prehistoric beginnings right up to today. There are also artifacts rescued from the Spanish Armada ships wrecked off the Irish coast in 1588 and a new Spanish Armada museum just opened in 2005. *Union Hall Place.* ☎ *028/7137-2411. Admission £4.20 adults, £2 students. July–Aug Mon–Sat 10am–5pm, Sun 2–5pm; Sept–June Tues–Sat 10am–5pm.*

FREE → **The Workhouse Museum and Library** Ever wondered if you'd have been tough enough to survive in a workhouse? Find out here. This museum tells a grim and moving tale of the Victorian workhouse, notorious for disease, misery, and death. Originally built to keep the poor from starving to death, workhouses were actually little more than concentration camps. It's all interesting stuff until the museum suddenly lurches off to include a bizarre exhibition on the Battle of the Atlantic, when Derry played a major role in the defeat of the Kriegsmarine, a German U-boat fleet that surrendered at Derry in 1945. Put it down to overenthusiasm. *23 Glendermott Rd., Waterside.* ☎ *028/7131-8328. Free admission. Year-round Tues–Sat 10am–4:30pm.*

➜ **Fifth Province** A multimedia exhibition whisking you through the history of Ireland's "Fifth Province," as it calls the world of the Celts. Travel in a "chariot" as the sexy Celtic warrior Calgach chats to you about the story of the Celts and famous Irish people who emigrated. By the end of all that enthusiastic brainwashing, you are thoroughly assimilated and profoundly believe that all the Irish must be geniuses. Time to go to the Genealogy museum and find out if you're one too. *4–22 Butcher St. Admission adults £3. Mon–Sat 9:30am–5pm.*

➜ **Genealogy Centre** If you think you might have a little bit of Northern Irish in you this is where to find out. Derry was one of the main ports for the exodus of thousands of emigrants to the New World in the 18th and 19th centuries. Ulster men and women became the second-most-numerous group in the colonial population, and played an important role in the settlement of the West. This heritage library and Genealogy Centre, in the heart of the old walled city, can help you research your Derry roots. *Heritage Library, 14 Bishop St. ☎ 028/7126-9792. www.irish roots.net/Derry.htm. £30 initial search fee. Mon–Fri 9am–5pm.*

HISTORIC BUILDINGS

MTV Best ➜ **The City Walls** A brilliant way to explore Derry is via its old stone walls. Climb to the top and you can circle the entire walled city in about 30 minutes. Start at the Diamond and walk down Butcher Street. You can climb the steps at Butcher's Gate—during the Troubles this was a security checkpoint between the Bogside and the city. Walk to the right past Castle Gate and Magazine Gate—once near a powder magazine. Shortly afterward you'll pass O'Doherty's Tower housing the five-star Tower Museum. From there you can see the brick walls of the Guildhall. Farther along you'll pass Shipquay Gate—once very near the port, back when the waters passed closer to the center. It's

uphill from there, past the Millennium Forum concert hall, to Ferryquay Gate. Here in 1689 local apprentice boys barred the gate against attacking forces, thus saving the town and leading to the siege. Next you'll pass Bishop's Gate. You should notice a tall brick tower just outside the gate—it's all that remains of the Old Gaol, where the rebel Wolfe Tone was imprisoned after his failed uprising in 1798. Farther along, the Double Bastion holds a military tower with elaborate equipment used to keep an eye on the Bogside—it's usually splashed by paint hurled at it by Republicans. From there you can easily access the serene churchyard of St. Columb's Cathedral. From the next stretch of wall you have a good view over the political murals of the Bogside down the hill. A bit farther along the wall an empty plinth stands where once there was a statue of Rev. George Walker, a governor of the city during the siege of 1699. It was blown up by the IRA in 1973. The small chapel nearby is the Chapel of St. Augustine (1872), and the building across the street from it with metal grates over the windows is the Apprentice Boys' Memorial Hall. Walk on a bit more and you're back to Butcher's Gate. *The City Walls. Open 24 hr.*

➜ **The Bogside** Just outside the walled city center, the Bogside developed in the 19th and early 20th centuries as a home to Catholic workers. By the 1960s it was overcrowded and rife with poverty and unemployment, making it ripe for revolution. In the late 1960s and 1970s, protests were regular events here, as Derry became the center of the Catholic civil rights movement. In 1969, protests morphed into riots, and the "Battle of the Bogside" unfolded over the course of 3 days, while fires burned and rocks were hurled at local police officers. At the end of it, the British government decided to base armed soldiers in Derry to keep the peace. By then relations between Catholics and the Protestant local government had broken down entirely. The 30,000 residents of the neighborhood declared their area as "Free Derry,"

Strut Your Stuff

Bet you didn't know Derry was once the epicenter of Victorian style. It's true. Back when Derry's elite lived inside the city walls and everyone else lived outside, a popular activity for the well-to-do ladies was to get dolled up in the latest fashions from London and parade around the walls all day, showing off their new duds. The disgruntled poor people down in the Bogside found this custom particularly offensive and got so fed up with it that they wrote to London newspapers, complaining about the shameless "cats" parading along the wall. The area around the wall became known as a "cat walk." Sound familiar? The expression stuck and is still used in the fashion world today.

independent of British and local government. They painted murals arguing their cause on the walls of their houses, and barricaded the soldiers and police out of the area. The Bogside was so dangerous for outsiders that even the military wouldn't go there without armored vehicles. Thus, in 1972, the civil rights march that attracted 20,000 marchers shouldn't have attracted particular attention, but for reasons still not fully understood, British troops opened fire on the marchers, in one of the worst atrocities of the Troubles (see "Sunday Bloody Sunday," above). Tensions remained through the 1970s and 1980s, but calmed in the 1990s. Most of the Bogside has been redeveloped now, with modern buildings replacing the old Victorian structures, and most of the population has moved elsewhere. But the Free Derry Corner remains near the house painted with the mural reading "You are Now Entering Free Derry." Near that is a memorial to those IRA members who died in hunger strikes in the 1970s.

A memorial stands on Rossville Street, where the Bloody Sunday shootings happened, commemorating those killed. *The Bogside.*

→ **Cathedral of St. Columb** An awesome Gothic building and the first cathedral to be built in Europe after the Reformation. Step inside to see scenes from the siege of Derry in 1688 and 1689 (King James II killed off loads of Derry citizens when he holed them up in the city walls until William of Orange came to the rescue) and the four original padlocks for the city gates. On the porch, a small stone inscribed "*In Templo Verus Deus Est Vereo Colendus*" (The true God is in His temple and is to be truly worshipped) is part of the original church built on this site in 1164. There's an old mortar shell on the porch as well—it was fired into the churchyard during the great siege; in its hollow core it held proposed terms of surrender. History at its most thrilling. *London St., Derry, County Derry.* ☎ *028/7126-7313. £1 donation requested. Mar–Oct Mon–Sat 9am–5pm; Nov–Feb Mon–Sat 9am–1pm and 2–4pm.*

FREE → **Guild Hall** Just outside the city walls, between Shipquay Gate and the River Foyle, this Tudor Gothic–style building looks much like its counterpart in London. The site's original structure was built in 1890, but it was rebuilt after a fire in 1908 and after a series of bombings in 1972. The hall is distinguished by its huge four-faced clock and its stained-glass windows, made by Ulster craftsmen, that illustrate almost every episode of note in the city's history. The hall is used as a civic and cultural center for concerts, plays, and exhibitions. *Shipquay Place, Derry, County Derry.* ☎ *028/7137-7335. Free admission. Mon–Fri 9am–5pm; Sat–Sun by appointment. Free guided tours July–Aug.*

FREE → **St. Eugene's Cathedral** Designed in the Gothic Revival style, this is Derry's Catholic cathedral, nestled in the heart of the Bogside district just beyond the city walls. The foundation stone was laid in

1851, but work continued until 1873. The spire was added in 1902. It's built of local sandstone and is known for stained-glass windows by the famed makers of stained glass, Meyer and Co. of Munich, depicting the Crucifixion. *Fransic St., Derry, County Derry. Free admission. Mon–Sat 7am–9pm; Sun 7am–6:30pm.*

PLAYING OUTSIDE

BICYCLING   Whether you want to rent a bike and do your own thang or sign up for a herd tour of County Derry and County Donegal, **An Mointean Rent-a-Bike and Cycle Tours** (245 Lone Moor Rd.; ☎ **028/7128-7128**), offers sound service. Rental of mountain or touring bikes costs £10 a day, £45 a week.

HORSEBACK RIDING   Ardmore Stables (8 Rushall Rd., Ardmore; ☎ **028/7134-5187**), offers lessons, trail rides, and pony trekking. Across the border, only 6.5km (4 miles) from Derry in County Donegal, **Lenamore Stables** (Muff, Inishowen; ☎ **077/718-4022;** lenamorestable@eircom.net), also offers lessons and trekking, and somewhere to stay.

WALKING   Just outside the city, off the main Derry-Belfast road, the Ness Woods have beautiful walks, nature trails, and the North's highest waterfall.

WATERSPORTS   Perched above the city, **Creggan County Park** (☎ **028/7136-3133;** www.creggancountrypark.com) can sort out your need to get wet. Canoeing, sailing, kayaking, and windsurfing are all available as is the no-skill-needed banana boat ride, or even pier jumping. On land is the "gorge walk"—a chance to get really dirty and soaked, scrambling over rocks and wading through ravines. The activity center itself has showers, a cafe, and a sweet store, all under a turf roof with power partly provided by a wind turbine, *and* environmental angels can rest even easier as all the center's CO_2 emissions are neutralized.

12 Hours In . . . Derry (Walking Tour)

Wake up at dawn and have the city walls all to yourself. OK, wake up a little later and join a Free Derry tour to get the lowdown on the Republican battle. Take a stroll along the River Foyle and get lunch at Sandino's. Explore the interior of the Walled City in the afternoon making sure to stop off at The Nerve Centre to find out what's going down this evening. Pop into Derry's top shops Trip and Flip (no, it's not a joke) before getting some serious mind stimuli at the Void gallery.

SHOPPING

The city center is a mixture of the usual drab chains—largely housed in the two ugly shopping centers—and the odd little nugget of pure shopping gold. Most stores are open Monday to Saturday 9am to 5:30pm. Shops in shopping centers are open Monday to Wednesday and Saturday 9am to 5:30pm, Thursday and Friday 9am to 9pm. In the summer, some shops are open on Sunday.

General

→ **Austin & Co., Ltd**   No, you're probably not going to swoon with excitement when you see this department store's collections of perfumes, china, crystal, and linens, but it is Ireland's oldest department store, established in 1839, so definitely worth a quick browse. Plus, their coffee shop has while-away-a-couple-of-hours panoramic views over the city. *The Diamond.* ☎ *028/7126-1817.*

→ **Derry Craft Village**   Derry's old quarter packed with buildings from the 16th to the 19th centuries. Grab a secondhand book from Foyle books, find your inner yogi at Equilibrium alternative therapies center, or simply kit yourself out for Irish dancing—complete with blonde wig and leg warmers—from Fascinating Rhythm. Put on a show—or recover—in the tearoom. *Shipquay St. (enter on Shipquay or Magazine St.).* ☎ 028/7126-0329.

Books

→ **Bookworm Bookshop & Coffee Shop** The usual classics and fiction with a focus on Irish titles all wrapped up in an appealing old red building. Also offering a handy out-of-print search service for hunting down that elusive Victorian title on botany for the beginner. *18–20 Bishop St.* ☎ 028/7128-2727. *www.bookwormderry.com.*

Clothes

→ **Trip** Get the Derry look at Trip, an independent clothing company set up by two style-aware brothers. Squeeze in alongside Derry trendsetters and students to flick through clothes racks hanging everything from Carharrt, Criminal, Converse, and Roxy to small designers you've never heard of but wish you had. Most shoppers end up with a non-commercial blend of jeans and bright, clean tops with a bias toward streetwear. Not your style? There's just about enough on offer to buck the trend. *3–5 London St.* ☎ 028/7126-5554. *Sun opening 1–5:30pm.*

→ **Flip** This is where the cool kids come to buy their clothes. Run by Mark Kenny for over a decade, it has enough vintage and brand gear to live whatever life you'd like to lead. Wanna be an oh-so-cool biker? He's got vintage leather. A raging skinhead? Try on a Harrington jacket. A blissed out hippy? One of his funky floral dresses or shirts will get you to the Age of Aquarius in style. Need a style guru? Take a leaf from the drop-dead-gorgeous shop assistants. They're not only handsome, they're smart too. *29 Ferryquay St.* ☎ 028/7137-2382.

Music

→ **Cool Discs Music** Run by the Byronic Lee Mason, this shop has a mission, "to turn people on to as much music as we can." Hence the large shop floor is filled with everything

from dance to death metal with a noticeable commitment to underground tunes and the Irish scene. As Lee adds, "Once a record is numbered in the top 10 our job is done." The staff are hugely knowledgeable and usually DJs and musicians themselves. *6/7 Lesley House, Foyle St.* ☎ 028/7126-0770.

→ **Vinyl Junkie** If you hadn't guessed by the name it's all about the mighty beat in here, a tiny dance music den packed with breakz, trance, techno, house, and all that's in between. And there are no nasty surprises when you get home as there's a listening post in the corner. Owner Darren McMenamin, a regular Lush DJ, hopes his new venture will become a hangout for young dance obsessives. Looks likely. *11 Magazine St.* ☎ 028/7130-9077.

Causeway Coast & Glens of Antrim: Portrush

Portrush's star is on the rise. Once a faded beach resort with nothing more to recommend it than Barry's Big Dipper (Don't worry this fairground attraction is still there if you fancy a ride), Portrush is rapidly morphing into a hot destination for world-class surfing and Northern Irish food. A mighty fine combination. It's still not much to look at but behind that facade of prissy B&Bs Portrush's heart is pumping.

Because of its proximity to the big city, Portrush is a major party destination for university students from Belfast—and young people from every other town in the region—so the crowd here is much younger and more rockin' than in other mega-touristy Northern towns like, say, Newcastle. Come here during high season and you'll have a blast. Come here in low season and, well, you'll have a blast too.

What Portrush really excels at is being an orgiastic center of post-adolescent partying. If you're young, like to dance, and pour substances in your body that make you feel funny, this is the place to be. People here don't seem to acknowledge that it never gets much above 20°C (68°F) here. You'll see kids partying with their shirts off around bonfires at the beach in the middle of the chilly summer, and crazy surfers sealed tight inside rubber suits and masks in the middle of freakin' January going absolutely ape on their boards.

Whenever you're here, make sure you go to Kelly's (see "Partying," below), a giant estate of a club attracting all the international big guns to its multiple DJ stages.

GETTING THERE & GETTING AROUND

BY BUS **Ulsterbuses** (www.translink.co. uk) run to and from Belfast, Bushmills, Giant's Causeway, and Ballycastle from the station on Dunluce Street (☎ 028/7126-2261) at the south end of downtown.

BY TRAIN Catch a big steel ride out of town at the **Eglinton St. Station,** Eglinton St. (☎ 02870/822-395) with connections to and from Belfast and Derry by way of Coleraine, five to nine times a day.

ON FOOT Feet will mostly do the job; otherwise, **Portrush Taxis** (☎ 028/7082-3483) will get you out to Kelly's (see "Partying," below) and **Bicycle Doctor** (104 Lower Main St.; ☎ 028/7082-4340; £10 per day) is located downtown.

BASICS

EMERGENCY In an emergency call ☎ **999.** The local **police station** can be found at 81A Strand Rd. (☎ **0845 600 8000**). There are no hospitals in Portrush.

PHARMACY **Heron Chemists** (5/9 Main St., ☎ 028/7082-2324; daily 9am–6pm, till 10:30pm, July–Aug) is in the downtown area.

POST OFFICE The **post office** (23 Eglinton St.; ☎ 028/7082-3700; Monday to Friday 9am–12:30pm and 1:30–5:30pm, Saturday 9am–12:30pm) is at the intersection of Eglinton Street and Causeway Road downtown.

TOURIST INFORMATION You got questions? **Dunluce Center** (Sandhill Rd.; ☎ **028/7082-3333;** June to August daily 9am–7pm; April to May and September, Monday to Friday 9am–5pm, Saturday to Sunday noon–5pm; October to March, Saturday and Sunday noon–5pm) has answers.

SLEEPING

Crashing on the cheap in Portrush is easy. There is only one small hostel but dozens of B&B's line the streets along the peninsula. Even so, reserve in the summer and on weekends to avoid being shut out or paying a lot of dough.

Run by a delightful husband and wife team called Gary and Kirsty (and their dog Murphy), **Best Macool's Portrush Youth Hostel** (5 Causeway View Terrace; ☎ **028/7082-4845;** www.portrush-hostel. com; dorm beds £10, twin room £24; one double room £28) is small and friendly, and a real treat. The showers are hot ALL day and the beach is right behind the hostel. Dorms are a bit small and cramped, but the beds (there are 25) are noticeably bigger and more comfortable than most hostels. Bathrooms and common areas are clean and exceedingly comfortable. It feels more like staying at a friend's house than a hostel. The kitchen is spotless, and big jars of curry, oregano, and other spices make cooking here a real pleasure. Macool's can also hook you up with local surf schools or give you the lowdown on what to see in the area, together with a complete history of the various ruins, myths, and attractions you might spot on your travels. Internet access is also available at a cost of £4 per hour.

Kerr Street, on the west side of the peninsula, along the water, is packed with B&Bs, all virtually identical: clean, pretty cheap, and close to the water. A place unknown to most budget travelers, the **Alexander House B&B** (23 Kerr St.; ☎ **028/7082-4566;**

£10 per bed in four-bed room; £32 double, breakfast included) is the only B&B in town with hostel-priced accommodations. The place is clean and basic, nothing fancy, but totally comfy and friendly. Another good Kerr Street option, **Brae Mar B&B** (28 Kerr St.; ☎ 028/7082-5224; £25 single, £40 double) is as basic and clean as the Alexander, but a bit smaller and more intimate. **Rest-a-While B&B** (Atlantic Ave.; ☎ 028/7082-2827; £24 single, £45 double) gives good bed without the frills.

Another option, a little way back from the sea but still only a very short walk from all the goings on, is **Abercorn Guesthouse** (57 Coleraine Rd.; ☎ 028/7082-5014; www.abercornportrush.co.uk; £20 single; £40 double (£4.50 more per person during July and Aug). Rooms are very flowery and colorful but clean. Breakfasts are big. There are TVs in all rooms and the family running the place is extremely friendly.

EATING

Fish and chips used to be all a traveler could get to eat in Portrush. Not any more. Now it's gourmet all the way. Some of the new eateries do cost a little more but lunch menus are often cheaper and the grease shops continue churning out their wares across town. **558 North** (1 Causeway St.; ☎ 028/7082-2811; mains at dinner £6.50–£16, mains at lunch £4–£5) is a great place to get acquainted with the beauty of the Atlantic Ocean thanks to its position overlooking the sea. The interior is a mixture of Scandinavian light woods and urbane animal prints. Sounds out of place but it works, creating a serene spacious vibe in contrast to the raging sea behind. At night, mains such as seared scallops with roast tomato and rocket or Irish salmon with bacon and savoy cabbage—although still under a tenner—may be a bit of a stretch, but during the day fish pies, pasta, burgers, and soups go for under a fiver. However watch out for the extras when trying to total up the cost of your meal. This is one of those cheeky places charging extra for veg.

Ramore Wine Bar (The Harbour, off Kerr St.; ☎ 028/7082-4313; pizzas and pastas in Coast £4.25–£6.95, other mains to £13) is part of a groovy eating-drinking collective consisting of Coast serving contemporary pizzas and pastas; or posh steaks, burgers, fusion meats, and seafood served in the cozy harbor bistro at the back of the old pub (see "Partying," below) or in the glam wine bar looking out across the harbor. There's no fussy service here; it's all pay-at-the-bar-and-find-your-own-seat type dining. The food is all good value for what you get but maybe not every day eating unless the limit on Daddy's credit card is sky high.

Another doable option is **The Blue Duck** (mains £7.25–£13; lunch and dinner daily) upstairs from Rogues Bar (see "Partying," below) where the focus is on fish fresh from the ocean: halibut, salmon, sole, cod—mostly from Donegal. The interior is not as trendy as Ramore and 558 North, more a light-pine-meets-the-Mediterranean look but it's both bright, warm, and unbothersome in the way that neutral colors are. If fish isn't your thing there are duck breasts and steaks too.

Those on cheap street will find basic and tasty little sandwich combinations at **Bread Shop** (21 Eglinton St.; ☎ 028/7082-3722; under £4; no credit cards), as well as greasy and delicious cod and chips. And it's easy to find, right next to the post office (see "Basics," above).

Down near the tourist information center is the **Café in the Center** (Dunluce Ave.; ☎ 028/7082-4444; main courses £2–£5; no credit cards) a Victorian-theme bi-level restaurant with a menu including sandwiches, omelets, salads, pastas, and steaks, as well as sausage, beans, and "Ulster fry" (a cheese-and-onion pie).

Hey, nobody's saying they serve the greatest food in the world at **Lucky House**

Chinese (53 Eglinton Ave.; ☎ 028/7082-3855; mains £3–£8), but it's on the south end of downtown, open late, and there's nothing like eating fried wontons at two in the morning on a Saturday after a night of debauchery at a local pub or club.

PARTYING

The summer months sees her shores hopping with beach parties—sort of like a refrigerated "MTV Spring Break." And, don't fret when the weather gets cold, the pubs stay open late here. Closing time is officially 1am at most bars, but it's not uncommon to see people staggering home at 4am. If police roll up, Portrush pub staff can clear every drop of liquor off the tables in under a minute to avoid a beefy fine. It's quite a sight to see. As soon as the fuzz rolls on, the fun begins again. There are also a couple of clubs here that stay open all night—including Kelly's (see "Bars & Clubs")—they're always full of kids from Belfast. Unlike the pubs, these places are allowed to stay open.

Bars & Clubs

Are you so fabulous it's difficult finding a club big enough to contain your raging party fury? One that has more bars than you can count on your hand and big-time DJs like Digweed and Judge Jules to blow your mind with all-night grooves? Officially known as Beetles Bar and Disco, 🎬 Best **Kelly's Nightclub** (Bushmill's Rd., right outside of town; ☎ 028/7082-3539; www.kellysportrush.co. uk; cover £5–£12) could be your salvation. All the major disc-spinners, from London to Ibiza show up at Kelly's. Thousands of kids pack the place every weekend for Lush!—the biggest party in Ireland. All sorts of all ages come here to get down. Just one rule, and it's a biggie: No sneakers. Otherwise, it's usually easy to get in. The music is everything you could imagine, depending on which end of the club you're in. The biggest parties are usually the trance/rave ones. Not to be missed.

It'll seem a step down by comparison but **The Harbour Bar** (5 Harbour Rd.; ☎ 028/7082-2430) is a gorgeous old fishermen's pub attracting a diverse crowd of locals and tourists (and it stays open late). This is where you'll find that cute guy/girl you saw out on the waves earlier today as its surfers' territory. A post-surf, early-evening drink outside the pub doors, overlooking the harbor is a must in the summer. On cold evenings snuggle up beside the salty sea dogs propping up the ancient, fire-warmed bar inside.

Rogues (54 Kerr St.; ☎ 028/7082-2076) has more locals than other pubs in town, but they'll still chat to out-of-towners (as long as you're not tanked up and mouthing off). Just across from the Harbour Bar, it's where to watch all the big sport matches, play pool, tap those brown toes along to trad music 7 nights a week in summer (from Thurs–Sun in the winter) and generally drink and put the world to rights until the wee hours of the morning.

The latest spot in town is the **Harbour Lounge,** part of the Harbour Bar collective (see "Eating," above). The more sophisticated groovsters gather here when the madness of Lush has got too much. Only just opened in 2005, it's the town's latest hotspot, entertaining with funky live bands in sleek surrounds decked out in dark wood and red drapes. A luxe option, it feels decidedly hip for these surroundings, with video screens flashing pop lovelies at a crowd of well-dressed 20- and 30-somethings.

SIGHTSEEING

Yes, there is culture even in such a hedonistic party town. You just have to hike a bit to find it.

🎬 Best →**Dunluce Castle** The castle is best reached by a beautiful 5km (3-mile) walk up the beach from Portrush (then take the winding road that'll bring you right here). As the tourist brochure says, "Like something out of a Tolkien fantasy, the ruins of Dunluce Castle have a desolate, awe-inspiring grandeur as they rise dramatically from a precipitous basaltic rock standing over a hundred-foot sheer above the wild and chill northern sea." Hmmm. Anyway, the ruins are great. Really, really great. See them at sunset and they appear as if from a film set, teetering on the top of the cliffs, black against the orange sky. One night in 1639 in the middle of a dinner party at the castle, the kitchen fell off into the sea, proving that too many cooks in the kitchen really do spoil the broth . . . . Skip the boring stuff in the information center and make for the ruins. There are some wonderful, still intact archways and intricate carvings in the windows. *87 Dunluce Rd. (5.6km/3½ miles east of Portrush off A2), Bushmills, County Antrim.* ☎ *028/2073-1938. www.northantrim.com/ dunlucecastle.htm. Admission £2.50 adults. Apr–May and Sept Mon–Sat 10am–6pm, Sun 2–6pm; June–Aug Mon–Sat 10am–6pm, Sun noon–6pm; Oct–Mar Mon–Sat 10am–4pm, Sun 2–4pm. Last admission 30 min. before closing.*

Over in sibling surf town Portstewart the **Flowerfield Arts Centre** (185 Coleraine Rd.; ☎ 028/7083-1400; www.flowerfield.org) offers up small doses of culture in the form of exhibitions from genuinely exciting Irish artists, together with the occasional musical performance in the evening. A coffee shop on-site provides more practical sustenance.

SHOPPING

When too many chemicals begin to fry the brain **Blue Moon** (3 Causeway St.; ☎ 028/ 7082-5365) provides alternative healing treatments. Waft away that headache with crystals and dragon balm, or sit back and let a dreamcatcher direct sweeter thoughts into your mind while listening to a self-help tape. If that's not enough, there are tarot cards and hippy-dippy clothing. In fact, everything the alternative might require on a restorative break beside the sea.

Other than that, the only interesting shops in Portrush are of the watersports variety. **Woody's Surfshop** (102 Main St.; ☎ 028/ 7082-3273) hires out wetsuits, surfboards, and bodyboards for a fiver while stocking branded surf and street wear such as Killah, Roxy, Blu, Paul Frank, and Fenchurch. But the real place to go if you're even considering getting wet in Portrush is **Troggs** (88 Main St.; ☎ 028/7082-5476; www.troggs surfshop.co.uk), two floors of surf and skate gear for hard-core pros and hard-partying beginners. Run by local surf kings Ian and Andy Hill, all their boys in the shop possess a fearless addiction to some type of extreme sport—just look out for the ones with scars and limps. Good advice is guaranteed. They've taken the beatings so you don't have to. When it comes to getting kitted out for the next beach party, you're on your own— Quicksilver, Billabong, Animal, and Roxy brands are all represented here. If you're looking to stay in these parts a while, this is the biggest selection of boards and wetsuits in Ireland so a good place to buy.

PLAYING OUTSIDE

DIVING **Aquaholics** (14 Portmore Rd., 250m from Portstewart Harbor in the direction of Portrush; ☎ 028/7083-2584; www. aquaholics.org) is a five-star PADI center offering open water courses for £395 and diving trips to the numerous reefs and wrecks in the area from £35 (experienced divers only), as well as powerboating trips along the wild coastline for £95 per hour—you will get wet; waterproofs are provided.

HORSEBACK RIDING **Maddybenny Riding Centre** (Maddybenny Farmhouse, Atlantic Rd.; ☎ 028/7082-3394; www. maddybenny.freeserve.co.uk) offers hacks in the surrounding countryside for £10 per hour. Hugely friendly old-timers Eric and Rosemary, also run a renowned B&B in their 17th-century farmhouse. At £55 for a double, it's not quite hitting in the bargain basement arena but the house is gorgeous and the breakfasts—complete with Drambuie in the porridge—are legendary.

SURFING   Surfing has really taken off in Northern Ireland over the past decade. There are numerous places to let rip along this coastline and a beach for pretty much all conditions (check www.troggssurfshop.co.uk for a guide to eleven beaches in the area). The surf really starts to get exciting in September when the storms hitting the U.S. East Coast make their presence felt on the other side of the Atlantic in the form of a huge swell. Some people say it's as good as Hawaii—minus the tropical sun—but there's nobody fighting the fact it's world class.

The summer sees local Northern Irish surfers out on the waves while the winter attracts travelers and surfers from around the globe. Whatever level you're at, if you haven't been here before check in with the surf schools for advice on where's best to stay safe in the current conditions. If you're a novice don't even think about going out on the water without a lesson.

Alive Bodyboard and Surf School (☎ 028/2074-1662, 0774-386-0509; www.alivesurfschool.com) offers bodyboarding and surfing with eight times national champion Bryan McAuley, a man who's surfed around the globe and still rates the Northern Irish waves as some of the best. Tagging along on one of his daily sessions costs £20. **Troggs** (see "Shopping," above) also runs their own surf school. Those crazy madcap guys will get you out in the water in January if you're up for it.

SKYDIVING   Take to the sky—for a few brilliantly terrifying minutes—with 📺 (Best) **Wild Geese Parachute Company** (116 Carrowreagh Rd., Garvagh, Coleraine; from Portrush follow the A29 to Coleraine, then on as if to Derry, stopping at Garvagh where there are signposts to Wild Geese; ☎ 028/2995-8609; www.wildgeese.demon.co.uk; open all year

Sorry, what was That? I couldn't Hear a word you were Saying.

Don't spend a season in the Irish water without wearing earplugs. It's not because it's dirty—this water is lovely and clean—it's because it's cold. Really cold. Freezing cold. Northern Ireland doesn't benefit from the Gulf Stream that warms up the coast of much of the U.K. Consequently surfers are at risk of developing Surfer's Ear or Diffuse Exostosis, a bone growth that blocks up the ear canal and can lead to constant ear infections and even deafness.

except for 2 weeks around Christmas). A "self-opening" static-line jump from 450m (3,500 ft.) costs £170 (inclusive of one day's training) or jet straight up to 390m (13,000 ft.) for a tandem jump attached to an instructor for £225. Learn to free-fall in just six jumps for £270.

WAKEBOARDING   Ireland's ex-number-one wakeboarder Peter Stewart runs coaching sessions from Loughan Marina in Coleraine through **Irish Wakeboarding** (☎ 07890/543-231; www.irishwakeboarding.com). They also offer water-skiing, bare-footing, banana boating, tube rides, Canadian canoeing, and water trampolining. If after all that exertion you don't fancy trekking back to Portrush there are a number of four-bed chalets available overlooking the water.

Bushmills

This little town is primarily a Protestant enclave, but you've likely come here to worship at a different altar: the Old Bushmills' Distillery.

GETTING THERE

Buses go from Portrush or Ballycastle to Bushmills only a couple of times a day, so plan ahead. Call **Ulsterbus** (☎ **028/9035-1201**) for schedule info. Bushmills is a 15-minute ride from Portrush, even closer to the Giant's Causeway.

SLEEPING & EATING

If you need a place to line your tummy for the impending whiskey deluge, the distillery has a cafe serving up tea, cakes, and sandwiches, or you can try **Valerie's Pantry** (125 Main St; ☎ **028/2073-2660**) where they also dish out sandwiches and burgers.

If you get stuck here for the night, don't just pass out in the street— there's a fairly new hostel on the scene called **Bushmills** (Mill Rest, 49 Main St.; ☎ **028/2073-1222; dorms £12**). A snazzy exterior makes it look more like a modern villa on the Mediterranean than a wind-battered Irish hostel. Inside are 74 beds, mostly in four-bed dorms. All are en suite and—wait for it— some even have baths outside on a little garden patio. If hostels aren't your bag try **Ballyness Bed & Breakfast** (38 Castlecat Rd.; ☎ **028/2073-1438; doubles £46**), a centrally heated farmhouse just half a mile from the distillery itself, with en suite showers.

SIGHTSEEING

MTV Best ➔ **The Bushmills' Distillery**
The one highlight in this otherwise unfantastic little town. Licensed to distill spirits in 1608, but with hints they were cooking up the old moonshine here as far back as 1276, this is the oldest distillery in the world. Watch and learn as fresh water comes in from the nearby River Bush and turns into whiskey via distillation, fermentation, and bottling. For your money you get a tour of the old distillery and a much-coveted sample of this smooth, blended whiskey. At the end of the tour, they'll ask you who wants to taste five different flavors of Scotch. Don't raise your hand! It's a trick question. We're in Ireland,

not Scotland, remember? Wait till all the rubes are found out, then raise your hand when they ask who wants proper Irish whiskey and get five free samples. Yee-haw! *Main St., Bushmills, County Antrim. ☎ 028/2073-1521. www.bushmills.com. Admission £4 adults, £3.50 students. Apr–Oct tours offered frequently throughout the day Mon–Sat 9:30am–5:30pm, Sun noon–5:30pm (last tour leaves 4pm); Nov–Mar tours offered Mon–Sat at 10:30am, 11:30am, 1:30, 2:30, and 3:30pm, Sun at 1:30, 2:30, and 3:30pm. Closed Good Friday, July 12, Christmas, New Year's Day.*

The Giant's Causeway

At the foot of a cliff by the sea, this mysterious mass of tightly packed hexagonal basalt columns is incredible.

GETTING THERE

Take **Ulsterbus** (☎ **090/351201**) from Portrush or Ballycastle. Buses leave twice a day from both of these places taking you to within a stone's throw of the entrance. Belfast and Derry also have tourist buses making trips here several times a day. Check with the tourist offices in those cities or at any youth hostel for more info.

BASICS

TOURIST INFORMATION **The Causeway Visitor's Center** (at the car park at the entrance to the Causeway Trail; ☎ **028/2073-1855**; June, daily 10am–6pm; July to August, daily 10am–7pm; March to May and September, daily 10am–5pm; £3 parking; free admission) does the whole question-and-answer thing.

SLEEPING

If you want to stay here, your only option is the **Causeway Hotel** (40 Causeway Rd.; ☎ **028/2073-1226**; double £70–£80) where rooms are all en suite and all soulless. We recommend you make the commute to Portrush or Ballycastle where accommodation is cheaper and livelier.

The Water of Life

Monks did a lot for Ireland. They painstakingly crafted the Book of Kells. They protected Irish antiquities in their round towers during invasions. But ask your average man on the Irish street, and he may say that the best thing monks did for Ireland was invent whiskey.

You read that right—monks invented whiskey. In about the 6th century, missionary monks brought the secret of distillation home from the Middle East, forever changing the face of Ireland. Irish whiskey is known all over the world for its smoothness and quality, and it has brought Ireland huge revenues over the centuries. The original Gaelic term for whiskey, *uisce beatha* (pronounced *ish*-ka *ba*-ha) means "water of life."

Whiskey became more than just a home brew in 1608, when the world's first distillery license was given to Old Bushmills Distillery. Next came John Jameson & Son in 1780 and John Powers & Son in 1791. These licenses blew open the whiskey export trade in Ireland, and the world's love affair with Irish whiskey began. By the end of the 19th century, more than 400 brands were available in American alone.

Prohibition put an end to such shenanigans in 1919. Then bootleggers began distributing lousy liquor under the respected name of Irish whiskey, destroying its reputation.

Meanwhile, Ireland and England were engaged in an economic war and stopped buying each other's products completely. With Irish whiskey out of the picture, Scotch jumped in to fill the void. Only recently has Irish whiskey become internationally popular again.

If you want to talk poncey while you sup, you need to know Irish whiskey has a distinctive smoothness, resulting from its triple-distillation (American whisky is distilled only once and Scotch, twice).

Want to find out more? Three historic distilleries are open for tours: The Old Bushmills Distillery, Bushmills (see "Bushmills," above); The Old Jameson Distillery, Dublin (see Dublin chapter, p. 98); and the Old Midleton Distillery, Cork (see Cork chapter, p. 261).

EATING

If you want a bite, head for the **Causeway Hotel** (see "Sleeping," above), where you can get chips and chicken or fish for around £7—but do it before 6pm. You can also grab a light meal at the Tea Room in the **Causeway Visitor's Center** (see "Tourist Information," above). **The Nook** at the Giant's Causeway now serves rather fine meals stuffed with health and local produce, in the old Causeway School (48 Causeway Rd.; ☎ **028/2073-2993**) located at the entrance to the Causeway itself.

SIGHTSEEING

The 📺 (Best) **Giant's Causeway** shares the title "The Eighth Wonder of the World" with enormities found in America such as the "World's Largest Ball of Twine," and wrestling legend Andre the Giant. It's definitely the more deserving. Thousands of hexagonal basalt pillars jut out from the sea all along the shoreline. Together they make a huge plane of geometrically pleasing steps.

There's a scientific explanation for the existence of these pillars. Millions of years ago, as molten igneous basalt rose up from shallow fissures in the earth, its uneven cooling led to the natural emergence of a crystalline pattern. Got all that?

The mythic—and much more fun—explanation concerns the legendary Irish giant Finn McCool who wanted to see his Scottish girlfriend and built these stepping stones to skip over to Staffa Island (the only other place where these kinds of pillars exist) for the night. Why he'd need 37,000 steps is beyond modern explanation. *Causeway Rd. Bushmills, County Antrim.* ☎ *028/2073-1582. www.giantscausewayofficialguide.com. Apr–Sept daily 10am–6pm; Oct–Mar daily 10am–4:30pm.*

Ballintoy/Carrick-A-Rede Island

Between Ballycastle and Portrush sits the village of Ballintoy, and another must-see Antrim attraction, the Carrick-A-Rede Island rope bridge.

GETTING THERE

If you're driving or biking to Ballintroy, take the A2 onto the B15 between Portrush and Ballycastle. From Ballycastle, head west on the A2 and turn right onto the B15 about 3.2 km (2 miles) out of town then continue on for 8 km (5 miles). Generally car is the only way to get here, but in the summer a shuttle bus runs between The Giant's Causeway and the Carrick-A-Rede Island rope bridge.

SLEEPING & EATING

There is a little hostel in Ballintoy, the **Sheep Island View Hostel** (42 Main St.; ☎ **028/ 2076-2470;** www.sheepislandview.com; £10 en suite dorm), that is a standard issue hostel with lounge, kitchen, and Internet access. Pluses are the attached village store for provision purchases and roaring fires inside the main hostel. If you're planning on staying here phone ahead as they run a free pickup service from Portrush, Ballycastle, Bushmills, and The Giant's Causeway. There's camping outside in the adjacent field at a fiver per person, for which you can use all the hostel

facilities. Nearby is the **Whitepark Bay International Youth Hostel** (157 Whitepark Rd.; leave Ballycastle on coast road A2 towards Bushmills. Pass through Ballintoy and above is approx 3 miles on right. ☎ **028/2073-1745;** www.hini.org.uk; dorm £12) with a fab panoramic lounge overlooking a beach where few tourists wander. There are 54 beds here mostly in four-bed dorms. It attracts a lot of cyclists on the 93 national cycle route along the coast.

Teahouse (121a Whitepark Rd.; ☎ **028/ 2076-2178**) operates at the bridge in spring and summer, offering decent scones and warm drinks.

SIGHTSEEING

MTV Best ➔ **Carrick-A-Rede Rope Bridge** Carrick-A-Rede Island is connected to the mainland only by an 18m (60-ft.) long swaying rope bridge over a 24m (80-ft.) drop into the drink. It's not as sketchy as it sounds: The bridge is heavily reinforced with nylon cords and sturdy planks. Local fishermen put up the bridge each spring to allow access to the island's salmon fishery, but visitors can use it for a thrilling walk and the chance to call out to each other, "Don't look down!" (This is excellent advice.) If you are acrophobic, stay clear; if you don't know whether you are—or what the word means—the middle of the bridge is not the place to find out. *Larrybane, County Antrim.* ☎ *028/2073-1582. Admission £2.20 adults. Bridge, center, and tearoom Apr–June and early Sept daily 10am–6pm; July–Aug 10am–7pm. Depending on weather.*

PLAYING OUTSIDE

The 19km (12-mile) coastal cliff path from the Giant's Causeway to the rope bridge is always open and is well worth the exhaustion. The cliffs are huge and the views are extreme and rugged.

Ballycastle

Not as rowdy as its die-hard party-town cousin, Portrush, this cute little seaside town offers more relaxed charm. It's close to all the major attractions of the region, has some fine pubs, good nearby outdoor activities, and is overall a pleasant place to spend a day or two.

GETTING THERE

BY BUS **Ulsterbus** (☎ **028/9035-1201**) runs to and from Portrush and Belfast several times a day.

BASICS

EMERGENCY **Dalriada Hospital** (Colraine Rd.; ☎ **028/7076-2666**) is the local care facility.

PHARMACY **McMichael's** (10 Ann St.; ☎ **028/2076-3342**; Mon–Sat 9am–1pm and 2–6pm) is about the only pill source in town.

POST OFFICE The **post office** (3 Ann St.; ☎ **028/2076-2519**) is there whatever the weather, except on Wednesday afternoons, when it closes.

TOURIST INFORMATION The **Ballycastle Tourist Information Office** (7 Mary St.; ☎ **028/1076-2024**; July and Aug Mon–Fri 9:30am–7pm, Sat 10am–6pm, Sun 2–6pm; Sep–June Mon–Fri 9:30am–5pm) in Ballycastle is excellent with loads of printouts on what to do in the area, where to eat, and how to get there on public transport, plus the staff are really helpful. It may be small but it's one of the best in Northern Ireland. Refreshingly more interested in giving you info than selling you books.

ORIENTATION

Ballycastle is centered around one main street running in a southwesterly direction away from Ballycastle Bay, changing names a few times along the way. Starting at the water it is Quay Road, then Ann Street, then Castle Street. Most of what you'll visit in Ballycastle is along this stretch. Along the shore, Mary Road runs out to the southeast from the main street, while North Street goes to the northeast. The Diamond, a square formed at the

end of Ann Street by the intersection of several roads, acts as the tiny town's center.

SLEEPING

The most popular hostel in town is the **Castle Hostel** (62 Quay Rd.; ☎ **028/2076-2337**; www.castlehostel.com; £8 dorm; £20 double; £25 triple). It's big and bright and right in the middle of things, down by the bay. Outside is pink and Victorian. Inside is warm and filled with friendly people, usually gathered around the open fire. The staff is keen to take travelers along to local music sessions and the owners are proud of the romances quota among previous guests, even laying claim to one hostel baby. Don't say you haven't been warned.

Ballycastle Backpackers (4 North St.; ☎ **028/2076-3612**; £7 dorm) is another decent hostel option. It's also right on the water, and some rooms have a view of the sea. Dorms are a bit tiny for full-grown people, but comfortable enough.

Also handy to the waterfront, is **Glenluce Guest House** (42 Quay Rd.; ☎ **028/2076-2914**; £25 single, £50 double) which has loads of rooms, some en suite. They don't mind travelers checking in early if the room's free—handy when you've caught the first bus into town and don't want to haul your bags around all day. The breakfast is a buffet, not a stunner, but extra helpings compensate for the lack of taste.

EATING

The best cheap spot to eat in town has to be **The Park Deli** (5 Quay Rd.; ☎ **028/2076-8563**; mains £4.99, sandwiches from £2, paninis from £3.25) on the main road to the harbor. A fine array of European cheeses and salamis greets you on entering. And, if you've got an imagination when it comes to sandwiches, the staff will try to find the fillings to match. Larger stomachs are waved at by pies, quiches, wraps, lasagnas, and baked potatoes, while meals are rounded off with homemade cakes. A perfect place to shop for picnic provisions. In the evening it comes over all bistro.

Further cheap treats can be found up the road at **Donnelly's Coffee Shop** (28 Ann St.; ☎ 028/2076-3236; pastries 60p, pies £1.50) where lovely old ladies doll out all sorts of fattening cakes, pastries, and pies. Nearby **Heralds Restaurant** (22 Ann St., ☎ 028/2076-9064; mains £4–£5) has dozens of dishes for under a fiver including Irish stews, lasagnas, fry-ups, and curries.

For a splurge option try the **Cellar Restaurant** (11B The Diamond; ☎ 028/2076-3037; mains £10–£15) a surprisingly decent restaurant largely serving fish. The menu changes according to what's been landed that day by local fishing family The Mortons. It can include Dover sole, lobster, skate, crab, and wild salmon. Afters are homemade puddings such as pavlova. Eaters sit on wooden church pews, warming themselves by the wood-burning stove. Book if you want a table; this place starts to fill up from teatime with travelers from across the area.

PARTYING

Considering the size of this tiny town there is a high proportion of pubs. Locals say it's about one to every 250 people, and on some nights it can seem like they're all out on the town. Pubs shut down around midnight, but you can usually hang out for an hour more. In the summer, they'll be open longer.

There's trad and folk music at the **House of McDonnell** (71 Castle St.; ☎ 028/2076-2975) almost every day of the week, and sessions can be brilliant. It's a rather touristy spot, but it's got one of the biggest concentrations of people under 30 in town. And it's a lovely old pub. **McCarrolls** (5–7 Ann St.; ☎ 028/2076-2123) is similar: a good, basic pub serving properly poured pints of Guinness to tourists and locals of all ages in a rustic setting. **O'Connors** (5–7 Ann

St.; ☎ 028/2076-2123) has folk nights on a Thursday and a sociable beer garden for the summer months. The rest of the young'uns can be found at the most recently refurbished joint in town **The Central Bar** (12 Ann St.; ☎ 028/2076-3877), where a program of karaoke and trad squashes in and around the weekend. Otherwise there's always sky sports on the telly. Central Bar stays open late but you've got to get in before midnight.

FESTIVALS

Ballycastle dozes through most of the year, exploding into life for the **Ballycastle Fleadh** (☎ 028/7034-4723) on the third weekend of June, when trad music entertains travelers and locals on the Diamond by day, and in the pubs by night. A great excuse for downing copious amounts of ale. If you thought the Ballycastle natives had used up all their energy, you'd be wrong. The big Ballycastle party is the **Ould Lammas Fair** (☎ 028/2076-2024), one of the oldest country fairs in Ireland. Here livestock are traded, stalls are set up, music is played, and visitors get to chew on the two local products: yellowman (a sweet chewy toffee) and dulse (a dried edible seaweed).

SIGHTSEEING

Most travelers use Ballycastle as a chilling spot or a base for visiting sights along the Antrim coast including **Bushmills** (see above) and **The Giant's Causeway** (see above)

If you really need to see more old buildings, the tourist information center has a Ballycastle Heritage trail leaflet guiding visitors around the churches and historical buildings in town. There's nothing outstanding but it can fill an afternoon.

Far more exciting is **Rathlin Island,** a wild, isolated island just off the coast of Ballycastle, attracting a mix of artists, writers, nature lovers, and those who just want to be alone. Its claim to fame is the fact it's

Northern Ireland's only offshore inhabited island. Catch the ferry (running from Ballycastle harbor throughout the day from 10:30am–4pm, taking 45 min.; adult £8.80 return, bicycle £2; ☎ 028/2076-9299; www.calmac.co.uk)—don't be surprised if sheep are your only fellow passengers, this is a working island—once aground there's a boathouse with artifacts from shipwrecks in the area, a colony of seals in nearby Mill Bay, thousands of birds including the puffin, and miles and miles of nothing. A minibus (summer only) will take you from Church Bay to the West Light Platform and the Kebble Nature Reserve for roughly £3 for adults, round-trip. Bicycles can be rented from **Soerneog View Hostel** (☎ **028/2076-3954**) for £8 per day. History buffs might like to know the first ever commercial radio broadcast was made by Marconi here in 1898. There are also three lighthouses, including an upside-down one. See it and believe it. If you like it here, don't rush back, there are pubs and places to stay on the island, mainly around the harbor. Fingers crossed you'll get invited to one of the many ceilidhs taking place on Rathlin throughout the year. The islanders notoriously use any excuse for a party.

For more info on the island and its offerings, call ☎ **028/2076-3948** or surf over to www.island-trail.com.

PLAYING OUTSIDE

ADVENTURE SPORTS **The Ardclinis Activity Centre** (High St., Cushendall, County Antrim; ☎ **028/2177-1340;** www.ardclinis.com; the center is 15 miles south of Ballycastle but many of their activities take place at Watertop Farm, just 6 miles away; see website for directions) offers everything from rock climbing, and mountain biking to windsurfing, canoeing, and rafting. Half-day, full-day, and weeklong activities are offered, as well as certificates and leadership qualifications. Book well in advance. They'll help you find a local hostel.

HIKING Hardly a hike but a perfect "walk off your hangover" morning walk is the stroll along Ballycastle beach to Pan Rocks, an outcrop of granite jutting out into the sea—a huge fave with local fishermen. Beyond that is the Devil's Churn, a bizarre tunnel in the rocks, accessed by concrete stairs. Here the sea rushes in, filling up the tunnel and making a fantastic noise. Across the water is the Mull of Kintyre, a Scottish island made famous by ex-Beatle Paul McCartney.

Alternatively, explore Ballycastle forest, running up the slopes of Knocklayd Mountain. A signpost on the diamond points to the Glentaisie Trail, giving great views of Ballycastle and later of Rathlin Island. Return to town via a steep downward path or instead turn right to head up the hill and explore the higher parts of the forest. It's steep but rewards with stupendous views—of the Scottish isles of Jura and Islay on a clear day.

CYCLING **Castle Hire** (Castle Service Station, 36 Castle St.; ☎ **028/2076-2355**) does bikes at £10 per day including a helmet. A 380km (236 mile) cycle route connects Ballycastle to Ballyshannon, taking between 5 and 7 days (go to www.sustransshop.co.uk to buy the relevant map for £5), and giving riders a full mix of Northern Ireland's stunning scenery, from rolling lowlands to Atlantic rollers. Alternatively, for a day ride, head up into the glens via Ballypatrick Forest, and on to Cushenden. Or take the sea-view route via Torr Head—completely awe-inspiring and completely exhausting. Do not attempt this on a non-geared bicycle.

DIVING See "Powerboating," below.

DEEP-SEA FISHING The reason there are so many birds on Rathlin Island is because the sea round here is virtually a cold fish stew, filled with the wriggly critters. Hook one or two for yourself on a sea-fishing trip. If there's a group of six of you, **Paul Martin** (☎ **077/5429-4177**) will take you out for

3 hours for £15 per person. If you're alone turn up at the pier on Monday, Wednesday, or Friday for a 3-hour trip for £10 (rod hire, £5; instruction, free) with **Mr. McCaughan** in his Turbo-diesel mobile.

POWERBOATING **Aquasports** (4 Coleraine Rd.; ☎ 028/7083-3563) runs high-speed powerboating trips out around the island, when the weather's not too rough, taking in the wildlife and the towering cliffs, which look even huger from below (£15–£25 per person for trips to or round the island). Alternatively eco trips run to see whales or seals—so curious Alan has to try his best not to bump into them when they gather round the boat (£15 per person for a 1.5 hour trip to the east of Rathlin Island). He also arranges diving holidays (£50 per day) and power-boating courses (£150 for a 2-day course leaving you with an RYA level 1 or 2 certificate). **Sea Treks** (Ballycastle; ☎ 028/2076-2372; www.seatreks-ireland.com) offers various trips along the Antrim coast too from £20 per person.

SWIMMING   Ballycastle beach is perfectly safe to swim in, and many people do. It is also very, very cold. Even in mid-summer. Refreshing some might say. Painful others might add.

Mourne Mountains/Newcastle

Roughly translated "Mourne" means "Hikers' Paradise." Just kidding, but the ▧ Best **Mourne Mountains** are a stunning collection of twelve peaks over 2,000 feet including the hefty Slieve Donard, which at 2,796 feet is Northern Ireland's highest mountain. The surrounding granite countryside ranges from gentle rolling hills to lush majestic vistas, with more than enough barren stretches of uninhabited desolation to discover the poet within. For the outdoor lover this means there's everything from a 30-minute stroll from the car to a full-on multi-day trek, plus horse riding, canoeing, and mountain biking.

GETTING THERE

A good way in is via Newcastle, a lively beach resort, which also makes a good place to stay. **Ulsterbus** (5–7 Railway St.; ☎ 028/4372-296) runs directly to and from Belfast on an hourly basis (the trip takes 1 hour); to and from Dublin through Newry six to eight times a day (the trip takes 2 hours); or between Downpatrick and Strangford 12 times a day (20 min. to Downpatrick, 40 min. to Strangford).

There are three simple ways into the Mournes. To get to the Mournes from Newcastle, head down Central Promenade until you see signs for Donard Forest, a 280-hectare (690-acre) stretch of pine woodland on the slopes of Slieve Donard. Another place to duck in is Tollymore Forest Park, over 400 hectares (1,000 acres) of lush fields and forest.

Alternatively, to get there via Tollymore, on the northern side of the Mournes, head about 2 miles west of Newcastle on Tully-brannigan Road. You can take an Ulsterbus shuttle from Newcastle to Tollymore at 10am, noon, and 4:30pm and ask to be dropped off at the entrance to the park.

Lastly try Castlewellan Forest Park, about 5 miles from Newcastle in Castlewellan. Buses leave several times a day from Newcastle to Castlewellan and the park is accessed off Main St.

BASICS

INTERNET   There are no cybercafes to be found, but the library at the **East Down Institute** (Castlewellan Rd., Newcastle; ☎ 028/4372-2451; £5 per hour), a block from the bus station, has computers with Web access. Open Monday to Friday 8:30am–4:30pm.

TOURIST INFORMATION   For information in the Down District, stop into the **St. Patrick Visitor Centre** (53A Market St., Downpatrick, County Down; ☎ 028/4461-2233), open October to June, Monday to Friday 9am to

5:30pm, Saturday 9:30am to 5pm; July to September Monday to Saturday 9:30am to 6pm and Sunday 2 to 6pm. Downpatrick (see "Getting There," above) is a good gateway from which to head into the Mourne Mountains from Belfast.

There's also the **Newcastle Tourist Information Centre** (10–14 Central Promenade, Newcastle, County Down; ☎ 028/4372-2222). It's open Monday to Saturday 10am to 5pm and Sunday 2 to 6pm, with extended hours (daily 10am–7pm) in the summer. Or get information and maps at the **Mourne Heritage Trust Centre** (87 Central Promenade Newcastle, County Down; ☎028/4372-4059), open all year Monday to Friday 9am to 5pm. It offers guided mountain walks Mondays and Saturdays when the weather cooperates.

RECOMMENDED WEBSITE   www.mourne mountains.com.

SLEEPING
Camping

Camping is the best way to fully immerse in the beauty of the Mournes. Well-equipped sites (with heated toilet and shower blocks) that are open year-round can be found at **Castwellan Forest Park** (☎ 028/4377-8664) and **Tollymore Forest** (☎ 028/4372-2428).

Hostels

→ **Newcastle Youth Hostel** Newcastle's only hostel is a cheap—and occasionally cheerful—option. The rooms are a little stark but the kitchen is huge, and other travelers warm the place up. The small TV room gets smoky when full but it's still a fun place to relax in. Call ahead in summer as this hostel fills up quickly. *32 Downs Rd, Newcastle. (Head down Railway St. toward the water. and turn right onto Downs Rd.)* ☎ *028/4372-2133; £10 dorm. Amenities: Bike store; drying room; kitchen; laundry.*

Cheap/Doable

→ **Cherry Villa** An ordinary gray building it may be from the outside, but indoors are three warm, cozy rooms; two unsuited, one with private bathroom. All with a huge breakfast included in the price. It's centrally located and there's no ludicrous curfew, making it a good base for those keen to enjoy the pleasures of nocturnal Newcastle. *12 Bryansford Gardens, Newcastle.* ☎ *028/4372-4128. Double £36-40 (dependent on season). Amenities: Laundry; TV.*

→ **Golf Links House** The decor may have been hot in the 1970s but the views from the lounge have stood the test of time. Ignore the wood paneling and flowery bed sheets and enjoy the in-house bar and thoroughly decent owners. With pastas and stir-fries from around £5 in the restaurant, the Golf Links position on the edge of Newcastle isn't too much of a problem either. *109 Dundrum Rd., Newcastle.* ☎ *028/4372-2054. www.golflinks house.com. Single £35, double £50. Rates include breakfast. MC, V. Amenities: Lounge; TV.*

Self-Catering

→ **Hannas Close** Snub the Newcastle nightlife and discover silence in the Mourne Mountains. Hannas Close is an amazing restored *clachan,* or medieval-style extended-family settlement, founded in 1640 and refurbished in 1997. Built on a low hill above a chattering stream, facing the spectacular Mountains of Mourne, this born-again *clachan* is so quiet there's little to wake you other than birdsong. The cottages, which sleep from two to seven, have everything you'll need, including central heating and microwaves in the kitchen. And, all have an open fire or a wood stove. Go wild. *Aughna-hoory Rd., Kilkeel, County Down. Contact RCH at* ☎ *028/9024-1100. www.cottagesinireland. com. 7 cottages. £275-£450 per week. Also available for 2- to 3-day stays. Additional charge for heat and electricity. V. Amenities: Kitchen; washing machine.*

EATING
Cheap

There are a few cafes doing good lunches on Central Promenade including **The Strand** (53–55 Central Promenade; ☎ **028/4372-3472**) with a bakery and coffeehouse serving up plenty of cheap satisfying fuel from donuts to egg and chips or sirloin steak, with everything under a tenner (and most "and chips" meals for under a fiver).

➜ **Café Maud's** CAFE   A sunny cafe with tasty views of the river and the mountains, and a straightforward menu of coffee, scones, sweet rolls, salads, crepes, sandwiches, and pasta. A good value lunch stop. *106 Main St., Newcastle, County Down.* ☎ *028/4372-6184. Main courses £3–£6. No credit cards. Daily 9am–9:30pm.*

➜ **Seasalt** ECLECTIC   This bright and cheerful Newcastle bistro is a good place to go when you don't know what you want. During the day, it's a casual place serving soups made from organic vegetables and steak-and-Guinness pie made from local livestock. On weekend nights, though, you gotta book in advance, as things get fancy, with a fusion menu. *51 Central Promenade, Newcastle, County Down. Reservations recommended weekends.* ☎ *028/4372-5027. 3-course dinner £19 available Fri–Sat; lunch main courses £5–£7. MC, V. Tues–Sun 10am–6pm; dinner Fri–Sat 7pm and 9pm.*

Splurge

➜ **The Duke Restaurant** MODERN   Fancy a starter of seared chili beef with crunchy veggies and Thai rice? Or a filet of turbot with butternut squash risotto drizzled with balsamic vinegar? Here's where to get it. The creative chef Mr. Gallagher has been making a bit of a name for himself in these parts. Being right next to Kilkeel's fishing port, fresh seafood is a good option. Steaks are fabulous, too. The midweek three-course dinner special, offering four choices at each course, is one of the great dining values on this island. *Above the Duke Bar, 7 Duke St., Warrenpoint (10km/6 miles on A2 from Newry), County Down. Reservations recommended.* ☎ *028/4175-2084. 3-course dinner £12 available Tues–Thurs. Dinner main courses £12–£14. MC, V. Tues–Sat 6–10pm; Sun 5:30–9pm.*

PARTYING

Newcastle isn't really hip and doesn't have a great nightlife, but there are a few good pubs to unwind in after a day out in the hills. On summer weekends, the town buzzes at night with moms, dads, kids, and others wandering the streets, eating ice cream and browsing for souvenirs. It's good old-fashioned fun. Pubs are open daily and usually until 11:30pm. This is flexible, and you may find yourself getting kicked out around 1am on weekend nights. Pick up a *What's On in Down District* brochure from the tourist office for a monthly listing of live music and arts events.

One of the most lively pubs is **Quinn's Spirit Grocer** (62 Main St.; ☎ **028/4372-6400**). It has a 1950s Americana feel inside and live rock, trad, and jazz several nights a week and DJs on the weekend—although put away those hard-core and trance requests, this is strictly retro classics. Dress for conquest, not subtlety.

The Percy French (Downs Rd.; ☎ **028/4372-3175**) is a more upscale, faux-Tudor watering hole with lots of polished wood, perfect pints, and friendly bartenders. Named after a mushy old 19th-century Irish songwriter, it's a respite from the tackiness of Newcastle. The crowd is generally grayer, moneyed folks but it doesn't mean they don't like a laugh; there's live oldies (1960s–1980s) music on Saturday, and a disco every Friday.

If you're out hiking to or from Kilkeel, warm up at **Jacob Halls** (Greencastle St.; ☎ 028/4176-4751) where its three massive fires are set blazing for the smallest reason.

This is a well-worn pub with vintage imagery all over the walls and live music Thursday to Sunday. It makes a good lunch/rewarding pint stop.

SIGHTSEEING

→ **Castlewellan Forest Park**   This is the most aristocratic of parks; a magnificent private castle overlooks a fine trout lake and the whole place just begs for picnics and outdoor activities. There are woodland walks, a lakeside sculpture trail, and even an arboretum, begun in 1740 and now grown to 10 times its original size. The largest of its three greenhouses even features a way-out collection of aquatic plants and free-flying tropical birds. Those in need of a caffeine fix will find a coffeehouse on the grounds. *6.5km (4 miles) northwest of Newcastle on A50, The Grange, Castlewellan Forest Park, Castlewellan.* ☎ *028/4377-8664. Free admission. Parking £4. Daily 10am–dusk; coffeehouse open summer 10am–5pm.*

FREE → **Drumena Cashel (Stone Fort)**   An ancient stone-ring fort, used as a farm in the early Christian period and later restored in 1925. The T-shaped *souterrain* (underground stone tunnel) was likely used as a huge fridge originally, and perhaps provided a chilly hideout when the Vikings came calling. There were once tens of thousands of these fortifications all across Ireland. This is one of the better-looking ones in this area. *3km (2 miles) southwest of Castlewellan, off A25, County Down. Free admission.*

→ **Dundrum Castle**   This castle lies in ruins now but—with its striking hilltop setting—it is still a real beauty. Originally an early Irish fortification (not that you can see any of it now) the oldest visible parts of the current building are about 800 to 900 years old while the newest parts have had a couple of hundred birthdays. This was once the mightiest of the Norman castles along the Down coast. It still commands the imagination, if nothing else. *6.5km (4 miles) east of*

Newcastle, off A2, Dundrum. No phone. Admission £1 adults. Apr–Sept Tues–Sat 10am–1pm and 1:30–7pm, Sun 2–7pm; Oct–Mar Tues–Sat 10am–1pm and 1:30–4pm, Sun 2–4pm.

→ **Greencastle Fort**   The first castle on this site, built in 1261, faced its companion, Carlingford Castle, across the lough. It was a two-story rectangular tower surrounded by a curtain wall with corner towers. Very little survives. Most of what you see is from the 14th century, a fortress that fell to Cromwell in 1652, never to rise again. *6.5km (4 miles) southwest of Kilkeel, Greencastle, Cranfield Point, Mouth of Carlingford Lough. No phone. Admission £1 adults. No credit cards. Apr–Sept Tues–Sat 10am–1pm and 1:30–7pm, Sun 2–7pm; Oct–Mar Tues–Sat 10am–1pm and 1:30–4pm, Sun 2–4pm.*

→ **Murlough Nature Reserve**   Sand dunes, heath land, and forest, surrounded by estuary and sea, make for a brilliant outing on a clear bright day, and a wild adventure when the storms come in. Whatever the weather it's usually windy. Bring a picnic and feast on the wild strawberries strewn across the dunes in summertime. *On the main Dundrum-Newcastle road (A2), southeast of Dundrum, County Down.* ☎ *028/4375-1467. Free admission. Parking £2.*

→ **Silent Valley Mountain Park**   The 36km (22-mile) dry-stone Mourne Wall was built to enclose Silent Valley over 90 years ago. The 36km (22-mile) Mourne Wall trek now threads together 15 of the range's biggest peaks—more than most hikers are up for. Others can try the walk from the fishing port of Kilkeel to the Silent Valley and Lough Shannagh instead. Real softies drive to the Silent Valley Information Centre and take the shuttle bus to the touristy top of nearby Ben Crom. The bus runs daily in July and August, weekends only in May, June, and September, and costs £2 round-trip. *6km (3¾ miles) north of Kilkeel on Head Rd., Silent Valley, County Down.* ☎ *028/9074-6581. Admission £3 per car.*

Information Centre Easter–Sept daily 10am–6:30pm; Oct–Easter daily 10am–4:30pm.

➜ **Tollymore Forest Park** Tollymore House went a long time ago. What's left is a scrumptious 480-hectare (1,200-acre) wildlife and forest park. There are plenty of walks along the Shimna River, noted for its salmon, or up into the north slopes of the Mournes. The forest is brimming with wildlife, including badgers, foxes, otters, and pine martens. And don't miss the trees for the forest—there are some exotic species here, including magnificent Himalayan cedars and a 30m (100-ft.) tall sequoia in the arboretum. *Off B180, 3.2km (2 miles) northwest of Newcastle, Tullybrannigan Rd., Newcastle. ☎ 028/4372-2428. Free admission. Parking £4. Daily 10am–dusk.*

PLAYING OUTSIDE

BICYCLING The Mourne roads are one of Ireland's cycling treats: narrow roads often bordered by dry-stone walls with very little traffic. The stunning views are simply a cherry on top. The foothills of the Mournes around Castlewellan are ideal for cycling. In these parts, the perfect year-round outfitter is **Ross Cycles** (44 Clarkhill Rd., signposted from the Clough-Castlewellan road, .8km (½ mile) out of Castlewellan; ☎ **028/4377-8029**), which has light-frame, highly geared mountain bikes. All cycles are fully insured, as are their riders. You can park and ride, or request local delivery. Daily rates are £7 to £10. Weekly rates are available.

There's little **off-road mountain biking** in Ireland generally; there is however a small off-road track in the Mournes at Moneyscalp near Bryansford. Phone ☎ **028/4373-1850** for further info. The Mountain and Water Sports Centre in Castlewellan also offers guided bike and hiking tours into the Mourne Mountains from £250 for three days (see "Watersports," below).

CLIMBING *Narnia* creator C. S. Lewis had the Mournes down as "earth-covered potatoes" as all but two of these granite peaks are soft and rounded. Doesn't mean there aren't plenty of climbing opportunities. Dampness can be a problem but there are routes that dry out quickly. Take a look at www.mournemountains.com/climbing for what's about.

Not exactly outside but definitely play is the **Hotrock Climbing Wall** (☎ **028/4372-5354;** www.hotrockwall.com) at Tollymore Mountain Centre in Bryansford. There's a high wall with over 40 rope-climbing routes together with a smaller bouldering wall, plus a snack bar and changing rooms. Experienced climbers can hop on the wall for £4.50 per session. Coaching for beginners is provided free on Tuesday evenings during the winter, or for £45 per day ordinarily. All the wall-scaling gear (boots, harness, and belay belt) is provided at a cost of around £4.50. Call ahead. No credit cards.

HIKING Stop by the Mourne Heritage Trust (see "Tourist Information," above) to pick up maps and hike ideas. A good choice is the Mourne Country Outdoor Pursuits Map, published by the Ordnance Survey of Northern Ireland, which is a detailed topographical map with many trails marked. Also useful is the Mourne Mountain Walks, a pack of 10 laminated cards featuring maps and detailed instructions for 10 of the area's best hikes.

Recommended for car-drivers is the hike to Hare's Gap, a gentle, winding path uphill with a scramble over large boulders before you reach the gap and a section of the Mourne Wall. There are awesome views of the countryside as you go up, and the Hare's Gap is the start point for a number of other trails going higher and deeper into the mountains. Find the route at the parking lot along Trassey Road at the northern foot of Clonachullion Hill. Turn left upon exiting the parking lot, and you'll see the gate and stile marking the beginning of the hike. The round-trip hike should take about 3½ hours. Good shoes are essential. Other hikes are included in "Sightseeing," above.

HORSEBACK RIDING The **Mount Pleasant Trekking and Horse Riding Centre** (☎ 028/4377-8651) offers group trekking tours into Castlewellan Forest Park for around £11 an hour. For riding in the Tollymore Forest Park or on local trails, contact the **Mourne Trail Riding Centre** (96 Castlewellan Rd., Newcastle; ☎ 028/4372-4315). They have quality horses and offer beach rides for highly skilled riders. **The Drumgooland House Equestrian Centre** (29 Dunnanew Rd., Seaforde, Downpatrick, County Down; ☎ 028/4481-1956), also offers trail riding in the Mournes, including $2^{1}/_{2}$-hour trekking around Tollymore and Castlewellan Forest Parks from £30. Full equestrian holidays are also available.

SAILING For leisure sailing cruises—from sightseeing to a meal afloat—contact Pamela or Aidan Reilly at **Leisure Sailing Cruises** (5 Coastguard Villas, Newcastle; ☎ 028/4372-2882).

MICROLIGHTING 📺 Best **Fly NI Airsports** (☎ 07867/832185; www.flyni.co.uk) located just 24km (15 miles) from Newry will get up in a microlight. Described by Fly NI themselves as looking like "a go-kart with wings" and a bit like "riding a motorcycle in the sky," it's one of the cheapest ways to get airborne with flights from £50 for 30 minutes and training from £75 per hour. Trips across Lough Neagh and the Mournes can be arranged. All flights are weather permitting. Visa and Mastercard accepted.

WATERSPORTS The 📺 Best **Mountain and Water Sports Centre** in Castlewellan Forest Park (☎ 028/4377-0714; www.mountainandwater.com) is a highly organized outfit offering canoeing and kayaking on water as well as abseiling, rock climbing, bouldering, zip-lining, mountain biking, canyoning, and the hottest adventure activity, coasteering—a mixture of coastal scrambling, cliff jumps, and adventure swimming. Prices range from £15 to £54 and it is

also possible to rent out gear including kayaks and camping gear or organize group trips elsewhere in Northern Ireland. Discounts will be given to individuals brandishing the guide you are reading right now: *MTV Ireland, 1st edition.*

Sperrin Mountains

If you want full-on Ireland, go elsewhere. This is Ireland in a minor key. You'll be unlikely to find the tallest, oldest, deepest, or most famous of anything Irish here. What you will find is an area free from herds of day-trippers/foreign travelers and plenty of unspoiled countryside.

From the top of the Sperrin's highest point at Sawel you can see across the Foyle Estuary and across open land to Lough Neagh and the Mournes. You'll also probably spot some sheep. Thousands of them call these mountains home.

There are some good forest parks in the area and opportunities for non-hardcore cycling, hiking, and horse riding abound. To top it off there's plenty of standing stones, high crosses, dolmens, and hill forts. All have tales to tell.

GETTING THERE

By Bus Ulsterbus (☎ 028/9033-3000) provides regular coach service to Cookstown from Belfast and Derry. By car, take M1 from Belfast. From Derry, A5 and A6 are both good routes.

BASICS

TOURIST INFORMATION There are four tourist information centers in County Tyrone. **The Cookstown Centre** (48 Molesworth St., Cookstown; ☎ 028/8676-6727), is open weekdays 9am to 5:30pm, with weekend and extended hours Easter to September. **The Kilmaddy Centre** (Ballgawley Rd. [off A4], Dungannon; ☎ 028/8776-7259), is open Monday to Friday 9am to 5pm, Saturday 10am to 4pm. **The Omagh Centre** (1 Market St., Omagh; ☎ 028/8224-7831), is open Easter to September, Monday to Saturday 9am to

5pm; October to Easter, Monday to Friday 9am to 5pm. **The Strabane Centre** (Abercorn Square, Strabane; ☎ 028/7188-3735), is open April to October, Monday to Saturday 9:30am to 5pm.

RECOMMENDED WEBSITE   www.sperrins tourism.com has plenty of images of lush green hills and info on activities too.

SLEEPING
Hostels
→ **Omagh Hostel**   Down a quiet country lane, the ivy-clad Omagh Hostel is one of the best-kept hostels in Ireland. Don't come expecting wild nights out, however; this is a homey base for launching into the surrounding countryside. Owners Billy and Marella will ensure you leave healthier than when you arrived, with organic vegetables and outdoor activities both on the detox menu. And you can bring your horse too if you like. *9a Waterworks Rd., Omagh.* ☎ *028/8224-1973. www.omaghhostel.co.uk. Dorms £9, doubles £22, camping £7. Bike storage, kitchen, TV and video.*

→ **Gortin Accommodation Suite and Activity Centre**   Another activities launch-pad, this time with an activity center on-site. Beds are numerous—not quite as numerous as the 999,999,999 suggested on the Northern Ireland Tourist Information website but still plentiful, divided up into self-catering units (sleeping four to eight), bunk rooms (sleeping six), and family rooms (sleeping four). The vibe is practical, the rooms are clean, the look is pine, and open fires keep all the social rooms warm. Spend a night and you'll be supporting the local community too as all profits are invested in the area. *62 Main St., Gortin, Ormagh.* ☎ *028/ 8164-8346. www.gortin.net. Self-catering unit £60–£120 dependent on size (two or three bedrooms) and season; bunk rooms £13; family rooms £40–£50 (dependent on season); continental breakfast £3. Amenities: Bicycle*

hire; drying room; Internet; laundry; sports center; TV.

Doable
→ **Greenmount Lodge**   This large, first-rate guesthouse is set on a 60-hectare (148-acre) farm. All the rooms are clean and tidy, if not perhaps how you'd decorate them yourself. Mrs. Frances Reid, the friendly hostess, is a superb cook; both breakfasts and evening meals are a home-style feast. *58 Greenmount Rd. (13km/8 miles southeast of Omagh on A5), Gortaclare, Omagh, County Tyrone.* ☎ *028/ 8284-1325. 8 units. £40 double. Rates include full breakfast. Dinner £16. MC, V. Amenities: Guest laundry room; sitting room. In room: TV.*

Self-Catering
→ **Sperrin Clachan**   This restored *clachan,* or family cottage compound, sits beside the Sperrin Heritage Centre in the beautiful Glenelly Valley. It makes a great base for exploring the Sperrins. Each cottage has everything you'll need to set up house, including central heating and an open fireplace. There are four cottages in all; each sleeps two to five people. In addition to these, Rural Cottage Holidays offers a wide array of other trad cottages in the region. *Glenelly Valley, Cranagh, County Tyrone. Contact RCH at* ☎ *028/9024-1100. www.cottagesinireland. com. 4 cottages. £155–£240 per week. Also available for 2- or 3-day stays. Free parking. Amenities: Dishwasher; kitchen; fridge; microwave; oven/stove; washing machine. In room: TV.*

EATING
Doable
→ **Mellon Country Inn**   INTERNATIONAL This one's a bit of a treat for those with cars. Located 2km (1¼ miles) north of the Ulster-American Folk Park. An old-world country inn combining an Irish theme with a connection to the Mellons of Pennsylvania. One of the dining rooms, the Pennsylvania Room, has log-cabin-style decor. The menu includes

simple fare—burgers, soup, salads, and ploughman's platters—as well as fancy dishes such as lobster Newburg. The house specialty is Tyrone black steak, a locally bred hormone-free beef. Food is available all day on a hot and cold buffet, and you can also order a late breakfast or afternoon tea. *134 Beltany Rd., Omagh, County Tyrone.* ☎ *028/8166-1224. Dinner main courses £8–£14. Daily 8am–9pm.*

PARTYING

A meander around Omagh turns up various options. If you want to head somewhere specific try **Hogshead** (1 McConnell Place; ☎ **028/82242110**) or **Bogan's** (26 Market St.; ☎ **028/8224-2183**), both of which are popular with locals and have a lively atmosphere. As with most towns regular closing is 11:30pm but many hostelries have late licenses and club nights dotted throughout the week, and at the weekend when bars stay open until 2am.

SIGHTSEEING

➜ **An Creagán Visitors' Centre**   Blending in beautifully with the surrounding craggy countryside, this visitor center is an excellent place to get a sense of where you're at in the Sperrins. Besides exhibitions on the region, you can find cycling and trekking routes, rent bicycles, and have a meal in the restaurant. The center owns self-catering cottages nearby, which could make a great base. Call for more information. *A505 (20km/ 13 miles east of Omagh), Creggan, County Tyrone.* ☎ *028/8076-1112. www.an-creagan. com. Admission £1.50 adults, £1 children. Apr–Sept daily 11am–6:30pm; Oct–Mar Mon–Fri 11am–4:30pm.*

➜ **Beaghmore Stone Circles**   In 1945, six stone circles and a whole load of complicated cairns and alignments were discovered here, in remote moorland north of Evishbrack Mountain, near Davagh Forest Park on the southern edge of the Sperrins. Nobody knows what this strange collection of Bronze Age stonework was really for. Archaeologists in the know guess it may have been something to do with astronomical observation and calculation. *17km (11 miles) northwest of Cookstown, signposted from A505 to Omagh, County Tyrone.*

➜ **Gortin Glen Forest Park**   Nearly 400 hectares (988 acres) of conifers make up this nature park, established in 1967. But there's far more than just trees here; the woodlands are home to lots of wildlife, including a herd of Japanese silka deer. The park's 7km (4¹/₃-mile) forest drive offers some great views of the Sperrins if you're in a car. There is also a nature center, wildlife enclosures, trails, and a cafe. For those planning to arrive and leave on foot, the Ulster Way passes through the park. *B48 (11km/6³/₄ miles north of Omagh), Cullion, County Tyrone.* ☎ *028/8164-8217. Free admission. Parking £3. Daily 9am to 1 hr. before sunset. The Gortin Rambler bus is a hop-on-hop-off service running from Omagh to Gortin Glen Forest Park (and on to various villages in the area and the Ulster–American Folk Park) at various times throughout the day (*☎ *028/ 9066-6630).*

➜ **Plantation of Ulster Visitor Centre**   This center tells the story of the Ulster Plantation of 1610, which saw the end of the Elizabethan Conquest of Ireland. Something that happened 400 years ago might seem irrelevant to life today but it goes a long way to explaining the divisions in modern Ireland. An on-site restaurant serves home-style meals. *50 High St., Draperstown, County Derry.* ☎ *028/7962-7800. Admission £3.50 adults, £3 students. July–Sept Mon–Sat 10am–4pm, Sun 11am–4pm; Oct–June Mon–Fri 10am–4pm.*

➜ **Sperrin Heritage Centre**   A range of computerized presentations and other exhibits introduce the history, culture, geology, and wildlife of the region. This is a gold-mining area, and for a small additional fee (around 70p) you'll get a chance to try your hand at panning for gold. A cafeteria, craft shop, and nature trail share the grounds.

274 Glenelly Rd. (east of Plumbridge off B47), Cranagh, County Tyrone. ☎ 028/8164-8142. Admission £2.50 adults. Apr–Sept Mon–Fri 11:30am–5:30pm; Sat 11:30am–6pm; Sun 2–6pm.

➔ **Tyrone Crystal** With a 200-year-old tradition, this crystal factory is one of Ireland's oldest and best known. Visitors are welcome to tour the operation and see glass being blown and crafted, carved, and engraved by hand. A 25-minute audiovisual presentation tells the story of the development of Tyrone Crystal, a showroom displays the finished products, and a very good cafe adds sustenance. Oaks Rd. (3.2km/2 miles east of town), Killybrackey, Dungannon, County Tyrone. ☎ 028/8772-5335. Admission £2 adults, free for seniors and children. Craft shop Mon–Sat 9am–6pm. Tours all year at 11am, noon, 2pm, and 3pm. Year-round daily 9:30am–5pm.

➔ **Ulster-American Folk Park** This outdoor museum presents the story of emigration from this part of rural Ireland to America in the 18th and 19th centuries. There are reconstructions of the thatched cottages the emigrants left behind, and replicas of the log cabins that became their homes on the American frontier. The park developed around the homestead where Thomas Mellon was born in 1813. He emigrated to Pittsburgh and prospered to the point where his son Andrew became one of the world's richest men. The Mellon family donated part of the funding to build this excellent park. Walk-through exhibits include a forge, weaver's cottage, smokehouse, schoolhouse, post office, Sperrin Mountain Famine cabin, and full-scale replica of an emigrant ship in a dockside area that features original buildings from the ports of Derry, Belfast, and Newry. A self-guided tour of all the exhibits, which are staffed by interpreters in period costume, takes about 2 hours. Musical events tie in with the Ulster-American theme, such as a bluegrass music festival in September. Mellon Rd.

(4.8km/3 miles north of Omagh on A5), Castletown, Camphill, Omagh, County Tyrone. ☎ 028/8224-3292. www.folkpark.com. Admission £4.50 adults, £2.50 seniors and children 5–16, £11 families. Oct–Easter Mon–Fri 10:30am–5pm; Easter–Sept Mon–Sat 10:30am–6pm, Sun 11am–6:30pm. Last admission 1 hr. before closing.

➔ **Ulster History Park** Ireland's history from the Stone Age to the 17th-century plantation period is the focus of this outdoor theme park. There are full-scale models of homes, castles, and monuments through the ages, including a Mesolithic encampment, Neolithic dwelling, crannóg (fortified lake dwelling), church settlement with round tower, and motte-and-bailery type of castle common. The park also contains an audiovisual theater, gift shop, and cafeteria. Cullion (on B48, 11km/7 miles north of Omagh), Omagh, County Tyrone. ☎ 028/8164-8188. Admission £3.75 adults; £2.50 students. MC, V. Apr–June and Sept Mon–Sun 9:30am–5:30pm; July–Aug Mon–Sun 9:30am–6:30pm. Last admission 90 min. before closing. Closed Nov–Mar.

PLAYING OUTSIDE

BICYCLING The Sperrin countryside is ideal for cycling. Bicycles can be rented by the day or week from the **An Creagán Visitors' Centre** (see "Sightseeing," above). Bike rentals run roughly £8 a day or £34 a week.

HIKING Whether you're on foot, wheels, or horseback, be sure to traverse the Glenshane Pass between Mullaghmore (545m/1,788 ft.) and Carntogher (455m/1,492 ft.), and the Sawel Mountain Drive along the east face of the mountain. The vistas along these routes through the Sperrins will remind you of why you've gone out of your way to spend time in Tyrone. **The Sperrins Rambler** (☎ 028/9066-6630;** www.translink.co.uk) is a special bus service running between Magherafelt and Omagh several times a day offering a hop-on-hop-off service.

HORSEBACK RIDING   To rent by the hour or take a multiday journey through the mountains, contact the **Edergole Riding Centre** (70 Moneymore Rd., Cookstown; ☎ **028/8676-1133**).

Fermanagh Lakelands

Tucked in the extreme southwest corner of Northern Ireland, County Fermanagh is dominated by Lough Erne, a long lake dotted with 154 islands and rimmed by countless alcoves and inlets. It has 81km (50 miles) of cruising waters—the least congested in Europe—ranging from a shallow trickle in some places to an 8km (5-mile) wide channel in others.

The hub of this lakeland paradise, wedged between the upper and lower branches of Lough Erne, is Enniskillen, a rather posh town with some great pubs.

In medieval times, a chain of island monasteries stretched across the waters of Lough Erne, establishing it as a haven for contemplatives. It's still a great place to get away from it all.

GETTING THERE & GETTING AROUND

Ulsterbus (☎ **028/9033-3000**) provides regular coach service to Enniskillen from Belfast. **Bus Éireann** (☎ **01/836-6111**) offers daily service from Dublin and Sligo.

By car, take M1 from Belfast or A5 from Derry. The best way to get around Enniskillen and the surrounding lakelands of Lough Erne is by car or bicycle. The total signposted driving circuit around the lake is 105km (65 miles).

BASICS

TOURIST INFORMATION   Contact the **Fermanagh Tourist Information Centre** (Wellington Rd., Enniskillen, County Fermanagh; ☎ **028/6632-3110**). It's open weekdays, year-round, from 9am to 5:30pm (to 7pm July–Aug). From Easter to September it's also open on weekends, Saturday 10am to 6pm, and Sunday 11am to 5pm. For an introduction to the Fermanagh Lakelands on the Web, take a look at www.fermanagh-online.com.

SLEEPING

Hostels

➜ **The Bridges Youth Hostel**   Seventy beds spread over a variety of two-, four-, and six-bed rooms, all housed in a modern functional building with an impressive glass-sided quiet room looking out over the town's river below. Rooms are all en suite, and reminiscent of a new college block. The kitchen is a huge stainless-steel affair, and there's a great cafe downstairs for those nights when you just can't be bothered. *The Bridges, Belmore St.* ☎ *028/6634-0110. Dorm £13, private room, when available, £5 extra. MC, V. Amenities: Bicycle store; drying room; Internet; kitchen; laundry; TV.*

Doable

➜ **Belmore Court Motel**   If you're just looking for a bed on which to crash, this three-story motel offers a variety of accommodations, from single rooms to family rooms, at fairly cheap prices. It's the same motel principle as in the United States: bland decor, no amenities, but rates that can't be beat. Most rooms have kitchenettes, and about a third of the units have two bedrooms or a suite setup of bedroom and sitting room. Guest rooms are nondescript but inoffensive, done up with pastel colors, standard furnishings in light woods, floral fabrics, down comforters, and writing desks. The motel is on the east edge of town, within walking distance of all the major sights and shops. *Temp Rd., Enniskillen, County Fermanagh.* ☎ *028/6632-6633. www.motel.co.uk. 31 units. £45 double; £50 double with kitchenette; £68 family room (sleeps 5). Full breakfast £5; continental breakfast £3. AE, MC, V. In room: TV, kitchenette or tea/coffeemaker.*

Self-Catering

➔ **Corraquil Country Cottages** These comfortable traditional cottages, on the banks of the Shannon-Erne Waterway, are ideal for couples or groups wanting to cozy up in the countryside or get stuck into the activities on offer: hiking, fishing, boating, cycling. The cottages sleep four, five, and six. What's more, taking to the waterways could not be more convenient—a small fleet of day cruisers moors just beyond the front yard. You'll find everything you need, including washing machines. All cottages have an open fire as well as central heating. In addition to these six cottages, Lakeland Country Breaks (LCB) offers a surprisingly diverse and attractive selection of self-catering cottages, lodges, and estates throughout the Lakelands region. *Teemore, County Fermanagh. Contact LCB at* ☎ *01365/327205. www.lakelandbreaks. ie. 6 cottages. £250–£385 per week. Also available for 2- or 3-day stays. Additional charge for heat and electricity. MC, V. Amenities: TV; kitchen; washing machine.*

EATING

Cheap

➔ **Saddlers** IRISH/PUB GRUB It's all about horses at this restaurant over the Horse Show Bar. They're everywhere, except on the menu. Barbecued pork ribs, steaks, surf-and-turf (lobster and steak), burgers, and mixed grills are the big boy choices, along with local seafood, salads, pizzas, pastas, and a house special of sirloin Sandeman with bacon, shallots, peppercorns, and port-wine sauce. *66 Belmore St., Enniskillen, County Fermanagh.* ☎ *028/6632-6223. Lunch main courses £5–£7, dinner main courses £8–£14. Daily noon–4pm and 5:30–11pm.*

Doable

➔ **Franco's** INTERNATIONAL Next to the Butter Market in three converted and restored buildings that were once part of Enniskillen's working waterfront, this casual eatery combines old-world ambience and sea-faring history with contemporary recipes and fresh local ingredients. Choices might include filet of beef en croûte; black sole and salmon with sorrel sauce; lobster Thermidor; Lough Melvin salmon on a bed of spinach in pastry and saffron sauce; or duck breast in plum sauce. A variety of specialty pastas and pizzas round out the menu. Wednesday to Sunday, traditional music starts at 9pm. *Queen Elizabeth Rd., Enniskillen, County Fermanagh.* ☎ *028/6632-4424. Reservations not accepted. Dinner main courses £8–£15. Daily noon–11pm.*

PARTYING

The best spot in the lakes for a big night out is Enniskillen. Here, the most popular pubs skip the usual 11pm closing time and go on until 1 or 2am in the morning, especially on the weekends. Nights start out around the diamond, usually in Pat's Bar (see below) with splinter groups migrating onward to Blakes, Crowe's Nest, and Bush Bar.

➔ **Blakes** You've gotta love this place. One of the oldest bars in Northern Ireland, it is an endless catacomb of different places to eat and drink rising way beyond its small stone front. First up is The Hollow bar, divided up into various delicious dark-wood snugs—even one with a pool table. Expect impromptu traditional tunes here. Upstairs are The Atrium bars—the venues for live rock bands. Farther up still is the Tonic club, where it's dance, dance, dance all weekend. Down in the cellar is a bistro with doable-priced food and jazz on Saturdays, while Number 6 is the town's fine-dining establishment. Definitely worth the walk up the other end of town. *6 Church St.* ☎ *028/6632-0918.*

➔ **Bush Bar** A sleek minimalist bar decked out in neutral earthy tones with surrealist art on the walls and plenty of long, low seating. Snag a cocktail and settle in for some iPod-generated ear candy or MTV visuals displayed on plasma screens. Wednesday is student night (the drinks are cheap and the music is old skool), Thursday is karaoke, but Saturday is when it really kicks off, in the back room, accompanied by a commercial dance soundtrack. *26 Townhall St.* ☎ *028/6632-5210. Cover £5 for back room dance night.*

➜ **Crowe's Nest** By day it's a light-wood bar with a restaurant in the back serving up simple pub meals to shoppers. By night the cookers spin over and it becomes a heaving bar, where grannies and groovers all get down together. Tuesday is trad night, Wednesday attracts the students, and Sunday is notorious for its pop-tastic disco where any mention of Monday morning is strictly banned. Upstairs disco is over 21s only. *12 High St.* ☎ *028/6632-5252. Cover £3–£5 on Fri and Sat to access upstairs disco.*

➜ **Pat's Bar** The management may seem unfriendly and suspicious, the bar may look rundown and in good need of a clean, but, surprisingly, this is one of the busiest bars in town. Ok, so it's certainly not sophisticated but if you want to get hammered with other people who know their way around a pint glass, this is as good a place as any. Thursday is "Crazy Karaoke with Big Daddy." Friday and Saturday see rock and blues bands from around the region and DJs upstairs. *1–5 Townhall St.* ☎ *028/6632-7462. No cover for dance nights.*

SIGHTSEEING

➜ **Castle Coole** On the east bank of Lower Lough Erne, this quintessential neoclassical mansion was designed by James Wyatt for the earl of Belmore and completed in 1796. Its rooms include a lavish state bedroom hung with crimson silk, said to have been prepared for George IV. Other features include a Chinese-style sitting room, magnificent woodwork, fireplaces, and furniture

dating from the 1830s. A nearly 600-hectare (1,482-acre) woodland estate surrounds the house. If you like a bit of classical music a series runs from May to October. *2.4km (1½ miles) southeast of Enniskillen on the main Belfast-Enniskillen rd. (A4), County Fermanagh.* ☎ *028/6632-2690. House admission £3 adults; grounds £2 per car. Easter–May and Sept Sat–Sun 1–6pm; June–Aug Fri–Wed 1–6pm (last tour 5:15pm).*

➜ **Crom Estate** This nearly 800-hectare (1,976-acre) nature reserve is a splendid National Trust property, with forest, parks, wetlands, fen meadows, and an award-winning lakeshore visitor center. There are numerous trails, with hides for observing birds and wildlife, as well as a heronry and boat rental. The estate is also a great place to fish for bream and roach. Permits and day tickets are available at the gate lodge. During the summer, there are frequently special programs and guided nature walks on weekends. *Newtownbutler, County Fermanagh.* ☎ *028/6773-8118. Admission £3 per car or boat. Apr–Sept Mon–Sat 10am–6pm; Sun noon–6pm. 34km (21 miles) south of Enniskillen. Take A4 and A34 from Enniskillen to Newtownbutler, then take the signposted right turn onto a minor road.*

➜ **Devenish Island** This is the most extensive of the ancient Christian sites in Lough Erne. In the 6th century, St. Molaise founded a monastic community here, to which the Augustinian Abbey of St. Mary was added in the 12th century. In other words, this is hallowed ground, hallowed all the more by the legend that the prophet Jeremiah is buried somewhere nearby—if you can figure that one out. The jewel of Devenish is the perfectly intact 12th-century round tower, erected with Vikings in mind. The island is a marvelous mélange of remnants and ruins, providing a glimpse into the lake's mystical past. While you're in the spirit, be sure to explore Boa and White islands, with their extraordinary carved stone figures, and bring your camera. *2.4km (1½ miles) downstream from Enniskillen.* ☎ *028/6862-1588. Admission to round tower 80p. Ferry from Trory Point (6.5km/4 miles from Enniskillen on A32) Apr–Sept at 10am, 1pm, 3pm, and 5pm. Round-trip fare £2.50 adults.*

→ **Enniskillen Castle** Dating from the 15th century, this magnificent stone fortress sits overlooking Lough Erne on the western edge of Enniskillen. It incorporates three museums: the medieval castle, with its unique twin-turreted Watergate tower, once the seat of the Maguires, chieftains of Fermanagh; the county museum, with exhibits on the area's history, wildlife, and landscape; and the museum of the famous Royal Inniskilling Fusiliers, with a collection of uniforms, weapons, and medals dating from the 17th century. Other exhibits include life-size figurines and 3-D models of old-time castle life. *Castle Barracks, Enniskillen, County Fermanagh.* ☎ *028/6632-5000. Admission £2.50 adults. May–June and Sept Mon and Sat 2–5pm, Tues–Fri 10am–5pm; July–Aug Tues–Fri 10am–5pm, Sat–Mon 2–5pm; Oct–Apr Mon 2–5pm, Tues–Fri 10am–5pm.*

→ **Florence Court** One of the most beautifully situated houses in Northern Ireland, this 18th-century Palladian mansion is set among dramatic hills, 13km (8 miles) southwest of Upper Lough Erne and Enniskillen. Originally the seat of the earls of Enniskillen, its interior is filled with fancy rococo plasterwork and antique Irish furniture, while outside is a walled garden, an icehouse, and a water-wheel-driven sawmill. The forest park offers a number of trails, one leading to the top of Mount Cuilcagh (nearly 660m/2,165 ft.). There's also a tearoom. *Florence Court, off A32, County Fermanagh.* ☎ *028/6634-8249. Admission £4 adults. June Mon–Fri 1–6pm, Sat–Sun noon–6pm; July–Aug daily noon–6pm; Sept–May Sat–Sun noon–6pm.*

→ **Marble Arch Caves** West of Upper Lough Erne and 19km (12 miles) from Enniskillen near the Florence Court estate, these caves are among the finest in Europe for exploring underground rivers, winding passages, and hidden chambers. Electrically powered boat tours take visitors underground, and knowledgeable guides explain the origins of the amazing stalactites and stalagmites. Tours last 75 minutes and leave at 15-minute intervals. The caves are occasionally closed after heavy rains, so phone ahead before making the trip. *Marlbank, Florence Court, off A32, County Fermanagh.* ☎ *028/6634-8855. Admission £6 adults, £4 students. Reservations recommended. Late Mar to June and Sept daily 10am–4:30pm (last tour at 4:30pm); July–Aug daily 10am–5pm (last tour at 5pm).*

SHOPPING

Eniskillen has the usual array of chain stores and cafes you might expect in a small town smattered with the odd surprise.

→ **Triskele Tattoos** A distinctly non-grungy tattoo parlor located in a traditional Irish shop. Janine Ashton is the owner and tattooist in residence, an art school graduate who specializes in coverups and one-off custom designs. That doesn't mean you can't pick out something from her massive tattoo library. Polynesian tatts are particularly popular right now. And there's a good range of Celtic designs too. Prices stretch up from £25. Cash only. Body piercing is also available. Janine's been at this game for over 11 years so that pigment gun and your soft skin are both in safe hands. *26a Daling St.* ☎ *028/6634-0440. www.triskeletattoos.com.*

→ **Island Discs** Most of the latest mainstream and alternative CDs, plus those American country tracks you've been missing. And two sections of Irish folk, trad, and country. Don't fret, there's also dedicated areas for metal, punk, and indie freaks. Upstairs is more of a rock den, with T-shirts, posters, and comics too—including Thunder road, Spiderman and X-men, when it's open. *3 The Diamond.* ☎ *028/6632-4882.*

PLAYING OUTSIDE

BICYCLING Several of the watersports and activity centers in the area, such as Erne Tours and Lakeland Canoe Center (see "Watersports," below), also rent bicycles. Bicycles are also available from **Corralea Activity Centre** (Belcoo; ☎ **028/6638-6668**); and **Out & Out Activities** (501 Rosscor, Belleek; (☎ **028/6865-8105**). Daily bike rental runs £7 to £10. For cycle tours with **Kingfisher Cycle Trail,** contact Pat Collum at the Tourist Information Centre (Wellington Rd., Enniskillen; ☎ **028/6632-0121;** www. kingfishercycletrail.com).

BOATING Lough Erne is an explorer's dream, and you can take that dream all the way to the Atlantic if you want. The price range for fully equipped four- to eight-berth cruisers is £700 to £1,135 per week, including VAT, depending on the season and the size of the boat. The many local cruiser-hire companies include **Belleek Charter Cruising** (Belleek; (☎ **028/6865-8027;** www25.brinkster.com/belleekcruising); **Erne Marine** (Bellanaleck; ☎ **028/6634-8267**); and **Carrickcraft** (Lurgan; ☎ **028/3834-4993;** www.cruise-ireland.com).

On Lower Lough Erne, north of town, you can hire motorboats from **Manor House Marine** (Killadeas; ☎ **028/6862-8100**). Charges average £50 for a half-day, and £70 for a full day.

HORSEBACK RIDING The **Ulster Lakeland Equestrian Centre** (Necarne Castle, Irvinestown; ☎ **028/6862-1919**), is an international center that offers full equestrian holidays. Pony trekking and riding lessons are available from **Drumhoney Stables** (Lisnarick; ☎ **028/6862-1892**).

WALKING The southwestern branch of the Ulster Way follows the western shores of Lough Erne, between the lake and the border. The area is full of great walks. One excellent 11km (6³/₄-mile, 3–7 hr.) hike is from a starting point near Florence Court and the Marble Arch Caves (see "Sightseeing," above) to the summit of Mount Cuilagh (656m/2,152 ft.). A trail map is included in the Northern Ireland Tourist Board's *Information Guide to Walking.*

WATERSPORTS The **Lakeland Canoe Center** (Castle Island, Enniskillen; ☎ **028/6632-4250**), is a watersports center based on an island west of downtown. For a full day of canoeing and other sports, including archery, cycling, dinghy sailing, and windsurfing, prices start roughly at £15 per day. Camping and simple accommodations are also available at a modest cost. **The Share Holiday Village** (Smith's Strand, Lisnaskea; ☎ **028/6772-2122;** www.sharevillage.org), offers sailing, canoeing, windsurfing, and banana skiing. A single 2¹/₂-hour session, including instruction and equipment, costs £5 per person. Other watersports centers include the **Boa Island Activity Centre** (Tudor Farm, Kesh; ☎ **028/6863-1943**).

Appendix: Ireland in Depth

History 101

THE FIRST SETTLERS With some degree of confidence, we can place the date of the first human habitation of the island somewhere after the end of the last ice age, around the late 8000s B.C.

Ireland's first colonizers, Mesolithic Homo sapiens, walked, waded, or floated across the narrow strait from what is now Britain in search of flint and, of course, food.

The next momentous prehistoric event was the arrival of Neolithic farmers and herders, sometime around 3500 B.C. The Neolithic "revolution" was the first of many to come to Ireland a bit late, at least 5,000 years after its inception in the ancient Near East. The domestication of the human species—settled life, agriculture, animal husbandry—brought with it a radically increased population, enhanced skills, stability, and all the implications of leisure. Unlike Ireland's Mesolithic hunters, who barely left a trace, this second wave of colonizers began to transform the island at once. They came with stone axes that could fell a good-size elm in less than an hour. Ireland's hardwood forests began to recede to make room for tilled fields and pastureland. Villages sprang up, and more permanent homes, planked with split oak, appeared at this time.

Far more striking, though, was the appearance of massive megalithic monuments, including court cairns, dolmens (stone tables), round subterranean passage tombs and wedge tombs. There are thousands of these scattered around Ireland, and to this day only a small percentage of them have been excavated. These megalithic monuments speak volumes about the early Irish. To visit Newgrange and Knowth in the Boyne Valley and Carrowmore in County Sligo is to marvel at the mystical practices of the early Irish. Even today little is known about the meaning of these mysterious stone remnants of their lives. Early Celtic inhabitants of the island assumed the tremendous stones and mounds were raised by giants. They called them the people of the *sí*, who eventually became the *Tuatha Dí Danann,* and, finally, faeries. Over many generations of oral tradition, the mythical people were downsized into "little people," who were believed to have led a magical life, mostly underground, in the thousands of *raths,* or earthwork structures, coursing the island like giant mole works. All of these sites were believed to be protected by the fairies, and to tamper with them was believed to bring great bad luck, so nobody ever touched them. Thus they have lasted to this day—ungraffitied, undamaged, unprotected by any visible fences or wires, but utterly safe.

THE CELTS Of all the successive waves of outsiders who have, over the years, shaped, cajoled, and pockmarked the timeline of Irish history, none have made quite such a deep-seated impact as that of the Celts. They came in waves, the first perhaps as early as the 6th century B.C. and continuing until the end of the first millennium. They fled from the Roman invasion, and clung to the edge of Europe, Ireland being, at the time, about as far as you could go to elude a Roman force. In time, they controlled the island and absorbed into their culture everyone they found there. Their ways—and their genes—dominated. They brought iron weapons; chariots; cults and contests; and poetry, music, and artistic genius, all of which took root and flourished in Irish soil. Despite their cultural potency, however, the Celts developed little in the way of centralized government, existing instead in a near-perpetual state of division and conflict with one another. The island was divided among as many as 150 tribes, grouped under alliances to one of five provincial kings. The provinces of Munster, Leinster, Ulster, and Connaught date from this period. They fought fiercely among themselves over cattle (their "currency" and standard of wealth), land, and women. None among them ever ruled the entire island, though not for lack of trying. One of the most impressive monuments from the time of the warring Celts is the stone fortress of Dún Aengus, on the wind-swept hills of the Aran Islands.

THE COMING OF CHRISTIANITY The Celtic chiefs neither warmly welcomed nor violently resisted the Christians who came ashore beginning in the 5th century A.D. Although threatened, the pagan Celts settled for a bloodless rivalry with this new religion. In retrospect, this may have been a mistake.

Not the first, but eventually the most famous, of these Christian newcomers was a man called Maewyn Succat, a young Roman citizen torn from his Welsh homeland in a Celtic raid and brought to Ireland as a slave, where he was forced to work in a place called the forest of Foclut (thought to be around modern Country Antrim). He escaped on a ship bound for France, where he spent several years as a priest, before returning to Ireland as a missionary. He began preaching at sacred Celtic festivals, a tactic that frequently led to confrontations with religious and political leaders, but eventually he became such a popular figure with the people of Ireland that after his death in 461, a dozen clan chiefs fought over the right to bury him. His lasting legacy was, of course, the establishment in Ireland of one of the

Dateline

- c. 8000 B.C. Earliest known human settlers arrive in Ireland.
- 2000 B.C. First metalworkers come to Ireland.
- c.700 B.C. Celtic settlement of Ireland begins.
- c.100 A.D. The Gaels arrive in Ireland, naming one of their biggest settlements "Dubhlinn."
- A.D. 432 Traditional date of St. Patrick's return to Ireland as a Christian missionary.
- 500–800 Ireland becomes one of the largest centers of Christianity in Europe—often referred to as the "golden age."
- 795 First Viking invasion.
- 841 Vikings build a sea fort in the area of modern-day Dublin.
- 853 Danes take possession of the Norse settlement.
- 1014 Battle of Clontarf. High King of Ireland, Brian Boru, defeats the Vikings.
- 1167–71 Forces of the English King, Henry II, seize Dublin and surrounding areas.
- 1204 Dublin Castle becomes center of English power.

strongest Christian orthodoxies in Europe—an achievement for which he was later beatified as St. Patrick.

Ireland's conversion to Christianity was a somewhat negotiated process. The church at the time of St. Patrick was, like the man who brought it, Roman. To Ireland, an island then still without a single proper town, the Roman system of dioceses and archdioceses were mysterious and pointless. So the Irish adapted the church to their own situation. They built isolated monasteries with extended monastic "families," each more or less autonomous. The pope, like an Irish high king, was to them like an ordained prizefighter—he was expected to defend his title, one challenge after another, or lose it.

Ireland flourished in this fashion for several centuries and became a center of monastic learning and culture. Monks and scholars were drawn to it in droves, and they were sent out in great numbers as well to Britain and the Continent as emissaries for the island's way of thinking and praying. As the historian Thomas Cahill wrote in *How the Irish Saved Civilization*, "Wherever they went the Irish brought with them their books, many unseen in Europe for centuries and tied to their waists as signs of triumph, just as Irish heroes had once tied to their waists their enemies' heads." And they worked with a fervor, in fact, they worked so hard that the Irish penned more than half the biblical commentaries written worldwide between 650 and 850.

Like their megalithic ancestors, these monks left traces of their lives behind, and these have become enduring monuments to their spirituality. Early monastic sites like gorgeous Glendalough in County Wicklow, wind-swept Clonmacnois in County Offaly, and isolated Skellig Michael off the Kerry coast give you an idea of how they lived, while striking examples of their work can be seen at Trinity College (which houses the Book of Kells) and at the Chester Beatty museum at Dublin Castle.

THE VIKING INVASIONS The monastic city-states of early medieval Ireland might have continued to lead the world's intellectual process, but the Vikings came along and ruined everything. After centuries of relative peace, the first wave of Viking invaders arrived in A.D. 795. The wealthy non-violent Irish monasteries were among their first targets. Unprepared and unprotected, the Irish monasteries, which had amassed collections of gold, jewels, and art from followers and thinkers around the world, were decimated. The round towers to which the monks retreated for safety were neither high enough nor strong enough to protect them and their treasures from the onslaught. Once word spread of the wealth to be had on the small

APPENDIX:
IRELAND IN DEPTH

- **1297** First parliamentary sessions in Dublin.
- **1300s** First great plague kills a third of the population of Dublin.
- **1500s** English rule consolidated across Ireland. Henry III proclaims himself king of Ireland.
- **1534–52** Henry VIII begins suppression of Catholic Church in Ireland.

- **1558–1603** Reign of Elizabeth I. Ireland proclaimed an Anglican country. The "plantation" of Munster divides Ireland into counties.
- **1591** Trinity College founded.
- **1607** The flight of the Irish earls, marking the demise of the old Gaelic order.
- **1641** Irish Catholic revolt in Ulster led by Sir Phelim O'Neill ends in defeat.

- **1649** Oliver Cromwell invades and begins the re-conquest of Ireland.
- **1690** The forces of King James II, a Catholic, are defeated at the Battle of the Boyne, consolidating Protestant order in England.
- **1691** Patrick Sarsfield surrenders Limerick. He and some 14,000 Irish troops, the "Wild Geese," flee to the Continent.

island, the Scandinavian invaders just kept on coming, but much as they were experts in the arts of pillage and plunder, one thing of which they had no knowledge was literature. They didn't know how to read. Therefore, they paid scant attention to the magnificent books they came across, passing them over for more obvious riches. This fortunate quirk of history allowed the monks some means of preserving their dying culture—and their immeasurably valuable work—for the benefit of future generations.

Of course, the Vikings did more than hit and run. They settled down and took over much of the country—securing every major harbor on Ireland's east coast with a fortified town. These were the first real towns in Ireland: In addition to Dublin, they also founded Cork, Waterford, and the river city of Limerick. They had plundered the country fairly thoroughly by the time the Irish, always disinclined to unite, did so at last, and managed to push out the Vikings after a decisive military campaign lead by the army of Brian Boru in 1014. When the Vikings departed, they left their towns behind, forever altering the Irish landscape. The legacy of the Vikings in Ireland is complex, and a visit to Dublin's Wood Quay and the city walls of Waterford is a good introduction to their influence.

With the Vikings gone, Ireland enjoyed something of a renewal in the 11th and 12th centuries. Its towns grew, its regional kings made successive unsuccessful bids to unite the country under a single high kingship, and its church came under imcreased pressure to conform to the Vatican's rules. All of these factors would play a part in ripening Ireland for the next invasion. The Vikings may have been gone, but prosperous and factionalized Ireland made attractive prey to other nations, and it was, tragically, an Irish king who opened the door to the next predator. Diarmait Mac Murchada, king of Leinster, whose ambition was to be king of all of Ireland, decided he could do it with a little help. So he called on Henry II, the Norman King of England. Diarmait offered Henry a series of tantalizing incentives in return for military aid: Not only did he bequeath his eldest daughter to whoever led the army, but he also offered them overlordship of the Kingdom of Leinster. To put it bluntly, he made Henry an offer he couldn't refuse. So it was that an expeditionary force, led by the Earl of Pembroke, Richard de Clare—better known as Strongbow—was sent to Diarmait's aid. After the successful invasion and subsequent battles in which Strongbow emerged victorious, he remained in Ireland as governor, and thus gave the English their first

- **1704** Enactment of first Penal Laws. Apartheid comes to Ireland.
- **1778** The Penal Laws are progressively repealed.
- **1782** The Irish Parliament is granted independence.
- **1791** Wolfe Tone founds the Society of the United Irishmen.
- **1796–97** Wolfe Tone launches an invasion from France, fails, is taken

captive, and commits suicide.
- **1798** "The Year of the French." A French invasion force is defeated at Killala Bay. General Humbert surrenders to Cornwallis.
- **1801** The Irish Parliament is induced to dissolve itself. Ireland becomes part of the United Kingdom.
- **1803** 25-year-old Robert Emmet is hanged after his

uprising, of less than 100 men, is a tragic failure.
- **1829** Daniel O'Connell secures passage of the Catholic Emancipation Act. He is later named lord mayor of Dublin.
- **1845–48** The Great Famine. Two million Irish die or emigrate, mostly to the U.S.
- **1848** The revolt of the Young Irelanders ends in failure.

foothold in Ireland. What Diarmait did not realize, of course, was that they would never leave.

THE NORMAN INVASION In successive expeditions from 1167 to 1169, the Normans, who had already conquered Britain, crossed the Irish Sea from England with crushing force. The massive Norman fortifications at Trim are a powerful reminder of the sheer power the invaders brought with them. Across the next century, the Norman-English settled in, consolidating their power in new towns and cities. Indeed, many of the settlers grew attached to the island, and did their best to integrate with the local culture. Marriages between the native Irish and the invaders became commonplace. Over the next couple of centuries, they became more Irish and less English in their loyalties.

In 1314 Scotland's Robert the Bruce defeated the English at Bannockburn and set out to fulfill his dream of a united Celtic kingdom. He installed his brother Edward on the Irish throne, but the constant state of war took a heavy toll. Within 2 years, famine and economic disorder had eroded any public support Edward might have enjoyed. By the time he was defeated and killed at Dundalk in 1317, few were prepared to mourn him.

Over the next 2 centuries, attempts to rid Ireland of its English overlords were laudable but fell short. Independent Gaelic lords in the north and west continued to maintain their territories. By the close of the 15th century, English control of the island was effectively limited to the Pale, a walled and fortified cordon around what is now Greater Dublin. (The phrase "beyond the pale" comes from this—meaning anything that is uncontrollable or unacceptable.)

ENGLISH POWER & THE FLIGHT OF THE EARLS During the reign of the Tudor monarchs in England (1485–1603), the brutal reconquest of Ireland was set in motion. Henry VIII was the first to proclaim himself king of all Ireland—something even his warlike ancestors had stopped short of doing—but it wasn't until later that century that the claim was backed up by force. Elizabeth I, Henry's daughter, declared that all Gaelic lords in Ireland must surrender their lands to her, with the dubious promise that she would immediately grant them all back again—unsurprisingly, the proposition was hardly welcomed in Ireland, and a rebel army was raised by Hugh O'Neill and "Red" Hugh O'Donnell, two Irish Chieftains.

Despite significant victories early on in their decade-long campaign, most notably over a force led by the Earl of Essex, whom Elizabeth had personally sent to subdue them, by 1603 O'Neill was left with few allies and no option but to surrender, which he did

APPENDIX: IRELAND IN DEPTH

- **1858** The Irish Republican Brotherhood, a secret society known as the Fenians, is founded in New York.
- **1866** In an imaginative publicity stunt, a miniscule army of Fenians attempts to invade Canada.
- **1879** Michael Davitt founds the National Land League to support the claims of tenant farmers.

- **1879–82** The "land war" forces the enactment of reform. The tenant system unravels; land returns to those who work it.
- **1886** and 1894 Bills for Home Rule are defeated in Parliament.
- **1893** The Gaelic League is founded to revive the Irish language.
- **1904** The Abbey Theatre opens in Dublin.

- **1905–08** Founding of Sinn Fein, "we ourselves," with close links to the Irish Republican Brotherhood.
- **1912** Third Home Rule bill passes in the House of Commons and is defeated by the House of Lords.
- **1916** Patrick Pearse and James Connolly lead an armed uprising on Easter Monday to proclaim the

on March 23, the day before Elizabeth died. O'Neill had his lands returned, but constant harassment by the English prompted him, along with many of Ireland's other Gaelic lords, to sail for Europe on September 14, 1607, abandoning their lands and their aspirations for freedom.

THE COMING OF CROMWELL By the 1640s, Ireland was effectively an English plantation. Family estates had been seized and foreign (Scottish) labor brought in to work them. A systematic persecution of Catholics, which began with Henry VIII's split from Rome but did not die with him, barred Catholics from practicing their faith. Resentment against the English and their punitive laws led to fierce uprisings in Ulster and Leinster in 1641, and by early 1642 most of Ireland was again under Irish control. Unfortunately for the rebels, any hope of extending the victories was destroyed by internal disunion and by the eventual decision to support the Royalist side in the English civil war. In 1648 King Charles I of England was beheaded, and the victorious commander of the Parliamentary forces, Oliver Cromwell, was installed as ruler. Soon his supporters were taking on his enemies in Ireland. A year later, the Royalists' stand collapsed in defeat at Rathmines, just south of Dublin.

Defeat for the Royalist cause did not, however, mean the end of the war. Cromwell became paranoid that Ireland would be used to launch a French-backed insurgency if it was not brought to heel, and he detested the country's Catholic beliefs. So it was that as the hot, sticky summer of 1649 drew to a close, Cromwell set sail for Dublin, bringing with him an army of 12,000 men and a battle plan so ruthless that, to paraphrase another dark chapter in the history of warfare, it would live forever in infamy.

In the town of Drogheda, over 3,552 Irish soldiers were slaughtered in a single night. When a large group of men sought sanctuary in the local church, Cromwell ordered them to be burned alive—an act of such monstrosity that some of his own men risked a charge of mutiny and refused the order. On another day in Wexford over 2,000 were murdered, a large proportion of them civilians. The trail of destruction rolled on, devastating counties Galway and Waterford. When asked where the Irish citizens could go to be safe from him, Cromwell famously suggested they could go "to hell or Connaught"—the latter being the most far-flung, rocky, and unfarmable part of Ireland. After a rampage that lasted 7 months, Cromwell finally left Ireland and its shattered administration in the care of his lieutenants and returned to England. His memory lingers painfully in Ireland. In certain parts of the country, people still spit at the mention of Cromwell's name.

Irish Republic. Defeat is followed by the execution of 15 leaders of the revolt.

■ **1918** Sinn Fein wins a landslide election victory against the Irish Parliamentary Party.

■ **1919** Sinn Fein, led by Eamon de Valera, constitutes itself as the first Irish áil and declares independence.

■ **1919–21** The Irish War of Independence. Michael Collins commands the Irish forces.

■ **1921** Anglo-Irish Treaty. Ireland is partitioned. Twenty-six counties form the Free State; the other six remain a part of the U.K. The Free State adopts its first constitution a year later.

■ **1922–23** The Irish civil war, between the government of the Free State and those who opposed the Anglo-Irish treaty. Michael Collins is assassinated by the I.R.A., who saw the treaty as a sell-out.

■ **1932** Eamon de Valera leads Fianna Fáil to victory and becomes head of government.

THE PENAL LAWS   Cromwell died in 1658, and 2 years later the English monarchy was restored, but the anti-Catholic oppression continued apace. In 1685, though, something quite remarkable happened. Contrary to the efforts of the English establishment, the new King, James II, refused to relinquish his Catholic faith after ascending to the throne. It looked for a while as if things could change in Ireland, and that the Catholics might have found a new ally in the unlikeliest of quarters, but such hopes were dashed 3 years later when James was ousted from power and the Protestant William of Orange installed in his place.

James fled to France to raise support for a rebellion, then sailed to Ireland to launch his attack. He struck first at Derry, to which he laid siege for 15 weeks before finally being defeated by William's forces at the Battle of the Boyne. The battle effectively ended James's cause, and with it, the hopes of Catholic Ireland for the best part of a century.

After James' defeat, English power was once more consolidated across Ireland. Protestant landowners were granted full political power, while laws were enacted to effectively immobilize the Catholic population. Being a Catholic in late 17th century Ireland was not exactly illegal *per se*, but in practice life was all but impossible for those who refused to convert to Protestantism.

Catholics could not purchase land, and existing landholdings were split up unless the families who owned them became Protestants; Catholic schools were banned, as were priests and all forms of public worship. Catholics were barred from holding any office of state, practicing law, or joining the army. Those who still refused to relinquish their faith were forced to pay a tax to the Anglican church, and by virtue of not being able to own land, the few who previously had been allowed to vote, certainly were not any more.

The new British landlords settled in, planted crops, made laws, and sowed their own seeds. Inevitably, over time, the "Anglos" became the Anglo-Irish. Hyphenated or not, they were Irish, and their loyalties were increasingly unpredictable. After all, an immigrant is only an immigrant for a generation; whatever the birthright of the colonists, their children would be Irish-born and bred. And so it was that an uncomfortable sort of stability set in for a generation or three, albeit of a kind that was very much separate and unequal. There were the haves—the wealthy Protestants—and the have-nots—the deprived and disenfranchised Catholics.

A kind of unhappy peace held for some time. But by the end of the 18th century the appetite for rebellion was whetted again. To understand why, one need look no further

■ **1937** The Free States adopt a new constitution, abandoning membership of the British Commonwealth and changing the country's official name to Eire.

■ **1939** Dublin is bombed by Germany at start of World War II, but Ireland remains neutral.

■ **1948** The Republic of Ireland Act. Ireland severs its last constitutional links with Britain.

■ **1955** Ireland is admitted into the United Nations.

■ **1963** U.S. Pres. John F. Kennedy visits Dublin.

■ **1969** Violence breaks out in Northern Ireland. British troops are called in.

■ **1972** In Derry a peaceful rally turns into "Bloody Sunday." The Northern Irish Parliament is dissolved, and direct rule imposed from Britain.

■ **1973** Ireland joins the European Community.

■ **1986** The Anglo-Irish Agreement gives the Republic a say in the government of Northern Ireland.

■ **1990** Mary Robinson is elected Ireland's first female president.

than the intellectual hotbed that flourished among the coffee shops and lecture halls of Europe's newest boom town: Dublin.

**WOLFE TONE, THE UNITED IRISHMEN &
THE 1798 REBELLION** By the 1770s, Dublin was thriving like never before. As a center for culture and learning, it was rivaled only by Paris and London; while, thanks to the work of such architects as Henry Gratton (who designed Custom House, the Kings Inns, and the Four Courts), its very streets were being remodeled in a grand, neoclassical style that was more akin to the great cities of southern Italy than of southern Ireland. However, while the urban classes reveled in their new-found wealth, the stringent penal laws that had effectively cut off the Catholic workers from their own countryside forced many of them to turn to the city for work. Into Dublin's buzzing intellectual scene were poured rich seams of political dissent, and even after a campaign by Irish politicians lead to many of the penal laws being repealed in 1783, all the ingredients were there to make Dublin a breeding ground for radical thinking and political activism. The results were explosive.

When war broke out between Britain and France in the 1790s, the United Irishmen—a nonviolent society formed to lobby for admission of Catholic Irishmen to the Irish Parliament—sent a secret delegation to per-suade the French to intervene on Ireland's

behalf against the British. Their emissary in this venture was a Dublin lawyer named Wolfe Tone. In 1796 Tone sailed with a French force bound for Ireland, and deter-mined to defeat forces loyal to the English crown, but was turned back by storms.

In 1798, though, full-scale insurrection led by the United Irishmen did spread across much of Ireland, particularly the South-western counties of Kilkenny and Wexford, where a tiny Republic was briefly declared in June, before it was crushed by loyalist forces, which then went on a murderous spree, killing tens of thousands of men, women, and children, and burning towns to the ground. The nadir of the rebellion came when Wolfe Tone, having raised another French invasion force, sailed into Lough Swilley in Donegal but was promptly cap-tured by the British. At his trial, wearing a French uniform, Tone requested that he be shot, in accordance with the rights of a for-eign soldier, but when the request was refused, he suffered a rather more gruesome end. While waiting for the gallows, he slit his own throat in jail; however, he missed the jugular vein, instead severing his windpipe, leading to a slow and painful death 8 days later. His last words were reputed to have been: "It appears, sir, that I am but a bad anatomist."

- **1994** The I.R.A. announces a ceasefire, and the Protestant paramilitaries follow suit. Commencement of peace talks.
- **1995** The British and Irish governments issue "A New Framework for Agreement," and U.S. President Bill Clinton makes a historic visit to Ireland, speaking to large crowds in Belfast and Derry.

He is received with enthusi-asm in the Republic.
- **1996** The I.R.A. breaks its ceasefire. An I.R.A. bomb in Omagh kills 25. The North sees the worst rioting in 15 years.
- **1997** The I.R.A. declares a new ceasefire. Sinn Fein enters inclusive all-party peace talks designed to bring about a comprehen-sive settlement.

- **1998** The all-party peace talks conclude with the so-called Good Friday Agreement, later strongly supported in referendums held on the same day in the Republic and the North. John Hume and David Trimble are awarded the Nobel Peace Prize.
- **1999** The implementation of the Agreement is blocked by a Unionist demand—"in the

The rebellion was over. In the space of 3 weeks, more than 30,000 Irish had been killed. As a final indignity in what became known as "The Year of the French," the British tricked the Irish Parliament into dissolving itself, and Ireland reverted to strict British rule.

A CONFLICT OF CONFLICTS In 1828 a Catholic lawyer named Daniel O'Connell, who had earlier formed the Catholic Association to represent the interests of tenant farmers, was elected to the British Parliament as MP for Dublin. Public opinion was so solidly behind him that he was able to persuade the British Prime Minister that the only way to avoid a civil war in Ireland was to force the Catholic Emancipation Act through Parliament. He remained an MP until 1841, when he was elected lord mayor of Dublin, a platform he used to push for repeal of the direct rule imposed from London after the 1798 rebellion. He organized enormous rallies (nicknamed "monster meetings") attended by hundreds of thousands and provoked an unresponsive conservative government to such an extent that it eventually arrested him on charges of seditious conspiracy. The charges were dropped, but the incident—coupled with growing impatience toward his nonviolent approach of protest and reform—led to the breakdown of his power base. "The

Liberator," as he had been known, faded, his health failed, and he died on a trip to Rome.

THE GREAT HUNGER Even after the anti-Catholic legislation began to recede, the vast majority of farmland available to the poor, mostly Catholic population of the countryside was harsh and difficult to cultivate. One of the few crops that could be grown reliably was the potato, which effectively became the staple diet of the rural poor. So when, in 1845, a fungus destroyed much of the potato crop of Ireland, it is not difficult to understand the scale of the devastation this caused. However, to label the Great Irish Famine of 1845–61 as a "tragedy" would be an incomplete description. It was, of course, tragic—undeniably, overwhelmingly so—but at the same time, the word implies a randomness to the whole sorry, sickening affair that fails to capture its true awfulness. The fact is that what started out as a disaster, was turned into a devastating crisis by the callous response of a disinterested British establishment.

As the potato blight worsened, it became apparent to many landlords that their farm tenants would be unable to pay rent. In order to offset their financial losses, they continued to ship grain overseas, in lieu of rent from their now starving tenants. The British parliament, meanwhile, was reluctant to send aid, putting the reports of a

spirit" but contrary to the letter of the Good Friday Agreement—that I.R.A. decommissioning precede the appointment of a new Northern Ireland executive. The peace process stalls until November, when the new power-sharing Northern Ireland Executive is established.

■ **2000** The I.R.A. issues a statement saying it will

decommission its arms. In May, power is restored to the institutions established by the Good Friday Agreement.

■ **2001** David Trimble threatens to resign as Ulster Unionist party leader if the I.R.A. does not decommission as promised. The I.R.A. doesn't; Trimble resigns in June. Following a surge of feeling in the wake of the

September 11 terrorist attacks on the U.S., I.R.A. decommissioning begins.

■ **2002** Irish voters defeat a referendum that would further restrict the availability of abortion. The peace process continues amid sectarian violence on both sides.

■ **2004** Irish government passes smoking ban in all public indoor spaces. U.S.

crisis down to, in the words of Prime Minister Robert Peel, "the Irish tendency to exaggerate."

Of course, as people started to die by the thousands, it became clear to the government that something had to be done, and emergency relief was sent to Ireland in the form of cheap, imported Indian cornmeal. However, this contained virtually no nutrients, and ultimately contributed to the spread of such diseases as typhus and cholera, which were to claim more victims than starvation itself. To make matters worse, the cornmeal was not simply given to those in need of it. Fearful that handouts would encourage laziness among a population they viewed as prone to that malaise, the British government forced people to work for their food. Entirely pointless make-work projects were initiated, just to give the starving men something to do for their cornmeal; roads were built that lead nowhere, for instance, and elaborate follies constructed that served no discernible purpose, some of which still litter the countryside today, memorials to cruelty and ignorance.

One of the most difficult things for us to comprehend a century and a half later is the sheer futility of it all. For behind the statistics, the memorials, and the endless personal anguish, lies perhaps the most painful truth of all: that the famine was easily preventable.

Enormous cargos of imported corn sat in Irish ports for months, until the British government felt that releasing them to the people would not adversely affect market rates. Meanwhile, huge quantities of meat and grain were exported from Ireland. (Indeed, in 1847, cattle exports went up 33% from the previous year.)

THE STRUGGLE FOR HOME RULE   As the famine waned and life returned to something like normality, the Irish independence movement gained new momentum. New fronts opened up in the struggle for home rule, both violent and nonviolent, and, significantly, the Republicans now drew considerable support from overseas—particularly from America, where groups such as the Fenians fundraised and published newspapers in support of the Irish cause, while more audacious schemes, such as an 1866 "invasion" of Canada with less than 100 men, amounted to little more than publicity stunts, designed to raise awareness for the cause.

Back home in Ireland, partial concessions were won in parliament, and by the 1880s, nationalists such as the MP for Meath, Charles Stewart Parnell, were able to unite various factions of Irish nationalists (including the Fenian Brotherhood in America) to fight for home rule. In a tumultuous decade of legislation, he came close, but revelations about his long affair with Kitty O'Shea, the

President George W. Bush arrives for E.U.-U.S. Summit and is greeted with anti-Iraq War protests.
■ 2005 David Trimble loses his parliamentary seat, but hard-line parties Sinn Fein and the DUP do extremely well. The I.R.A. decommissioning process is officially declared complete, and the I.R.A. disbands as a paramilitary unit.

■ 2006 Peace holds, but the North has rarely been more polarized. The Gaeltacht movement spreads, and larger regions of the country are declared, in essence, Gaelic language only.

wife of a supporter, brought about his down-fall as a politician.

By 1912, a bill to give Ireland home rule was passed through the British House of Commons, but was defeated in the House of Lords. Many felt that the political process was still all but unstoppable, and that it was only a matter of time before the bill passed fully into law, and effective political inde-pendence for Ireland would be secured. However, when the onset of the First World War in 1914 forced the issue onto the back burner once again, many in the home rule movement grew tired of the political process.

THE EASTER REBELLION On Easter Monday 1916, a group of nationalists occu-pied the General Post Office in the heart of Dublin, from where they proclaimed the foundation of an Irish Republic. Inside were 1,500 fighters, led by the school teacher and Gaelic League member Patrick Pearse and Socialist leader James Connolly. The British, nervous at an armed uprising on its doorstep while it fought a massive war in Europe, responded with overwhelming force. Soldiers were sent in, and a battle raged in the streets of Dublin for 6 days before the leaders of the rebellion were captured and imprisoned. There are still bullet holes in the walls of the post office, and the buildings and statues up and down O'Connell Street. Pearse, Connolly, and 12 other leaders were imprisoned, secretly tried, and speedily executed.

Ultimately, though, the British reaction was as counter-productive as it was harsh. The totality with which those involved in organizing the rebellion were pursued and dispatched acted as a lightning rod for many of those who had been undecided about the effectiveness of a purely political struggle. Indeed, a fact that has become somewhat lost in the ensuing hundred or so years since Patrick Pearse stood on the steps of the Post Office early on that cold Monday morning reading a treatise on Irish independence is that a great many Irish didn't support the

rebellion at the time, either believing that the best course of action was to lie low until the war had ended, when concessions would be won as a result, or that it was simply the wrong thing to do, as long as there were sons of Ireland sacrificing their lives in the trenches of Europe. But however it is that we trace the path to violence, the aftermath of 1916 all but guaranteed, for better or for worse, that Ireland's future would be decided by the gun.

REBELLION A power vacuum was left at the heart of the nationalist movement after the Easter Rising, and it was filled by two men: Michael Collins and Eamon de Valera. On the surface both men had much in common; Collins was a Cork man who had returned from Britain in order to join the Irish Volun-teers (later to become the Irish Republican Army or I.R.A.), while de Valera was an Irish-American math teacher who came back to Ireland to set up a new political party, Sinn Fein.

When de Valera's party won a landslide victory in the general election of 1918, its MPs refused to sit in London, instead pro-claiming the first Dáil, or independent par-liament, in Dublin. De Valera went to rally support for the cause in America, while Collins stayed to concentrate on his work as head of the Irish Volunteers. Tensions inevitably escalated into violence, and for the next 2 years, Irish nationalists fought a tit-for-tat military campaign against the British in Ireland. The low point of the strug-gle came in 1920, when Collins ordered 14 British operatives to be murdered in their beds, in response to which British troops opened fire on the audience at a football game at Croke Park in Dublin, randomly killing 12 innocent people. A truce was even-tually declared on July 9, 1921, and 6 months later, the Anglo-Irish treaty was signed in London, granting legislative independence to 26 Irish counties (known together as the Irish Free State). The compromise through which that freedom was won, though, was that six counties in the north would remain part of the United Kingdom. Collins knew that compromise would not be accepted by the more strident members of his rebel group. And he knew they would blame him for agreeing to it in the first place. When he signed the treaty he told the people present, "I am signing my own death warrant."

As he feared, nationalists were split between those who accepted the treaty as a platform on which to build and those, led by the nationalist de Valera, who saw it as a betrayal and would accept nothing less than immediate and full independence at any cost. Even the withdrawal of British troops from Dublin for the first time in nearly 800 years did not quell their anger. The result was an inexorable slide into civil war. The flashpoint came in April 1922, when violence erupted around the streets of the capital and rolled on for 8 days until de Valera's supporters were forced to surrender. The government of the fledgling Free State ordered that Republicans be shot on sight, leading to the deaths of 77 people. And Collins had been right about his own fate: 4 months later he was assassinated while on a visit to his childhood home.

The fallout from the civil war dominated Irish politics for the next decade. De Valera split from the republicans to form another party, Fianna Fail (meaning "the warriors of Ireland"), which won the election of 1932 and governed for 17 years. Despite his continuing dedication to the republican ideal, however, de Valera was not the one who finally declared Ireland a republic in 1948; ironically, that distinction went to a coalition led by de Valera's opponent, Douglas Hyde, whose victory in the election of 1947 was attributed to the fact that de Valera had become too obsessed with abstract republican ideals to govern effectively.

STUCK IN NEUTRAL   One of the more controversial, not to say morally ambiguous,

decisions that Eamon de Valera made while in office was to stay neutral during World War II despite the best efforts of Winston Churchill and Franklin Roosevelt to persuade him otherwise. The basis for his decision—a combination of Ireland's size and economic weakness and the British presence in Northern Ireland—may have made sense to some extent, but it left Ireland in the peculiar position of openly favoring one side in a war but refusing to help it. His reticence didn't find much favor among the Irish population, and as many as 300,000 Irish men found ways to enlist in the British or U.S. armies. In the end, more than 50,000 Irish soldiers died in the war their country never joined.

TROUBLE ON THE WAY   After the war, 2 decades passed without violence in Ireland, until the late 1960s once more saw the outbreak of sectarian conflict in the North. What started out as a civil rights movement to demand greater equality for Catholics within Northern Ireland soon escalated into a cycle of violence that lasted for 30 years. It would be a terrible over-simplification to say that the Troubles were merely a clear-cut struggle between those who wanted to complete the process of Irish unification and those who wanted to remain part of the United Kingdom, although that was, of course, the crux of the conflict. Factors such as organized crime and terrorism, together with centuries-old conflicts over religion, land, and social issues, make the conflict even harder for outsiders to understand.

The worst of the Troubles came in the 1970s. In 1972, British troops inexplicably opened fire on a peaceful demonstration in Derry, killing 12 people—many of whom were shot while they tended to the wounds of the first people injured. The I.R.A. took advantage of the mood of public outrage and began a civilian bombing campaign on the British mainland. The cycle of violence continued for 20 years, inexorably and depressingly, while all the while none of the myriad sides in the conflict would talk to each other. Finally, in the early 1990s, secret talks were opened between the British and the I.R.A., leading to an I.R.A. cease-fire in 1994 (although the cease-fire held only shakily—an I.R.A. bomb in Omagh 4 years later killed 29, the most to die in any single incident of the Troubles).

The peace process continued throughout the 1990s, helped significantly by the mediation efforts of U.S. President Bill Clinton, who arguably became more involved in Irish affairs than any president before him until, on Good Friday 1998, a peace accord was finally signed in Belfast. The agreement committed all sides to a peaceful resolution of the conflict in Northern Ireland and included the reinstatement of full self-government for the region in a power-sharing administration. It stopped short of resolving the territorial issue once and for all—in other words, Northern Ireland is still part of the U.K. and will be for the foreseeable future. On the contrary, to some extent the conflicts rage more bitterly and more divisively than ever before, the difference being that, with notable exceptions, they are fought through the ballot box rather than the barrel of a gun. As a coda, in 2005 the I.R.A. fully decommissioned its weapons, and officially dissolved itself as a paramilitary unit.

While the North of Ireland is still struggling to recover from years of conflict, the Republic of Ireland continues to flourish. The 1990s brought unprecedented wealth and prosperity to the country, thanks in part to European Union subsidies and partly to a thriving economy, which acquired the nickname "The Celtic Tiger" for its new global strength. It has also become a more socially liberal country over the last 20 years or so—although it has to be said, Ireland is still a long way behind much of the western world over attitudes towards divorce, homosexuality, and abortion.

And so it is that Ireland in the early 21st century faces up to the latest battle in its long, long history: a democratic battle with itself to decide just what kind of a country it will be.

Ireland Today

Proving wrong those who said the Irish boom economy of the late 1990s was only a short-lived bubble has been one of Ireland's great pleasures in recent years. The economy was dubbed the "Celtic Tiger" in the international press, and other nations looked on enviously as Ireland decided what to do with its new-found wealth. It verged on silly money, as the E.U. lavished one of its poorest members with subsidies so vast that, at times, the Irish government seemed not to know precisely what to do with it all. Sometimes they made bad decisions—building bridges, statues, and clocks while traffic in Dublin and Galway City ground to a standstill, brought to inertia by roads too old and narrow to handle the modern traffic. And as hospitals crumbled, parents put their children in private schools to save them from the inadequacies of the state-funded versions.

In recent years, though, the country seemed to get a handle on its new situation and poured money into infrastructure—developing a new tram system in Dublin and widening roads around the country. Today, the dumptruck seems to be the national symbol of Ireland, as the huge vehicles trundle along by the dozen, each carrying tons of gravel and sand to be used building, building, building: building new roads, widening old roads, building new houses, expanding old houses, building structures in ugly, boxlike shapes helter-skelter along the edges of old villages, towns, and suburbs that seem to be free of the pesky limitations of zoning ordinances. The chatter of jackhammers forms a constant aural background in virtually every town in the Republic. The sound of hammer hitting nail has replaced the bodhran and tin whistle.

It is, I suppose, the sound of success and progress. But it is changing Ireland rapidly— has changed Ireland already. Everytime I visit a part of the country I haven't seen in a few months, I am astonished by the new apartment complexes and businesses thrown up in the meantime—so many of them with no character or charm. One worries that architects go begging in Ireland today as construction companies flourish.

All of this doesn't come cheap, and housing prices in Ireland are shocking. You would pay hundreds of thousands of euro for even the most isolated, unrenovated cottage. To peruse the property pages in the *Irish Times* is to marvel that anybody can afford to own a home. And many cannot. Property prices have made millions of people millionaires on paper, while making it virtually impossible for young people to buy homes or to live in city centers. Those who didn't own property before the boom cannot afford to buy now, particularly in Dublin and Galway, where most of the workers come into town every day from small homes in the distant suburbs. This has lead to a paradoxical situation familiar to many "wealthy" nations—wealth has been accompanied by rising crime, drug abuse, and urban homelessness—but it is new to Ireland, and it has come as a shock.

Added to this is a worrying growth in overall inflation—in 2006 inflation in Ireland exceeded 4 percent, double the inflation rate in other European nations such as Germany and Britain. Property prices (combined with soaring fuel costs) were primarily to blame. Is the Irish economic bubble yet to burst? Or has the Celtic Tiger only just hit its stride?

Only time will tell.

Still, it's not all bad news. While the Irish find themselves adjusting to the problems of having, to some extent, too much wealth, they've also relished the biggest side effect of a strong economy—peace.

In recent years, the violence in the north has calmed, and a recognizable democratic debate grips the land. There is much disagreement still between those who think it should stay as it is—with the North still under U.K. control and the Republic a fully independent and part of the European Union of nations—and those who believe it should be united. There is also still tension between Catholics and Protestants, who are learning not to greet each other's divergent religious views with violence, but who still whisper the words "Catholic" and "Protestant" when talking in a public place. With all of the changes and recent peace, this is still the kind of place where you look over your shoulder when you talk, even in the most inoffensive terms, about religion or Irish politics.

But that is something the Irish themselves seem not even to notice. To them, looking over their shoulders when talking about religion is nothing compared to the past, when they waited for bullets to fly or bombs to explode. For them, this is real democratic peace. And there is so much joy in the Republic of Ireland right now about its prosperity, and a kind of intense pride that has not been seen in this country in some time about its independence, its strong economy, and its place within the EU, that the North could be forgiven for feeling a bit of jealousy about that. For while the Republic has grown richer, the North has stayed—at least economically—the same.

At the moment both the North and the Republic are working through these growing pains, and even when the Irish complain about the changes in their country over the last few years, they do so with a kind of heartwarming pride. Heart-warming because, for so very long, there was little to be proud of in an Ireland torn apart by violence and perennially threatened by its own intrinsic inability to ever give way, even to itself.

Now the Irish have learned what you will find out for yourself on any visit here, that the new Ireland is not yet incompatible with the old. The country has thus far maintained and preserved its beautiful old buildings and quiet country lanes, while also growing and changing into a place that *it* can love. It is a difficult—even tense—balancing act. Modern new supermarkets stand beside Georgian town houses, and many of the old Irish shops have been replaced by European and British chain stores. But the Irish always find a way to sell their wares in small boutiques and shops around the country, and to make the old new again (one of the most popular Irish chains—Avoca Weavers—uses old methods to make intensely modern products from Irish wool and clay).

Yes, the old Irish spirit is still here, beneath its new facade, behind the coffee shops, the juice bars, the pricey restaurants, and expensive cars. You'll find it in the pubs and when walking in the hills, or sharing a laugh with someone in the post office, or as you stand under an awning in the rain.

INDEX